A REFERENCE PUBLICATION IN LITERATURE
Marilyn Gaull, *Editor*

William Wordsworth:
A Reference Guide to
British Criticism, 1793-1899

N. S. Bauer

G. K. Hall & Co., 70 Lincoln Street, Boston, Mass.

80-6

Copyright © 1978 by N. S. Bauer

Library of Congress Cataloging in Publication Data

Bauer, Neil Stephen, 1943-
    William Wordsworth : a reference guide.

    (Reference publications in literature)
    Includes index.
    1. Wordsworth, William, 1770-1850--Bibliography.
I. Series.
Z8985.B38 [PR5881]   016.821'7   77-23883
ISBN 0-8161-7828-3

This publication is printed on permanent/durable acid-free paper
MANUFACTURED IN THE UNITED STATES OF AMERICA

Contents

Introduction

Critics in the nineteenth century were themselves preoccupied with the history of Wordsworth's critical reception and the underlying question of how a reader should approach Wordsworth's poems. On the most obvious level, their concern manifested itself in discussions, as early as the second decade of the century, of the harsh reviews of his works; by the 1830's it had become common for writers to cite as one of Wordsworth's virtues that he had calmly persevered in his poetic mission, despite hostile criticism, eventually to triumph. His triumph was so marked that as early as 1835 a writer was complaining that Wordsworth was now overly praised. These two themes, that Wordsworth persevered confident in his mission and that he was either overly damned or overly praised, continued to be voiced to the end of the century.

The thrust of the early critical attack was that Wordsworth failed to consider the poetic predispositions of his reader. In response, several critics, such as Coleridge and John Wilson, defended Wordsworth by arguing, from a close examination of the texts, that his poems were indeed conventionally understandable. Their discussions, in turn, provided the critical assumptions that enabled essayists later in the century to discuss seriously Wordsworth's philosophical ideas.

Another common defense against the early attackers, however, was the positive assertion, typified by J. H. Reynolds' arguments in the Champion, that Wordsworth wrote a special kind of poetry for a special kind of reader predisposed to appreciate it. These defenders, in other words, accepted the premise of the early attackers, but shifted the blame for the unintelligibility of Wordsworth's poems from the poet to the reader. As the notion became more and more prevalent that Wordsworth was writing for a select group of initiates, the critics' role of necessity became less and less important: the poet, calmly persevering, need not be tutored; the reader, if a Wordsworthian, needed no instruction and if not a Wordsworthian could not be made one by a critic. Perhaps these critical assumptions account for what to us is apt to seem the abundance of inconsequential criticism in the last third of the century: writers providing background

Introduction

information for confirmed Wordsworthians--tracing Wordsworth's path
down the Duddon, indexing his references to birds, and so forth.

The two critical responses joined in the later critics' concern
for establishing Wordsworth's text and in studying his life. By 1840
the myth of Wordsworth's ideal life had become firmly established:
Wordsworth was the aged poet, living happily amidst his family, re-
mote from the problems of society, untouched by personal sorrow.
Wordsworth's life and poetry were serene, and it was this serenity
that gave his poems their unique healing power. One might expect
Wordsworth's attraction to the Victorians to lie in his example of a
man who had overcome sorrow: but most preferred to see him as a man
who had not known it. Both Arnold's and Ruskin's admiration, for
example, was based on the prevalent view that Wordsworth lacked
knowledge of suffering: to Arnold, "Wordsworth's eyes avert their
ken / From half of human fate," yet he "made us feel"; Ruskin cher-
ished Wordsworth's asserting that "We live by Admiration, Hope, and
Love" even when he came to quarrel with Wordsworth as "a measured
mind, and calm; innocent, unrepentant, helpful to sinless creatures."
Wordsworth's healing and fortifying power came from his innocence,
not his experience.

To survey Victorian criticism in such a way is to say that that
criticism has an historical interest; and such an interest is not un-
important. It is worthwhile to study how a figure influences different generations and how critical knowledge of his poems evolves. As
Coleridge's and Lamb's letters, for example, came gradually to be published, the educated reader had a shifting foundation of basic critical knowledge with which to approach Wordsworth's poems. The entire
concept of the evolving availability of critical knowledge as well as
Wordsworth's philosophical and artistic importance to the Victorians,
can be much more carefully studied than it has been.

But what the early critics of Wordsworth had to say is worthwhile
not only historically but in its own right. Critics in the twentieth
century have indeed advanced in psychological insight and the vocabulary of precise literary analysis. But they have touched on few areas
that were not studied by the Victorian critics we, confident in our
superiority, tend to ignore. To cite but three examples: Even at
the beginning of the century critics were writing that Wordsworth's
role in the poetic revolution at the end of the eighteenth century
had been overrated, that he had followed, rather than initiated, a
change in literary taste. From the late 1870's critics became preoccupied with the question of Wordsworth as poet versus Wordsworth as
philosopher: was Wordsworth championed as a poet only because readers
found his ideas acceptable? And throughout the century critics
raised the issue of Wordsworth's dependence upon or transcendence of
the natural world: Leigh Hunt, for example, in 1819 noted that in
"Malham Cove" Wordsworth paradoxically forsakes the visible world he
would have us love, while Hall Caine in 1883 argued that Wordsworth's
"mind never went to work on its own vision." The relevance of such

Introduction

observations to the concerns of twentieth-century critics need not be emphasized to anyone who has surveyed Wordsworth's critical reception since the turn of the century.

The present bibliography ends with 1899 in the belief that twentieth-century criticism has been thoroughly surveyed by James V. Logan in Wordsworthian Criticism: A Guide and Bibliography (1947; reprinted Columbus: Ohio State Univ. Press, 1961), Elton F. Henley and David H. Stam in Wordsworthian Criticism 1945-1964: An Annotated Bibliography (revised edition, New York: New York Public Library, 1965), and David H. Stam in Wordsworthian Criticism 1964-1973 . . . (New York: New York Public Library and Readex Books, 1974). In contrast, no comprehensive annotated bibliography of nineteenth-century criticism has hitherto been compiled. The best modern bibliographies are those of William S. Ward, recently reprinted in Literary Reviews in British Periodicals 1798-1820: A Bibliography: With a Supplementary List of General (Non-Review) Articles on Literary Subjects (2 vols., New York and London: Garland, 1972), which unfortunately ends with 1820 and is not annotated, John O. Hayden's extension of Ward's listing of reviews to 1824 in The Romantic Reviewers 1802-1824 (Chicago: Univ. of Chicago Press, 1968), and the catalogue of The Cornell Wordsworth Collection . . . , compiled by George Harris Healey (Ithaca: Cornell Univ. Press, 1957), the most extensive listing but one limited to the holdings of the collection. To all the above lists I am deeply indebted, as well as to the bibliographies published during the nineteenth century and included below--principally that published by William Knight in The Poetical Works of William Wordsworth (London and New York: Macmillan, 1896).

In going beyond existing bibliographies and searching through periodicals and critical studies for references to Wordsworth, I have had to rely more than is prudent on indices and tables of contents. Hence although I have tried to make the following Guide as complete as possible, I am well aware I have overlooked much. In addition, I have been forced, by the sheer bulk of the material, to omit many minor references that ought perhaps to have been included. I have tried to make the list as comprehensive as possible for the first third of the century, when Wordsworth's fame was first developing. But even the briefest biographical sketch in the 1890's can be of interest for the writer's choice of poems by which to identify Wordsworth; so I have included some representative short notices (for example, notes to selections in school texts) throughout the century. Discussions of the Lake Poets have generally been omitted unless specific reference to Wordsworth is made. I have included only the most detailed or important discussions of Wordsworth in critical studies of his contemporaries: scarcely a biographical notice of Coleridge, for example, fails to mention Wordsworth, and the student who wishes to locate every possible reference to Wordsworth should use this Guide in collaboration with bibliographies of other major nineteenth-century poets. I have also been especially selective in

including notices of Wordsworth in guides to the Lake District and
poems of tribute: routine descriptions of Wordsworth's associations
with Grasmere and Rydal, as well as routine poetic expressions of
gratitude, have been omitted unless the writers go further to include
extended or unique details. What follows is a guide to references
about Wordsworth's life or work: hence I have not recorded the appearance of extracts from his poems unaccompanied by critical text,
nor of items, such as announcements of meetings of committees to
erect monuments to Wordsworth, that say nothing significant about his
life or work; similarly, in including reviews of editions of Wordsworth's poems, I have annotated only the reviewer's comments about
Wordsworth, not about the quality of the editing. Because of their
importance, however, I have made exceptions to include selected notices of the activities of the Wordsworth Society and some reviews of
editions late in the century that record the controversy between
William Knight, Edward Dowden, and Thomas Hutchinson over the
handling of Wordsworth's texts.

Each entry lists material not previously published. If a periodical article is revised and reprinted by its author, the revision is
annotated as a separate entry; if it is reprinted by its author without change (most commonly in a volume of collected essays), the first
such reprinting is noted, by short title and date, in the annotation
of the original periodical article unless the volume containing the
reprinted material is annotated because it contains other new essays,
in which case the reprinting is noted by means of a cross-reference
in the original annotation. If a book is later revised by its author,
the revision is annotated as a separate entry. Therefore, if subse-
quent nineteenth-century reprintings or editions of an item are not
listed, one may assume they contain no revisions from the original
text. If one encounters in a particular volume material about Wordsworth that is not annotated, he may assume that material has been
previously published and locate that publication with the help of the
index.

Reviews of essays about Wordsworth have been included only if the
reviewer adds new criticism of his own to that summarized from the
work he is reviewing.

In annotating entries, I have included in the annotation the
titles of Wordsworth's poems most extensively discussed by the critic;
but since it is clearly impossible to list every poem to which a pass-
ing comment is made, the reader interested in tracking down all references to a particular poem should consult all reviews of the volume
in which the poem first appeared, even if the title is not mentioned
in the annotation. In annotating anthologies, I have similarly included the titles of poems most thoroughly dealt with in the editor's
notes; but in annotating large selections and complete editions I
have obviously been unable to list every title, so that again the
reader wishing to be thorough should check these volumes for critical
comments about poems even though the titles have not been listed in

the annotation. Also, many of the discussions I have noted as containing "a biographical sketch" contain, in addition to an account of
Wordsworth's life, a sketch of his poetic career and a discussion of
his principal poems.

Page numbers listed in an entry refer to the inclusive pagination
of the periodical article or section of a book, followed in parenthe-
ses by the numbers of those pages containing references to Wordsworth.
When a book contains no distinct divisions, the pages listed are those
simply throughout the book on which references may be found. In all
cases, page numbers are given only for the references annotated, and
an essay may in addition contain other, minor references. When an
essay printed over several issues in a periodical is annotated as one
entry, page numbers are included in the annotation to mark the divisions between installments. Likewise, when several distinct sections
of a book are annotated, page numbers have been inserted in the annotations to mark the divisions between sections. Titles and line numbers of Wordsworth's poems have been standardized to those given in
Wordsworth: Poetical Works, edited by Thomas Hutchinson and Ernest de
Selincourt (London, Oxford, and New York: Oxford Univ. Press, 1969).

Although I have tried to list the first appearance of each item,
I have been unable to trace the original publication of several essays, especially those that were later collected from provincial journals. As scholarly activity on nineteenth-century criticism of Wordsworth increases, one would hope that many of these earlier printings
can be identified, as well as provincial journals themselves, often
extremely inaccessible, searched more thoroughly. One trusts as well
that in the future more of the essays may be attributed to specific
writers. I am indebted for attributions to the standard editions and
bibliographies of the writer in question, to standard bibliographies
and studies of the periodical involved, or to the first two volumes
of The Wellesley Index to Victorian Periodicals 1824-1900, edited by
Walter E. Houghton, et al. (Toronto: Univ. of Toronto Press; London:
Routledge & Kegan Paul, 1966-72). Attributions taken from other than
these standard, recognized sources are noted in the annotations.

The largest task facing future bibliographers not only of Wordsworth but of Victorian culture in general is the cataloguing of references in the daily press. Except when they have been reprinted in
non-daily periodicals or books, such references have been omitted
from the present Guide. Important notices of Wordsworth in the London
papers do exist, ranging from Daniel Stuart's notes on the Lyrical
Ballads in the Morning Post and Courier, to Leigh Hunt's comments in
the Tatler in 1831, to discussions such as that surrounding Thomas
Wakley's attack on Wordsworth's poetry in the House of Commons in
1842, to notices of events in Wordsworth's life and of his death, to
the extended criticism that appeared in the Westminster Gazette at
the end of the century. To survey such criticism thoroughly will require an immense, coordinated effort on the part of a large number of
researchers.

INTRODUCTION

I have included as "British criticism" works by those born in the British Isles even though published elsewhere. For the sake of convenience, I have also included remarks on Wordsworth originally published in British periodicals, regardless of the nationality of the author: foreign reprintings of periodical articles by non-British writers have, however, not been noted.

Entries are grouped by year of publication and listed alphabetically under the categories of "Books" and "Shorter Writings." Anonymous entries and entries by the same author within any given year are listed chronologically. An asterisk precedes those entries, listed in previous bibliographies, that I have been unable to locate.

I am indebted to many libraries for small but essential favors. I wish, however, especially to thank the libraries at Dove Cottage, Columbia, Cornell, and Yale for allowing me to consult their collections and to thank for their patience the staffs at the Bodleian Library, the British Library, and The New York Public Library, where most of my research has been conducted. To my wife Helen, and to Carl Woodring, Richard and Josephine Haven, and Marilyn Gaull, I am deeply grateful for substantial help and encouragement.

Writings about William Wordsworth, 1793-1899

<u>1793 A   BOOKS - NONE</u>

<u>1793 B   SHORTER WRITINGS</u>

1   ANON.   Review of <u>Descriptive Sketches</u>. <u>Analytical Review</u>, 15
    (March), 294-96.
       Wordsworth presents diversified pictures of nature,
    though the poem suffers from lack of narrative and from
    artificial and hence obscure expression.

2   ANON.   Review of <u>An Evening Walk</u>. <u>Analytical Review</u>, 15
    (March), 296-97.
       The poem is written by a diligent observer and copyist
    of nature.

3   ANON.   Review of <u>An Evening Walk</u>. <u>Critical Review</u>, NS 8
    (July), 347-48.
       The poem, though obscure because of harshness in con-
    struction and versification, contains new and picturesque
    imagery.

4   ANON.   Review of <u>Descriptive Sketches</u>. <u>Critical Review</u>, NS 8
    (August), 472-74.
       Wordsworth's "lines are often harsh and prosaic; his
    images ill-chosen, and his descriptions feeble."

5   ANON.   Review of <u>An Evening Walk</u>. <u>European Magazine</u>, 24
    (September), 192-93.
       Wordsworth's description is minute, accurate, pathetic.

6   [HOLCROFT, THOMAS].   Review of <u>Descriptive Sketches</u>. <u>Monthly
    Review</u>, NS 12 (October), 216-18.
       Quarrels with Wordsworth's diction.

7   [HOLCROFT, THOMAS].   Review of <u>An Evening Walk</u>. <u>Monthly
    Review</u>, NS 12 (October), 218.
       The poem includes figurative language no poetical li-
    cense can justify.

1794

1794 A BOOKS - NONE

1794 B SHORTER WRITINGS

1   PEREGRINATOR. Review of An Evening Walk. Gentleman's
      Magazine, 64 (March), 252-53.
          Recommends the poem to visitors to the Lakes for its ac-
      curate description not of particular spots but of the
      country in general.

1796 A BOOKS - NONE

1796 B SHORTER WRITINGS

1   COLERIDGE, S.[AMUEL] T.[AYLOR]. "Notes," in Poems on Various
      Subjects. London: Robinsons; Bristol: Cottle, pp. 177-88
      (185-86).
          Wordsworth, "whose versification is occasionally harsh
      and his diction too frequently obscure," is unrivalled in
      "manly sentiment, novel imagery, and vivid colouring."

1798 A BOOKS - NONE

1798 B SHORTER WRITINGS

1   ANON. Review of Lyrical Ballads (1798). Monthly Mirror, 6
      (October), 224-25.
          Approves of the author's experiment in poetic language.

2   ANON. Review of Lyrical Ballads (1798). Analytical Review,
      28 (December), 583-87.
          Finds Wordsworth's remarks in the Advertisement "sen-
      sible"; admires the simplicity and tenderness of some poems.

3   ANON. "Half-yearly Retrospect of Domestic Literature."
      Monthly Magazine, 6 (Suppl.), 493-521 (514).
          The author of Lyrical Ballads (1798) imitates the style
      of old English versifiers with success.

4   [SOUTHEY, ROBERT]. Review of Lyrical Ballads (1798).
      Critical Review, NS 24 (October), 197-204.
          Though the author ranks with the best of living poets,
      his experiment fails, not because he adopts the language of
      conversation, but because he chooses uninteresting subjects
      (e.g., in "The Idiot Boy," "The Thorn," "Goody Blake and
      Harry Gill"). "Tintern Abbey" is superior to the rest of
      the volume.

1799 A   BOOKS - NONE

1799 B   SHORTER WRITINGS

1   ANON. Review of Lyrical Ballads (1798). New London Review, 1
     (January), 33-35.
         In contrast to the author's view in the Advertisement,
     the language of conversation of the lower classes can never
     be the language of poetry; one cannot dismiss one's past
     definitions of poetry; rudeness is not the same as simpli-
     city. In many of the poems, however, the author does not
     follow his own principles.

2   ANON. Review of Lyrical Ballads (1798). Naval Chronicle, 2
     [September?], 328-30; [October?], 418-20.
         Praises the author's harmonious rhythm and original
     thought.

3   ANON. Review of Lyrical Ballads (1798). British Critic, 14
     (October), 364-69.
         The author of the laudable volume attains a "judicious
     degree of simplicity." Regretfully, he aims in "The Female
     Vagrant" to expose evils no man can prevent. The poems con-
     tain only minor instances of enmity to present institutions.
     (For a discussion of the traditional attribution of this
     review to Francis Wrangham, see R. S. Woof, "John Stoddart,
     'Michael' and Lyrical Ballads," Ariel, 1, no. 2 [1970], 19.)

4   ANON. "Preface." British Critic, 14 (July-December), i-xviii
     (xv).
         The author of Lyrical Ballads (1798) does not descend to
     conversational language as often as he threatens to in the
     Advertisement.

5   ANON. "Domestic Literature Of the Year 1798." New Annual
     Register . . . For the Year 1798, 19:[215]-[317] ([309]-
     [10]).
         The author of Lyrical Ballads (1798) has considerable
     talent, though his genius has been misemployed on some
     poems.

6   [BURNEY, CHARLES]. Review of Lyrical Ballads (1798). Monthly
     Review, NS 29 (June), 202-10.
         The author's return to the uncouth practices of the past
     degrades poetry; his delineations of passions and characters
     are interesting, though overly gloomy; his "painting" re-
     calls Rembrandt and Michelangelo. Questions the social and
     political implications of "The Female Vagrant," "Goody Blake

and Harry Gill," "The Last of the Flock," "Animal Tran-
quillity and Decay," and "Tintern Abbey."

7   Q. Letter to the Editor. Ipswich Magazine, April,
    pp. 105-106.
        Points out the application of the moral in "Goody Blake
    and Harry Gill" to the present scarcity of coal.

1800 A   BOOKS - NONE

1800 B   SHORTER WRITINGS

1   [HEATH, WILLIAM]. Review of Lyrical Ballads (1798). Anti-
    jacobin Review and Magazine, 5 (April), 334 [misprint for
    434].
        Recommends the volume. Attribution: John O. Hayden,
    The Romantic Reviewers 1802-1824 (Chicago: Univ. of
    Chicago Press, 1968), p. 296.

1801 A   BOOKS - NONE

1801 B   SHORTER WRITINGS

1   ANON. Review of Lyrical Ballads (1800). Monthly Mirror, 11
    (June), 389-92.
        The poems reveal energy of thought, pathos, and dis-
    criminately selected imagery, but are marked by obscurity,
    arising from a search for simplicity, studied abruptness,
    a "monotony of woe," and "a wayward spirit of discontent."
    Wordsworth's moral force approaches Cowper's.

2   ANON. "Preface." British Critic, 17 (January-June), i-xix
    (xiii).
        Though Wordsworth's simplicity in Lyrical Ballads
    (1800) is sometimes disappointing, his preference for
    truth over hollow argument is salutary.

3   RUSTICUS. "Barham Downs; or, Goody Grizzle and Her Ass: A
    Lyrical Ballad, in the Present Fashionable Stile."
    European Magazine, 40 (September), 201-202.
        A burlesque.

4   [STODDART, JOHN]. Review of Lyrical Ballads (1800). British
    Critic, 17 (February), 125-31.
        Wordsworth's style has changed wholly from the obscure
    and inflated diction of Descriptive Sketches and An Evening
    Walk. Wordsworth has deeply studied human nature. His

subjects are worthy, though they may not at first appear so. The title of the volume is objectionable. Attribution: see The Letters of William and Dorothy Wordsworth, edited by Ernest de Selincourt, 2nd ed.: The Early Years 1787-1805, revised by Chester L. Shaver (Oxford: Clarendon Press, 1967), p. 320n.

5   STODDART, JOHN. Remarks on Local Scenery and Manners in Scotland during the Years 1799 and 1800. 2 vols. London: Miller, I:68; II:30.
    Commends Wordsworth's description of bells in Descriptive Sketches and his consulting of Nature.

6   THELWELL, JOHN. "Lines, written at Bridgewater, in Somersetshire, on the 27th of July, 1797; during a long excursion, in quest of a peaceful retreat," in Poems chiefly written in Retirement. . . . London: Phillips, and Ridgeway; Dublin: Stockdale, pp. 126-32 (130-31).
    Voices his desire for the fellowship of Dorothy and William, "Allfoxden's musing tenant."

1802 A BOOKS - NONE

1802 B SHORTER WRITINGS

1   ANON. Review of Lyrical Ballads (1800). Monthly Review, NS 38 (June), 209.
    Wordsworth is a "natural, easy, and sentimental Bard," though he has a somewhat peculiar imagination.

2   ANON. "Marriages." Gentleman's Magazine, 72 (Suppl.), 1223-24 (1224).
    Records Wordsworth's marriage.

3   [JEFFREY, FRANCIS]. Review of Southey's Thalaba. Edinburgh Review, 1 (October), 63-83 (63-72).
    The "modern school of poetry" is not original but derived from the writings of Rousseau, Kotzebue, Schiller, Cowper, Philips, Quarles, and Donne. It is characterized by meanness of language and subjects, attempts at sublimity, and discontent with existing institutions of society.

4   WARNER, THE REV. RICHARD. A Tour through the Northern Counties of England, and the Borders of Scotland. 2 vols. London: Robinson, II:101-102.
    Lyrical Ballads "breathe the true, nervous, and simple spirit of poetry."

1803

1803 A BOOKS - NONE

1803 B SHORTER WRITINGS

 1 BAYLEY, PETER, JR. "The Fisherman's Wife" (poem), in Poems.
        London: Miller, pp. 193-206.
          Parody of "The Idiot Boy."

 2 N., T. "Observations on the Corruptions of Literature."
        Edinburgh Magazine, or Literary Miscellany, NS 22 (July),
        23-27 (26-27).
          The poems of Wordsworth and his school incite discontent
        with the allotments of Providence, display unbounded
        benevolence.

1805 A BOOKS - NONE

1805 B SHORTER WRITINGS

 1 ANON. Review of Southey's Metrical Tales. Literary Journal,
        5 (February), 157-65 (160).
          Wordsworth does not understand the capacities of common
        readers.

1806 A BOOKS - NONE

1806 B SHORTER WRITINGS

 1 ANON. Review of Southey's Madoc. General Review, 1 (June),
        505-26 (509-10).
          Wordsworth, Coleridge, and Southey revived poetry by
        appealing to Nature and simplicity, though they have at
        times gone to extremes.

 2 [CAURTIER, PETER L.]. "William Wordsworth," in The Lyre of
        Love. 2 vols. London: Sharpe, II:127.
          Wordsworth possesses a beautiful wife, "his union with
        whom was characterised by that eccentric enthusiasm which
        constitutes the charm of his poetry." Attribution:
        Dictionary of Anonymous and Pseudonymous English Literature
        (Samuel Halkett and John Laing), new ed., 9 vols. (Edin-
        burgh: Oliver and Boyd, 1926-62), III:411.

1807 A   BOOKS - NONE

1807 B   SHORTER WRITINGS

1   ANON. Review of Poems (1807). Critical Review, 3rd ser., 11
(August), 399-403.
Laments Wordsworth's squandering of his genius, evident
in Lyrical Ballads, on the trivial subjects in the present
volume.

2   ANON. Review of Poems (1807). Le Beau Monde, 2 (October),
138-42.
Wordsworth expresses feeling for unworthy objects; he has
extended the puerile errors rather than the beauties of
Lyrical Ballads, especially in "To the Daisy" ("In youth
from rock to rock I went"). Most of the poems lack meaning.

3   ANON. Review of Poems (1807). Literary Annual Register, or
Records of Literature, 1 (October), 468-69.
The poems are obscure, prosaic.

4   ANON. Review of Poems (1807). Satirist, 1 (November), 188-91.
Wordsworth presumptuously proposed a new system of poetry
in the Preface to Lyrical Ballads, but when he forgot his
system he displayed genuine talent. In Poems (1807), however, he writes egotistical, poorly rhymed nursery poems.

5   [BYRON, LORD]. Review of Poems (1807). Monthly Literary
Recreations, 3 (July), 65-66.
Lyrical Ballads received deserving applause. Though of
less merit, Poems (1807) contains poems of natural elegance.
Wordsworth ceases to please when he abandons his mind to
commonplace ideas, expressed in puerile language, as in the
"Moods of My Own Mind."

6   EVANS, JOHN. Note, in The Parnassian Garland; or, Beauties of
Modern Poetry. . . . Edited by John Evans. London:
Cundee, p. 80.
Commends the simplicity of the subject of "Song for the
Wandering Jew."

7   [JEFFREY, FRANCIS]. Review of Poems (1807). Edinburgh Review,
11 (October), 214-31.
The Lake School is dangerous because its bad taste is
combined with genius. Lyrical Ballads was, in spite of its
occasional vulgarity, popular; Poems (1807), however, is
marked more strongly by Wordsworth's particularities, his
denial of the pleasure that arises from the propriety and

1807

associations of poetic diction and his connecting of lofty
conceptions with objects his readers will think low, silly,
or uninteresting. Wordsworth does write well when he
abandons his system, especially in his sonnets.

1808 A BOOKS - NONE

1808 B SHORTER WRITINGS

1   [AIKIN, LUCY]. Review of Poems (1807). Annual Review . . .
    for 1807, 6:521-29.
         Wordsworth's argument in the Preface to Lyrical Ballads
    in favor of meter could equally support the use of poetic
    diction; his definition of the poet ignores the inventive
    faculty that gives rise to good poetic diction. Judged by
    his own theories, the poems (e.g., "Fidelity") are failures.
    The sonnets, though stiff, are commendable. Wordsworth's
    mistaken theories arise from his solitary life.
    Attribution: John O. Hayden, The Romantic Reviewers 1802-
    1824 (Chicago: Univ. of Chicago Press, 1968), p. 297.

2   ANON. Review of Poems (1807). Cabinet, 3 (April), 249-52.
         Wordsworth had nearly established a theory of poetic
    simplicity in Lyrical Ballads; but through lack of taste he
    has now degenerated to writing contemptible puerilities.

3   ANON. "Domestic Literature of the Year 1807." New Annual
    Register . . . For the Year 1807, 28:[321]-[79] ([378]).
         Poems (1807) is marked by Wordsworth's "common ease and
    simplicity."

4   [DU BOIS, EDWARD] **. "Simplicity." Monthly Mirror, NS 3
    (April), 326-27.
         Includes "Fair women win the hearts of men" (poem), a
    parody of "Foresight." Attribution: D. B. Green, "Words-
    worth and Edward Du Bois," Philological Quarterly, 33
    (1954), 436.

5   [JEFFREY, FRANCIS]. Review of Crabbe's Poems. Edinburgh
    Review, 12 (April), 131-51 (132-37).
         Crabbe's characters are taken from common observation;
    Wordsworth's (e.g., in "The Thorn") are "aberrations from
    ordinary nature." Reprinted with minor addition in
    1844.B24.

6   [MANT, RICHARD]. The Simpliciad; a Satirico-Didactic Poem:
    Containing Hints for the Scholars of the New School. . . .
    London: Stockdale, passim.

Ridicules Wordsworth's writing of low and ordinary subjects in the lisping accents of the nursery. Attribution:
Bodleian catalogue.

7   [MONTGOMERY, JAMES]. Review of Poems (1807). Eclectic
     Review, 4 (January), 35-43.
         In Lyrical Ballads Wordsworth was a bold and fortunate
     innovator; though he went too far in rejecting, in the
     Preface, all embellished diction, in the poems themselves
     he rose above his theory. He has taught us new sympathies.
     The blank verse was the glory of Lyrical Ballads; in Poems
     (1807) Wordsworth gives but trifles. The sonnets are often
     obscure and heavy; "Ode: Intimations of Immortality" re-
     gretfully preaches pre-existence. Wordsworth's talent is
     personal description (e.g., in "Resolution and Independ-
     ence"). Attribution: John O. Hayden, The Romantic Review-
     ers 1802-1824 (Chicago: Univ. of Chicago Press, 1968),
     p. 297.

8   R.[OBINSON], H.[ENRY] C.[RABB]. "Remarks on the Genius and
     Writings of Herder." Monthly Repository, 3 (April),
     173-79 (177).
         Reports Herder's admiration of Lyrical Ballads.

1809 A   BOOKS - NONE

1809 B   SHORTER WRITINGS

1   ANON. Review of The Simpliciad. British Critic, 33
     (February), 180-81 (180).
         Wordsworth carries his pursuit of simplicity too far.

2   ANON. Review of The Simpliciad. Eclectic Review, 5
     (February), 192-93.
         Poems (1807) "may be regarded as the suicide of the
     'new school.'"

3   ANON. Review of Poems (1807). British Critic, 33 (March),
     298-99.
         Except in "Character of the Happy Warrior," Wordsworth
     expresses flimsy, puerile thoughts in feeble, halting
     verse.

4   ANON. "Preface." British Critic, 33 (January-June), iii-xix
     (xvii).
         Wordsworth "is often too simply simple" in Poems (1807).

1809

5   ANON. Review of Concerning . . . the Convention of Cintra.
     British Critic, 34 (September), 305-306.
         Though Wordsworth pushes some of his arguments and
     principles to extremes, his enthusiasm in the cause of an
     oppressed people is praiseworthy.

6   [BYRON, LORD]. English Bards, and Scotch Reviewers: A Satire
     (poem). London: Cawthorn [1809], pp. 11-13, 49.
         Satirizes "The simple Wordsworth," who proves "That
     prose is verse" and writes poems such as "The Idiot Boy."

7   [COLERIDGE, SAMUEL TAYLOR]. Introductory Essay. Friend,
        no. 1 (1 June), pp. 2-13 (13).
         Praises "one" (presumably Wordsworth) as a poet. Re-
     printed in The Friend (1812).

8   [COLERIDGE, SAMUEL TAYLOR]. "To My Readers." Friend, no. 2
        (8 June), pp. 17-32 (20).
         Notes his attachment to Wordsworth, "a superior mind."
     Reprinted in The Friend (1812).

9   [COLERIDGE, SAMUEL TAYLOR]. "On the Communication of Truth
        and the Rightful Liberty of the Press in Connection with
        It." Friend, no. 3 (10 August), pp. 33-48 (37).
         Praises Wordsworth's thought and feeling in "My heart
     leaps up when I behold." Reprinted in The Friend (1812)
     and 1818.B6.

10   [COLERIDGE, SAMUEL TAYLOR]. "Essay IV: On the Principles of
        Political Philosophy." Friend, no. 7 (28 September),
        pp. 98-112 (111-12).
         Commends Concerning . . . the Convention of Cintra.
     Reprinted in The Friend (1812) and 1818.B6.

11   [COLERIDGE, SAMUEL TAYLOR]. Note, "Satyrane's Letters:
        Letter III" (signed "Satyrane"). Friend, no. 18
        (21 December), pp. 273, 276-88 (278-88).
         Praises "Thought of a Briton on the Subjugation of
     Switzerland." Reprinted in The Friend (1812) (273). Re-
     counts his and Wordsworth's visits with Klopstock, including
     Wordsworth's conversation on Shakespeare, eighteenth-
     century poets, and rhyme. Reprinted in The Friend (1812)
     and 1817.B5 (278-88).

12   [COLERIDGE, SAMUEL TAYLOR]. Untitled Essay, "Christmas Out of
        Doors." Friend, no. 19 (28 December), pp. 291-300 (299),
        301-304 (303).

Praises Wordsworth's reply to Mathetes. Reprinted in
The Friend (1812) (299). Gives passage praising The Prelude from "To William Wordsworth: Composed on the Night
after his recitation of a Poem on the Growth of an Individual Mind" (poem) (see 1817.B6). Reprinted in The Friend
(1812) and 1818.B6 (303).

13 [JEFFREY, FRANCIS]. Review of Cromek's Reliques of Robert
Burns. Edinburgh Review, 13 (January), 249-76 (276).
Burns portrays characters with true simplicity; Wordsworth describes "fantastical personages" in a "nurserymaid's
vocabulary." Reprinted in 1844.B24.

14 [MANNERS, GEORGE]. "The Bards of the Lake." Satirist, 5
(December), 548-56 (548-50).
Includes burlesque, "The Hermit and the Snail" (poem).
Attribution: P. M. Zall, "Sam Spitfire; or, Coleridge in
The Satirist," Bulletin of The New York Public Library, 71
(1967), 240.

15 MATHETES. See 1809.B19.

16 [MONTGOMERY, JAMES]. Review of Concerning . . . the Convention
of Cintra. Eclectic Review, 5 (August), 744-50.
Wordsworth's language is at once splendid and obscure,
the sentiments too dark and too bright; but the spirit of
philanthropy and patriotism pervades the pamphlet. Wordsworth has formed his opinions removed from the practical
world. His arguments on intellectual courage are the best
in the work. Attribution: John O. Hayden, The Romantic
Reviewers 1802-1824 (Chicago: Univ. of Chicago Press,
1968), p. 267.

17 ROBINSON, H.[ENRY] C.[RABB]. Review of Concerning . . . the
Convention of Cintra. London Review, 2 (November), 231-75.
Concerning . . . the Convention of Cintra is "an ethic
essay on a political subject" in which moral principles are
applied to the conduct of nations. Wordsworth's originality
includes his combining love of liberty, patriotism, and
contempt towards Napoleon, and his regarding of the French
aggression as insult rather than injury. Wordsworth lacks
Burke's ability in irony and playfulness; he is more intense, self-centered, and careless of his audience.

18 SATYRANE. See 1809.B11.

19 [WILSON, JOHN and ALEXANDER BLAIR] MATHETES. Letter to the
Editor. Friend, no. 17 (14 December), pp. 257-68 (266-67).

1809

Many have benefited from Wordsworth's teaching. Reprinted in The Friend (1812) and 1818.B6.

1810 A BOOKS - NONE

1810 B SHORTER WRITINGS

1   [COLERIDGE, SAMUEL TAYLOR]. "Sketches and Fragments of the
        Life and Character of the late Admiral Sir Alexander Ball."
        Friend, no. 21 (25 January), pp. 340-50 (343, 346).
            Records Ball's appreciation of the psychological insight
        of Peter Bell. Reprinted in The Friend (1812) and, with
        additions, in 1818.B6.

2   [COLERIDGE, SAMUEL TAYLOR]. "On the Law of Nations." Friend,
        no. 24 (15 February 1809 [misprint for 1810]), pp. 385-400
        (393).
            Praises Wordsworth's characterization of men in
        "Michael." Reprinted in The Friend (1812) and 1818.B6.

3   [SCOTT, SIR WALTER]. "Of the Living Poets of Great Britain."
        Edinburgh Annual Register, for 1808, 1-2:417-43 (419,
        426-30).
            Wordsworth's seclusion betrays him into focusing on the
        particular rather than the general in nature and into
        giving too much importance to his own peculiar observations.
        Though he stoops to vulgar language, he is to be praised
        for "interesting the feelings." Attribution: The Letters
        of Sir Walter Scott 1808-1811, edited by H. J. C. Grierson
        (London: Constable, 1932), p. 283.

1811 A BOOKS - NONE

1811 B SHORTER WRITINGS

1   ANON. Review of Poems (1807). Poetical Register . . . for
        1806-1807, 6:540-41.
            Wordsworth sacrifices his genius to his system, and so
        often writes "drivelling nonsense."

2   EXPLORATOR. "Cobbett and Wordsworth." Satirist, 8 (June),
        486-88.
            Includes burlesque, "Lines originally intended to have
        been inserted in the last Edition of Wordsworth's Poems."

3   [HUNT, LEIGH] ☞ . "The Feast of the Poets" (poem).
     Reflector, no. 4, pp. 313-23 (319).
        Wordsworth's second childhood followed "close on the
     first." Revised in 1814.B9.

4   [JEFFREY, FRANCIS]. Review of The Dramatic Works of John
     Ford. Edinburgh Review, 18 (August), 275-304 (283).
        Wordsworth's style is imitative, hence artificial; yet
     he is a poet of feeling and imagination. Reprinted in
     1844.B24.

5   SEWARD, ANNA. Letters of Anna Seward: Written between the
     Years 1784 and 1807. 6 vols. Edinburgh: Constable;
     London: Longman, Miller, and Murray, VI:258-61, 366-67.
        Wordsworth, often meanly familiar, turgid, and obscure,
     extends the use of common language too far. He is an
     "egotistic manufacturer of metaphysic importance upon
     trivial themes" in poems like "I wandered lonely as a
     cloud," though when he writes "naturally" in Poems (1807)
     he writes well.

6   [TALFOURD, THOMAS NOON]. "Notes," in Poems, on Various
     Subjects. . . . London: Longman; Reading: Rusher,
     pp. 223-44 (229-30).
        Criticizes Wordsworth's sophistry in discussing Dr.
     Bell's plan of education. Attribution: British Museum
     catalogue.

1812 A BOOKS - NONE

1812 B SHORTER WRITINGS

1   ANON. Review of Wilson's The Isle of Palms. Glasgow Magazine,
     3 (February), 131-41 (131).
        Wordsworth, a poet of simplicity, works to overturn the
     established rules of poetry.

2   ANON. "The Story of Doctor Pill and Gaffer Quake, after the
     most approved modern Style, And containing Words worth
     imitation." Satirist, 10 (May), 354-58.
        Parody of "Goody Blake and Harry Gill."

3   ANON. "The Rejected Bards--Genus Irritabilé" (poem).
     Satirist, 11 (November), 375-83 (377, 382).
        Mocks Wordsworth's "baby lispings."

1812

4   J., M. Review of Wilson's The Isle of Palms. Glasgow
     Magazine, 3 (May), 382-90 (387, 389-90).
          One can praise pieces like "The Old Cumberland Beggar"
     while admitting Wordsworth descends too low in "Goody Blake
     and Harry Gill."

5   [JEFFREY, FRANCIS]. Review of Wilson's The Isle of Palms.
     Edinburgh Review, 19 (February), 373-88 (373-76).
          Criticizes Wordsworth's choice of ordinary subjects, for
     which most people cannot feel the emotion he does.

6   [JEFFREY, FRANCIS]. Review of Rejected Addresses. Edinburgh
     Review, 20 (November), 434-51 (434, 438).
          The author imitates Wordsworth's "maukish affectations
     of childish simplicity and nursery stammering." Reprinted
     in 1844.B24.

7   [SMITH, JAMES]. "The Baby's Debut" (poem), in Rejected
     Addresses: or The New Theatrum Poetarum. [By James and
     Horace Smith.] London: Miller, pp. 5-10.
          A burlesque, signed "W. W."

8   WILSON, JOHN. "The Angler's Tent" (poem), in The Isle of
     Palms, and Other Poems. London: Longman; Edinburgh:
     Ballantyne; Glasgow: Smith, pp. 181-219.
          Records a fishing expedition with Wordsworth, including
     the group's appreciation of nature; praises Wordsworth's
     singing of earth's "unseen grandeur."

1813 A BOOKS - NONE

1813 B SHORTER WRITINGS

1   [AGG, JOHN] HUMPHREY HEDGEHOG. "Specimen the Fourth: Written
     During a Tour" (poem), in Rejected Odes; or Poetical Hops,
     Steps, and Jumps of a Dozen Popular Bards, for the Obtain-
     ment of the Situation of Poet Laureat. London: Johnson,
     pp. 23-31.
          Parody of "Alice Fell." Attribution: British Museum
     catalogue.

2   ANON. "British Mecaenases, and Fashionable Writers." Town
     Talk; or, Living Manners, 4 (May), 257-62 (258-59).
          Wordsworth, a poetic success, receives distinctions
     while surfeiting the public with "unintelligible balder-
     dash."

14

3 ANON. "Applications for the Laureatship." Satirist, 13
(September), 241-56 (247-48).
Parodies, in a mock letter to the Lord Chamberlain
signed "W. Wordsworth."

4 [BOWRING, JOHN]. "On Mr. Wordsworth's Appointment to the
Office of Stamp Distributor for the County of Westmoreland"
(poem). Examiner, no. 278 (25 April), p. 265.
Can Wordsworth "eat Corruption's bread, / And still con-
tinue unpolluted"? Reprinted from the Morning Chronicle of
20 April. Attribution: Bowring, in 1877.B11; tentatively
attributed to Hazlitt by John Kinnaird, "Hazlitt as Poet:
The Probable Authorship of Some Anonymous Verses on Wordsworth's Appointment as Stamp-Distributor," Studies in
Romanticism, 12 (1973), 426-35.

5 HEDGEHOG, HUMPHREY. See 1813.B1.

6 Q., Q. and W. W. See 1813.B7.

7 [REYNOLDS, JOHN HAMILTON] Q. Q. and W. W., eds. Leaves of
Laurel; or New Probationary Odes, for The Vacant Laureat-
ship. London: Becket and Porter, pp. 13-15.
Includes burlesque, "Hush a Bye! Baby Bye!" (poem),
signed "W. W." Attribution: Dictionary of Anonymous and
Pseudonymous Literature (Samuel Halkett and John Laing),
new ed., 9 vols. (Edinburgh: Oliver and Boyd, 1926-62),
IX:169.

1814 A BOOKS - NONE

1814 B SHORTER WRITINGS

1 ANON. Review of Hunt's The Feast of the Poets. Critical
Review, 4th ser., 5 (March), 293-303 (302-303).
Even to delineate primitive feelings, as Wordsworth does,
a poet should not withdraw from the bustle of the world.

2 ANON. Review of The Excursion. New Monthly Magazine, 2
(September), 157.
The poem is ponderous, overly metaphysical, and written
in hobbling verse.

3 ANON. "Mr. Wordsworth." Variety, no. 1 (10 September),
pp. 5-6.
In The Excursion Wordsworth perseveres in his extraordinary style of composition.

1814

4   ANON. Modern Parnassus; or, the New Art of Poetry, A Poem,
     Designed to Supersede the Rules of Aristotle, Horace,
     Longinus, Vida, Boileau, and Pope. London: Johnson,
     especially pp. viii-ix, xiii, 46-52.
          Satirizes Wordsworth's poetry of the low and simple.

5   ANON. Sortes Horatianae: A Poetical Review of Poetical
     Talent. London: Hamilton, pp. 12, 86-94.
          Mocks Wordsworth as a writer of simplistic lullabies.

6   [COLERIDGE, JOHN TAYLOR]. Review of Coleridge's Remorse.
     Quarterly Review, 11 (April), 177-90 (177-83).
          The Lake Poets force the reader to exercise his own men-
     tal powers. Though they minutely analyze slight, transient
     emotions not shared by most readers and give a moral anima-
     tion to nature, they excel in writing of domestic virtues,
     women, and love purified from gross passion. Attribution:
     John O. Hayden, The Romantic Reviewers 1802-1824 (Chicago:
     Univ. of Chicago Press, 1968), p. 278.

7   H.[AZLITT], W.[ILLIAM]. "Character of Mr. Wordsworth's New
     Poem, The Excursion." Examiner, no. 347 (21 August),
     pp. 541-42; no. 348 (28 August), pp. 555-58; no. 353
     (2 October), pp. 636-38.
          If Wordsworth's choice of materials had been equal to his
     genius and more readily communicable, The Excursion would
     seem less a half-finished structure. The poem resembles
     the majestic countryside in which the scene is laid. Words-
     worth's mind is "coeval with the primary forms of things."
     "His thoughts are his real subject": "an intense intellec-
     tual egotism swallows up every thing." The dialogues are
     all spoken by one character (541-42). The narratives and
     descriptions hinder the effect of Wordsworth's reflections.
     His comments on Voltaire evidence a narrow spirit; his op-
     timism that one day virtue will totally triumph is un-
     founded. He correctly points out the origins of Greek myth
     and the egotism of philosophical pursuits (555-58). Though
     he possesses the highest powers of feeling, he is deficient
     in fanciful invention to embody them. His poems resemble
     Rembrandt's landscapes in deriving effects from barest ma-
     terials. Wordsworth ignores the facts of country life when
     he makes rustics the interpreters of his sentiments (636-38).
     Revised in 1817.B12.

8   [HUNT, LEIGH] 👉. "Note upon Note." Examiner, no. 346
     (14 August), pp. 525-26 (525).
          Wordsworth is the "greatest poet of the present time."

9   [HUNT, LEIGH]. "Preface," "The Feast of the Poets" (poem),
    "Notes on the Feast of the Poets," in The Feast of the
    Poets, with Notes, and Other Pieces in Verse. By the
    Editor of the Examiner. London: Cawthorn, pp. ix-xiv (x),
    1-21 (12-14), 23-133 (77-109, 125).
        Repents his earlier attack on Wordsworth (x). Revised
    from 1811.B3. Wordsworth changed "his harp for a whistle,"
    models his verse on children's ballads. Revised in
    1815.B22 (12-14). Wordsworth's governmental office ties up
    his independence. He has abused his genius. His practice
    does not live up to his theories in the Preface to Lyrical
    Ballads: he gives us affectation for nature. Feeling
    giving importance to action has dangerous consequences. He
    denies the possibility of artful style. Revised in
    1815.B22 (77-109, 125).

10 [JEFFREY, FRANCIS]. Review of The Excursion. Edinburgh
    Review, 24 (November), 1-30.
        The case of Wordsworth is now hopeless; habits of seclu-
    sion and ambition of originality can alone account for the
    combination in Wordsworth of bad taste and genius. The Ex-
    cursion depends for its success on Wordsworth's system; it
    is a long, wordy, obscure, tediously minute "tissue of moral
    and devotional ravings," devoid of incident, in which Words-
    worth indecorously makes a pedlar the spokesman of virtue.
    The doctrine Wordsworth preaches is but the familiar one of
    a belief in a beneficent Being pervading the universe and
    supporting man in affliction. Wordsworth does succeed,
    however, in his forceful moral declarations, pathetic nar-
    ratives, perception of the springs of emotion, energetic
    description, and elegant single images. He gives an im-
    pressive appeal on the injury done by industrialism and on
    the need for education among the lower orders. Reprinted
    with omissions and an added note in 1844.B24.

11 [LAMB, CHARLES and WILLIAM GIFFORD]. Review of The Excursion.
    Quarterly Review, 12 (October), 100-11.
        The charm of the poem arises from the mixture of conver-
    sation and description, tale and setting. Nature, to Words-
    worth, presents not symbols but insights into man's inner
    life. Wordsworth's creed resembles "an expanded and gener-
    ous Quakerism." The tale of Margaret might have been post-
    poned until the reader had been better prepared for Words-
    worth's views. The moral argument of Book IV is excellent;
    the anecdote of the Jacobite and Hanoverian exhibits a
    "thoughtful playfulness" reminiscent of Cowper. Wordsworth
    is not popular because his genius is bold and original.
    The Excursion contains few of the imperfections that

1814

characterize Wordsworth's shorter poems; if one objects to
the lowness of the Pedlar, one can substitute "Palmer" or
"Pilgrim."

12 O'DONOVAN, P. M. See 1814.B13.

13 [PEACOCK, THOMAS LOVE] P. M. O'DONOVAN. Sir Proteus: A
Satirical Ballad. London: Hookham, passim.
A burlesque.

14 STRADA. "Portraits of Authors: No VII: Mr. Wordsworth."
Champion, no. 73 (29 May), pp. 174-75.
Despite occasional babyisms, Wordsworth's profound
thought, intense feeling, and sublime moral sense elevate
him above Coleridge and Southey. His best poems contradict
his poetic theory; common incidents do not suggest to him
common sentiments or language.

1815 A BOOKS - NONE

1815 B SHORTER WRITINGS

1 [ALLEN, WILLIAM]. Review of The Excursion. Philanthropist,
5:342-63.
Wordsworth aims at the moral improvement of his readers.
His choice of a pedlar as philosophical spokesman is proper.
The tales and descriptions in the poem are characterized by
simplicity, pathos, and truth. Attribution: Donald H.
Reiman, ed., The Romantics Reviewed, 3 parts (New York and
London: Garland, 1972), Part A, p. 802.

2 ANON. Review of The Excursion. Monthly Magazine, 38 (Suppl.,
30 January), 638-49.
Despite his solemnity, mysticism, and mistaken politics,
Wordsworth has written an admirable poem.

3 ANON. "Spoils of Literature." Scourge, 9 (March), 220-25.
Attacks Wordsworth's greed in publishing The Excursion
in an expensive quarto volume.

4 ANON. Review of The Excursion. British Critic, NS 3 (May),
449-67.
Wordsworth's poetry is "metaphysical," though it has only
superficial analogues with Donne's. It is based on the
principle, argued by Christian writers and previous poets,
that descriptive verse should illustrate how all sensuous
impressions are capable of spiritual associations. The only

faults in The Excursion arise from Wordsworth's being too
intent on this principle to see that his associations are
often too personal. The poem encourages men to progress
from meditation to active virtue.

5   ANON. Review of The Excursion. La Belle Assemblée, NS 11
     (May), 224–25.
        The sentiments and descriptions in The Excursion are
     skillfully done.

6   ANON. Review of The White Doe of Rylstone. Theatrical
     Inquisitor, 6 (June), 445–50.
        Wordsworth's poems are characterized by a perverseness
     of taste, sickliness of sentiment, affectation of excessive
     feeling, and appearance of meaning, but also by high feeling
     and knowledge of the human heart. In The White Doe of
     Rylstone the language is too exquisite for the subject.

7   ANON. Review of Byron's Hebrew Melodies. New Universal
     Magazine, 3 (July), 37–38 (38).
        "The insipid puerilities of Wordsworth" are "occasionally
     illuminated by some flashes of genius."

8   ANON. Review of The White Doe of Rylstone. British Lady's
     Magazine, 2 (July), 33–37.
        The name of no living poet is better known than Words-
     worth's; but his works, if read, are misunderstood. His
     system of poetry is not peculiar to him; rather, he has re-
     turned to the principles of the greatest poetry of the past.
     The White Doe of Rylstone should help his popularity.

9   ANON. Review of The White Doe of Rylstone. La Belle
     Assemblée, NS 12 (July), 31–33.
        A "pleasing poem."

10   ANON. Review of The White Doe of Rylstone. New Monthly
     Magazine, 3 (July), 546.
        The volume is costly.

11   ANON. Review of Poems (1815), The Excursion, and The White
     Doe of Rylstone. Augustan Review, 1 (August), 343–56.
        Although Wordsworth's language is generally prosaic, his
     simplicity of style does have a happy effect in his poems
     on childhood and in The White Doe of Rylstone. The Excur-
     sion would have been improved by the use of rhyme and a
     less ambitious design; it illustrates Wordsworth's lack of
     classic taste, though its moral tendency is admirable. If
     he would abandon meter, Wordsworth could become a respec-
     table essayist.

1815

12   ANON. Review of The Excursion. British Review, 6 (August),
      50-64.
          Wordsworth's lack of popularity stems from readers' re-
      fusing to approach his poems in his own frame of mind.
      More than one style of poetry should be tolerated. In The
      Excursion Wordsworth's elevated thoughts and power to make
      characters and scenes appear real are praiseworthy; the
      role of the pedlar can be justified, but the negative view
      of the French Revolution is one-sided.

13   ANON. Review of Poems (1815). Monthly Review, NS 78
      (November), 225-34.
          Wordsworth's poetical character is marked by a strong
      admiration of the beauties of nature, growing out of a re-
      clusive life. Wordsworth wastes his genius. In the arro-
      gant Essay (1815) and Preface (1815), with its "pompous
      classification of trifles," he gives fresh evidence that
      he wishes to found a poetic system. His pompous prose
      contrasts markedly with the frolicsome language of his
      poems, poems characterized by silliness of system, want of
      harmony, and vacancy of thought.

14   ANON. Review of The White Doe of Rylstone. British Review,
      6 (November), 370-77.
          Wordsworth must overcome the prejudices of readers, es-
      pecially when he writes with a simplicity too extreme. The
      White Doe of Rylstone contains examples of natural and pa-
      thetic narration and of Wordsworth's peculiar power of con-
      veying an impression of sadness. The title of "The Force
      of Prayer" is misleading.

15   ANON. Review of The White Doe of Rylstone. Monthly Review,
      NS 78 (November), 235-38.
          The poem contains Wordsworth's usual defects. The de-
      picting of human affairs is inferior to the describing of
      the doe.

16   ANON. Review of The White Doe of Rylstone. Gentleman's
      Magazine, 85-2 (December), 524-25.
          In the poem Wordsworth artlessly displays richness of
      fancy and tenderness of feeling; he cannot in this instance
      be censured for homeliness.

17   C. "Modern Poets.--No. III: Wordsworth." Scourge, 10
      (October), 266-75.
          Wordsworth perversely ignores man's cultural advances
      and chooses to write primitively. Yet his contemplating of
      the ideal and natural worlds, his appeal to the reader's

20

fancy, and his linking of the earthly with the immortal,
deserve praise.

18 [HAZLITT, WILLIAM]. "Theatrical Examiner." Examiner, no. 389
(11 June), pp. 381-82 (382).
Mocks Wordsworth's praise of the king in "November,
1813." Reprinted with slight omissions as "Comus" in A View
of the English Stage (1818).

19 H.[AZLITT], W.[ILLIAM]. "The Round Table." Examiner, no. 399
(20 August), pp. 541-42 (542).
Wordsworth's blank verse is "mere lumbering prose." Reprinted as "On Milton's Versification" in 1817.B12.

20 [HAZLITT, WILLIAM] S. T. "The Round Table." Examiner,
no. 400 (27 August), pp. 554-56 (556).
Attacks Wordsworth's quarrel with the gypsies in "Gipsies." Reprinted as "On Manner" in 1817.B12.

21 [HAZLITT,] W.[ILLIAM]. "The Round Table" ["Parallel Passages
in Various Poets"]. Examiner, no. 417 (24 December),
825-27 (826-27).
Wordsworth's style was anticipated by Wither.

22 HUNT, LEIGH. "Preface to the Second Edition," "The Feast of
the Poets" (poem), "Notes on the Feast of the Poets," in
The Feast of the Poets, with Other Pieces in Verse. Second
edition, amended and enlarged. London: Gale and Fenner,
pp. vii-x (ix-x), 1-25 (13-18, 21), 27-131 (77-111, 123).
Wordsworth's beauties are more noteworthy than his defects, which result from theory rather than incapacity
(ix-x). Revised from 1814.B9. Wordsworth sings exquisitely, despite imperfections, of nature's power to restore our
hearts. Revised in 1832.B19 (13-18, 21). Revised from
1814.B9. Wordsworth claims his governmental office does not
tie up his independence, has retracted his former thoughts
on meter. The Excursion "is a succession of noble reveries"
(77-111, 123).

23 [JEFFREY, FRANCIS]. Review of The White Doe of Rylstone.
Edinburgh Review, 25 (October), 355-63.
In the poem, which contains all of his faults and none
of his beauties, Wordsworth unnaturally combines mystical
wordiness with the bad features of ancient ballads. He re-
gretfully focuses on the doe rather than on the tragic interest in Francis. Reprinted in 1844.B24.

1815

24   [LYALL, WILLIAM ROWE]. Review of Poems (1815) and The White
     Doe of Rylstone. Quarterly Review, 14 (October), 201-25.
         Wordsworth lacks moderation in his attacks on his critics
     in Essay (1815). The question is not whether, as Wordsworth
     argues in the Preface to Lyrical Ballads, the language and
     subjects of low life are more instructive, but whether they
     are more pleasing and are capable of being understood by
     the reader. Wordsworth does not choose subjects of general
     interest but writes of his own feelings about objects inci-
     dental to his own particular and uncommon way of life. The
     White Doe of Rylstone exhibits tenderness and a simplicity
     that is pleasing except when it is artificial or lacks
     precision.

25   [MERIVALE, JOHN HERMAN]. Review of The Excursion. Monthly
     Review, NS 76 (February), 123-36.
         Wordsworth has now made a full exposition of his creed,
     the commonplace one that a soul animates all nature. That
     creed spoils the otherwise fine descriptive passages for
     readers who are not predisposed to accept it. Though the
     pedlar's undignified station in life is not objectionable,
     his unnatural language is. The Excursion is Wordsworth's
     smaller poems, less their infantine simplicity, writ large.
     His defects stem from an overly enthusiastic pursuit of his
     excellencies: his powerful imagination and sensibility,
     and his devotion to the beautiful works of nature. He has
     affinities with Crabbe, Cowper, and Milton.

26   [MONTGOMERY, JAMES]. Review of The Excursion. Eclectic
     Review, NS 3 (January), 13-39.
         Though fallen into sin, man can still glimpse forms of
     grace in the universe; Wordsworth points out even the most
     unexpected of these forms, though it is sometimes difficult
     to distinguish the reverence he pays them from what should
     be due to God alone. In The Excursion his system is splen-
     didly, if not clearly and fully, unfolded: by conversing
     with the soul of the natural world, man becomes regenerate;
     but Wordsworth fails to stress sufficiently the necessity
     of Christ's sacrifice to man's redemption. He subdues the
     most untractable thoughts, in an intellectual language op-
     posed to his theories in the Preface to Lyrical Ballads.
     He succeeds in his daring experiment of making a pedlar his
     hero; the Wanderer is as ideal as Homer's Achilles. Words-
     worth, in contrast to Crabbe and Cowper, casts the hue of
     thought over his delineations of the poor. Attribution:
     John O. Hayden, The Romantic Reviewers 1802-1824 (Chicago:
     Univ. of Chicago Press, 1968), p. 297.

27 R.[EYNOLDS, JOHN HAMILTON]. "Mr. Wordsworth's Poetry."
    Champion, no. 153 (9 December), p. 398.
        Wordsworth calls forth "retired thoughts and fleeting
    recollections" from those like himself. He observes nature
    closely. The Excursion is above both the pockets and under-
    standings of common readers.

28 S*. "Modern Poetry." Champion, no. 149 (12 November),
    pp. 366-67 (366).
        Wordsworth's poems are characterized by elevated
    thoughts, the union of "energy, sanctity, and beauty of
    poetical feeling."

29 [SCOTT, JOHN]. "Mr. Wordsworth's Poems." Champion, no. 129
    (25 June), pp. 205-206.
        The narration in The White Doe of Rylstone is not suc-
    cessful; the most beautiful passages center around the doe.
    Wordsworth's fame rests on his early poetry, which, con-
    trary to the critic of the Edinburgh Review, does contain
    elegant diction. He should, however, exercise a stricter
    principle of selection, recognizing he cannot successfully
    convey all that he feels. Attribution: John O. Hayden,
    The Romantic Reviewers 1802-1824 (Chicago: Univ. of
    Chicago Press, 1968), p. 297.

30 T., S. See 1815.B20.

31 TALFOURD, T.[HOMAS] N.[OON]. "An Attempt to Estimate the
    Poetical Talent of the Present Age. . . ." Pamphleteer, 5,
    no. 10, 413-71 (435, 462-67).
        Wordsworth, a deep thinker, suffers critical abuse be-
    cause of his indifference to applause, his apparently
    trifling effusions, and his personal themes.

1816 A BOOKS - NONE

1816 B SHORTER WRITINGS

 1 AMATEUR, AN. See 1816.B20.

 2 ANON. Review of Cowper's Poems. Monthly Repository, 11
    (March), 161-66 (161).
        The language of the lower classes is not suitable for
    poetry.

 3 ANON. Review of The White Doe of Rylstone. European
    Magazine, 69 (March), 237-39.
        The poem is a nobly pathetic tale, in the manner of
    Scott.

 4 ANON. Review of A Letter to A Friend of Robert Burns.
    Monthly Review, NS 80 (June), 221-22.
        Agrees with Wordsworth about the revealing of biographi-
    cal information.

1816

5   ANON.   Review of A Letter to A Friend of Robert Burns.
      Critical Review, 5th ser., 4 (July), 51-58.
            Wordsworth's remarks on biography are just; his vindi-
      cation of Burns is understandable when one considers the
      resemblance between the two poets' minds and styles.

6   ANON.   Review of Coleridge's Christabel. Augustan Review, 3
      (July), 14-24 (14-18).
            Though the principles of the Lake School are enchanting,
      Wordsworth has erred in taking the vulgarisms of dalesmen
      for poetry.

7   ANON.   Review of Thanksgiving Ode. British Critic, NS 6
      (September), 313-15.
            The poems exhibit admirable piety and fewer of Words-
      worth's former peculiarities of expression.

8   ANON.   "Wordsworth's White Doe, of Bolton Priory." Amusing
      Chronicle, 1 (3 October), 44-46; (10 October), 54-56;
      (17 October), 67-69.
            Wordsworth "satisfactorily explains" why the doe visits
      the churchyard.

9   ANON.   Review of Byron's Childe Harold's Pilgrimage: Canto
      the Third. Critical Review, 5th ser., 4 (November),
      495-506 (505).
            Points out Byron's plagiarism from "Tintern Abbey."

10   ANON.   Review of Taylor's Essays in Rhyme. Augustan Review,
      3 (November), 459-73 (473).
            Talent cannot render mean and ludicrous things poetical.

11   ANON.   Review of Thanksgiving Ode. Dublin Examiner, 2
      (November), 18-25.
            Finds fault with the lowness of Wordsworth's subjects
      and, in Thanksgiving Ode, with his optimistic prophecies
      and the absence of rapid narration that characterizes
      Scott's poems.

12   ANON.   Review of The Poetic Mirror. Critical Review, 5th ser.,
      4 (November), 456-71 (466-68).
            Rejoices in the improved reputation of Wordsworth, a
      poet of thought as opposed to hollow eloquence.

13   ANON.   Review of Byron's Childe Harold's Pilgrimage: Canto
      the Third. Portfolio, no. 5 (30 November), pp. 97-102
      (102).
            Notes Byron's debt to Wordsworth's view of nature in
      "Tintern Abbey."

14   ANON. Review of Byron's The Prisoner of Chillon. Critical
      Review, 5th ser., 4 (December), 567-81 (567-69, 573, 576).
         Byron's conversion from misanthropy is due to Words-
      worth's poems, the reading of which expands one's faculties.
      In The Prisoner of Chillon Byron imitates Wordsworth's use
      of natural language and borrows a simile from "I wandered
      lonely as a cloud."

15   ANON. Review of The Poetic Mirror. Augustan Review, 3
      (December), 556-78 (566-71, 576).
         A "paltry ambition" led Wordsworth to found a sect based
      on "the happy imbecility and the quiet thoughtlessness of
      infantine simplicity." Wordsworth's system obscures his
      true pathos.

16   ANON. "Domestic Literature for the year 1815." New Annual
      Register . . . For the Year 1815, 36:[364]-[432] ([430]).
         The Excursion and The White Doe of Rylstone contain oc-
      casional veins of touching simplicity and tenderness im-
      bedded in rubbish.

17   [CONDER, JOSIAH]. Review of The White Doe of Rylstone.
      Eclectic Review, NS 5 (January), 33-45.
         Not all can converse with Wordsworth's mind and so sym-
      pathize fully with his poems. His poems, like Milton's,
      lack the universality of Scott's; they combine the sensi-
      bility of the metaphysical poets with minute observations
      of nature. In The White Doe of Rylstone Wordsworth should
      have better prepared the reader to receive the feeling of
      contemplative melancholy he conveys. The story, more suit-
      able for a ballad, has too few incidents. Attribution:
      John O. Hayden, The Romantic Reviewers 1802-1824 (Chicago:
      Univ. of Chicago Press, 1968), p. 297.

18   [CONDER, JOSIAH]. Review of Southey's The Poet's Pilgrimage
      to Waterloo and Thanksgiving Ode. Eclectic Review, NS 6
      (July), 1-18 (1-8).
         As opposed to Southey and Milton, Wordsworth is always
      metaphysical, losing himself in abstraction; only rarely do
      his poems come within the reach of ordinary readers. In
      Thanksgiving Ode his praise of England is too general to be
      correct; his praise of military virtues is execrable. The
      poem is desultory and irregular. Attribution: John O.
      Hayden, The Romantic Reviewers 1802-1824 (Chicago: Univ.
      of Chicago Press, 1968), p. 297.

19   D., S. N. See 1816.B43.

1816

20   [HAZLITT, WILLIAM] AN AMATEUR. "The Round Table." <u>Examiner</u>,
        no. 423 (4 February), pp. 77-78 (78).
           Wordsworth's praise of the king in "November, 1813"
        represents "literary prostitution." (Reference omitted
        when essay reprinted as "On Beauty" in <u>The Round Table</u>
        [1817].)

21   H.[AZLITT], W.[ILLIAM]. "The Round Table." <u>Examiner</u>, no. 428
        (10 March), pp. 157-59 (157).
           Notes that a certain "poetical enthusiast" (presumably
        Wordsworth) would have passed his life contemplating "his
        own idea, if he had not been disturbed in his reverie by
        the Edinburgh Reviewers." Reprinted as "The Same Subject
        ["On Pedantry"] Continued" in 1817.B12.

22   H.[AZLITT], W.[ILLIAM]. "The Round Table." <u>Examiner</u>, no. 433
        (14 April), pp. 237-38 (238).
           Wordsworth and Rousseau wrote about themselves, Words-
        worth unfortunately having to add imaginative color because
        he was writing in verse. Reprinted as "On the Character of
        Rousseau" in 1817.B12.

23   [HAZLITT, WILLIAM]. "Theatrical Examiner." <u>Examiner</u>, no. 436
        (5 May), p. 286.
           Wordsworth does not understand his sentiments on kings
        perishing in <u>The Excursion</u> (Book VII). Reprinted as "Mr.
        Kemble's Sir Giles Overreach" in <u>A View of the English</u>
        <u>Stage</u> (1818).

24   [HAZLITT, WILLIAM]. "The Round Table." <u>Examiner</u>, no. 441
        (9 June), pp. 361-63 (362).
           Criticizes Wordsworth as "an exciseman." (Reference
        omitted when essay reprinted as "On Good Nature" in <u>The</u>
        <u>Round Table</u> [1817].)

25   [HAZLITT, WILLIAM]. "Literary Notices, No. 9." <u>Examiner</u>,
        no. 452 (25 August), pp. 538-41 (540).
           Wordsworth should stick to his excise; "the world have
        had enough of his <u>simplicity</u> in poetry and politics."

26   [HAZLITT, WILLIAM]. "Literary Notices, No. 13." <u>Examiner</u>,
        no. 457 (29 September), pp. 616-18.
           <u>Concerning . . . the Convention of Cintra</u> is remarkable
        for "the profound egotism of the style."

27   [HAZLITT, WILLIAM]. "Literary Notices: No. 19: Illustrations
        of The Times Newspaper: On Modern Apostates." <u>Examiner</u>,
        no. 468 (15 December), pp. 785-87 (785, 787).

Remarks Wordsworth's political apostasy in "November, 1813." Reprinted with minor omission in Political Essays (1819).

28 [HAZLITT, WILLIAM]. "Literary Notices: No. 20: Illustrations of The Times Newspaper: On Modern Lawyers and Poets." Examiner, no. 469 (22 December), pp. 801-803 (803).
    Wordsworth's "lyrical poetry was a cant of humanity about the commonest people to level the great with the small; and his political poetry is a cant of loyalty to level Bonaparte with kings." "He sees nothing but himself and the universe." Reprinted in Political Essays (1819).

29 [HOGG, JAMES]. "The Stranger; Being A Further Portion of 'The Recluse,' A Poem," "Further Extract from 'The Recluse,' A Poem: The Flying Tailor," "Still Further Extract from 'The Recluse,' A Poem: James Rigg," in The Poetic Mirror, or The Living Bards of Britain. London: Longman; Edinburgh: Ballantyne, pp. 131-53, 155-70, 171-87.
    Parodies of The Excursion, announced as by "W. Wordsworth."

30 HORNE, THOMAS HARTWELL. The Lakes of Lancashire, Westmorland, and Cumberland. London: Cadell, and Davies, pp. 12, 27.
    Suggests Wordsworth, "the admired author of The Excursion," may have been picturing the church at Bowness in The Excursion (Book V).

31 [HUNT, LEIGH]. "Heaven Made a Party to Earthly Disputes--Mr. Wordsworth's Sonnets on Waterloo." Examiner, no. 425 (18 February), pp. 97-99.
    Criticizes Wordsworth's political views in "Occasioned by the Battle of Waterloo: February, 1816" ("Intrepid sons of Albion! not by you"); "Occasioned by the Battle of Waterloo: February, 1816" ("The Bard--whose soul is meek as dawning day"); and "Siege of Vienna Raised by John Sobieski: February, 1816."

32 [HUNT, LEIGH]. "Literary Notices: No. 12." Examiner, no. 456 (22 September), pp. 602-603 (603).
    Wordsworth's character "as a poet is also his own"; "Wordsworth will never be a narrative poet."

33 [JEFFREY, FRANCIS]. Review of Byron's Childe Harold's Pilgrimage: Canto the Third and The Prisoner of Chillon. Edinburgh Review, 27 (December), 277-310 (277-78).
    Though Byron has imitated Wordsworth, he has not copied Wordsworth's lack of sense, lofty flights on mean subjects, or verbosity. Reprinted in 1844.B24.

1816

34   PEPPERPOD, PETER. The Literary Bazaar; or, Poets' Council.
         London: Harper, Richardson, and Allman, passim.
         Includes "The Lay of Rylstone," a burlesque.

35   R.[EYNOLDS], J.[OHN] H.[AMILTON]. "Sonnet: To Wordsworth."
         Champion, no. 163 (18 February), p. 54.
         Wordsworth's poems have calmed a troubled heart.

36   R.[EYNOLDS], J.[OHN] H.[AMILTON]. "The Pilgrimage of Living
         Poets to the Stream of Castaly." Champion, no. 170
         (7 April), p. 110.
         All nature comes alive to reverence Wordsworth. See
         1820.B40.

37   R.[EYNOLDS], J.[OHN] H.[AMILTON]. "The Reader: No. V."
         Champion, no. 178 (2 June), pp. 173-74 (174).
         The moods of Wordsworth's mind "are valuable at all
         times."

38   [REYNOLDS, JOHN HAMILTON]. "The Exeter Theatre." Champion,
         no. 192 (8 September), p. [285].
         Wordsworth's poetry catches the inspiration of the
         mountains and lakes.

39   [REYNOLDS, JOHN HAMILTON]. "Popular Poetry--Periodical
         Criticism, &c." Champion, no. 197 (13 October), 326-27
         (326).
         Criticizes attacks on Wordsworth in the Edinburgh Review.

40   [REYNOLDS, JOHN HAMILTON]. Review of Thanksgiving Ode.
         Champion, no. 198 (20 October), pp. 334-35.
         Wordsworth's devout and patriotic hymn is not occasional;
         it proceeds from his imagination. Reading the poem aloud
         should convince one of Wordsworth's merits. One's mind
         must be brought into full participation with his poems.

41   R.[EYNOLDS], J.[OHN] H.[AMILTON]. "Boswell's Visit."
         Champion, no. 206 (15 December), pp. 397-98 (398).
         Characters praise Wordsworth.

42   SHELLEY, PERCY BYSSHE. "To Wordsworth" (poem), in Alastor;
         or, the Spirit of Solitude: And Other Poems. London:
         Baldwin, Cradock, and Joy, and Carpenter, pp. 67-68.
         Mourns Wordsworth's deserting of truth and liberty.

43   [TALFOURD, THOMAS NOON?] S. N. D. "On Poetical Scepticism."
         Monthly Repository, 11 (April), 217-20 (217-18); (May),
         278-80.

28

Objects to Wordsworth's statement in Essay (1815) that a religion based on the understanding is one based on pride (217-18). Calvinism renders impossible a poetry celebrating the joy of childhood (such as "Ode: Intimations of Immortality") and human virtue (such as "The Old Cumberland Beggar") (278-80).

44 [WATKINS, JOHN, FREDERICK SHOBERL (and WILLIAM UPCOTT?)].
A Biographical Dictionary of the Living Authors of Great Britain and Ireland. London: Colburn, p. 399.
Wordsworth heads a school of poetry characterized by simplicity. Attribution: Bodleian catalogue.

1817 A BOOKS - NONE

1817 B SHORTER WRITINGS

1 ANON. Review of Thanksgiving Ode. Monthly Review, NS 82 (January), 98-100.
Thanksgiving Ode is uninteresting and harmless, written in a conversational and insipid manner.

2 ANON. "On Modern Poets--Mr. Southey." Literary Gazette, no. 14 (26 April), pp. 210-11 (211).
Mocks Wordsworth's use of low subjects.

3 ANON. Musomania; or Poets' Purgatory (poem). London: Baldwin, Cradock, and Joy, pp. 50, 108.
Ridicules the puerile absurdity of "Alice Fell" and the ponderousness of The Excursion. (Dedication signed "Jeremiah Jingle.")

4 B. "On the Present State of English Poetry." Literary Gazette, no. 26 (19 July), pp. 40-41.
Poetry has become marked by barbarisms and affected simplicity.

5 COLERIDGE, S.[AMUEL] T.[AYLOR]. Biographia Literaria; or Biographical Sketches of My Literary Life and Opinions. 2 vols. London: Fenner, especially I:52-53, 56 (Chapter iii), 71-91 (Chapter iv), 178 (Chapter x), 282-84 (Chapter xii); II:1-5 (Chapter xiv), 34-95, 104-17, 123-24, 128-82 (Chapters xvii-xxii), 236-53.
Had Wordsworth omitted "less than an hundred lines" and his Preface, Lyrical Ballads would not have attracted criticism. Wordsworth's original genius was evident in the language and images of Descriptive Sketches and in the

imaginative transformation of common objects in "Guilt and
Sorrow." Wordsworth never troubled himself with politics
when living at Alfoxden. Objects to Wordsworth's discussion
of imagination and fancy in Preface (1815). Outlines plan
for Lyrical Ballads: Wordsworth was "to give the charm of
novelty to things of every day." Objects to Wordsworth's
arguments in the Preface to Lyrical Ballads on the use of
the language of rustics and on poetry versus prose, and to
F. Jeffrey's reviewing of Wordsworth's poems. The defects
of Wordsworth's poems include uneven style, "a matter-of-
factness," poorly executed dramatic form, disproportionate
feeling towards objects, and "thoughts and images too great
for the subject"; the excellencies include "a perfect appropriateness of the words to the meaning," sane thoughts,
strong and original single passages, true natural descriptions, "a meditative pathos," and imagination. Reprints
"Satyrane's Letters: Letter III" from 1809.B11.

6   COLERIDGE, S.[AMUEL] T.[AYLOR]. "To a Gentleman: Composed on
     the night after his recitation of a Poem on the Growth of
     an Individual Mind" (poem), "Dejection: An Ode," in
     Sibylline Leaves. London: Fenner, pp. 197-203, 237-43.
          Hails Wordsworth's mental growth as outlined in The Pre-
     lude. Wordsworth exists "in the choir / Of ever-enduring
     men." (Later entitled "To William Wordsworth. . . .")
     See 1810.B12 and 1883.B25 (197-203). Manuscript version of
     poem addressed specifically to Wordsworth: see 1883.B25
     and 1895.B13; originally published, with variants, in the
     Morning Post, 4 October 1802: "Edmund" (Wordsworth) is
     raised from care by seeing good everywhere (237-43).

7   D. See 1817.B28.

8   E., J. "Polite Literature." Literary Gazette, no. 17
     (17 May), pp. 257-58.
          A reply to 1817.B2 and 1817.B24. Wordsworth's writing
     is manly, dignified.

9   [HAZLITT, WILLIAM]. "The Times Newspaper: On the Connection
     between Toad-eaters and Tyrants." Examiner, no. 472
     (12 January), pp. 26-28 (27-28).
          "Simon Lee" is a tale of these times. Criticizes Words-
     worth's praise of kingship. Reprinted with omissions in
     Political Essays (1819).

10   [HAZLITT, WILLIAM]. "The Courier and 'The Wat Tyler.'"
     Examiner, no. 483 (30 March), pp. 194-97 (196).

Since Wordsworth gave up his Jacobin principles and poems, his poetical powers have flagged. Reprinted in Political Essays (1819).

11 [HAZLITT, WILLIAM]. "Political Examiner: No. 470: Sketch of the History of the Good Old Times." Examiner, no. 484 (6 April), pp. 209-11 (210); no. 485 (13 April), 228-30 (228-29).
Attacks Wordsworth's politics.

12 HAZLITT, WILLIAM. "On Milton's Versification," "On Manner," "The Same Subject ["On Pedantry"] Continued," "On the Character of Rousseau," "Observations on Mr Wordsworth's Poem, 'The Excursion,'" "The Same Subject Continued," in The Round Table: A Collection of Essays on Literature, Men, and Manners. 2 vols. Edinburgh: Constable; London: Longman, I:102-10 (110), 111-24 (120-22); II:36-45 (36-37), 45-55 (54-55), 95-112, 112-22.
Reprinted from 1815.B19 (I:110). Reprinted from 1815.B20 (120-22). Reprinted from 1816.B21 (II:36-37). Reprinted from 1816.B22 (54-55). Abridged from 1814.B7, first two installments (95-112). Revised from 1814.B7, third installment (112-22).

13 HAZLITT, WILLIAM. "Romeo and Juliet," in Characters of Shakespear's Plays. London: Hunter, and Ollier, pp. 135-52 (139-41).
In "Ode: Intimations of Immortality" Wordsworth idly attributed the vivid impressions of childhood to a pre-existent state.

14 [HAZLITT, WILLIAM and FRANCIS JEFFREY]. Review of Coleridge's Biographia Literaria. Edinburgh Review, 28 (August), 488-515 (488-89, 491, 495, 502, 507-12).
Wordsworth errs in confining the language of poetry to that of the lower orders. Includes a note by Jeffrey (signed "F. J.") reviewing and reaffirming his criticism of the Lake School.

15 [HUNT, LEIGH]. Review of Keats's Poems. Examiner, no. 492 (1 June), p. 345; no. 497 (6 July), pp. 428-29 (429).
Wordsworth has advanced beyond the extremes of the early Lake poetry to open up "a fund of thinking and imagination" (345). Keats's allusion to the origin of mythology corresponds to Wordsworth's in The Excursion (429).

16 K., E. See 1817.B23.

1817

17   KEATS, JOHN. "Addressed to the Same" (i.e., Haydon) (poem), in Poems. London: Ollier, p. 92.
      A poet (presumably Wordsworth) "of the cloud, the cataract, the lake," "Catches his freshness from Archangel's wing."

18   N. See 1817.B27.

19   [PEACOCK, THOMAS LOVE]. Melincourt. By the Author of Headlong Hall. 3 vols. London: Hookham, and Baldwin, Cradock, and Joy, II:201-203, 210-11 (Chapter xxviii); III:119-55 (Chapter xxxix).
      Introduces Wordsworth as Mr. Paperstamp, "chiefly remarkable for an affected infantine lisp," self-esteem, place-seeking, and apostasy.

20   [REYNOLDS, JOHN HAMILTON]. "Covent Garden Theatre: The Ravens; or, the Force of Conscience." Champion, no. 213 (2 February), p. 38.
      Wordsworth is wrong in "Ode to Duty."

21   [REYNOLDS, JOHN HAMILTON]. "The Arithmetic of Poetry." Champion, no. 215 (16 February), p. 54.
      Mocks Wordsworth's use of arithmetic in his poems.

22   [REYNOLDS, JOHN HAMILTON]. Review of Coleridge's Zapolya. Champion, no. 254 (16 November), p. 365.
      Wordsworth, like Milton, "set himself in early youth, a great task."

23   [SHELLEY, PERCY BYSSHE] E. K. "Literary Notices: No. 37: Godwin's Mandeville." Examiner, no. 522 (28 December), pp. 826-27.
      Wordsworth's fame would have suffered as Godwin's has but that Wordsworth's dissent is too easily reconcilable with prevailing opinion.

24   T., H. "Modern Poets: Defence of Coleridge." Literary Gazette, no. 15 (3 May), p. 227.
      A reply to 1817.B2. Criticizes Wordsworth's "babyism" and "inane prosing"; he should not be coupled with Coleridge.

25   T.[ALFOURD], T.[HOMAS] N.[OON]. "Sonnets: Supplementary to Wordsworth's Sonnets to Liberty." Monthly Repository, 12 (June), 370-71 (370).
      Praises the "majestic simplicity and natural grandeur" of Wordsworth's sonnets.

26   [WILSON, JOHN]. "Observations on Mr Wordsworth's Letter
      Relative to a New Edition of Burns' Works." [Blackwood's]
      Edinburgh Monthly Magazine, 1 (June), 261-66.
          Wordsworth's zeal to give advice on a subject about which
      he is not qualified and his opinion unnecessary, is moti-
      vated by his own egotism, as evidenced by his attack on
      the editor of the Edinburgh Review. His accusations against
      Dr. Currie are false.

27   [WILSON, JOHN] N. "Vindication of Mr Wordsworth's Letter to
      Mr Gray, on a New Edition of Burns." Blackwood's Edinburgh
      Magazine, 2 (October), 65-73.
          A reply to 1817.B26. Defends both Wordsworth and
      Jeffrey as an appreciative critic. Though he has made mis-
      takes, Wordsworth has brought about a revolution in poetry
      without ever violating the principles of taste or reason.

28   [WILSON, JOHN] D. "Letter Occasioned by N.'s Vindication of
      Mr Wordsworth in Last Number." Blackwood's Edinburgh
      Magazine, 2 (November), 201-204.
          A reply to 1817.B27. Wordsworth published A Letter to A
      Friend of Robert Burns to strike back at the Edinburgh Re-
      view. A "half-parson sort of gentleman," he is unfit to
      judge the jolly Burns. His poems are not widely known in
      Scotland.

1818 A   BOOKS - NONE

1818 B   SHORTER WRITINGS

1   ANON. Review of Hunt's Foliage. Eclectic Review, NS 10
     (November), 484-93 (487-88).
         Praises Wordsworth's use of mythology in The Excursion
     (Book IV).

2   ANON. Review of Moore's A Selection of Irish Melodies.
     Monthly Review, NS 87 (December), 419-33 (427).
         Accuses Wordsworth of debasing language by using parti-
     ciples instead of nouns.

3   ANON. "Literary Retrospect." New Annual Register . . . For
     the Year 1817, 38:[1]-[81] ([45]-[49]).
         In contrast to the social poetry of Burns and Cowper,
     Wordsworth's poems arise from the contemplations of the
     poet's own mind. The Lake Poets share a benevolent faith
     in the happiness of man.

1818

4　ANON. Prodigious!!! or, Childe Paddie in London. 3 vols.
London: privately printed, II:112-21, 135-36, 142-43;
III:225.
　　By his "affectation, his pertinaciousness of system, his
defiance of censure, his childishness amounting to babyism,"
and his choice of low subjects Wordsworth hides his talent.

5　[BARTON, BERNARD]. "Verses, Addressed to Wm. Wordsworth,
Esq.: Being a Parody on the Stanzas Prefixed to the 'White
Doe,'" in Poems. By An Amateur. London: privately
printed, pp. 10-14.
　　Records his appreciation of Wordsworth's poems in his
youth.

6　COLERIDGE, S.[AMUEL] T.[AYLOR]. The Friend: A Series of
Essays, in three Volumes, to Aid in the Formation of Fixed
Principles in Politics, Morals, and Religion, with Literary
Amusements Interspersed. A new edition. London: Fenner,
especially I:58-59, 212, 316-17; II:189, 325; III:22-24,
243-44, 296, 302-303.
　　Reprinted with additions from 1809.B9-B10, B12, B19;
1810.B1-B2. Praises the "wise and high-minded author" of
"November, 1806." Records Baron von Humboldt's praise of
"Ode: Intimations of Immortality."

7　D. See 1818.B23.

8　F., J. "Imitation of Living Poets. No. IV." Letter-Box,
no. 13 (16 May), pp. 199-208.
　　Includes "The Old Tolbooth" (poem), a burlesque signed
"Wm. W----ds----th."

9　☞. "On the Lake School of Poetry." Portfolio: A Weekly
Paper, on Criticism and Manners, 1 (26 November), 21-23.
　　Wordsworth explores, without ornament, the mind and
human nature.

10　[HAZLITT, WILLIAM]. "The Press--Coleridge, Southey, Wordsworth, and Bentham." Yellow Dwarf, no. 1 (3 January),
pp. 4-5.
　　After his earlier enthusiasm for liberty, Wordsworth is
now silent, busy in his stamp office.

11　[HAZLITT, WILLIAM] X. "On the Clerical Character." Yellow
Dwarf, no. 6 (7 February), pp. 44-46 (46).
　　Criticizes Wordsworth's opinion "that the press ought to
be shackled." Reprinted in Political Essays (1819).

12   [HAZLITT, WILLIAM]. Review of The Fudge Family in Paris.
      Yellow Dwarf, no. 17 (25 April), pp. 132-35 (132).
         Wordsworth is "a mouthing sycophant." Reprinted in
      Political Essays (1819).

13   [HAZLITT, WILLIAM]. Review of Byron's Childe Harold's
      Pilgrimage: Canto the Fourth. Yellow Dwarf, no. 18
      (2 May), pp. 142-44 (142).
         Wordsworth, in his egotism, creates interest out of
      nothing; Byron would destroy our interest in all things.
      Byron's abuse of Napoleon is worthy of Wordsworth's "place-
      hunting Muse."

14   [HAZLITT, WILLIAM] T. T. "On the Ignorance of the Learned."
      Edinburgh Magazine, and Literary Miscellany, 3 (July),
      55-60 (58).
         Attacks Wordsworth's vanity. (Reference omitted when
      essay reprinted in Table-Talk [1821].)

15   [HAZLITT, WILLIAM] PETERKINS. "Mr. Wordsworth and the
      Westmorland Election." Examiner, no. 549 (5 July), p. 427.
         A Letter to A Friend of Robert Burns is dull and con-
      temptible. Attacks Wordsworth's participation in the West-
      morland election.

16   [HAZLITT, WILLIAM] M. N. "Thoughts on Taste." Edinburgh
      Magazine, and Literary Miscellany, NS 3 (October), 308-11
      (310-11).
         Attacks Wordsworth's criticism of Voltaire. Wordsworth's
      muse lacks "sweetness of expression as well as regularity
      of outline." For continuation, see 1819.B36.

17   [HAZLITT, WILLIAM]. Review of Letters from the Hon. Horace
      Walpole to George Montagu, Esq. Edinburgh Review, 31
      (December), 80-93 (84).
         In The Excursion "we are talked to death by an arrogant
      old proser."

18   HAZLITT, WILLIAM. "On Shakespeare and Milton," "On Swift,
      Young, Gray, Collins, &c.," "On Burns, and the Old English
      Ballads," "On the Living Poets," in Lectures on The English
      Poets: Delivered at the Surrey Institution. London:
      Taylor and Hessey, pp. 86-134 (104-105, 123-24), 206-44
      (227, 234-35, 242-43), 245-82 (255-63), 283-331 (295,
      306-24).
         To Wordsworth nothing is interesting but the moods of
      his own mind (104-105, 123-24). The Excursion is dull
      (227, 234-35, 242-43). Wordsworth champions himself, not

1818

Burns, in A Letter to A Friend of Robert Burns. As opposed
to Burns, he moralizes on life without entering into it
(255-63). Wordsworth's poetry contrasts with Scott's: it
is internal, the poetry of mere sentiment. Wordsworth, as
The Excursion proves, "is totally deficient in all the ma-
chinery of poetry." Many of the Lyrical Ballads possess
beauty, originality, and pathos. The Lake School had its
origin in the French Revolution (295, 306-24).

19 [HODGSON, FRANCIS]. Childe Harold's Monitor; or Lines
Occasioned by the Last Canto of Childe Harold, including
Hints to Other Contemporaries. London: Porter, passim.
Wordsworth, led by vanity to choose the novelty of lowness as the way to greatness, writes obscure, prosaic, and
puerile poems and prefaces. Attribution: British Museum
catalogue.

20 [HUNT, LEIGH]. "Living Authors," in The Literary Pocket-book;
or Companion for the Lover of Nature and Art [for] 1819.
London: Ollier [1818], pp. 160-63 (163).
Lists "Wordsworth (William) poetry and politics."
Attribution: British Museum catalogue.

21 HUNT, LEIGH. "Preface, including Cursory Observations on
Poetry and Cheerfulness," in Foliage; or Poems Original and
Translated. London: Ollier, pp. 9-39 (10-11, 13-14).
Considering the novelty of his poetical system and the
errors of his moral one, Wordsworth has succeeded quite
well. Reports Byron's appreciation of Wordsworth's school
of poetry.

22 [LOCKHART, JOHN GIBSON] Z. "Cockney School of Poetry: No IV."
Blackwood's Edinburgh Magazine, 3 (August), 519-24 (520).
Wordsworth is the purest, loftiest, most classical of
living poets.

23 [MOREHEAD, THE REV. ROBERT] D. "Observations on the Poetical
Character of Dante." Edinburgh Magazine, and Literary
Miscellany, NS 3 (September), 223-29 (226-28).
Wordsworth exhibits, in a less admirable way, aspects of
poetry that characterize Dante: rejection of older poets,
plain language, close observation of nature, and metaphysical discussion. Attribution: 1875.B12, pp. 167-71.

24 N., M. See 1818.B16.

. 25 [NAPIER, MACVEY]. Hypocrisy Unveiled, and Calumny Detected:
in a Review of Blackwood's Magazine. Edinburgh: Pillans,
pp. 24-26.

1818

Attacks the inconsistent treatment of Wordsworth in
Blackwood's Edinburgh Magazine. Attribution: Dictionary
of Anonymous and Pseudonymous Literature (Samuel Halkett
and John Laing), new ed., 9 vols. (Edinburgh: Oliver and
Boyd, 1926-62), III:126.

26   P.[ATMORE], P.[ETER] G.[EORGE]. "Sonnets to Mr Wordsworth."
      Blackwood's Edinburgh Magazine, 2 (February), 512-13.
          Wordsworth's pure, naked poetry breaks up the mists of
      doubt.

27   PETERKINS. See 1818.B15.

28   [PROCTOR, BRYAN WALLER] [***]. "Original Poetry: For St.
      Cecilia's Day." Literary Gazette, no. 88 (26 September),
      p. 618.
          Wordsworth, a "philosophic bard," communes with lonely
      nature. Attributed and reprinted in 1853.B12, III:337-41.

29   Q IN THE CORNER. Letter to the Editor. Man of Kent, 1
      (24 October), 93-94.
          Ridicules Wordsworth's use of personification.

30   READER, A CONSTANT. Letter to the Editor. Edinburgh
      Reflector, no. 10 (2 September), p. 77.
          Points out a similarity between "Composed upon West-
      minster Bridge" and a passage from Wilson's City of the
      Plague.

31   [REYNOLDS, JOHN HAMILTON]. "Literature: The Quarterly
      Review--Mr. Keats." Alfred, West of England Journal, and
      General Advertiser, 4 (6 October), p. [4].
          Wordsworth "lost himself by looking at his own image."

32   T., T. See 1818.B14.

33   [WILSON, JOHN]. "Essays on the Lake School of Poetry, No. I:
      Wordsworth's White Doe of Rylstone." Blackwood's Edinburgh
      Magazine, 3 (July), 369-81.
          In contrast to Scott and Byron, Wordsworth is the philoso-
      pher of the elementary laws of our nature, confident of the
      prevalence of virtue over vice in the human and natural
      worlds. The White Doe of Rylstone will not be appreciated
      by readers who demand violent excitement.

34   [WILSON, JOHN]. "Essays on the Lake School of Poetry, No. II:
      On the Habits of Thought, inculcated by Wordsworth."
      Blackwood's Edinburgh Magazine, 4 (December), 257-63.

37

1818

> Wordsworth's poems are vehicles for currently unfashion-
> able doctrines: like Platonic and Hindu philosophers, he
> attempts to awaken men through contemplation to the silent
> workings of moral laws in the universe and to the beauties
> of the human affections. His poems convey more exalted
> meaning than Milton's; they form a consistent whole. He
> presents the external world as the creation of his mind.
> Because he dwells on the natural world, his poetry is joy-
> ful; when he turns to man, he exhibits Christian sorrow.
> He may be considered the Rousseau of present times.

35 X. See 1818.B11.

36 Z. See 1818.B22.

1819 A BOOKS

1 ANON. Benjamin the Waggoner, A Ryghte merrie and conceitede
   Tale in Verse: A Fragment. London: Baldwin, Cradock, and
   Joy, 96 pp.
       Parody of Peter Bell. (Sometimes attributed to John
   Hamilton Reynolds.)

2 ANON. The Dead Asses: A Lyrical Ballad. London: Smith and
   Elder, 24 pp.
       A burlesque.

3 [REYNOLDS, JOHN HAMILTON]. Peter Bell: A Lyrical Ballad.
   London: Taylor and Hessey, 37 pp.
       A burlesque.

1819 B SHORTER WRITINGS

1 ANON. "Memoir of William Wordsworth, Esq." New Monthly
   Magazine, 11 (February), 48-50.
       A biographical sketch.

2 ANON. Review of Coleridge's Biographia Literaria. Monthly
   Review, NS 88 (February), 124-38 (132-38).
       Wordsworth lacks merit and originality as a "rustic ego-
   tistical metaphysician." He is capricious in his criticism
   of Gray's sonnet in the Preface to Lyrical Ballads.

3 ANON. "Another Peter Bell!" Edinburgh Magazine and Literary
   Miscellany, NS 4 (May), 427-29.
       Assumes Wordsworth's poem is also an impertinent imita-
   tion of the true Peter Bell.

4   ANON. Review of <u>Peter Bell</u>. <u>Blackwood's Edinburgh Magazine</u>,
        5 (May), 130-36.
            <u>Peter Bell</u> admirably illustrates Wordsworth's principle
        that emotions can make even homely circumstances poetical.
        Its chief fault is a "dallying prolixity." The characters
        are but vehicles to portray the true subject of the poem:
        the relation of feelings within the human mind.

5   ANON. Review of <u>Peter Bell</u>. <u>Gentleman's Magazine</u>, 89-1
        (May), 441-42.
            The "pleasingly melancholy" tale is one of Wordsworth's
        brightest gems.

6   ANON. Review of <u>Peter Bell</u>. <u>Theatrical Inquisitor</u>, 14 (May),
        369-76; (June), 441-46.
            Wordsworth's poems are marked by an unfortunately "in-
        tricate metaphysic" reminiscent of Cowley and an affectation
        of simple diction (369-76). In <u>Peter Bell</u>, the story lacks
        anything to arrest the reader's attention or to convey a
        particular lesson. One cannot sympathize with Peter. The
        fine passages are those in which Wordsworth abandons his
        extreme simplicity (441-46).

7   ANON. Review of <u>Peter Bell</u>. <u>Literary Gazette</u>, no. 119
        (1 May), pp. 273-75.
            The story is too mean for dignity, too insignificant for
        sustained pathos; it is filled with inconsistencies in dic-
        tion and description. Wordsworth's system of poetry is
        radically wrong.

8   ANON. Review of <u>Peter Bell</u>. <u>Literary Chronicle</u>, 1 (29 May),
        20-21.
            The simplicity in <u>Peter Bell</u> is ridiculous, fit only for
        the nursery.

9   ANON. "New Books Published in May." <u>Monthly Magazine</u>, 47
        (June), 440-48 (442).
            "<u>Peter Bell</u> is all puerility."

10 ANON. Review of <u>Peter Bell</u>. <u>British Critic</u>, NS 11 (June),
        584-603.
            Though Wordsworth writes with admirable Petrarchan sim-
        plicity, he has gone too far in thinking that the commonest
        external things are more fit for, rather than simply capable
        of, spiritual association; in so far as he neglects to con-
        sider that communication in poetry depends on the predis-
        position of the reader, he diminishes his power of doing
        good. Most persons will be repulsed by the inappropriate,

1819

base language in Peter Bell. Wordsworth's playfulness fails. He succeeds in his portrayal of the changes in Peter's mind, his picturesque drawing, and his pathetic narration.

11   ANON. Review of [Reynolds's] Peter Bell. Theatrical Inquisitor, 14 (June), 449-50.
Wordsworth "seldom puts forth a note, or a line of preface, in which he does not" declare "that his writings are the best of the day." His "exquisite touches of genuine poetry," however, atone for his defects.

12   ANON. Review of The Waggoner. Blackwood's Edinburgh Magazine, 5 (June), 332-34.
The poem shows an unexpected, playful side of Wordsworth's muse.

13   ANON. Review of The Waggoner. European Magazine, 75 (June), 531-33.
The Waggoner suffers in comparison with Peter Bell. The subject is not adapted to Wordsworth's talents; both it and the execution are fit for a nursery song. But the description of the jollity at the inn is worthy of Burns.

14   ANON. Review of The Waggoner. General Review, or Weekly Literary Epitome, 1 (June), 36-46.
Wordsworth, whose name stands high, has perverted his powers in The Waggoner.

15   ANON. Review of The Waggoner. Theatrical Inquisitor, 14 (June), 447-49.
Wordsworth attaches too great an importance to Peter Bell. In it he shows deep feeling, but also an affected expression and attempted elevation of a low subject that contrasts unfavorably with Bloomfield's treatment of rustics. The Waggoner is destitute of all interest.

16   ANON. Review of The Waggoner. Literary Gazette, no. 125 (12 June), pp. 369-71.
Though the waggoner is a more natural character than Peter Bell, The Waggoner is characterized by lack of sense, unintelligible and nasty images, trite vulgarity of language, and bad grammar. The description of jollity at the inn shows that Wordsworth could write well if he would choose worthy subjects.

17   ANON. "New Books Published in June." Monthly Magazine, 47 (July), 539-46 (540).

The sonnets in The Waggoner prove Wordsworth can command respect when he is serious; but he plays the fool when he tries to be merry.

18 ANON. Review of Peter Bell and The Waggoner. Eclectic Review, NS 12 (July), 62-76.
Wordsworth lacks a sense of the ludicrous, because to him all things are equally worthy of serious regard. A solemn man fails if he tries to be comic. The allegory of the Prologue in Peter Bell is not well managed; the poem itself is vulgar, though the inclusion of the Methodist preacher and the pathos are pleasing. The Waggoner lacks a significant catastrophe. Wordsworth above all exhibits bad taste; his fame depends on his best poems being judiciously selected and published in one volume.

19 ANON. Review of Peter Bell. New British Lady's Magazine, 3rd ser., 3 (July), 34-35.
Peter Bell will rank among Wordsworth's best poems. Wordsworth is more admired than read: his subjects are too humble, his style not bold or varied.

20 Review of [Reynolds's] Peter Bell. New British Lady's Magazine, 3rd ser., 3 (July), 35-36.
Wordsworth conceives of his own work too seriously to satirize himself.

21 ANON. Review of Peter Bell and The Waggoner. Literary and Statistical Magazine for Scotland, 3 (August), 314-19.
Wordsworth brings the practices of the metaphysical poets down to the level of ordinary men. His writings are mystical rather than philosophical--he traces the tie between the emotions and objects of the external senses. Yet he cultivates an eccentricity deliberately designed to disgust the reader (e.g., in the Prologue to Peter Bell and in the feeling directed towards the ass). The Waggoner is even more barren of incident than Peter Bell; its subject is too undignified for poetry.

22 ANON. Review of Peter Bell. Monthly Review, NS 89 (August), 419-22.
The poem is lisping drivel, suitable for the nursery or a Cheap Repository Tract. Wordsworth gives a ludicrous, unfaithful portrait of nature.

23 ANON. Review of The Waggoner. Fireside Magazine, 1 (August), 303-304.

1819

> Though the poem represents much ado about nothing, Wordsworth does maintain interest (by leading the reader to expect a dread catastrophe) and describes well.

24   ANON. Review of The Waggoner. Gentleman's Magazine, 89-2
(August), 143-44.
> The poem, written in an unaffected style, is not less
meritorious than Peter Bell.

25   ANON. Review of The Waggoner. New British Lady's Magazine,
3rd ser., 3 (August), 85-86.
> The plot and structure of The Waggoner are not suited to
Wordsworth's peculiar talents.

26   ANON. Review of The Waggoner. New Monthly Magazine, 12
(August), 81.
> The poem is disappointing.

27   ANON. Review of The Dead Asses. Literary Chronicle, 1
(28 August), 232.
> Wordsworth has disgraced his muse by writing Peter Bell
and The Waggoner.

28   ANON. Review of The Waggoner. Monthly Review, NS 90
(September), 36-40.
> Wordsworth seems determined to see how far he can degrade
poetry. Praises Wordsworth's irony in The Waggoner; quarrels with the diction of the sonnets.

29   ANON. Review of The Waggoner. British Critic, NS 12
(November), 464-79.
> Wordsworth's novelty in The Waggoner consists in treating
a plain subject as it is, not heightened by exaggeration or
excess passion or reduced by irony. The interest in such a
poem lies in the artistry and the moral sympathy of the
poet. The faults of The Waggoner lie in the confused
images, the sailor's inappropriate language, and the initial
description of the sailor; the beauties lie in the descriptions, especially of the fellowship at the inn.

30   ANON. Review of Peter Bell and The Waggoner. Edinburgh
Monthly Review, 2 (December), 654-61.
> Wordsworth ought to exert his talents in a manner likely
to gratify public taste. The two volumes exhibit unequalled
lowness and affected simplicity. The ass is the hero of
Peter Bell.

31   B., J. Review of Peter Bell. European Magazine, 75 (May),
445-48.

> Wordsworth is in the first rank of poets of the present
> day. He sees familiar things with a microscopic eye, de-
> spising the common machinery of poetry and trusting in his
> own original genius.

32   [BYRON, LORD]. Don Juan. London: privately printed, pp. 48
     (Canto i, Stanzas xc-xci), 105 (ccv), 114 (ccxxii).
        Wordsworth's poems are unintelligible; Wordsworth is
     "crazed beyond all hope."

33   [COLERIDGE, JOHN TAYLOR]. Review of Shelley's Laon and Cythna
     and The Revolt of Islam. Quarterly Review, 21 (April),
     460-71 (461-62).
        The pure philosophy of the "mountain poet" (presumably
     Wordsworth) is perverted by atheists and pantheists such as
     Shelley. Attribution: John O. Hayden, The Romantic Re-
     viewers 1802-1824 (Chicago: Univ. of Chicago Press, 1968),
     p. 291.

34   G., R. "Peter Bell, Junior: A Simple Story" (poem).
     Kaleidoscope, 1 (8 June), 184.
        A burlesque.

35   [HAZLITT, WILLIAM]. "Death of John Cavanagh." Examiner,
     no. 580 (7 February), pp. 94-95 (94).
        Wordsworth's epic poetry lumbers. Reprinted as "The
     Indian Jugglers" in 1821.B20.

36   [HAZLITT, WILLIAM] M. N. "Thoughts on Taste." Edinburgh
     Magazine, and Literary Miscellany, NS 5 (July), 13-16 (15).
        A continuation of 1818.B16. Records Wordsworth's praise
     of Milton.

37   [HAZLITT, WILLIAM] X. Y. Z. "Character of the Country People."
     Examiner, no. 603 (18 July), pp. 450-52 (451).
        Records Cumberland peasants' laughing when read Words-
     worth's poems.

38   HAZLITT, WILLIAM. A Letter to William Gifford, Esq. London:
     Miller, pp. 50, 56.
        States that his objection to "Ode: Intimations of Im-
     mortality" in 1817.B13 was to Wordsworth's doctrine, not
     his poetical conceit.

39   [HODGSON, FRANCIS]. Saeculomastix; or, the Lash of the Age We
     Live In; A Poem, in two Parts. By the Author of "Childe
     Harold's Monitor." London: Porter, pp. 43-44, 90-91.

1819

Wordsworth writes with prosaic obscurity, having borrowed from Coleridge his "one idea," that man colors the external world with his own mind.

40   [HUNT, LEIGH]. Review of Peter Bell. Examiner, no. 592
(2 May), pp. 282-83.
Peter's reformation is based on a weak and vulgar philosophy of violence and fear. Some of Wordsworth's descriptions are as true as Crabbe's, but Wordsworth should never affect vivacity. In "Malham Cove" he paradoxically forsakes the visible world he would have us love.

41   [HUNT, LEIGH] 👉 . Review of Shelley's Rosalind and Helen.
Examiner, no. 593 (9 May), pp. 302-303 (302).
Wordsworth's "administrations of melancholy" make men timid and servile. The egotistical Wordsworth, in contrast with Shelley, "has become hopeless of this world."

42   [HUNT, LEIGH]. "Fatal Mistake of Nervous Disorders for Insanity." Indicator, no. 7 (24 November), pp. 53-56 (55).
Wordsworth "has written an idle couplet about the insanity of poets" in "Resolution and Independence." Reprinted in The Indicator, and The Companion (1834).

43   [KEATS, JOHN]. Review of [Reynolds's] Peter Bell. Examiner,
no. 591 (25 April), p. 270.
The writer "has felt the finer parts of Mr. Wordsworth's poetry."

44   KEMPFHERHAUSEN, PHILLIP. See 1819.B55.

45   [LOCKHART, JOHN GIBSON?] Z. "On the Cockney School of Poetry: No. V." Blackwood's Edinburgh Magazine, 5 (April), 97-100
(97).
As opposed to Hunt's, Wordsworth's egotism is pardonable because he is rejected by the "fine" world, which cannot understand his characters.

46   [LOCKHART, JOHN GIBSON and JOHN WILSON]. Peter's Letters to
His Kinsfolk. Second edition [actually the first]. 3 vols.
Edinburgh: Blackwood; London: Cadell, and Davies;
Glasgow: Smith, I:118, 121-24, 140-41, 179-80, 259,
304-305; II:143-44, 219, 309-12, 337-39; III:130.
Notes Jeffrey's prejudices against Wordsworth; Wordsworth's poems should appeal to all men. The pedlar in The Excursion seems modelled upon James Hogg. Praises the invocation in the Preface to The Excursion. The reading public of Edinburgh think Wordsworth "a mere old sequestered

hermit, eaten up with vanity and affectation." Wordsworth thinks and in conversation speaks of nothing but poetry. Describes Wordsworth's head. Praises "From the dark chambers of dejection freed." (Dedication signed "Peter Morris.") Attribution: British Museum catalogue.

47 [MAGINN, WILLIAM] M. N. "Don Juan Unread" (poem). Blackwood's Edinburgh Magazine, 6 (November), 194-95.
   Parody of "Yarrow Unvisited."

48 [MOIR, DAVID MACBETH] MORGAN ODOHERTY. "Letter from Mr Odoherty, enclosing Three Articles." Blackwood's Edinburgh Magazine, 5 (July), 433-43 (433-34).
   Includes burlesque, "Billy Routing, A Lyrical Ballad" (poem), signed "W. W."

49 N., M. See 1819.B36, B47.

50 ODOHERTY, MORGAN. See 1819.B48.

51 P., E. "Remarks Philosophical and Literary." Gentleman's Magazine, 89-2 (November), 397-400 (398).
   Wordsworth's and Coleridge's native talent is hidden beneath littleness and absurdities.

52 [TERROT, CHARLES HUGHES]. Common Sense: A Poem. Edinburgh: Brown; London: Allman, pp. 8-10, 16.
   Though Wordsworth's lays are of "spotless tenor," they are deficient in rhyme, sense, diction, and fancy. Wordsworth errs in choosing common language and subjects. "Few poets have been more reviewed, or less read." Because they are concerned with psychology, Wordsworth and Coleridge are inferior to Crabbe. Attribution: Bodleian catalogue.

53 TURNER, SHARON. "Prolusion on Modern Poets and Poetry" (poem), in Prolusions on the Present Greatness, of Britain; on Modern Poetry; and on the Present Aspect of the World. London: Longman, pp. 85-134 (115-21).
   Though his "ethic purpose" is admirable, Wordsworth errs in tying his thoughts to humble men and the natural world.

54 [WILSON, JOHN]. "Three Original Sonnets of Wordsworth; Suggested by Westall's Views of the Caves in Yorkshire." Blackwood's Edinburgh Magazine, 4 (January), 471.
   Praises Wordsworth as an "illustrious author."

55 [WILSON, JOHN] PHILLIP KEMPFHERHAUSEN. "Letters from the Lakes . . . : Letter III." Blackwood's Edinburgh Magazine, 4 (March), 735-44 (739-44).

1819

Describes Rydal Mount, Wordsworth's appearance and his behavior towards his family. Walks with Wordsworth through the scenes of Wordsworth's inspiration; reports the respect Wordsworth received from the peasants, his views on poetry, his praise of A. W. and Friedrich von Schlegel and of Coleridge, his contempt of periodical criticism, and his despair over Napoleon.

56   [WILSON, JOHN]. "Observations on Mr Campbell's Essay on English Poetry, &c." Blackwood's Edinburgh Magazine, 5 (May), 217-31 (230-31).
       Wordsworth is not the poet of the passions of real life.

57   [WILSON, JOHN]. Review of Crabbe's Tales of the Hall. Blackwood's Edinburgh Magazine, 5 (July), 469-83 (469-71).
       Burns, Wordsworth, and Crabbe choose subjects from the British people; hence their poetry is deeply felt. Though he looks into the human soul, Wordsworth stands aloof from the objects of his description, especially in The Excursion. He deals too exclusively with perverted passions. Yet he gives us a cheering faith in the goodness of the Deity.

58   [WILSON, JOHN]. "Opinion on Kempferhausen's [sic] Article." Blackwood's Edinburgh Magazine, 5 (September), 654.
       Records incident of Wordsworth being mistaken for a horse dealer.

59   Z. See 1819.B45.

60   Z., X. Y. See 1819.B37.

1820 A   BOOKS

1   ANON. The Battered Tar, or, the Waggoner's Companion: A Poem, with Sonnets, &c. London: Johnston; Simpkin and Marshall; Sherwood, Neely, and Jones; Clarke [1820], 46 pp.
     Includes "The Battered Tar," a parody of The Waggoner, and four sonnets and a poem ridiculing Wordsworth's confidence in his fame and his attitude toward gypsies in "Gipsies."

1820 B   SHORTER WRITINGS

1   ANON. Review of The River Duddon. Literary Gazette, no. 166 (25 March), pp. 200-203.

46

Though the poems contain a few unnatural expressions, the volume, and especially "Vaudracour and Julia," is unstained by Wordsworth's previous puerilities and serves to rank Wordsworth among the foremost bards of the age.

2   ANON. Review of The River Duddon. European Magazine, 77 (June), 523-25.
      Though Wordsworth is not appreciated by all, he is equalled by few of his contemporaries. The prose in The River Duddon is almost as interesting as the poetry.

3   ANON. Review of The River Duddon. London Magazine; and Monthly Critical and Dramatic Review, 1 (June), 618-27.
      Wordsworth's poems combine the meditative spirit of the metaphysical poets with the simplicity and love of nature of the Elizabethans. The Excursion is the touchstone of his talent; the lowly subjects and language in Lyrical Ballads, though justly chosen, understandably alienate most readers. In accurate and minute--sometimes too minute-- description he is unrivalled. The River Duddon contains fewer of his peculiarities, and more of his modest philosophical beauties, than any earlier work; the sonnets beautifully adapt morality to description. The attacks in the Edinburgh Review and the prejudices of readers keep Wordsworth's poems from being popular.

4   ANON. "Sonnet to Wordsworth." Edinburgh Magazine and Literary Miscellany, NS 6 (June), 504.
      Wordsworth's song gives peace, pride in humanity.

5   ANON. "Extract from Mr Wordsworth's Last Volume.--Memoir of the Reverend Robert Walker." Edinburgh Magazine and Literary Miscellany, NS 7 (July), 38-43.
      Chooses to quote from the memoir, rather than the poems in The River Duddon, as more to the level of his vulgar capacities.

6   ANON. Review of Spence's Anecdotes. Quarterly Review, 23 (July), 400-43 (410-11).
      Wordsworth errs in his theory of nature versus the artificial.

7   ANON. "The Lion's Head." London Magazine, 2 (July), 3-8 (7-8).
      Except for the "sportive imitation" of Milton in "On the Detraction which Followed the Publication of a Certain Poem," Wordsworth does not in The River Duddon, as he had in the past, violate the principles of selection and harmony essential to poetry.

1820

8   ANON. Review of The River Duddon. Literary Chronicle, 2
        (1 July), 420-22.
            Though typically choosing for his title an insignificant
        river with a barbarous name, Wordsworth exhibits few of his
        characteristic defects in The River Duddon.

9   ANON. Review of The River Duddon. Eclectic Review, NS 14
        (August), 170-84.
            Wordsworth, in writing "On the Detraction which Followed
        the Publication of a Certain Poem," misunderstands Milton's
        sonnet. The prose of the volume proves that Wordsworth
        should have treated more of his subjects in prose rather
        than poetry. His blank verse is his best, though the Duddon
        sonnets contain noble descriptions. In "Whence that low
        voice?--A whisper from the heart," he confounds the figura-
        tive with the physical. The enigmatical odes and "The
        Prioress' Tale" are the least pleasing in the volume; what
        was meant by Chaucer for satire, might be mistaken by Words-
        worth for pathos. The volume atones for Peter Bell and The
        Waggoner.

10 ANON. Review of The River Duddon. Ladies' Monthly Museum,
        3rd ser., 12 (August), 95.
            Wordsworth has abandoned the affected simplicity of Peter
        Bell and The Waggoner to write with true simplicity.

11 ANON. Review of The River Duddon. Literary and Statistical
        Magazine for Scotland, 4 (August), 323-28.
            Though the stanzas on the Duddon are uninteresting, the
        sketch of Robert Walker is moving.

12 ANON. Review of The River Duddon. British Review, 16
        (September), 37-53.
            In the Duddon sonnets Wordsworth brings intensity and
        originality of natural expression to the imbuing of external
        description with interior feelings. In some poems (e.g.,
        "Vaudracour and Julia," "The Pilgrim's Dream"), however, he
        becomes too prosaic. The essay on the Lakes is valuable as
        an illustration of the poems and in its own right.

13 ANON. "Lake School of Poetry.--Mr. Wordsworth." New Monthly
        Magazine, 14 (October), 361-68.
            Wordsworth's faults include writing with obscurity and
        false simplicity in poems like "The Idiot Boy" and "Goody
        Blake and Harry Gill."

14 ANON. Review of The River Duddon. Gentleman's Magazine, 90-2
        (October), 344-46.

The poems are written with Wordsworth's customary ease and elegant simplicity.

15   ANON. Review of The River Duddon. Monthly Review, NS 93 (October), 132-43.
      In the volume Wordsworth recants his theory of poetic language. The best poems are the miscellaneous pieces; in "The Pass of Kirkstone" he does not forget Dr. Johnson's advice and gives a general view of nature. But in "Vaudracour and Julia" he uses prosaic language, treats inanimate objects as if alive, and portrays immorality. In the sonnets he exhibits his peculiar ability to make nonsense seem wisdom.

16   ANON. Review of Miscellaneous Poems (1820). Literary Gazette, no. 194 (7 October), p. 641.
      Though he is mistaken in relishing what is mean, affected, and puerile, Wordsworth has made amends with The River Duddon.

17   ANON. "Contemporary Authors--No. 9: Wordsworth, and the Lake School of Poets." Monthly Magazine, 50 (November), 307-10.
      In his political apostasy, Wordsworth is well-meaning and honest, though deficient in judgment. He is a true revolutionist. He had exhibited his natural literary style in An Evening Walk and Descriptive Sketches but gave it up when he discovered it would not make him popular. He now writes monotonous, prosaic philosophical verse, though Coleridge is too severe in his censure of Wordsworth's subjects.

18   ANON. Review of The Excursion (second edition). Literary Gazette, no. 206 (30 December), p. 837.
      In its new format, The Excursion will be universally read and duly appreciated.

19   BARTON, BERNARD. "To William Wordsworth; On the Publication of his Poem, Entitled 'Peter Bell'" (poem), in Poems. London: Harvey and Darton, pp. 106-12.
      The tale of Peter Bell is worthy of a more simple, primal age of feeling, an age analogous to one's youth.

20   BYRONIUS. "Longinus o'er a Bottle: Canto II" (poem). London Magazine; and Monthly Critical and Dramatic Review, 1 (March), 329-30 (329).
      Mocks and burlesques Wordsworth's plain style.

1820

21   C.[AREY], D.[AVID]. "The Mansion of the Poets," in <u>Beauties</u>
      <u>of the Modern Poets</u>. Edited by David Carey. London:
      Wright, pp. v-xxv (xx).
        Wordsworth is characterized by simplicity, withdrawal.

22   [CAREY, DAVID?]. "The Water Melon" (poem), in <u>Beauties of the</u>
      <u>Modern Poets</u>. Edited by David Carey. London: Wright,
      p. 319.
        A burlesque, signed "Wordsworth."

23   CORCORAN, PETER. <u>See</u> 1820.B41.

24   ETONIAN, AN. Letter to the Editor. <u>Salt-Bearer</u>, no. 24,
      pp. 278-83.
        A reply to 1820.B35. "To H. C.," "She was a Phantom of
      delight," and <u>Peter Bell</u> illustrate Wordsworth's unintelli-
      gibility.

25   [GOSNELL, WILLIAM and WILLIAM MAGINN]. "Daniel O'Rourke, an
      Epic Poem." <u>Blackwood's Edinburgh Magazine</u>, 8 (November),
      155-61 (159).
        "Cheer up, Great Poet, loud thy fame will swell, /
      When thy detractors' name shall be unknown."

26   [HAZLITT, WILLIAM]. "The Drama: No. IV." <u>London Magazine</u>, 1
      (April), 432-40 (435-36).
        Wordsworth would be unlikely to succeed in writing drama:
      he cannot go outside of himself; he is not interested in
      the goings on of life.

27   [HAZLITT, WILLIAM] T. "Table-Talk: No. I: On the Qualifica-
      tions Necessary to Success in Life." <u>London Magazine</u>, 1
      (June), 646-54 (646-50).
        Wordsworth's reputation illustrates the fact that merit
      is not rewarded. Reports Wordsworth's remark that great
      poets have been more healthy and handsome than ingenious
      ones. Reprinted with minor omissions in 1826.B10.

28   [HAZLITT, WILLIAM] T. "Table-Talk: No. III: On the Conver-
      sation of Authors." <u>London Magazine</u>, 2 (September), 250-62
      (261).
        Wordsworth "sometimes talks like a man inspired on sub-
      jects of poetry (his own out of the question)." Reprinted
      as "The Same Subject ["On the Conversation of Authors"]
      Continued" in 1826.B10.

29   [HUNT, LEIGH]. "Spring.--Daisies.--Gathering Flowers."
      <u>Indicator</u>, no. 28 (19 April), pp. 217-24 (220-22).

Quarrels with Wordsworth's description of the daisy in "To the Same Flower" ("With little here to do or see"). Reprinted in The Indicator, and The Companion (1834).

30 LANDOR, SAVAGIUS. "De Cultu Atque Usu Latini Sermonis et Quamobrem Poetae Latini Recentiores Minus Legantur," in Idyllia Heroica Decem. . . . Pisa: Nistrium, pp. 167-258 (215).
    Praises Wordsworth, whom greatness did not preserve from critical attacks. (In Latin.)

31 [MAGINN, WILLIAM]. "Extract from Poems of the Apprehension." Literary Gazette, no. 180 (1 July), p. 427.
    Parody of "My heart leaps up when I behold." Attribution: R. S. Mackenzie in 1855.B6, II:263.

32 [MAGINN, WILLIAM and JOHN GIBSON LOCKHART?]. "'Luctus' on the Death of Sir Daniel Donnelly." Blackwood's Edinburgh Magazine, 7 (May), 186-201 (187, 189-92).
    Rebukes Wordsworth for distinguishing between fancy and imagination. Includes "Letter from Mr W. W. to Mr Christopher North" ridiculing Wordsworth's attitude, in Essay (1815), towards periodical criticism and enclosing burlesques: "Extract from my Great Auto-biographical Poem" and "Sir Daniel Donnelly.--A Ballad."

33 [MAGINN, WILLIAM (and JOHN WILSON?)]. "Boxiana, No. VIII: The Sable School of Pugilism." Blackwood's Edinburgh Magazine, 8 (October), 60-67 (61-64).
    Contains Maginn's "Sonnet: On the Battle between Mendoza and Tom Owen, at Banstead Downs, July 4th, 1820: By W. W.," a burlesque, the epigraph parodying "Yarrow Visited."

34 M.[ONTGOMERY], G.[ERARD]. See 1820.B35.

35 [MOULTRIE, JOHN] G.[ERARD] M.[ONTGOMERY]. "On Wordsworth's Poetry." Etonian, 1 (November), 99-104; (December), 217-25.
    Wordsworth has survived the abuse of the Edinburgh Review; he possesses the powers of invention and imitation, and the command of language, of a genuine poet (99-104). He presents impressions produced by common objects and feelings that demand a corresponding sensibility in the reader. Because he is a lover of the Universe as the symbol of God, he cannot neglect even the lowest part of it. But, as opposed to Burns, Bloomfield, and Clare, he does not simply make verse of common objects; he works upon them with his fancy and imagination. He has faith in the intrinsic

1820

godliness of the soul (e.g., in "Ode: Intimations of Immortality"). Popularity is not a test of poetic merit
(217-25). Attribution: Charles Knight in 1864.B8, I:298.

36   N.   Review of Evening Hours. London Magazine; and Monthly
Critical and Dramatic Review, 1 (January), 49-54 (49-51).
     "Wordsworth's braying of pedlars' asses" has degraded
poetry.

37   N., D.   "Essay on Poetry." London Magazine, and Monthly
Critical and Dramatic Review, 2 (November), [470]-74
([470]); (December), 557-62 (559).
     Wordsworth, a poet of imagination rather than fancy
([470]), benevolently depicts "the amiable sensibilities of
mankind." His poetry cannot be appreciated in passages,
but only as a whole (559).

38   [PEACOCK, THOMAS LOVE].   "The Four Ages of Poetry." Olliers
Literary Miscellany, no. 1, pp. 183-200 (195-98).
     Wordsworth's poetry consists of "phantastical parturi-
tion[s] of the moods of his own mind."

39   QUIZ, SAM.   "Immortality in Embryo; or, Genius in its Night-
gown." London Magazine; and Monthly Critical and Dramatic
Review, 2 (July), 39-43 (39-41).
     Mocks Wordsworth as founder of a new, mystical poetic
system and compatriot of Coleridge. Includes burlesque,
"To the Muse" (poem).

40   [REYNOLDS, JOHN HAMILTON].   "Living Authors, A Dream."
Edinburgh Magazine and Literary Miscellany, NS 7 (August),
133-40 (133-34, 140).
     Wordsworth "would be greater, if he did not think him-
self the greatest." He calumniated nature's favors by "fits
of childishness and vanity." Recast from 1816.B36.

41   [REYNOLDS, JOHN HAMILTON] PETER CORCORAN.   "Introduction" to
"King Tims the first: an American Tragedy," "Peter Bell v.
Peter Bell" (poem), in The Fancy, a Selection from the
Poetical Remains of the late Peter Corcoran. London:
Taylor & Hessey, pp. 3-12 (5), 86-87.
     Wordsworth's pedlars "talk a linsey-woolsey philosophy
in uninhabited woods" (5). Snipes at "Simplicity's Poet"
(86-87).

42   [SCOTT, JOHN].   "Living Authors: No. II: Wordsworth."
London Magazine, 1 (March), 275-85.

Wordsworth's works exhibit a genuine communion with moral and physical beauty. Unlike Teniers in his paintings, Wordsworth does not excel in presenting literal truth but in giving thoughts the literal facts suggest; his poetical characters are marked by his own character; his subjects, when he writes well, are hence only superficially simple, contrary to the opinions expressed in the Edinburgh Review. But he perverts the sound aspects of his theory when, as in "The Idiot Boy" and "The Sailor's Mother," he focuses on the mere accidental circumstances attending his subjects, without integrating them to his own or his reader's character. Attribution: B. W. Procter in 1866.B13, pp. 149-50.

43 [SCOTT, JOHN]. "Blackwood's Magazine." London Magazine, 2 (November), 509-21 (512-13).
    Wordsworth has expressed contempt of both the vilifications and praises by Wilson in Blackwood's Edinburgh Magazine. Attribution: Walter Graham, English Literary Periodicals (New York: Nelson, 1930), p. 281.

44 [SCOTT, JOHN]. "The Mohock Magazine." London Magazine, 2 (December), 666-85 (673-74).
    Attacks Wilson's writings on Wordsworth in Blackwood's Edinburgh Magazine. Attribution: Walter Graham, English Literary Periodicals (New York: Nelson, 1930), p. 281.

45 SHELLEY, PERCY BYSSHE. "An Exhortation" (poem), in Prometheus Unbound: A Lyrical Drama in Four Acts with Other Poems. London: Ollier, pp. 186-87.
    Laments that a desire for fame forces poets to change their opinions. See 1859.B19.

46 T. See 1820.B27-B28.

47 [TALFOURD, THOMAS NOON]. "Modern Periodical Literature." New Monthly Magazine, 14 (September), 304-10 (305-306, 308, 310).
    Wordsworth, Coleridge, and Southey do not form a poetic school. The Edinburgh Review dwells on a few of Wordsworth's simplicities, ignoring his beauties.

48 T.[ALFOURD], T.[HOMAS] N.[OON]. "On the Genius and Writings of Wordsworth." New Monthly Magazine, 14 (November), 498-506; (December), 648-55.
    It is unfair to judge Wordsworth by his theories rather than by the poems themselves, though his choices of language and subjects can be justified. His genius is evident in his descriptions, his probings of the quiet passions and of the interactions of mind and nature (e.g., in "Yew-trees")

53

1820

(498-506), his perceptions of moral beauty, his contempla-
tions of "the grand abstractions of humanity" (e.g., in
"Ode: Intimations of Immortality"), his delineations of
individuals (especially in The White Doe of Rylstone), and
his handling of mythological stories (648-55).

49   [TALFOURD, THOMAS NOON]. Review of Wallace's Various Prospects
      of Mankind, Nature, and Providence. Retrospective Review,
      2:185-206 (197, 201).
            Wordsworth's "divine philosophy" is equalled by no other
      poet. He goes beyond Cowper, Goldsmith, Collins, and Burns
      to discover new insights. He should not be classed with
      Coleridge or Southey.

50   TICKL'EM, TOBY. "The Centinel." Lonsdale Magazine, 1
      (November), 482-87 (484-87).
            To exhibit his talents in reviewing, first praises and
      then damns Wordsworth's delineation of character and simple
      style in Peter Bell.

51   [WADE, JOHN]. The Black Book; or, Corruption Unmasked! . . . .
      2 vols. London: Fairburn, I:89.
            Lists Wordsworth as distributor of stamps. Attribution:
      British Museum catalogue. For Volume III, see 1823.B30.

52   [WILSON, JOHN or JOHN GIBSON LOCKHART?]. Review of The River
      Duddon. Blackwood's Edinburgh Magazine, 7 (May), 206-13.
            Critics have failed to check Wordsworth's fame. In The
      River Duddon his customary singularities of style are less
      prominent. Had critics been silent over his few trivial
      poems, he may have written fewer in that class and more
      like the stately "Dion."

1821 A   BOOKS - NONE

1821 B   SHORTER WRITINGS

1   ANON. "The Nose-Drop; a Physiological Ballad." Academic,
      no. 1 (15 January), pp. 15-20.
            A burlesque, "by the late W. W."

2   ANON. Review of The River Duddon. British Critic, NS 15
      (February), 113-35.
            Because Wordsworth writes on a system, it is unfair to
      judge him on the basis of extracts or opinions of critics
      who do not understand that system. Wordsworth's qualifica-
      tions to be a poet include his perception of moral truth,

his reasoning power, his diction (which is not so low as
his subjects), his metrical excellence in blank verse
(though not in the lyric), his knowledge (including knowledge of Horace), his observation of external nature and the
human heart, and his worthy notion of his art. His failings
include evidences of indistinctness of idea (e.g., in "On
the Death of His Majesty [George the Third]"), too rapid a
transition in thought (e.g., in "To the Rev. Dr. Wordsworth"), imperfect description (e.g., in "Ode to Lycoris"),
a notion of pre-existence (in "Ode: Intimations of Immortality"), lack of dramatic skill (e.g., in "Dion"), and
idiosyncratic habits of mind. The River Duddon has fewer
of his peculiarities than any preceding volume.

3   ANON. Review of Southey's A Vision of Judgment. Gold's London
     Magazine, 3 (April), 393-401 (393).
          Wordsworth is not a deep thinker; he abstracts the book
     of nature for his own use.

4   ANON. Review of Leigh's The View. Gold's London Magazine, 4
     (July), 85-91 (85, 87-88).
          Wordsworth's followers have imbibed his occasional vul-
     garisms and obscurity, not his purity and sublimity.

5   ANON. "Byron versus Wordsworth." Examiner, no. 712
     (26 August), p. 540.
          Though a backslider from liberty, Wordsworth is a noble
     poet.

6   ANON. "To Mrs. Hannah More, from W------ W--ds--th" (poem)
     and Note, in Lost Valentines Found; with Other Trifles in
     Rhyme. London: Allman, pp. 44-53, 94-95.
          A burlesque.

7   ARISTARCHUS. "Vindication of Lord Byron's Poetry." Imperial
     Magazine, 3 (September), 810-12; (November), 1016-24.
          A reply to 1821.B26. Attacks the elevation of Words-
     worth at the expense of Byron (810-12). A reply to
     1821.B24, B27. Attacks Wordsworth's simplicity (1016-24).

8   ATKINS, LEONARD. See 1821.B9.

9   [BRIGGS, JOHN] LEONARD ATKINS. "Letters from the Lakes:
     Letter VII." Lonsdale Magazine, 2 (July), 243-48 (243,
     245).
          Wordsworth is "easily understood." His image of viewing
     the Lakes as spokes in A Description of the Scenery of the
     Lakes is not original.

1821

10   BULL, JOHN. <u>See</u> 1821.B25.

11   [BYRON, LORD]. <u>Don Juan, Cantos III, IV, and V</u>. London:
        privately printed, pp. 55-58 (Canto iii, Stanzas xciii-xcv,
        xcviii-c), 125 (Canto iv, Stanza cix).
           Wordsworth, unhired, "Season'd his pedlar poems with
        democracy." Mocks the length and unintelligibility of <u>The</u>
        <u>Excursion</u>, Wordsworth's low subjects (e.g., in <u>Peter Bell</u>),
        and his arguments about poetic fame.

12   BYRON, THE RIGHT HON. LORD. <u>Letter to **** ******, on the</u>
        <u>Rev. W. L. Bowles' Strictures on the Life and Writings of</u>
        <u>Pope</u>. London: Murray, pp. 24, 28-29; Addenda p. 4.
           Mocks Wordsworth's use of low subjects. (Addenda added
        in second issue.)

13   CHRISTIANUS. "Wordsworth." <u>Imperial Magazine</u>, 3 (November),
        393.
           A reply to 1821.B26. Attacks as blasphemous "Occasioned
        by the Battle of Waterloo" ("The Bard--whose soul is meek
        as dawning day").

14   COLERIDGE, S.[AMUEL] T.[AYLOR]. "Selection from Mr Coleridge's
        Literary Correspondence with Friends, and Men of Letters:
        No. I." <u>Blackwood's Edinburgh Magazine</u>, 10 (October),
        243-62 (255-56, 259).
           Includes letters in which Coleridge comments on the salu-
        tary influence of Wordsworth's minor poems.

15   [DE QUINCEY, THOMAS]. "Confessions of an English Opium-Eater:
        Being an Extract from the Life of a Scholar." <u>London</u>
        <u>Magazine</u>, 4 (September), 293-312 (293); (October), 353-79
        (355, 370, 374).
           Praises Wordsworth's poems and reading of his own verses.
        Reprinted in <u>Confessions of an English Opium-Eater</u> (1822)
        and <u>De Quincey's Writings</u> (1850-59); expanded in 1856.B5.

16   ETHERIDGE [misprinted "Coleridge"], MARK. "Byron and
        Wordsworth.--Wordsworth Vindicated." <u>Imperial Magazine</u>, 3
        (December), 1122-24.
           Attacks 1821.B7. (Misprint corrected, <u>Imperial Magazine</u>,
        4 [1822], 421.)

17   F., F. F. "On the Respective Merits of Byron and Wordsworth."
        <u>Imperial Magazine</u>, 4 (May), 421-23.
           Praises 1821.B26-B28; attacks 1821.B35, B37.

18   [HAZLITT, WILLIAM] T. "Table-Talk: No. VII: On Reading Old
      Books." London Magazine, 3 (February), 128-34 (132, 134).
           Notes his debt to Wordsworth and Coleridge's admiration
      of an Essay on Marriage by Wordsworth. Reprinted in Table-
      Talk (Paris, 1825) and 1826.B10.

19   [HAZLITT, WILLIAM] T. "Table Talk: No. XII: On Consistency
      of Opinion." London Magazine, 4 (November), 485-92
      (487-88).
           Though he does not renounce his past poetic theories,
      Wordsworth incongruously degrades rustics by his actions in
      Westmorland politics. Records incident of Wordsworth's
      frugality (see 1885.B48).

20   HAZLITT, WILLIAM. "Essay III: On the Past and Future,"
      "Essay V: The Same Subject ["On Genius and Common Sense"]
      Continued," "Essay VII: On People with One Idea," "Essay
      IX: The Indian Jugglers," in Table-Talk; or, Original
      Essays. 2 vols. London: Warren, I:43-64 (49), 91-111
      (97-100), 135-58 (149, 155-56), 179-208 (203).
           Remarks Wordsworth's attitude towards the past (49).
      Wordsworth is an original poet because he is a great ego-
      tist; he relates everything to himself (97-100). The Ex-
      cursion does not sell. Wordsworth admits of no merit but
      his own (149, 155-56). Reprinted from 1819.B35 (203).
      For Volume II, see 1822.B34.

21   HOGG, JAMES, the Ettrick Shepherd. "Memoir of the Life of
      James Hogg," in The Mountain Bard; Consisting of Legendary
      Ballads and Tales. Third edition, enlarged: to which is
      prefixed a Memoir of the Author's Life, Written by Himself.
      Edinburgh: Oliver & Boyd, pp. ix-lxxvii (lvii-lix).
           Records his account of Wordsworth's sending, and after-
      wards reclaiming, his contribution to The Poetic Mirror.
      Reprinted in 1832.B17.

22   HUNT, LEIGH. Note to "Literary Notices: No. 47." Examiner,
      no. 695 (29 April), p. 269.
           Clarifies Byron's opinion of Wordsworth as he had re-
      ported it in 1818.B21.

23   [HUNT, LEIGH]   . "Sketches of the Living Poets: No. 4.--
      Mr. Coleridge." Examiner, no. 720 (21 October), pp. 664-67
      (665).
           Attacks Wordsworth's pride and his position as distribu-
      tor of stamps.

1821

24   J., G. "Vindication of Wordsworth's Poetry." *Imperial
     Magazine*, 3 (October), 923-26.
          Supports 1821.B26; attacks 1821.B7. Prefers the puerili-
     ties of Wordsworth to the obscenities of Byron.

25   [LOCKHART, JOHN GIBSON] JOHN BULL. *Letter to the Right Hon.
     Lord Byron*. London: Wright, pp. 11-20, 43, 46, 49-50, 52.
          Wordsworth thinks no one thought a tree beautiful until
     he announced his own perceptions. He is now best known as
     a stamp-master.

26   M., G. "On the Genius and Writings of Wordsworth." *Imperial
     Magazine*, 3 (July), 598-602.
          Wordsworth's system has been misrepresented. His great-
     ness lies in his calling forth of man's holiest sympathies,
     his majestic and pure feelings, and his noble depicting of
     both simple and lofty subjects. No living poet depends so
     much upon the "bare strength of his own powers." The fame
     of his benevolent poetry is rising, while that of Byron's
     misanthropic poetry is falling.

27   M., G. "Defence of Wordsworth." *Imperial Magazine*, 3
     (October), 885-87.
          A reply to 1821.B7. All the great poets of the age have
     honored Wordsworth.

28   M., G. "Byron and Wordsworth.--Wordsworth Vindicated."
     Imperial Magazine, 3 (December), 1118-22.
          A reply to 1821.B7.

29   M., M. "Observations on Lord Byron and Wordsworth." *Imperial
     Magazine*, 3 (November), 978-83.
          A reply to 1821.B7. Byron's writings are not calculated
     to make men better, are immoral and plagiarized; Words-
     worth's are the opposite.

30   [MOIR, DAVID MACBETH] △ . "Sonnet to Wordsworth."
     Blackwood's Edinburgh Magazine, 8 (February), 542.
          Men in cities feel the innocence of Wordsworth's musings
     in solitude.

31   [MOIR, DAVID MACBETH] MORGAN ODOHERTY. "Familiar Letter from
     the Adjutant." *Blackwood's Edinburgh Magazine*, 9 (May),
     131-40 (138-40).
          Includes "The Kail Pot" and "Billy Blinn" (poems),
     burlesques.

32   MONTGOMERY, GERARD. See 1821.B33.

58

33 [MOULTRIE, JOHN] GERARD MONTGOMERY. "On Coleridge's Poetry."
    Etonian, 1 (February), 307-18.
        Compares Wordsworth and Coleridge. There is nothing that
    can be called love in Wordsworth's poems. Attribution:
    Charles Knight in 1864.B8, I:298.

34 ODOHERTY, MORGAN. See 1821.B31.

35 PHILO-ARISTARCHUS. "Byron and Wordsworth.--Byron Vindicated."
    Imperial Magazine, 3 (December), 1115-18.
        Defends 1821.B7.

36 Q. "Prospective Letter Concerning Poetry." Blackwood's
    Edinburgh Magazine, 10 (September), 125-27 (126-27).
        Wordsworth's writing is not free from a "puritanical
    grudge," evidence of his taking too great a pleasure in his
    own accomplishment.

37 SCRUTATOR. "Byron and Wordsworth.--Byron Vindicated."
    Imperial Magazine, 3 (December), 1113-15.
        Defends 1821.B7; attacks 1821.B26-B27.

38 ST. JOHN, H. "Peter Bell." Kaleidoscope, NS 1 (6 March),
    285-86.
        The Prologue lacks sense; the poem is ridiculous rubbish.

39 SUBSCRIBER, A. "Byron and Wordsworth.--Wordsworth Vindicated."
    Imperial Magazine, 3 (December), 1124.
        A reply to 1821.B7. Wordsworth has made amends for his
    early puerilities.

40 T. See 1821.B18-B19.

41 [TALFOURD, THOMAS NOON]. Review of Lloyd's Desultory Thoughts
    in London. London Magazine, 3 (April), 406-13 (406-407).
        Contrasts Wordsworth with Coleridge, Southey, and Lloyd
    in choice of subjects, egotism, and intensity.

42 [WATTS, ALARIC A.]. "Lord Byron's Plagiarisms." Literary
    Gazette, no. 217 (17 March), pp. 168-70 (168-69).
        Wordsworth is the most original of modern poets. Attri-
    bution: Literary Gazette, no. 214 (24 February), p. 121.

1822

1822 A BOOKS - NONE

1822 B SHORTER WRITINGS

1   ANON. "Ballad Poetry." Literary Speculum, 1 (January),
       161-64 (162-64).
           Wordsworth is ready to burst into tears at the simple
       sights of nature but passes unheeded the miseries of man.

2   ANON. "Hapless Ellen." Examiner, no. 730 (20 January),
       pp. 42-43; no. 731 (27 January), pp. 58-59.
           That Wordsworth is neglected shows the public wants
       taste (42-43). The expensive, bulky format of The Excursion
       has hindered its sale (58-59).

3   ANON. "The White Doe." Examiner, no. 735 (24 February),
       p. 126.
           Welcomes the announcement of small-sized editions of
       Wordsworth's poems that the public can afford.

4   ANON. Review of Ecclesiastical Sketches. Literary Gazette,
       no. 271 (30 March), pp. 191-92.
           Wordsworth again sinks into weakness and doating, choos-
       ing a prosaic subject and an absurd plan. He shuns what he
       can do well to turn to what no talent can render acceptable.
       The sonnets contain errors in diction and unintelligible
       thoughts.

5   ANON. Review of Memorials of a Tour on the Continent.
       Literary Gazette, no. 271 (30 March), p. 192.
           The volume possesses greater variety than Ecclesiastical
       Sketches.

6   ANON. "Lyrical Ballad" (poem). Country Constitutional
       Guardian, 1 (April), 367-68.
           Parody of "Resolution and Independence."

7   ANON. Review of Memorials of a Tour on the Continent.
       Literary Gazette, no. 272 (6 April), pp. 210-12.
           The volume contains "teemings of egotistical compla-
       cency," few poetical ideas, infelicitous diction and imag-
       ery, and "namby-pamby and doggrel."

8   ANON. "New Books Published in April." Monthly Magazine, 53
       (May), 340-47 (343-44).
           Wordsworth describes "any trait of feeling or pathos
       with peculiar force." Ecclesiastical Sketches is less in-
       teresting than Memorials of a Tour on the Continent.

9   ANON. Review of Ecclesiastical Sketches. General Weekly
     Register (5 May), pp. 184-85.
          The reputation of the Lake School, of which Coleridge is
     the metaphysician and Wordsworth the philosopher, is de-
     clining. In Ecclesiastical Sketches Wordsworth abandons
     the divinity of nature for that of "painted wood, gilt
     crosses, and priestcraft."

10   ANON. Review of Memorials of a Tour on the Continent.
     Literary Museum, no. 4 (18 May), pp. 52-53.
          Because Wordsworth himself gives value to the external
     objects he observes, one must approach his poems with his
     predispositions. Memorials of a Tour on the Continent con-
     tains not the grander flights of Wordsworth's imagination,
     but passing musings.

11   ANON. Review of Ecclesiastical Sketches. Monthly Literary
     Register, no. 2 (1 June), pp. 88-89.
          The volume cannot revive the declining reputation of the
     Lake School, of which Wordsworth is the philosopher. Words-
     worth champions clerical power.

12   ANON. "The Augustan Age in England." Album, 1 (July),
     183-234 (215-16).
          Wordsworth martyrs his genius to the hypotheses of the
     Preface to Lyrical Ballads.

13   ANON. Review of Ecclesiastical Sketches. Christian's Pocket
     Magazine, 7 (September), 128-30.
          Dullness and insipidity characterize Wordsworth's poems.

14   ANON. Review of Ecclesiastical Sketches and Memorials of a
     Tour on the Continent. British Critic, NS 18 (November),
     522-31.
          Ecclesiastical Sketches fails in method; the sonnets
     fail as sonnets, though they are delightful poems. In
     Memorials of a Tour on the Continent Wordsworth exhibits
     wise tolerance, true philanthropy, and ardent patriotism.
     He has retreated from his untenable peculiarities.

15   ANON. "Strictures on the Poets of the Present Day: No. 5.--
     William Wordsworth." La Belle Assemblée, NS 26 (November),
     440-43.
          Wordsworth has written too much to write uniformly well;
     he should publish less. He indulges in tedious details and
     "the perpetual and futile analysis of every common operation
     of the mind."

1822

16   ANON. "Wordsworth's Excursion to the Top of Scawfell."
        Lonsdale Magazine, 3 (30 November), 429-30.
            A Description of the Scenery of the Lakes is "a very in-
        teresting little work."

17   ANON. Review of Memorials of a Tour on the Continent.
        British Review, 20 (December), 459-66.
            The poems contain thoughtful, fresh observation. Words-
        worth should not squander his powers on sonnets.

18   ANON. Review of Ecclesiastical Sketches. Literary Chronicle,
        4 (14 December), 791.
            Wordsworth has made sad work of an unfortunate task.

19   ANON. Review of Memorials of a Tour on the Continent.
        Literary Chronicle, 4 (14 December), 791.
            The volume contains "pure and unadulterated nonsense."

20   ANTI-BYRON. "On the Respective Merits of Byron and Wordsworth."
        Imperial Magazine, 4 (May), 423.
            Notes that G. M. and Etheridge have refuted Aristarchus.
        See 1821.B7, B16, B26-B28. Does not really like either
        Byron or Wordsworth.

21   ARISTARCHI AMICUS. "On the Respective Merits of Byron and
        Wordsworth." Imperial Magazine, 4 (May), 437-39.
            A reply to 1821.B7, B29. Criticizes Wordsworth's in-
        ferior intellect and effeminate style.

22   ARISTARCHUS. "Remarks on Byron and Wordsworth." Imperial
        Magazine, 4 (July), 628-50.
            Sums up the correspondence in the Imperial Magazine on
        Byron and Wordsworth: a final repeating of the charge of
        simplicity against Wordsworth.

23   [BOWRING, JOHN?]. Review of Ecclesiastical Sketches and
        Memorials of a Tour on the Continent. Monthly Repository,
        17 (June), 360-65.
            Wordsworth has little success with sonnets. In writing
        of the past, he records the interests of the lowly; but
        since he changed his politics, he ignores the plight of the
        oppressed in his writings about today. In Ecclesiastical
        Sketches his sympathies are not dependent on facts or con-
        victions, but on prejudices and passions. Memorials of a
        Tour on the Continent contains much exquisite pathos and
        description. Wordsworth's spirit has dominated the age.

24   BYRONIS POEMATUM ADMIRATOR. "On the Respective Merits of
      Byron and Wordsworth." Imperial Magazine, 4 (May), 435-36.
         A reply to 1821.B7, B26-B28. Attacks Wordsworth's
      simplicity.

25   [COLERIDGE, HARTLEY] THERSITES. "On the Poetical Use of the
      Heathen Mythology." London Magazine, 5 (February), 113-20
      (113).
         Notes Wordsworth's "fondness, of late, for classical
      tales and images." Reprinted in 1851.B16.

26   D.[OUBLEDAY], T.[HOMAS]. "How Far is Poetry an Art?"
      Blackwood's Edinburgh Magazine, 11 (February), 153-59
      (156-57).
         Wordsworth unites poetical with metaphysical talent,
      writing about the things he lives amidst.

27   ELIA. See 1822.B40.

28   EPSILON. "On the Respective Merits of Byron and Wordsworth."
      Imperial Magazine, 4 (May), 424-31.
         A reply to 1821.B7, B35, B37. Defends Wordsworth's sim-
      plicity and blank verse, and the imaginative beauty, gran-
      deur, classic dignity, and moral truth of his poems. Words-
      worth transmutes and exalts all that he observes.

29   ETHERIDGE, MARK. "On the Respective Merits of Byron and
      Wordsworth." Imperial Magazine, 4 (May), 419-21.
         A reply to 1821.B35, B37.

30   H. "On the Poetical Writings of Wordsworth." Literary
      Speculum, 1 (May), 433-44.
         Though characterized by much puerility and dullness,
      Wordsworth's poems are redeemed by their pathos and pictures
      of the natural world and of man's affections. Especially
      praiseworthy are The Excursion, The Waggoner, and Peter
      Bell, though these works have faults, as does The White Doe
      of Rylstone.

31   H., W. "Modern Plagiarism." Kaleidoscope, NS 2 (5 March),
      278-79 (278).
         Notes verbal similarities between Byron's "Darkness" and
      "The Dream," and The Excursion.

32   [HARLEY, JAMES]. The Press, or Literary Chit-chat: A Satire
      (poem). London: Relfe, pp. 24, 50.
         Wordsworth, living in a "modest mansion," is the "sport
      of every thought," yet often paints truly. Attribution:

1822

The English Catalogue of Books . . . 1801-1836, edited by
P. A. Peddie and Q. Waddington (London: Publishers'
Circular, 1914), p. 468.

33 [HAZLITT, WILLIAM]. "Table Talk: No. III: On Milton's
Sonnets." New Monthly Magazine, [NS] 4 [March], 238-43
(239).
In contrast to Milton's, Wordsworth's sonnets to liberty
are insincere. Expanded in 1822.B34.

34 HAZLITT, WILLIAM. "Essay II: On Milton's Sonnets," in
Table-talk; or, Original Essays. 2 vols. London: Colburn,
II:17-32 (22-23).
Expanded from 1822.B33. It is no criticism of Words-
worth to call him a lesser man and poet than Milton. For
Volume I, see 1821.B20.

35 I. "Whoso attemps to imitate Bob Southey" (poem). Argo,
no. 1 (25 November), pp. 6-7.
Wordsworth labors like a bee at works that come to
nothing.

36 INA. Review of A Description of the Scenery of the Lakes.
New European Magazine, 1 (December), 490-97.
Admires the work, especially Wordsworth's remarks on
new buildings.

37 J., G. "On the Respective Merits of Byron and Wordsworth."
Imperial Magazine, 4 (May), 417-19.
A reply to 1821.B7.

38 J., J. See 1822.B48.

39 [JEFFREY, FRANCIS]. Review of Memorials of a Tour on the
Continent. Edinburgh Review, 37 (November), 449-56.
Since Wordsworth has exchanged the company of leech-
gatherers for that of tax-gatherers, his poetry has become
characterized by feebleness of thought disguised under a
sententious manner and a verbose, obscure style. In
Memorials of a Tour on the Continent he seizes upon trivial
subjects (e.g., in "The Column Intended by Buonaparte for
a Triumphal Edifice in Milan") and ignores facts (e.g., in
"The Germans on the Heights of Hochheim," "The Last Supper,
by Leonardo da Vinci," and his remarks on the triumph of
the late Queen).

40 [LAMB, CHARLES] ELIA. "A Complaint of the Decay of Beggars in
the Metropolis." London Magazine, 5 (June), 532-36 (536).

1822

Notes a proper use of artificial language, contrary to
Wordsworth's theory. (Reference omitted when essay reprinted in Elia [1823].)

41 LAMBDA. "On the Respective Merits of Byron and Wordsworth."
Imperial Magazine, 4 (May), 431-35.
     A reply to 1821.B7. Though some parts of his poems are
mean and obscure, Wordsworth puts his ability to better use
than Byron: he aims at improving man.

42 M., G. "On Modern Poetry." Imperial Magazine, 4 (April),
338-46 (342-43).
     Milton is the only poet with whom Wordsworth can be
compared.

43 [MAGINN, WILLIAM]. "Noctes Ambrosianae: No. IV." Blackwood's
Edinburgh Magazine, 12 (July), 100-14 (102).
     Characterizes Ecclesiastical Sketches as being about
Roman Catholic emancipation.

44 [MAGINN, WILLIAM and OTHERS] PADDY. "Metricum Symposium
Ambrosianum, Seu Propinatio Poetica Northi" (poem).
Blackwood's Edinburgh Magazine, 12 (July), 79-83 (80).
     Mocks Wordsworth, "so wise and so wordy," "Who in vain
blows the bellows of Milton's old organ."

45 [MOIR, DAVID MACBETH] △ . "Peter Ledyard,--A Lyrical
Ballad" (poem). Blackwood's Edinburgh Magazine, 12
(August), 145-47.
     An imitation (burlesque?).

46 [MOIR, DAVID MACBETH and WILLIAM MAGINN?]. C. N. "New-Year's
Day Congratulations." Blackwood's Edinburgh Magazine, 11
(January), 180-19 (113-15).
     Includes burlesque, "Tokens of Natural Affection" (poem).

47 N., C. See 1822.B46.

48 [OLLIER, CHARLES] J. J. "London Chit-chat." Blackwood's
Edinburgh Magazine, 11 (March), 331-34 (333).
     Wordsworth has been "miserably misrepresented" in the
Edinburgh Review.

49 PADDY. See 1822.B44.

50 R., N. "Epistle to W. W." (poem). Edinburgh Magazine and
Literary Miscellany, NS 11 (September), 312-15.
     Wordsworth sheds a new light of love on the natural
world.

1822

51   THERSITES. <u>See</u> 1822.B25.

52   W., W. Letter to the Editor. <u>Brighton Magazine</u>, 1 (May),
      483-84.
          Includes burlesque, "The Cursed Tree" (poem).

53   [WILSON, JOHN]. "Noctes Ambrosianae: No. II." <u>Blackwood's
      Edinburgh Magazine</u>, 11 (April), 475-89 (483).
          Attacks Wordsworth's egotism.

54   [WILSON, JOHN]. Review of Green's <u>The Tourist's New Guide</u>.
      <u>Blackwood's Edinburgh Magazine</u>, 12 (July), 84-90 (87).
          Though <u>A Description of the Scenery of the Lakes</u> is fine,
      the best book on the Lakes is <u>Lyrical Ballads</u>.

55   [WILSON, JOHN]. Review of <u>Ecclesiastical Sketches</u> and
      <u>Memorials of a Tour on the Continent</u>. <u>Blackwood's
      Edinburgh Magazine</u>, 12 (August), 175-91.
          Wordsworth broods in solitude, not caring to write for
      his own age. His poetry is felt as a religion. He has had
      a greater influence over English poetry than any other in-
      dividual: he was the first to impregnate descriptions of
      nature with passion; he vindicated the native dignity of
      human nature; he knew the real province of language. He is
      the most original poet of the age, to whom Scott, Byron, all
      other poets are indebted. <u>Ecclesiastical Sketches</u>, indi-
      vidually and as a series, are "magnificent," carry an im-
      portant lesson for the present day on the power of religion,
      and complement Wordsworth's sonnets on liberty. Words-
      worth's sonnets are superior to Milton's. In <u>Memorials of
      a Tour on the Continent</u> Wordsworth takes his household gods
      with him into foreign lands; especially effective are "The
      Italian Itinerant," "The Three Cottage Girls," and "The
      Eclipse of the Sun, 1820."

56   [WILSON, JOHN?]. "Noctes Ambrosianae: No. [V]." <u>Blackwood's
      Edinburgh Magazine</u>, 12 (September), 369-91 (372-73).
          Challenges Wordsworth's discussion of Ossian in Essay
      (1815).

57   Y. Letter to the Editor. <u>Inquisitor</u>, no. 11 (30 January),
      pp. 81-88.
          Affectation of simplicity has its origin in lack of
      ability. Includes burlesque by H. A., "The Mendicant Tar"
      (poem).

1823 A BOOKS - NONE

1823 B SHORTER WRITINGS

1   ANON. Review of <u>Memorials of a Tour on the Continent</u> and
    <u>Ecclesiastical Sketches</u>. <u>Monthly Censor</u>, 2 (March),
    324-35.
       Wordsworth has ceased to pursue the offensive peculiari-
    ties that made <u>Lyrical Ballads</u> unpopular. His poetry is
    chiefly characterized by its centering around the poet him-
    self. Wordsworth is above all a moral poet.

2   ANON. Review of Baillie's <u>A Collection of Poems</u>. <u>Literary
    Register</u>, no. 42 (19 April), pp. 241-42 (242).
       "Dr. Diaphanous Wordsworth" has of late put forth "unin-
    telligible rubbish."

3   ANON. Review of Byron's <u>Don Juan: Cantos VI.--VII.--and VIII.</u>
    <u>Literary Examiner</u>, no. 1 (5 July), 6-12 (8).
       Wordsworth's gentle portraiture (e.g., in "Alice Fell")
    is preferable to Byron's constant satiric dwelling upon
    man's wickedness.

4   ANON. "Life and Adventures of Peter Wilkins." <u>Retrospective
    Review</u>, 7:120-83 (128-30).
       Because he figures predominantly in the revolution by
    which nature replaced art in poetry, Wordsworth should be
    forgiven his indiscretion in choosing low subjects.

5   ANON. "Donne's Poems." <u>Retrospective Review</u>, 8:31-55 (49).
       Wordsworth's language and versification are but a return
    to Donne's.

6   ANON. "William Wordsworth, Esq.," in <u>Public Characters of All
    Nations. . . .</u> Illustrated. 3 vols. London: Phillips,
    III:630-32.
       A biographical sketch.

7   BURTON, CHARLES. <u>The Bardiad, A Poem</u>. Second edition.
    London: Longman; Manchester: Gleave, p. 20.
       Wordsworth, poet of sentiment, writes pure images, is
    not so simple.

8   [BYRON, LORD]. "The Blues." <u>Liberal</u>, no. 3 [26 April],
    pp. 1-21 (2, 13-15, 17-18 [Eclogue i, Lines 9-10; Eclogue
    ii, Lines 47-63, 97-110]).
       Mocks Wordsworth as stamp distributor, poet of low
    subjects.

1823

9   [BYRON, LORD]. Don Juan: Cantos VI.--VII.--and VIII. London:
     Hunt, pp. 115, 183 (Canto viii, Stanza ix and note).
        Mocks Wordsworth's statement that "Carnage is thy
     daughter" in "Ode: 1815."

10   [BYRON, LORD]. Don Juan: Cantos IX.--X.--and XI. London:
     Hunt, p. 132 (Canto xi, Stanza lix).
        Wordsworth has "two or three" supporters.

11   [DE QUINCEY, THOMAS] X. Y. Z. "Letters to a Young Man Whose
     Education Has Been Neglected: By the Author of the Con-
     fessions of an English Opium-Eater: No. III: On
     Languages." London Magazine, 7 (March), 325-35 (332-33).
        Notes his debt to Wordsworth for the distinction between
     knowledge and power. Reprinted in De Quincey's Writings
     (1850-59) and Letters to a Young Man Whose Education Has
     Been Neglected [De Quincey's Works, Volume XIV] (1860).

12   [DE QUINCEY, THOMAS] X. Y. Z. "Notes from the Pocket-book of
     a late Opium-Eater: No. III: English Dictionaries . . .
     To the Lakers. . . ." London Magazine, 8 (November),
     493-501 (495, 497-98).
        Wordsworth has been "attentive to the scholar-like use
     of words." Notes Wordsworth's objection to geologists in
     The Excursion (Book III). Partially reprinted in De Quin-
     cey's Writings (1850-59).

13   ELIA. See 1823.B22.

14   H.[AZLITT], W.[ILLIAM]. "My First Acquaintance with Poets."
     Liberal, no. 3 [23 April], pp. 23-46 (30, 36-44).
        Records visit to Alfoxden: Wordsworth's appearance, his
     recognition of the pathos of Lyrical Ballads, Coleridge's
     criticism of the "matter-of-fact-ness" of Wordsworth's de-
     scriptive poetry.

15   [HAZLITT, WILLIAM]. "Table-Talk: No. VII: On Londoners and
     Country People." New Monthly Magazine, [NS] 8 [August],
     171-79 (179).
        Wordsworth, in the Preface to The Excursion, incorrectly
     presents men in cities as evil spirits without natural af-
     fections. Reprinted in 1826.B10.

16   [HAZLITT, WILLIAM]. "Common Places." Literary Examiner,
     no. 15 (11 October), pp. 239-40 (240).
        Wordsworth requires a "midwife to bring his works to
     light."

17   [HAZLITT, WILLIAM and FRANCIS JEFFREY?]. Review of Moore's
     Loves of the Angels and Byron's Heaven and Earth.
     Edinburgh Review, 38 (February), 27-48 (30).
         Wordsworth relies too exclusively on petty and repulsive
     subjects.

18   HERBERT, EDWARD. See 1823.B28.

19   IRVING, THE REV. EDWARD. "Of Judgment to Come," in For the
     Oracles of God, Four Orations; For Judgment To Come, An
     Argument, in Nine Parts. London: Hamilton, pp. 99-548
     (504-505).
         One man today (presumably Wordsworth), living a reclu-
     sive, god-like life of virtue, modesty, and common house-
     hold truth, has been rewarded with new knowledge of nature
     and nature's God. But this Epicurean age rejects and
     abuses him.

20   JOHNSTON, CHARLES. "To W. Wordsworth, Esq." (poem), in
     Sonnets, Original and Translated. London: Murray, p. 53.
         Defends summer as a poetic season in response to "Septem-
     ber, 1815" ("While not a leaf seems faded; while the
     fields").

21   JOYEUSE, VYVYAN. See 1823.B27.

22   [LAMB, CHARLES] ELIA. "Letter of Elia to Robert Southey,
     Esquire." London Magazine, 8 (October), 400-407 (402).
         Praises his friend Wordsworth.

23   [LANDOR, WALTER SAVAGE]. "Imaginary Conversation between Mr.
     Southey and Professor Porson." London Magazine, 8 (July),
     5-9.
         The characters discuss Wordsworth's verbosity, his chal-
     lenging of readers to admire his poems, his simplicity, and
     his imitation of the ancients (e.g., in "Laodamia"). Re-
     printed with verbal changes in Imaginary Conversations of
     Literary Men and Statesmen (1824); revised in 1826.B14.

24   [LOCKHART, JOHN GIBSON]. "Letters of Timothy Tickler, Esq.,
     to Eminent Literary Characters, No. X." Blackwood's
     Edinburgh Magazine, 14 (September), 312-29 (317-18).
         Defends Wordsworth's holding of the stamp office.

25   [LOCKHART, JOHN GIBSON]. Reginald Dalton. By the Author of
     Valerius, and Adam Blair. 3 vols. Edinburgh: Blackwood;
     London: Cadell, I:153-54 (Book I, Chapter xii), 229
     (Book II, Chapter iii).

1823

Characters praise "She was a Phantom of delight" and Wordsworth.

26 [PATMORE, PETER GEORGE] VICTOIRE, COUNT DE SOLIGNY. Letters on England. 2 vols. London: Colburn, II:7-20.
In contrast to Byron, Wordsworth is a poet of lofty contemplation. Wordsworth's intellectual poetry refreshes and restores man to his basic human nature; it creates in the reader the faculties by which it is appreciated. His shorter poems are unequalled in their variety. Attribution: British Museum catalogue.

27 [PRAED, WINTHROP MACKWORTH] VYVYAN JOYEUSE. "What You Will." Knight's Quarterly Magazine, 1 (June), 215-26 (220-21).
Includes "Imitation of The Excursion," signed "Hamilton Murray" [i.e., Henry Malden], a parody of The Excursion. Attributions: Charles Knight in 1864.B8, I:298.

28 [REYNOLDS, JOHN HAMILTON] EDWARD HERBERT. "The Literary Police Office, Bow-Street." London Magazine, 7 (February), 157-61 (157-58, 161).
Mocks Wordsworth, "a pedlar by trade, that hawks about shoe-laces and philosophy."

29 SOLIGNY, VICTOIRE, COUNT DE. See 1823.B26.

30 [WADE, JOHN]. The Black Book: Supplement to the Black Book; or, Corruption Unmasked!! 2 vols. London: Fairburn, II:330.
"There is a W. Wordsworth, Distributor of Stamps, and what is called a Lake Poet." Attribution: British Museum catalogue. For Volume I, see 1820.B51.

31 [WILSON, JOHN (and JOHN GIBSON LOCKHART?)]. "Noctes Ambrosianae: No. XII." Blackwood's Edinburgh Magazine, 14 (October), 484-503 (486-87, 494-95).
The characters criticize Wordsworth's egotism, wordiness, and prose writings, praise his painting of female characters and his imagination.

32 Z., X. Y. See 1823.B11-B12.

1824 A BOOKS - NONE

1824 B SHORTER WRITINGS

1   ANON. "The Fashionable and Unfashionable Writers of the
        Present Day." Oriental Herald, 1 (April), 575-83 (582).
        Wordsworth is unpopular because he is too deep for the
        multitude.

2   ANON. "Lectures on Poetry delivered at the Metropolitan
        Literary Institution in May and June, 1823: By the Honorary
        Secretary.--Lecture III." Metropolitan Literary Journal,
        no. 4 (August), pp. 301-17 (312).
        "Wordsworth is excellent in descriptive poetry."

3   ANON. "On the Poetry of Southey." Knight's Quarterly
        Magazine, 3 (August), 156-64.
        Wordsworth's poetry, as opposed to Southey's, is homo-
        geneous. Lyrical Ballads ranks higher than The Excursion.

4   ANON. Review of Medwin's Journal of the Conversations of Lord
        Byron. Gentleman's Magazine, 94-2 (November), 434-42 (438).
        Contrary to Byron's opinion, Wordsworth is not a
        hireling.

5   BRYDGES, SIR [SAMUEL] EGERTON. Gnomica: Detached Thoughts,
        Sententious, Axiomatic, Moral and Critical: But especially
        with Reference to Poetical Faculties, and Habits. Geneva:
        privately printed, pp. 315-17, 320-24.
        Praises Wordsworth's arguments on popularity not being
        a sign of poetic merit and on the purpose of poetry being
        to treat of things as they appear.

6   [DEACON, WILLIAM FREDERICK]. "Old Cumberland Pedlar" (poem),
        Notes, in Warreniana; with Notes, Critical and Explanatory.
        By the Editor of a Quarterly Review. London: Longman,
        pp. 17-24, 189-208 (191-92).
        A burlesque, signed "W. W.," with notes by "W. G."

7   DIBDIN, THE REV. T.[HOMAS] F.[ROGNALL]. The Library Companion;
        or, the Young Man's Guide, and the Old Man's Comfort, in the
        Choice of a Library. London: Harding, Triphook, and
        Lepard, and Major, pp. 736, 738.
        Tenderness, lofty and just moral and religious views,
        and sweetness of diction pervade Wordsworth's poems.

8   EDGAR. "My Common Place Book: No. II: Poetry--Wordsworth."
        Mirror of Literature, Amusement, and Instruction, 3
        (5 June), 375-77.

1824

The writer, who reads poetry to escape from the everyday world, admires Wordsworth.

9   [FOX, WILLIAM JOHNSON]. Review of Boone's Men and Things in 1823. Westminster Review, 1 (January), 1-18 (12-13).
    Wordsworth resists the spirit of the age: rather than write for the people, he tells "the initiated few that the many should be sung to."

10 [HAZLITT, WILLIAM]. Review of Landor's Imaginary Conversations. Edinburgh Review, 40 (March), 67-92 (80-81).
    Wordsworth contrasts with Shakespeare, exhibits little "variety of powers." "Laodamia" is the positive result of the earlier harsh criticism of Wordsworth.

11 [HAZLITT, WILLIAM]. Review of Shelley's Posthumous Poems. Edinburgh Review, 40 (July), 494-514 (502).
    Notes "the labour and throes of parturition of Wordsworth's blank-verse."

12 [HAZLITT, WILLIAM]. "The Political Examiner: Character of Mr. Canning." Examiner, no. 858 (11 July), pp. 433-35 (433).
    Notes Canning's visit to Wordsworth. Reprinted in The Spirit of the Age (Paris, 1825).

13 HAZLITT, WILLIAM. "Preface," "A Critical List of Authors Contained in This Volume," in Select British Poets, or New Elegant Extracts from Chaucer to the Present Time, with Critical Remarks. Edited by William Hazlitt. London: Hall, pp. i-iv (iv), v-xv (xiii).
    Wordsworth's poems are characterized by his "thoughtful humanity" (iv), his "power of raising the smallest things in nature into sublimity by the force of sentiment" (xiii).

14 [LOCKHART, JOHN GIBSON]. "Noctes Ambrosianae: No. XV." Blackwood's Edinburgh Magazine, 15 (June), 706-24 (712, 714-15).
    Wordsworth and Scott are the two original writers of the day. Wordsworth, as opposed to Scott and Byron, is the philosophic contemplator of the Age of Revolution.

15 [LOCKHART, JOHN GIBSON, WILLIAM MAGINN, and JOHN WILSON]. "Noctes Ambrosianae: No. XVII." Blackwood's Edinburgh Magazine, 16 (November), 585-601 (592-93).
    The character Hogg recounts the visits of himself and Byron to Wordsworth: Wordsworth's egotism.

16   [MACAULAY, THOMAS BABINGTON] T.[RISTRAM] M.[ERTON]. "Criti-
      cisms on the Principal Italian Writers: No. II: Petrarch."
      Knight's Quarterly Magazine, 2 (April), 355-68 (356).
         Wordsworth's intense egotism has procured him a set of
      enthusiastic worshippers. Attribution: Charles Knight in
      1864.B8, I:298.

17   M'DERMOT, M.[ARTIN]. "Preliminary View of the Literature of
      the Age," in The Beauties of Modern Literature. London:
      Sherwood, Jones, pp. ix-civ (x-xiv, xxvi-xxxvi, xlii-xlviii).
         Modern poets have abandoned reason for feeling and sim-
      plicity. Wordsworth's arguments in the Preface to Lyrical
      Ballads reflect his imperfect knowledge of human nature.

18   MEDWIN, THOMAS. Journal of the Conversations of Lord Byron:
      Noted during a Residence with his Lordship at Pisa, in the
      Years 1821 and 1822. London: Colburn, pp. 192-95.
         Records Byron's recognition of his debt to Wordsworth
      (acquired through Shelley) and his remark that Wordsworth
      lost his poetic ability when he became a hireling.

19   M.[ERTON], T.[RISTRAM]. See 1824.B16.

20   WATT, ROBERT. Bibliotheca Britannica; or A General Index to
      British and Foreign Literature. 4 vols. Edinburgh:
      Constable; London: Longman, II:983.
         A primary bibliography.

1825 A BOOKS - NONE

1825 B SHORTER WRITINGS

1   ANON. "On the Genius and Poetry of Wordsworth." Literary
      Magnet, 3 (January), 26-29; (March), 67-72; (May), 156-60.
         Supports Wordsworth's poetic principles (26-29, 67-72).
      Wordsworth aims to evoke pity, especially by his use of
      animals. His poems, which most resemble Cowper's, are su-
      perior to his prefaces. He must be content with readers
      who share his own environment (156-60).

2   BOWLES, THE REV. WM. L. A Final Appeal to the Literary
      Public, relative to Pope. . . . London: Hurst, Robinson,
      p. 149.
         Boasts of Wordsworth's admiration of his poems.

3   [CARLYLE, THOMAS]. The Life of Friedrich Schiller: Compre-
      hending an Examination of His Works. London: Taylor and
      Hessey, pp. 265-66.

1825

Wordsworth's rustic characters are "whining drivellers" beside Schiller's.

4   [HAZLITT, WILLIAM]. "Novelty and Familiarity." New Monthly Magazine, [NS] 13 [February], 129-40 (135).
    Records Wordsworth's admiration of the grandeur in the sleep of infancy. Expanded in 1826.B10.

5   [HAZLITT, WILLIAM]. "Lord Byron," "Mr. Wordsworth," in The Spirit of the Age: or Contemporary Portraits. London: Colburn, pp. 157-81 (168, 171-72), 229-50.
    Contrasts Byron's poetry with that of Wordsworth, who creates sentiments out of nothing (168, 171-72). Wordsworth's genius expresses the revolutionary spirit of the age: he delivers household truths; his muse is a levelling one; he rejects art--perhaps because he was "prevented by native pride and indolence from climbing the ascent of learning or greatness." He has associated his own feelings with pastoral scenes, interesting the lonely student of nature. His later philosophic poems (e.g., "Laodamia") are classical and courtly. In The Excursion he repeats the same conclusions until they become insipid; his mind is not analytic, but synthetic, not theoretical, but reflecting. Describes Wordsworth's appearance, conversation, opinion of other writers, and admiration of Poussin and Rembrandt. Had he been a more liberal critic, he would have been a better writer. He has been soured by criticism (229-50).

6   [HOOD, THOMAS]. "Ode to Mr. Graham, the Aeronaut," in Odes and Addresses to Great People. London: Baldwin, Cradock, & Joy, pp. 1-13.
    Parody of Peter Bell.

7   [JEWSBURY, MARIA JANE]. "To William Wordsworth, Esquire" (poem, signed "M. J. J."), "Cursory Remarks on Modern Ballads as Compared with the Old Ones," in Phantasmagoria; or, Sketches of Life and Literature. 2 vols. London: Hurst, Robinson; Edinburgh: Constable, I:[v]; II:1-27 (10, 21-22).
    Wordsworth's poems give a "deep quiet gladness" (I:[v]). Wordsworth and other modern poets have imitated the use of two single-syllable epithets in old ballads. "Ruth," "Laodamia," and "She was a Phantom of delight" combine the excellencies of ancient and modern writing in their simplicity of feeling and strength of thought (II:10, 21-22). Attribution: British Museum catalogue.

8 [LOCKHART, JOHN GIBSON] PHILLIPUS. "Midsummer Madness and
   Mr Martin." Blackwood's Edinburgh Magazine, 18 (October),
   497-99 (497).
        A defense of 1825.B13. The criticism of Wordsworth was
   merely "jocular."

9 [O'SULLIVAN, SAMUEL]. College Recollections. London:
   Longman, p. 51.
        Wordsworth has the reputation of being one who "babbles
   about green fields." Attribution: British Museum catalogue.

10 P., P. "Letter from an Absent Contributor on Hazlitt's Spirit
   of the Age." London Magazine, NS 2 (June), 182-89 (184,
   187).
        Crabbe's writings will outlast Wordsworth's.

11 PHILLIPUS. See 1825.B8.

12 [WILSON, JOHN]. "Noctes Ambrosianae: No. XIX." Blackwood's
   Edinburgh Magazine, 17 (March), 366-84 (366, 375).
        Characters mock Wordsworth's contempt for his age, criti-
   cize the "nerveless laxity" of the language of The Excursion.

13 [WILSON, JOHN]. "Noctes Ambrosianae: No. XXI." Blackwood's
   Edinburgh Magazine, 18 (September), 378-92 (380-83).
        Praises Wordsworth's statements on the nature of poetry,
   but laments he has made so little out of them. Discusses
   Wordsworth's appearance and his vanity. See 1825.B8.

1826 A BOOKS - NONE

1826 B SHORTER WRITINGS

1 ANON. "Wordsworth." Literary Magnet, NS 1 (January), 17-22;
   (February), 68-76.
        Wordsworth's poems were initially unpopular principally
   because they require study. His peculiar genius lies in
   his celebration of the happiness of man, in his just portrayal of women (17-22), in his moral use of the natural
   world (in which he contrasts with Byron), and in his precise diction (68-76).

2 ANON. "A Parady [sic] on a Sonnet by Wordsworth" (poem).
   Elector's Guide, no. 3 (18 February), pp. 47-48.
        Parody of "She dwelt among the untrodden ways."

1826

3   ANON. "Gazette Extraordinary." Wasp, 1 (18 November), 128.
        Wordsworth, as stamp distributor, is in prosy circum-
        stances and unable to finish The Excursion.

4   [COLERIDGE, DERWENT]. "A Lecture on Wordsworth." Metropolitan
        Quarterly Magazine, no. 2, pp. 457-79.
            "Delivered at a Provincial Institution--February 24th,
        1825." Laments the state of Wordsworth's reputation. Ap-
        proves of Wordsworth's use of language and of his "greatness
        of intention" in the poems of his middle years, including
        the lyrical ballads, the sonnets, and The Excursion (in
        which he well describes the Solitary's disease, but not the
        cure). Defends "Ode: Intimations of Immortality" against
        the charge of obscurity. Attribution: Peter Allen and
        Cleve Want, "The Cambridge 'Apostles' as Student Journal-
        ists: A Key to Authorship in the Metropolitan Quarterly
        Magazine (1825-6)," Victorian Periodicals Newsletter, 6,
        nos. 3-4 (1973), 27.

5   C.[OLERIDGE], D.[ERWENT]. "An Essay on the Poetic Character
        of Percy Bysshe Shelley, and on the Probable Tendency of
        His Writings." Metropolitan Quarterly Magazine, no. 3,
        pp. 191-203 (192, 196-200).
            For Wordsworth and Shelley, bettering man's lot was a
        living hope, not a Utilitarian calculation. Wordsworth's
        verses that are weak in thought are not rescued by their
        diction, as are Shelley's. Attribution: Peter Allen and
        Cleve Want, "The Cambridge 'Apostles' as Student Journal-
        ists: A Key to Authorship in the Metropolitan Quarterly
        Magazine (1825-6)," Victorian Periodicals Newsletter, 6,
        nos. 3-4 (1973), 29.

6   [DE QUINCEY, THOMAS] THE ENGLISH OPIUM-EATER. "Gallery of the
        German Prose Classics: No. I.--Lessing." Blackwood's
        Edinburgh Magazine, 20 (November), 728-44 (737-38).
            "Upon the Sight of a Beautiful Picture" and "Essay upon
        Epitaphs" illustrate the agreement of Wordsworth and
        Lessing: Wordsworth stresses "the continuous self-repeating
        nature" of the picture in the poem. Reprinted in De Quin-
        cey's Writings (1850-59). Revised as "Lessing" in 1859.B9.

7   ENGLISH OPIUM-EATER, THE. See 1826.B6.

8   [HAZLITT, WILLIAM] J. B. R. "Boswell Redivivus.--No. 1."
        New Monthly Magazine, [NS] 17 [August], 113-18 (116).
            Discusses Wordsworth's popularity. Reprinted as "Conver-
        sation the First" in Conversations of James Northcote
        (1830).

9   [HAZLITT, WILLIAM]. "Chapter IX," in <u>Notes of a Journey</u>
     <u>through France and Italy</u>. London: Hunt and Clarke,
     pp. 114-28 (124).
         Criticizes Wordsworth for his reproach of the French in
     "Great men have been among us; hands that penned." (Re-
     printed from the <u>Morning Chronicle</u> of 17 November 1824.)

10   [HAZLITT, WILLIAM]. "Essay IV: The Same Subject ["On the
     Conversation of Authors"] Continued," "Essay VII: On
     Londoners and Country People," "Essay X: On Envy (A
     Dialogue)," "Essay XII: Whether Genius is Conscious of Its
     Powers?", "Essay I: On the Qualifications Necessary to
     Success in Life," "Essay III: On Reading Old Books,"
     "Essay IX: On Novelty and Familiarity," "Essay X: On Old
     English Writers and Speakers," in <u>The Plain Speaker:</u>
     <u>Opinions on Books, Men, and Things</u>. 2 vols. London:
     Colburn, I:77-97 (92), 153-79 (177), 229-53 (242-47), 279-
     303 (289-90); II:1-33 (6, 16, 20), 61-83 (76, 81), 239-76
     (259, 275), 277-307 (298).
         Reprinted from 1820.B28 (I:92). Reprinted from 1823.B15
     (177). Wordsworth is narrow in taste "because he sees
     every thing from a single and original point of view"
     (242-47). Reports remark (presumably by Wordsworth) that
     all Claude's pictures are the same (289-90). Reprinted
     with minor omissions from 1820.B27 (II:6, 16, 20). Re-
     printed from 1821.B18 (76, 81). Expanded from 1825.B4.
     Records Wordsworth's opinion that as man grows older he
     gains in variety and richness of experience what he loses
     in intensity (259, 275). Praises Wordsworth's subtle sense
     of beauty (e.g., in "Laodamia") (298).

11   HEMANS, F.[ELICIA]. "To the Author of The Excursion and The
     Lyrical Ballads" (poem). <u>Literary Magnet</u>, NS 1 (April),
     169-70.
         Wordsworth's poems are best read in their appropriate
     natural settings. Reprinted with minor changes as "To
     Wordsworth" in <u>Records of Woman</u> (1828).

12   [JAMESON, ANNA BROWNELL]. <u>A Lady's Diary</u>. London: Thomas,
     p. 95.
         Carlo Dolci's <u>La Poesia</u> presents the personified genius
     of Wordsworth's poetry. Attribution: British Museum
     catalogue.

13   J.[EWSBURY], M.[ARIA] J.[ANE]. "A Poet's Home" (poem).
     <u>Literary Magnet</u>, NS 2 (July), 42-43.
         Portrays Rydal Mount, "Low, and white, yet scarcely
     seen."

1826

14   LANDOR, WALTER SAVAGE. "Conversation IV: Southey and Porson,"
      in Imaginary Conversations of Literary Men and Statesmen.
      Volume I. Second edition, corrected and enlarged. London:
      Colburn, pp. 49-95 (51-52, 57, 59, 65-66, 74-78, 87-91).
          Reprinted with additions from 1823.B23. Revised in
      1846.B10.

15   MALAGROWTHER, MALACHI. See 1826.B21.

16   M.[AURICE, JOHN FREDERICK DENISON]. "The New School of
      Cockneyism: No. I." Metropolitan Quarterly Magazine,
      no. 1, pp. 34-62 (36).
          The "Lake School was a mere fiction of Jeffrey's brain."
      Attribution: Peter Allen and Cleve Want, "The Cambridge
      'Apostles' as Student Journalists: A Key to Authorship in
      the Metropolitan Quarterly Magazine (1825-6)," Victorian
      Periodicals Newsletter, 6, nos. 3-4 (1973), 27.

17   [MAURICE, JOHN FREDERICK DENISON] R. R. "The Age of Folly:
      No. II." Metropolitan Quarterly Magazine, no. 2, pp. 257-79
      (261, 264-67, 269, 277-78).
          Wordsworth's egotism is indispensable to his poetic aims;
      yet it has led him to overvalue his own feelings and under-
      value those of others. Attribution: Peter Allen and Cleve
      Want, "The Cambridge 'Apostles' as Student Journalists: A
      Key to Authorship in the Metropolitan Quarterly Magazine
      (1825-6)," Victorian Periodicals Newsletter, 6, nos. 3-4
      (1973), 28.

18   R., D. L. "Gems of Poetry." Inspector, 1 (September), 271-75.
          Prints a series of "images" and "thoughts" from Words-
      worth's poems to win the reader to Wordsworth.

19   R., J. B. See 1826.B8.

20   R., R. See 1826.B17.

21   [SCOTT, SIR WALTER] MALACHI MALAGROWTHER. Letter to the
      Editor. Edinburgh Weekly Journal, 29 (1 March), 67-[70]
      (67).
          Includes "Whate'er the Minister could say" (poem), a
      parody of "We Are Seven." Reprinted in A Second Letter to
      the Editor of the Edinburgh Weekly Journal, from Malachi
      Malagrowther, Esq. (1826).

22   [WILSON, JOHN]. "Cottages." Blackwood's Edinburgh Magazine,
      19 (March), 241-66 (247, 263-64).

Wordsworth touches sympathies too profound to be general.
He always shows feeling for, and accurate knowledge of, the
natural world. A Description of the Scenery of the Lakes
is heavy, even as a philosophical essay. Reprinted with
omissions in 1842.B33.

23 [WILSON, JOHN]. "Noctes Ambrosianae: No. XXVI." Blackwood's
Edinburgh Magazine, 19 (June), 737-56 (742).
Take Wordsworth out of the Lake Country and his prattle
is tedious.

24 [WILSON, JOHN]. "Hints for the Holidays: No. II."
Blackwood's Edinburgh Magazine, 20 (August), 255-80 (258-59).
Describes Rydal. Revised as "Stroll to Grassmere: First
Saunter" in 1842.B33.

25 [WILSON, JOHN]. "Hints for the Holidays: No. III."
Blackwood's Edinburgh Magazine, 20 (September), 397-426
(410-11).
Wordsworth communes with Nature. Disagrees with his
opinion of Ossian. Partly reprinted as "The Moors" in
1842.B33.

26 [WILSON, JOHN]. "A Glance over Selby's Ornithology."
Blackwood's Edinburgh Magazine, 20 (November), 657-80 (667).
Mocks Wordsworth's blank verse. Reprinted as "Christo-
pher in his Aviary: Third Canticle" in 1842.B33.

1827 A BOOKS - NONE

1827 B SHORTER WRITINGS

1 ANON. Review of Poetical Works (1827). London Weekly Review,
1 (9 June), 5-6.
Wordsworth's passions are too civilized, his reason too
weak, his imagination too bounded. His poetry is homely,
soft, and tame; though wanting in force, it abounds in
sweetness and in the celebration of the minor virtues. A
political renegade, Wordsworth has an arrogant opinion of
his own worth. "Laodamia" is his best poem.

2 ANON. Review of Heber's Hymns and Keble's The Christian Year.
British Critic, 4th ser., 2 (October), 443-53 (449).
Though his language is pure and accurate, Wordsworth often gives mere hieroglyphics of the thought he wishes to
express.

1827

3   ANON. Review of Montgomery's The Pelican Island. Westminster
Review, 8 (October), 303-28 (305-308, 324).
The clamor raised against Wordsworth excited discussion
and procured him disciples; yet he is not appreciated by the
multitude. But it is not true, as Wordsworth argues in
Essay (1815), that the multitude automatically prefer the
worst writing. Recommends Wordsworth's shorter poems for
inclusion in anthologies for schools.

4   ANON. "Contributions by distinguished Contemporaries: No. I:
W---W---, Esq." Inspector, 2:102.
"The Bridge" (poem), a parody of "We Are Seven."

5   ANON. "Odds and Ends." Inspector, 2:40.
Includes "He dwelt amid the untrodden ways" (poem) [by
Hartley Coleridge], a parody of "She dwelt among the un-
trodden ways."

6   [DE QUINCEY, THOMAS]. "Literary and Scientific Notices:
No. 40.--Blackwood's Magazine.--No. CXXXI." Edinburgh
Saturday Post, no. 21 (29 September), p. 166.
Recounts Hartley Coleridge's reporting of Wordsworth's
conversation about buttered toast.

7   [HARE, AUGUSTUS WILLIAM and JULIUS CHARLES]. Guesses at Truth.
By Two Brothers. 2 vols. London: Taylor, especially
I:252-54.
Wordsworth often (e.g., in "French Revolution, as it
Appeared to Enthusiasts at its Commencement") roughly inter-
jects reflections rather than weaving them imaginatively
into the context.

8   [HERAUD, JOHN ABRAHAM]. "Historical Romance." Quarterly
Review, 35 (March), 518-66 (518-19).
Wordsworth and Milton cannot be popular poets because
they demand that the reader share their individual associations.

9   M., T. Q. "Notes on a Tour, Chiefly Pedestrian, from Skipton
in Craven, Yorkshire, to Keswick, in Cumberland." Table
Book, no. 36, pp. 271-84 (271, 275-81).
Recounts the local peasantry's good opinion of Wordsworth
and his participation in the rush-bearing procession.

10   MONTGOMERY, JAMES. "A Theme for a Poet: 1814" (poem), in The
Pelican Island, and Other Poems. London: Longman,
pp. 213-18 (215).
Wordsworth's genius possesses us, until we are "strangely
pleased" to find his thoughts our own.

11   [MONTGOMERY, ROBERT]. The Age Reviewed: A Satire: in Two
     Parts (poem). London: Carpenter, pp. 134–36.
        Wordsworth writes whimpering, prosy verse and in The Ex-
     cursion sleep-inducing trash. Attribution: Dictionary of
     Anonymous and Pseudonymous Literature (Samuel Halkett and
     John Laing), new ed., 9 vols. (Edinburgh: Oliver and Boyd,
     1926–62), I:49.

12   SCRIBBLER, A. The Critics and Scribblers of the Day: A
     Satire (poem). London: Washbourn, pp. 19, 38.
        Wordsworth imparts to the reader of The Excursion a love
     of all nature and of God; yet one rarely finds him praised
     in journals.

13   TAYLOR, JOHN. "To William Wordsworth, Esq." (poem), in Poems
     on Various Subjects. 2 vols. London: Payne and Foss;
     Longman; Richardson; and Murray, I:191.
        Wordsworth finds morals in all of nature's various
     scenes.

14   [WILSON, JOHN]. "Noctes Ambrosianae: No. XXXII." Blackwood's
     Edinburgh Magazine, 21 (April), 473–89 (475).
        Wordsworth in The Excursion lacks invention of character.

15   [WILSON, JOHN]. Review of Aird's Religious Characteristics.
     Blackwood's Edinburgh Magazine, 21 (June), 677–94 (677).
        Wordsworth ignores the comforts of Christianity in tell-
     ing the story of Margaret in The Excursion.

16   [WILSON, JOHN]. Review of Montgomery's The Pelican Island.
     Blackwood's Edinburgh Magazine, 22 (October), 491–511
     (493–95, 498–99, 501, 510–11).
        Wordsworth suffers from having investigated the laws of
     poetry. Many read his poetry for its religion of the woods.
     He is a master of blank verse, except when art smothers na-
     ture in The Excursion. Partially reprinted as "Sacred
     Poetry: Chapter II" in 1842.B33.

17   [WILSON, JOHN]. "A Preface to a Review of the Chronicles of
     the Canongate." Blackwood's Edinburgh Magazine, 22
     (November), 531–56 (539–40).
        Contrasts Crabbe's, Burns's, and Wordsworth's use of
     common life in poetry.

18   Z., Y. Letter to the Editor. Sphynx, no. 19 (10 November),
     p. 301.
        Notes parallels between a poem by Barton and "On the Ex-
     tinction of the Venetian Republic."

1828

1828 A BOOKS - NONE

1828 B SHORTER WRITINGS

1   ALCIPHRON. "Some Speculations on Literary Pleasures--No.
        VIII." Gentleman's Magazine, 98-1 (May), 398-401 (399-400).
        Wordsworth copies Erasmus Darwin's verbosity and, like
        Sterne, extracts sentiment from unusual sources.

2   ANGLER, AN. See 1828.B7.

3   ANON. "A Memoir of Mr. Wordsworth." Lady's Magazine, NS 9
        (January), 47-48.
        A biographical sketch. The chief feature of Lyrical
        Ballads is irregularity. Wordsworth's more recent publica-
        tions redeem his poetic credit lost with the publication of
        Peter Bell and The Waggoner.

4   ANON. "Living Poets: No. 1: Wordsworth." Leodiensian, 1
        (January), 84-87; (February), 93-97.
        Hails Wordsworth's exalting, purifying, calming poetry.
        Because an innovator, he has been scorned (84-87). He re-
        sembles Milton and expresses the German transcendental
        philosophy (93-97).

5   ANON. "The Annuals for 1829." Edinburgh Literary Journal,
        no. 1 (15 November), pp. 2-9 (4).
        Wordsworth's contributions to The Keepsake (1829) give
        evidence of the feebleness of advancing life.

6   ANON. Review of Barton's A New-Year's Eve. Athenaeum, no. 58
        (3 December), pp. 917-18 (917).
        A reply to 1828.B19. Wordsworth deserves praise for ex-
        pressing religion divorced from theology and dogma.

7   [DAVY, HUMPHREY] AN ANGLER. Salmonia: or Days of Fly Fishing:
        in a Series of Conversations. . . . London: Murray, p. 6
        and passim.
        Notes Wordsworth loves to fish. Character of Poietes
        perhaps based on Wordsworth (see 1828.B18).

8   [DE QUINCEY, THOMAS]. "Elements of Rhetoric." Blackwood's
        Edinburgh Magazine, 24 (December), 885-908 (886, 906).
        Wordsworth "has paid an honourable attention to the pur-
        ity and accuracy of his English." Reprinted in De Quincey's
        Writings (1850-59) and with minor addition as "Rhetoric" in
        Critical Suggestions on Style and Rhetoric [De Quincey's
        Works, Volume XI] (1859).

1828

9   H.[AZLITT], W.[ILLIAM]. "On the Causes of Popular Opinion."
    London Weekly Review, 2 (16 February), 106-107 (106).
    Discusses "Michael."

10 [HAZLITT, WILLIAM]. "Byron and Wordsworth." London Weekly
    Review, 2 (5 April), 220.
    Wordsworth, in contrast to Byron, describes his own pe-
    culiar feeling about common objects.

11 [HAZLITT, WILLIAM]. Review of Landor's Imaginary Conversa-
    tions. London Weekly Review, 2 (14 June), 372-74 (373).
    Attacks the sympathy with oppressors of "some of our
    pensioned Sonnetteers" (presumably referring to Wordsworth).

12 [HEWITT, JOHN]. "Wm. Wordsworth." Phoenix, or Manchester
    Literary Journal, no. 6 (9 August), pp. 88-91.
    Despite the efforts of the Edinburgh Review Wordsworth
    is the first of living poets--not for Lyrical Ballads, in
    which he adopts the affected language of the nursery, but
    for the later poems, including Peter Bell and The Waggoner,
    which Wordsworth writes with true simplicity. Attribution:
    British Museum copy.

13 HUNT, LEIGH. Lord Byron and Some of His Contemporaries; with
    Recollections of the Author's Life, and of his Visit to
    Italy. London: Colburn, pp. 4, 30, 77, 128-29, 132, 150,
    153, 157-58, 252, 260, 262, 464-65.
    Recounts his praise of Wordsworth in the Examiner. Notes
    Byron pretended to think worse of Wordsworth than he did.
    Wordsworth's "sullen ebullition" in "Ode: 1815" illustrates
    how little he understands Goethe. Includes letters in which
    Byron states that Wordsworth's performance has not lived up
    to his ability, calls Wordsworth an "arch-apostle of mystery
    and mysticism," and objects to his descriptions of Greece
    and Turkey. Records Wordsworth's reaction to Keats and his
    criticism of repetition in Shakespeare.

14 [JEFFREY, FRANCIS]. Review of Atherstone's The Fall of
    Nineveh. Edinburgh Review, 48 (September), 47-60 (47).
    Wordsworth is "burnt out."

15 [MAURICE, JOHN FREDERICK DENISON]. "Sketches of Contemporary
    Authors: No. V.--Mr. Wordsworth." Athenaeum, no. 8
    (19 February), pp. 113-15.
    Wordsworth's poems require the exercise of more feeling
    and reason than are found in ordinary men. Wordsworth
    headed the literary revolution of the age. He has been
    criticized mainly for his plain language and heroes; but he

1828

writes in elevated as well as plain language, and, unlike Crabbe, he observes humble men not as individuals but as representatives of humanity in general. His writings encourage men to see their common nature rather than their differences, a lesson men need in the present day. His poems, in contrast to Goethe's, rescue men from the social concerns of everyday life.

16   M.[AURICE, JOHN FREDERICK DENISON]. "Lord Byron's Monument." Athenaeum, no. 49 (1 October), pp. 767-68.
        Wordsworth belongs to future ages, not to the present.

17   [WILSON, JOHN]. Review of Hunt's Lord Byron and Some of His Contemporaries. Blackwood's Edinburgh Magazine, 23 (March), 362-408 (371).
        Praises Wordsworth's dedications of The Excursion and Poems (1815).

18   [WILSON, JOHN]. Review of Salmonia. Blackwood's Edinburgh Magazine, 24 (August), 248-72 (254-55, 261-62).
        Notes Wordsworth is "unused to the laughing mood." Suggests he may have been Davy's model for Poietes in Salmonia. Reprinted with omissions as "Christopher in his Aviary: Second Canticle" in 1842.B33.

19   [WILSON, JOHN]. "Sacred Poetry." Blackwood's Edinburgh Magazine, 24 (December), 917-38 (925-28).
        The defect in Wordsworth's system of thought is the absence of revealed religion. Wordsworth is not a Christian poet; his religion is but the religion of the woods. In The Excursion the characters "may all, for anything that appears to the contrary, be--deists." The absence of religion in the tale of Margaret makes Wordsworth's "Church-of-Englandism" absurd. Even in Ecclesiastical Sketches the essential doctrines of Christianity are rarely brought forth. Nevertheless, the Wordsworth of the woods is to be preferred to the Wordsworth of the cathedral. Revised in 1842.B33.

1829 A   BOOKS - NONE

1829 B   SHORTER WRITINGS

1   ANON. Review of The Keepsake, etc. Monthly Repository, NS 3 (January), 53-54 (54).
        Commends "A Gravestone upon the Floor in the Cloisters of Worcester Cathedral."

2   ANON. "On the Genius of Professor Wilson." <u>Edinburgh Literary</u>
      <u>Gazette</u>, 2 (2 January), 1-3.
        The "mysticism and exaggeration of sentiment" of the
      Lake Poets is atoned for by Wordsworth's "pastoral freshness
      and high-toned morality." Compares Wordsworth's poems with
      Wilson's.

3   ANON. "The Present State of Poetry." <u>Leeds Monthly Magazine</u>,
      1 (March), 4-13 (5, 12-13).
        Wordsworth speaks "severe truth and moral censure" to an
      irreligious age.

4   ANON. "Literary Reminiscences." <u>Edinburgh Literary Gazette</u>,
      1 (18 July), 145-47 (146).
        Recalls his initial reaction to Wordsworth's lack of
      judgment and the "wild sing-song" in <u>Lyrical Ballads</u>.

5   ANON. "On the Genius of Wordsworth." <u>Edinburgh Literary</u>
      <u>Gazette</u>, 1 (8 August), 193-94.
        Contrasts Wordsworth with Scott and discusses the philo-
      sophical basis of Wordsworth's appeal to readers. He sacri-
      fices too much for the sake of his system; his innocent view
      of the world arises from his own seclusion.

6   ANON. Review of Johnstone's <u>Specimens of the Lyrical,</u>
      <u>Descriptive, and Narrative Poets of Great Britain.</u>
      <u>Eclectic Review</u>, NS 30 (October), 368-75 (370-71).
        Wordsworth lacks Chaucer's sense of humor.

7   ANON. "On the Cycles of English Literature." <u>Edinburgh</u>
      <u>Literary Gazette</u>, 1 (26 December), 513-14.
        Contrasts Wordsworth with Southey and Erasmus Darwin;
      approves of Wordsworth's poetic language but not of his
      subjects.

8   BAINES, EDWARD, JR. <u>A Companion to the Lakes of Cumberland,</u>
      <u>Westmoreland, and Lancashire. . . .</u> London: Hurst, Chance;
      Liverpool: Wales and Baines; Leeds: Baines, pp. 98-99,
      265-66; Itinerary, p. 20.
        Wordsworth's "deep seclusion may have tended to confirm"
      his eccentricities. He writes "pure morality, and exalted
      philosophy."

9   BALFOUR, ALEXANDER. "On Reading Wordsworth's 'Excursion'"
      (poem). <u>Edinburgh Literary Gazette</u>, 1 (31 October), 397.
        Wordsworth's song is like a purified landscape. Re-
      printed in <u>Weeds and Wild Flowers</u> (1830).

1829

10 [DE QUINCEY, THOMAS]. "Sketch of Professor Wilson: (In a
Letter to an American Gentleman)." Edinburgh Literary
Gazette, no. 4 (6 June), pp. 49-51 (49-50).
Recounts Wordsworth's introducing him to J. Wilson.

11 [ELLIOTT, EBENEZER]. The Village Patriarch: A Poem. London:
Bull, p. 59 (Book IV, Line 32).
Wordsworth's "thoughts acquaint us with our own."

12 [HAZLITT, WILLIAM]. "Autographs." Atlas, 4 (28 June), 424.
Wordsworth's autograph is plain, rustic.

13 [HAZLITT, WILLIAM]. "Phrenological Fallacies." Atlas, 4
(12 July), 456-57 (457).
In Wordsworth's poems "time--the recurrence of impres-
sions--is every thing; the object itself is almost indif-
ferent."

14 [JAMESON, ANNA BROWNELL]. The Loves of the Poets. By the
Author of the "Diary of an Ennuyée." 2 vols. London:
Colburn, II:342-44, 351, 354.
Wordsworth's portraits of women are just.

15 PARSON, WM. and WM. WHITE. History, Directory, and Gazetteer,
of the Counties of Cumberland and Westmorland. . . .
Leeds: White, pp. 617, 620.
Wordsworth's "house and gardens are in the best taste."

16 S., M. "Percy Bysshe Shelley." Literary Phoenix, no. 1
(November), pp. 14-18 (15).
Wordsworth writes insipid nursery trash.

17 SOUTHEY, ROBERT. Sir Thomas More: or, Colloquies on the
Progress and Prospects of Society. 2 vols. London:
Murray, I:367; II:152-53.
Wordsworth departs from legend in "For the Spot where
the Hermitage Stood on St. Herbert's Island, Derwent-water."
Praises "Song at the Feast of Brougham Castle."

18 [TOWNSHEND, CHAUNCEY HARE]. "An Essay on the Theory and the
Writings of Wordsworth." Blackwood's Edinburgh Magazine,
26 (September), 453-63; (October), 593-609; (November),
774-88; (December), 894-910.
The peculiarity of Wordsworth's poetry is the mixture of
philosophy with low subjects. When he writes well, Wordsworth forgets the theories of the Preface to Lyrical Ballads. What is good in his theory--his thoughts on the real
language of men--is not new, and what is new--his preference

for low and rural subjects, and his assertions about the
language of prose, the inferiority of poetic language to
that of real life, and meter--is not good. He has given
his own peculiar feelings as representative of those belong-
ing to man as a species. He attacks a poetic diction
founded on a mechanical abuse of language, ignoring a poetic
diction founded on the imaginative use of language (453-63).
If he was truly writing of men to men, he should have become
popular, his arguments in Essay (1815) not withstanding.
But he rarely uses the real language of men. And his theory
that feeling gives importance to action results in his expressing feeling for unworthy objects in magnificent language (e.g., in "The Wild Duck's Nest," "There was a Boy,"
The Waggoner), and feeling for worthy objects in insufficient language (e.g., in "The Idiot Boy," Peter Bell, "Goody
Blake and Harry Gill"). His errors derive from his attach-
ing too great importance to his own feelings, as he himself
makes clear in the Preface (1815). Yet his disciples insist
he can do no wrong (593-609). He cannot be classed among
the highest poets because: 1) his system is advanced mys-
teriously and unfortunately in poems such as "My heart leaps
up when I behold," "Ode: Intimations of Immortality," and
The Excursion; 2) rather than molding the spirit of the age,
he is a perverted production of it; he argues too much for
his own merit, singularity, and originality; 3) he has no
style of his own: that there is no continuity between the
style of An Evening Walk and Descriptive Sketches, of Lyrical Ballads, and of his later poems, shows that he merely
adopted changing styles in search of popularity; 4) his
writing is unequal, even within single poems (e.g., "Louisa") (774-88). Nevertheless, he has been underrated when
one considers: 1) his powers of description of external
nature, especially mountain scenery (e.g., in The Excursion,
The Waggoner, "A Night-piece"), internal passion (e.g., in
The Excursion, "Influence of Natural Objects"), and human
appearance as indicative of human character (e.g., in Peter
Bell, The Excursion); 2) his ability to move the affections
by simple pathos (e.g., in "The Complaint of a Forsaken
Indian Woman," poems about love); 3) his attaining of a
classical dignity (e.g., in "London, 1802"); 4) his illus-
tration of religious and moral truth (e.g., in "Resolution
and Independence"); 5) his excellence in the sonnet. Those
who admire Byron also honor Wordsworth's genius, to which
Byron is indebted (894-910).

19 WILLCOCKS, THE REV. T.[HOMAS] and THE REV. T.[HOMAS] HORTON.
    "Preface," in Moral and Sacred Poetry. Edited by the Rev.
    T. Willcocks and the Rev. T. Horton. Devonport: privately
    printed, pp. [iii]-[vi] ([vi]).

1829

        Wordsworth's musings are beautiful though occasionally obscure.

20   [WILSON, JOHN]. "Noctes Ambrosianae: No. XLII." Blackwood's Edinburgh Magazine, 25 (April), 525-48 (538-39).
        Criticizes Wordsworth's prejudice against the Scottish, especially Adam Smith.

21   [WILSON, JOHN]. "Noctes Ambrosianae: No. XLVII." Blackwood's Edinburgh Magazine, 26 (December), 845-78 (855).
        Criticizes Wordsworth's contempt for others' poetry.

1830 A BOOKS - NONE

1830 B SHORTER WRITINGS

1   ANON. Review of The Poetical Works of S. T. Coleridge. Westminster Review, 12 (January), 1-31 (2).
        Wordsworth is a sound reasoner. For discussion of attribution, see Richard Haven et al., eds., Samuel Taylor Coleridge: An Annotated Bibliography of Criticism and Scholarship, Volume I (Boston: G.K. Hall, 1976), p. 67.

2   ANON. "On Language and Style, as Poetical Vehicles." Edinburgh Literary Gazette, 2 (16 January), 33-35 (33-34).
        Uneducated peasants are not closer to nature and hence better poetic subjects than educated, upper-class men. Wordsworth's practice does not correspond to his theory about the use of simple language. Crabbe delineates life; Wordsworth uses it for imaginative or thematic purposes.

3   ANON. "A Visit to the Grand National Cemetery in the Year 2000." British Magazine: a Monthly Journal of Literature, Science, and Art, 1 (May), 337-44 (342-43).
        Includes verse testimony: Wordsworth's poems "Gladden the spirit and keep green the mind."

4   HALLAM, A.[RTHUR] H.[ENRY]. "Meditative Fragments: in Blank Verse," "Sonnet: (Written in the Pass of Killiecrankie, and alluding to that written by Mr. Wordsworth in the same place)," in [Poems. n.p., privately printed, 1830], pp. 41-61 (56-59), 107.
        Pays tribute to Wordsworth's tales of quiet tenderness and poems of lofty thought. Wordsworth believed all things reveal the divine (56-59). Criticizes Wordsworth for his celebration of a war-making murderer in "Sonnet: In the Pass of Killicranky" (107).

5 [HAZLITT, WILLIAM]. "Specimens of a Dictionary of Definitions:
     The Ideal." Atlas, 5 (10 January), 25-26 (25).
       Praises "Laodamia."

6 HAZLITT, WILLIAM. The Life of Napoleon Buonaparte. 4 vols.
     London: Wilson, and Chapman and Hall, IV:455.
       Wordsworth seems to have forgotten that the French Revo-
     lution ever occurred.

7 JEWSBURY, MARIA JANE. The Three Histories. London: Westley,
     and Davis, pp. 23-24.
       A character admires Wordsworth's portrait of a wife in
     "To a Young Lady who had been Reproached for Taking Long
     Walks in the Country," but feels she would not look divine
     but beggarly.

8 [MACNISH, ROBERT] A MODERN PYTHAGOREAN. "Poetical Portraits."
     Blackwood's Edinburgh Magazine, 27 (April), 632-33 (632).
       Celebrates Wordsworth as a philosopher, poet of Nature.
     Attribution: William Cushing, Initials and Pseudonyms:
     A Dictionary of Literary Disguises (New York: Crowell,
     1885), p. 196.

9 MOORE, THOMAS, ed. Letters and Journals of Lord Byron: with
     Notices of His Life. 2 vols. London: Murray, I:117, 170,
     316, 575, 578-79; II:26, 87, 117, 149, 318, 442, 526.
       Reports Byron's notation that his comments on Wordsworth
     in English Bards, and Scotch Reviewers were unjust, and
     Shelley's praising of Wordsworth to Byron. Includes letters
     in which Byron comments on the length of The Excursion, and
     commends and attacks Wordsworth. Includes "Versicles"
     (poem), ridiculing The White Doe of Rylstone, and lines
     mocking Wordsworth as "the grand metaquizzical poet."

10 NORTH, CHRISTOPHER. See 1830.B18.

11 PYTHAGOREAN, A MODERN. See 1830.B8.

12 W., J. "Scraps from a Note-Book." Gentleman's Magazine,
     100-2 (July), 23-25 (24).
       Objects, on the basis of fact, to Wordsworth's use of
     "Lothbury" in "The Reverie of Poor Susan."

13 WARNER, THE REV. RICHARD. Literary Recollections. 2 vols.
     London: Longman, II:154.
       Briefly notes his visit to the philosophical Wordsworth
     in 1801.

1830

14   [WILSON, JOHN]. "Moore's Byron." Blackwood's Edinburgh
      Magazine, 27 (February), 389-420 (393, 395); (March),
      421-54 (425-26, 436, 440).
            Though usually meek, Wordsworth can give way to anger
      (393, 395). He conceives the mountains of Switzerland to
      be his private domain; he at times becomes prosy. Eclipsed
      by Byron's fame, he declared Byron had no genius (425-26,
      436, 440).

15   [WILSON, JOHN]. Review of Atherstone's The Fall of Nineveh.
      Blackwood's Edinburgh Magazine, 27 (February), 137-72
      (146-47, 170-71).
            Analyzes Wordsworth's Miltonic invocation in The Recluse
      (quoted from the Preface to The Excursion); discusses Words-
      worth's religion of the woods.

16   [WILSON, JOHN]. Review of Bowles's Days Departed. Blackwood's
      Edinburgh Magazine, 27 (February), 279-305 (280, 285-88,
      302-303).
            Wordsworth frequently lapses into bald prosaic lines.

17   [WILSON, JOHN]. "Noctes Ambrosianae: No. L." Blackwood's
      Edinburgh Magazine, 27 (June), 917-48 (929-30, 933).
            Characters recount Wordsworth's remarks on the cowardice
      of poets, criticize "Resolution and Independence."

18   [WILSON, JOHN] CHRISTOPHER NORTH. "Winter Rhapsody."
      Blackwood's Edinburgh Magazine, 28 (December), 863-94
      (873-77).
            Attacks Wordsworth's arguments in Essay (1815) on the
      reputation of Thomson and the imagery of eighteenth-century
      poems. Revised as "A Few Words on Thomson" in 1842.B33.

1831 A BOOKS - NONE

1831 B SHORTER WRITINGS

1   ANON. Review of Selections from the Poems of William
      Wordsworth. Literary Gazette, no. 750 (4 June), p. 360.
            The editor shows a want of taste by choosing poems in
      which Wordsworth sacrifices poetry to a poetical theory.
      Wordsworth inspires enthusiasm because of the humanizing
      spirit of his poems.

2   ANON. Review of Selections from the Poems of William
      Wordsworth. Examiner, no. 1219 (12 June), p. 373.

No poet profits more by judicious selection than Wordsworth. "Power of Music" "is a Hogarth in verse."

3   ANON. Review of Selections from the Poems of William
     Wordsworth. Literary Beacon, no. 1 (18 June), p. 8.
        Wordsworth's poetry "is of a nature calculated to find
     admirers among all classes," though his language and choice
     of subjects are frequently infelicitous.

4   ANON. "Journal of Literature." Englishman's Magazine, 1
     (July), 524-30 (527-28).
        The goals of the editor of Selections from the Poems of
     William Wordsworth are worthy: Wordsworth's feelings are
     intelligible to all; the poems are particularly fit, be-
     cause they trace the spirit of good, for training young
     minds. The editor has chosen too heavily from Wordsworth's
     earlier, vulgar poems.

5   ANON. Review of Selections from the Poems of William
     Wordsworth. New Monthly Magazine, [NS] 33 (July), 304.
        Wordsworth's cheerful, consoling spirit elevates and en-
     larges the mind and improves the heart.

6   ANON. "The Dissecting Room: Mr. Wordsworth." Literary
     Beacon, no. 4 (9 July), pp. 61-63.
        Points out the "puerilities and absurdities" in Peter
     Bell.

7   ANON. Review of Selections from the Poems of William
     Wordsworth. Lady's Magazine, improved series, 4 (August),
     104.
        A good heart and benevolent temper have rendered Words-
     worth a universal favorite with children.

8   ANON. Review of Selections from the Poems of William
     Wordsworth. Monthly Review, [4th ser.,] 2 for 1831
     (August), 602.
        Wordsworth's natural imagery, simple diction, and fer-
     vent thoughts deserve admiration, though not idolatry.

9   ANON. Review of Selections from the Poems of William
     Wordsworth. Metropolitan, 2 (September), 16.
        The selections are not judiciously chosen.

10   ANON. "Coronation Lays." New Monthly Magazine, [NS] 32
     (October), 327-35 (331-32).
        Includes burlesques, "Sonnets on the Coronation" (three
     sonnets: "National Happiness," "Effects of Rain at a
     Coronation," "The Subject Continued").

1831

11   ANON. "New Peers!" National Omnibus, 1 (4 November), 156-57
     (157).
         Includes "A driver of a rattling Cab" (poem), a parody
     of "We Are Seven."

12   [BULWER-LYTTON, EDWARD]. "To Wordsworth" (poem), in The
     Siamese Twins: A Satirical Tale of the Times: with Other
     Poems. By the Author of "Pelham," &c. &c. London:
     Colburn and Bentley, pp. 371-73.
         Wordsworth, living a beautiful retired life, wrote lines
     of "Man in his simple grandeur."

13   BYRON, LORD. "Hints from Horace" (poem), in The Works of
     Lord Byron. 6 vols. London: Murray, V:273-327 (302).
         To be a poet, "Write but like Wordsworth, live beside a
     lake."

14   [DE QUINCEY, THOMAS]. "Dr Parr and His Contemporaries."
     Blackwood's Edinburgh Magazine, 29 (February), 376-91
     (384); (May), 763-82 (778-79, 781).
         Praises Wordsworth's "accurate valuation of words" in
     "To the Right Honourable William, Earl of Lonsdale, K.G."
     ("Oft, through thy fair domain, illustrious Peer!") (384).
     Notes Wordsworth followed his advice in omitting quotation
     marks in "Ode: Intimations of Immortality." Praises
     "Essay upon Epitaphs" (778-79, 781). Reprinted in De Quin-
     cey's Writings (1850-59) and with minor verbal changes and
     addition as "Whiggism in Its Relations to Literature" in
     1857.B6.

15   [HALLAM, ARTHUR HENRY]. "On Some of the Characteristics of
     Modern Poetry, and on the Lyrical Poems of Alfred Tennyson."
     Englishman's Magazine, 1 (August), 616-28 (616-20).
         Wordsworth correctly argues against immediate popularity
     as a test for poetry. As opposed to Hunt, Shelley, Keats,
     and Tennyson, he writes poems of thought rather than of
     beauty: they are good philosophy but bad poetry.

16   HAZLITT, WILLIAM. "The Letter-bell." Monthly Magazine, NS 11
     (March), 280-83 (280-81).
         Brands Wordsworth a political recreant.

17   HINE, JOSEPH. "Preface," in Selections from the Poems of
     William Wordsworth, Esq.: Chiefly for the Use of Schools
     and Young Persons. Edited by Joseph Hine. London: Moxon,
     pp. v-xii.
         Records his students' appreciation of Wordsworth; ap-
     plauds the moral purity of the poems.

18   HOWITT, WILLIAM. The Book of the Seasons; or the Calendar of
      Nature. London: Colburn and Bentley, pp. xxii, 45, 84,
      271.
           Wordsworth has "retired to the perpetual contemplation"
      of nature. Notes Wordsworth's descriptions of nature.

19   [JEWSBURY, MARIA JANE]. Review of Selections from the Poems
      of William Wordsworth. Athenaeum, no. 191 (25 June),
      pp. 404-405.
           The number of Wordsworth's unlettered admirers proves
      that the main qualification for approaching his poems is an
      honest heart; his detractors are mainly "clever" men.
      Though children cannot comprehend "Lucy Gray," "We Are
      Seven," or "The Pet-lamb," they will benefit from Words-
      worth's unswerving regard for the dignity and happiness of
      man.

20   [JEWSBURY, MARIA JANE]. "Shelley's 'Wandering Jew.'"
      Athenaeum, no. 194 (16 July), pp. 456-57 (457).
           Wordsworth is the poet of the royalist and ecclesiastical
      past.

21   [MACAULAY, THOMAS BABINGTON]. Review of Moore's Letters and
      Journals of Lord Byron. Edinburgh Review, 53 (June),
      544-72 (564-65, 568-69).
           Byron made Wordsworth's perception of nature popular with
      the multitude. The minuteness of Wordsworth's descriptions
      diminishes their effect. Reprinted in Critical and Histori-
      cal Essays (1843).

22   [MAGINN, WILLIAM and OTHERS?]. "Coronation Coronal; or,
      Verses on the Coronation of Their Majesties, King William
      IV. and Queen Adelaide." Fraser's Magazine, 4 (October),
      375-86 (375).
           Includes "Thoughts on the Coronation" (poem), an imita-
      tion/burlesque.

23   MILLIGEN, JULIUS. Memoirs of the Affairs of Greece; containing
      an Account of the Military and Political Events, which
      Occurred in 1823 and following Years: with various Anec-
      dotes relating to Lord Byron, and an Account of his last
      Illness and Death. London: Rodwell, p. 11.
           Byron in Greece voiced bitter sarcasms against Words-
      worth.

24   MONTGOMERY, JAMES. "A View of Modern English Literature."
      Metropolitan, 2 (November), 305-11 (308-309); (December),
      349-57 (349-50).

1831

Cowper and the French Revolution prepared the way for
Wordsworth and the Lake School; but their simplicity was
too often mixed with coarseness. Wordsworth seeks and finds
good and beauty everywhere (308-309). He can reach the
peak of his excellence only by sacrificing his merely good,
common thoughts and concentrating on his peculiar genius
(349-50). Expanded in 1833.B16.

25   NORTH, CHRISTOPHER. See 1831.B29.

26   [PEACOCK, THOMAS LOVE]. Crotchet Castle. By the Author of
      Headlong Hall. London: Hookham, p. 84 (Chapter v).
          Introduces Wordsworth as Mr. Wilful Wontsee, whose greed
      motivated his apostasy.

27   [POWELL, THOMAS] PIERCE PUNGENT. "Literary Characters: No.
      III: Mr. Wordsworth." Fraser's Magazine, 3 (June),
      557-66.
          Wordsworth's followers, with their sectarian spirit, de-
      prive Wordsworth of the fair reputation he deserves by
      praising his faults. Both his faults and beauties stem
      from his "enthusiasm." He has shown littleness of mind by
      carrying his system of plainness too far, by founding his
      system on negatives, and in the egotism of his long self-
      justifications in the Preface to Lyrical Ballads, Preface
      (1815), and Essay (1815). His poetry is justly charged
      with affectation, maudlin sentimentality, mysticism, ab-
      surdity, childish dawdle, wordiness, and striving after
      originality (especially in "Power of Music," "Glen Almain,"
      and "A slumber did my spirit seal"). Yet he is a great and
      original poet, even in The Excursion but especially in
      "Laodamia," in his moral and pathetic thoughts and in his
      investigation of those emotions that give a soul to external
      nature.

28   PUNGENT, PIERCE. See 1831.B27.

29   [WILSON, JOHN] CHRISTOPHER NORTH. "Winter Rhapsody."
      Blackwood's Edinburgh Magazine, 29 (February), 287-327
      (296, 309-10).
          Wordsworth's opinion in Essay (1815) not withstanding,
      Thomson's style possesses an enthusiasm Wordsworth's lacks.
      Wordsworth celebrates the Platonic concept of reminiscence
      in "Ode: Intimations of Immortality." Revised with omis-
      sions as "A Few Words on Thomson" and "The Snowball Bicker
      of Pedmount" in 1842.B33.

30   [WILSON, JOHN]. "Noctes Ambrosianae: No. LVI." Blackwood's
        Edinburgh Magazine, 29 (April), 688-720 (693-96, 700-701).
            The characters discuss The Excursion--its failure because
        Wordsworth cannot conceive an overall plan, its differences
        from Paradise Lost and The Task, its use of a pedlar as nar-
        rator--and the Quakers' appreciation of Wordsworth's poems.

31   [WILSON, JOHN]. "Sotheby's Homer: Critique III." Blackwood's
        Edinburgh Magazine, 30 (July), 93-125 (93-94, 104, 108).
            Rebukes Wordsworth for his attacks on the Scottish and
        on Pope's translation of Homer; commends his diction in
        "Rob Roy's Grave."

32   [WILSON, JOHN]. Review of Audubon's Ornithological Biography.
        Blackwood's Edinburgh Magazine, 30 (August), 247-80 (251-53).
            Wordsworth stooped to study the poor, hence the success
        of his poems about them.

33   [WILSON, JOHN]. "An Hour's Talk about Poetry." Blackwood's
        Edinburgh Magazine, 30 (September), 475-90 (477-79, 481,
        489).
            Wordsworth's glory lies in embuing nature with spiritual-
        ities. But he has not written one Great Poem: The Excur-
        sion is a series of poems. Byron imitates Wordsworth in
        Childe Harold's Pilgrimage (Canto iii). Wordsworth improves
        upon Spenser's picture of Una in "Personal Talk." Reprinted
        in 1842.B33.

1832 A   BOOKS - NONE

1832 B   SHORTER WRITINGS

    1   ANON. "Mysticism of Modern Poetry." Aberdeen Magazine, 2
            (March), 115-23 (119-20).
                Passages from "To H. C.," The Waggoner, and "Glen Almain"
            illustrate Wordsworth's unintelligibility.

    2   ANON. "Popular Information on Literature." Chambers'
            Edinburgh Journal, 1 (28 April), 99-100 (99).
                Wordsworth, "a quiet, retired, old gentleman," "made a
            great mistake in the beginning of his career" and never
            recovered.

    3   ANON. Review of Lewis's Use and Abuse of Political Terms.
            Tait's Edinburgh Magazine, 1 (May), 164-72 (164-65).
                Reports Wordsworth's opinion in conversation that the
            foundation of poetry is logic.

1832

4   ANON. "The Rambler: Authors Continued." <u>National Omnibus</u>, 2
(22 June), 193-94; (29 June), 201-202 (202).
     Commends the wisdom and truth of Wordsworth's poems, es-
pecially his portrayal of nature (193-94). The poets of
the Lake School seek to replace affectation with truth and
simplicity (202).

5   ANON. "The Summer." <u>National Omnibus</u>, 2 (29 June), 205-206
(206).
     Includes burlesque, "The Butter Woman!" (poem).

6   ANON. Review of <u>Selections from the Poems of William
Wordsworth</u>. <u>Academic Correspondent</u>, 1 (July), 29-31.
     The volume is recommended for use in schools; also it is
"better adapted for general perusal than the formidable
quartos from which it is derived."

7   ANON. "The Spinning-wheel." <u>Schoolmaster, and Edinburgh
Weekly Magazine</u>, 1 (18 August), 38.
     Praises "Grief, thou hast lost an ever-ready friend."

8   ANON. "Jeremy Bentham." <u>Schoolmaster, and Edinburgh Weekly
Magazine</u>, 1 (8 September), 81-83 (81).
     Wordsworth "is, in approaching blindness, completing his
resemblance to Milton, in life as in spirit."

9   ANON. Review of <u>Selections from the Poems of William
Wordsworth</u>. <u>Monthly Review</u>, [4th ser.,] 3 for 1832
(November), 365-71.
     Though his poetry is admirable, Wordsworth often exhibits
"an obstinate perversion of taste": he gives a false impression of society by choosing lowly characters and giving
them incongruous attributes; his language belongs to no
class of society; his associations are sometimes too personal and local. The poems perpetuate religious intolerance.

10   BYRON, GEORGE GORDON NOEL. "Observations upon 'Observations':
A Second Letter to John Murray, Esq. on the Rev. W. L.
Bowles's Strictures on the Life and Writings of Pope,"
Note, in <u>The Works of Lord Byron: with his Letters and
Journals and his Life, by Thomas Moore</u>. 17 vols. London:
Murray, VI:382-416 (410, 413); X:287.
     Wordsworth has observed Nature widely. He is never vul-
gar (VI:410, 413). In manuscript note to "Churchill's
Grave," states his admiration and imitation of Wordsworth
(X:287). For Volumes XV-XVI, <u>see</u> 1833.B5.

11   CORNWALL, BARRY. <u>See</u> 1832.B22.

12   ETTRICK SHEPHERD, THE. See 1832.B16.

13   GREAT UNMENTIONABLE, THE. "The Lake Poets,--Wilson, Southey,
     Coleridge, and Wordsworth," in The Poetical March of
     Humbug! being Burlesque Imitations of the Principal Poets
     of the Day. . . . London: Gilbert, pp. 18-24 (18-19,
     21-22).
          Includes "Dusty Bob" (poem), a burlesque.

14   [HERAUD, JOHN ABRAHAM]. "German Poetry: No. III." Fraser's
     Magazine, 5 (April), 280-94 (283-84, 286).
          Wordsworth has realized his theory of diction only in
     Lyrical Ballads. In his celebrating of the lowly he con-
     trasts with Bürger.

15   [HERAUD, JOHN ABRAHAM]. Review of Poetical Works (1832).
     Fraser's Magazine, 6 (November), 607-25.
          Wordsworth's poetry, in contrast to Byron's, is charac-
     terized by perpetual elevation of the material to the
     spiritual world: hence Wordsworth's interest in the act of
     dreaming and in lowly men (perhaps too lowly in "The Idiot
     Boy"), animals, and natural objects. Wordsworth is the
     poet of the intellect, celebrating what is excellent in
     man; Burns is the poet of feeling, constructing poetry out
     of man's infirmities. The Waggoner can be compared with
     "Tam o'Shanter." Wordsworth's works, as opposed to Schil-
     ler's, successfully unite philosophy and poetry. His dic-
     tion is in practice not low; it is sprinkled with classical
     allusions. The diction of "Laodamia" recalls that of Dante.
     Wordsworth's textual alterations in the present volume are
     generally unfortunate. His sonnets, especially Ecclesiasti-
     cal Sketches, are good. He has demonstrated that it is
     possible to write fine poetry without the aid of super-
     natural or artificial machinery.

16   [HERAUD, JOHN ABRAHAM and WILLIAM MAGINN?]. "Lord Byron's
     Juvenile Poems." Fraser's Magazine, 6 (September), 183-204
     (186-89).
          Attacks Coleridge's criticism of "Ode: Intimations of
     Immortality."

17   [HOGG, JAMES] THE ETTRICK SHEPHERD. "Memoir of the Author's
     Life," "Reminiscences of Former Days," in Altrive Tales:
     Collected among the Peasantry of Scotland, and from Foreign
     Adventurers. Illustrated by George Cruikshank. London:
     Cochrane, pp. i-xciii (lxiv-lxix), xciv-cli (cxxiv-cxxx).
          Reprinted from 1821.B21 (lxiv-lxix). Records his first
     meeting and tour of Scotland in 1814 with Wordsworth:

1832

Wordsworth's sentient conversation, kindness; recalls his anger at Wordsworth's affront to him as a poet. Notes "the richness of his works for quotations" (cxxiv-cxxx).

18 [HUNT, LEIGH] A LOVER OF BOOKS. "The World of Books." Tait's Edinburgh Magazine, 1 (May), 145-50 (149).
    Wordsworth undervalues the real scene in the Yarrow poems. Reprinted in Men, Women, and Books (1847).

19 HUNT, LEIGH. "Preface," "The Feast of the Poets" (poem), in Poetical Works. London: Moxon, pp. v-lviii (xvii-xviii, lii), 139-58 (150-51, 155).
    Praises Wordsworth's prose essays (xvii-xviii, lii). Abridged from 1815.B22; reprinted in 1844.B23; revised in 1860.B11 (150-51, 155).

20 LOVER OF BOOKS, A. See 1832.B18.

21 [MAGINN, WILLIAM]. "Gallery of Literary Characters: No. XXIX: William Wordsworth, Esq." Fraser's Magazine, 6 (October), 313.
    Byron and the critics in the Edinburgh Review had their effect, though Wordsworth's fame will increase as poems like "The Idiot Boy" are forgotten. Yet these are the poems Wordsworth defends most strenuously. Wordsworth "is a good sturdy Tory, a most exemplary man in all the relations of life, and a stamp-master void of reproach."

22 MICHELL, NICHOLAS. Living Poets and Poetesses; a Biographical and Critical Poem. London: Kidd, pp. 66-73.
    Satirizes Wordsworth's obscurity, his choice of simple subjects and language.

23 MOTHERWELL, WILLIAM. "Tim the Tacket: A Lyrical Ballad, supposed to be written by W. W." (poem), in Poems Narrative and Lyrical. Glasgow: Robertson; Edinburgh: Oliver and Boyd; London: Longman, pp. 149-54.
    A burlesque. Also issued anonymously as Tim the Tackit, Paisley: privately printed (n.d.), 4 pp.

24 [PROCTOR, BRYAN WALLER] BARRY CORNWALL. "Introduction," in English Songs, and Other small Poems. London: Moxon, pp. v-xvi (xi).
    Sentiment alone, without elaborate expression, is sufficient in Wordsworth's poems.

25 SOUTHEY, ROBERT. "Two Letters Concerning Lord Byron: 1822-1824," in Essays, Moral and Political. 2 vols. London: Murray, II:181-205 (202-204).

98

Denies, in a letter dated 8 December 1824 originally
published in the Courier, that he and Wordsworth were offended by Byron's attack in a letter to Hogg.

26 TAYLOR, JOHN. Records of My Life. 2 vols. London: Bull,
    II:287-88.
       Records receiving Lyrical Ballads (1800), with a request
    for his opinion of the poems; records meeting Wordsworth in
    London.

27 WATTS, ALARIC A. "Sketches of Modern Poets: I: Wordsworth"
    (poem), in The Literary Souvenir. Edited by Alaric A.
    Watts. London: Longman, pp. 289-90.
       Wordsworth's poems contain "lessons of wisdom" for all.

28 [WILSON, JOHN]. "Noctes Ambrosianae: No. LXI." Blackwood's
    Edinburgh Magazine, 31 (April), 693-720 (695-97).
       The Germans esteem some of Lyrical Ballads, but few have
    read more than extracts from The Excursion.

29 [WILSON, JOHN]. Review of Tennyson's Poems. Blackwood's
    Edinburgh Magazine, 31 (May), 721-41 (passim).
       Praises Wordsworth.

30 [WILSON, JOHN]. "Christopher at the Lakes: Flight First."
    Blackwood's Edinburgh Magazine, 31 (June), 857-80 (871-77).
       Had Wordsworth written nothing else but his sonnets, in-
    cluding those in The River Duddon, his fame would be im-
    mortal.

31 [WILSON, JOHN]. Review of Michell's Living Poets and
    Poetesses. Blackwood's Edinburgh Magazine, 31 (June),
    957-64 (958, 960, 962-64).
       Defends Wordsworth against the attack in 1832.B22.

32 [WILSON, JOHN]. "Christopher at the Lakes: Flight Second."
    Blackwood's Edinburgh Magazine, 32 (July), 121-38 (126,
    134).
       When he wishes, Wordsworth writes with Doric simplicity.
    Pokes fun at Wordsworth's prose in A Description of the
    Scenery of the Lakes.

33 [WILSON, JOHN]. "Noctes Ambrosianae: No. LXIV." Blackwood's
    Edinburgh Magazine, 32 (November), 846-74 (854).
       Describes Wordsworth's appearance.

1833

1833 A   BOOKS - NONE

1833 B   SHORTER WRITINGS

1   ANON. Review of Taylor's The Life of William Cowper. British
     Critic, 4th ser., 14 (July), 26-45 (44).
          Wordsworth is indebted to Cowper for his style and his
     manner of looking equally upon the lowly and the sublime
     objects of nature.

2   ANON. "A Brief Survey of the History of English Poetry,"
     "William Wordsworth," in Readings in Poetry: A Selection
     from the Best English Poets. . . . London: Parker,
     pp. 3-14 (12), 213.
          Wordsworth's efforts to revive British literature have
     been successful (12). He depicts scenery faithfully, ap-
     peals to the heart, inculcates philanthropy, and teaches
     devout morality (213).

3   ANTIQUUS. See 1833.B15.

4   BULWER[-LYTTON], EDWARD LYTTON. England and The English.
     2 vols. London: Bentley, II:52, 69, 96-104, 112, 129.
          Wordsworth's conservative genius resembles Goethe's,
     contrasts with Shelley's. In "studying to be simple, he
     becomes often artificial." His poetry has been influential
     in opposing materialism.

5   BYRON, GEORGE GORDON NOEL. "Some Observations upon an Article
     in Blackwood's Magazine, No. XXIX, August, 1819," "Dedica-
     tion" to Don Juan (poem), Notes to Don Juan, in The Works
     of Lord Byron: with his Letters and Journals, and his
     Life, by Thomas Moore. 17 vols. London: Murray, XV:55-98
     (76-88, 98); 101-108 (102-104); 327, 334, XVI:51.
          Records Wordsworth's depreciation of Southey, Hunt's
     praise of Wordsworth; attacks Wordsworth's prose: his
     criticism of eighteenth-century poets, his arguments about
     poetic reputation (XV:76-88, 98). Mocks the incomprehensi-
     bility of The Excursion, Wordsworth's "place in the Excise"
     (102-104). Notes include manuscript readings of passages
     in Don Juan about Wordsworth (327, 334, XVI:51). For
     Volumes VI and X, see 1832.B10.

6   COLERIDGE, HARTLEY. "Sonnet XV: To Wordsworth," in Poems.
     Volume I. Leeds: Bingley; London: Baldwin and Cradock,
     pp. 15, 147.
          Wordsworth celebrates "the thoughts that make / The life
     of souls," is priest "Of Nature's inner shrine." Reprinted
     in 1851.B17.

7   CUNNINGHAM, ALLAN. "Biographical and Critical History of the
    Literature of the Last Fifty Years: Wordsworth."
    Athenaeum, no. 313 (26 October), p. 718.
        Summarizes Wordsworth's life and works, stressing the
    unfair attacks in the Edinburgh Review. Reprinted in Bi-
    ographical and Critical History of the British Literature
    of the Last Fifty Years (1834).

8   DYCE, THE REV. ALEXANDER. Dedication, Preface, "Notes," in
    Specimens of English Sonnets. London: Pickering,
    pp. [iii], [v]-vi (vi), 211-24 (222).
        Expresses his esteem for Wordsworth ([iii]). Praises
    Wordsworth's success with the sonnet (vi, 222).

9   EARLY RISER, AN. See 1833.B21.

10 ELLISON, HENRY. "After Reading Wordsworth's Laodamia" (poem),
    "Wordsworth and Byron," in Madmoments: or First Verseat-
    tempts. . . . 2 vols. [Malta: privately printed],
    II:16-17, 399-400.
        Reading Wordsworth results in "a placid Light thrown
    over all I see" (16-17). Wordsworth sends us into the
    world with expansive hearts. "Laodamia" breathes the
    spirit of Sophocles (399-400).

11 [EMPSON, WILLIAM]. Review of Hayward's translation of Faust.
    Edinburgh Review, 57 (April), 107-43 (115-21).
        Wordsworth insists too exclusively on equating the lan-
    guages of poetry and prose. To be consistent, he must also
    renounce the use of meter.

12 HUNT, LEIGH. "The Townsman, No. XII: Names of Streets.--A
    Walk to Chelsea (Continued)." Weekly True Sun, NS no. 12
    (17 November), pp. 93-94 (94).
        Wordsworth's criticism of the French in "Great men have
    been among us; hands that penned" is unworthy of his genius.

13 JERDAN, WILLIAM. "William Wordsworth, Esq.," in National
    Portrait Gallery of Illustrious and Eminent Personages of
    the Nineteenth Century. 5 vols. London: Fisher, Fisher,
    and Jackson, IV:1-14 (each portrait paged individually).
        A biographical sketch. Wordsworth has led an ideal,
    benevolent existence, which is reflected in his works. His
    poems contrast with Byron's. The worst fault of The Excur-
    sion is that it requires too much study.

14 M.[ERRYWEATHER, MRS.] I. A. "To Wordsworth" (poem), in The
    Hermit of Eskdaleside, with Other Poems. Whitby: Kirby,
    p. 117.

1833

        Wordsworth's poems calm, refresh, and elevate. Attribution: British Museum catalogue.

15   [MILL, JOHN STUART] ANTIQUUS. "The Two Kinds of Poetry."
      Monthly Repository, NS 7 (October), 714-24 (717-22, 724).
        Wordsworth's poetry is that of a cultivated but not of a
      naturally, spontaneously poetic mind, like Shelley's: the
      ultimate end of the feeling Wordsworth portrays is thought.
      He is never entirely given up to emotion. Hence his genius
      is unlyrical. Reprinted with minor additions as "Thoughts
      on Poetry and Its Varieties" in Dissertations and Discussions (1859).

16   MONTGOMERY, JAMES. Lectures on Poetry and General Literature,
      Delivered at The Royal Institution in 1830 and 1831.
      London: Longman, especially pp. 112-13, 134-41, 368-72,
      376-78.
        Expanded from 1831.B24. Wordsworth achieves harmony and
      strong sentiment and feeling while adhering to the strict
      form of the sonnet in "Feelings of the Tyrolese." He faces
      the difficulty of trying to convey his own particular, uncommon experience. Though he unqualifiedly rejects elevated
      diction in the Preface to Lyrical Ballads, he fortunately
      does not limit himself in practice to following his theory.

17   P., T. "Poets" (poem). Tourist, 1 (Suppl., 28 January), 187.
        Hails Wordsworth as a poet who refuses to sell or profane
      his poetic gifts for "lusts or lies."

18   [SMITH, HORACE]. "Preface to the Eighteenth Edition," in
      Rejected Addresses: or, The New Theatrum Poetarum. [By
      Horace and James Smith.] Eighteenth edition, revised.
      London: Murray, pp. vii-xxi (xii-xiii).
        Adds, to 1812.B7, a preface noting the injustice of burlesquing Wordsworth's simple ballads while ignoring the wisdom of his loftier writings. Attribution: James Smith and
      Horace Smith, Rejected Addresses: or, The New Theatrum
      Poetarum, 24th ed. (London: Murray, 1855), p. x.

19   W., G. "The Lakes and the Lake Poets." Cobbett's Magazine, 2
      (August), 1-6 (3-6); (November), 320-26 (321-22).
        Recounts visits to Rydal and Wordsworth: Wordsworth's
      appearance, reaction to Jeffrey, refusal to consider Hogg
      a poet. His faults are his persisting in his early puerilities and his ties with Lord Lonsdale and the stamp office.
      Praises A Letter to A Friend of Robert Burns.

20 [WILSON, JOHN]. Review of Motherwell's Poems. Blackwood's
   Edinburgh Magazine, 33 (April), 668-81 (668).
   Interprets "Ode to Duty."

21 [WILSON, JOHN] AN EARLY RISER. "Morning Monologues: No. I."
   Blackwood's Edinburgh Magazine, 34 (October), 429-39
   (434-35).
   The present age has not been unjust to Wordsworth. Reprinted in 1842.B33.

22 [WILSON, JOHN]. "Spenser." Blackwood's Edinburgh Magazine,
   34 (November), 824-56 (824-25, 843).
   Contrasts Wordsworth's and Spenser's use of natural
   imagery. Wordsworth is the apostle of endurance, resigna-
   tion, and faith. "Resolution and Independence" resembles
   Daphnaida.

1834 A BOOKS - NONE

1834 B SHORTER WRITINGS

1 A'BECKETT, WILLIAM, JR. "Wordsworth (William)," in A Universal
   Biography. . . . 3 vols. London: Isaac [1834?],
   III:995-96.
   A biographical sketch.

2 ANON. "The Supper and Flight of the Poets" (poem). Cambridge
   Quarterly Review, 2 (January), 19-33 (20, 27, 29-31).
   Agrees with Wordsworth's own opinion of his worth;
   praises the Lucy poems.

3 ANON. "A Few Words on Reviewing." Oxford University Magazine,
   1 (March), 92-95 (93-94).
   Because Jeffrey reviewed as a lawyer, the multitude dislike Wordsworth.

4 ANON. "On a Stone." Leigh Hunt's London Journal, 1
   (9 April), 9-10 (9).
   Praises the image of the stone in "She dwelt among the
   untrodden ways."

5 ANON. "Hogarth and His Works--No. V." Penny Magazine, 3
   (30 August), 329-30 (330).
   Analyzes "Resolution and Independence": the leech-
   gatherer is a useful member of society.

1834

6   ANON. "Law and Music." Examiner, no. 1393 (12 October),
     pp. 641-42 (641).
        "Power of Music" shows how the benevolent Wordsworth
     contemplates an act of vagrancy.

7   ANON. "Biographical Memoir of the Late Samuel Taylor
     Coleridge." Analyst, no. 2, pp. 148-52 (149-51).
        Coleridge attacked the fallacies of Wordsworth's poetic
     theory relating to low life.

8   ANON. The Georgian Era: Memoirs of the Most Eminent Persons,
     Who Have Flourished in Great Britain, from the Accession of
     George the First to the Demise of George the Fourth.
     4 vols. London: Vizetelly, Branston, III:422-23.
     A biographical sketch.

9   BARNETT, JOHN. "Ossian's Glen, Descriptive Canzona for Tenor
     or Soprano," in Lyric Illustrations of the Modern Poets.
     London: D'Almaine [1834], pp. 52-55.
     Uses the text of "Glen Almain."

10   C., E. W. "William Wordsworth." Bath and Bristol Magazine, 3
     (January), 82-87.
        Wordsworth's poems celebrate England, thoughts connected
     with a faithful portrayal of nature, benevolence, and the
     virtue of the poor.

11   [CHATTO, WILLIAM ANDREW] STEPHEN OLIVER, THE YOUNGER. Scenes
     and Recollections of Fly-fishing, in Northumberland,
     Cumberland, and Westmorland. London: Chapman and Hall,
     pp. 32-33, 158.
        Praises Wordsworth's description of trout in The Excur-
     sion. Wordsworth is "eloquent in truth's simplest and
     purest language." Attribution: British Museum catalogue.

12   [CRAIK, GEORGE L.]. Review of Coleridge's Poetical Works.
     Printing Machine, 1 (16 August), 275-79 (278).
        Their "homely every-day truth" makes Wordsworth's poems
     proverbs. Attribution: Craik, in 1845.B6; VI:141.

13   [DE QUINCEY, THOMAS] THE ENGLISH OPIUM-EATER. "Samuel Taylor
     Coleridge." Tait's Edinburgh Magazine, NS 1 (September),
     509-20 (509-10, 517, 520); (October), 588-96.
        Recounts his initial reaction to Lyrical Ballads: their
     freshness (509-10, 517, 520). Discusses Wordsworth as he
     touches Coleridge's life; compares Wordsworth and Southey
     (588-96). Reprinted in De Quincey's Writings (1850-59);
     reprinted with minor changes in 1854.B4.

14 DE VERE, SIR AUBREY. "On a Visit to Wordsworth, after a
    Mountain Excursion" (poem), in The Literary Souvenir.
    Edited by Alaric A. Watts. London: Longman, p. 178.
        Wordsworth is "the Poet of the age and land." Reprinted
    with verbal changes as "Rydal with Wordsworth" in 1842.B18.

15 DOYLE, FRANCIS HASTINGS. "Sonnet Written in the First Page of
    Wordsworth's Poems," in Miscellaneous Verses. London:
    Taylor, p. 59.
        Calm and lofty of soul, Wordsworth writes verse full of
    hope and immortality.

16 ELLIOTT, EBENEZER. "Preface," in The Village Patriarch, Love,
    and Other Poems. Volume II [of Poetical Works, in 3 vols.].
    London: Steill, pp. 1-7 (1-2).
        As opposed to Crabbe, Wordsworth only meets a humble
    subject "half-way, and with his hinder-end towards it."

17 ENGLISH OPIUM-EATER, THE. See 1834.B13.

18 HEMANS, FELICIA. Dedication, in Scenes and Hymns of Life,
    with Other Religious Poems. Edinburgh: Blackwood; London:
    Cadell, p. [v].
        Testifies to her respect for Wordsworth's character and
    gratitude for his moral and intellectual teaching. See
    1839.B12.

19 [HERAUD, JOHN ABRAHAM]. "Reminiscences of Coleridge,
    Biographical, Philosophical, Poetical, and Critical."
    Fraser's Magazine, 10 (October), 379-403 (386-93).
        Discusses Wordsworth's and Coleridge's lives in the west
    of England. In "The Idiot Boy" the ideal is hidden within
    the idiot's mind.

20 HERAUD, JOHN A.[BRAHAM]. An Oration on the Death of Samuel
    Taylor Coleridge, Esq.: Delivered at the Russell Institu-
    tion, On Friday, August 8, 1834. London: Fraser, p. 15.
        Wordsworth's merits are now acknowledged, thanks to
    Coleridge's critique in Biographia Literaria.

21 LANDOR, W.[ALTER] S.[AVAGE]. "To Wordsworth" (poem).
    Athenaeum, no. 327 (1 February), p. 88.
        Praises Wordsworth's use of "skilful eye and fit device."
    Reprinted with minor verbal changes as "An Ode" in [J.
    Ablett,] Literary Hours (1837) and 1846.B10.

22 LANDOR, WALTER SAVAGE. "Ode to a Friend." Leigh Hunt's
    London Journal, 1 (3 December), 282.

1834

        Hails Wordsworth as a creator "of immortal things." Re-
printed as "To Joseph Ablett" in 1835.B2; as "An Ode: 1832"
in [J. Ablett,] Literary Hours (1837); as "To Joseph Ablett"
in 1846.B10.

23   [MUDFORD, WILLIAM] GEOFFREY OLDCASTLE. "The late S. T.
       Coleridge, Esq." Canterbury Magazine, 1 (September),
       121-31 (126).
         Prints letter in which Coleridge blames Wordsworth for
adverse criticism in the periodicals. Attribution: William
Cushing, Initials and Pseudonyms: A Dictionary of Literary
Disguises, Second series (New York: Crowell, 1888), p. 110.

24   OLDCASTLE, GEOFFREY. See 1834.B23.

25   OLIVER, STEPHEN, THE YOUNGER. See 1834.B11.

26   [SORTAIN, JOSEPH]. Review of The Poetical Works of S. T.
       Coleridge. British Critic, 4th ser., 16 (October), 393-417
       (393-96).
         Wordsworth's "dignified apology" for his poems in the
Preface to Lyrical Ballads is deficient in that it sees
only social changes as the cause of the present deteriorated
taste in literature. Wordsworth's poems are calm, Coleridge's tumultuous; Wordsworth observes the mind's phe-
nomena, Coleridge probes their latent causes. Attribution:
Richard Haven et al., eds., Samuel Taylor Coleridge: An
Annotated Bibliography of Criticism and Scholarship,
Volume I (Boston: G.K. Hall, 1976), p. 84.

27   [TAYLOR, HENRY]. Review of Poetical Works (1832) and
       Selections from the Poems of William Wordsworth (1834).
       Quarterly Review, 52 (November), 317-58.
         As a result of Wordsworth's poems more than his pre-
faces, poetry is now plain-spoken, though a new false diction has arisen. Wordsworth weakened his immediate influence by deliberately antagonizing his critics on unim-
portant points (e.g., by announcing a serious purpose in
"The Idiot Boy" and by adopting a militant attitude towards
his theory of diction and hence sometimes writing with a
forced simplicity). He has not put forth a new philosophical system but has, rather, modified philosophical ideas by
his own temperament, as illustrated by his treatment of
pride in "Lines Left upon a Seat in a Yew-tree," a treatment that contrasts with Burns's, and by his reaction to
the beauty of nature, including his attributing human
properties to inanimate objects. A sense of the dignity of
his calling pervades his writings; they have a sanative

influence, giving the reader a sense of "freedom of the
heart" (best defined in "Ode to Duty"). In narrative poems
such as "Michael" and "The Female Vagrant" he is able to
make the plain realities of life interesting by convincing
the reader of the power of the poet's mind and of his
familiarity with his subjects. His sonnets (especially
"Scorn not the Sonnet; Critic, you have frowned" and the
sonnets connected with Napoleon) are "exquisitely chiselled,"
free from false effects. In The Excursion he rightly mixes
poetical and unpoetical passages. Despite criticism, he has
steadfastly kept his faith in his poetry, poetry which constitutes a personal tie between himself and his admirers.
Revised in 1849.B13.

28   [WILSON, JOHN]. "Poetry of Ebenezer Elliott." Blackwood's
      Edinburgh Magazine, 35 (May), 815-35 (816-19).
          Wordsworth is a poet of, but not for, the poor.

29   [WILSON, JOHN]. "Spenser." Blackwood's Edinburgh Magazine,
      36 (September), 408-30 (410, 421); (November), 681-714
      (683, 708).
          Wordsworth's prayer for fame in "Personal Talk" will be
      answered (410, 421). He dedicated himself to his high
      calling (683, 708).

30   [WILSON, JOHN]. Review of Coleridge's Poetical Works.
      Blackwood's Edinburgh Magazine, 36 (October), 542-70
      (passim).
          Wordsworth "has illustrated the Faith of Universal Feel-
      ing." The movements in "Ode: Intimations of Immortality"
      are too laborious; "Dion" lacks impetuosity.

1835 A BOOKS - NONE

1835 B SHORTER WRITINGS

1   ALFORD, HENRY. "Recollections of Wordsworth's 'Ruth'" (poem),
     in The School of the Heart and Other Poems. 2 vols.
     London: Longman; Cambridge: Deighton, I:18.
         Wordsworth is the "most pure of Poesy-gifted Men." Re-
     printed in 1853.B1.

2   ANON. "Mr Landor's Ode to a Friend." Leigh Hunt's London
     Journal, 2 (15 April), 113-14 (113).
         The critics of the Edinburgh Review no longer quarrel
     "with the illustrious Muse of the Lakes." Reprints
     1834.B22 as "To Joseph Ablett."

1835

3   ANON. Review of <u>Yarrow Revisited</u>. <u>Athenaeum</u>, no. 390
     (18 April), pp. 293-94.
       Welcomes Wordsworth's elevated thoughts and undiminished
     power.

4   ANON. Review of <u>Yarrow Revisited</u>. <u>Literary Gazette</u>, no. 953
     (25 April), pp. 257-58.
       The volume is a diary in which Wordsworth chronicles his
     benevolent thoughts and feelings. "Criticism is an imper-
     tinence to such poems."

5   ANON. Review of <u>Yarrow Revisited</u>. <u>Examiner</u>, no. 1421
     (26 April), pp. 259-60.
       Wordsworth has worthily achieved fame. He goes among
     the poor not as a companion but as a moralist; he delineates
     nature truly, however. The execution of "The Egyptian Maid"
     is brilliant.

6   ANON. "Wordsworth's New Poems." <u>New Monthly Magazine</u>, [NS]
     44 (May), 12-16.
       Wordsworth's genius results from an egotistical involve-
     ment in his writings; his egotism, however, differs from
     Rousseau's: it elevates nature, even if it prevents Words-
     worth, except in <u>Peter Bell</u>, from giving true-to-life por-
     traits (in the manner of Crabbe and Teniers) divorced from
     his philosophy. In <u>Yarrow Revisited</u>, only a few political
     remarks are offensive; Wordsworth avoids extreme simplicity.
     He chooses the sonnet form so the poem will owe its success
     to nothing but himself.

7   ANON. Review of <u>Yarrow Revisited</u>. <u>Printing Machine</u>, 3
     (2 May), 281-85.
       Wordsworth's life has been favored. Praises the Yarrow
     poems, sonnets, and "The Egyptian Maid."

8   ANON. Review of <u>Yarrow Revisited</u>. <u>Mirror of Literature,
     Amusement, and Instruction</u>, 25 (Suppl., 23 May), 346-48.
       Variety, originality, simplicity, and grandeur charac-
     terize Wordsworth's poetry. The sifting of Wordsworth's
     sublime from his ridiculous poems will improve his popular-
     ity.

9   ANON. Review of <u>Yarrow Revisited</u>. <u>Spectator</u>, 8 (23 May),
     493-94.
       Wordsworth's simplicity was not designed to gain him
     popularity. His peculiar power lies in blending description
     with reflection.

10   ANON. Review of Yarrow Revisited. Dublin University Magazine,
      5 (June), 680-705.
          Questions Wordsworth's arrangement of his poems, the con-
      tents and printing of the Preface to Lyrical Ballads and
      Essay (1815), and the alterations of earlier texts; compares
      Wordsworth with Aikenside, Macpherson, and Cowper; criti-
      cizes the Yarrow poems. Wordsworth's failure in writing
      dramatic and narrative poetry accounts for his difficulty
      in pleasing most readers.

11   ANON. Review of Yarrow Revisited. Christian Remembrancer, 17
      (July), 413.
          Wordsworth recommends not only religion and morality,
      but Church institutions.

12   ANON. Review of Montgomery's A Poet's Portfolio and Yarrow
      Revisited. Monthly Review, [4th ser.,] 2 for 1835
      (August), 605-17 (605-606, 612-17).
          Wordsworth retains all his power, in a more hallowed
      tone.

13   ANON. Review of Cattermole's Sacred Poetry of the Seventeenth
      Century. Examiner, no. 1444 (4 October), pp. 627-28 (628).
          Wordsworth's poetry was anticipated by Wither.

14   ANON. Review of Southey's "Life of Cowper." Examiner,
      no. 1450 (15 November), pp. 724-25 (724).
          Wordsworth's thoughts in "Resolution and Independence"
      lack his usual depth of philosophy.

15   ANON. "The Ettrick Shepherd." Newcastle Journal, 4
      (5 December), [3].
          Wordsworth is one of England's "best and most loyal
      subjects."

16   ANON. "Wordsworth on the Death of the Ettrick Shepherd."
      Court Journal, no. 346 (12 December), p. 789.
          In "Extempore Effusion upon the Death of James Hogg"
      Wordsworth's sympathy is "rendered more affecting by the
      self-reference which is here and there betrayed."

17   ANON. "Wordsworth." Fraser's Literary Chronicle, no. 3
      (19 December), pp. 42-43.
          Draws attention to the noble sympathy and resignation
      with which Wordsworth has regarded the sufferings and
      deaths of his great contemporaries.

1835

18   ANON. "Rydal Lake, and Residence of the Poet Wordsworth,
      Westmorland." Mirror of Literature, Amusement, and
      Instruction, 26 (26 December), 433-35.
          Wordsworth lives amidst congenial scenery.

19   ANON. "Wordsworth." Fraser's Literary Chronicle, no. 4
      (26 December), pp. 60-62.
          Admires Wordsworth's saving creed of healthful, manly,
      and natural feeling; cites the Yarrow poems to show the con-
      sistency of Wordsworth's poetic character over the years.

20   ANON. "William Wordsworth, Esq." Mirror of Literature,
      Amusement, and Instruction, 26 (Suppl.), v-viii.
          A biographical sketch. Wordsworth is "the Reformer of
      Poetry," having improved poetic diction and associated
      poetry with philosophy. He excels in writing sonnets.

21   ANON. Some Remarks on the Preface to Philip van Artevelde.
      London: privately printed, pp. 6-7.
          Wordsworth is totally absorbed in his own poetry.

22   ANON. The World: A Poem. London: Hurst, pp. 60-61.
          Wordsworth, a true domestic poet, is the bard both of
      sweet enjoyment and high philosophy. Scorned by his age,
      he lives in sweet retirement.

23   B.[AILEY, BENJAMIN?]. "Sonnets: Bard of the Lake and
      Mountain! I should grieve," "Written in Continuation of
      the first Sonnet of the second part of Wordsworth's
      Miscellaneous Sonnets, beginning 'Scorn not the Sonnet'"
      (poem), "Written in the first blank leaf of Wordsworth's
      'Yarrow Revisited, and Other Poems'" (poem), "Written in
      the last blank leaf of the same Volume" (poem), "Lines
      Written on a Page of 'The Italian Itinerant and the Swiss
      Goatherd,'" "On a Portrait of Wordsworth" (poem), in Lines
      Addressed to William Wordsworth Esq. Colombo: privately
      printed, pp. 8, 9, 10, 11, 12, 13.
          Hails Wordsworth as Nature's poet (8), writer of sonnets
      (9), whose poems recall the "dawn of youth" (10), soothe
      the soul "to wisest melancholy" (11), and express benevo-
      lence (12). His portrait reveals a face of deep, serene
      thought (13). Attribution: British Museum catalogue.

24   BELL, GEORGE. "Rydal Mount" (poem), in Descriptive and Other
      Miscellaneous Pieces, in Verse. Penrith: privately
      printed, p. 112.
          Wordsworth's poems combine deep thoughts and joy.

25   [COLERIDGE, HENRY NELSON]. Review of Yarrow Revisited.
     Quarterly Review, 54 (July), 181-85.
          The volume "is almost without the reach of periodical
     criticism"; it "supports an established fame." Wordsworth's
     poems exhibit nobleness of thought expressed in appropriate
     language, sculptural precision, completeness, pensive tints
     of the autumn of the poet's life, and patriotism. The
     Postscript offers the profound insight of one who knows
     the poor.

26   [COLERIDGE, HENRY NELSON, ed.]. Specimens of the Table Talk
     of the late Samuel Taylor Coleridge. 2 vols. London:
     Murray, I:101, 266; II:69-72, 117, 270-71, 300.
          Records Coleridge's wish that Wordsworth had published
     the first two books of The Excursion separately and had
     never "abandoned the contemplative position," and his under-
     standing of Wordsworth's plan for his philosophical poem.
     Records Coleridge's remarks that Wordsworth, like Goethe,
     feels for, not with, his characters, and that Wordsworth's
     poems were laughed at "because of some few wilfulnesses."

27   [DANIEL, GEORGE]. Note to "The Modern Dunciad," in The Modern
     Dunciad[,] Virgil in London and Other Poems. London:
     Pickering, p. 38.
          Wordsworth perversely provokes ridicule when he might
     command applause. Attribution: British Museum catalogue.

28   [DE QUINCEY, THOMAS] AN ENGLISH OPIUM EATER. "Sketches of
     Life and Manners; from the Autobiography of an English
     Opium Eater: Oxford." Tait's Edinburgh Magazine, NS 2
     (August), 541-50 (543).
          Recounts his early appreciation of Wordsworth and the
     progress of Wordsworth's reputation.

29   DEWHURST, H. W. "The Yew-tree." Mirror of Literature,
     Amusement, and Instruction, 25 (21 February), 119-21.
          Wordsworth "ranks with the finest poets of our own
     times."

30   ENGLISH OPIUM EATER, AN. See 1835.B28.

31   [FOX, WILLIAM JOHNSON?]. Review of Yarrow Revisited. Monthly
     Repository, NS 9 (June), 430-34.
          Wordsworth, having overcome obstacles, now receives in-
     discriminate homage as he had before received indiscriminate
     ridicule. He is frequently philosophical at the expense of
     his poetry, and vice versa. In politics and religion, he
     is the poet of the past. Yarrow Revisited contains scarcely

1835

any of his former peculiarities. The poems describing
Scottish scenery "want peculiarity and appropriateness";
the ballads and narratives are best.

32 [GILLIES, ROBERT PEARSE]. "Recollections of Sir Walter
    Scott." Fraser's Magazine, 12 (December), 687-703 (693).
       Records Scott's praise of Wordsworth. Reprinted in
    Recollections of Sir Walter Scott (1837).

33 [HERAUD, JOHN ABRAHAM?]. Review of Yarrow Revisited.
    Fraser's Magazine, 11 (June), 689-707.
       Wordsworth is a fit guide for young people: he cor-
    rected the false taste of the last century. He invests the
    meanest subjects with dignity, yet is also equal to the most
    important arguments. He takes care in the arrangement of
    his poems. He sympathizes with the poor. "Stanzas Sug-
    gested in a Steamboat Off Saint Bees' Heads" reminds us to
    endeavor to make Protestantism more catholic and apostolic
    in spirit; "The Egyptian Maid" can be compared with Cole-
    ridge's "The Rime of the Ancient Mariner." Wordsworth was
    originally, like Byron, a poet of nature and actual life,
    though Wordsworth was the poet of a nature purified by his
    own mind (e.g., in "Gold and Silver Fishes in a Vase"); he
    has now become a religious poet as well (e.g., in "On the
    Power of Sound"). His powers are not declining.

34 HOUSMAN, ROBERT FLETCHER. "Notes," in A Collection of English
    Sonnets. Edited by Robert Fletcher Housman. London:
    Simpkin, Marshall; Lancaster: Willan [1835], pp. 301-[352]
    (327-33).
       Prints letter in which Mrs. Hemans expresses her admira-
    tion of Wordsworth as a poet of "home-affections," eloquent
    political poems, and powerful single lines.

35 HOWITT, WILLIAM. "The Great Modern Poets Great Reformers."
    Tait's Edinburgh Magazine, NS 2 (March), 157-67 (157-58,
    165-67).
       Wordsworth's writings, especially his admiration of
    Milton in his sonnets, are Radical, despite the Toryism of
    his personal life caused by a desire for advancement.

36 [HUNT, LEIGH]. "Ice,--With Poets upon It." Leigh Hunt's
    London Journal, 2 (28 January), 25-26 (25).
       Wordsworth writes vigorously about ice skating because
    he is himself a skater. Reprinted in The Seer (1841).

37 [HUNT, LEIGH]. "Chat with the Magazines: Wordsworth's
    Sonnets." Leigh Hunt's London Journal, 2 (20 May), 153-54.

Wordsworth's productivity and facility with language are admirable. In contrast with Milton, he is narrow-minded, retrospective, lacking in sympathy, and melancholy. Reprinted as "Wordsworth and Milton" in The Seer (1840).

38 MACKINTOSH, ROBERT JAMES, ed. Memoirs of the Life of the Right Honourable Sir James Mackintosh. Edited by his Son. 2 vols. London: Moxon, I:409-10.
    Includes journal entry in which J. Mackintosh notes that Wordsworth's poems provide escape from the vexations and dangers of the world.

39 [MOIR, GEORGE?]. Review of Glassford's Lyrical Compositions. Edinburgh Review, 60 (January), 353-63 (356-57).
    Though negligent in following the rhymes of Italian models, Wordsworth does in his sonnets develop one idea into a polished whole.

40 MOXON, EDWARD. "Sonnet XVI," in Sonnets. Part second. London: privately printed, p. 22.
    Wordsworth has brought the light of truth from unknown sources, enlarging our perceptions.

41 R., W. "Stanzas," in Lines Addressed to William Wordsworth Esq. Colombo: privately printed, pp. 3-7.
    Hails Wordsworth as a poet of liberty.

42 T.[ALFOURD] T.[HOMAS] N.[OON]. "Preface," in Ion; A Tragedy, in Five Acts. London: privately printed [1835], pp. vii-xvii (xii-xiii).
    Testifies to Wordsworth's influence on his own literary development. In addition to purifying current literature, Wordsworth provides a new insight into enjoying the literature of the past by his tracing of the lowly and the good.

43 [WALLACE, WILLIAM]. "State of English Literature." British and Foreign Review, 1 (July), 190-217 (210-16).
    Wordsworth is not a poet of the first order, as shown by the fact that he is cried up by a clique. There is a perverse egotism in his exalting of unpoetical commonplaces by pompous language. Attribution: Richard Haven et al., eds., Samuel Taylor Coleridge: An Annotated Bibliography of Criticism and Scholarship, Volume I (Boston: G.K. Hall, 1976), p. 92.

44 [WILSON, JOHN]. Review of Roscoe's Poems. Blackwood's Edinburgh Magazine, 37 (February), 153-60 (155, 157).
    Notes Wordsworth's debt to Percy's Reliques.

1835

45 [WILSON, JOHN]. Review of Mant's The British Months.
Blackwood's Edinburgh Magazine, 37 (April), 684-98 (684).
Ecclesiastical Sketches, fine illustrations of Christianity, are far better than Wordsworth's earlier religion of
the woods.

46 [WILSON, JOHN]. Review of Yarrow Revisited. Blackwood's
Edinburgh Magazine, 37 (May), 699-722.
Wordsworth has triumphed over his Scottish critics. He
is a poet for older men as well as youth. There is wisdom
for the present day in Ecclesiastical Sketches. Memorials
of a Tour on the Continent surpasses all prose tours; "The
Eclipse of the Sun, 1820" is the finest lyrical effusion
ever written. In his poems on Scotland Wordsworth captures
the Scottish spirit while retaining his own originality.
He is best when dealing with the common goings-on of life
(e.g., in "Stepping Westward"). He excels Milton as a
writer of sonnets.

47 [WILSON, JOHN]. "Anglimania." Blackwood's Edinburgh Magazine,
38 (August), 145-66 (146-47).
Wordsworth's "feelings are always healthful," especially
when he recalls childhood.

1836 A BOOKS - NONE

1836 B SHORTER WRITINGS

1 [ALLSOP, THOMAS, ed.]. Letters[,] Conversations and
Recollections of S. T. Coleridge. 2 vols. London: Moxon,
I:105-107, 205, 207, 218, 222-25; II:5-7, 114, 127, 166,
228.
Wordsworth was a poet "in whom the repressive faculty
was predominant"; people mistook The Excursion for a touring
book. Includes Coleridge's remarks that many of Wordsworth's
striking passages mean less than they seem; that Wordsworth
mistakenly makes the soul dependent upon accidents of birth
and abode, confuses God with the world; that his introduction of religion in his later works suggests worldly pru-
dence; that Longman's reported that seafaring men purchased
Lyrical Ballads, thinking it a naval song book; and that
Wordsworth possesses little "femineity in his mind." Records Wordsworth's comment that when he is a good man he is
a good Christian, and Byron's ridiculing of Wordsworth.

2 ANON. "A New Year's Gift." Fraser's Literary Chronicle,
no. 5 (2 January), pp. 71-74 (73).

Includes "Brandy Untasted" (poem), a parody of "Yarrow Unvisited."

3 ANON. Review of Housman's <u>A Collection of English Sonnets</u>.
   <u>Kendal Mercury</u>, no. 90 (30 January), p. [4].
      Extracts from Wordsworth will spread his fame. Reprints
   letter from the <u>Lancaster Gazette</u> in which R. F. Housman
   states Wordsworth's approval of the inclusion of his sonnets
   in Housman's anthology.

4 ANON. "Wordsworth and the Poor." <u>Fraser's Literary Chronicle</u>,
   no. 14 (5 March), pp. 219-20.
      Wordsworth, in Postscript (1835), reasons soundly in
   pleading the cause of the poor.

5 ANON. "Béranger and Wordsworth." <u>Fraser's Literary Chronicle</u>,
   no. 19 (9 April), pp. 297-98.
      Compares the treatment of infancy by Béranger and Words-
   worth.

6 ANON. "Wordsworth: Resolution and Independence." <u>Fraser's
   Literary Chronicle</u>, no. 21 (23 April), pp. 326-28.
      Wordsworth, Coleridge, and Southey do not, as was claimed
   in the <u>Edinburgh Review</u>, form one poetic school. A man must
   have suffered to understand the feeling and moral grandeur
   of "Resolution and Independence."

7 ANON. Review of the <u>London and Westminster Review</u> (January-
   April 1836). <u>Fraser's Literary Chronicle</u>, no. 22
   (30 April), pp. 341-42.
      A reply to 1836.B15. the shorter poems, not <u>The Excur-
   sion</u>, provide the chief statements of Wordsworth's intellectual character.

8 ANON. "Afterthoughts." <u>Chambers' Edinburgh Journal</u>, 5
   (21 May), 129-30 (129).
      Wordsworth correctly views afterthoughts and lying in
   "Anecdote for Fathers."

9 ANON. "A Contrast from Wordsworth." <u>Fraser's Literary
   Chronicle</u>, no. 26 (28 May), p. 412.
      Points out contrasting versification within "Song at the
   Feast of Brougham Castle."

10 ANON. Review of <u>Poetical Works</u> (1836-37, Volume I).
    <u>Examiner</u>, no. 1502 (13 November), p. 724.
       Human hopes and the human heart are the staples of Words-
    worth's poems. Wordsworth has endured strife and achieved
    glory.

1836

11   ANON. Dedication, in Attempts at Verse. London: Mann,
      p. [iii].
           A tribute to Wordsworth as "high-priest."

12   CARLYON, CLEMENT. Early Years and Late Reflections.   4 vols.
      London: Whittaker, I:116-19, 196-98.
           Recalls visit to Wordsworth in 1801 and account of Words-
      worth and Coleridge journeying together in Germany without
      Dorothy.   For Volume II, see 1843.B6.

13   CHAMBERS, ROBERT. History of the English Language and
      Literature. Edinburgh: Chambers, pp. 199-200.
           A biographical sketch.   Wordsworth has retained many
      poems in manuscript, believing the public of the present
      age cannot appreciate them.   He breaks his own poetic rules;
      his later, meditative poems deserve praise.

14   CHORLEY, HENRY F., ed. Memorials of Mrs. Hemans: with
      Illustrations of her Literary Character from her Private
      Correspondence. 2 vols.   London: Saunders and Otley,
      I:166-67, 173-76; II:43, 107-49 (passim), 252, 289, 352.
           Records Hemans's admiration of Wordsworth, and her visit
      to Rydal Mount in 1830:   Wordsworth's "lurking love of mis-
      chief," "patriarchal simplicity," impulsive conversation,
      earnest reading of his poems, criticism of Burns, reading
      Schiller.   Records M. J. Jewsbury's friendship with Words-
      worth.

15   D. "The Poets of Our Age, Considered as to Their Philosophic
      Tendencies." London and Westminster Review, 3 and 25
      (April), 60-71.
           A scepticism lurks at the foundation of The Excursion;
      Wordsworth bases his argument not on an absolute first
      truth, but on man.   There is little of substance in the ad-
      vice of the Wanderer and Pastor.   As a philosophical poet,
      Wordsworth contrasts with Shelley.   Ecclesiastical Sketches
      show him in utter despair of a topic.   He and Coleridge, in
      contrast to Shelley, cling to the principles of the past.

16   ED. "Winander Lake and Mountains, and Ambleside Fall: By
      John Keats." Western Messenger; Devoted to Religion and
      Literature, 1 (June), 772-77 (774-75).
           Prints letter in which Keats records his disappointment
      at Wordsworth's political activities in 1818.

17   H.[ORNE], R.[ICHARD] H.[ENGIST]. "Sonnet to Wordsworth."
      Monthly Repository, NS 10 (July), 424.
           Wordsworth, the poet of virtue, makes the human heart
      lie bare.

18 LAMB, CHARLES. "To Dora W---, On Being Asked by Her Father to Write in Her Album" (poem), in The Poetical Works of Charles Lamb. A new edition. London: Moxon, p. 170.
  Praises the "intelligential Orchard" of Wordsworth's mind.

19 LANDOR, WALTER SAVAGE. A Satire on Satirists, and Admonition to Detractors (poem). London: Saunders and Otley, pp. 25-34.
  Mocks Wordsworth's politics and egotism in preferring his own poetry. Discusses Wordsworth's borrowing of the image of the shell in The Excursion (Book IV). Partially reprinted, with minor verbal changes, as "To an Aged Poet" in 1846.B10. Minor manuscript variants printed in Literary Anecdotes, edited by Nicoll and Wise (1895).

20 [MAGINN, WILLIAM and FRANCIS MAHONY]. "Report on Fraser's Magazine." Fraser's Magazine, 13 (January), 1-79 (26-27).
  Poets such as Wordsworth write for men of their own moral and intellectual calibre. For Wordsworth all power proceeds from God rather than from the people.

21 R., N. "On Wordsworth's Poems" (poem), "On a Collection of Modern Poems" (poem). Scottish Monthly Magazine, 1 (December), 866.
  Wordsworth's poems vivify, chase woe.

22 RICHARDSON, D.[AVID] L.[ESTER]. Literary Leaves or Prose and Verse. Calcutta: Smith, pp. 6, 66, 134-35, 138, 162-63, 205-208, 221-22, 293, 394, 397-98.
  The "querulous melancholy" in his prefaces shows that Wordsworth's repose has been destroyed by hostile criticism. Wordsworth has failed to discipline his poetic powers, is an egotist. Both ear and mind are satisfied by the concluding image in "Composed upon Westminster Bridge." Wordsworth sometimes sacrifices a poem to a theory. The Excursion is a soliloquy; he cannot construct a narrative or a drama. His daily life is pure. He contrasts with Campbell. Praises "Ode: Intimations of Immortality." Wordsworth is indebted to Anne Finch, Countess of Winchelsea, in "Written in Very Early Youth." (Reprinted from periodicals not located.) Expanded in 1840.B16.

23 W., R. "English Literature of 1835." London and Westminster Review, 3 and 25 (April), 234-64 (262).
  Yarrow Revisited presents a variety of pleasures.

1836

24 [WILLMOTT, ROBERT ELDRIDGE ARIS]. "The Poet Wordsworth and
   Professor Smythe," in Conversations at Cambridge. London:
   Parker, pp. 235-52.
      Discusses Wordsworth's opinions on poets of the eight-
   eenth century, especially Gray, and on poetic theory and
   technique. Attribution: British Museum catalogue.

25 [WILSON, JOHN]. Review of Alford's School of the Heart.
   Blackwood's Edinburgh Magazine, 39 (May), 577-93 (579,
   583-85, 592).
      Notes Alford's admiration of Wordsworth.

1837 A BOOKS - NONE

1837 B SHORTER WRITINGS

1 ANON. Review of Poetical Works (1836-37, Volumes I-III).
   Athenaeum, no. 484 (4 February), p. 83.
      Wordsworth seems to have published the volumes to pro-
   tect the copyright.

2 ANON. "Wordsworth and His Poetry." Chambers' Edinburgh
   Journal, 6 (4 March), 47-48.
      A biographical sketch. A meditative poet, Wordsworth
   waited patiently for his readers to be converted to his
   poetic theories. The Excursion, "Laodamia," and the sonnets are characteristic of his genius.

3 ANON. Review of Poetical Works (1836-37). Athenaeum,
   no. 499 (20 May), pp. 359-60.
      Wordsworth writes with "force and freshness" in "To the
   Moon: Composed by the Seaside,--on the Coast of Cumberland."

4 ANON. Review of Poetical Works (1836-37, Volume V).
   Metropolitan Magazine, 19 (June), 40.
      Wordsworth's poems do not need praise; they serve to
   bring man up to a higher state.

5 ANON. Review of Poetical Works (1836-37, Volume V). Monthly
   Review, [4th ser.,] 2 for 1837 (June), 304-306.
      Wordsworth's spirit is bathed in warmth when he contem-
   plates the moon in "To the Moon: Composed by the Seaside,--
   on the Coast of Cumberland."

6 ANON. Review of Lyra Apostolica. Christian Observer,
   no. 427 (July), pp. 460-79 (470-71).
      Wordsworth exaggerates facts in "To Joanna."

118

7 ANON. Review of <u>The Literary Remains of Samuel Taylor
Coleridge</u>, etc. <u>Church of England Quarterly Review</u>, 2
(July), 24-56 (34-35, 40).
Wordsworth abandoned his objections to poetic diction,
regrets having written literary criticism. "Ode: Intima-
tions of Immortality" surpasses all contemporary lyrics.

8 ANON. "English Lake Scenery: Wordsworth's Residence at Rydal
Water." <u>Saturday Magazine</u>, 11 (8 July), 15-16.
Wordsworth's poetry, which casts a halo over Rydal, has
simple yet majestic beauty.

9 ANON. "Canute and his Courtiers." <u>Penny Magazine</u>, 6
(30 September), 376.
Wordsworth uses the story of Canute to inculcate "a
great moral lesson" in "A Fact, and an Imagination."

10 B.[ULWER-LYTTON], E.[DWARD]. Review of Talfourd's <u>The Letters
of Charles Lamb</u>. <u>London and Westminster Review</u>, 5 and 27
(July), 229-43 (230-31, 233).
Wordsworth did not regenerate poetry; he did not mean-
ingfully influence his contemporaries. His poems are too
divorced from the life of the passions to be popular.

11 COTTLE, JOSEPH. <u>Early Recollections; Chiefly Relating to the
late Samuel Taylor Coleridge, during his long residence in
Bristol</u>. 2 vols. London: Longman, I:250-53, 282, 298-99,
307-25; II:21, 23-27.
Includes letters from Coleridge and Cottle's recollections on Wordsworth's genius, life in Somerset and Germany,
and the publication of <u>The Borderers</u>, Wordsworth's poems,
and <u>Lyrical Ballads</u> (1798). Wordsworth attributed the slow
sale of <u>Lyrical Ballads</u> (1798) to "The Rime of the Ancient
Mariner" and unfavorable reviews. Expanded in 1847.B13.

12 CROSSLEY, THOMAS. "The Muse of Wordsworth" (poem), "To
Wordsworth" (poem), in <u>Flowers of Ebor: Poems</u>. London:
Longman; Halifax: Leyland, pp. 46-47, 176.
Wordsworth's poems, devoid of art, calm and elevate the
soul (46-47). They are "sweetly simple 'midst sublimity"
(176).

13 [DE QUINCEY, THOMAS] AN ENGLISH OPIUM-EATER. "Autobiography
of an English Opium-Eater: Literary Connexions or
Acquaintances." <u>Tait's Edinburgh Magazine</u>, NS 4 (February),
65-73 (68, 71); (March), 169-76 (172, 174-75).
<u>A Letter to A Friend of Robert Burns</u> contains embittered
feeling against Jeffrey but profound criticism on biography

(68, 71). Notes Wordsworth's acceptance in aristocratic
circles; records his presence at a gathering in the Courier
office. Records Mrs. Grant's objections to, and his justi-
fication of, "The Redbreast Chasing the Butterfly" (172,
174-75). Reprinted in De Quincey's Writings (1850-59).

14 ENGLISH OPIUM-EATER, AN. See 1837.B13.

15 HAMILTON, SIR WILLIAM [ROWAN]. "Lines, Addressed to the Poet
Wordsworth," in The Tribute: A Collection of Miscellaneous
Unpublished Poems. Edited by Lord Northampton. London:
Murray, and Lindsell, pp. 34-35.
      Pays tribute to Wordsworth's conversation on the lowly
and on God.

16 HERAUD, JOHN A. Substance of a Lecture on Poetic Genius as a
Moral Power: Delivered 2nd October, 1837, at the Milton
Institution. . . . London: Fraser, pp. 38, 44-48.
      Wordsworth rejoices in the ideal, "which he sometimes
represents under the Platonic form of pre-existence."

17 [HERAUD, JOHN ABRAHAM (and WILLIAM MAGINN?)]. "One or Two
Words on One or Two Books." Fraser's Magazine, 15 (April),
498-514 (501-504).
      Wordsworth has praised contemporary poets, including
Southey. He has not plagiarized from Landor.

18 [LOCKHART, JOHN GIBSON]. Memoirs of the Life of Sir Walter
Scott, Bart. 7 vols. Edinburgh: Cadell; London: Murray,
and Whittaker, especially I:402-407; II:70-71, 129, 132-33,
235, 301; V:40-41; VI:78-79.
      Records the visits of Wordsworth with Scott in 1803,
1805, and 1825. Includes letters in which Scott records
praising Wordsworth to Jeffrey, notes that Wordsworth's
lesser poems "ought to have been more cautiously hazarded,"
agrees with Wordsworth in Concerning . . . the Convention
of Cintra, and praises Wordsworth's lofty genius while
lamenting he sometimes chooses "to crawl upon all fours."
For Volume VII, see 1838.B20.

19 MACKENZIE, R.[OBERT] SHELTON. "Sonnet on First Meeting Southey
and Wordsworth." Metropolitan Magazine, 18 (February), 129.
      Wordsworth draws from nature "high converse all unknown
before."

20 [PEACOCK, THOMAS LOVE]. "Paper Money Lyrics, No. IV: A Mood
of My Own Mind" (poem). Guide, no. 7 (4 June), p. 50.

A burlesque, attributed to "W. W., Esq., Distributor of Stamps." Reprinted in Paper Money Lyrics (1837).

21 [SMITH, WILLIAM HENRY]. Review of Landor's Imaginary Conversations, etc. Quarterly Review, 58 (February), 108-48 (134-35, 143).
   Defends "Laodamia" and Wordsworth's friendship with Southey against Landor's attacks. Wordsworth uses the image of the shell in The Excursion to make a moral point; Landor simply describes.

22 SOUTHEY, ROBERT. "Preface," in The Poetical Works of Robert Southey, Collected by Himself. 10 vols. London: Longman, I:v-xii (x).
   Records his friendship with Wordsworth. For Volumes IV and IX, see 1838.B24.

23 TALFOURD, THOMAS NOON. A Speech Delivered by Thomas Noon Talfourd, Sergeant at Law, in the House of Commons, on Thursday, 18th May, 1837, on Moving for Leave to Bring in A Bill to Consolidate the Law relating to Copyright, and to Extend the Term of Its Duration. London: Moxon, pp. 13-14.
   Wordsworth persevered to triumph over his critics; he has opened a new vein of sentiment and thought and "supplied the noblest antidote to the freezing effects of the scientific spirit of the age."

24 TALFOURD, THOMAS NOON, ed. The Letters of Charles Lamb, with A Sketch of his Life. 2 vols. London: Moxon, passim.
   Wordsworth's genius more fitly traces the springs of heroic passion than the resulting action. Records his admiration of Wordsworth. Records Lamb's admiration of and correspondence with Wordsworth; includes letters in which Lamb details his effort to buy books for Wordsworth and his showing Wordsworth "Bartlemy fair," notes parallel between a poem by Vincent Bourne and "Power of Music" and between himself and The Waggoner, and records Manning's praise of The White Doe of Rylstone.

25 TEGG, THOMAS. Remarks on the Speech of Sergeant Talfourd, on Moving for Leave to Bring in A Bill to Consolidate the Laws relating to Copyright, and to Extend the Term of Its Duration. London: Tegg, pp. 17-18.
   A reply to 1837.B23. The public does not yet share Talfourd's estimate of Wordsworth's merit.

26 [WILSON, JOHN]. "Our Two Vases." Blackwood's Edinburgh Magazine, 41 (April), 429-48* (439, *447); 42 (October), 548-72 (551).

1837

> Wordsworth recites his own poetry magnificently; he has restored the sonnet to its place in poetry (439, *447). Wordsworth never will--never can--die (551).

27   [WILSON, JOHN]. "Poetry by our New Contributor." Blackwood's Edinburgh Magazine, 42 (November), 573-98 (577-78, 580). Mocks Wordsworth.

1838 A BOOKS - NONE

1838 B SHORTER WRITINGS

1   ANON. Review of Miscellaneous Poems (1820), The Excursion, Ecclesiastical Sketches, Yarrow Revisited, etc. Church of England Quarterly Review, 4 (July), 139-86 (139-43, 151-74, 186).
     Wordsworth must create in the reader the taste by which his poems are to be enjoyed. His initial unpopularity was largely due to extrinsic circumstances. A humanizing spirit, a pious and rational serenity, mark his poems, especially his characteristic ones on childhood and humble subjects and The Excursion; they contain the suggestive power to awaken the reader's imagination. Wordsworth is the Milton of the nineteenth century, though contrasting with him in many points.

2   ANON. "Local Intelligence." Newcastle Journal, 7 (7 July), p. [3]; (28 July), p. [3].
     Records visit to Newcastle and Durham of Wordsworth, "one of the most virtuous as well as the most loyal of her Majesty's subjects."

3   ANON. "Spectator's Library." Spectator, 11 (14 July), 660-64 (663).
     "Protest against the Ballot (1838)" "is sheer absurdity"; Wordsworth's relegating his attack on Grote (in "Said Secrecy to Cowardice and Fraud") to the notes is hypocritical.

4   ANON. Review of The Sonnets of William Wordsworth. Examiner, no. 1589 (15 July), 436.
     Wordsworth's sonnets are incomparable, though "Protest against the Ballot (1838)" is absurd.

5   ANON. "University Intelligence." Durham Advertiser, no. 1247 (27 July), p. [3].
     Reports Wordsworth's receiving of an honorary degree and Professor Jenkyns's commending of the simple truth, deep thought, and pure feelings of Wordsworth's poems.

6   ANON. Review of Barrett's The Seraphim. Metropolitan
     Magazine, 22 (August), 97-101 (97).
          E. Barrett's poems echo those of "the great and good
     Wordsworth."

7   ANON. Review of The Sonnets of William Wordsworth. Literary
     Gazette, no. 1127 (25 August), 540.
          Ever since he threw off his simplicity, Wordsworth has
     earned our admiration.

8   ANON. Review of Montgomery's Poetical Works and Lectures.
     Wesleyan-Methodist Magazine, 3rd ser., 17 (November),
     828-36 (832).
          Objects to poets (identified in the index to the volume
     as referring to Wordsworth) who confuse pleasure in nature
     with adoration towards God.

9   ANON. Observations on the Law of Copyright; in Reference to
     the Bill Introduced into the House of Commons by Mr.
     Sergeant Talfourd. . . . London: Scott, Webster, and
     Geary, p. 39.
          The many cannot read Wordsworth's poems at their present
     price.

10   B., A. Letter to the Editor. Kendal Mercury, no. 205
     (14 April), p. [3].
          Did Wordsworth ever complain of his works being included
     in an anthology?

11   CHORLEY, HENRY F. The Authors of England: A Series of
     Medallion Portraits of Modern Literary Characters, Engraved
     from the Works of British Artists, by Achille Collas: with
     Illustrative Notices. London: Tilt, pp. 87-93.
          A biographical sketch. As Wordsworth was before too
     derided, he is today too revered. Expanded in 1861.B5.

12   [DE QUINCEY, THOMAS] AN ENGLISH OPIUM-EATER. "Autobiography
     of an English Opium-Eater: Recollections of Charles Lamb."
     Tait's Edinburgh Magazine, NS 5 (April), 237-47 (237,
     240-46); (June), 355-66 (362, 365).
          Records his early admiration of Wordsworth's poems.
     Wordsworth's judging of the human face was faulty; he
     craves the visual forms of nature. "Written after the
     Death of Charles Lamb" clarifies Lamb's checkered life
     (237, 240-46). The "pensive morality" of "The Oak and the
     Broom" contrasts with the levity of La Fontaine (362, 365).
     Reprinted in De Quincey's Writings (1850-59).

1838

13   ENGLISH OPIUM-EATER, AN. See 1838.B12.

14   GUEST, EDWIN. A History of English Rhythms. 2 vols. London:
       Pickering, I:89, 182.
             False accentuation creates ambiguity in The White Doe of
       Rylstone. Wordsworth uses archaic pronunciations.

15   HALL, S.[AMUEL] C.[ARTER]. "Wordsworth," in The Book of Gems:
       The Modern Poets and Artists of Great Britain. Edited by
       S. C. Hall. London: Whittaker, p. 2.
             A biographical sketch. Despite criticism, Wordsworth
       has led a serene life, certain of ultimate success.

16   [HARE, AUGUSTUS WILLIAM and JULIUS CHARLES]. Guesses at Truth.
       By Two Brothers. Second edition. First series. London:
       Taylor and Walton, pp. v-viii, 138.
             Includes dedication, "To William Wordsworth," signed
       Julius Charles Hare: Wordsworth and Coleridge came forth
       in a worldly age as the regenerators of poetry and philoso-
       phy. Wordsworth, usually conscientiously scrupulous in the
       use of words, misuses "individual."

17   HOWITT, WILLIAM. The Rural Life of England. 2 vols. London:
       Longman, especially I:85-87, 163-64, 222-23, 254-55, 297;
       II:34-37.
             Commends Wordsworth's objections to larches in A Guide
       through the District of the Lakes and his painting of "clas-
       sical and enduring specimens of rustic heart and mind"
       taken from the Cumberland hills.

18   JAMES, ROBERT. "Parodied from Wordsworth's Lines on Aloys
       Reding" (poem), "On the Same" (poem), Note, in Poems.
       Cambridge: privately printed, pp. 8, 9, 20.
             Burlesques.

19   [LANDOR, WALTER SAVAGE] RODNEY RAIKES. "High and Low Life in
       Italy." Monthly Repository, [3rd ser.,] 1 (January),
       22-39 (26-29).
             Includes "Attempts at Simplicity," signed J. J. Stivers,
       consisting of three poems ("Beck: A Tale," "An Eclogue of
       Canton," and "I found a little flower, so small") bur-
       lesquing Wordsworth and parodying "We Are Seven."

20   [LOCKHART, JOHN GIBSON]. Memoirs of the Life of Sir Walter
       Scott, Bart. 7 vols. Edinburgh: Cadell; London: Murray,
       and Whittaker, especially VII:5-6, 25, 309-11.
             Includes remarks from his journal in which Scott criti-
       cizes Wordsworth for choosing subjects men do not sympathize

with. Records Wordsworth's visit with Scott in 1831. For
Volumes I-VI, see 1837.B18.

21 MILNES, RICHARD MONCKTON. "To a Certain Poet" (poem), in
    Poems of Many Years. London: Moxon, p. 132.
    Wordsworth feeds the multitude.

22 [NEAVES, CHARLES] ISAAC TOMKINS. "Letter from Tomkins--Bagman
    versus Pedlar." Blackwood's Edinburgh Magazine, 44
    (October), 508-23.
        A reply to 1838.B32. Attacks Wordsworth's use of the
    pedlar in The Excursion; includes "'You all have heard'"
    (poem), a parody of The Excursion, and "The Bagman to His
    Bag" (poem), a burlesque.

23 RAIKES, RODNEY. See 1838.B19.

24 SOUTHEY, ROBERT. "Preface" to Volume IV, "Preface" to Volume
    IX, in The Poetical Works of Robert Southey, Collected by
    Himself. 10 vols. London: Longman, IV:ix-xiv (xiv);
    IX:ix-xx (xviii, xx).
        Protests the unfairness of associating himself, Words-
    worth, and Coleridge as Lake Poets (IV:xiv). Includes let-
    ters in which J. Hogg quotes Jeffrey's comment in 1814 about
    Wordsworth's conceit and refers to his "crushing review"
    and in which Southey defends The Excursion (IX:xviii, xx).
    For Volume I, see 1837.B22.

25 STUART, DANIEL. Letter to the Editor. Gentleman's Magazine,
    NS 9 (May), 485-92 (486); (June), 577-90 (577, 580-81);
    NS 10 (July), 23-27 (27).
        Wordsworth contributed nothing to the Morning Post in
    1798; records Coleridge's praise of Wordsworth (486). Later
    Wordsworth contributed some political sonnets but no prose
    to the Morning Post; he received no money from it or the
    Courier. Prints letters in which Coleridge discusses
    Stuart's loan to Wordsworth and the Scotch tour (577,
    580-81). Repeats that he never gave Wordsworth money (27).

26 TALFOURD, THOMAS NOON. A Speech Delivered by Thomas Noon
    Talfourd, Sergeant at Law, in the House of Commons, on
    Wednesday, 25th April, 1838, on Moving the Second Reading
    of the Bill to Amend the Law of Copyright. London: Moxon,
    pp. 10, 21.
        Wordsworth, having labored to create the taste by which
    he is appreciated, is in the dawn of his fame; he has
    emerged from his seclusion to declare his support for the
    bill.

1838

27 TOMPKINS, ISAAC. See 1838.B22.

28 [WEBSTER, DR. G.]. Observations on the Law of Copyright; in Reference to the Bill Introduced into the House of Commons by Mr. Sergeant Talfourd. . . . London: Scott, Webster, and Geary, p. 39.
The many can never read Peter Bell at its present price. Attribution: Dictionary of Anonymous and Pseudonymous Literature (Samuel Halkett and John Laing), new ed., 9 vols. (Edinburgh: Oliver and Boyd, 1926-62), IV:221.

29 WILBERFORCE, ROBERT ISAAC and SAMUEL. The Life of William Wilberforce. By His Sons. 5 vols. London: Murray, IV:260, 388-90, 395-96.
Includes references in his diary in which W. Wilberforce notes his pleasure with Wordsworth's company in 1815 (Wordsworth was "independent almost to rudeness") and records visiting Rydal in 1818.

30 [WILSON, JOHN]. "Our Two Vases." Blackwood's Edinburgh Magazine, 43 (May), 577-706 (685, 687).
The Solitary's confession of his sins and sorrows sets him above the pompous Pedlar in The Excursion.

31 [WILSON, JOHN]. "Christopher in His Cave." Blackwood's Edinburgh Magazine, 44 (August), 268-84 (268).
Notes ambiguous meaning in "Nutting."

32 [WILSON, JOHN]. "Christopher among the Mountains." Blackwood's Edinburgh Magazine, 44 (September), 285-316 (290-97, 299-304).
Defends the Pedlar in The Excursion. Byron strains to imitate Wordsworth's communion with nature. Revised as "The Moors" in 1842.B33.

33 [WILSON, JOHN]. "Our Pocket Companions." Blackwood's Edinburgh Magazine, 44 (November), 573-96 (585, 590).
Rebukes Wordsworth for withholding The Prelude. Wordsworth writes to counteract the practical, active spirit of the age. In "The Old Cumberland Beggar" he is indebted to Cowper.

1839 A   BOOKS - NONE

1839 B   SHORTER WRITINGS

1   ANON. "Wordsworth and His Contemporaries." London Saturday
     Journal, 1 (9 February), 81-84.
          Wordsworth, the quietist of poetry who wrote of the hu-
     man heart, was in advance of his time.

2   ANON. A Few Words on the Copyright Question, Shewing it to be
     one of Public Interest: with Some Objections to Mr. Ser-
     geant Talfourd's Bill to Change the Present Law of Copy-
     right. London: Scott, Webster, and Geary [1839], pp. 15,
     27-28.
          Until Wordsworth's poems are sold more cheaply, they
     will be read only by the higher ranks of society.

3   ANON. "Sketches of Distinguished Public Characters of the
     Regency and Reign of George the Fourth: . . . Letter III:
     Coleridge.--Wordsworth," in Diary Illustrative of the Times
     of George the Fourth. . . . Edited by John Galt. 4 vols.
     London: Colburn, IV:179-82 (181-82).
          In detached passages Wordsworth is a thinker of the
     highest order.

4   [DE QUINCEY, THOMAS] THE ENGLISH OPIUM-EATER. "Lake
     Reminiscences, from 1807 to 1830: No. I[-III]--William
     Wordsworth." Tait's Edinburgh Magazine, NS 6 (January),
     1-12; (February), 90-103; (April), 246-54.
          Records his initial shyness in meeting Wordsworth, and
     his first visit in 1807. Mary Wordsworth's "repose of mind"
     was perfectly suited to Wordsworth. Dorothy tempered Words-
     worth's stern intellect with a sense of beauty. Words-
     worth's "self-consuming style of thought" led to an appear-
     ance of premature old age. He did not return friendship.
     His life was insulated from worldly cares (1-12). An ex-
     tensive biographical sketch. Records Wordsworth's psycho-
     logical explanation of observing a star after listening for
     the carrier and of "There was a Boy." The dream of the
     Arab in The Prelude illustrates "the eternity and the in-
     dependence of all social modes." Gives Wordsworth's account
     of his development from The Prelude (90-103). Wordsworth
     could not have been a passionate lover of his wife. The
     circumstances of his life were marked by good luck. Praises
     Dorothy (246-54). Reprinted in De Quincey's Writings
     (1850-59). Revised with omissions as "William Wordsworth"
     in 1854.B4.

1839

5   [DE QUINCEY, THOMAS] THE ENGLISH OPIUM-EATER. "Lake
     Reminiscences, from 1807 to 1830: No. IV.--William
     Wordsworth and Robert Southey." Tait's Edinburgh Magazine,
     NS 6 (July), 453-64.
          Continues account of his visit to Wordsworth in 1807
     (see 1839.B4): Wordsworth's "honourable poverty," lack of
     true regard for Southey, irreverence for new books, disap-
     pointing conversation and marginalia. Southey was more
     amiable, but less a good companion, than Wordsworth. Re-
     printed in De Quincey's Writings (1850-59). Reprinted with
     omissions as "William Wordsworth and Robert Southey" in
     1854.B4.

6   [DE QUINCEY, THOMAS] THE ENGLISH OPIUM-EATER. "Lake
     Reminiscences, from 1807 to 1830: No. V.--Southey,
     Wordsworth, and Coleridge." Tait's Edinburgh Magazine,
     NS 6 (August), 513-17.
          Wordsworth's use of books contrasted with Southey's.
     Wordsworth shunned political economy. Reprinted in De
     Quincey's Writings (1850-59). Reprinted with omissions as
     "William Wordsworth and Robert Southey" in 1854.B4.

7   [DE QUINCEY, THOMAS] AN ENGLISH OPIUM-EATER. "Sketches of
     Life and Manners; from the Autobiography of an English
     Opium-Eater: Recollections of Grasmere." Tait's Edinburgh
     Magazine, NS 6 (September), 569-81 (569-78).
          Recounts the Wordsworths' involvement in the tragedy of
     George and Sarah Green. Reprinted in De Quincey's Writings
     (1850-59). Revised as "Early Memorials of Grasmere" in
     1854.B4.

8   [DE QUINCEY, THOMAS] AN ENGLISH OPIUM-EATER. "Sketches of
     Life and Manners, from the Autobiography of an English
     Opium-Eater: The Saracen's Head." Tait's Edinburgh
     Magazine, NS 6 (December), 804-808.
          Continues recounting his visit with Wordsworth in 1807
     (see 1839.B4-B5). Wordsworth exercised a "keen spirit of
     business" in dealing with the landlord of Allan Bank. Re-
     printed in De Quincey's Writings (1850-59).

9   ENGLISH OPIUM-EATER, AN. See 1839.B7-B8.

10   ENGLISH OPIUM-EATER, THE. See 1839.B4-B6.

11   [HOOD, THOMAS]. "Literary Reminiscences: No. IV," in Hood's
     Own: or, Laughter from Year to Year: Being former
     Runnings of his Comic Vein, with an Infusion of New Blood
     for General Circulation. London: Baily, pp. 545-68
     (552-53).

Despite his "Betty Foy-bles" and baby poetry, Wordsworth "has furnished strong meat for men." Records meeting Wordsworth and Wordsworth's praise of Shelley.

12 [HUGHES, HARRIET]. "Memoir of Mrs. Hemans," in The Works of Mrs. Hemans; with a Memoir by her Sister. 6 vols. Edinburgh: Blackwood; London: Cadell, I:1-315 (145-47, 206-15, 270-72, 301-302).
Records M. J. Jewsbury's and Felicia Hemans's enthusiasm for Wordsworth's poems, and Mrs. Hemans's visit to Rydal Mount in 1830. Prints text of original dedication to Wordsworth of Scenes and Hymns of Life (1834).

13 J., B. R. "Lines in Imitation of Wordsworth." Cambridge University Magazine, 1 (November), 197-98.
An imitation/parody of "Resolution and Independence."

14 L.[ANDON], L.[ETITIA] E.[LIZABETH]. "On Wordsworth's Cottage, near Grasmere Lake" (poem), in The Zenana and Minor Poems of L. E. L. London and Paris: Fisher [1839], pp. 270-76.
Wordsworth's poems give serenity, freshness, hope.

15 [NEWMAN, JOHN HENRY]. Review of Revival of Popery, etc. British Critic, [4th ser.,] 25 (April), 395-426 (400).
Wordsworth, a poet of "philosophical meditation," led his readers toward Catholic truth. Quoted in Part V of Apologia Pro Vita Sua (1864); reprinted as "Prospects of the Anglican Church" in Essays Critical and Historical (1871).

16 SHELLEY, MRS. [MARY]. "Note on Queen Mab," "Note on the Early Poems," "Note on the Poems of 1817," in The Poetical Works of Percy Bysshe Shelley. Edited by Mrs. Shelley. 4 vols. London: Moxon, I:96-106 (102); III:15-17 (17), 68-72 (71).
Records Shelley's reading of Wordsworth.

17 [SMITH, WILLIAM HENRY]. "A Prosing upon Poetry." Blackwood's Edinburgh Magazine, 46 (August), 194-202 (200).
Wordsworth extends our sympathies in "The Old Cumberland Beggar."

18 TALFOURD, SERGEANT [THOMAS NOON]. "Speech, &c," in Sergeant Talfourd's Speech on the Copyright Question, Delivered in the House of Commons, February 27, 1839; to which is Added Mr. Tegg's Letter to "The Times" on Copyright Monopoly. London: Foster and Hextall, pp. 3-11 (8, 11).
Notes Wordsworth's petition on behalf of the copyright bill.

1839

19 TEGG, THOMAS. "Mr. Tegg's Letter to 'The Times,'" in Sergeant
Talfourd's Speech on the Copyright Question, Delivered in
the House of Commons, February 27, 1839; to which is Added
Mr. Tegg's Letter to "The Times" on Copyright Monopoly.
London: Foster and Hextall, pp. 12-16 (13).
Notes the "produce of copyright" from Moxon's republica-
tion of Wordsworth's works was 1,000 guineas.

20 W. "To the Poet Wordsworth" (poem). Cambridge University
Magazine, 1 (March), 69.
Nature has unlocked her secrets for Wordsworth.

21 [WILSON, JOHN]. "Christopher in His Alcove." Blackwood's
Edinburgh Magazine, 45 (April), 538-70 (538, 551-53).
Examines Wordsworth's description of the Pedlar in The
Excursion. Praises "To the Moon: Composed by the Seaside,
--on the Coast of Cumberland." Revised as "The Moors" in
1842.B33.

22 [WILSON, JOHN]. "Have You Read Ossian?" Blackwood's
Edinburgh Magazine, 46 (November), 693-714 (693-94).
Quarrels with Wordsworth's criticism of Macpherson.

1840 A BOOKS - NONE

1840 B SHORTER WRITINGS

1 [ALFORD, HENRY]. "Chapters on Poetry and Poets . . . . :
Wordsworth." Dearden's Miscellany, 3 (February), 93-108.
The whole of Wordsworth's poetry illustrates principles
laid down in the Preface to Lyrical Ballads. The Excursion
is not without Christianity. Attribution: See 1873.B2,
p. 115.

2 [ALFORD, HENRY]. "Chapters on Poetry and Poets . . . . :
Wordsworth's Sonnets, &c." Dearden's Miscellany, 3
(April), 245-53.
Wordsworth is true to his poetic creed in his sonnets.
"Ode: Intimations of Immortality" acquaints "us with new
and shadowy realms of thought." In his later poems his
power has not declined. Attribution: See 1873.B2, p. 115.

3 ALISON, ARCHIBALD. History of Europe from the Commencement of
the French Revolution in MDCCLXXXIX to the Restoration of
the Bourbons in MDCCCXV. 10 vols. Edinburgh: Blackwood;
London: Cadell, VIII:7.
Wordsworth, "profound and contemplative," clothed the
lessons of wisdom" in simple verse.

4   ANON. Review of Pindari Carmina. British and Foreign Review,
     11:510-42 (514).
        Wordsworth's form in "Ode: Intimations of Immortality"
     is perfect, though his subject is unintelligible.

5   B., G. "Sonnet to Wordsworth." Saturday Magazine, 17
     (4 July), 8.
        Wishes Wordsworth good health.

6   B.[ROWN], C.[HARLES] A.[RMITAGE]. "Walks in the North, During
     the Summer of 1818." Plymouth and Devonport Weekly Journal,
     no. 1085 (8 October), p. [3].
        Records his and Keats's visit to Rydal in 1818 when
     Wordsworth was absent. Attribution: Hyder Edward Rollins,
     ed., The Letters of John Keats 1814-1821, 2 vols. (Cam-
     bridge, Mass.: Harvard Univ. Press), I:421.

7   ELLIOTT, EBENEZER. "A Defence of Modern Poetry; Written for
     the Sheffield Mechanics' Institution." Tait's Edinburgh
     Magazine, NS 7 (May), 309-14 (310-11).
        Wordsworth's egotism is not selfish.

8   [DE QUINCEY, THOMAS] AN ENGLISH OPIUM-EATER. "Sketches of
     Life and Manners, from the Autobiography of an English
     Opium-Eater: Westmoreland and the Dalesmen." Tait's
     Edinburgh Magazine, NS 7 (January), 32-39.
        Wordsworth's opinion to the contrary, Westmorland cottage
     architecture does not derive from the dalesmen's superior
     taste. Records Wordsworth's and M. Simond's mutual dislike
     of each other. Reprinted in De Quincey's Writings (1850-59).

9   [DE QUINCEY, THOMAS] AN ENGLISH OPIUM-EATER. "Sketches of
     Life and Manners, from the Autobiography of an English
     Opium-Eater." Tait's Edinburgh Magazine, NS 7 (March),
     159-67 (161-62); (June), 346-56 (350, 352-56); (August),
     525-32 (525, 527-29); (October), 629-37 (632-36);
     (December), 765-76 (765, 771-72).
        Recalls Wordsworth's arrogance (161-62), his admiration
     of T. Wilkinson (but not of De Quincey) and of the Sympsons,
     and his hatred of larches (350, 352-56). Wordsworth did not
     live amidst a circle of admirers. Records his grief at the
     death of Catherine Wordsworth (525, 527-29). Wordsworth's
     pride and one-sidedness make familiar intercourse with him
     impossible (632-36). Records Talfourd's and J. Clare's ad-
     miration of Wordsworth's poems (765, 771-72). Reprinted in
     De Quincey's Writings (1850-59).

1840

10   DOYLE, FRANCIS HASTINGS. "Sonnet: Written in the First Page
of Wordsworth's Poems," in Miscellaneous Verses. London:
Saunders and Otley, p. 136.
Wordsworth's "soul is calm and lofty," his verse "full
of hope, and immortality."

11   ENGLISH OPIUM-EATER, AN. See 1840.B8-B9.

12   HOWITT, WILLIAM. Visits to Remarkable Places: Old Halls,
Battle Fields, and Scenes Illustrative of Striking Passages
in English History and Poetry. Illustrated by Samuel
Williams. London: Longman, pp. 171, 198-231.
Wordsworth's life has no "stamp of poverty about it";
"his poetry is become fashionable!" Describes the setting
of The White Doe of Rylstone and "Song at the Feast of
Brougham Castle." Had he earlier chosen romantic and his-
toric subjects, Wordsworth, the philosophic poet of the affections, would have sooner gained popularity.

13   [KING, HENRY]. "Thoughts upon Asses." Blackwood's Edinburgh
Magazine, 47 (January), 57-64 (62-64).
In Peter Bell Wordsworth recognized the moral dignity of
the ass.

14   [NEAVES, CHARLES]. "On Personification." Blackwood's
Edinburgh Magazine, 47 (June), 798-815 (798-99).
Peter Bell's moral deficiency is shown by his inability
to personify the natural world.

15   RICHARDSON, DAVID LESTER. "Biographical and Critical Notices,"
in Selections from the British Poets from the Time of
Chaucer to the Present Day: with Biographical and Critical
Notices. Edited by David Lester Richardson. Calcutta:
Committee of Public Instruction, pp. i-cxxviii (xcii-cxx
[passim]).
A biographical sketch, partially adapted from 1836.B22.
Wordsworth is a narrow-minded, pompous egotist whose poems
want force and precision but contain golden images and noble
soarings. He is not likely to become popular. His life
and poetry shared an Arcadian simplicity and quietude.
Partially reprinted in 1852.B25.

16   RICHARDSON, DAVID LESTER. Literary Leaves or Prose and Verse
Chiefly Written in India. Second edition, with additions.
2 vols. London: Allen, passim.
Expanded from 1836.B22. Wordsworth's high reputation
"has been forced upon the public by the critics." His sonnets, exquisite in thought and diction, occasionally lack

unity and point. He was a poor critic of other poets. His
simplicity, often too bare, is not novel. He remains con-
vinced of his genius, though he is anything but popular.
He should judiciously edit his works. Expanded in 1852.B25.

17 [SEWELL, WILLIAM]. Review of Carlyle's Critical and
    Miscellaneous Essays, etc. Quarterly Review, 66
    (September), 446-503 (447-48).
        Wordsworth and Coleridge began a philosophical revolu-
    tion. Wordsworth's poetry is quiet, pure, and sober, yet
    not superficial. He taught the value of little things.

18 SHELLEY, MRS. [MARY]. "Note on the Poems of 1819," in The
    Poetical Works of Percy Bysshe Shelley. Edited by Mrs.
    Shelley. London: Moxon, pp. 251-53 (253).
        Shelley admired Wordsworth; he does not criticize him
    personally in "Peter Bell the Third."

19 SHELLEY, PERCY BYSSHE. Essays, Letters from Abroad,
    Translations and Fragments. Edited by Mrs. [Mary] Shelley.
    2 vols. London: Moxon, II:337.
        Wordsworth's thought in "French Revolution as it Appeared
    to Enthusiasts at its Commencement" is "demoniacal."

20 SHELLEY, PERCY BYSSHE. "Peter Bell the Third" (poem), "To
    Mary, (On Her Objecting to the Following Poem, Upon the
    Score of its Containing No Human Interest)" (poem), in The
    Poetical Works of Percy Bysshe Shelley. Edited by Mrs.
    [Mary] Shelley. London: Moxon, pp. 236-46, 268.
        A parody of Peter Bell, including criticism of Words-
    worth's political apostasy (236-46). Attacks Wordsworth's
    "slow, dull care" in retouching Peter Bell (268).

21 TEGG, THOMAS. Extension of Copyright, Proposed by Serjeant
    Talfourd. [London: privately printed, 1840], p. 3.
        Notes that Wordsworth received £1050 for Moxon's repub-
    lication of his works, and that his works cost less in
    America.

1841 A BOOKS - NONE

1841 B SHORTER WRITINGS

1 ANON. Review of The Poems of Geoffrey Chaucer, Modernized.
   Athenaeum, no. 693 (6 February), pp. 107-108.
       Wordsworth is "a worshipper of genius and a true poet."

1841

2   ANON. Review of The Poems of Geoffrey Chaucer, Modernized.
     Church of England Quarterly Review, 9 (April), 500.
         Wordsworth's modernizations are well done.

3   ANON. "Chapters on English Poetry: On Its Progress: on Our
     Late Poets, Individually and Collectively: and on Its
     Present Condition." Tait's Edinburgh Magazine, NS 8 (May),
     303-13 (306-307, 313).
         The gravity with which Wordsworth considered "Throned in
     the Sun's descending car" "jars unpleasantly with our faith
     in the expansiveness of the poetic creed which he pro-
     pounded." Descriptive Sketches is "cold and correct."

4   ANON. "Narrow Escape of Wordsworth the Poet." Annual
     Register, or a View of the History, and Politics, of the
     Year 1840, [82]:107-108.
         Describes Wordsworth's "providential" escape in the col-
     lision with the mail coach.

5   ANON. Review of Trench's Poems. British and Foreign Review,
     12:180-97 (180-84, 192).
         Wordsworth's example as a lyric and reflective poet has
     been largely salutary for imitators.

6   BENNOCH, FRANCIS. "To Wordsworth" (poem), in The Storm, and
     Other Poems. London: Smith; Edinburgh: Tait; Dumfries:
     Sinclair, p. 130.
         Wordsworth's poems exalt virtue, purify.

7   BON GAULTIER. See 1841.B13.

8   [COLERIDGE, HENRY NELSON]. Review of Baillie's Fugitive
     Verses. Quarterly Review, 67 (March), 437-52 (437-38).
         The Preface to Lyrical Ballads represented an "unevade-
     able protest and manifesto."

9   [DE QUINCEY, THOMAS]. "Style: No. IV." Blackwood's
     Edinburgh Magazine, 49 (February), 214-28 (221).
         Commends Wordsworth's remark that language is "'the in-
     carnation of thoughts.'" Reprinted in De Quincey's Writings
     (1850-59) and Critical Suggestions on Style and Rhetoric
     [De Quincey's Works, Volume XI] (1859).

10   [GRIMES, J. A.]. Review of The Poems of Geoffrey Chaucer,
     Modernized. Monthly Magazine, [3rd ser.,] 5 (January),
     71-102 (80-81, 83-84).
         Wordsworth's translation of "The Cuckoo and the Night-
     ingale" is faithful and felicitous, though lacking metrical

variety. "Troilus and Cresida" is less faithful. Attribution: Monthly Magazine, [3rd ser.,] 5 (March), 250.

11   HORNE, R.[ICHARD] H.[ENGIST]. "Introduction," in The Poems of
     Geoffrey Chaucer, Modernized. Edited by R. H. Horne.
     London: Whittaker, pp. v-cv (x, xxix, lxii-lxv).
         Commends "the severe poetical fidelity" of Wordsworth's
     "The Prioress' Tale." Wordsworth restored Milton's varied
     accents and pauses to blank verse.

12   LANDOR, WALTER SAVAGE. "The Descent of Orpheus." Examiner,
     no. 1759 (16 October), p. 663.
         Condemns Wordsworth's translation of Vergil.

13   [MARTIN, THEODORE] BON GAULTIER. "Illustrations of the
     Thieves' Literature.--No. 1: Flowers of Hemp; or, the
     Newgate Garland." Tait's Edinburgh Magazine, NS 8
     (April), 215-23 (218).
         Includes "Great men have been among us,--names that
     lend," a parody of "Great men have been among us; hands
     that penned," and "Turpin! thou shouldst be living at this
     hour!", a parody of "London, 1802." Attribution: The Book
     of Ballads, edited by Bon Gaultier, new ed. (Edinburgh and
     London: Blackwood, 1903), p. xiv.

14   [QUIN, MICHAEL JOSEPH]. Review of Doyle's Miscellaneous
     Verses, etc. Dublin Review, 10 (February), 254-76 (255-60).
         Wordsworth's poems, meandering and dull, are now
     fashionable.

15   [SMITH, WILLIAM HENRY]. "Wordsworth." Blackwood's Edinburgh
     Magazine, 49 (March), 359-71.
         The Excursion, not the affectedly homely Lyrical Ballads
     and Peter Bell, is a model of pure diction; Wordsworth is
     justly charged with prolix and prosaic writing, especially
     in the sonnets, though he is not obscure. In contrast with
     Byron and Shelley, he is the poet of peaceful reflection,
     of the beauty of nature, of stoic duty and of pathos. He
     studies humanity rather than man.

16   [TAYLOR, HENRY]. Review of The Sonnets of William Wordsworth.
     Quarterly Review, 69 (December), 1-51.
         Wordsworth's greatness as a philosophic poet stems from
     a life led in the love of truth. In his political sonnets
     he realizes that liberty must rest on morals rather than
     politics. In his itinerary sonnets, he is seldom purely
     descriptive; he does not disparage science. In the Sonnets
     Upon the Punishment of Death he takes an enlarged view of

1841

a fit subject for poetic treatment. Discusses in detail Wordsworth's probing of the demands of liberty in "Nuns fret not at their convent's narrow room"; his statement in "From the dark chambers of dejection freed" that poetry is not founded on melancholy; his versification and diction in The River Duddon, and his use of pagan superstition in "The world is too much with us; late and soon." Revised in 1849.B13.

1842 A BOOKS - NONE

1842 B SHORTER WRITINGS

1   ANON. "Wordsworth: Poems of the Fancy: Poems of the Imagination." Gentleman's Magazine, NS 17 (January), 3-17 (3, 12-17).
        Discusses Wordsworth's definitions of fancy and imagination.

2   ANON. Review of Poems, Chiefly of Early and Late Years. Church of England Quarterly Review, 11 (April), 481-87.
        Wordsworth enjoys immortality in his lifetime. He blends the practical and poetical. Commends the sympathy of "At the Grave of Burns," the political economy of the sonnets, and the deep probing of "Elegiac Verses in Memory of My Brother, John Wordsworth." The Sonnets Upon the Punishment of Death are written on a subject unfit for poetry.

3   ANON. Review of Poems, Chiefly of Early and Late Years. Examiner, no. 1787 (30 April), p. 275.
        The Borderers lacks action. The volume is entitled to respect.

4   ANON. "Wakley on Wordsworth." Dublin University Magazine, 19 (May), 688-90.
        Ridicules Thomas Wakley's criticism in the House of Commons of Wordsworth's poetry as childish and worthless. Wordsworth's poetry is not fit for the coffee-house. Records reaction of the London daily papers to Wakley's speech.

5   ANON. "Wordsworth's New Poems." Chambers' Edinburgh Journal, 11 (14 May), 134.
        The majority of Wordsworth's poems are "modelled after the loftiest exemplars of our language."

1842

6   ANON. "Wordsworth's Poems of Early and Late Years."
     Spectator, 15 (28 May), 522.
          The Borderers is improbable, undramatic. "Guilt and
     Sorrow" is effective.

7   ANON. "New Poems." Tait's Edinburgh Magazine, NS 9 (June),
     407-409 (407-408).
          The Borderers is a "deep study of the human heart, in its
     most hidden weakness and perversity."

8   ANON. Review of Poems, Chiefly of Early and Late Years, etc.
     Christian Remembrancer, NS 3 (June), 655-71 (655-69); NS 4
     (July), 42-58 (43, 47).
          Wordsworth's later work still requires vindication. His
     poetry is now exactly what it should be in his old age, his
     style having progressed from its earlier periods. He should
     not, however, now revise his earlier poems (655-69). Words-
     worth interested himself in men and his country (43, 47).

9   ANON. Review of Poems, Chiefly of Early and Late Years.
     Monthly Review, [4th ser.,] 2 for 1842 (June), 270-83.
          Wordsworth requires patience, earnestness, religious re-
     flection, and an understanding of language by the reader.
     He perfectly adapts words to sentiments. His moral purity
     never degenerates into prudery or sickly sentimentality.
     His religion goes beyond the Church of England. The Bor-
     derers is non-dramatic.

10   ANON. Review of The Poems of Geoffrey Chaucer, Modernized.
     Church of England Quarterly Review, 12 (July), 26-49 (45-46).
          Commends Wordsworth's "The Prioress' Tale."

11   ANON. Review of Poems, Chiefly of Early and Late Years.
     Eclectic Review, 4th ser., 12 (November), 568-79.
          Though Wordsworth carried his early poetic theories to
     excess, he has now justly achieved fame; however, he still
     lapses into the trivial, lacks a "thorough abandonment of
     himself to his own emotions," and cannot construct a narra-
     tive. His role as a poetic revolutionary is overrated. He
     should publish only a judicious selection from his work.
     He voices "pernicious" religious doctrines.

12   ANON. Review of Hegel's Vorlesungen über die Aesthetik, etc.
     British and Foreign Review, 12:1-49 (10, 12, 14, 16-17).
          Wordsworth's descriptions are often nothing more than
     catalogues; his commonplace names excite the ludicrous.

1842

13   ANON. "Essay on the English Poetry of the Nineteenth Century,"
      "William Wordsworth," in Book of the Poets: The Modern
      Poets of the Nineteenth Century. London: Scott, Webster &
      Geary, pp. 9-32 (15-19, 28), 102.
            Wordsworth perceived the true poetry of external and in-
      ner nature. He persevered in his revolt despite laughter
      (15-19, 28). A biographical sketch. Wordsworth has finally
      triumphed over his critics (102).

14   B., C. "Lines on Wordsworth's Great Sonnet Written on
      Westminster Bridge." Tait's Edinburgh Magazine, NS 9
      (July), 457.
            Wordsworth instantly understood and expressed the mystery
      of the sight he describes in "Composed upon Westminster
      Bridge."

15   B., J. "The 'Childe Harold,' and the 'Excursion.'" London
      University Magazine, 1 [April], 31-63.
            Wordsworth and Byron represent opposing schools of taste
      and morals, though The Excursion and Childe Harold's Pil-
      grimage contain some similarities: The Excursion contains
      more original thought, higher moral principle and natural
      feeling, and finer execution.

16   [BARRETT, ELIZABETH B.]. Review of Poems, Chiefly of Early
      and Late Years. Athenaeum, no. 774 (27 August), pp. 757-59.
            Wordsworth was chief in the movement to return literature
      to nature. In contrast with Byron, he knows grief by sym-
      pathy rather than by suffering. His "eye is his soul." He
      is a true Christian poet, his works united by his life,
      though he is at times "over-rustic." Except for the Sonnets
      Upon the Punishment of Death, Poems, Chiefly of Early and
      Late Years is a worthy volume. Though faulty in action and
      unity, The Borderers is Greek in intention. Wordsworth's
      life offers a moral example to men, especially poets. Re-
      printed with omissions in The Greek Christian Poets and the
      English Poets (1863).

17   BARRETT, ELIZABETH B. "Sonnet: On Mr. Haydon's Portrait of
      Mr. Wordsworth." Athenaeum, no. 783 (29 October), p. 932.
            Celebrates Wordsworth as "poet-priest." Reprinted with
      minor verbal changes in 1844.B10.

18   DE VERE, SIR AUBREY. "To William Wordsworth," "Rydal with
      Wordsworth" (poem), in A Song of Faith[,] Devout Exercises
      and Sonnets. London: Pickering, pp. v, 208.
            Wordsworth's name is "the noblest of modern literature"
      (v). Reprinted with verbal changes from 1834.B14 (208).

19   FABER, FREDERICK WILLIAM. Sights and Thoughts in Foreign
      Churches and Among Foreign Peoples. London: Rivington,
      pp. [v], 99, 161, 626-32.
          Testifies to Wordsworth's "personal kindness" and "con-
      versations on the rites, prerogatives, and doctrines" of
      the Church. Wordsworth is a "sage and high-souled bard"
      and "a reverent, cautious Christian." The Excursion re-
      sembles Homer's Odyssey, with the addition of Christianity.

20   GREEN, THOMAS. "Diary of a Lover of Literature." Gentleman's
      Magazine, NS 17 (February), 139-42 (141-42); (May), 472-77
      (472-73).
          Wordsworth's affected homeliness is disgusting (141-42),
      though he has "a fine strain of pure moral feeling" (472-73).

21   HARCOURT, MAURICE. "Winderemere and Wordsworth." Bradshaw's
      Journal, 4 (December), 1-6.
          Describes visit to Rydal Mount in 1841: Wordsworth's
      hearty frankness, praise of Southey, Hartley Coleridge,
      Hunt, and E. Elliott.

22   HOWITT, WILLIAM. Visits to Remarkable Places: Old Halls,
      Battle Fields, and Scenes Illustrative of Striking Passages
      in History and Poetry: Chiefly in the Counties of Durham
      and Northumberland. Second series. Illustrated by
      Carmichael, Richardsons, and Taylor. London: Longman,
      pp. 111-12.
          Records incident of Wordsworth visiting Finchall Priory.

23   [LANDOR, WALTER SAVAGE]. Review of Theocritus, Bio, et
      Moschus. Foreign Quarterly Review, 30 (October), 161-90
      (180-83).
          Wordsworth "is deficient in the delineation of charac-
      ter"; some beautiful idylls might be extracted from The Ex-
      cursion. Includes "'Twas in the year of ninety-five" and
      "I very much indeed approve," poems burlesquing the school
      of Wordsworth. "I very much indeed approve" reprinted as
      "New Style" in 1846.B10.

24   LANDOR, WALTER SAVAGE. "Imaginary Conversation: Southey and
      Porson." Blackwood's Edinburgh Magazine, 52 (December),
      687-715.
          Attacks Wordsworth's impatience at criticism and lack of
      grammar and sense, especially in "Great men have been among
      us; hands that penned," Lyrical Ballads (including "Anec-
      dote for Fathers"), and "Laodamia." Includes burlesque,
      "Hetty, old Dinah Mitchell's daughter" (poem). Revised,
      with omissions, in 1846.B10.

1842

25   [MERIVALE, HERMAN]. Review of The Poetical Works of Thomas
        Moore. Edinburgh Review, 75 (April), 162-87 (167-68).
            Wordsworth's distinction between imagination and fancy
        in the Preface (1815) is unsound.

26   POWELL, THOMAS. "To Wordsworth" (poem), "On a Portrait of
        Wordsworth, Painted by Miss Margaret Gillies" (poem), "To
        Wordsworth" (poem), in Poems. London: Wilson, pp. 177,
        283, 318.
            Praises Wordsworth as nature's priest (172) and as poet
        of thought and song (283) and of God (318).

27   S., J. "A Chapter on Poetry and Poets." Cambridge University
        Magazine, 2 (October), 606-16 (606-608).
            Praises Poems, Chiefly of Early and Late Years, and
        Wordsworth's "vivid, although miniature, picturing" of
        nature.

28   SEDGWICK, A.[DAM]. "Three Letters on the Geology of the Lake
        District," in A Complete Guide to the Lakes, Comprising
        Minute Directions for the Tourist, with Mr. Wordsworth's
        Description of the Scenery of the Country, &c. and Three
        Letters upon the Geology of the Lake District, by the Rev.
        Professor Sedgwick. Edited by the Publishers [John Hudson].
        Kendal: Hudson and Nicholson; London: Longman, and
        Whittaker; Liverpool: Webb; Manchester: Simms, pp. 3-55
        (3, 54-55).
            Commends Wordsworth's view on science, his interpretation
        of nature. Expanded in 1853.B29.

29   [STERLING, JOHN]. Review of Tennyson's Poems. Quarterly
        Review, 70 (September), 385-416 (389, 394-95, 398, 401-402,
        415-16).
            Wordsworth is interested in daily life only as it "suits
        his spirit of ethical meditation." "Ode: Intimations of
        Immortality" is comparable to "the Portland funeral vase,"
        admitting endless interpretations. Wordsworth's feelings
        are always strictly watched by his meditative conscience.

30   STORY, ROBERT. Love and Literature; Being the Reminiscences,
        Literary Opinions, and Fugitive Pieces, of a Poet in Humble
        Life. London: Longman, pp. 183-86, 190-91.
            The Excursion is "besprinkled with thoughts and phrases
        of the purest beauty."

31   W., S. "Contributions of William Wordsworth to the Revival of
        Catholic Truths." Christian's Miscellany, 2 [September],
        185-206.

The tone of Wordsworth's writings has done more to restore religious truth than his direct allusion to Catholic
doctrines. His influence in the Catholic movement is great.

32   [WILLMOTT, ROBERT ELDRIDGE ARIS?]. "New Edition of Campbell's
      Poets." Fraser's Magazine, 25 (March), 353-62 (353-54).
      Wordsworth's works can not please the multitude; his
      career provides an example of perseverance. His best poems
      follow the manner of the old masters rather than his own
      rules.

33   [WILSON, JOHN]. "Morning Monologue," "Cottages," "An Hour's
      Talk about Poetry," "The Moors," "Sacred Poetry: Chapter
      II," "Christopher in his Aviary: Second Canticle,"
      "Christopher in his Aviary: Third Canticle," "A Few Words
      on Thomson," "The Snowball Bicker of Pedmount," "Stroll to
      Grassmere: First Saunter," in The Recreations of Christo-
      pher North. 3 vols. Edinburgh and London: Blackwood,
      I:154-78 (165-67), 200-66 (217), 267-342 (274-76, 279-80,
      288, 341); II:1-190 (7-29, 34-36, 182-84), 342-72 (344-70);
      III:42-76 (53-54), 77-99 (83), 229-58 (234-35, 245, 248-56),
      259-74 (272-73), 336-76 (357-69).
      Reprinted from 1833.B21 (I:156-67). Reprinted with
      omissions from 1826.B22 (217). Reprinted from 1831.B33
      (274-76, 279-80, 288, 341). Revised from 1826.B25,
      1838.B32, and 1839.B21 (II:7-29, 34-36, 182-84). Revised
      from 1827.B16 and 1828.B19. Though Christianity is absent
      from The Excursion, much of Wordsworth's subsequent poetry,
      including the Ecclesiastical Sonnets and "The Eclipse of
      the Sun, 1820," is truly religious. Compares Wordsworth
      as a religious poet with J. Montgomery (344-70). Reprinted
      with omissions from 1828.B18 (III:53-54). Reprinted from
      1826.B26 (83). Revised from 1830.B18 and 1831.B29 (234-35,
      245, 248-56). Revised with omissions from 1831.B29 (272-
      73). Revised from 1826.B24. Wordsworth is of all poets
      the most truthful and the most idealizing. He has tri-
      umphed over his critics, as befits one who has benefitted
      humanity by purifying and calming men's passions (357-69).

1843 A   BOOKS - NONE

1843 B   SHORTER WRITINGS

1   ANON. "Wordsworth--The New Poet Laureate." Illustrated
      London News, 2 (15 April), 259.
      Wordsworth's poems are hallowed by gentleness of heart.

WRITINGS ABOUT WILLIAM WORDSWORTH, 1793 - 1899

1843

2 ANON. "Promotions, Preferments, &c." Gentleman's Magazine,
       NS 19 (May), 526-28 (526).
          Records Wordsworth's appointment as Poet Laureate.

3 ANON. Review of Poems, Chiefly of Early and Late Years.
       British and Foreign Review, 14:1-28.
          Wordsworth expects each of his poems to be viewed in its
       relation to all the rest. His literary life consists of
       educational (1793-97, including "Guilt and Sorrow" and The
       Borderers), poetical (1798-1803), and philosophical (1803-
       42) periods. His best poems contain tender feeling and
       solemn sweetness; in his later ones he changes from uncon-
       scious to conscious philosopher. He has always been in op-
       position to his age.

4 ANON. "Advertisement," in Select Pieces from the Poems of
       William Wordsworth. London: Burns [1843], pp. [vii-x].
          Commends Wordsworth's ministering to the beauty of the
       material and spiritual world, his purity and command of
       language.

5 BON GAULTIER. See 1843.B11.

6 CARLYON, CLEMENT. Early Years and Late Reflections. 4 vols.
       London: Whittaker, II:93-97.
          Briefly notes Coleridge's reverence for Wordsworth,
       Wordsworth's for Scott. For Volume I, see 1836.B12.

7 [GRIFFIN, DANIEL]. Life of Gerald Griffin Esq. By his
       Brother. London: Simpkin and Marshall; Dublin: Cumming;
       Edinburgh: Bell and Bradfute, pp. 274-76.
          Records G. Griffin's mocking, in conversation, prose,
       and verse, the studied obscurity of the Lake School, in-
       cluding Wordsworth.

8 J., H. "A Concert of the Poets." Chambers's London Journal,
       3 (27 May), 167.
          Reports a dream in which Wordsworth, looking "something
       like a Methodist preacher," retires in a pet when his play-
       ing is not appreciated but silences his critics with Mil-
       tonic peals.

9 LESLIE, C.[HARLES] R.[OBERT]. Memoirs of the Life of John
       Constable, Esq. R.A.: Composed Chiefly of his Letters.
       London: Carpenter, pp. 36, 40, 88.
          Includes letters in which Constable praises Wordsworth
       and the landscape descriptions in The Excursion.

142

10   [LORDAN, CHRISTOPHER L.]. Colloquies, Desultory and Diverse,
      but chiefly upon Poetry and Poets: Between an Elder,
      Enthusiastic, and an Apostle of the Law. Romsey: Lordan,
      especially pp. 54-68, 156, 165-66, 188-89.
           Characters discuss Wordsworth, noting he is either loved
      or despised, his "philanthropic aim . . . to purify . . .
      the cotter's mind," his tearing the veil of indifference
      from Nature, his optimism, and his "theory of a sentient
      principle in plants"; his doctrines need to permeate our
      being and grow with us. Attribution: Preface to the
      volume. Revised and expanded in 1844.B26.

11   [MARTIN, THEODORE and W. E. AYTOUN] BON GAULTIER. "Lays of
      the Would-be Laureates." Tait's Edinburgh Magazine, NS 10
      (May), 273-76*.
           Includes "The Laureates' Tourney," mocking Wordsworth's
      appointment as Poet Laureate, and "Bays, which in former
      years have graced the brow" (by Martin alone), a burlesque
      "apostrophe of conscious greatness." Reprinted with addi-
      tions in 1845.B11. Attributions: The Book of Ballads,
      edited by Bon Gaultier, new ed. (Edinburgh and London:
      Blackwood, 1903), p. 155.

12   QUILLINAN, EDWARD. "Imaginary Conversation, between Mr Walter
      Savage Landor and the Editor of Blackwood's Magazine."
      Blackwood's Edinburgh Magazine, 53 (April), 518-36
      (528-36).
           A reply to 1842.B24. The character "Christopher North"
      defends the treatment of Wordsworth in Blackwood's Edin-
      burgh Magazine and attacks Landor's criticism, especially
      concerning Wordsworth's opinion of Southey and his debt to
      Landor in The Excursion.

13   ROBBERDS, J.[OHN] W.[ARDEN], ed. A Memoir of the Life and
      Writings of the late William Taylor of Norwich. . . .
      2 vols. London: Murray, passim.
           Includes letters in which Southey gives Lyrical Ballads
      (1798) mixed praise, confesses in 1803 that Wordsworth is
      a stranger to him, praises Wordsworth's modernization of
      Chaucer, notes Wordsworth's grief over the death of his
      brother John and his own task of reviewing Wordsworth's
      poems, and praises Concerning . . . the Convention of Cintra
      and The Excursion. Includes letters in which Coleridge
      transcribes Wordsworth's opinion of Bürger and Taylor re-
      cords his own admiration of Wordsworth's poems (though
      Wordsworth magnifies trifles) and an enthusiastic lecture
      on Wordsworth by "our Octagon minister, Mr. Madge."

1843

14 [RUSKIN, JOHN]. Modern Painters. . . . By a Graduate of
    Oxford. London: Smith, Elder, pp. 4 (Part I, Section I,
    Chapter i, Paragraph 2), 144-45 (Part II, Section II,
    Chapter iii, Paragraph 5), 185 (Section III, Chapter i,
    Paragraph 7), 191-92 (Paragraph 15), 200-201 (Chapter ii,
    Paragraph 9), 419 (Section VI, Chapter iii, Paragraph 23).
        To the vulgar, it is a labor to read Wordsworth. Praises
    Wordsworth's seeing the essential in nature (as does Turner).
    Revised in 1846.B12.

15 SHELDON, FREDERICK. Mieldenvold, the Student; or, the
    Pilgrimage through Northumberland, Durham, Berwickshire,
    and the Adjacent Counties (poem). Berwick-upon-Tweed:
    Warder Office, etc., p. ix.
        "That priest of Nature--Wordsworth's almost done."

1844 A BOOKS - NONE

1844 B SHORTER WRITINGS

1 ANON. Review of Select Pieces from the Poems of William
    Wordsworth. Church of England Quarterly Review, 15
    (January), 245.
        Wordsworth expresses his healing power in language in-
    debted to Cowper.

2 ANON. Review of Select Pieces from the Poems of William
    Wordsworth. Gentleman's Magazine, NS 21 (January), 63.
        The volume contains admirable poems by "the great poet
    of the Lakes."

3 ANON. Review of Select Pieces from the Poems of William
    Wordsworth. Metropolitan Magazine, 39 (January), 23.
        Wordsworth's poems have been met with a wide diversity
    of opinion.

4 ANON. Review of "Testimonies of W. Wordsworth and of S. T.
    Coleridge to Catholic Truth," etc. Christian Remembrancer,
    NS 7 (February), 163-83 (171-74).
        Wordsworth has promoted the cause of Catholicity not by
    scattered statements of doctrine but by his early, seemingly
    pantheistic poems.

5 ANON. Review of Select Pieces from the Poems of William
    Wordsworth. Gentleman's Magazine, NS 21 (March), 284.
        The volume is full of images of beauty and lessons of
    truth.

1844

6   ANON.   Review of <u>Select Pieces from the Poems of William Wordsworth</u>. <u>New Monthly Magazine</u>, NS 71 (May), 142.
         The poems, from a <u>"most elegant</u>, and <u>now</u> most popular" poet, are suitable for ladies.

7   ANON.   Review of <u>A New Spirit of the Age</u> (ed. Horne). <u>Church of England Quarterly Review</u>, 16 (July), 161-74 (163).
         Wordsworth, by defending his own childish poems, hinders his reputation. He is a spectator of life rather than an actor.

8   ANON.   "Poetry and Railways." <u>Spectator</u>, 17 (14 December), 1187-88.
         Though his verse is worthy, Wordsworth argues poorly in his first letter on the Kendal and Windermere Railway.

9   ANON.   "Miscellaneous." <u>Spectator</u>, 17 (21 December), 1206-07 (1207).
         Wordsworth's second letter on the Kendal and Windermere Railway is not much better than the first.

10   BARRETT, ELIZABETH BARRETT. "On a Portrait of Wordsworth, by R. B. Haydon" (poem), "Lady Geraldine's Courtship" (poem), in <u>Poems</u>. 2 vols. London: Moxon, I:125, 209-50 (225).
         Reprinted with minor verbal changes from 1842.B17 (125). Refers to Wordsworth as the poet of "solemn-thoughted idyl" (225).

11   "BETA." "Modern Poets." <u>Athenaeum</u>, no. 856 (23 March), pp. 270-71.
         Wordsworth heads a group of cold and unimpassioned poets; his sonnets would not arouse men to oppose an invasion.

12   BETA. "Hasty Suggestions on Modern Poetry, and Hints for a Vindication of Public Taste: By One of the Public." <u>Athenaeum</u>, no. 860 (20 April), pp. 357-58 (357).
         Wordsworth's works excell those of his followers.

13   BETA. "Suggestions on Modern Poetry; with Hints for a Vindication of Public Taste." <u>Athenaeum</u>, no. 864 (18 May), pp. 453-55 (454).
         Byron, rather than Wordsworth, writes true simple pathos.

14   CHAMBERS, ROBERT [and ROBERT CARRUTHERS]. "William Wordsworth," in <u>Cyclopaedia of English Literature</u>. Edited by Robert Chambers. 2 vols. Edinburgh: Chambers, II:322-33.
         A biographical sketch. In discussing the influence of nature upon man, Wordsworth is "sometimes unintelligible

from his idealism." Though in simplicity inferior to earlier poets, he has triumphed in spite of his theory. In The Excursion he preaches enlightened humanity, though with a pedlar incongruously as moralist. Wordsworth's system of classifying his poems is capricious. He is too intellectual, his sensibilities too peculiar, to become generally popular. His power is best displayed in his sonnets. "Vaudracour and Julia" is written in the style of Ford or Massinger. Wordsworth's retirement leads both to his inability to discriminate among his own works and to his originality. Attribution: The Dictionary of National Biography . . . , ed. Stephen and Lee (Oxford: Oxford Univ. Press, 1921-22), III:1093. Revised in 1860.B7.

15 COLERIDGE, HARTLEY. Letter to the Editor: "Windermere Railway." Kendal Mercury, no. 550 (23 November), p. [3].
"Wordsworth does not wish to keep the Lakes to himself."

16 ELLISON, HENRY. "To Wordsworth" (poem), in The Poetry of Real Life. A new edition, much enlarged and improved. First series. London: privately printed, p. 7.
Wordsworth has "made day for all men to partake."

17 [FABER, FREDERICK W.]. "The Life of St. Bega," in Lives of the English Saints: No. VI: . . . St. Bega. [Edited by John Henry Newman.] London: Toovy, pp. 135-87 (181-87).
"Stanzas Suggested in a Steamboat off Saint Bees' Heads" anticipates the revival of Catholic doctrines. Though "very little in sympathy with Roman doctrine on the whole," Wordsworth revered the Catholic past.

18 GRANT, J.[OHN] P., ed. Memoir and Correspondence of Mrs. Grant of Laggan. Edited by her Son. 3 vols. London: Longman, II:59-60, 224-25, 281-82.
Includes letters in which Mrs. Grant notes that Wordsworth's piety in The Excursion is too pantheistic, that Wordsworth talks incessantly, that he is always morally right, though his writing is often too metaphysical or childish, and that the Pedlar in The Excursion reflects the realities of Scottish life.

19 HALL, S.[AMUEL] C.[ARTER]. Note, in The Book of British Ballads. Edited by S. C. Hall. Second series. London: How, pp. 313-14.
A biographical sketch. "Ruth" is natural, true, moral. Wordsworth is a firm friend of virtue.

20 HAYDON, B.[ENJAMIN] R.[OBERT]. Dedication, in Lectures on
    Painting and Design. . . . Illustrated. London: Longman,
    p. v.
        Expresses his admiration for Wordsworth.

21 HERBST, OSWALD. "Oswald Herbst's Letters from England:
    Letter II.--To Carl Frühling." Tait's Edinburgh Magazine,
    NS 11 (October), 641-45 (642-45).
        A unity of purpose pervades Wordsworth's writings, which
    are best read in the Lake District. His poems are deficient
    in dramatic variety and too abstract. Records visit to
    Wordsworth at Rydal Mount: Wordsworth's evaluation of
    Scott and Coleridge. Records J. Wilson's praise of
    Wordsworth.

22 HORNE, R.[ICHARD] H.[ENGIST]. "William Wordsworth and Leigh
    Hunt," "Alfred Tennyson," "Henry Taylor and the Author of
    'Festus,'" in A New Spirit of the Age. Edited by R. H.
    Horne. Second edition. 2 vols. London: Smith, Elder,
    I:305-32 (305-15, 321-32); II:1-32 (8, 11-12), 281-310
    (284-86, 301-302).
        Wordsworth was a determined advocate of the natural in
    poetry. He absorbed the natural world into himself. He is
    deficient in passion. As a teacher and poet he both com-
    pares and contrasts with Hunt (I:305-15, 321-32; written in
    collaboration with E. B. Barrett [see 1877.B24]). Thought,
    rather than simplicity, is the secret of Wordsworth's po-
    etry (II:8, 11-12). Others should imitate Wordsworth's
    grander poems rather than those on mean subjects (284-86,
    301-302).

23 HUNT, LEIGH. "Preface," "The Feast of the Poets" (poem),
    "Lines on the Birth of the Princess Alice" (poem), in The
    Poetical Works of Leigh Hunt: Containing Many Pieces Now
    First Collected. London: Moxon, pp. iii-x (vii, x),
    79-88 (83-84, 86), 164-65 (164).
        Notes his fighting for Wordsworth's reputation (vii, x).
    Reprinted from 1832.B19; revised in 1860.B11 (83-84, 86).
    Wordsworth's "calm and stately" verse makes him a fit laure-
    ate. Reprinted with added note in 1860.B11 (164).

24 JEFFREY, FRANCIS. "The Dramatic Works of John Ford,"
    "Reliques of Robert Burns," "Poems: By the Reverend George
    Crabbe," "Childe Harold's Pilgrimage, Canto the Third,"
    "The Excursion," "The White Doe of Rylstone," "Rejected
    Addresses," in Contributions to the Edinburgh Review.
    4 vols. London: Longman, II:284-314 (294-95), 389-421
    (421); III:3-23 (6-11), 164-98 (165-66), 233-68, 269-79;
    IV:470-86 (471, 475).

1844

Reprinted from 1811.B4 (II:294-95). Reprinted from
1809.B13 (421). Reprinted with minor addition from 1808.B5
(III:6-11). Reprinted from 1816.B33 (165-66). Reprinted,
with omissions and an additional note, from 1814.B10. Ad-
mits he attacked Wordsworth too bitterly, though he remains
intolerant of certain poems (233-68). Reprinted from
1815.B23 (269-79). Reprinted from 1812.B6 (IV:471, 475).

25 KEBLE, JOANNE. De Poeticae Vi Medica: Praelectiones
    Academicae Oxonii Habitae, Annis MDCCCXXXII......MDCCCXLI.
    2 vols. Oxford: Parker, I:[iii]; II:615-16, 789.
        Wordsworth raises up men's hearts to holy things, cham-
    pioned the cause of the poor and simple. Praises "Ode:
    Intimations of Immortality." (In Latin.)

26 [LORDAN, CHRISTOPHER L.]. Colloquies Desultory, but Chiefly
    upon Poetry and Poets; between an Elder, Enthusiastic, and
    an Apostle of the Law. London: Orr, and Houlston and
    Stoneman; Romsey: Lordan, especially pp. 63-80, 187,
    197-98, 221.
        Revised and expanded from 1843.B10. Wordsworth labored
    "to make conspicuous disregarded things."

27 M.[ILNES], R.[ICHARD] M.[ONCKTON]. "Projected Railways in
    Westmorland: in Answer to Mr Wordsworth's Late Sonnet"
    (poem). Whitehaven Herald, no. 691 (30 November), p. [3].
        Rebukes Wordsworth for his opposition to the railway in
    "On the Projected Kendal and Windermere Railway." Reprinted
    with verbal changes in Selections from the Poetical Works
    of Richard Monckton Milnes, Lord Houghton (1863).

28 [MONCREIFF, JAMES]. Review of Jeffrey's Contributions to the
    Edinburgh Review. North British Review, 1 (May), 252-84
    (272-74).
        Wordsworth's willful obscuring of his strong poetic
    powers by an indefensible affectation deserved Jeffrey's
    severe rebuke.

29 PARKINSON, RICHARD. The Old-Church Clock. Second edition.
    London: Rivington; Manchester: Simms and Dinham, p. xxvii.
        Praises Wordsworth's "prose scenery-painting" in the
    notes to The River Duddon.

30 STANLEY, ARTHUR PENRHYN. The Life and Correspondence of
    Thomas Arnold, D.D. 2 vols. London: Fellowes, I:16-17,
    63, 284, 322; II:130, 157.
        Records Arnold's appreciation of Wordsworth's poems. In-
    cludes letters in which Arnold expresses his friendship for

Wordsworth and notes Wordsworth's reception at Oxford in
1839. Expanded in 1844.B31.

31 STANLEY, ARTHUR PENRHYN. The Life and Correspondence of
    Thomas Arnold D.D. Second edition. 2 vols. London:
    Fellowes, I:16-17, 68, 313, 357; II:133, 160.
        Expanded from 1844.B30. Includes letter in which Arnold
    details his visit to Wordsworth in 1832: their friendship,
    despite arguing over the Reform Bill.

32 TALFOURD, T.[HOMAS] N.[OON]. "On the Reception of the Poet
    Wordsworth at Oxford" (poem), in Tragedies; to Which Are
    Added a Few Sonnets and Verses. London: Moxon, p. 246.
        Hails the tribute of England's Youth to "Her once neg-
    lected bard."

33 TAYLOR, HENRY. "Notes," in Philip Van Artevelde; A Dramatic
    Romance: In two Parts. Third edition. London: Moxon,
    pp. 283-307 (285).
        Acknowledges that some parts of the Preface to the volume
    were borrowed from Wordsworth's conversations.

34 THETA. "Modern Poetry." Athenaeum, no. 867 (8 June),
    pp. 525-26 (525).
        A reply to 1844.B11. Though Wordsworth fails in so far
    as he relies on mere abstract assertion instead of dramatic
    representation, he does stir passion.

1845 A BOOKS - NONE

1845 B SHORTER WRITINGS

1   ANON. Review of Keble's De Poeticae Vi Medica. Eclectic
    Review, NS 17 (January), 22-42 (29-30, 39-40).
        Wordsworth is now justly admired; the language of poetry
    may differ from that of prose.

2   ANON. Review of Poems, Chiefly of Early and Late Years.
    Gentleman's Magazine, NS 24 (December), 555-75.
        Wordsworth has worked to correct the errors of false po-
    etic taste. In The Borderers he adheres to nature, analyzes
    the mind under the influence of passion. In his sonnets he
    occasionally alters the established rules.

3   ANON. Review of Poems (1845). Examiner, no. 1977
    (20 December), 804.
        The volume is a tribute to Wordsworth's simplicity,
    purity, and wisdom.

1845

4   BON GAULTIER. See 1845.B11.

5   BROWNING, ROBERT. "The Lost Leader" (poem), in Bells and
    Pomegranates: No. VII: Dramatic Romances and Lyrics.
    London: Moxon, p. 8.
        Criticizes a poet, presumably Wordsworth (see 1876.B12;
    1891.B35), for abandoning the side of freedom "for a handful
    of silver."

6   CRAIK, GEORGE L. Sketches of the History of Literature and
    Learning in England. . . . 6 vols. London: Knight,
    VI:67, 114-40, 148-53, 160-61, 205.
        Quarrels with Wordsworth's definition of poetic language
    in the Preface to Lyrical Ballads and with his alterations
    to "Laodamia." Wordsworth, influenced by the Germans,
    widened the domain of poetry to include common life. His
    later poetry is not obscure. His, Coleridge's, and Southey's
    earlier poems contrast; in their later works Wordsworth and
    Coleridge become more alike. Briefly expanded in 1861.B9.

7   [DE QUINCEY, THOMAS]. "Coleridge and Opium-Eating."
    Blackwood's Edinburgh Magazine, 57 (January), 117-32 (129,
    131).
        Wordsworth's self-mastery of Latin is remarkable. Re-
    printed in De Quincey's Writings (1850-59); reprinted with
    minor addition in 1859.B10.

8   DE QUINCEY, THOMAS. "On Wordsworth's Poetry." Tait's
    Edinburgh Magazine, NS 12 (September), 545-54.
        By writing the Preface to Lyrical Ballads, Wordsworth
    compelled critics to notice his theory of poetic diction.
    He does not deal with passion directly but "when passing
    under the shadow of some secondary passion." His poems re-
    pel ordinary readers because their subjects fail to interest
    them. In The Excursion the incidents and characters in the
    tale of Margaret are contrived and dubiously pathetic; the
    Solitary's restoration must be implausible. The Excursion
    has an undulatory, colloquial character dangerous to a
    philosophic discussion. Wordsworth's greatness lies in the
    truth and novelty of his observations of the natural world.
    Reprinted in De Quincey's Writings (1850-59); reprinted
    with verbal changes and minor revisions in 1857.B6.

9   GILFILLAN, GEORGE. "William Wordsworth," in A Gallery of
    Literary Portraits. Edinburgh: Tait; London: Simpkin,
    Marshall; Dublin: Cumming, pp. 307-20.
        Wordsworth lives in seclusion, unmoved by criticism; his
    mission was to raise the mean. His poetry is microscopic,

magnifying that which is small. Though they have faults, Lyrical Ballads and The Excursion contain admirable pathos and philosophy. (First published in the Dumfriesshire and Galloway Herald.)

10   HUGHES, JOHN. "Poetry," in Encyclopaedia Metropolitana; or, Universal Dictionary of Knowledge. . . . Edited by the Rev. Edward Smedley, the Rev. Hugh James Rose, and the Rev. Henry John Rose. 26 vols. London: Fellowes, etc.; Oxford: Parker, and Laycock; Cambridge: Deighton, V:651-84 (655).
        Wordsworth's speculation about the child's mind in "Ode: Intimations of Immortality" is "somewhat fanciful." (Issued in parts, 1817-45.)

11   [MARTIN, THEODORE and W. E. AYTOUN] BON GAULTIER. "The Laureates' Tourney" (poem), in The Book of Ballads. Illustrated by Alfred Crowquill. London: Orr, pp. 23-29.
        Reprinted with additional note from 1843.B11. Wordsworth is "full of the serene consciousness of superiority."

12   PAYNE, JOSEPH. Notes, in Studies in English Poetry. . . . Edited by Joseph Payne. London: Relfe and Fletcher, pp. 18-19, 101-102, 109-10, 195, 226-27.
        Critical notes to the poems selected, including "To the Cuckoo" ("O blithe New-comer! I have heard"), "To a Sky-lark" ("Ethereal minstrel! pilgrim of the sky!"), "Three years she grew in sun and shower," "She was a Phantom of delight," "To May."

13   THOM, JOHN HAMILTON, ed. The Life of the Rev. Joseph Blanco White, Written by Himself; with Portions of his Correspondence. 3 vols. London: Chapman, II:297-99.
        Includes extract from his journals in which White complains that "Wordsworth is too frequently a party poet" who publishes too much and is cried up by a coterie.

14   WHEWELL, WILLIAM. Dedication, in The Elements of Morality, including Polity. 2 vols. London: Parker, I:[iii].
        Wordsworth's poems raised readers above the moral temper of the times.

15   [WILSON, JOHN]. "North's Specimens of the British Critics: No. VI." Blackwood's Edinburgh Magazine, 58 (July), 114-28 (125-28).
        Wordsworth's translation of "The Cuckoo and the Nightingale" lacks the spirit of Chaucer.

1846

1846 A   BOOKS - NONE

1846 B   SHORTER WRITINGS

1   ANON. "Past and Present Condition of British Poetry."
    Fraser's Magazine, 33 (May), 577-90 (584-86, 590); (June),
    708-18 (708-12, 718).
        An Evening Walk exhibits originality and keen observa-
    tion. In 1798 few read, liked, or understood Lyrical Bal-
    lads (584-86, 590). Records Hogg's story of Wordsworth's
    refusal to consider others as poets (708-12, 718).

2   ANON. Review of Mackay's The Scenery and Poetry of the
    English Lakes. Examiner, no. 2027 (5 December), p. 774.
        Wordsworth "terribly disappoints those who go to hear
    him"; he opposes all progress.

3   ANON. "Bull in the Printing Office" (poem), in The Comic
    Almanack, for 1846. . . . By Rigdum Funnidos, Gent.
    Illustrated by George Cruikshank. London: Bogue, p. 15.
        Poem, signed "W. Wordsworth, Poet Laureate," mocking
    Wordsworth's complaints about the unpopularity of his poems.

4   BRYDGES, SIR [SAMUEL] EGERTON. "To W. W. and R. S. (William
    Wordsworth and Robert Southey)" (poem), in Human Fate, and
    An Address to the Poets Wordsworth & Southey: Poems.
    Great Totham: privately printed, pp. [20-21].
        Pays tribute to the poets of virtue, spiritual truth,
    sympathy with human misery, and life's daily tasks.

5   [BULWER-LYTTON, EDWARD]. The New Timon: A Romance of London
    (poem). London: Colburn, p. 51.
        Speaks of poets "Outbabying Wordsworth." (Reference
    omitted in revised edition, 1846.)

6   [DIX, JOHN]. Pen and Ink Sketches of Poets, Preachers, and
    Politicians. London: Bogue, pp. 122-29, 135, 201-203,
    218-19.
        Records visit to Rydal Mount and Wordsworth's conversa-
    tion on his poetry ("The Thorn" and the tenets of his new
    "school"), his reception (by Jeffrey and in Blackwood's
    Edinburgh Magazine), Milton, and Byron. Wordsworth owed
    his favorable early reputation to J. Wilson. Records see-
    ing Wordsworth at the theater: "he looked more like a man
    borne down by some heavy grief, than a profound thinker."
    Recounts the circumstances behind Wordsworth's writing of
    "When Severn's sweeping flood had overthrown." Attribution:
    Bodleian catalogue.

7 HARVEY, THOMAS. "Introduction," "Wordsworth," in The Poetical
 Reader; A Selection from the Eminent Poets of the Last
 Period of English Literature. . . . Edited by Thomas
 Harvey. Geneva: Kessmann; Paris: Derache, pp. xiii-xxxii,
 148-54.
 Wordsworth, the meditative head of the Lake School, had
 a high sense of his mission (xiii-xxxii). He is a good
 Christian, appeals too constantly to nature (148-54).

8 HAYNES, HENRY W. "Dedication," in The Pleasures of Poesy: A
 Poem in two Cantos. London: Yates, p. [v].
 Venerates Wordsworth's character and writings.

9 HOWITT, WILLIAM. "William Wordsworth." People's Journal, 1
 (24 January), 43-45.
 Wordsworth withdrew from the throng in order to labor
 most effectively for it. He pointed out the need for general education and the lot of farmers and child workers in
 factories, though he mistakenly opposes the Windermere
 railway.

10 LANDOR, WALTER SAVAGE. "Southey and Porson," "Southey and
 Porson: Second Conversation," "Southey and Landor: Second
 Conversation," "CCXLII: New Style" (poem), "CCLXVI" ("One
 tooth has Mummius; but in sooth") (poem), "CCLXXXIX: To
 Wordsworth" (poem), "CCXCVI: To Andrew Crosse" (poem),
 "CCCXV: To Joseph Ablett" (poem), "CCCXVI: To an Aged
 Poet" (poem), in The Works of Walter Savage Landor.
 2 vols. London: Moxon, I:11-20, 68-84; II:154-74 (156),
 660-61, 664, 667, 668-69, 673-74 (673), 674.
 Revised from 1826.B14. Wordsworth and Coleridge are
 dissimilar (I:11-20). Revised, with omissions, from
 1842.B24 (68-84). In his best verses Wordsworth reverts to
 the influence of paganism (II:156). Reprinted from
 1842.B23 (660-61). Mocks Wordsworth; reprinted, identifying
 Wordsworth as the subject, in 1863.B12 (664). Reprinted
 with minor verbal changes from 1834.B21 (667). "Hoarse
 whistles Wordsworth's watery flute" that once indignately
 mourned in "To Toussaint L'Ouverture" (668-69). Reprinted
 from 1834.B22 (673). Comprised of lines reprinted with
 minor verbal changes from 1836.B19 (674).

11 [NEWMAN, JOHN HENRY]. Review of Lyra Innocentium. Dublin
 Review, 20 (June), 434-61 (447).
 Notes that in much of the poetry of the day (presumably
 including "Ode: Intimations of Immortality") poets extol
 the divine nature of infancy without acknowledging its
 source in baptism. Reprinted as "John Keble" in Essays
 Critical and Historical (1871).

1846

12   [RUSKIN, JOHN]. Modern Painters: Volume I: Containing
       Part I. and II. By a Graduate of Oxford. Third edition,
       revised. London: Smith, Elder, pp. 3 (Part I, Section I,
       Chapter i, Paragraph 2), 82 (Part II, Section I, Chapter
       vii, Paragraph 10), 174-75 (Section II, Chapter iii, Para-
       graph 5), 204 (Section III, Chapter i, Paragraph 7), 209
       (Paragraph 15), 217-18 (Chapter iii, Paragraph 9).
           Revised from 1843.B14. Praises Wordsworth's "foreground
       painting" in "So fair, so sweet, withal so sensitive."

13   [RUSKIN, JOHN]. Modern Painters: Volume II: Containing
       Part III: Section 1 and 2: Of the Imaginative and
       Theoretic Faculties. By a Graduate of Oxford. London:
       Smith, Elder, pp. 36 (Section I, Chapter v, Paragraph 2),
       61-62 (Chapter vii, Paragraphs 2, 4), 86-87 (Chapter xii,
       Paragraphs 2-3), 188-92 (Section II, Chapter iv, Paragraphs
       5-8), 216 (Addenda).
           Commends Wordsworth's authority in questions relating to
       the influence of external things on the soul, his imagina-
       tive portrayal of repose, his love of all creatures and
       plants, his illustrations of fancy and imagination, and his
       opposition to the Kendal railway. Expanded in 1883.B54.

1847 A   BOOKS - NONE

1847 B   SHORTER WRITINGS

1   ANON. "Walks in Westmoreland." Chambers' Edinburgh Journal,
       NS 7 (10 April), 225-28 (225, 227-28).
           Wordsworth and Rydal Mount are fit for each other. In-
       cludes tribute to Wordsworth's "sacred joy," "Sonnet Written
       in Wordsworth's Window."

2   ANON. "Our Weekly Gossip." Athenaeum, no. 1028 (10 July),
       pp. 734-35 (735).
           Wordsworth "was awakened from his long sleep" to write
       "Ode on the Installation of His Royal Highness Prince
       Albert."

3   ANON. "The Installation Ode." Chambers' Edinburgh Journal,
       NS 8 (7 August), 93-94.
           No one can read "Ode on the Installation of His Royal
       Highness Prince Albert" without pitying Wordsworth.

4   ANON. "Literary and Scientific Institution." Reading Mercury,
       125 (23 October), p. [3]; (30 October), p. [3].

Reports first and second lectures by T. N. Talfourd on
the "Genius of Wordsworth": traces Wordsworth's poetic
career.

5   ANON. "Lecture by Mr. Serjeant Talfourd." Reading Mercury,
125 (13 November), p. [3].
    Reports Talfourd's third lecture: Wordsworth's poetry
consists chiefly in the communion of man and nature; hence
his poems are religious but not theological.

6   ANON. "William Wordsworth, Esq." London Journal, 6
(27 November), 205-206.
    A biographical sketch. Wordsworth devoted his entire
life to poetry--an ideal lot. He propounds a "poetic
Quakerism."

7   ANON. "Mr. Wordsworth's Ode, on the Installation of H. R. H.
Prince Albert at Cambridge, June, 1847" (poem). Man in the
Moon, no. 6 [1847], pp. 349-50.
    A parody of "Ode on the Installation of His Royal High-
ness Prince Albert."

8   ANON. "Poets of the Age." Eton School Magazine, no. 2
[1847], pp. 41-46 (43, 45).
    The age now appreciates the "chaste simplicity and de-
votional spirit" of the Lake School.

9   ANON. Hand-book to the English Lakes. Kendal: Atkinson;
London: Hamilton, Adams, pp. 33-34.
    Describes Rydal Mount, where Wordsworth, surrounded by
beauty and domestic happiness, writes poems that are universally applauded.

10 ANON. Lectures on the English Poets. London: Earle,
pp. 109-15.
    Wordsworth now receives exaggerated praise. Early in
life he planned to participate in the pantisocracy scheme.
His poems incongruously combine simplicity of style with
lofty sentiment. His tales in The Excursion are not equal
to Crabbe's in pathos; his philosophy is overrated.

11 COLERIDGE, HENRY NELSON. Notes, in Biographia Literaria: or
Biographical Sketches of My Literary Life and Opinions. By
Samuel Taylor Coleridge. Second edition. Edited by Henry
Nelson Coleridge and his widow [Sara Coleridge]. 2 vols.
London: Pickering, passim.
    Includes critical notes (signed "Ed."): Wordsworth was
defrauded of profit from his works because of the attacks
in the Edinburgh Review.

1847

12 COLERIDGE, SARA. Dedication, "Introduction," Notes, in
    Biographia Literaria: or Biographical Sketches of My
    Literary Life and Opinions. By Samuel Taylor Coleridge.
    Second edition. Edited by Henry Nelson Coleridge and his
    widow [Sara Coleridge]. 2 vols. London: Pickering, I:i,
    v-clxxxvii (cxxxiii, clviii-clxiii, clxvii-clxviii), passim.
        Expresses her wish for the association together of Words-
    worth's and Coleridge's names (i). The spirit of Christian-
    ity pervades Wordsworth's poetry. Most who laughed at his
    poems knew them only through the biased Edinburgh Review.
    He has borrowed from others less than any other great poet
    (cxxxiii, clviii-clxiii, clxvii-clxviii). Includes critical
    notes (signed "S. C."): Wordsworth's early unpopularity
    arose from the novelty of his poems, not from the attacks
    in the Edinburgh Review; criticizes his textual revisions
    in "There was a Boy," "The Blind Highland Boy," and "Gip-
    sies"; compares The Excursion (Book I) with a passage by
    Goethe; praises the transitions in "Song at the Feast of
    Brougham Castle"; Poems of the Fancy are much more than
    fanciful; Wordsworth's sonnets may be grouped in pairs;
    praises the lightness of The Waggoner (passim).

13 COTTLE, JOSEPH. Reminiscences of Samuel Taylor Coleridge and
    Robert Southey. London: Houlston and Stoneman, pp. 260,
    407-408, 413, 418-19, 443, 450, 469.
        Expanded from 1837.B11. Records Arch's expectations of
    losing money on Lyrical Ballads (1798), Hannah More's
    praise of the volume, Southey's statement in 1836 that
    Wordsworth did not know of Coleridge's later criticism of
    him, Southey's approval of Wordsworth's portrait, Words-
    worth's description of Southey in 1841, and Coleridge's
    opinions on Wordsworth (including Lyrical Ballads [1800]
    and Wordsworth's devotion to "his great work").

14 DE QUINCEY, THOMAS. "Notes on Savage Landor." Tait's
    Edinburgh Magazine, NS 14 (February), 96-104 (97-98).
        Wordsworth, who was only once tipsy, never met Porson.
    Reprinted in De Quincey's Writings (1850-59) and Leaders in
    Literature: with a Notice of Traditional Errors Affecting
    Them [De Quincey's Works, Volume IX] (1858).

15 DE QUINCEY, THOMAS. "Milton versus Southey and Landor."
    Tait's Edinburgh Magazine, NS 14 (April), 253-59 (254-56).
        A reply to "Southey and Landor: Second Conversation" in
    1846.B10. Discounts Landor's report of Wordsworth's criti-
    cism of Keats and objects to Landor's judgment of Words-
    worth's best poems. Though proud, Wordsworth was not en-
    vious. He does not celebrate paganism. Reprinted in De
    Quincey's Writings (1850-59) and 1859.B10.

16 HEATON, WILLIAM. "Stanzas: To William Wordsworth, Esq.,"
   "To William Wordsworth; The Poet Laureate to Her Majesty"
   (poem), in The Flowers of Calder Dale: Poems. London:
   Longman; Halifax: Leyland, pp. 19-20, 84.
      Wordsworth is guarded from earthly strife (19-20). Hails
   Wordsworth's varied Muse (84).

17 HOWITT, WILLIAM. Homes and Haunts of the Most Eminent British
   Poets. Illustrated by W. and G. Measom. 2 vols. London:
   Bentley, especially II:91-93, 99-101, 232, 257-91.
      A biographical sketch. Wordsworth's poems are indis-
   solubly tied to the Lake Country. His life has been for-
   tunate. He preaches "a poetic Quakerism," especially in
   The Excursion. He quietly enjoys being beseiged by visitors
   at Rydal Mount.

18 KNIGHT, CHARLES. Note, in Half-hours with the Best Authors.
   Edited by Charles Knight. Illustrated. 4 vols. London:
   Knight [1847], I:144.
      The "vulgar" do read Wordsworth. The secret of his suc-
   cess is his universality. Revised in 1854.B7.

19 MEDWIN, THOMAS. The Life of Percy Bysshe Shelley. 2 vols.
   London: Newby, I:243; II:24-26.
      Records Shelley's "drenching" Byron with Wordsworth,
   laughing over Peter Bell, and praising Wordsworth's earlier
   poems (but not his odes).

20 W., J. "The Lecture on the Poetry of Mr. Wordsworth."
   Reading Mercury, 125 (13 November), p. [1].
      Talfourd in his lecture (see 1847.B5) seeks to find re-
   ligion not in the Bible but in the sentimental poetry of
   Wordsworth.

1848 A BOOKS - NONE

1848 B SHORTER WRITINGS

1 [CHRISTIE, WILLIAM DOUGAL]. Review of Cottle's Reminiscences
   of Samuel Taylor Coleridge and Robert Southey. Edinburgh
   Review, 87 (April), 368-92 (378-82, 387).
      Notes Wordsworth's relations with Coleridge and his in-
   difference to Southey's poetry.

2 COLLINS, EDWARD [JAMES] M.[ORTIMER]. "Windermere" (poem) and
   "Notes," "The Terrace at Rydal" (poem), in Windermere; A
   Poem: and Sonnets. Kendal: Atkinson; London: Hamilton,
   Adams, pp. 1-14 (7, 13-14), 17.

1848

> Wordsworth, priest of Nature, "has been victor o'er a
> recreant age" (7, 13-14) with his "holy musing" (17).

3   DE QUINCEY, THOMAS. "Protestantism." Tait's Edinburgh
     Magazine, NS 15 (February), 84-88 (85).
     Recounts incident of his accusing Wordsworth of express-
     ing incorrect Anglican doctrine in The Excursion (Book V).
     Reprinted in De Quincey's Writings (1850-59); reprinted with
     verbal changes in Essays Sceptical and Anti-Sceptical on
     Problems Neglected or Mis-conceived [De Quincey's Works,
     Volume VIII] (1858).

4   [DE QUINCEY, THOMAS]. Review of Talfourd's Final Memorials of
     Charles Lamb. North British Review, 10 (November), 97-116
     (114).
     Longmans's editions of Wordsworth were slovenly produced.
     Records Lamb's jollity at the expense of Wordsworth's
     "boots." Reprinted in De Quincey's Writings (1850-59).
     Reference omitted when article revised as "Charles Lamb" in
     Leaders in Literature: with a Notice of Traditional Errors
     Affecting Them [De Quincey's Works, Volume IX] (1858).

5   GRANT, JAMES GREGOR. Dedication, "On the First Perusal and
     Study of Wordsworth's Poetry: 1832" (poem), "Rydal.--
     Wordsworth" (poem), "Bruges: Approach.--Recollection of
     Wordsworth's Sonnet" (poem), in Madonna Pia, and Other
     Poems. 2 vols. London: Smith, Elder, I:[iii], 204;
     II:87, 278.
     Testifies to his appreciation of Wordsworth (I:[iii],
     204; II:278) and to Wordsworth's freshness in age (87).

6   [HARE, AUGUSTUS WILLIAM and JULIUS CHARLES]. Guesses at Truth.
     By Two Brothers. Second edition. Second series. London:
     Taylor and Walton, especially pp. 108-33, 159-60, 165.
     Notes Wordsworth amended the passage in "French Revolu-
     tion, as it appeared to Enthusiasts at its Commencement"
     criticized in 1827.B7. But Wordsworth perhaps follows too
     much the advice of others, for his alterations (e.g., in
     "The Blind Highland Boy," "Gipsies," and "Laodamia") have
     been unfortunate--though he has lately restored some ori-
     ginal readings. Eminently the poet of his age, he exhibits
     its proneness to reflection in his psychological analysis
     in "The Brothers" and "To ---" ("Let other bards of angels
     sing"). His interest in the least objects of nature results
     not from natural sympathy but from an act of will; because
     he caters to modern tastes, his poems express sentiment
     rather than feeling.

7   HARE, JULIUS CHARLES. "Sketch of the Author's Life," in
    Essays and Tales. By John Sterling. Edited by Julius
    Charles Hare. 2 vols. London: Parker, I:i-ccxxxii
    (xxvi-xxviii, lxxvii, clxx, ccxvi-ccxvii).
        Records Sterling's impression of Wordsworth's lack of
    pretension and "companionable sympathies" upon meeting
    Wordsworth in 1828, and his admiration for Wordsworth's
    poems, especially their "strong sense of righteousness."

8   LESTER, JOHN W. Criticisms. Second edition, revised and
    enlarged. London: Longman; Cambridge: Deighton,
    pp. 97-99.
        Wordsworth's poems are remarkable for their clear, puri-
    fying spirituality.

9   MILNES, RICHARD MONCKTON, ed. Life, Letters, and Literary
    Remains, of John Keats. 2 vols. London: Moxon, I:xii-xv,
    28-29, 40-41, 55, 58, 80, 84-87, 105, 135-40, 152-55,
    217-21, 266; II:63.
        Commends Wordsworth's remarks on biography in A Letter
    to A Friend of Robert Burns. Records Keats's intercourse
    with Wordsworth in London and disappointment in not seeing
    him at Rydal. Includes letters in which Keats expresses
    his reverence for Wordsworth, complains of the "palpable
    design" his poems have upon the reader, questions whether
    he martyrs his epic passions in favor of the human heart,
    which he explores more deeply than Milton, and speaks of
    "the Wordsworthian, or egotistical sublime."

10 RICHARDSON, DAVID LESTER. Literary Chit-chat: with
    Miscellaneous Poems and an Appendix of Prose Papers.
    Calcutta: D'Rozario, passim.
        Suggests Wordsworth criticized Pope out of envy of his
    popularity; Wordsworth excels Byron in philosophy but is
    verbose and feeble compared to Milton. He will not be popu-
    lar; he is best when majestic, not simple. Criticizes his
    odes, sonnets, and blank verse. Jeffrey's criticism of
    The Excursion is sagacious; now Wordsworth is considered
    faultless. Though excelling as a meditative and descriptive
    poet, he lacks largeness of mind, versatility, and critical
    judgment of his own powers. He gives false importance to
    trivial facts, and often inserts prosaic matter into ele-
    vated passages. (Reprinted from a Calcutta periodical not
    located.) Expanded in 1852.B25.

11 TALFOURD, THOMAS NOON, ed. Final Memorials of Charles Lamb:
    Consisting Chiefly of His Letters not before Published,
    with Sketches of Some of His Companions. 2 vols. London:
    Moxon, passim.

1848

Expresses his friendship for Wordsworth and admiration of his poems; records Lamb's championing of Wordsworth's genius. Includes letters in which Lamb records his delight in Wordsworth's poems; criticizes individual poems in Lyrical Ballads; objects to Wordsworth's revisions in Poems (1815) (including to "The Blind Highland Boy"), to "Yarrow Visited," and to "The Reverie of Poor Susan"; praises "Essay upon Epitaphs," "The Force of Prayer" and The Excursion; records Gifford's alterations in his review of The Excursion; records proofreading for Wordsworth; and complains of the forced humor and style of Peter Bell.

12   TOOVY, ALFRED DIXON. "Preface," in Biographical and Critical Notices of the British Poets of the Present Century, with Specimens of their Poetry. London: Kent and Richards, pp. i-xii (iii-x).
Wordsworth, in his simplicity, has given a healthy tone to poetry, though his poems are frequently too abstract and devoid of human interest.

1849 A BOOKS - NONE

1849 B SHORTER WRITINGS

1   ANON. "William Wordsworth." Hogg's Instructor, NS 3:353-54.
A biographical sketch. Wordsworth's merits have now overcome the critics' ridicule. His poetic theories formed no part of his genius. His "life has been a poetic reverie."

2   [BARTON, LUCY, ed.]. Selections from the Poems and Letters of Bernard Barton. Edited by his Daughter. London: Hall, Virtue, pp. 8, 79, 109.
Includes letters in which B. Barton refers to Wordsworth as "Daddy" and Southey describes Wordsworth as an admirable man, conversationalist, and poet.

3   [CHRETIEN, CHARLES PETER]. Review of Tennyson's The Princess. Christian Remembrancer, NS 17 (April), 381-401 (381, 395-96).
Wordsworth and Tennyson agree on the vocation of a poet. Wordsworth's poems do not exemplify the Preface to Lyrical Ballads. Attribution: Isobel Armstrong, Victorian Scrutinies: Reviews of Poetry 1830-1870 (London: Athlone Press of Univ. of London, 1972), p. 200.

4   [DE VERE, AUBREY THOMAS]. Review of Taylor's The Eve of the Conquest. Edinburgh Review, 89 (April), 352-80 (359, 369).

Wordsworth feels "more for man than for men"; the natural
world he celebrates is unfallen. His poetry is impassioned.

5   [DE VERE, AUBREY THOMAS]. Review of Tennyson's The Princess,
     The Poetical Works of Percy Bysshe Shelley, and Life,
     Letters, and Literary Remains of John Keats. Edinburgh
     Review, 90 (October), 388-433 (418).
          Wordsworth and Coleridge are poets of thought; in Words-
     worth the meditative prevails. Both lack versatility. Con-
     densed and recast as "The Two Chief Schools of English Po-
     etry" in 1887.B19.

6   FRANK, PARSON. "On Wordsworth's 'Lucy.'" People's & Howitt's
     Journal, [NS 1 (November 1849),] 292-94.
          Wordsworth, the poet of common life, blends the ideal
     and the real in his portraits of women, especially in the
     pathetic "She dwelt among the untrodden ways."

7   [GIBSON, ALEXANDER CRAIG]. The Old Man; or Ravings and
     Ramblings Round Conistone. London: Whittaker; Kendal:
     Hudson, passim.
          Admits Wordsworth "is a true poet, with all his whims,"
     but objects to his opinions, including those on whitewash,
     industry, and Robert Walker. His portraits of dalesmen are
     fanciful rather than true. (Originally published serially
     in the Kendal Mercury.)

8   LANDOR, WALTER SAVAGE. "To the Author of Festus, on the
     Classick and Romantick" (poem). Examiner, no. 2187
     (29 December), p. 821.
          "Wordsworth, in sonnet, is a classick," though his longer
     poems are tedious. Reprinted with additions in 1853.B17.

9   [MOGRIDGE, GEORGE]. Loiterings among the Lakes of Cumberland
     and Westmoreland. By the Author of "Wanderings in the Isle
     of Wight." London: Religious Tract Society [1849],
     especially pp. 27-30, 35-36, 45-48, 157.
          Characters discuss and praise Wordsworth's descriptions
     of scenes in the Lake District, recount meeting Wordsworth.
     Attribution: British Museum catalogue.

10   POWELL, THOMAS. The Living Authors of England. New York:
     D. Appleton; Philadelphia: Geo. S. Appleton, pp. 9, 25-30.
          His poetry did not contain sufficient philosophy to en-
     able Wordsworth to account for the failure of the French
     Revolution. In his later poetry Wordsworth indulges in re-
     grets; he is incapable of humor. Includes a brief primary
     bibliography.

1849

11 SHAW, THOMAS B. Outlines of English Literature. London:
    Murray, pp. 518-26.
        The poets of the Lake School are poetic Quakers. With
    Wordsworth, aesthetics and ethics are inseparable. He
    preaches a Christianized Platonic belief in the life of
    nature. He abandoned in practice his theory of poetic lan-
    guage. His odes are too obscure; The Excursion, though
    lofty, lacks dramatic interest, credible moral spokesmen,
    and variety of language; The White Doe of Rylstone has an
    affected air. "Laodamia" and the sonnets are unsurpassed.
    Revised in 1864.B13.

12 [SMITH, WILLIAM HENRY]. "Tennyson's Poems." Blackwood's
    Edinburgh Magazine, 65 (April), 453-67 (453).
        That Wordsworth is prosaic, especially when writing on
    ecclesiastical themes, no longer disturbs critics; his fame
    is secure.

13 TAYLOR, HENRY. "The Poetical Works of Mr. Wordsworth," "Mr.
    Wordsworth's Sonnets," in Notes from Books: In Four Essays.
    London: Murray, pp. 1-90, 91-186.
        Revised from 1834.B27 (1-90). Revised from 1841.B16
    (91-186). Again revised in 1878.B25.

14 [WILSON, JOHN]. "Dies Boreales: No. I." Blackwood's
    Edinburgh Magazine, 65 (June), 742-67 (764-66).
        Opposes Wordsworth's argument in the Preface to Lyrical
    Ballads on meter and the language of poetry. Wordsworth,
    uniquely, has made one song of his life.

15 WOODWARD, THE REV. THOMAS. "Memoir," in Sermons, Doctrinal
    and Practical. By the Rev. William Archer Butler. Edited
    by the Rev. Thomas Woodward. Dublin: Hodges and Smith,
    pp. i-xlix (xxvii-xxx, xxxv).
        Includes letter from R. P. Graves describing Butler's
    visit with Wordsworth in 1844, and Wordsworth's praise of
    Byron and Shelley.

1850 A BOOKS - NONE

1850 B SHORTER WRITINGS

1 ANON. "Wordsworth the Poet." Chambers' Edinburgh Journal,
   NS 13 (9 February), 96.
       Only once was Wordsworth's sense of smell awakened.

1850

2   ANON. "Death of the Poet Wordsworth." Illustrated London
    News, 16 (27 April), 296.
        A biographical sketch. Like his writings, Wordsworth's
    life was blameless.

3   ANON. "Death of William Wordsworth." Examiner, no. 2204
    (27 April), p. 265.
        A biographical sketch.

4   ANON. "Death of Wordsworth." Examiner, no. 2204 (27 April),
    p. 259.
        "Rarely has a human life closed on purposes so fully ac-
    complished." Only a few are still living who felt Words-
    worth's power when he was scoffed at by critics.

5   ANON. "William Wordsworth." Athenaeum, no. 1174 (27 April),
    pp. 447-48.
        A biographical sketch. Wordsworth's admirers have
    carried their idolatry too far; but Wordsworth's style and
    his sonnets deserve praise.

6   ANON. "William Wordsworth." Literary Gazette, no. 1736
    (27 April), p. 299.
        The difference between Wordsworth, Coleridge, and Southey
    was great. Wordsworth possessed "an undergrowth of
    pleasantry."

7   ANON. Review of Poetical Works (1849-50). Christian Observer,
    NS no. 149 (May), pp. 307-20.
        Wordsworth, earnest and serious in purpose, exquisitely
    adapts scene and character to his thoughts in The Excursion,
    though the poem raises questions that demand a higher solu-
    tion than they receive.

8   ANON. "Wordsworth." Democratic Review of British and Foreign
    Politics, History, & Literature, 1 (May), 473.
        Wordsworth dies unregretted by those "who have no tears
    for the salaried slave of Aristocracy and pensioned parasite
    of Monarchy."

9   ANON. "William Wordsworth." Critic: the London Literary
    Journal, NS 9 (1 May), 230-31.
        A biographical sketch and obituary, reprinted from the
    Morning Chronicle of 25 April.

10   ANON. "Funeral of the Poet Laureate." Court Journal,
    NS no. 112 (11 May), p. 294.
        "A long procession of carriages and horsemen" attended
    Wordsworth's funeral.

1850

11   ANON. "William Wordsworth." London Journal, 11 (25 May), 190.
      A biographical sketch. Wordsworth aimed to revive a
      taste for the simple and artless, portrayed childhood with
      rare sympathy.

12   ANON. "Religious Character of Wordsworth's Poetry."
      Christian Observer, NS no. 150 (June), pp. 381-82.
      Wordsworth's genius was always pure, serious, and noble.
      Includes letter in response to 1850.B7 pointing out that
      Wordsworth did add Christian references to the text of The
      Excursion printed in 1846.

13   ANON. Review of The Life and Correspondence of Robert Southey.
      Gentleman's Magazine, NS 33 (June), 611-19 (617-18).
      Records Canning's opinion of the eloquence of Concerning
      . . . the Convention of Cintra. Campbell has not borrowed
      from Wordsworth in Gertrude of Wyoming.

14   ANON. "William Wordsworth, Esq." Gentleman's Magazine,
      NS 33 (June), 668-72.
      A biographical sketch, including encomium reprinted from
      the Times of 25 April: Wordsworth has purified and ele-
      vated humanity.

15   ANON. Editor's Note. Chambers' Edinburgh Journal, NS 13
      (8 June), 366.
      Wordsworth is singularly deficient in "kindness of
      heart": his poems are purely intellectual.

16   ANON. "The Poetry of Wordsworth" (poem). Dublin University
      Magazine, 36 (July), 52.
      Praises Wordsworth's "holy tranquillizing power."

17   ANON. "William Wordsworth." Tait's Edinburgh Magazine,
      NS 17 (July), 393-98.
      Wordsworth's mind was more one-sided, more based in ex-
      perience, than Goethe's. Wordsworth confused the true
      limits of poetry and prose. He was ruled by "educated im-
      pulses" rather than "scholarlike objective criticism" of
      his art, by didactic rather than artistic motives. The Ex-
      cursion exhibits no powers not equally prominent in his
      shorter poems, which center around "simple but unexpected
      association." In The White Doe of Rylstone he traces a
      simple picture of female purity confronted by real life.

18   ANON. Review of The Prelude. Examiner, no. 2217 (27 July),
      pp. 478-79.

1850

Wordsworth was a true poet despite his poetic theory.
He lacked sympathy with and knowledge of men. There is
real vitality in the theme of The Prelude. Wordsworth's
muse was Jacobinical; when his politics changed, his poetry
fell off.

19   ANON. "A Visit to the Lakes." Ainsworth's Magazine, 18
      (August), 137-45 (137, 140-42).
          Describes meeting Wordsworth and the tourists' passion
      for seeing him.

20   ANON. "Wordsworth's Posthumous Poem." Fraser's Magazine, 42
      (August), 119-32.
          In The Prelude Wordsworth writes of trite subjects con-
      cerning London. His poetry has purified public taste. His
      earliest works tend to pantheism. His prose in Concerning
      . . . the Convention of Cintra is majestic and elevated.

21   ANON. Review of The Prelude. Athenaeum, no. 1188 (3 August),
      pp. 805-807.
          The Prelude exhibits Wordsworth's "easy and somewhat
      amusing egotism" and the influence of Milton.

22   ANON. Review of The Prelude. Literary Gazette, no. 1750
      (3 August), 513-15.
          Wordsworth studies nature, not man, the real, not the
      ideal. The Prelude contains the "playful feature" distinc-
      tive of Wordsworth.

23   ANON. Review of The Prelude. Spectator, 23 (3 August),
      738-39.
          The Prelude would have benefitted from shortening and
      the inclusion of more real biographical facts.

24   ANON. Review of The Prelude. Critic: the London Literary
      Journal, NS 9 (15 August), 402-404.
          The Prelude, more than The Excursion, is complete in it-
      self, Wordsworth's greatest work. His genius was reflec-
      tive.

25   ANON. Review of The Prelude. Tait's Edinburgh Magazine,
      NS 17 (September), 521-27.
          In The Prelude Wordsworth is prolix, careless of phrase,
      and trivial in subjects. He dwells long on the sports of
      childhood, but inconsistently dismisses the pleasures of
      later youth. As a poet he lacked versatility, yet his
      gentle concerns soothe the troubled spirit.

165

1850

26 ANON. "The New Poem by Wordsworth." Dublin University
    Magazine, 36 (September), 329-37.
       Public appreciation of Wordsworth's poems has grown
    slowly. Wordsworth teaches that simple circumstances can
    be noble. The Prelude is at times prosaic and solemn; it
    does not reveal how Wordsworth's poetic mind was formed.
    Wordsworth never expected his pantheism to take the place
    of Christianity. He differs from Burns and Scott. The
    Prelude abounds with instructive and elevated poetry.

27 ANON. Review of The Prelude. Christian Remembrancer, NS 20
    (October), 332-73.
       Wordsworth has advanced the cause of common brotherhood
    and raised us above ourselves towards God: The Prelude,
    though a noble search into the mysterious sources of power,
    shows us nothing new about Wordsworth. One must doubt the
    propriety of such a self-analysis that ends in self-appre-
    ciation.

28 ANON. "The Poetry of Wordsworth." Wesleyan-Methodist
    Magazine, 4th ser., 6 (October), 1074-83; (November),
    1192-99; (December), 1305-13.
       Wordsworth's higher efforts have failed because of his
    didactic purpose (1074-83). The Excursion fails because of
    its philosophic character, its imperfect fable, and its
    prosaic blank verse. Wordsworth often utters "semi-heathen
    sentiments" (1192-99). His smaller poems exhibit "variety
    of sentiment and corresponding interest of character,"
    though in some he mistakes the vulgar and the trivial for
    the universal and the true. He succeeds in "The Old Cum-
    berland Beggar," his classical poems, and his sonnets
    (1305-13).

29 ANON. Review of The Prelude. Eclectic Review, 4th ser., 28
    (November), 550-62.
       Wordsworth's autobiography contrasts with that in Sartor
    Resartus. Wordsworth's "sole sin lies in loving nature too
    well"; they who now criticize Wordsworth are misguided. In
    The Prelude his purpose is more metaphysical than biographi-
    cal. He subordinates the materials of art to art itself.
    He is both like and unlike Milton.

30 ANON. "Wordsworth's Autobiographical Poem." Gentleman's
    Magazine, NS 34 (November), 459-68.
       The Prelude, which must be approached as a product of
    the past, contains Wordsworth's characteristic defects:
    laxity of phrase, want of precision in form, and absence of
    vital sympathy with men. It resembles Cowper's The Task.

1850

31 ANON. Review of The Prelude. British Quarterly Review, 12
      (1 November), 549-79.
        The lack of description in The Prelude of his school life
      indicates Wordsworth's early sternness. Wordsworth mistook
      his own genius for a type; he defined nature too narrowly.
      The chief novelty in The Prelude lies in the Books about
      France. Wordsworth possessed a mind more meagre and didac-
      tic than Goethe's.

32 ANON. "Wordsworth's 'Prelude.'" Ainsworth's Magazine, 18
      (December), 558-59.
        Wordsworth is the greatest of the metaphysical poets,
      especially in The Excursion.

33 ANON. "Gems of Modern English Poetry: Peter Bell." Hogg's
      Instructor, NS 5:321-23.
        In Peter Bell the "large-hearted Wordsworth" speaks a
      familiar truth: that sorrow redeems man; he presents half
      the theme of Coleridge's "The Rime of the Ancient Mariner."

34 ANON. "Recent Poetry: Kingsley; Trench; Burbidge and Clough."
      Prospective Review, 6:112-37 (123, 127, 132-33).
        Though lacking poetical gifts, Wordsworth threw off ele-
      vated thoughts, arising from his innocent and holy life.

35 ANON. Review of The Prelude. Sharpe's London Journal,
      12:185-92.
        Wordsworth's poetic theories, centered upon the vulgar,
      have been salutary. The Prelude contains excellent single
      passages, though much of the later books is flat and
      common-place.

36 ANON. "William Wordsworth." Chambers's Papers for the
      People, 5, no. 40.
        A biographical sketch. Wordsworth lacks a sense of
      smell and the stronger passions. His life was a continuous
      development of a passion for nature. Reprinted in 1887.B9.

37 ANON. "William Wordsworth." Sharpe's London Journal,
      11:349-53.
        Records meeting Wordsworth and his "quiet satisfaction"
      at his poetic success. His life and writings were in har-
      mony. A biographical sketch.

38 ANON. "Notes," in The Prelude, or Growth of a Poet's Mind;
      An Autobiographical Poem. By William Wordsworth. London:
      Moxon, pp. 373-74.
        Brief critical notes to The Prelude.

1850

39   ANON. "Rydal Head.--Windermere" (poem), "Rydal.--April 23,
      1850" (poem), "Rydal Head from Windermere.--1847" (poem),
      in Hand-book of Verse for the English Lakes. London:
      Rivington [1850], pp. 6-7, 141-42, 150-51.
          Wordsworth "wrote no line he need to blot" (6-7). His
      life was peaceful, though shaken by sorrow (141-42); he
      has persisted, in lonely strength, to be revered at last
      (150-51).

40   A.[RNOLD, MATTHEW]. "Memorial Verses: April 27, 1850."
      Fraser's Magazine, 41 (June), 630.
          Wordsworth's poems shed a "healing power," the "freshness
      of the early world," and made men feel. Reprinted with
      verbal changes and omissions in 1852.B7.

41   ATKINSON, GEORGE. The Worthies of Westmorland: or, Notable
      Persons Born in That Country since The Reformation.
      2 vols. London: Robinson, II:346-48.
          Corrects the story of Wordsworth and Coleridge trying
      to puzzle John Gough over the identification of a plant.

42   BIGG, J. STANYAN. "Death of the Poet Laureate." Soulby's
      Ulverston Advertiser, no. 90 (25 April), p. 3.
          A biographical sketch. Wordsworth saw nature as the
      revelation of God.

43   BUSSEY, G. MOIR. "William Wordsworth." People's & Howitt's
      Journal, [NS] 2 [May 1850], 277-80.
          A biographical sketch. Wordsworth chose not to sacri-
      fice his beliefs to obtain poetic fame.

44   [CARTER, JOHN]. "Advertisement," in The Prelude, or Growth
      of a Poet's Mind; An Autobiographical Poem. By William
      Wordsworth. London: Moxon, pp. v-viii.
          The materials that would have formed the third part of
      "The Recluse" have been incorporated in Wordsworth's other
      poems written after The Excursion.

45   [COLERIDGE, SARA]. "Introduction," in Essays on His Own
      Times: Forming a Second Series of The Friend. By Samuel
      Taylor Coleridge. Edited by his Daughter. 3 vols.
      London: Pickering, I:xix-xciii (lxii-lxiii).
          Praises Postscript (1835).

46   COOPER, THOMAS. "A Reminiscence of Wordsworth." Cooper's
      Journal, 1 (11 May), 291-92; (25 May), 324-25.
          Records visit with Wordsworth in 1846: Wordsworth's
      conversation supporting Chartism but opposed to physical

force, his jealousy of Byron (291-92), his discussion of
French politics, and his praise of Tennyson (324-25). Reprinted in The Life of Thomas Cooper (1872).

47 CORNLAW RHYMER, THE. See 1850.B51, B68.

48 COSMOPOLITAN, A. See 1850.B49.

49 [DIX, JOHN] A COSMOPOLITAN. "A Sketching Party: No. II,"
in Pen and Ink Sketches of Eminent English Personages.
London: Pratt, pp. 85-93 (92-93).
Records meeting Wordsworth during a visit to Goodrich
Castle; criticizes him for his reported rudeness to Ameri-
can visitors. (Originally published in the Boston Atlas.)
Attribution: Bodleian catalogue.

50 E*. Review of The Prelude. Westminster and Foreign Quarterly
Review, 54 (October), 271-77.
Wordsworth in The Prelude characteristically presents,
in the manner of a metaphysician rather than a poet, the
truth "that the earth is adorned with beauty to win man to
good." Wordsworth finds good even in pain.

51 [ELLIOTT, EBENEZER] THE CORNLAW RHYMER. "A Lecture on the
Principle that Poetry is Self-Communion: Written for the
Hull Mechanics' Institute," "A Lecture on the Poets who
Succeeded Milton, and Preceded Cowper and Burns: Written
for the Sheffield Mechanics' Institution," "A Lecture on
Cowper and Burns, the two Earliest Great Poets of the
Modern School: Written for the Sheffield Mechanics' Institution," in More Verse and Prose. 2 vols. London:
Fox, II:125-57 (139, 148-50), 158-90 (161, 172, 181),
191-220 (195-96).
Wordsworth's practice refutes his theory in Essay (1815)
that poetry should represent not things as they are but as
they seem to be. His descriptions "express the very soul
of the scenes described" (139, 148-50). He erred in "London, 1802": Milton did not dwell apart from the great men
of his time. His poetry is both literal and ideal; he has
succeeded more than other poets in telling a tale of common
life in rhyme (161, 172, 181). His simplicity is affected
(195-96).

52 F., R. "Visit to Wordsworth's Grave." Literary Gazette,
no. 1754 (31 August), p. 641.
Describes rush-bearing ceremony and visit to Wordsworth's grave.

1850

53   [GILFILLAN, GEORGE]. Review of The Poetical Works of William
       Wordsworth. Eclectic Review, 4th ser., 28 (July), 56-68.
         Wordsworth's spiritual transfiguration of nature must
       not be confounded with pantheism. His poems are fragmen-
       tary, leaving much untold. He should not have tried to
       justify his works in prefaces. He did not sympathize suf-
       ficiently with modern life. Attribution: George Harris
       Healey, ed., The Cornell Wordsworth Collection . . .
       (Ithaca: Cornell Univ. Press, 1957), p. 155.

54   HOLT, DAVID. "Lines on the Death of Wordsworth," in A Lay of
       Hero Worship and Other Poems. London: Pickering,
       pp. 120-22.
         Wordsworth, a poet of "sublime simplicity," has given
       "The lofty moral of thy spotless life."

55   HUNT, LEIGH. The Autobiography of Leigh Hunt; with
       Reminiscences of Friends and Contemporaries. 3 vols.
       London: Smith, Elder, I:49; II:41, 103-104, 112, 163-67,
       208, 320, 323, 326-28.
         Records his opinions of Wordsworth (including his move-
       ment from detraction, in "The Feast of the Poets," to ad-
       miration upon reading the poems for himself), his visits
       with Wordsworth in 1815 and the 1840's (Wordsworth's criti-
       cism of his contemporary poets), and his feeling that Words-
       worth never reciprocated his aid. Revised with omissions
       in 1860.B10.

56   HUNTER, JOSEPH. "The Genealogical Oak Press in the Possession
       of the Poet Wordsworth." Gentleman's Magazine, NS 34
       (July), 43-44.
         Describes the oak press and Wordsworth's taking posses-
       sion of it.

57   [KINGSLEY, CHARLES]. "Tennyson." Fraser's Magazine, 42
       (September), 245-55 (246-47, 249).
         Though he believed Nature revealed the divine, Wordsworth
       did not always "leave her to reveal her own mystery." It
       is remarkable that he rose so high, "considering the level
       on which his taste was formed." "Like all fanatics, Words-
       worth was better than his own creed." Tennyson's descrip-
       tion excels Wordsworth's. Reprinted in Miscellanies
       (1859).

58   LANDOR, WALTER SAVAGE. "English Hexameters" (poem). Fraser's
       Magazine, 42 (July), 62-63 (63).
         Wordsworth stands out, though he is at times wordy,
       feeble, and too tame. Expanded in 1853.B17.

59   LANDOR, WALTER SAVAGE. "Walter Savage Landor, Esq. to the
      Rev. C. Cuthbert Southey, Curate of Plumbland." Fraser's
      Magazine, 42 (December), 647-50 (648-49).
          Wordsworth is less philosophical and more narrow than
      Southey, excels in description, may be compared with Cow-
      per. The Excursion is a collection of small poems. Re-
      printed with brief addition as "To the Reverend Charles
      Cuthbert Southey on his Father's Character and Public Ser-
      vices" in 1853.B17.

60   [LANDOR, WALTER SAVAGE]. Review of Lumley's The Burden of the
      Bell. Examiner, no. 2236 (7 December), pp. 782-83 (783).
          Wordsworth's works are not incomparable.

61   MARTINEAU, HARRIET. The History of England during the Thirty
      Years' Peace: 1816-1846. 2 vols. London: Knight,
      II:545-46, 702.
          If he were to die, Wordsworth would be deprived by the
      existing copyright law of all benefits from sales of his
      works. He rescued poetry from "a misleading conventional-
      ism."

62   [MASSON, DAVID]. Review of Poetical Works (1849-50). North
      British Review, 13 (August), 473-508.
          Wordsworth's theory of diction errs by exaggeration.
      His poetry, a revolt from that of the previous age, is dis-
      tinguished by imagination, sensibility to external nature,
      intellectual vigor blended with a contemplative, religious
      tone, a sense of tradition, and mastery of language. Yet
      Wordsworth lacked the highest intellect, humor, and ener-
      getic passion. Reprinted in Essays, Biographical and Criti-
      cal (1856) and Wordsworth, Shelley, Keats, and Other Essays
      (1874).

63   P., L. "On Reading in India of the Death of Wordsworth"
      (poem). Examiner, no. 2218 (3 August), p. 495.
          Wordsworth's teaching melts hearts.

64   R., C. "Wordsworth and His Poetry." Chambers' Edinburgh
      Journal, NS 13 (8 June), 363-66.
          A biographical sketch. Wordsworth's own efforts should
      have convinced him of the impracticability of his poetic
      theory; he lived with a sense of morbid disappointment at
      its failure. His subject is not nature but himself. He is
      either too plain or too deep to be popular.

65   SCRYMGEOUR, DANIEL. "William Wordsworth," in The Poetry and
      Poets of Britain, from Chaucer to Tennyson. . . . Edited
      by Daniel Scrymgeour. Edinburgh: Black, pp. 368-76.

1850

Wordsworth's perseverance against ridicule has been re-
warded. In The Excursion Wordsworth aims "to encourage the
hopes of the wretched beyond the grave"; the thought is often obscure but the pictures of solitude are beautiful. In
his poetry "the soul of man animates nature." Includes
critical notes to "'Weak is the will of Man, his judgment
blind,'" and "Ode: Intimations of Immortality." Revised
in 1852.B27.

66   SEDGWICK, ADAM. A Discourse on the Studies of the University
      of Cambridge. Fifth edition. London: Parker; Cambridge:
      Deighton, pp. 315-18.
          Wordsworth effected a revolution in taste; his natural,
      lofty poetry gives happiness to its readers. His judgments
      of Cambridge in The Prelude were not wise ones. He did not
      forget nature's God. He was consoled in old age by knowing
      his poems do not pander to base passions.

67   SOUTHEY, THE REV. CHARLES CUTHBERT, ed. The Life and
      Correspondence of Robert Southey. Edited by his Son.
      6 vols. London: Longman, II-VI (passim).
          Records Southey's intercourse with Wordsworth. Includes
      letters in which Southey praises the plain and wholesome
      Lyrical Ballads, questions if Wordsworth's associations are
      not too particular, records that Wordsworth was considered
      a dangerous Jacobin in 1805, praises Poems (1807), comments
      that Wordsworth fails in Concerning . . . the Convention of
      Cintra because of his admiration of Milton and his habit of
      dictating, praises The Excursion, and records Wordsworth's
      political fears in 1832 and his participation in the Mars-
      den case in 1836. Includes Shelton Mackenzie's recollec-
      tions of the Marsden case.

68   SOUTHEY, ROBERT. "Critique, Written by the Late Robert
      Southey for the Quarterly Review, but Rejected by the
      Editor, after the Author had Corrected a Proof for the
      Press," in More Verse and Prose. By the Cornlaw Rhymer
      [Ebenezer Elliott]. 2 vols. London: Fox, II:81-116
      (86, 90).
          "No other poet ever produced so great an effect upon the
      style of his contemporaries, and the mind of the rising
      generation," as Wordsworth.

69   TUPPER, MARTIN F. "Wordsworth" (poem). Court Journal,
      NS no. 112 (11 May), p. 294.
          Wordsworth communed with nature in love, taught men to
      turn from lurid passion to pure, lowly things.

1851

70   W.(L.). "Translations of Juvenal--Wordsworth." Notes and
     Queries, 2 (3 August), 145-46.
          Records Wordsworth's praise of Dryden's translation of
     Juvenal. Wordsworth admitted the absurdity of the "party
     in a parlour" stanza in Peter Bell.

71   [WEIR, WILLIAM]. "William Wordsworth." Household Words, 1
     (25 May), 210-13.
          A biographical sketch. In contrast to the stirring age
     in which he lived, Wordsworth's poetry is passionless.
     Peter Bell and The Waggoner, though written in "genuine
     racy English," differ from the mode of Burns. Wordsworth's
     genius was moralizing and reflective; his blank verse was
     imperfect.

72   [WILSON, JOHN]. "Dies Boreales: No. VIII." Blackwood's
     Edinburgh Magazine, 68 (October), 479-98 (490).
          Criticizes Wordsworth's statement that poetry should have
     good sense.

1851 A BOOKS

1   WORDSWORTH, CHRISTOPHER. Memoirs of William Wordsworth.
     2 vols. London: Moxon, 469 pp; 532 pp.
          A full "biographical manual, designed to illustrate the
     poems." Includes accounts by Dr. James Satterthwaite of
     Wordsworth's fall from his horse in 1822; by the Rev. R. P.
     Graves of Wordsworth's reaction to Coleridge's death and of
     his conversation on sacred poetry, the reality of the ex-
     ternal world, and other poets; by John Taylor Coleridge of
     Wordsworth in 1836; by H. C. Robinson of Wordsworth's tour
     of Italy in 1837; by Lady Richardson of Wordsworth on
     Goethe, literary criticism, marriage, the separation of
     rich and poor, Coleridge, Scott, and Burns, and of Words-
     worth's birthday celebration in 1844 and visits with Words-
     worth in 1844-46; by Mrs. Davy of Wordsworth's remarks in
     the 1840's on college habits, Coleridge, and Christianity;
     by Christopher Wordsworth of Wordsworth's conversation on
     literary subjects; and by Ellis Yarnall of a visit to Rydal
     in 1849, including Wordsworth's conversation on his life in
     France. Includes annotations by the Rev. Alexander Dyce,
     the Rev. Henry Alford, and John Peace of their letters to
     Wordsworth. Prints extracts from Dorothy Wordsworth's let-
     ters and journals; poem by S. T. Coleridge addressed to
     Wordsworth, "William, my teacher, my friend! dear William
     and dear Dorothea!": calls Wordsworth "my head and my
     heart!"; letter of C. J. Fox expressing his pleasure at

1851

> Lyrical Ballads; Robert Montgomery's verse testimony to
> Wordsworth's unlocking of the spiritual and moral signifi-
> cance of nature, "Lines Written after a Visit to Words-
> worth"; and an excerpt from John Keble's oration when Words-
> worth received his honorary degree at Oxford in 1839, in
> which Keble praises Wordsworth's portrayal of the poor.

1851 B SHORTER WRITINGS

1 ANON. Review of C. Wordsworth's Memoirs of William Wordsworth.
   Examiner, no. 2255 (19 April), pp. 244-46.
     Wordsworth does not display ordinary egotism. His ear-
   lier political views will outlive his later ones. He lacked
   contact with men.

2 ANON. "Dr. Wordsworth's Memoirs of William Wordsworth."
   Spectator, 24 (26 April), 399-400.
     A biographical sketch. Wordsworth's life was uneventful,
   preoccupied with poetry. Wordsworth's originality lies not
   in his opposition to certain practices of eighteenth-century
   poets but in his fresh observation, deep feelings and sympathies, felicitous language, and "recognition of humanity
   in the human creature."

3 ANON. Review of C. Wordsworth's Memoirs of William Wordsworth.
   Athenaeum, no. 1226 (26 April), pp. 445-47; no. 1227
   (3 May), pp. 475-77.
     Wordsworth should not be likened to Milton (445-47). He
   was especially stung to self-defense by charges of care-
   lessness of diction. Though he seldom wrote, his letters
   are as carefully composed as poems. He argued with limited
   success on social topics (475-77).

4 ANON. Review of C. Wordsworth's Memoirs of William Wordsworth.
   Literary Gazette, no. 1788 (26 April), pp. 293-95.
     Wordsworth's life was uneventful, visited by few calami-
   ties; his correspondence is uninteresting. He failed to
   recognize poetic genius different from his own.

5 ANON. Review of C. Wordsworth's Memoirs of William Wordsworth.
   Critic: the London Literary Journal, NS 10 (15 May),
   226-28.
     Wordsworth, not a man of the world or a vivacious writer
   of letters, provides little material for a biography. A
   biographical sketch. His later political conservatism was
   never rancorous.

6   ANON. Review of C. Wordsworth's Memoirs of William Wordsworth.
     Tait's Edinburgh Magazine, NS 18 (June), 368-70.
         Wordsworth's life was the very type of respectability.
     His prose is even more prosaic than his poetry. Wordsworth
     clung with unworthy tenacity to his political and religious
     prejudices.

7   ANON. "Wordsworth's Life." Dublin University Magazine, 38
     (July), 77-94.
         Wordsworth has exercised greater influence on English
     poetry than any of his contemporaries. A biographical
     sketch.

8   ANON. "William Wordsworth." Gentleman's Magazine, NS 36
     (August), 107-16.
         Wordsworth's life was poetic, content. Wordsworth spoke
     coldly of his contemporary poets, protested too much
     against his critical reception. He did lose his early po-
     litical and religious hopes.

9   ANON. "Poetry--Sacred and Profane." Nottinghamshire Guardian,
     no. 291 (30 October), p. 2.
         Wordsworth ministers to our pure delight; it is unfair
     to dwell on his early puerilities.

10   ANON. "Wordsworth: The Prelude." Prospective Review,
     7:94-131.
         In Wordsworth "the Poet and the Philosopher are never
     wholly blended" (e.g., in The Excursion). He lacked suf-
     ficient knowledge of man's heart and reverence for God.
     His boyhood compares with Lamartine's. Though often prosy,
     The Prelude reveals an uncharacteristic "fulness of life,"
     "vividness of thought" and "potency of passion."

11   ANON. "William Wordsworth." Poetic Companion, for the
     Fireside, the Fields, the Woods and the Streams, 1:168-73.
         Wordsworth has written with unity of purpose, to ennoble
     simple wisdom. He teaches the intimate relation between
     nature and man. His poetry is serene.

12   ANON. "Wordsworth, William," in The National Cyclopaedia of
     Useful Knowledge. 12 vols. London: Knight, XII:967-68.
         A biographical sketch.

13   [BRIMLEY, GEORGE]. "Wordsworth." Fraser's Magazine, 44
     (July), 101-18 (101-102, 106-18); (August), 186-98.
         A biographical sketch. Wordsworth's pure poetry re-
     vealed the glory of the material world and man's high moral

175

function. It works to obliterate distinctions between rich
and poor. Wordsworth asserts "a science of appearances,
speaking through the senses to the heart, acting on and
acted upon by the imagination." He would have understood
men better had he partaken more in the pleasures of the
world. Those few of his poems in which he does follow the
theories of the Preface to Lyrical Ballads are his poorest
(101-102, 106-18). His range of reading was limited. He
was not the negative character portrayed by C. Wordsworth
(186-98).

14 C. "Influence of Higher upon Inferior Natures." Christian
    Observer, NS no. 160 (April), 219-25 (219-20).
        In The White Doe of Rylstone Wordsworth brings an in-
    ferior animal too nearly up to the level of man.

15 [COLERIDGE, DERWENT]. "Memoir of Hartley Coleridge," in
    Poems. By Hartley Coleridge. With a Memoir of His Life by
    his Brother. 2 vols. London: Moxon, I:ix-ccxv (passim).
        Records Wordsworth's intercourse with and influence on
    Hartley Coleridge. Includes C. H. Townshend's reminiscences
    of Hartley's reciting of "Resolution and Independence."

16 COLERIDGE, HARTLEY. "On the Poetical Use of the Heathen
    Mythology," "Marginalia," in Essays and Marginalia. Edited
    by his Brother [Derwent Coleridge]. 2 vols. London:
    Moxon, I:18-39 (18); II:3-359 (8, 18-21, 29-30, 101, 110,
    164-65).
        Reprinted from 1822.B25 (I:18). Commends Wordsworth's
    revisions of "The Blind Highland Boy." (In an editorial
    note, Derwent Coleridge disagrees.) Notes parallels in the
    careers of Wordsworth and Milton. Wordsworth's arguments on
    poetic fame are not satisfactory (II:8, 18-21, 29-30, 101,
    110, 164-65).

17 COLERIDGE, HARTLEY. "To Wordsworth" (poem), "To William
    Wordsworth" (poem), "To the Same" (poem), "Rydal" (poem),
    "The Celandine and the Daisy" (poem), "To W. W., on his
    Seventy-fifth Birthday" (poem), in Poems. With a Memoir of
    His Life by his Brother. 2 vols. London: Moxon, I:19,
    158; II:18, 19, 20, 99, 160.
        Reprinted from 1833.B6 (I:19, 158). Wordsworth's poetry
    unites souls, proves "that purest joy is duty" (II:18); it
    binds men together in love (19). His "prose and rhyme" are
    "Too strong for aught but Heaven itself to tame" (20).
    Praises "one mighty bard" (presumably Wordsworth) (99).
    Wordsworth "Sought in all shapes the very form of beauty,"
    wisely pruned his early rash works (160).

1851

18   [CROLLY, GEORGE]. Review of C. Wordsworth's Memoirs of William
      Wordsworth and Poetical Works (1849-50). Dublin Review, 31
      (December), 313-65.
          Wordsworth had the consolation of his family's love dur-
      ing his early unpopularity. His style is sometimes obscure,
      his diction and subjects too plain. He never entirely loses
      touch with reality in his imaginative raptures. He could
      not appreciate poetry unlike his own. A biographical
      sketch. Emily, in The White Doe of Rylstone, should have
      devoted herself to a religious order rather than to the doe.
      Wordsworth recognized the merits of the Roman Catholic
      church.

19   FRANK, PARSON. "'Memoirs of Wordsworth.'" People's and
      Howitt's Journal, NS 4 [May 1851], 289-93.
          A biographical sketch. Despite criticism, Wordsworth
      did not abate in his belief in himself.

20   GILLIES, R.[OBERT] P.[EARSE]. Memoirs of A Literary Veteran;
      including Sketches and Anecdotes of the Most Distinguished
      Literary Characters from 1794 to 1849. 3 vols. London:
      Bentley, I:228-30; II:137-73, 185; III:331.
          Recalls the ridicule that greeted Lyrical Ballads in
      Edinburgh, Wordsworth's visit to Edinburgh in 1814 (Words-
      worth's conviviality, conversation on poets and poetry, and
      criticism of Byron), and Wordsworth's friendship.

21   [GLADSTONE, WILLIAM E.]. Review of C. Wordsworth's Memoirs of
      William Wordsworth. Scottish Ecclesiastical Journal,
      no. 7 (17 July), pp. 151-52.
          His biography testifies to Wordsworth's high purpose.
      Wordsworth quickly transformed observed incidents into
      poems, yet judged them calmly before publishing them. His
      letters show him to be a true Christian, prophetic, leading
      an unblemished life. Attribution: Charles Wordsworth in
      1891.B50, p. 93.

22   GORTON, JOHN. A General Biographical Dictionary. A new
      edition. 4 vols. London: Bohn, IV:481.
          A biographical sketch.

23   HENRY, JAMES. "Wordsworth's Horse" (poem), "Wordsworth and
      the Pig" (poem), in The Unripe Windfalls in Prose and
      Verse. . . . Dublin: University Press, pp. [39-40], [41-42].
          Ridicules Wordsworth's finding poetry in everything.
      Reprinted in 1853.B9.

1851

24   MACKAY, CHARLES. The Scenery and Poetry of the English Lakes:
      A Summer Ramble. Illustrated by Harvey, et al. London:
      Longman, especially pp. 19-45.
        Wordsworth's poems are "meditative, passionless, equable,
      and sometimes elegant: but very often tame." Recounts
      visit to Wordsworth: his conversation on Southey's illness.

25   MAUNDER, SAMUEL. "Wordsworth, William," in The Biographical
      Treasury; A Dictionary of Universal Biography. Seventh
      edition, revised. London: Longman, p. 885.
        A biographical sketch. Briefly expanded in 1866.B9.

26   MEREDITH, GEORGE. "The Poetry of Wordsworth" (poem), in
      Poems. London: Parker [1851], p. 24.
        Wordsworth's poetry is sublime in conception, yet simple.

27   MOIR, D.[AVID] M.[ACBETH]. Sketches of the Poetical Literature
      of the Past Half-Century in Six Lectures Delivered at the
      Edinburgh Philosophical Association. Edinburgh and London:
      Blackwood, pp. 59-82, 89, 91, 129, 160-67, 255-56, 313-14.
        Surveys Wordsworth's life and work. Lyrical Ballads con-
      tains eccentricities and excellencies. "Goody Blake and
      Harry Gill" and "Resolution and Independence" resemble
      paintings. His self-devotion enabled Wordsworth to re-
      store poetry to truth and nature, but hindered him from
      seeing his own failings, including his verbose, exaggerated,
      and silly manner. Like Turner, he leaves out the obvious
      to present the eccentric. He had no prototype; he is his
      own subject. In his pictures he defies perspective, as
      much pleased with the small as the great. The Prelude will
      be remembered not for its philosophy but for the beauty of
      its descriptions. Wordsworth contrasts with Coleridge, in-
      fluenced Byron, must share his claim to originality with
      Joanna Baillie. The Pedlar in The Excursion is incongru-
      ously both pedlar and philosopher.

28   [RUSKIN, JOHN]. Pre-Raphaelitism. By the Author of "Modern
      Painters." London: Smith, Elder, pp. 23, 67-68.
        Wordsworth's self-confidence stiffens his thoughts in
      his prefaces into defiance. In The Excursion (Book III) he
      writes ignorantly of men of science.

29   RUSKIN, JOHN. The Stones of Venice: Volume the First: The
      Foundations. Illustrated by the Author. London: Smith,
      Elder, pp. 240-41 (Chapter xxi, Paragraph 18).
        Commends Wordsworth's observation of the sun rising be-
      hind pine trees.

30   [SMITH, WILLIAM HENRY]. "Mr Ruskin's Works." Blackwood's
      Edinburgh Magazine, 70 (September), 326-48 (346).
          Wordsworth, in contrast to Ruskin, recognizes that all
      natural beauty need not lead to thoughts of God.

31   TENNYSON, ALFRED. "To the Queen" (poem), in Poems. Seventh
      edition. London: Moxon, pp. vii-viii (vii).
          Wordsworth "utter'd nothing base."

32   WRIGHT, JOHN. "Introduction," "The Cat and Kittens: In
      Imitation of Wordsworth" (poem), "On a Fly: In Imitation
      of Wordsworth" (poem), "An Epigram on the Late Poet
      Laureate," "Pastimes with the Late Poet Laureate,
      Wordsworth" (poem) and Notes, in Poetry Sacred and Profane.
      London: Longman, pp. v-xxix, 283-87, 288-89, 289, 290-311,
      336-41.
          "Resolution and Independence" "abounds with self-contra-
      dictions, absurdities, and silly iterations." Wordsworth
      "plodded on in pursuit of his favourite amusement, until
      his claims to preferment could be no longer resisted." His
      poems lack intense, disciplined feeling (e.g., the elegiac
      poems) and solid instruction (e.g., "The Thorn," "Anecdote
      for Fathers"). His knowledge of plants is inaccurate and
      his similies are distasteful. He "exhibits humanity in its
      worst phase." Reprinted in 1853.A1 (v-xxix). Burlesques
      (283-87, 288-89, 290-311, 336-41). Wordsworth's "Works set
      forth / A claim to 'Words,' but none to 'Worth'" (289).

1852 A BOOKS

1   [PHILLIPS, GEORGE SEARLE] JANUARY SEARLE. Memoirs of William
      Wordsworth, Compiled from Authentic Sources. . . . London:
      Partridge & Oakey, 312 pp.
          Wordsworth retired amongst the mountains, regardless of
      censure, to fulfill his mission of winning men back to the
      natural and the common. A full biography. Attribution:
      British Museum catalogue.

2   SEARLE, JANUARY. See 1852.A1.

1852 B SHORTER WRITINGS

1   ALISON, SIR ARCHIBALD. History of Europe from the Fall of
      Napoleon in MDCCCXV to the Accession of Louis Napoleon in
      MDCCCLII. 8 vols. Edinburgh and London: Blackwood,
      I:434-35.
          Less discursive but more profound than Southey, Words-
      worth is less imaginative than Goethe.

1852

2   ANON. Review of Wright's Poetry. Critic, London Literary
     Journal, NS 11 (15 January), 37.
          Wordsworth incongruously mingles ludicrous images with
     the tenderest emotions, lacks narrative and dramatic power,
     classifies his poems whimsically, and is too metaphysical;
     yet he celebrates liberty, writes glorious sonnets and
     other poems when he forgets his theories.

3   ANON. Review of The Poetical Works of Henry Wadsworth
     Longfellow, etc. Church of England Quarterly Review, 31
     (April), 309-27 (312-13).
          Wordsworth typifies the Lake Poets, who affect profundity
     in an obscure or puerile style.

4   ANON. "Bird's-eye View of English Literature in the Nineteenth
     Century." Hogg's Instructor, NS 9:41-42.
          Wordsworth's mind was democratic.

5   ANON. "William Wordsworth." Lives of the Illustrious (The
     Biographical Magazine), 2:1-20.
          A biographical sketch. "Wordsworth's life was eminently
     beautiful and poetic"; he rebelled against the poetry of
     the eighteenth century and persevered, careless of criti-
     cism.

6   ANON. Letters of Percy Bysshe Shelley. With an Introductory
     Essay by Robert Browning. London: Moxon, pp. 82-84.
          Points out the influence of Wordsworth on Childe Harold's
     Pilgrimage (Canto iii). (A forgery; not by Shelley.)

7   A.[RNOLD, MATTHEW]. "Memorial Verses: April, 1850,"
     "Stanzas in Memory of the Author of 'Obermann,'" "The Youth
     of Nature" (poem), in Empedocles on Etna, and Other Poems.
     London: Fellowes, pp. 157-61, 184-95 (187-89), 209-16.
          Reprinted with verbal changes and omissions from 1850.B40
     (157-61). Wordsworth's "eyes avert their ken / From half
     of human fate" (187-89). Wordsworth "Felt the dissolving
     throes / Of a social order he lov'd"; he was the priest
     "Of the wonder and bloom of the world" (209-16).

8   [BAGEHOT, WALTER]. Review of Life of Lord Jeffrey. Inquirer:
     a weekly journal of Religion, Politics, and Literature, 11
     (10 April), 226-27 (227).
          Wordsworth received "the fond enthusiasm of secret stu-
     dents, the lonely rapture of lonely minds"; "he is now
     principally forgotten."

9   [BAGEHOT, WALTER]. Review of H. Coleridge's Lives of the
     Northern Worthies. Prospective Review, 8 (October), 514-44
     (515, 519, 531, 539-42).
          Wordsworth was a heretic, teaching not Anglicanism but
     the sacredness of rugged hills. Reprinted in Estimates of
     Some Englishmen and Scotchmen (1858).

10   [BENNETT, WILLIAM COX]. Verdicts (poem). London: Wilson,
     pp. 43-51.
          Wordsworth, "a genuine reformer and poet," was too
     zealously damned, then too zealously praised. The Excursion
     and the sonnets are dull. Living remote from the world,
     his heart grew cold. Attribution: British Museum catalogue.

11   BURKE, JAMES. The Life of Thomas Moore. . . . Dublin:
     Duffy, p. 60.
          Prints Moore's toast in 1818 to Wordsworth, "a poet,
     even in his puerilities."

12   [CAMPBELL, GEORGE DOUGLAS,] HIS GRACE THE [EIGHTH] DUKE OF
     ARGYLL. "Address Delivered to the Members of the Glasgow
     Athenaeum, On the 21st January, 1851," in The Importance of
     Literature to Men of Business: A Series of Addresses
     Delivered at Various Popular Institutions. London: J.
     Griffin; Glasgow: R. Griffin, pp. 253-78 (271-73).
          Wordsworth never uttered anything that may not nourish
     men's hearts.

13   [CHICHESTER, FREDERICK RICHARD,] EARL OF BELFAST. Poets and
     Poetry of the XIXth Century: a Course of Lectures. London:
     Longman, pp. 9, 13, 20, 35-56.
          Wordsworth's poetry contains at once much to admire and
     to condemn. Wordsworth did not profit from early criticism
     to reform his absurdities, but accepted it with calm indif-
     ference. His life and poetry were pure--perhaps too re-
     moved from passion. He excelled in imagination and fancy,
     and in the study of man and nature, but is too didactic.

14   COCKBURN, [HENRY THOMAS,] LORD [COCKBURN]. Life of Lord
     Jeffrey with a Selection from his Correspondence. 2 vols.
     Edinburgh: Black, I:291-93, 322; II:293.
          Jeffrey was not obstinate or unkind in his treatment of
     Wordsworth. Records Jeffrey's friendship with Wordsworth
     in 1831 and Jeffrey's attack, in a letter of 1837, on Words-
     worth's idealized conception of poverty.

15   COLERIDGE, DERWENT and SARA COLERIDGE. "Notes," in The Poems
     of Samuel Taylor Coleridge. A new edition. Edited by

1852

Derwent and Sara Coleridge. London: Moxon, pp. 379-88
(381, 383-84).
Prints the Rev. Alexander Dyce's recollections of Wordsworth's conversation about his contributions to "The Rime
of the Ancient Mariner."

16 DALLAS, E.[NEAS] S.[WEETLAND]. Poetics: An Essay on Poetry.
London: Smith, Elder, pp. 191-92, 198-205.
Wordsworth has the Ossianic habit "of laying out the
mind as so much ground." Wordsworth's concept of the
imagination is narrow.

17 DE QUINCEY, THOMAS. "Sir William Hamilton, with a Glance at
his Logical Reforms." Hogg's Instructor, NS 9:273-77
(274-75).
Records Wordsworth's curiosity for seeing Belzoni. Reprinted in De Quincey's Writings (1850-59).

18 [ELWIN, WHITWELL]. Review of C. Wordsworth's Memoirs of
William Wordsworth and Searle's Memoirs of William
Wordsworth. Quarterly Review, 92 (December), 182-236.
An extended biographical sketch. Wordsworth descends to
irrelevant trivialities; his portraits of the poor do not
give their true emotions; he is never carried away by his
sympathies. But he does bring man's mind into union with
the inanimate world. For Wordsworth the sonnet becomes a
lute rather than a trumpet. His faulty meter and rhymes
arise from an insufficient command of language. He did not
initiate but followed a literary revolution begun by
eighteenth-century poets; his own particular theories remain universally condemned.

19 [JONES, JOHN] TALHAIARN. Letter to the Editor. Carnarvon and
Denbigh Herald, 22 (6 November), p. 3.
Records visit to Wordsworth in 1844, including pheno-
logical analysis of Wordsworth's head.

20 KNIGHT, CHARLES. "Lecture Delivered at the Opening of the
Sheffield Athenaeum, On the 5th May, 1847," in The
Importance of Literature to Men of Business: A Series of
Addresses Delivered at Various Popular Institutions.
London: J. Griffin; Glasgow: R. Griffin, pp. 158-80
(179).
Wordsworth is the poet of the people.

21 LANDOR, WALTER SAVAGE. "Written at Herstmonceux, On reading
a poem of Wordsworth's" (poem). Examiner, no. 2322
(31 July), p. 485.
Hails Wordsworth. Reprinted in 1853.B17.

182

22 [MASSON, DAVID]. Review of Reynolds's Discourses on the Fine
    Arts, etc. British Quarterly Review, 16 (1 August),
    197-220 (201-207, 213).
        The pre-Raphaelites' innovation in art parallels Words-
    worth's in poetry. Attribution: James Sambrook, Pre-
    Raphaelitism: A Collection of Critical Essays (Chicago and
    London: Univ. of Chicago Press, 1974), p. 71.

23 MITFORD, MARY RUSSELL. Recollections of a Literary Life; or,
    Books, Places, and People. 3 vols. London: Bentley,
    III:19-20.
        Praises the personifications in "Yew-trees."

24 PALMER, ROUNDELL. The Connection of Poetry with History: A
    Lecture, Delivered on Thursday, January 8th, 1852, before
    the Members of the Plymouth Mechanics' Institute. London:
    Whittaker; Plymouth and Devonport: Lidstone, pp. 28-29.
        Wordsworth extracts the good from Rousseau's system; he
    harmonizes the philosophy of sentiment with natural reli-
    gion.

25 RICHARDSON, DAVID LESTER. Literary Recreations or Essays[,]
    Criticisms and Poems Chiefly Written in India. London:
    Thacker, passim.
        Revised and expanded from 1840.B15-B16 and 1848.B10.
    Wordsworth never forgave Jeffrey's good-natured laugh at
    his stylistic peculiarities. His vanity accounts for his
    work being unequal. The Prelude is prosaic.

26 ROBERTSON, THE REV. FRED. W. Two Lectures on the Influence of
    Poetry on the Working Classes, Delivered before the Members
    of the Mechanics' Institution, February, 1852. Brighton:
    King; London: Hamilton, Adams, passim.
        Wordsworth's "mystic obscurity" is a "witness for the
    infinite in the soul of man." He is too calm to be popular.
    As opposed to Shakespeare and Tennyson, he gives "us human-
    ity stript of its peculiarities." Reprinted in 1858.B13.

27 SCRYMGEOUR, DANIEL. "William Wordsworth," in The Poetry and
    Poets of Britain, from Chaucer to Tennyson. . . . Fourth
    edition. Edited by Daniel Scrymgeour. Edinburgh: Black,
    pp. 368-76.
        A biographical sketch, revised from 1850.B65.

28 [SMITH, WILLIAM HENRY]. "Miss Mitford's 'Recollections.'"
    Blackwood's Edinburgh Magazine, 71 (March), 259-72 (268-69).
        Wordsworth shared the desponding spirit of the age but
    overcame it; one rightly deserts Byron for Wordsworth.

1852

29 [SMITH, WILLIAM HENRY]. "Jeffrey: Part II." <u>Blackwood's</u>
    <u>Edinburgh Magazine</u>, 72 (October), 461-78 (461-70).
        Jeffrey's criticism of Wordsworth is just but incomplete,
    though its tone is unpardonable. Wordsworth's alleged ob-
    scurity results from his complex, transcendental philosophy.
    In <u>The Excursion</u> and the Ecclesiastical Sonnets he preaches
    a humanizing and liberalizing creed in which all men can
    unite.

30 TALHAIARN. <u>See</u> 1852.B19.

31 TILLOTSON, JOHN. "William Wordsworth," in <u>Lives of Eminent</u>
    <u>Men: or, Biographical Treasury. . . .</u> <u>Illustrated.</u>
    London: Holmes [c. 1852], pp. 252-63.
        A biographical sketch.

1853 A BOOKS

1 WRIGHT, JOHN. <u>The Genius of Wordsworth Harmonized with the</u>
   <u>Wisdom and Integrity of his Reviewers</u>. London: Longman,
   134 pp.
        A reply to 1851.B9. Reprints "Introduction" from
   1851.B32. Wordsworth confers little honor upon Lucy in
   "She dwelt among the untrodden ways." His intellectual perversion is evident in "Ode: Intimations of Immortality."
   His natural descriptions are vague, his inductions absurd,
   especially in "If this great world of joy and pain," "It
   was an April morning: fresh and clear," "Desponding
   Father! mark this altered bough," and <u>The Excursion</u>. His
   theory of poetic diction and imagery in the Preface to
   <u>Lyrical Ballads</u> is wrong; yet when he does attempt figura-
   tive language, he fails. His purpose in writing was noble,
   though better carried out living in a city. He tolerated
   the vulgar's worst vices. He "wrongly estimated the moral
   susceptibilities of our nature," was insensible to Divine
   truth. It is difficult to determine what he meant by
   "Nature." Bloomfield's poetry is superior to Wordsworth's.

1853 B SHORTER WRITINGS

1 ALFORD, HENRY. "Recollection of Wordsworth's 'Ruth'" (poem),
   "Rydal Mount: June, 1838" (poem), in <u>The Poetical Works</u>
   <u>of Henry Alford</u>. Boston: Ticknor, Reed, and Fields,
   pp. 126, 410.
        Reprinted from 1835.B1 (126). The deep calm of Rydal
   Mount is fitting for Wordsworth (410).

Writings about William Wordsworth, 1793 - 1899

2   ANON. Note. <u>Beautiful Poetry: Selected by the Editors of</u>
    <u>The Critic,</u> <u>London Literary Journal</u>, no. 3 (15 February),
    p. 71.
        Wordsworth sang of the soul of Nature.

3   ANON. Note. <u>Beautiful Poetry: Selected by the Editors of</u>
    <u>The Critic,</u> <u>London Literary Journal</u>, no. 4 (1 March), p. 85.
        Wordsworth does not appeal to the young and impulsive
    but to the reflective.

4   ANON. "What Constitutes a Poet?" <u>Hogg's Instructor</u>,
    NS 10:609-13 (610).
        Wordsworth's calm, self-complacent soliloquies show his
    lack of earnestness and sympathy with men.

5   ANON. "William Wordsworth," in <u>The Book of English Poetry</u>.
    London and Edinburgh: Nelson, pp. 24-25.
        A biographical sketch.

6   AUSTIN, WILTSHIRE STANTON and JOHN RALPH. <u>The Lives of the</u>
    <u>Poets-Laureate: With an Introductory Essay on the Title</u>
    <u>and Office</u>. London: Bentley, pp. 396-428.
        A biographical sketch. Wordsworth's self-reliance and
    sense of mission led both to his beauties and faults. He
    was willful, impulsive, lacking in the critical faculty,
    and original.

7   DE QUINCEY, THOMAS. "Chapter III: Infant Literature," in
    <u>Autobiographic Sketches</u>. [<u>De Quincey's Works</u>, Volume I.]
    London: Hogg, pp. 114-29 (114-15).
        Wordsworth was the first to notice infancy's closeness
    to truth and to the natural world.

8   EDGAR, JOHN G. <u>The Boyhood of Great Men: Intended as an</u>
    <u>Example to Youth</u>. Illustrated by Birket Foster. New
    edition. London: Bogue, pp. 19-25.
        A biographical sketch. Wordsworth acquired from local
    scenery his enthusiasm for his calling as a poet.

9   HENRY, JAMES. "Past twelve at night; upon my bed" (poem),
    "Wordsworth's Horse" (poem), "Wordsworth and the Pig"
    (poem), in <u>My Book</u>. Dresden: privately printed,
    pp. [137-43], [157-58], [159-60].
        Ridicules "drowsy Wordsworth" ([137-43]). Reprinted from
    1851.B23 ([157-58], [159-60]).

10 HOLT, DAVID. "A Pathway at Rydal" (poem), "At the Grave of
    Wordsworth, in Grasmere Churchyard" (poem), in <u>Janus, Lake</u>

1853

        Sonnets, Etc. And Other Poems. London: Pickering, and
        Bell, pp. 32, 35-36.
           Wordsworth's benediction shall endure (32); his immor-
        tality is fixed (35-36).

11   [HUDSON, JOHN, ed.]. A Complete Guide to the Lakes, Comprising
        Minute Directions for the Tourist; with Mr. Wordsworth's
        Description of the Scenery of the Country, Etc.: and Five
        Letters on the Geology of the Lake District, by the Rev.
        Professor Sedgwick. Fourth edition. Edited by the
        Publisher. Kendal: Hudson; London: Longman, and
        Whittaker; Liverpool: Webb; Manchester: Simms, pp. 50-58.
           Describes Rydal Mount, Wordsworth's grave, and Dove
        Cottage.

12   JERDAN, WILLIAM. The Autobiography of William Jerdan, with
        his Literary, Political, and Social Reminiscences and
        Correspondence during the last Fifty Years. 4 vols.
        London: Hall, Virtue, III:337-41; IV:237-40.
           See 1818.B28 (III:337-41). Describes visit to Wordsworth
        at Rydal Mount. In London, Wordsworth's conversation, in-
        cluding his criticism of Turner, was lively and entertaining
        (IV:237-40).

13   JOHNSTON, WILLIAM. "Memoir of Edward Quillinan," in Poems.
        By Edward Quillinan. London: Moxon, pp. xi-xlvi.
           Discusses Wordsworth as he figured in Quillinan's life.

14   [KINGSLEY, CHARLES]. "Alexander Smith and Alexander Pope."
        Fraser's Magazine, 48 (October), 452-66 (456, 460).
           Wordsworth fell into puerility by indulging false the-
        ories on descriptive poetry. Reprinted in Miscellanies
        (1859).

15   [KINGSLEY, CHARLES]. "Thoughts on Shelley and Byron."
        Fraser's Magazine, 48 (November), 568-76 (568-69).
           Wordsworth declared, "a little too noisily" the glory of
        naturalness and the dignity of simple human relationships.
        Reprinted in Miscellanies (1859).

16   L., M---A. "Passage in Wordsworth." Notes and Queries, 7
        (22 January), 85.
           Notes source of a phrase in "Walton's Book of Lives."

17   LANDOR, WALTER SAVAGE. "Archdeacon Hare and Walter Landor,"
        "To the Reverend Charles Cuthbert Southey on his Father's
        Character and Public Services," "XXXVIII" ("Matthias,
        Gifford, men like those") (poem), "XLVII" ("We know a poet

rich in thought, profuse") (poem), "LXIV" ("People may
think the work of sleep") (poem), "CLXXVIII: English Hexameters" (poem), "CCXXXVI: Written at Hurstmonceaux: on
Reading a Poem of Wordsworth's" (poem), "CCXXXVIII: To the
Author of 'Festus': on the Classick and Romantick" (poem),
in The Last Fruit Off an Old Tree. London: Moxon,
pp. 97-131 (110-11, 116-18, 121-23), 332-38 (332-35), 372,
374, 377, 410-12 (411-12), 450, 451-55 (454).
   Though inexact in "She dwelt among the untrodden ways,"
Wordsworth excels in The Prelude (Book III). Notes Wordsworth's debt to him, and Wordsworth's tameness; praises his
rural delineations. Wordsworth does not equal Milton. Reports Coleridge regretted Wordsworth followed his advice in
calling the poems Lyrical Ballads (110-11, 116-18, 121-23).
Reprinted with brief addition from 1850.B59 (332-35). Criticizes those who find in Wordsworth "but a husky wheeze"
(372). His works went winnowing (374). Criticizes a poet's
(presumably Wordsworth's) works as wheezy (377). Expanded
from 1850.B58 (411-12). Reprinted from 1852.B21 (450).
Expanded from 1849.B8 (454).

18   LE GRICE, C.[HARLES] V. "Sonnet: On my first and only visit
     to the Poet Wordsworth. . . ." Gentleman's Magazine,
     NS 39 (February), 129.
        Records visit to Wordsworth, "bard of the heart."

19   LE GRICE, C.[HARLES] V. "A Sonnet, Tributary to the Poet
     Wordsworth." Gentleman's Magazine, NS 40 (December), 578.
        Wordsworth drinks deeply of the soul of things.

20   LYNCH, THOMAS T. Essays on Some of the Forms of Literature.
     London: Longman, pp. 16, 144-45.
        Wordsworth benefitted from criticism of his simplicities.

21   [MASSON, DAVID]. Review of Dallas's Poetics and Smith's Poems.
     North British Review, 19 (August), 297-344 (298, 301,
     306-307, 311-13, 327, 343).
        In the Preface to Lyrical Ballads Wordsworth reverts "to
     the imitation-theory of Aristotle." Reprinted in Essays,
     Biographical and Critical (1856) and Wordsworth, Shelley,
     Keats, and Other Essays (1874).

22   N., W. L. "Passage in Wordsworth." Notes and Queries, 7
     (19 February), 191.
        A reply to 1853.B16. Notes source of a phrase in "Wal-
     ton's Book of Lives."

1853

23   P.[ALGRAVE], F.[RANCIS] T.[URNER]. "Method of Lectures on
     English Literature." Educational Expositor, 1 (May),
     119-22; (June), 176-80.
        The character "Wordsworth" advocates life amidst nature
     as opposed to cities, discusses "Coleridge's" lecturing.

24   QUILLINAN, EDWARD. "Suspiria: I.--Wordsworth's Home" (poem),
     "On the Reported Visit of Queen Adelaide to Wordsworth"
     (poem), in Poems. London: Moxon, pp. 71, 139-40.
        Reflects on Wordsworth's affection for Dora (71), his
     power to move men's consciences to good (139-40).

25   [RICHARDSON, LADY MARY]. "William Wordsworth." Sharpe's
     London Magazine, NS 2:148-55.
        A biographical sketch. Wordsworth's life was pure, un-
     worldly, gentle, illustrating ideal domestic relations in
     his affection for Dorothy. His mind was humble, forbearing.
     His effect on readers is comparable to Jane Austen's. At-
     tribution: George Harris Healey, ed., The Cornell Words-
     worth Collection . . . (Ithaca: Cornell Univ. Press, 1957),
     p. 161.

26   ROBERTSON, FRED. W. Letter to the Editor. Brighton Guardian,
     no. 1363 (9 March), p. 1.
        Wordsworth balanced High Church and pantheistic ten-
     dencies.

27   RUSKIN, JOHN. The Stones of Venice: Volume the Third: The
     Fall. Illustrated by the Author. London: Smith, Elder,
     p. 127 (Chapter iii, Paragraph 26).
        Wordsworth plays wisely.

28   RUSSELL, THE RIGHT HONOURABLE LORD JOHN, ed. Memoirs, Journal,
     and Correspondence of Thomas Moore. 8 vols. London:
     Longman, III:159-63; IV:47-49, 334-35.
        Includes Moore's notations, in his diary, of his inter-
     course with Wordsworth: Wordsworth holds forth in conver-
     sation and is rather dull; notes Byron's debt to Wordsworth
     in Childe Harold's Pilgrimage, Wordsworth's high opinion of
     himself, his lack of an ear for music, and Scott's descrip-
     tion of "Wordsworth's manly endurance of his poverty." For
     Volume V, see 1854.B12; for Volume VII, see 1856.B14.

29   SEDGWICK, A.[DAM]. "Geology of the Lake District," in A
     Complete Guide to the Lakes, Comprising Minute Directions
     for the Tourist; with Mr. Wordsworth's Description of the
     Scenery of the Country, Etc.: and Five Letters on the
     Geology of the Lake District, by the Rev. Professor

Sedgwick. Fourth edition. Edited by the Publisher [John
Hudson]. Kendal: Hudson; London: Longman, and Whittaker;
Liverpool: Webb; Manchester: Simms, pp. 167-258 (257-58).
  Expanded from 1842.B28, adding a tribute to Wordsworth:
he never let his communion with nature lead him to panthe-
ism and a degrading of man's social and religious duties.

30 SPALDING, WILLIAM. The History of English Literature. . . .
    Edinburgh: Oliver & Boyd, pp. 362-63, 374-79.
      The Excursion evidences Wordsworth's inattention to sym-
    metry of plan. Wordsworth is didactic everywhere. He is
    now overly praised. He is characterized by a delight in
    rural scenery and an unimpassioned and self-absorbed temper-
    ament alien to dramatic and narrative verse. He is a
    philosophical poet, rightly insisting on the importance of
    poetic pleasure though sometimes becoming too mean and
    trivial. The blank verse of The Excursion deserves praise.
    Revised in 1870.B15.

31 TAYLOR, TOM, ed. Life of Benjamin Robert Haydon, Historical
    Painter, from His Autobiography and Journals. 3 vols.
    London: Longman, I:124-25, 274-76, 300-302, 353-57;
    II:10-11, 72-73, 277-78; III:126-28, 146-48, 199-204,
    276-79, 298.
      Records Haydon's intercourse with Wordsworth; Sir George
    Beaumont's warning in 1809 of Wordsworth's "'terrific demo-
    cratic notions'"; Haydon's opinion that Wordsworth's great-
    ness lay in his descriptions of men's feelings about exis-
    tence before birth and after death, and his reverence for
    Wordsworth as a purified being; Hunt's respect for Words-
    worth; Haydon's dinner for Wordsworth in 1817 (Wordsworth's
    good humor); Wordsworth's egotism, in contrast with Scott;
    Haydon's going to church with Wordsworth; Wordsworth's ex-
    traordinary knowledge of art; and Haydon's criticism of
    Wordsworth for going to Court in 1845. Includes letter in
    which Keats notes that "Wordsworth has damned the Lakes."

32 W., A. "Wordsworth." Notes and Queries, 8 (23 July), 77.
      Notes source in the epitaph of the Empress Matilda of
    lines in "Lament of Mary Queen of Scots."

1854 A BOOKS - NONE

1854 B SHORTER WRITINGS

  1 ADMIRER OF WORDSWORTH AND HIS POETRY, AN. See 1854.B9.

1854

2   ANON. "Protestant Alliance: Lecture on the Reformation."
       Westmorland Gazette, 37 (2 December), 5.
          Reports lecture by George Henry Davis: Wordsworth's
       "writings were one of the principal causes of the late
       great revival of ceremonial and priestly religion."

3   [BAYNE, PETER]. "Thomas De Quincey and His Works." Hogg's
       Instructor, 3rd ser., 3 (July), 1-15 (9-10, 14).
          Wordsworth "is, of all poets, the furthest removed from
       the practical world." Reprinted in 1857.B3.

4   DE QUINCEY, THOMAS. "Chapter III: Early Memorials of
       Grasmere," "Chapter IV: Samuel Taylor Coleridge,"
       "Chapter V: William Wordsworth," "Chapter VI: William
       Wordsworth and Robert Southey," in Autobiographic Sketches:
       with Recollections of the Lakes [De Quincey's Works,
       Volume II]. London: Hogg, pp. 104-41 (104-33), 142-226
       (passim), 227-314, 315-45.
          Revised from 1839.B7. Clarifies his grief over the
       death of Catherine Wordsworth (104-33). Reprinted with
       minor changes from 1834.B13 (142-226). Revised with omis-
       sions from 1839.B4 (227-314). Combined with omissions from
       1839.B5-B6 (315-45).

5   HUNT, LEIGH. "An Organ in the House." Musical Times, and
       Singing Class Circular, 6 (1 September), 159-62 (162).
          Praises Wordsworth's description of the organ in "Ode:
       1815."

6   JAMESON, MRS. [ANNA BROWNELL]. A Commonplace Book of Thoughts,
       Memories, and Fancies, Original and Selected. London:
       Longman, especially pp. vii, 3-6, 15-16, 86-89, 321-22,
       337-39.
          "Character of the Happy Warrior" applies to any unselfish
       man--or woman. In The Excursion (Book IX) Wordsworth anti-
       cipates Ruskin's comments in The Stones of Venice on sepa-
       rating thinking from working. He is only partly correct in
       thinking that action is nobler than thought. His remark
       that Sir Joshua Reynolds lived too much for his own age is
       unjust. The alterations of "Laodamia" are unfortunate.

7   KNIGHT, CHARLES. Note, in Half-hours with the Best Authors.
       Third edition. Edited by Charles Knight. 4 vols. London:
       Routledge, I:97-98.
          Revised from 1847.B18. Adds a biographical sketch.

8   PATMORE, P.[ETER] G.[EORGE]. My Friends and Acquaintance:
       Being Memorials, Mind-Portraits, and Personal Recollections

of Deceased Celebrities of the Nineteenth Century: with
Selections from their Unpublished Letters. 3 vols. London:
Saunders and Otley, I:19, 28, 45, 118-19, 300; II:134,
262-63; III:140-44, 148-54, 224-28.
   Records his opinion that Lamb altered his wardrobe because of Wordsworth's description in "A Poet's Epitaph,"
Wordsworth's taking extra sugar in his tea, Hazlitt's malice
towards Wordsworth, and L. Blanchard's admiration of Wordsworth. Wordsworth's poems affect us as a personal matter
between the poet and ourselves; they make us happier.
Wordsworth can feel nothing but contempt for his late fame.

9   [PEARSON, WILLIAM] AN ADMIRER OF WORDSWORTH AND HIS POETRY.
      "Correspondence: Was Wordsworth a Protestant?" Westmorland
      Gazette, 37 (23 December), 5.
         A reply to 1854.B2. Though charitable towards what is
      good in Roman Catholicism, Wordsworth was a Protestant.
      Attributed and reprinted in 1863.B14.

10   PENDENNIS, ARTHUR. See 1854.B15.

11   [ROBY, ELIZABETH RYLAND]. "Sketch of the Literary Life and
      Character of John Roby," in The Legendary and Poetical
      Remains of John Roby . . . with a Sketch of his Literary
      Life and Character by his Widow. London: Longman,
      pp. 3-118 (60-62).
         Includes letter in which Mrs. Roby recounts a visit to
      Wordsworth in 1849: Wordsworth's enthusiasm and warm
      manner.

12   RUSSELL, THE RIGHT HONOURABLE LORD JOHN, ed. Memoirs, Journal,
      and Correspondence of Thomas Moore. 8 vols. London:
      Longman, V:292-93.
         Includes Moore's reference in his diary to breakfasting
      with Wordsworth. For Volumes III-IV, see 1853.B28; for
      Volume VII, see 1856.B14.

13   SCOTT, WILLIAM BELL. "Wordsworth: On Reading the Memoirs by
      Dr. C. Wordsworth" (three poems), in Poems. London:
      Smith, Elder, pp. 172-74.
         Wordsworth's life contains too much of tours and nature,
      not enough concern for the cares of the age. He announced
      truisms sententiously, never doubted; but he is justly
      praised.

14   SPALDING, WILLIAM. "Wordsworth, William," in Cyclopaedia of
      Biography: Embracing a Series of Original Memoirs of the

1854

Most Distinguished Persons of All Times. Edited by Elihu
Rich. London and Glasgow: Griffin, pp. 849-51.
A biographical sketch. It is important to note that
many passages incorporated in The Excursion were written
early. Wordsworth's eccentric judgment of his own work
lingered all his life.

15 [THACKERAY, WILLIAM MAKEPEACE] ARTHUR PENDENNIS, ed. "Chapter
XXI: Is Sentimental But Short," in The Newcomes: Memoirs
of a Most Respectable Family. Illustrated by Richard Doyle.
London: Bradbury and Evans, no. 7 (April), p. 198.
The old Colonel finds the new reverence for Wordsworth
puzzling.

1855 A BOOKS - NONE

1855 B SHORTER WRITINGS

1 ANON. "William Wordsworth." Leisure Hour, 4 (12 July),
439-42.
A biographical sketch. Wordsworth stirs our hidden affinities with nature; he wrote calmly, unmoved by critical
abuse. His abandoning of mistaken youthful opinions provides a positive lesson.

2 ANON. "Tennyson's Maud." National Review, 1 (October),
377-410 (passim).
To the end of his days Wordsworth moved in a world of
child-like vision (like that, suggested by Vaughan, described in "Ode: Intimations of Immortality"). Wordsworth
and Tennyson use nature in different ways. Wordsworth
failed to discriminate among his works.

3 [BAGEHOT, WALTER]. "William Cowper." National Review, 1
(July), 31-72 (59-63).
Wordsworth's "dreary intercourse" is dreary because he
lacks a sense of the ludicrous. To Cowper, nature is a
background; to Wordsworth, it is a religion. Reprinted in
Estimates of Some Englishmen and Scotchmen (1858).

4 [BAGEHOT, WALTER]. "The First Edinburgh Reviewers." National
Review, 1 (October), 253-84 (274-75).
Adapted from 1852.B8. For "the lovers of polished Liber-
alism," Wordsworth will not do. Reprinted in Estimates of
Some Englishmen and Scotchmen (1858).

1856

5   HOLLAND, JOHN and JAMES EVERETT. Memoirs of the Life and
     Writings of James Montgomery. . . . 7 vols. London:
     Longman, II:137, 211; IV:57.
         Records Wordsworth's admiration for Montgomery. For
     Volumes V-VII, see 1856.B10.

6   MACKENZIE, DR. [ROBERT] SHELTON. Note, in The Odoherty Papers.
     By the late William Maginn. Edited by Dr. Shelton Mac-
     kenzie. 2 vols. New York: Redfield, II:55.
         Records Wordsworth's amusement at 1820.B32.

7   MASSEY, GERALD. "The Poetry of Alfred Tennyson." Hogg's
     Instructor, 3rd ser., 5 (July), 1-14 (2, 4, 6-7).
         In contrast to Tennyson, Wordsworth is content to write
     down what first comes into his mind. Wordsworth's world
     has the appearance of health and eternity.

8   OXONIAN. "A Few Words on Sonnets and Sonnet-Writers." Hogg's
     Instructor, 3rd ser., 4 (June), 494-97.
         In his sonnets Wordsworth avoided antithesis, worked to
     produce a general harmony. He maintained the sonnet's
     unity, despite his multiplicity of subjects; his sonnets
     illustrate his theory of diction.

1856 A BOOKS

1   HOOD, EDWIN PAXTON. William Wordsworth; a Biography. London:
     Cash; Edinburgh: Menzies; Dublin: Hodges & Smith, 517 pp.
         A full biographical and critical study, written with
     "affectionate reverence" to present "a coherent view of the
     life of the Poet, from his own records of thoughts and emo-
     tions."

1856 B SHORTER WRITINGS

1   ALFORD, HENRY. "English Descriptive Poetry: A Lecture," in
     Evening Recreations; or, Samples from the Lecture Room.
     Edited by John Hampden Gurney. London: Longman, pp. 1-27
     (11).
         Wordsworth atoned in his later poems for his early ex-
     treme simplicity.

2   ANON. "Conversation and Poetry of Rogers." National Review,
     2 (April), 387-412 (390-92, 395, 398-405).
         Wordsworth "did not build up a true theory of expression,"
     but destroyed a false one.

1856

3   [BAGEHOT, WALTER]. "Percy Bysshe Shelley." National Review,
      3 (October), 342-79 (372-73).
         Wordsworth described the inexorable facts of life;
      Shelley struggled to change them. Reprinted in Estimates
      of Some Englishmen and Scotchmen (1858).

4   COLLIER, J.[OHN] PAYNE. "Preface," in Seven Lectures on
      Shakespeare and Milton. By the late S. T. Coleridge. . . .
      London: Chapman and Hall, pp. i-cxx (xxxii-xxxix, xlix-lvi).
         Records references, from his diary, to Wordsworth's
      praise of Spenser and initial ignorance of Fairfax's trans-
      lation of Tasso, his depreciation of "The Female Vagrant"
      and rhymed stanzas, his praise of eighteenth-century poets
      and of "To the Cuckoo" ("O blithe New-comer! I have
      heard"), his fondness for talking about his own poetry, and
      his efforts to help Coleridge in 1817. Records Coleridge's
      remark that Wordsworth desired popularity but would not
      receive it.

5   DE QUINCEY, THOMAS. Confessions of an English Opium-Eater.
      . . . Revised and enlarged. [De Quincey's Works, Volume
      V.] London: Hogg, pp. 6, 35, 74-76, 97-98, 122, 194, 223,
      226, 254, 264, 286-90.
         Expanded from 1821.B15. "Ruth" is founded upon fact.
      Records his early veneration of Wordsworth and his efforts
      to convert other readers. Wordsworth is "a truth-speaker
      of the severest literality." His greatness was not ac-
      knowledged until the early 1830's. He drew auguries of im-
      mortality in "We Are Seven" and "Ode: Intimations of
      Immortality."

6   [DODGSON, CHARLES L.]. "Upon the Lonely Moor" (poem). Train,
      2 (October), 255-56.
         Parody of "Resolution and Independence." Revised in
      1872.B12.

7   [DYCE, ALEXANDER, ed.]. Recollections of the Table-talk of
      Samuel Rogers: to which is Added Porsoniana. 2 vols.
      Illustrated. London: Moxon, I:passim.
         Includes Rogers's and Dyce's reports of Wordsworth's de-
      preciation of Gray, Southey, Scott, Darwin, and Campbell;
      of C. J. Fox's introduction to Wordsworth; of Wordsworth's
      praise of T. Tickell, Coleridge's conversation, Cary, and
      Bowles; of Wordsworth's and Coleridge's tour of Scotland in
      1803; and of Wordsworth's account of the origins of Byron's
      hatred of Wordsworth. Includes Rogers's comments that the
      sonnet form saved Wordsworth from wordiness and that Words-
      worth had no ear for music.

8   F., M. E. "Wordsworth v. Campbell." Notes and Queries, NS 1
     (3 May), 351.
        Wordsworth was ignorant of geography in criticizing
     Campbell.

9   [FINLASON, WILLIAM FRANCIS]. Review of Poems of William
     Wordsworth and Cardinal Wiseman's On the Perception of
     Natural Beauty. Dublin Review, 40 (June), 338-91.
        Those who attack Wordsworth's poems have narrowed their
     definitions of poetry. Wordsworth's mind tended naturally
     towards Roman Catholicism; but when he wrote directly on
     religion, he was vague and dreamy. Though his poems are
     morally pure, he did not properly see God as the cause and
     cure of evils he portrayed. Praises "Ode: Intimations of
     Immortality," Peter Bell, and The White Doe of Rylstone.

10   HOLLAND, JOHN and JAMES EVERETT. Memoirs of the Life and
     Writings of James Montgomery. . . . 7 vols. London:
     Longman, V:200-203, 328-30, 407-408; VI:106-107, 125, 160,
     162, 303; VII:17, 35-36, 174.
        Records Wordsworth's admiration of Montgomery and Mont-
     gomery's admiration of Wordsworth, including his verse
     tribute "To William Wordsworth, Esq.," and Montgomery's
     opinions that Wordsworth's poems often depart from his
     theories, that to enjoy them one must enter into Words-
     worth's spirit, and that his poems are devoid of spiritual
     allusions. Includes John Dix's recollections of Words-
     worth's revising of "When Severn's sweeping flood had over-
     thrown." For Volumes II and IV, see 1855.B5.

11   LANDOR, W. S. Letter from W. S. Landor to R. W. Emerson.
     Bath: Williams [1856], pp. 11-15.
        Wordsworth ignorantly criticized Byron and Scott. Re-
     cords Hazlitt's comparing of Wordsworth's appearance to
     that of a horse, and his own visits with Wordsworth. In-
     cludes verse urging poets to leave behind "Asthmatic Words-
     worth." (Line incorporated in "To Recruits" in 1858.B10.)

12   [OLIPHANT, MARGARET]. "Modern Light Literature--Poetry."
     Blackwood's Edinburgh Magazine, 79 (February), 125-38
     (128-29).
        Wordsworth is responsible for our now viewing the poet
     as a being withdrawn from common existence.

13   RUSKIN, JOHN. Modern Painters: Volume III: Containing Part
     IV: Of Many Things. London: Smith, Elder, pp. 12 (Chap-
     ter i, Paragraph 14), 137-38 (Chapter x, Paragraph 9), 161
     (Chapter xii, Paragraph 6), 170 (Paragraph 15), 259 (Chapter

xvi, Paragraph 10), 265-67 (Paragraphs 23-26), 276 (Paragraph 38), 287 (Chapter xvii, Paragraphs 2-3), 290-95 (Paragraphs 6-11), 299 (Paragraphs 22-23), 304 (Paragraph 29).

Commends Wordsworth's power of exciting one's feelings; criticizes him as a judge of painting. Ellen in The Excursion does not allow emotion to affect her reason. Wordsworth was not so sure of his religion. His self-complacency and affected simplicity mark a second-rate intellect. He "understands how to be happy, but yet cannot altogether rid himself of the sense that he is a philosopher, and ought always to be saying something wise." He errs in his analysis of the feelings, did not understand the value of dissecting nature to examine it. His love of nature is his weakness; his strength lies in warring with pomp and pretense. He did not originate the school of simplicity.

14 RUSSELL, THE RIGHT HONOURABLE LORD JOHN, ed. Memoirs, Journals, and Correspondence of Thomas Moore. 8 vols. London: Longman, VII:69-73, 85, 197-98.

Includes Moore's notations, in his diary, of his intercourse with Wordsworth: Wordsworth's objections to "English as a poetical language," praise of Coleridge, debt to coach passengers for subjects for poems, and deliberately writing dull letters. For Volumes III-IV, see 1853.B28; for Volume V, see 1854.B12.

15 W., T. "A Lesson for Laureates." Notes and Queries, NS 2 (20 December), 487.

Prints what Wordsworth attested to be his "favourite autograph for ladies."

16 WARTER, JOHN WOOD, ed. Selections from the Letters of Robert Southey, &c.&c.&c. Edited by his Son-in-law. 4 vols. London: Longman, passim.

Includes letters in which Southey praises Lyrical Ballads and notes he scarcely has any acquaintance with Wordsworth in 1803, records in 1806 "that Wordsworth went in powder, and with a cocked hat under his arm" to a rout, praises Poems (1807) and Poems (1815), notes Landor's praise of Wordsworth, and records his intercourse with Wordsworth. Includes letter in which Landor criticizes Wordsworth's unevenness.

17 WISEMAN, [NICHOLAS PATRICK STEPHEN] HIS EMINENCE CARDINAL. "Lecture I," in On the Perception of Natural Beauty by the Ancients and the Moderns: Rome, Ancient and Modern: Two Lectures Delivered on the 10th of December, 1855, and on

the 31st of January, 1856. London: Burns and Lambert, and
Shean, pp. 1-34 (3, 6, 13-14, 24-25).
   Wordsworth's love of nature "was sound, noble and moral";
his poems appeal to like love in the reader. He tied the
virgin snows with Mary. Includes sonnet, "Wordsworth!
some men have said thou art not drest."

1857 A   BOOKS - NONE

1857 B   SHORTER WRITINGS

  1   ANON. Review of The Poetical Works of William Wordsworth and
       The Earlier Poems of William Wordsworth. Athenaeum,
       no. 1526 (24 January), pp. 109-10.
          Wordsworth's annotations to his own poems are valuable
       and necessary; his egotism is never offensive.

  2   ANON. "Coleridge and Wordsworth" (poem), in Peripatetic
       Papers: Being a Volume of Miscellanies by the Members of
       a Literary Society. Edited by John M'Gilchrist. London:
       Blackwood, pp. 202-204.
          Wordsworth was the "calm rivulet" compared to Coleridge,
       the torrent.

  3   BAYNE, PETER. "Thomas De Quincey and His Works," "Tennyson
       and His Teachers," in Essays in Biography and Criticism.
       First series. Boston: Gould and Lincoln; New York:
       Sheldon, Blakeman; Cincinnati: Blanchard, pp. 15-49 (35-36,
       47), 50-145 (55-58, 67, 70, 72, 113-14).
          Reprinted from 1854.B3 (35-36, 47). Wordsworth owed his
       influence, including that on Tennyson, to the moral eleva-
       tion of his poetry. He lacked wit and imagination; his
       subjects are limited. Expanded in 1859.B6 (55-58, 67, 70,
       72, 113-14).

  4   BLACKIE, JOHN STUART. "Lays and Legends: Introduction"
       (poem), in Lays and Legends of Ancient Greece, with Other
       Poems. Edinburgh: Sutherland and Knox; London: Simpkin,
       Marshall, pp. 1-14 (2).
          "Lone in far mountains" Wordsworth "hums a thoughtful
       lay."

  5   BREEN, HENRY H. Modern English Literature: Its Blemishes &
       Defects. London: Longman, pp. 87, 251-53.
          Criticizes "Carnage is thy daughter" in "Ode: 1815."
       Wordsworth's plagiarisms are not numerous.

1857

6   DE QUINCEY, THOMAS. "Preface," "Whiggism in Its Relations to
     Literature," "On Wordsworth's Poetry," in Sketches:
     Critical and Biographic. [De Quincey's Works, Volume VI.]
     London: Hogg, pp. i-ix (ii-iv), 30-193 (94, 142-44, 149,
     170), 234-68.
         Wordsworth and Coleridge differed in defining imagination
     and poetic diction. Wordsworth shared Euripides's views on
     poetic diction, but failed to establish his theory and mis-
     understood his own meaning (ii-iv). Reprinted with minor
     verbal changes and addition from 1831.B14 (94, 142-44, 149,
     170). Reprinted with verbal changes and minor revisions
     from 1845.B8 (234-68).

7   GASKELL, E.[LIZABETH] C. The Life of Charlotte Brontë.
     2 vols. London: Smith, Elder, I:162-65.
         Includes Branwell Brontë's letter to Wordsworth testify-
     ing to his admiration of Wordsworth's poems.

8   [HUTTON, RICHARD HOLT]. "William Wordsworth." National
     Review, 4 (January), 1-30.
         The most striking characteristic of Wordsworth's mind
     and poetry is simplicity. In contrast with Coleridge and
     Tennyson, Wordsworth "withdraws his imagination from the
     heart of his picture to contemplate it in its spiritual re-
     lations." He cannot structure his poems. His mind was
     rigid. He did not paint nature but interpreted its spir-
     itual expressions. Revised as "Wordsworth and His Genius"
     in 1871.B7.

9   JOHNSTON, WILLIAM. "Preface," Notes, in The Earlier Poems of
     William Wordsworth. Edited by William Johnston. London:
     Moxon, pp. vii-xxvi, passim.
         One today may not realize the resistance Wordsworth's
     unconventional poems first met. Wordsworth revised his
     poems for the better in Poems (1815). He discovered a new
     meaning in nature, finding moral sentiments in ordinary,
     familiar incidents. His poems were unpopular because they
     present unadorned truth, addressed to the reflective part
     of man's nature. But no ordinary reader can read them with-
     out being made more thoughtful, gentle, dutiful, and kind
     (vii-xxvi). Includes brief textual and critical notes
     throughout the volume (passim).

10   NATHANIEL, SIR. "Notes on Note-Worthies, of Divers Orders,
     Either Sex, and Every Age: VI.--William Wordsworth."
     New Monthly Magazine, NS 109 (April), 379-92.
         Wordsworth, confident of his powers, waited for public
     approval. His power of sight was keen, his sense of smell
     non-existent.

1858

11 SYMINGTON, ANDREW JAMES. The Beautiful in Nature, Art, and
    Life. 2 vols. London: Longman, especially I:175-83,
    401-402, 408-409; II:176.
        Wordsworth acknowledges the beauty of the world; his
    poems abound in "quotable felicitous condensations." He is
    the greatest contemplative teacher of the century.

1858 A BOOKS - NONE

1858 B SHORTER WRITINGS

1 ANON. "St. Martin's School of Art." Building News, 4
   (23 April), 428-30 (429).
       Reports lecture by Ruskin: Wordsworth was not the first
   to introduce simple language. "Efforts now being made to
   depreciate" him should not succeed.

2 ANON. "Preface," in Lectures and Addresses on Literary and
   Social Topics. By the late Rev. Frederick W. Robertson.
   London: Smith, Elder, pp. vii-xxxviii (xix-xxii).
       Prints letter in which Robertson defends Wordsworth's
   "pantheism."

3 ANON. "Publisher's Advertisement," in The Poetical Works of
   William Wordsworth. London and New York: Routledge,
   p. iii.
       Wordsworth "bravely and perseveringly contended" against
   hostile criticism and neglect, never wavering, certain of
   eventual triumph. He has now a hundred readers where
   twenty-five years ago he had one.

4 ANON. "Wordsworth, William," in The English Cyclopaedia: A
   New Dictionary of Universal Knowledge. Edited by Charles
   Knight. Biography.--6 vols. London: Bradbury and Evans,
   VI:808-12.
       A biographical sketch. (The six volumes were also issued
   with an alternate title-page as Cyclopaedia of Biography.
   The article was also published in 1858 in The Second Supple-
   ment to the Penny Cyclopaedia of the Society for the Diffu-
   sion of Useful Knowledge [London: Knight], pp. 774-76.)

5 [CRAIK, GEORGE LILLIE and CHARLES Mac FARLANE]. The Pictorial
   History of England: Being a History of the People as Well
   as a History of the Kingdom. Illustrated. New edition,
   revised and extended. 7 vols. London and Edinburgh:
   Chambers, VI:858, 883-87.

1858

A German influence is marked in Wordsworth. His theories
in the Preface to Lyrical Ballads refute themselves and are
refuted by his own practice. He is the poet of common life,
though he lacks humor. He fails in the formal qualities of
his poetry. Attribution: British Museum catalogue.

6 DAVY, JOHN, ed. Fragmentary Remains, Literary and Scientific,
   of Sir Humphry Davy, Bart. . . . Edited by his Brother.
   London: Churchill, pp. 77-78, 81-89, 102, 109-10.
      Includes letters in which Coleridge discusses Words-
   worth's plans to publish Lyrical Ballads (1800) and "The
   Pedlar," Wordsworth's health, and his plans to live with
   Calvert. Wordsworth modelled a sketch in The Excursion
   (Book VII) upon Thomas Wedgwood.

7 [DE VERE, AUBREY THOMAS]. Review of Patmore's The Angel in the
   House. Edinburgh Review, 107 (January), 121-33 (122).
      Wordsworth pleaded on behalf of humble life rather than
   English life. But in actual simple life he saw nothing
   worthy of song.

8 DE VERE, AUBREY [THOMAS]. Notes, in Select Specimens of the
   English Poets, with Biographical Notices, &c. Edited by
   Aubrey De Vere. London: Burns and Lambert, pp. 189-90,
   207.
      A biographical sketch. Wordsworth's life was happy and
   virtuous; his poetry is imaginative and meditative, characterized by broad sympathy with human nature in its ideal.
   Many poems express a Catholic tone. He at times becomes
   diffuse. He differs from Coleridge.

9 HOGG, THOMAS JEFFERSON. The Life of Percy Bysshe Shelley.
   2 vols. London: Moxon, II:11, 386-88.
      Records Shelley's praise of Wordsworth's poems and a
   banker's attesting to Wordsworth's writing his poems in bed
   at night.

10 LANDOR, WALTER SAVAGE. "No. 121: A Poet Sleeping" (poem),
   "No. 126: To Recruits" (poem), in Dry Sticks, Fagoted.
   Edinburgh: Nichol; London: Nisbet, pp. 69, 71.
      Notes a poet's (presumably Wordsworth's) verses are
   wheezy (69). Reprints line about "Asthmatic Wordsworth"
   from 1856.B11 (71).

11 PEACOCK, T.[HOMAS] L.[OVE]. "Memoirs of Percy Bysshe Shelley."
   Fraser's Magazine, 57 (June), 643-59 (644, 657).
      Records Shelley's fondness for Wordsworth's "To the
   Cuckoo" ("O blithe New-comer! I have heard") and "Stanzas

1859

Written in My Pocket-copy of Thomson's 'Castle of Indolence.'"

12 R., W. "The Life of Wordsworth," in The Poetical Works of William Wordsworth. London and New York: Routledge, pp. v-xiv.
      A biographical sketch. Wordsworth directed his entire life towards poetry, and his life itself became poetic. He owes the elevation and depth in his poetry to Dorothy. He had too high an opinion of himself, and overrated the value of simplicity. His small poems are his best. Though annoyed by public neglect, he persevered.

13 ROBERTSON, THE LATE REV. FREDERICK W. "Two Lectures on the Influence of Poetry," "Lecture on Wordsworth," in Lectures and Addresses on Literary and Social Topics. London: Smith, Elder, pp. 91-200 (passim), 201-56.
      Reprinted from 1852.B26 (91-200). A lecture "delivered to the Members of the Brighton Athenaeum, on February 10th, 1853": To sympathize with Wordsworth, one must share his unworldliness and truth and depth of feeling. His life was a life of contemplation, not of action; he calls men away from the idolatry of wealth. He was true to himself, consistent in his inner life, and the poet of human liberty. (Lecture reported in the Brighton Herald of 12 February 1853) (201-56).

14 TRELAWNY, E.[DWARD] J.[OHN]. Recollections of the Last Days of Shelley and Byron. London: Moxon, pp. 4-8.
      Records meeting Wordsworth in Switzerland in 1820: Wordsworth, self-confident and dogmatic in opinion, laments the presence of carriages in the mountains, dismisses Shelley as a poet. Later in life he admitted Shelley's greatness.

1859 A BOOKS

1 ANON. Catalogue of the Varied and Valuable Historical, Poetical, Theological, and Miscellaneous Library of the late Venerated Poet-Laureate, William Wordsworth . . . which will be sold by Auction, by Mr. John Burton . . . at . . . Rydal Mount, near Ambleside, Windermere, On Tuesday the 19th, Wednesday the 20th, and Thursday the 21st, days of July, 1859. Preston: privately printed [1859], 59 pp.
      Wordsworth's library shared in his characteristic plainness. Lists books to be sold.

1859

1859 B   SHORTER WRITINGS

1   ANON. "Crabbe." National Review, 8 (January), 1-32 (3, 25).
    The speakers in The Excursion are mouthpieces for Words-
    worth. One finds depth beneath Wordsworth's apparent plati-
    tude, harmony under his seeming ungainliness.

2   ANON. "William Wordsworth." Christian Observer, 58 (March),
    156-72.
    Though mistaken in his handling of homely subjects and
    language, Wordsworth rightly conceived of the poet's mis-
    sion and wrote in the spirit of a Christian.

3   ANON. "Memoirs of the Authors," in Favourite English Poems of
    the Two Last Centuries Unabridged. London: Sampson Low,
    pp. xii-xx (xx).
    A biographical sketch.

4   ANON. "The Life of William Wordsworth," in The Poetical Works
    of William Wordsworth. Edinburgh: Gall & Inglis [1859],
    pp. iii-xiv.
    A biographical sketch. Wordsworth came later in life to
    realize that his early principles of diction could not be
    pressed to the extreme, and so he revised some bald pas-
    sages. When Wordsworth is successful, the reader forgets
    the poet and becomes absorbed in the description itself.
    Even now Wordsworth is not a popular poet. His political
    and religious narrow-mindedness is unworthy of him and per-
    haps resulted from his spite at the multitude's rejection
    of his poems. The Prelude can be neither interesting nor
    intelligible to those who have no experience in analyzing
    mental states. Wordsworth's career is instructive for all
    men: he triumphed over the difficulties all reformers must
    overcome.

5   [BAGEHOT, WALTER]. "Tennyson's Idylls." National Review, 9
    (October), 368-94 (369, 390-93).
    Early in the century, "Wordsworthians were considered a
    kind of Quakers in literature"; some of the defects in
    Wordsworth's poems may be traced to his writing for such a
    sect of readers. Wordsworth dealt with elemental passions
    and a spiritual conception of the universe. Tennyson excels
    Wordsworth in that Wordsworth does not make fun nor deline-
    ate a general picture of human life.

6   BAYNE, PETER. "Elementary Principles of Criticism," "Tennyson
    and His Teachers," in Essays, Biographical, Critical, and
    Miscellaneous. Edinburgh and London: Hogg, pp. 144-201
    (147-48, 175), 202-80 (229).

Intensity of feeling cannot prevent Wordsworth from being commonplace in Peter Bell (147-48, 175). Expanded from
1857.B3. Wordsworth taught Tennyson the majesty of man and
to observe nature (229).

7   BLACKBURNE, THOMAS. "A Talk about Rydal Mount." Once a Week,
    1 (6 August), 107-109.
        Describes Grasmere, Rydal, and Rydal Mount.

8   CURTIS, GEORGE WILLIAM. "Notes of Charles Lamb to Thomas
    Allsop." Harper's New Monthly Magazine, 20 (December),
    88-97 (88-90, 92, 94).
        Prints letters from Lamb noting Wordsworth's presence in
    London.

9   DE QUINCEY, THOMAS. "Lessing," in Speculations Literary and
    Philosophic. [De Quincey's Works, Volume XIII.] London:
    Hogg, pp. 230-303 (253-56).
        Revised from 1826.B6.

10 DE QUINCEY, THOMAS. "Prefatory Note," "Coleridge and Opium-
    Eating," "Milton versus Southey and Landor," in Speculations
    Literary and Philosophic: with German Tales and Other
    Narrative Papers. [De Quincey's Works, Volume XII.]
    London: Hogg, pp. v-vii, 71-111 (102, 106, 108), 176-98
    (182-87).
        Notes Wordsworth and Coleridge were of identical height:
    5'10" (v-vii). Reprinted with minor addition from 1845.B7
    (102, 106, 108). Reprinted from 1847.B15 (182-87).

11 GRINSTED, T. P. Relics of Genius: Visits to the Last Homes
    of Poets, Painters, and Players, with Biographical Sketches.
    Illustrated. London: Kent, pp. 48, 204-207.
        A biographical sketch. Wordsworth "was not to be de-
    terred from his purpose" by hostile criticism. His poetic
    characters lack reality, his poems "the earnestness of in-
    spiration."

12 HEY, REBECCA. "On Visiting Wordsworth's Grave in Grasmere
    Churchyard, 1850" (poem) and note, in Holy Places, And
    other Poems. London: Hatchard, pp. 105-107, 156-57.
        Nature and men mourn Wordsworth. Laments tourists at
    Wordsworth's grave.

13 [HUNT, LEIGH]. "The Occasional: No. II." Spectator, 31
    (Suppl., 22 January), 101-102 (101).
        Wordsworth could have used more of Burns's enlarged sym-
    pathies. "To the Sons of Burns" is an ungracious lecture.

14   HUNT, LEIGH. "English Poetry <u>versus</u> Cardinal Wiseman."
      <u>Fraser's Magazine</u>, 60 (December), 747-66 (759, 764-65).
            Cardinal Wiseman's opinion notwithstanding, Wordsworth
      expresses anti-Roman Catholic sentiments.

15   LANDOR, WALTER SAVAGE. Note to "Gebir," in <u>The Hellenics of</u>
      <u>Walter Savage Landor; comprising Heroic Idyls, &c.</u> New
      edition, enlarged. Edinburgh: Nichol; London: Griffin,
      p. 100.
            Notes Wordsworth's borrowing of the image of the shell
      in <u>The Excursion</u> (Book IV).

16   LUDLOW, J.[OHN] M.[ALCOLM]. "Moral Aspects of Mr. Tennyson's
      'Idylls of the King.'" <u>Macmillan's Magazine</u>, 1 (November),
      63-72 (68).
            Wordsworth's sense of duty counteracts his tendency to-
      wards pantheism. Wordsworth views man too coldly to be of
      much help to those struggling through life.

17   [MOIR, GEORGE and W. E. AYTOUN?] G. M.--R. and W. E. A.
      "Poetry," in <u>The Encyclopaedia Britannica, or Dictionary of</u>
      <u>Arts[,] Sciences, and General Literature.</u> Eighth edition.
      21 vols. Edinburgh: Black, XVIII:91-127 (93-94, 126).
            Commends Wordsworth's definition of Fancy in the Preface
      (1815). His poetry is contemplative; his fame rests upon
      his minor poems, not the tedious <u>The Excursion</u>. His lack
      of humor and his belief in his own powers led to the
      critics' ridicule.

18   PAYN, JAMES. <u>A Handbook to the English Lakes</u>. London:
      Whittaker; Longman; Simpkin, Marshall; Hamilton, Adams;
      Windermere: Garnett [1859], pp. 20-21.
            Wordsworth's poetry is too philosophic to be popular; he
      knew fine scenery "in an intenser sense" than other poets.

19   SHELLEY, LADY [JANE], ed. <u>Shelley Memorials: From Authentic</u>
      <u>Sources. . . .</u> London: Smith, Elder, pp. 121, 124, 139,
      141.
            Includes letters in which Shelley notes that he, Byron,
      and Wordsworth all reflect the spirit of their age, re-
      quests his publisher delete the name Emma from "Peter Bell
      the Third," and suggests he excuses Wordsworth in a poem
      of his (provisionally identified as "An Exhortation" [<u>see</u>
      1820.B45] by W. M. Rossetti in 1870.B12 and by Frederick L.
      Jones, <u>The Letters of Percy Bysshe Shelley</u> [2 vols., Ox-
      ford: Clarendon Press, 1964], I:195<u>n</u>).

1860

20   [SWAYNE, GEORGE C.]. "Sentimental Physiology." Blackwood's
     Edinburgh Magazine, 86 (July), 87-98 (93-94).
         Wordsworth paints women truly as pictures of health and
     activity.

21   WILLMOTT, ROBERT ARIS. "Preface," in Poems of William
     Wordsworth. Edited by Robert Aris Willmott. London and
     New York: Routledge, pp. [iii-vi].
         A biographical sketch.

1860 A   BOOKS - NONE

1860 B   SHORTER WRITINGS

1   ANON. Review of Collected Works of William Wordsworth and
     The Prelude. British Quarterly Review, 31 (1 January),
     79-117.
         Because the beauties are latent rather than dazzling,
     Wordsworth's poems initially repel the reader. They combine
     sublime passages with lines in which Wordsworth carries his
     poetic theories too far. He lacked rapidity of thought.
     His poems, combining simple diction with philosophic reflec-
     tions, awaken thought in the reader. He surpassed all po-
     ets, except Byron whom he taught, in contemplating nature
     reflectively.

2   ANON. "Richard Baxter Paraphrased by Wordsworth." Leisure
     Hour, 9 (26 April), 272.
         Wordsworth borrowed Baxter's language and thought in
     The Excursion.

3   ANON. "Deaths." Annual Register, or a View of the History
     and Politics of the Year 1859, [101]:406-99 (497-99).
         An obituary of Mary Wordsworth, including an abridged
     version of H. Martineau's biographical sketch. See
     1869.B17.

4   ANON. Evenings with the Poets and Sketches of Their Favourite
     Scenes. By the Author of "Success in Life," "Memorials of
     Early Genius," Etc. London, Edinburgh, and New York:
     Nelson, pp. 280-85.
         A biographical sketch. Wordsworth inaugurated a new era
     of poetry.

5   ASPLAND, [T.] LINDSEY. Notes, in The Excursion: A Poem. By
     William Wordsworth. Windermere: Garnett; London:

1860

Whittaker; Longman; Simpkin, Marshall; Hamilton, Adams
[1860], passim.
    Topographical notes.

6   [CARRUTHERS, ROBERT] R. C.--S. "Wordsworth, William," in The
     Encyclopaedia Britannica, or Dictionary of Arts, Sciences,
     and General Literature. Eighth edition. 21 vols.
     Edinburgh: Black, XXI:929-32.
        Wordsworth, "a philosophical and patriotic English poet,"
     was long ridiculed but lived to see his creed firmly es-
     tablished. His taste was not equal to his genius. A bio-
     graphical sketch. Attribution: W. Knight in 1896.B36,
     VIII:353.

7   CHAMBERS, ROBERT [and ROBERT CARRUTHERS]. Cyclopaedia of
     English Literature. 2 vols. London and Edinburgh:
     Chambers, II:279-91.
        A biographical sketch, revised from 1844.B14. Attribu-
     tion: see 1844.B14.

8   DULCKEN, H.[ENRY] W.[ILLIAM]. Note, in Pearls from the Poets:
     Specimens from the Works of Celebrated Writers. Edited by
     H. W. Dulcken. With a Preface by the Rev. Thomas Dole.
     London: Ward and Lock [1860], pp. 22-23.
        A biographical sketch. The chief charm of his poems
     lies in Wordsworth's appreciation of natural beauty.

9   HUGHES, T. "Wordsworth Travestie." Notes and Queries, NS 9
     (12 May), 365.
        Partially prints, and queries source of, poetic bur-
     lesque of Wordsworth beginning "Did you never hear the
     story."

10 HUNT, LEIGH. The Autobiography of Leigh Hunt. New edition,
     revised by the Author; with further revision, and an in-
     troduction, by his eldest son [Thornton Hunt]. London:
     Smith, Elder, pp. 37, 191, 219, 224, 247-49, 269-70.
        Revised with omissions from 1850.B55.

11 HUNT, LEIGH. "The Feast of the Poets" (poem) and note,
     "Lines on the Birth of the Princess Alice" (poem) and note,
     in The Poetical Works of Leigh Hunt: Now Finally Collected,
     Revised by Himself. Edited by His Son, Thornton Hunt.
     Illustrated by Corbould. London and New York: Routledge,
     Warne, and Routledge, pp. 194-201 (197, 199) and 441-42,
     307 and 451.
        Revised from 1844.B23. Apologizes for his initial at-
     tack on Wordsworth, though tempers the praise given

Wordsworth in earlier revisions of the poem (197, 199, 441-42). Reprinted with note identifying Wordsworth as the subject of the lines from 1844.B23 (307, 451).

12   PEACOCK, T.[HOMAS] L.[OVE]. "Unpublished Letters of Percy Bysshe Shelley." Fraser's Magazine, 61 (March), 301-19 (302).
      Includes letter in which Shelley in 1818 exclaims, about the apostate Wordsworth: "That such a man should be such a poet!" See 1877.B16.

13   S.[OTHEBY], H.[ANS] W.[ILLIAM]. "Life and Writings of Thomas De Quincey." Fraser's Magazine, 62 (December), 781-92 (787-90).
      Recounts De Quincey's relations with Wordsworth.

1861 A   BOOKS - NONE

1861 B   SHORTER WRITINGS

1   ANON. "The Life and Genius of Wordsworth," in The Poetical Works of William Wordsworth. London, Edinburgh, and New York: Nelson, pp. iii-xix.
      A biographical sketch: notes the "remarkable purity" of Wordsworth's early life, and the influence of Dorothy; praises the moral purity of his works, his attitude towards the poor, and his revisions of many of the particular associations and the prosy language in early poems; criticizes his narrow, Church-of-England Christianity and his later political conservatism. Wordsworth wrote, determinedly in the face of ridicule, not for the bustling generation, but for their children.

2   ATHOR. "Wordsworth and Campbell." Notes and Queries, NS 11 (27 April), 326.
      Had Wordsworth been better acquainted with Milton, he would not have criticized lines from Campbell.

3   BEETON, S.[AMUEL] O.[RCHART] and JOHN SHERER. Beeton's Dictionary of Universal Information. London: Beeton [1861], p. 1388.
      A biographical sketch.

4   BENNETT, W.[ILLIAM] C.[OX]. "So this is yours, our Wordsworth's pictured face" (poem), in The Worn Wedding-Ring, And other Poems. London: Chapman and Hall, p. 136.
      Wordsworth stills the fever of our lives with the peace of nature.

1861

5   CHORLEY, HENRY F. The Authors of England: A Series of
     Medallion Portraits of Modern Literary Characters, Engraved
     from the Works of British Artists by Achille Collas: with
     Illustrative Notices. New edition, revised. [Edited by
     G. B.] London: Griffin, Bohn, pp. 72-77.
          Expanded (by "G. B."--see Preface) from 1838.B11. Words-
     worth was honored in old age.

6   CHURTON, EDWARD, ed. Memoir of Joshua Watson. 2 vols.
     Oxford and London: Parker, especially I:5, 307, 324;
     II:1-3, 45, 51-53, 220.
          Records Watson's visits and correspondence with Words-
     worth; notes Wordsworth's refusing in 1831 to write upon
     politics, and his entertaining callers at Rydal Mount.
     Wordsworth's poems imaged his life; he upheld freedom,
     education.

7   COLLIER, WILLIAM FRANCIS. A History of English Literature, in
     a Series of Biographical Sketches. London, Edinburgh, and
     New York: Nelson, pp. 453-60.
          A biographical sketch. The Lakists' poetic theory was
     healthy, though carried too far. The Excursion is "written
     only for the thinking few."

8   [CONNINGTON, JOHN]. Review of The Works of Virgil. Quarterly
     Review, 110 (July), 73-114 (102-103).
          "Translation of Part of the First Book of the Aeneid"
     lacks rapidity of movement.

9   CRAIK, GEORGE L. A Compendious History of English Literature,
     and of The English Language, from The Norman Conquest:
     with Numerous Specimens. 2 vols. London: Griffin, Bohn,
     II:397-98, 435-56, 463-67, 473, 518.
          Briefly expanded from 1845.B6. Readers of all classes
     may understand The Prelude.

10   DE VERE, AUBREY [THOMAS]. "Composed at Rydal: Sept. 1860"
     (poem), "To Wordsworth: On Visiting the Duddon" (poem), in
     The Sisters, Inisfail, and Other Poems. London: Longman;
     Dublin: Mc Glashan and Gill, pp. 104, 105-106.
          Wordsworth, "True bard, because true man," was a poet of
     insight and wide sympathies (104), "last poet of the great
     old race" (105-106).

11   [KEBBEL, THOMAS EDWARD]. Review of Selections, Grave and Gay,
     from Writings . . . by Thomas De Quincey. Quarterly Review,
     110 (July), 1-35 (20, 30-31).

Wordsworth and Euripides occupied parallel positions, though not, as De Quincey suggests, in their use of common language.

12   LANDRETH, P. "Wordsworth's 'Peter Bell,'" in Studies and Sketches in Modern Literature: Periodical Contributions. Edinburgh: Oliphant; London: Hamilton, Adams, pp. 134–43.
     Wordsworth argued, erroneously, that "simple nature and plain man" are the only proper poetic materials. His characters, as opposed to Byron's, are real men and women. He harmonizes all elements of his poems. Peter is convincingly converted in Peter Bell. (Dated 1852; reprinted from a periodical not identified.)

13   [PALGRAVE, FRANCIS TURNER]. Review of Bell's Annotated Series of British Poets. Quarterly Review, 110 (October), 435–59 (447–50).
     Wordsworth, in contrast with earlier poets, connects a natural scene with a universal moral rather than with individual feeling.

14   PALGRAVE, FRANCIS TURNER. "Notes," in The Golden Treasury of the Best Songs and Lyrical Poems in the English Language. Edited by Francis Turner Palgrave. Cambridge and London: Macmillan, pp. 308–23 (322–23).
     Suggests a comparison between "Elegiac Stanzas Suggested by a Picture of Peele Castle" and Shelley's Prometheus Unbound; praises the exaltation of "To the Cuckoo" ("O blithe New-comer! I have heard"). Expanded in 1884.B21.

1862 A   BOOKS – NONE

1862 B   SHORTER WRITINGS

1   ANON. "Life of William Wordsworth," in Select Poems. By William Wordsworth. With Life of the Author. London: Milner [c. 1862], pp. v–xxiv.
     A biographical sketch.

2   ANON. The Poet of the Age: A Satirical Poem. London: Hardwicke, pp. 121–25, 131, 143–44.
     Wordsworth fails because he chooses inconsequential heroes (especially the pedlar in The Excursion) and because he makes poetry the vehicle for his peculiar theories and so can be appreciated only by the disciples of his own sect.

1862

3   ANON. "Wordsworth, William," in The Popular Encyclopedia; or, Conversations Lexicon: Being a General Dictionary of Arts, Sciences, Literature, Biography, History, and Politics; with Preliminary Dissertations by Distinguished Writers. New and revised edition. Illustrated. 7 vols. Glasgow, Edinburgh, and London: Blackie [1862], VII:892-94.
    A biographical sketch. Revised in 1877.B5.

4   ARNOLD, MATTHEW. On Translating Homer: Last Words: A Lecture Given at Oxford. London: Longman, pp. 22, 29-30, 57-62.
    In The Prelude ("at the Hoop alighted") Wordsworth sinks "with his subject by resolving not to sink with it." In "Michael" his simplicity is natural. In "Ruth" the gravity of his subject forces him to expand the ballad form.

5   ARNOLD, THOMAS. A Manual of English Literature, Historical and Critical: with an Appendix on English Metres. London: Longman, especially pp. 217, 229-33, 314, 338-39, 407.
    A biographical sketch. Wordsworth's system of classifying his poems illustrates the self-conscious spirit of modern times. The lyrical ballads are not lyrical, because they contain not passion but reflection. The Excursion is the most important English philosophical poem. Wordsworth's frequent introduction in The Excursion of lines with only three accents is not pleasing.

6   GORDON, MRS. [MARY], ed. "Christopher North": A Memoir of John Wilson . . . Compiled from Family Papers and other Sources. By his Daughter. 2 vols. Edinburgh: Edmonston and Douglas, I:39-48, 125-35, 199-200, 211; II:142.
    Recounts Wilson's opinion of Lyrical Ballads and The White Doe of Rylstone and his associations with Wordsworth in the Lake District. Prints letters in which F. Jeffrey responds to Wilson's defense of Wordsworth and in which A. Cunningham complains of Wordsworth's attitude towards the annuals.

7   GRATTAN, THOMAS COLLEY. Beaten Paths; And Those Who Trod Them. 2 vols. London: Chapman and Hall, II:107-45.
    Describes meeting and touring with Wordsworth and Coleridge in Belgium in 1828: Wordsworth's coarse appearance, absence of egotism, commonplace conversation, searching for tombstones, bad French, and criticism of Byron and Scott.

8   [HUNT, THORNTON, ed.]. The Correspondence of Leigh Hunt. Edited by his Eldest Son. 2 vols. London: Smith, Elder, I:92, 206, 217, 262, 265, 317; II:92-93.

Includes letters in which Hunt acknowledges Wordsworth's
merits, notes that Wordsworth's poetry is not musical, and
calls Wordsworth "a kind of puritan retainer of the Estab-
lishment." Includes letter from L. Blanchard reporting
Wordsworth's admiration of Hunt, and letter from T. Moore
lamenting that Wordsworth's absurdities were so rudely
handled by critics.

9   [INGLIS, ROBERT]. "William Wordsworth," in Gleanings from the
     English Poets, Chaucer to Tennyson. [Edited by Robert
     Inglis.] Edinburgh: Gall & Inglis; London: Houlston &
     Wright [1862], pp. 362-63.
        A biographical sketch. Attribution: Bodleian catalogue.

10   KENT, W.[ILLIAM] CHARLES. "Wordsworth at Rydal" (poem), in
     Dreamland: with Other Poems. London: Longman, pp. 97-100.
        Wordsworth, "of Nature's homeliest mould," "broods on
     Earth's neglected things."

11   PATTERSON, ALEXANDER S. Poets and Preachers of the Nineteenth
     Century: Four Lectures, Biographical and Critical, on
     Wordsworth, Montgomery, Hall, and Chalmers. Glasgow:
     Murray; Edinburgh: Paton and Ritchie; London: Hall,
     Virtue, pp. 3-46.
        A biographical sketch. To Wordsworth the outward as-
     pects of nature and men were morally suggestive. His po-
     litical, religious, and literary views were narrow.

12   WORSLEY, P.[HILIP] S.[TANHOPE]. "Stanzas to Wordsworth."
     Blackwood's Edinburgh Magazine, 92 (July), 92-93.
        Wordsworth teaches one the "remedial virtue" of rapture
     with nature. Reprinted in Poems and Translations (1863).

1863 A   BOOKS - NONE

1863 B   SHORTER WRITINGS

1   ANON. "The Poems of Hood and of Wordsworth." Christian
     Observer, 62 (September), 677-97.
        A biographical sketch. Wordsworth's poetry had its
     sources in Wordsworth's friends and the circumstances of
     his life.

2   ANON. "Life of William Wordsworth," in The Poetical Works of
     William Wordsworth. Illustrated by Keeley Halswelle.
     Edinburgh: Nimmo, pp. iii-xiv.
        A biographical sketch.

1863

3   ARNOLD, MATTHEW. "Dante and Beatrice." Fraser's Magazine, 67
     (May), 665-69 (665-66, 669).
         Contrasts Dante's conception of Beatrice with Words-
     worth's portrait in "She was a Phantom of delight."

4   ARNOLD, MATTHEW. "Heinrich Heine." Cornhill Magazine, 8
     (August), 233-49 (242-43).
         Wordsworth "voluntarily cut himself off from the modern
     spirit." Reprinted in 1865.B4.

5   BYRNE, THE REV. JAMES. "The Influence of National Character
     on English Literature," in The Afternoon Lectures on English
     Literature: Delivered in the Theatre of the Museum of
     Industry, S. Stephen's Green, Dublin, in May and June,
     1863. London: Bell and Daldy; Dublin: Hodges and Smith,
     and Mc Gee, pp. 1-40 (24-26).
         Wordsworth's inspiration as prophet of nature was
     heightened by the mood of the times and his personal crisis
     of faith during the French Revolution.

6   C.[OLERIDGE], D.[ERWENT]. "Introduction," in The Wanderer:
     Being the First Book of The Excursion. By William
     Wordsworth. London: Moxon, pp. iii-vii.
         A biographical sketch. Wordsworth's poetry is well
     suited for the purposes of instruction: in the present
     case, for the structure of the language. Attribution:
     British Museum catalogue.

7   FERRIER, J. F. "Wordsworth, William," in The Imperial
     Dictionary of Universal Biography: A Series of Original
     Memoirs of Distinguished Men of All Ages and All Nations.
     Edited by John Francis Waller. 3 vols. London, Glasgow,
     Edinburgh, etc.: Mackenzie [1863], III:932-34.
         A biographical sketch. Commends Wordsworth's "spell-
     like originality."

8   GILCHRIST, ALEXANDER. Life of William Blake, "Pictor Ignotus,"
     with Selections from his Poems and Other Writings.
     Illustrated by W. J. Linton. 2 vols. London and Cambridge:
     Macmillan, I:1-2, 27, 73-74, 104, 120-23, 343-47.
         Records Wordsworth's admiration for Blake and compares
     Blake's career with Wordsworth's. Wordsworth's matter, not
     manner, was obnoxious to critics. Includes H. C. Robinson's
     reminiscences of Blake's rapture over "Ode: Intimations of
     Immortality" and his view that Wordsworth's worship of na-
     ture constituted atheism. Prints Blake's marginalia to
     Poems (1815): Wordsworth "'must know that what he writes
     valuable is not to be found in nature'"; Wordsworth's
     prefaces contradict his poems.

9 GRANT, ALEXANDER H. "W. Wordsworth," in Half-Hours with Our
   Sacred Poets. Edited by Alexander H. Grant. Illustrated
   by H. S. Marks. London: Hogg [1863], pp. 318-19.
   A biographical sketch. Of modern poems, Wordsworth
   valued only his own.

10 [HUTTON, RICHARD HOLT]. "Shelley's Poetical Mysticism."
    National Review, 16 (January), 62-87 (63-65).
    Wordsworth's meditative mysticism, based on the real
    earth, differs from Shelley's. Reprinted in 1871.B7.

11 [JERDAN, WILLIAM]. "Men I Have Known: William Wordsworth."
    Leisure Hour, 12 (3 October), 628-31.
    Wordsworth's poetry is characterized by the mixing of
    the affected with the natural, by minute observation and
    studied simplicity of language, by trying to make too much
    of small subjects, and by morality. Records visit to Rydal
    Mount; Wordsworth was "facile and courteous" and witty when
    in London. Reprinted in Men I Have Known (1866).

12 LANDOR, WALTER SAVAGE. "Squibs, crackers, serpents, rockets,
    Bengal lights" (poem), "Come lads, the day is all before
    ye" (poem), "To a Poet" (poem), "One tooth has Wordsworth,
    but in sooth" (poem), in Heroic Idyls, with Additional
    Poems. London: Newby, pp. 181, 187, 247, 274.
    Notes Wordsworth's poems put him to sleep (181). Words-
    worth writes "curds and whey" (187). Wishes Wordsworth
    "would forbear / From sticking pins into my chair" (247).
    Reprinted, with verbal change identifying Wordsworth, from
    1846.B10 (274).

13 [PEARSON, ANN]. "Memoir of William Pearson," in Papers Letters
    and Journals of William Pearson. Edited by his Widow.
    London: privately printed, pp. 3-174 (13, 27-106, 137-73).
    James Patrick was the prototype of the Wanderer in The
    Excursion. Includes account of G. Dawe's admiration of
    Wordsworth's poems, of Wordsworth's presence in 1812 at a
    wrestling match, of Pearson's early appreciation of Words-
    worth's poems, and of Wordsworth's intervention with the
    Colonial Office in 1827 on behalf of a friend. Includes
    letters to Pearson from T. Smith on the cost of purchasing
    Wordsworth's poems and on his admiration for Wordsworth,
    correspondence concerning Wordsworth's composing an epitaph
    for Smith's wife and preparing a new edition of his poems
    in 1826, and miscellaneous letters, chiefly from Dorothy
    Wordsworth, concerning daily life at Rydal Mount from the
    1820's onward. Records a visit to Rydal in 1844, corre-
    spondence with Wordsworth in 1849, and correspondence with

1863

> R. P. Graves in 1854 over Wordsworth's role in the Oxford
> Movement. Prints Pearson's account of his visit in 1855 to
> Wordsworth's grave.

14   PEARSON, WILLIAM. "Wordsworth's Protestantism," "To Words-
     worth" (poem), in Papers Letters and Journals of William
     Pearson. Edited by his Widow [Ann Pearson]. London:
     privately printed, pp. 295-99, 324.
           Reprinted from 1854.B9 (295-99). Wordsworth reveals the
     depths of feeling, heals our doubts and griefs (324).

15   ROBINSON, THE REV. H.[UGH] G.[EORGE]. "Notes," in The First
     Book of The Excursion: The Wanderer. . . . By William
     Wordsworth. Edinburgh: Gordon; London: Hamilton Adams,
     pp. 39-47.
           Brief critical notes.

16   RUSHTON, WILLIAM. "The Classical and Romantic Schools of
     English Literature: As Represented by Spenser, Dryden,
     Pope, Scott, and Wordsworth," in The Afternoon Lectures on
     English Literature: Delivered in the Theatre of the Museum
     of Industry, S. Stephen's Green, Dublin, in May and June,
     1863. London: Bell and Daldy; Dublin: Hodges and Smith,
     and Mc Gee, pp. 41-92 (81-87).
           Wordsworth offended critics by going out of his way to
     introduce trivial language and by assuming a dogmatic tone
     in the Preface to Lyrical Ballads. He was more successful
     in turning men to nature, and in his sonnets.

1864 A   BOOKS - NONE

1864 B   SHORTER WRITINGS

1   ARNOLD, MATTHEW. "The Function of Criticism at the Present
     Time." National Review, NS no. 1 (November), pp. 230-51
     (230-31, 233-34).
           Wordsworth, himself a great critic, exaggerated his dis-
     paragement of literary critics. He would have been a
     greater poet had he read more. Expanded in 1865.B4.

2   B.[AGEHOT], W.[ALTER]. "Wordsworth, Tennyson, and Browning;
     or, Pure, Ornate, and Grotesque Art in English Poetry."
     National Review, NS no. 1 (November), pp. 27-67 (29, 39-41,
     44-45).
           Wordsworth, in his pure style, writes precisely, without
     anything unnecessary; yet he lacks spontaneity.

3   BROMBY, THE REV. C.[HARLES] H.[ENRY]. Notes, in The First
    Book of Wordsworth's Excursion. Edited by the Rev. C. H.
    Bromby. London: Longman, passim.
        Brief critical notes.

4   [BROWN, JOHN TAYLOR]. Review of Mémoires d'un Bibliophile and
    The Book-Hunter. North British Review, 40 (February),
    70-92 (78, 84-88).
        Describes Wordsworth's autographs and annotations in
    copies of Drayton and Scriptores de Re Rustica, and Sara
    Coleridge's manuscript criticisms of "The Blind Highland
    Boy" and "Gipsies." Reprinted in "Bibliomania" (1867).

5   COLQUHOUN, JOHN CAMPBELL. Scattered Leaves of Biography.
    London: Macintosh, pp. 137-221.
        A full biographical and critical sketch, designed "to do
    right to a reputation which has been wronged" by previous
    biographers. Wordsworth's observations are minutely accur-
    ate, though he was misled by his theory of poetry and his
    writing is marred by long words and hazy ideas. His poetry
    is Christian in spirit. Wordsworth failed not so much in
    his choice of inferior subjects as in his handling of them.
    The greatness of his poetry rises from its appeal to man's
    inner sense.

6   FOWLER, FRANK. Last Gleanings. With a Preface by a Friend.
    London: Sampson Low, Son, and Marston, p. 234.
        Wordsworth's calm, clear style approaches the naked
    grandeur of the Greek lyrists.

7   GARNETT, R.[ICHARD]. "Letters from Coleridge to William
    Godwin." Macmillan's Magazine, 9 (April), 524-36 (passim).
        Includes letters in which Coleridge discusses The Bor-
    derers and praises Wordsworth.

8   KNIGHT, CHARLES. Passages of a Working Life during Half a
    Century: with A Prelude of Early Reminiscences. 3 vols.
    London: Bradbury & Evans, I:174, 206, 221, 289; II:54.
        Around 1818 Wordsworth's higher poetry was scarcely
    known popularly. His universality has sent his poems into
    the homes of the poor and lowly. Records H. N. Coleridge's
    defense of Wordsworth. For Volume III, see 1865.B13.

9   LE BRETON, PHILIP HEMERY, ed. Memoirs, Miscellanies and
    Letters of the late Lucy Aikin: including those Addressed
    to the Rev. Dr. Channing from 1826 to 1842. London:
    Longman, pp. 223, 229-30.

1864

Includes letters in which Lucy Aikin reports Wordsworth's conversation against general education and the Reform Bill, and notes that though Wordsworth advances as a poet in Yarrow Revisited, the volume shows his dread of innovation.

10   LOWNDES, WILLIAM THOMAS and HENRY G. BOHN. The Bibliographer's Manual of English Literature. . . . New edition, revised, corrected, and enlarged. Part X. London: Bohn, pp. 2992-93.
A primary bibliography.

11   MORLEY, HENRY. "Introduction: The Four Periods of English Literature," in English Writers: The Writers before Chaucer; with an Introductory Sketch of the Four Periods of English Literature. London: Chapman and Hall, pp. 1-116 (104-106).
"The introspective spirit of Goethe was in Wordsworth healthier for its English setting."

12   [SHAIRP, JOHN CAMPBELL]. "Wordsworth: The Man and the Poet." North British Review, 41 (August), 1-54.
An extended biographical sketch and survey of Wordsworth's poems. Wordsworth's popularity is now at the ebb. The reader must reenact Wordsworth's thinking to understand his poems. His imagination possessed itself of the life of whatever it dealt with, though its interest in human life was limited in his early years. His Christian faith grew over the years. Revised and expanded in 1868.B14.

13   SHAW, THOMAS B. The Student's Manual of English Literature: A History of English Literature. A new edition, enlarged and rewritten. Edited by William Smith. London: Murray, pp. 446-51.
Revised from 1849.B11. Adds a biographical sketch.

1865 A   BOOKS - NONE

1865 B   SHORTER WRITINGS

1   ANGUS, JOSEPH. The Handbook of English Literature. London: Religious Tract Society [1865], especially pp. 233-34, 256-59, 275.
A biographical sketch. Wordsworth excels in "ethical wisdom," meditative and descriptive poetry. The experiment of Lyrical Ballads failed: the volume did not sell. Wordsworth's early, middle, and late works must be judged separately. His poems rank with Cowper's in naturalness; though

religious, they are not specifically Christian. His use of only four accented syllables per line in The Excursion is offensive.

2   ANON. Letters and Remains of Arthur Hugh Clough. London: privately printed, pp. 39, 57–58, 69.
    Includes letter in which Clough comments on Wordsworth at Oxford in 1839 and an account by J. C. Shairp of Clough's defending Wordsworth in an Oxford debate.

3   ANON. "William Wordsworth: 1770–1850," in Chambers's Readings in English Poetry. London and Edinburgh: Chambers [1865], p. 131.
    A biographical sketch.

4   ARNOLD, MATTHEW. "The Function of Criticism at the Present Time," "Heinrich Heine," in Essays in Criticism. London and Cambridge: Macmillan, pp. 1–41 (2–4, 7), 151–86 (171).
    Expanded from 1864.B1. Wordsworth's works had their source in a great movement of feeling, not of mind (2–4, 7). Reprinted from 1863.B4 (171).

5   [AYTOUN, WILLIAM EDMONSTOUNE]. "Sir E. Bulwer Lytton's Poems." Blackwood's Edinburgh Magazine, 97 (March), 330–41 (331).
    Wordsworth's simpler ballads have outlived The Excursion.

6   BROOKE, STOPFORD A., ed. Life and Letters of Frederick W. Robertson. . . . Illustrated. 2 vols. London: Smith, Elder, I:22–24, 46–47, 176–77, 351–53; II:173–83, 205, 224.
    Records Robertson's veneration for Wordsworth. Includes letters in which Robertson records Wordsworth's reception at Oxford in 1839 and his comments that in The Prelude Wordsworth shows, in clear and pure diction, how a pure character is built up out of a life apparently monotonous. Records the controversy over Robertson's discussion of Wordsworth's pantheism and religion in his lecture on Wordsworth.

7   C. "Two Poets of England." Temple Bar, 16 (December), 106–16 (106–109, 115–16).
    Describes visit to Wordsworth at Rydal Mount. "Conscious that his attempts to be lyrical were clumsy and awkward, he preferred the sonnet" for his occasional poems.

8   C., G. A. "Preface," in Poems. By the late Edmund J. Armstrong. London: Moxon, pp. iii–li (viii, xlix–l).
    Includes Joseph Napier's recollections of the spiritual strength Armstrong found in Wordsworth's poems.

1865

9   [CLOUGH, ARTHUR HUGH]. Review of The Works of William
        Wordsworth. North American Review, 100 (April), 508-21.
            A biographical sketch. Wordsworth influenced and was in-
        fluenced by his contemporary poets. His chief charm derives
        from his style, which is in opposition to the principles of
        his prefaces. He wrote too much. His writing is charac-
        terized by elevation, moral selectivity, evasion of the
        actual world, false "positiveness," and mawkishness.

10   DENNIS, JOHN, ed. Evenings in Arcadia. London: Moxon,
        pp. 13, 103-107, 160-61, 184-85, 221-63.
            Wordsworth succeeds in his translation of "The Cuckoo
        and the Nightingale." In his descriptions he gives not a
        literal copy but the thoughts and images the scene suggested
        to him. His arguments on Thomson's fame in Essay (1815) are
        faulty. He seldom read other poets. His power lies in the
        beauty of detached thoughts and single lines, in his son-
        nets, and in his accurate observations of nature. He grows
        feeble when he follows his critical tenets. The pathos of
        his pastorals is painful. His influence is profound but
        not universal. His poetry is at once spiritual and pic-
        toral.

11   FANSHAWE, MISS CATHERINE MARIA. "Fragment in imitation of
        Wordsworth" (poem), in Memorials of Miss Catherine Maria
        Fanshawe. [Edited by William Harness.] [London:]
        privately printed [1865], pp. 49-51.
            An imitation/burlesque.

12   JACOX, FRANCIS. "The Child is Father of the Man: A Cue from
        Wordsworth." New Monthly Magazine, [NS] 133 (March),
        289-302 (289, 292, 296).
            Wordsworth is metaphysical in "My heart leaps up when
        I behold."

13   KNIGHT, CHARLES. Passages of a Working Life during Half a
        Century: with A Prelude of Early Reminiscences. 3 vols.
        London: Bradbury & Evans, III:27-29.
            Records visit with Wordsworth in 1849: the cottagers
        greeted Wordsworth with familiar respect; he was not in-
        terested in modern books. For Volumes I-II, see 1864.B8.

14   [LEIGH, HENRY S.]. "Only Seven: A Pastoral Story, After
        Wordsworth" (poem). Fun, NS 2 (11 November), 81.
            Parody of "We Are Seven." Reprinted in Carols of
        Cockayne (1869).

15   LEWES, GEORGE HENRY. "The Principles of Success in Literature."
     Fortnightly Review, 1 (15 July), 572–89 (580–82);
     (1 August), 697–709 (708).
          Wordsworth's description in The Prelude is imaginative,
     accurate (580–82). His poems affect us because he puts in
     them things he has seen (708).

16   PALGRAVE, FRANCIS TURNER. "Biographical Preface," in A
     Selection from the Works of William Wordsworth. Edited by
     Francis Turner Palgrave. London: Moxon, pp. iii–xxi.
          A biographical sketch. Wordsworth's view of nature pro-
     gressed from an idealistic one to one of Christian panthe-
     ism. The republicanism of his early subjects and style
     gave way to greater floridity and more direct moralizing as
     he became more conservative.

17   RUSKIN, JOHN. "Lecture II.--Lilies: Of Queens' Gardens," in
     Sesame and Lilies: Two Lectures Delivered at Manchester in
     1864: 1. Of Kings' Treasuries, 2. Of Queens' Gardens.
     London: Smith, Elder, pp. 119–96 (151–54, 166).
          Wordsworth, a poet distinguished "by exquisite right-
     ness," perfectly describes womanly beauty in "Three years
     she grew in sun and shower" and "She was a Phantom of de-
     light."

18   [SHAIRP, JOHN CAMPBELL]. "Samuel Taylor Coleridge." North
     British Review, 43 (December), 251–322 (253–91 [passim]).
          Discusses Wordsworth's life and work as they touch Cole-
     ridge's. Reprinted with minor additions in 1868.B14.

19   TRENCH, RICHARD CHENEVIX. "Sonnet" ("A counsellor well fitted
     to advise"), in Poems. Collected and arranged anew.
     London and Cambridge: Macmillan, p. 83.
          Hails a poet (presumably Wordsworth) as a fit counsellor
     in daily life.

1866 A   BOOKS - NONE

1866 B   SHORTER WRITINGS

1   ANON. "Mr. Swinburne, His Crimes and His Critics." Eclectic
     Review, [8th ser.,] 11 (December), 493–508 (496–97, 505).
          Swinburne is blind to Wordsworth's moral grandeur.
     Wordsworth persevered to triumph over his critics.

2   ASKEW, JOHN. A Guide to the Interesting Places in and around
     Cockermouth, with an Account of its Remarkable Men and
     Local Traditions. Cockermouth: Evening, pp. 22–24.

1866

        Recounts humorous encounter of Wordsworth with three
drunken rustics near Brigham.

3   CORNWALL, BARRY. <u>See</u> 1866.B13.

4   DALLAS, E.[NEAS] S.[WEETLAND]. <u>The Gay Science</u>. 2 vols.
        London: Chapman and Hall, I:50-51, 127, 292-93, 320-24.
        Wordsworth harped incessantly on the opposition between
nature and humanity. He wrote for the few. Peter Bell
fails to see the primrose as a type. Because it appeals to
the hidden soul, some of Wordsworth's poetry is rightly
without analyzable meaning.

5   DAWSON, JAMES, JR. "Wordsworth and Hartley Coleridge: In
        Grasmere Churchyard, Westmoreland" (poem). <u>Macmillan's</u>
        <u>Magazine</u>, 13 (January), 232.
        Salutes Wordsworth and Hartley Coleridge, two poets
"whom nothing could divide."

6   FITZHOPKINS. "Notes on Fly-leaves: Peter Bell." <u>Notes and</u>
        <u>Queries</u>, 3rd ser., 9 (10 February), 127.
        Reynolds and Wordsworth were friends until the publica-
tion of Reynolds's parody of <u>Peter Bell</u>.

7   HALL, S.[AMUEL] C.[ARTER] and MRS. S. C. HALL. "Memories of
        the Authors of the Age: . . . William Wordsworth." <u>Art-</u>
        <u>Journal</u>, NS 5 (August), 245-49; (September), 273-77.
        A biographical and character sketch; prints Sir John
Mac Neill's testimony to Wordsworth's expounding of God's
goodness, and letters of Southey (criticizing Wordsworth's
straining to examine the minute in nature) and Hunt (ex-
plaining that Wordsworth's lack of popularity arose from
the taste of the times and his own excesses). Wordsworth
was pleased by the large sale of Galignani's pirated edition. Includes verse tribute by John Dillon: thought to
Wordsworth was feeling, earth a heaven (245-49). Describes
a tour of Grasmere, Rydal, and the Lake District. <u>A Guide</u>
<u>through the District of the Lakes</u> is dull (273-77). Ex-
panded in 1871.B6; recast as 1883.B29.

8   HANNAY, JAMES. <u>A Course of English Literature</u>. London:
        Tinsley, pp. 12-13, 202-203, 228-31.
        Outlines a course of reading in Wordsworth, a poetic
reformer.

9   MAUNDER, SAMUEL and WILLIAM L. R. CATES. "Wordsworth, William,"
        in <u>The Biographical Treasury; A Dictionary of Universal</u>
        <u>Biography</u>. Thirteenth edition, revised. London: Longmans,
        pp. 1110-11.

1866

Briefly expanded by Cates from 1851.B25. A biographical
sketch. Recast in 1867.B8.

10   NOEL, RODEN. "On the Use of Metaphor and 'Pathetic Fallacy'
in Poetry." Fortnightly Review, 5 (1 August), 670-84
(677-79).
Wordsworth speaks unguardedly when discussing the alter-
ing power of imagination in the Preface (1815). Incorporated in "On the Poetic Interpretation of Nature" in
1886.B36.

11   PALGRAVE, F.[RANCIS] T.[URNER]. "Descriptive Poetry in
England from Anne to Victoria." Fortnightly Review, 5
(15 June), 298-320 (300, 302, 306-308, 314-20).
Wordsworth evenly unites the poetry of man and of nature.
His poetry reflects his life.

12   [PATER, WALTER]. Review of Conversations, Letters, and
Recollections of S. T. Coleridge. Westminster Review,
NS 29 (1 January), 106-32 (108-10).
In partial contrast with Coleridge, Wordsworth engaged
in "a reflective, but altogether unformulated, analysis"
of the affinities between nature and man. Recast as
"Coleridge" in 1889.B49.

13   [PROCTER, BRYAN WALLER] BARRY CORNWALL. Charles Lamb: A
Memoir. London: Moxon, especially pp. 51, 53, 83-88, 143,
147.
Even Wordsworth was indebted to Coleridge. Wordsworth's
longer poems contain barren wastes; yet his genius and influence are great. His battle for fame has been perilous.
Records his impressions upon meeting Wordsworth: Wordsworth's fondness for reciting his own poetry. Records
Lamb's friendship with Wordsworth.

14   [SAUNDERS, FREDERICK]. Festival of Song: A Series of
Evenings with the Poets. Illustrated. New York: Bunce
and Huntington, pp. 265-72.
Wordsworth decks his themes with "roseate tints and
aromatic odours." Revised in 1887.B47.

15   SILAX. "Notes on Fly-leaves: Peter Bell." Notes and Queries,
3rd ser., 9 (10 February), 127.
Byron, indebted to Wordsworth, was dishonest in ridiculing him.

16   SWINBURNE, ALGERNON CHARLES. "Preface," in A Selection from
the Works of Lord Byron. Edited by Algernon Charles
Swinburne. London: Moxon, pp. v-xxix (v, xi, xxvii).

1866

> Wordsworth used nature "as a vegetable fit to shred into his pot and pare down . . . for didactic and culinary purposes." Expanded in 1875.B20.

17   [THOMSON, JAMES] B. V. "The Poems of William Blake."
      National Reformer, NS 7 (14 January), 22-23 (23);
      (4 February), 70-71 (70).
          Wordsworth "was a good, conscientious, awkward pedagogue, who, charmed by the charms of childhood, endeavoured himself to play the child."

18   THOMSON, THE REV. THOMAS. "Biographical Sketch of the Ettrick Shepherd," in The Works of the Ettrick Shepherd: Poems and Life. A new edition. Edited by the Rev. Thomas Thomson. Illustrated. [2 vols.] London, Glasgow, and Edinburgh: Blackie, [II:]ix-lvi (xxxii-xxxiii, xxxviii, 1-li).
          Recounts Hogg's relationship with Wordsworth.

19   V., B. See 1866.B17.

20   Z., X. Y. "Notes on Fly-leaves." Notes and Queries, 3rd ser., 9 (20 January), 66-67.
          Describes Reynolds's parody of Peter Bell. (A reply to J. B., "Notes on Fly-leaves," Notes and Queries, 3rd ser., 8 [23 December 1865], 522.)

1867 A   BOOKS - NONE

1867 B   SHORTER WRITINGS

1   ANON. "Wordsworth," in The Royal Dictionary-Cyclopaedia, for Universal Reference. Edited by Thomas Wright. Illustrated. 5 vols. London and New York: London Printing and Publishing [1867], V:936.
          A biographical sketch.

2   [BULWER-LYTTON, EDWARD]. Review of Talfourd's Final Memorials of Charles Lamb, etc. Quarterly Review, 122 (January), 1-29 (3, 6-7, 21).
          The Cockney School paved the way for the appreciation of Wordsworth. Reprinted in Miscellaneous Prose Works (1868).

3   DIXON, J. H. "Wordsworth and the 'Pet Lamb.'" Notes and Queries, 3rd ser., 11 (27 April), 330.
          Barbara Lewthwaite, a plain girl, was not involved in the incident recorded in "The Pet-lamb."

Writings about William Wordsworth, 1793 - 1899

1867

4 GRAVES, THE VERY REV. CHARLES. "Address." Proceedings of the
Royal Irish Academy, 9:307-16 (312-13).
W. R. Hamilton was responsible for raising Wordsworth's
estimate of science.

5 HUNT, LEIGH. "An Essay on the Cultivation, History, and
Varieties of the Species of Poem Called the Sonnet," Notes,
in The Book of The Sonnet. Edited by Leigh Hunt and S.
Adams Lee. 2 vols. Boston: Roberts, I:3-91 (6, 82-86),
226-27, 235-38, 240, 242.
Wordsworth does not exhibit Milton's independence of
mind; Sonnets upon the Punishment of Death are deplorable
(6, 82-86). Many of those Wordsworth describes in "Nuns
fret not at their convent's narrow room" do indeed protest
their loss of liberty. In "London, 1802" he takes liberties
with Milton's name. Praises Wordsworth's description in "A
Parsonage in Oxfordshire"; suggests an Italian source for
"Methought I saw the footsteps of a throne" (226-27, 235-38,
240, 242).

6 JACOX, FRANCIS. "About Peter Bell and Primroses: A Cue from
Wordsworth." New Monthly Magazine, [NS] 141 (October),
161-73.
Peter Bell is typical in his attitude towards primroses.
Reprinted with omissions in Cues from All Quarters (1871).

7 LARKINS, WILLIAM GEORGE. A Handbook of English Literature:
Poets. London: Routledge, pp. 150-53.
A biographical sketch. The Excursion is becoming in-
creasingly popular. Wordsworth followed, rather than initiated, a change in literary taste.

8 [MAUNDER, SAMUEL and WILLIAM L. R. CATES]. "Wordsworth,
William," in A Dictionary of General Biography. . . .
Edited by William L. R. Cates. London: Longmans,
pp. 1246-47.
A biographical sketch, recast from 1866.B9.

9 [MILNES, RICHARD MONCKTON,] LORD HOUGHTON, ed. The Life and
Letters of John Keats. A new edition. London: Moxon,
p. 57.
Adds to previously published Keats correspondence letter
in which Keats defends and criticizes "Gipsies."

10 PAYN, JAMES. The Lakes in Sunshine: Being Photographic and
Other Pictures of the Lake District of Westmorland and
North Lancashire. Windermere: Garnett, pp. 17, 26, 32-54,
67, 70, 84, 90-91.

1867

Solemn Wordsworth believed in his calling; he strangely, for one who preferred solitude, entitled his principal poem The Excursion. He prospered financially, though the local people preferred Hartley Coleridge's poems. Wordsworth's descriptions in The Prelude of his schooltime are as minute as Rousseau's, though Wordsworth has no weaknesses to confess. His descriptions in The Excursion (Book I), The River Duddon, and "Resolution and Independence" are true to nature.

11 SWINBURNE, ALGERNON CHARLES. "Mr. Arnold's New Poems." Fortnightly Review, NS 2 (1 October), 414-45 (424-29, 440). Wordsworth, a "great poet, perverse theorist, and incomplete man," influenced men, including M. Arnold, because of his power of will, his genius, and his "invincible Philistinism." Wordsworth's pathos is trenchant, not tender. Reprinted in 1875.B20.

12 [SYMONDS, JOHN ADDINGTON]. "Blank Verse." Cornhill Magazine, 15 (May), 620-40 (637-38). Wordsworth's blank verse is tediously heavy. Reprinted in Sketches and Studies in Italy (1879).

13 TRENCH, RICHARD CHENEVIX. "The History of the English Sonnet," in The Afternoon Lectures on Literature and Art: Delivered in the Theatre of the Museum of Industry, S. Stephen's Green, Dublin, in April and May, 1866. Fourth series. London: Bell and Daldy; Dublin: Hodges and Smith, and Mc Gee, pp. 133-66 (136, 153-58). Commends Wordsworth's originality in the use of the sonnet sequence, and his sonnets to liberty. Reprinted in The Sonnets of William Wordsworth (1884).

1868 A BOOKS - NONE

1868 B SHORTER WRITINGS

1 ALEXANDER, PATRICK PROCTOR. "Memoir," "Appendix: Plagiarisms of Alexander Smith" (unsigned), in Last Leaves: Sketches and Criticisms. By Alexander Smith. Edited by Patrick Procter Alexander. Edinburgh: Nimmo, pp. v-cxxiii (xxi), 315-34 (319-27, 333). Records Smith's opinion that nothing but Lake water came from Wordsworth (xxi). Notes parallel passages in Wordsworth and Milton, and in Wordsworth and later nineteenth-century poets (319-27, 333).

2   ANON. Catalogue of the Third and Concluding Exhibition of
     National Portraits Commencing with the Fortieth Year of the
     Reign of George the Third and Ending with the Year
     MDCCCLXVII: on Loan to the South Kensington Museum:
     April 13, 1868. London: Science and Art Department of
     the Committee of Council on Education, pp. 52, 55-56.
     Describes paintings of Wordsworth.

3   ANON. "Wordsworth, William," in Chambers's Encyclopaedia: A
     Dictionary of Universal Knowledge for the People. [Edited
     by Andrew Findlater.] Illustrated. 10 vols. London and
     Edinburgh: Chambers, X:272-74.
        A biographical sketch. Wordsworth added philosophic
     meditation to the movement towards truth and simplicity
     initiated by Cowper and Burns. The early ridicule of his
     poems was deserved.

4   ANON. "Wordsworth, William," in The National Encyclopaedia:
     A Dictionary of Universal Knowledge. By Writers of
     Eminence in Literature, Science, and Art. 13 vols.
     London, Glasgow, Edinburgh: Mackenzie [1868], XIII
     (Part 65):959-61.
        A biographical sketch. Wordsworth does not merely de-
     scribe but shows the inner relations of nature. Revised
     and expanded in 1888.B40.

5   BUCHANAN, ROBERT [WILLIAMS]. "The Poet, or Seer," "On My Own
     Tentatives," in David Gray, and Other Essays, Chiefly on
     Poetry. London: Sampson Low, Son, and Marston, pp. 3-60
     (28-32, 56-58), 289-318 (294-95).
        Wordsworth's "emotional meditation" in "Tintern Abbey"
     succeeds as poetry, while that in a passage from The Prelude
     fails (28-32, 56-58). Wordsworth dissected "silent endur-
     ance with iron pathos"; his pictures of life are often too
     cold and disinterested (294-95).

6   BUNSEN, BARONESS FRANCES. A Memoir of Baron Bunsen. . . .
     2 vols. London: Longmans, II:137, 234.
        Wordsworth in 1849 was "utterly broken in spirit" by the
     loss of Dora. Includes letter in which Baron Bunsen notes
     that the performance of "Ode on the Installation of His
     Royal Highness Prince Albert" was "affecting."

7   CARPENTER, J.[OSEPH] E.[DWARDS]. A Handbook of Poetry. . . .
     London: Sampson Low, Son, and Marston, pp. 53-54.
        Wordsworth alone advocates using ordinary language for
     poetry, but he does not follow his own theory.

1868

8   [CONWAY, MONCURE D.]. "The Culture of Emerson." Fraser's
    Magazine, 78 (July), 1-19 (7).
        Wordsworth's pantheism was unconscious, overpowering his
    intellectual beliefs. Records Emerson's praise of Words-
    worth in lectures.

9   [GREEN, THOMAS HILL]. "Popular Philosophy in its Relation to
    Life." North British Review, 48 (March), 133-62 (156-58).
        Though his creative power had neither wide range nor
    spontaneity, Wordsworth delivered literature from bondage
    to a philosophy resting on passivity and individuality.

10 [HAZLITT, WILLIAM CAREW and G. A. SALA, eds.]. The Complete
    Correspondence and Works of Charles Lamb: With an Essay on
    his Life and Genius by George Augustus Sala. Volume I.
    London: Moxon, pp. 291, 402.
        Prints passages deleted in previous editions of his let-
    ters in which Lamb records that Hazlitt "goes on lecturing
    against W. W." and Wordsworth's opinion that he could write
    like Shakespeare if he wished. Attribution: W. C. Hazlitt
    in 1874.B24, p. 15.

11 [HUTTON, RICHARD HOLT?]. "Aristocratic and Democratic Poetry."
    Spectator, 41 (11 April), 431-32.
        Wordsworth's poetry changed with his politics. His
    poetry is rooted in "hardy mountaineer individualism."

12 MACDONALD, GEORGE. England's Antiphon. 3 parts. [London:]
    Macmillan, Part III (December), pp. 255-56, 261-62, 303-307.
        Compares Vaughan's "The Retreat" with "Ode: Intimations
    of Immortality." After the failure of the French Revolu-
    tion, the power of God came upon Wordsworth.

13 [MOZLEY, JOHN RICKARDS]. Review of The Poems of Samuel Taylor
    Coleridge. Quarterly Review, 125 (July), 78-106 (78, 83,
    91-99, 104).
        Wordsworth, in contrast with Coleridge, narrowed his
    mind to achieve his ends; he lost his communication with
    men. His prose criticism has been an essential element in
    his influence. His and Coleridge's sympathetic vision con-
    trasts with Byron's and Shelley's passion.

14 SHAIRP, J.[OHN] C.[AMPBELL]. "Preface," "Wordsworth,"
    "Coleridge," in Studies in Poetry and Philosophy.
    Edinburgh: Edmonston and Douglas, pp. v-x (vi-viii),
    1-115, 116-266 (120-99 [passim]).
        Wordsworth and Coleridge spoke of the soul to a sense-
    bound age. They serve as a lesson on how to discover faith

in an age of change. Reprinted in 1872.B27 (vi-viii). Revised and expanded from 1864.B12. The reader must be sub-
consciously atuned to Wordsworth's poems; Wordsworth does
not invest nature with his own feelings but draws out nature's own essence. Reprinted with verbal changes and additions in 1872.B27 (1-115). Reprinted with minor additions
from 1865.B18; reprinted in 1872.B27 (120-99).

15   TRENCH, RICHARD CHENEVIX. "Preface," "Notes," in A Household
      Book of English Poetry. Edited by Richard Chenevix Trench.
      London: Macmillan, pp. v-xii (ix), 389-415 (396, 406,
      408-10).
          "Tintern Abbey" and "Elegiac Stanzas Suggested by a Pic-
      ture of Peele Castle" are most characteristic of Wordsworth.
      Reprinted in 1870.B16 (ix). Notes similarities between
      Vaughan's "The Retreat" and "Ode: Intimations of Immortal-
      ity" and precedents for "To the Cuckoo" ("O blithe New-
      comer! I have heard") and the Yarrow poems. Revised in
      1870.B16 (396, 406, 408-10).

1869 A BOOKS - NONE

1869 B SHORTER WRITINGS

1   [ADAMS, W. H. DAVENPORT]. Notes, in The Household Treasury of
     English Song. Edited by W. H. Davenport Adams. London,
     Edinburgh, and New York: Nelson, pp. 144-63.
         A biographical sketch. Wordsworth's poems combine depth
     of thought with splendor of language. Brief critical notes
     to the poems selected, including "To the Same Flower"
     ("With little here to do or see"), "To the Small Celandine"
     ("Pansies, lillies, kingcups, daisies"), and "Simon Lee."

2   ANON. Review of Shairp's Studies in Poetry and Philosophy.
     Christian Observer, 68 (May), 344-55 (347-54).
         Wordsworth and Coleridge would have been more effective
     had they based their thought more fully on Christianity.

3   ANON. "Notes of a Lecture by George Macdonald," in The Old
     College: Being The Glasgow University Album for MDCCCLXIX.
     Edited by Students. Glasgow: Maclehose, pp. 290-305.
         "Wordsworth got amusement out of nature." He sneers at
     all worldlings and is blind to the ludicrous.

4   ANON. "Wordsworth, William," in Cassell's Biographical
     Dictionary. Edited by T. Teignmouth Shore. Part 36.

1869

London and New York: Cassell, Petter, and Galpin [1869],
pp. 1154–55.
A biographical sketch.

5   BAGEHOT, WALTER. "Henry Crabb Robinson." Fortnightly Review,
NS 6 (August), 179–88 (186).
Wordsworth's poems can only be truly felt in solitude.
Testifies to Clough's veneration of Wordsworth's poems.

6   BOWDEN, JOHN EDWARD. The Life and Letters of Frederick William
Faber, D.D. London, Dublin, and Derby: Richardson,
especially pp. 70, 113–14, 129–31, 134.
Discusses Faber's associations with and admiration of
Wordsworth. Includes extracts from his journal in which
Faber notes that in The Excursion (Book IV) Wordsworth
speaks not as a topographer but as a scholar and that his
poems produce happiness, quiet, and good resolves.

7   BRISBANE, THE REV. T.[HOMAS]. The Early Years of Alexander
Smith, Poet and Essayist. . . . London: Hodder &
Stoughton, pp. 17, 27, 72, 170.
Records Smith's early reading of Wordsworth. Includes
letter in which Smith records seeing Wordsworth's grave and
Dorothy Wordsworth.

8   CARPENTER, J.[OSEPH] E.[DWARDS]. Note, in The Public School
Speaker and Reader: A Selection of Prose and Verse. . . .
Edited by J. E. Carpenter. London: Warne [1869], p. 134.
A biographical sketch.

9   COLERIDGE, SIR J.[OHN] T.[AYLOR]. A Memoir of the Rev. John
Keble. Oxford and London: Parker, pp. 17–18, 247–50.
Recalls Keble's admiration for Wordsworth and his poetry;
corrects C. Wordsworth (see 1851.A1) concerning Keble's
presenting of Wordsworth at Oxford in 1839.

10 DOYLE, SIR F.[RANCIS] H.[ASTINGS]. Lectures Delivered before
the University of Oxford 1868. London: Macmillan, pp. 16,
101–105.
That Wordsworth wrote poor poems such as "Ellen Irwin"
does not cancel his good ones. In contrast to Newman,
Wordsworth sees life in nature; he unites passion with
thought.

11 FORSTER, JOHN. Walter Savage Landor: a Biography. 2 vols.
London: Chapman and Hall, passim.
Includes letters in which Landor praises Wordsworth for
avoiding "street-and-house language," criticizes a line in

228

1869

"To the Right Honourable William, Earl of Lonsdale, K.G."
("Oft through thy fair domains, illustrious Peer!"), praises
"Laodamia," objects to the opening of Peter Bell, urges
Wordsworth to complete The Recluse, and discusses dedicating
Imaginary Conversations to Wordsworth. Includes letters in
which Walter Birch comments on being unable to procure The
Excursion, Southey praises Wordsworth, Wordsworth reveals
his appreciation of and friendship with Landor, and Julius
Hare notes Wordsworth's alarm over the Reform Bill. Records
Landor's visit to Wordsworth in 1832 (Wordsworth's egotism)
and prints "Glorious the names that cluster here," a verse
tribute to Wordsworth. Discusses Landor's criticism of
Wordsworth's attitude towards Southey. Includes "Byron's
sharp bark and Wordsworth's long-drawn wheese" (poem),
praising Wordsworth as a guide.

12 [FRISWELL, JAMES HAIN]. Essays on English Writers. By the
    Author of "The Gentle Life." London: Sampson Low, Son,
    and Marston, pp. 307-12, 321-22, 325, 328-34.
        Wordsworth worships the inner worth in man and God's
    manifestations in nature. His thoughts have filtered down
    to purify many men. He devoted himself to "the proper cul-
    tivation of self." A biographical sketch. Attribution:
    British Museum catalogue.

13 G., F. J. "William Wordsworth," in The Old College: Being
    The Glasgow University Album for MDCCCLXIX. Edited by
    Students. Glasgow: Maclehose, pp. 243-59.
        Wordsworth's idealism was the most absolute and permanent
    among his contemporary poets. Nature was but the mirror for
    his soul. His poetry lacks variety of content.

14 GRAVES, ROBERT PERCEVAL. "Recollections of Wordsworth and the
    Lake Country," in The Afternoon Lectures on Literature &
    Art: Delivered in the Theatre of the Royal College of
    Science, S. Stephen's Green, Dublin, in the Years 1867 &
    1868. Dublin: Mc Gee; London: Bell and Daldy,
    pp. 275-321.
        Wordsworth manifested a lively interest in Ireland. A
    pure and healthful moral atmosphere pervaded his home. One
    must approach his poems in the spirit in which they were
    written. He exhibited ability in many subjects, except
    science, but chose to dedicate himself to poetry. His fond-
    ness for his own works was not egotism. He was not cold to-
    wards his friends. In politics, religion, and poetry he
    dealt with first principles. He actively carried out the
    benevolence expressed in his poems. He believed in a per-
    sonal God.

1869

15   [HUTTON, RICHARD HOLT?]. "Can the Poet, as Such, Have a
     Creed?" Spectator, 42 (10 April), 446-48 (447).
         An intellectual creed lies at the heart of Wordsworth's
     poetry.

16   MAKROCHEIR. "Wordsworth's 'Lucy.'" Notes and Queries,
     4th ser., 4 (24 July), 85-86.
         Identifies Hartley Coleridge as the author of a parody
     of "She dwelt among the untrodden ways." (A reply to query
     by G. E., "Wm. Wordsworth," Notes and Queries, 4th ser., 3
     [19 June], 580.)

17   MARTINEAU, HARRIET. "Mrs. Wordsworth," in Biographical
     Sketches. London: Macmillan, pp. 402-408.
         With Mary Wordsworth's death an era closes. The defect
     of Wordsworth's circle was its exclusiveness. Reprinted
     from the Daily News of 20 January 1859; appeared abridged
     in 1860.B3.

18   SADLER, THOMAS, ed. Diary, Reminiscences, and Correspondence
     of Henry Crabb Robinson, Barrister-at-law, F.S.A. 3 vols.
     London: Macmillan, passim.
         Records, via letters, diaries, and reminiscences, Robin-
     son's and other contemporaries' intercourse with and
     opinions of Wordsworth and Wordsworth's views on his con-
     temporaries, his own work, political, social, and philosoph-
     ical topics. Expanded in 1869.B19.

19   SADLER, THOMAS, ed. Diary, Reminiscences, and Correspondence
     of Henry Crabb Robinson, Barrister-at-law, F.S.A. 3 vols.
     Second edition. London: Macmillan, passim.
         Slightly expanded from 1869.B18; expanded in 1872.B26.

20   SEELEY, PROFESSOR [JOHN ROBERT]. "Milton's Poetry."
     Macmillan's Magazine, 19 (March), 407-21 (411).
         Wordsworth, a prophet, could not illustrate his beliefs
     from general experience; hence his poetry becomes autobi-
     ographical or abstract. Reprinted in Lectures and Essays
     (1870).

21   [SIDGWICK, HENRY]. Review of The Poems and Prose Remains of
     Arthur Hugh Clough. Westminster and Foreign Quarterly
     Review, NS 36 (1 October), 363-87 (367, 383-85).
         Clough's simplicity and attitude towards nature are de-
     rived from Wordsworth. Attribution: Isobel Armstrong,
     Victorian Scrutinies: Reviews of Poetry 1830-1870 (London:
     Athlone Press of Univ. of London, 1972), p. 288.

22   SWINBURNE, ALGERNON. "Essay on Coleridge," in Christabel and
     the Lyrical and Imaginative Poems of S. T. Coleridge.
     Edited by Algernon Charles Swinburne. London: Sampson
     Low, Son, and Marston, pp. v-xxiii (v, xvii, xix).
         Contrasts "hysterical verses" by Coleridge with Words-
     worth's "majestic and masculine" ones. Wordsworth is the
     lesser poet, though possessing "a harder and sounder mind."
     Reprinted in 1875.B20.

23   WELLS, THORNTON. See 1869.B25.

24   WILKINS, J. "Wordsworth." Notes and Queries, 4th ser., 3
     (15 May), 455.
         Wordsworth reveals his ignorance of reaping in "The
     Brothers."

25   [WILLIAMS, T.] THORNTON WELLS. "To the Daisy" (poem), "To the
     Memory of Wordsworth" (poem), in Poems. London: Longmans,
     pp. 43-46 (45), 110-12.
         Hails Wordsworth as good and sage (45), who instills
     pure precepts and spreads a spirit of innocence (110-12).
     Attribution: British Museum catalogue.

1870 A   BOOKS - NONE

1870 B   SHORTER WRITINGS

1   ANON. "Wordsworth at Work." Chambers's Journal, 4th ser., 7
    (16 April), 247-51.
        Wordsworth loved nature, composed amidst nature.

2   ANON. "Illustrated Gift-Books." Athenaeum, no. 2252
    (24 December), pp. 838-41 (839-40).
        Wordsworth's verses are "as severe, delicate, and
    finished, as antique gems."

3   ANON. "Life of Wordsworth," in Wordsworth's Excursion:
    Book I.--The Wanderer. London and Edinburgh: Chambers
    [1870], pp. 1-2.
        A biographical sketch. The Excursion contains "views at
    once comprehensive and simple."

4   ARNOLD, THOMAS. Chaucer to Wordsworth: A Short History of
    English Literature, From the Earliest Times to the Present
    Day. London: Murby [1870], pp. 396-403.
        Lyrical Ballads (1798) reveals Wordsworth's shift from
    an interest in politics to poetry. To him, life was a

1870

continual rapture. The Excursion presents a philosophical consolation available only to the cultured few. A biographical sketch.

5   COLLINS, [EDWARD JAMES] MORTIMER. "Coleridge's Country." Belgravia, NS 2 (August), 197-203 (200-203).
    Wordsworth in his younger days (e.g., in Peter Bell) had "a touch of humour, grim and grotesque." Records visit with Wordsworth in 1848: Wordsworth's boyish delight, opinion of Southey and Macaulay.

6   G., W. "Drayton and Wordsworth." Notes and Queries, 4th ser., 5 (14 May), 464-65.
    Notes echo of Drayton in "To Joanna."

7   GILFILLAN, THE REV. GEORGE. Life of Sir Walter Scott, Baronet. Edinburgh: Oliphant, pp. 70, 77, 114, 191-94, 334, 344-45.
    Though mixed in their admiration of each other, Scott and Wordsworth shared a love of the primitive, the antique, and domestic virtues.

8   L'ESTRANGE, THE REV. A. G., ed. The Life of Mary Russell Mitford, Related in a Selection from her Letters to her Friends. 3 vols. London: Bentley, especially I:289, 303; II:10-11, 18, 43-44, 61-63, 73-74, 108; III:44, 53, 173-74.
    Includes letters in which Mitford laments Wordsworth's wasting his talents upon a pedlar, notes that "the cleverest young men in London" in 1817 worshipped Wordsworth, relates anecdotes of Wordsworth's personal habits, her and her acquaintances' criticisms of Wordsworth's poems, and her meetings with Wordsworth.

9   MACKENZIE, R.[OBERT] SHELTON. Life of Charles Dickens. . . . Philadelphia: Peterson [1870], p. 243.
    Wordsworth and Dickens shared a mutual contempt.

10 MORLEY, HENRY. Tables of English Literature. London: Chapman and Hall, Table 8, Plate 1.
    Brief primary bibliography.

11 PAYN, JAMES. The Lakes in Sunshine: Being Photographic and Other Pictures of the Lake District of Cumberland. London: Simpkin, Marshall; Windermere: Garnett, pp. 19-20, 88-89.
    Wordsworth helped men appreciate natural beauty. Recounts fishing expedition of Wordsworth and John Wilson in Wastdale; Wordsworth did not get on with his fellow men as Wilson did.

1870

12 ROSSETTI, WILLIAM MICHAEL. "Notes," in The Poetical Works of
    Percy Bysshe Shelley: Including Various Additional Pieces
    from MS. and Other Sources. Edited by William Michael
    Rossetti. 2 vols. London: Moxon, II:543-602 (543-47,
    564).
        Shelley both attacked Wordsworth in "Peter Bell the
    Third" and admired him at the same time.

13 ROSSETTI, WILLIAM MICHAEL. "Prefatory Notice," in The Poetical
    Works of William Wordsworth. Edited by William Michael
    Rossetti. Illustrated by Edwin Edwards. London: Moxon
    [1870], pp. xv-xxiv.
        A biographical sketch. Wordsworth was quite content to
    lead an ordinary, uneventful life; "he was eminently a
    mental man." Today the phrase Lake School has become in-
    significant; Ruskin is Wordsworth's most influential cham-
    pion. Wordsworth should not be damned for his political
    tergiversation, though "a certain crust of 'Respectability'"
    tainted his thought. This respectability, combined with
    his contemplativeness, kept him from being a magnetic man
    and hence a magnetic poet: he is too self-conscious for a
    poet. Briefly expanded in 1878.B18.

14 [SAUNDERS, FREDERICK]. Evenings with the Sacred Poets: A
    Series of Quiet Talks about the Singers and their Songs.
    New York: Randolph, pp. 363-69.
        Wordsworth's life was "beautiful and poetic"; a "mystic
    spiritualism" imbues his poetry. Attribution: Library of
    Congress catalogue.

15 SPALDING, WILLIAM. The History of English Literature. . . .
    Eleventh edition. Edinburgh: Oliver and Boyd; London:
    Simpkin, Marshall, pp. 361-62, 373-78.
        Revised from 1853.B30. Wordsworth was the apostle of a
    poetic revival that grew not so much from him as from the
    times. Reprinted with verbal changes in A History of Eng-
    lish Literature (new edition, 1883).

16 TRENCH, RICHARD CHENEVIX. "Preface," "Notes," in A Household
    Book of English Poetry. Edited by Richard Chenevix Trench.
    Second edition, revised. London: Macmillan, pp. v-xii
    (ix), 391-423 (399, 410-11, 413-16).
        Reprinted from 1868.B15 (ix). Revised from 1868.B15.
    Notes Wordsworth did own Vaughan's works (399, 410-11,
    413-16).

17 WHATELY, THE REV. EDWARD. "Personal Recollections of the Lake
    Poets." Leisure Hour, 19 (8 October), 651-53.

1870

> Wordsworth's character, writing, and habits contrast with Southey's. Wordsworth's conversation was characterized by common sense. He was a student rather than a friend of children.

1871 A BOOKS

1 ANON. Rydal Mount, near Lake Windermere: Catalogue of the Household Furniture . . . which will be Sold by Auction by Messrs. Furher, Price & Furher . . . on Tuesday, the 15th of August, 1871. . . . [No place: privately printed, 1871].
  A catalogue.

1871 B SHORTER WRITINGS

1 C., T. W. "'Pen of an Angel's Wing': Wordsworth, Constable, etc." Notes and Queries, 4th ser., 7 (8 April), 312.
  Notes parallel between John Evelyn and a line in "Walton's Book of Lives."

2 COLLIER, JOHN PAYNE. An Old Man's Diary, Forty Years Ago; for the First Six Months of 1832. London: privately printed, pp. 7, 88-90.
  Describes an evening with Wordsworth in 1832: Wordsworth's appearance, complaint against De Quincey, praise of H. Coleridge, Collier, Brydges, and Dryden, and testimony to being affected by a tale as a boy.

3 COLLIER, JOHN PAYNE. An Old Man's Diary, Forty Years Ago; for the Last Six Months of 1832. London: privately printed, p. 47.
  Records Wordsworth's dislike of Sotheby's Homer.

4 DE QUINCEY, THOMAS. "Memorial Chronology on a New and More Apprehensible System: in a Series of Letters to a Lady," in Suspiria De Profundis: Being a Sequel to the Confessions of an English Opium-Eater and Other Miscellaneous Writings. [De Quincey's Works, Volume XVI (Supplementary).] Edinburgh: Black, pp. 51-96 (63-64).
  Notes the unpopularity of The Excursion with an Edinburgh librarian.

5 ELWIN, THE REV. WHITWELL. Notes, in The Works of Alexander Pope. New edition. . . . [Edited by the Rev. Whitwell Elwin and William John Courthope.] 10 vols. London: Murray, I:334-35; II:142, 208-209.

Writings about William Wordsworth, 1793 - 1899

1871

Speculates on passages in Pope praised by Wordsworth in
Essay (1815). Notes Wordsworth's debt to Pope, his perfect
description in "Hart-leap Well."

6   HALL, S.[AMUEL] C.[ARTER]. A Book of Memories of Great Men
     and Women of the Age, from Personal Acquaintance. London:
     Virtue, pp. 287-318.
         Slightly expanded from 1866.B7.

7   HUTTON, RICHARD HOLT. "Wordsworth and His Genius," "Shelley's
     Poetical Mysticism," in Essays: Theological and Literary.
     2 vols. London: Strahan, II:101-46, 147-89 (147-52).
         Revised from 1857.B8. Wordsworth's spiritual courage and
     frugality keep him from becoming a dreamer (101-46). Re-
     printed from 1863.B10 (147-52).

8   KETTLE, R.[OSA] M.[ACKENZIE], ed. Memoirs and Letters of
     Charles Boner, . . . with Letters of Mary Russell Mitford
     to him during ten Years. 2 vols. London: Bentley,
     I:59-65, 129-30, 198.
         Records Boner's visit to Rydal Mount in 1844. Includes
     letters from Mitford in which she reports Ruskin's opinion
     that Wordsworth does not understand Switzerland, and criti-
     cizes The Prelude as long, prosy.

9   [KNIGHT, WILLIAM]. "Theism--Desiderata in the Theistic
     Argument." British Quarterly Review, 54 (1 July), 34-76
     (71-73).
         In nature Wordsworth sees not "the ghostly forms of his
     own imagination" but "real existence." Reprinted with ver-
     bal changes in 1879.B16.

10   METEYARD, ELIZA. A Group of Englishmen (1795 to 1815): Being
     Records of the Younger Wedgwoods and Their Friends. . . .
     London: Longmans, pp. 75-79, 98-99, 188.
         A biographical sketch of Wordsworth's life in the west
     of England. Notes Wordsworth's debt to Thomas Wedgwood in
     connection with the trip to Germany in 1798-99.

11   [OLIPHANT, MARGARET]. "New Books." Blackwood's Edinburgh
     Magazine, 109 (April), 440-64 (444-47).
         In contrast with Goethe, Wordsworth is moral, bound by
     rule; both poets focus upon themselves. Wordsworth's po-
     etry can be understood only when one considers his unim-
     passioned nature.

12   [OLIPHANT, MARGARET]. "A Century of Great Poets, from 1750
     Downwards: No. II.--Walter Scott." Blackwood's Edinburgh
     Magazine, 110 (August), 229-56 (237, 240-41).

235

1871

> Wordsworth's poetry is well-trained, useful, and deep,
> Scott's wayward, bright, and superficial. <u>See</u> 1882.B46.

13 [OLIPHANT, MARGARET]. "A Century of Great Poets, from 1750
    Downwards: No. III.--William Wordsworth." <u>Blackwood's
    Edinburgh Magazine</u>, 110 (September), 299-326.
        A full biographical sketch. Without Cowper, Wordsworth
    could not have been. Wordsworth's constant effort to jus-
    tify suffering stems from his experience of the French Revo-
    lution. He lacked the critical ability to see that the
    merit of <u>Lyrical Ballads</u> (especially "The Idiot Boy") and
    <u>Peter Bell</u> lay not in their inane simplicities but in their
    insights into human nature. The Lucy poems work together
    as do the poems in Tennyson's <u>Maud</u>. Though Wordsworth's
    egotism is more innocent than Goethe's, <u>The Prelude</u> is
    founded on mistaken self-importance. That the hero of <u>The
    Excursion</u> is a pedlar is irrelevant; the poem exhibits a
    solemn yet cheerful calm, though Wordsworth fails in por-
    traying Margaret. Despite his power, Wordsworth rarely
    moves readers profoundly because he is not a poet of pas-
    sion. <u>See</u> 1882.B46.

14 [OLIPHANT, MARGARET]. "A Century of Great Poets, from 1750
    Downwards: No. IV.--Samuel Taylor Coleridge." <u>Blackwood's
    Edinburgh Magazine</u>, 110 (November), 552-76 (564-66, 569).
        Discusses Wordsworth, Coleridge, and <u>Lyrical Ballads</u>.
    <u>See</u> 1882.B46.

15 PALGRAVE, FRANCIS TURNER. "William Wordsworth: 1845" (poem),
    in <u>Lyrical Poems</u>. London and New York: Macmillan,
    pp. 127-29.
        Praises Wordsworth's insight into unseen worlds, his
    "sanity of soul."

16 S., T. C. "Wordsworth: Constable, etc." <u>Notes and Queries</u>,
    4th ser., 7 (18 March), 233.
        Notes sources for "Walton's Book of Lives."

17 SPROAT, GILBERT MALCOLM. <u>Sir Walter Scott as a Poet</u>.
    Edinburgh: Edmonston & Douglas, p. 67.
        Wordsworth's descriptions of scenery are sterile.

18 YOUNG, JULIAN CHARLES. <u>A Memoir of Charles Mayne Young,
    Tragedian, with Extracts from his Son's Journal</u>. 2 vols.
    London and New York: Macmillan, I:171-85.
        Recounts meetings with Wordsworth, Coleridge, and Dora
    Wordsworth in July 1828 in Godesberg: Wordsworth's balanced
    principles, interest in the smallest natural objects, and

opinion of Coleridge. Relates incidents of Wordsworth lis-
tening to the organ at Haarlem and giving his poems to a
girl in London.

1872 A BOOKS

1 NEAVES, [CHARLES,] LORD. A Lecture on Cheap and Accessible
   Pleasures: With a Comparative Sketch of the Poetry of Burns
   and Wordsworth: Delivered at Haltwhistle in Connection with
   the Enlargement of the Mechanics' Institute There on 4th
   April 1872. Edinburgh and London: Blackwood, 32 pp.
       Wordsworth's life and poems contrast with Burns's.
   Wordsworth worshipped nature at the expense of man and
   adopted a patronizing tone toward the poor. He wrote no
   songs. Burns's frailties attract our sympathies, Wordsworth's do not. Wordsworth's shorter poems would be popular if separated from his philosophical ones and his critical prefaces. In "Ode: Intimations of Immortality" Wordsworth deals too fancifully with a solemn subject.

1872 B SHORTER WRITINGS

1 ANON. "Wordsworth Impartially Weighed." Temple Bar, 34
   (February), 310-30.
       One may extol Wordsworth without depreciating the
   eighteenth-century poets; he was an innovator. He invented
   a poetic theory to cover his own unsatisfactory performance.
   "By writing about everything when there was nothing to say,
   Wordsworth came to be often unable to say anything when
   there was everything to write about." He suffered from
   having the leisure to devote himself solely to poetry.
   The Excursion is pious and pure, but monotonous.

2 ANON. "Memoir," in The Poetical Works of Wordsworth: A
   Reprint of the 1827 Edition. London: Warne; New York:
   Scribner, Welford and Armstrong [1872], pp. xxiii-xxxix.
       A biographical sketch. Wordsworth wrote and published
   undeterred by his hostile critical reception.

3 BAGEHOT, WALTER. Physics and Politics: or Thoughts on the
   Application of the Principles of 'Natural Selection' and
   'Inheritance' to Political Society. London: King,
   pp. 34-35.
       In the Preface to Lyrical Ballads Wordsworth explains,
   "in a kind of vexed way," that he will not write as he is
   expected to.

1872

4   BRADBURY, JOHN. The English Lakes: How to See Them for Five
     and a Half Guineas. London: Simpkin, Marshall; Manchester:
     Heywood [1872], pp. 61–67, 82.
          A biographical sketch and description of Rydal Mount and
     Grasmere. No poet except Shakespeare is more quoted than
     Wordsworth.

5   CARROLL, LEWIS. See 1872.B12.

6   CHORLEY, HENRY, ed. Letters of Mary Russell Mitford. Second
     series. 2 vols. London: Bentley, especially I:285;
     II:152.
          Includes letters in which Mitford notes that in 1841
     Wordsworth is "at the height of fashion" though little read,
     and records her disappointment in The Prelude.

7   COLLIER, JOHN PAYNE. An Old Man's Diary, Forty Years Ago; for
     the Last Six Months of 1833. London: privately printed,
     pp. 38, 72–74.
          Records Wordsworth's presence at the Court of Inquiry
     into the Convention of Cintra, and Wordsworth's description
     of Dryden's mode of translating.

8   [COURTHOPE, WILLIAM JOHN]. Review of Swinburne's Songs before
     Sunrise, etc. Quarterly Review, 132 (January), 59–84
     (61–62, 81–83).
          Wordsworth's aristocratic definition of a poet in the
     Preface to Lyrical Ballads "subordinates the qualities of
     the poet, as a master of language, to his qualities as a
     man."

9   DE MORGAN, AUGUSTUS. A Budget of Paradoxes. London:
     Longmans, p. 435.
          Reports conversations in which Wordsworth praises Byron,
     Byron Wordsworth.

10   [DENNIS, JOHN]. "English Rural Poetry." Cornhill Magazine,
     25 (February), 164–76 (173–76).
          Wordsworth, like Tennyson, never forgets man in his
     nature poetry. Reprinted in Studies in English Literature
     (1876).

11   [DENNIS, JOHN]. "The English Sonnet." Cornhill Magazine, 25
     (May), 581–98 (595–97).
          Wordsworth's sonnets lack intensity, excel in purity of
     language, variety, and association of human emotion with
     aspects of nature. Abridged in English Sonnets (1873);
     reprinted with minor addition in Studies in English Litera-
     ture (1876).

12 [DODGSON, CHARLES L.] LEWIS CARROLL. "I'll tell thee every-
    thing I can" (poem), in Through the Looking-Glass, and What
    Alice Found There. Illustrated by John Tenniel. London:
    Macmillan, pp. 177-81.
        Parody of "Resolution and Independence," revised from
    1856.B6.

13 G., W. "Wordsworth's 'Primrose.'" Notes and Queries, 4th
    ser., 9 (6 April), 289.
        A reply to 1872.B18. Discusses parallels to the "prim-
    rose" passage in Peter Bell.

14 HALES, J.[OHN] W.[ESLEY]. "William Wordsworth," in Longer
    English Poems. Edited by J. W. Hales. London: Macmillan,
    pp. 390-97.
        A biographical sketch. Wordsworth's genius was intro-
    spective and interpretative. Wordsworth was a conscious
    artist. Includes critical notes to "Ode: Intimations of
    Immortality" and "Laodamia."

15 HARE, AUGUSTUS J. C. Memorials of a Quiet Life. 2 vols.
    London: Strahan, I:194, 210; II:85-88, 273-74.
        Julius Hare was one of the first of a circle to uphold
    Wordsworth at Cambridge c. 1820. He preserved throughout
    his life an admiration for Wordsworth. Includes letters in
    which Augustus William Hare testifies in 1819 to Words-
    worth's interest "in the common concerns of life" and Maria
    Hare testifies in 1844 to Wordsworth's kind-heartedness and
    simplicity. For continuation, see 1876.B13.

16 HOLLAND, SIR HENRY. Recollections of Past Life. London:
    Longmans, pp. 205-206, 209.
        Recalls Wordsworth's fondness for praise and his own
    poems.

17 [HUTTON, RICHARD HOLT]. "The Poetry of Matthew Arnold."
    British Quarterly Review, 55 (1 April), 313-47 (313-22,
    328, 341).
        Wordsworth, in his later phase a conscious artist as
    well as poet, influenced Arnold. Wordsworth "steeped him-
    self in the rapture of a meditative solitude which puts him
    at a distance from all mankind." He does not restore us to
    the freshness of our youth but "baptizes us in his own
    strong and unique spirit." Reprinted in Essays in Literary
    Criticism ([1876]) and Essays: Theological and Literary
    (1877).

1872

18   JACKSON, STEPHEN. "Wordsworth's 'Primrose.'" Notes and
      Queries, 4th ser., 9 (9 March), 197.
          Suggests Wordsworth was indebted to a German song for
      the "primrose" passage in Peter Bell.

19   L., W. "The Yarra-Yarra Unvisited" (poem). Month, 16 (May-
      June), 425-27.
          An imitation/parody of the Yarrow poems.

20   [MALLOCK, WILLIAM HURRELL] A NEWDIGATE PRIZEMAN. Every Man
      His Own Poet: or, The Inspired Singer's Recipe Book.
      Oxford: Shrimpton, p. 6.
          Wordsworth's choice of subjects gives his poems a "vege-
      table tone." Attribution: Bodleian catalogue.

21   NEWDIGATE PRIZEMAN, A. See 1872.B20.

22   [OLIPHANT, MARGARET]. "A Century of Great Poets, from 1750
      Downwards: No. VII.--Lord Byron." Blackwood's Edinburgh
      Magazine, 112 (July), 49-72 (51).
          Some will always doubt Wordsworth's greatness. Words-
      worth, not Shakespeare, is the representative of poetry
      among ordinary men. See 1882.B46.

23   [OLIPHANT, MARGARET]. "A Century of Great Poets, from 1750
      Downwards: No. VIII.--Johann Wolfgang Goethe."
      Blackwood's Edinburgh Magazine, 112 (December), 675-97
      (679).
          Wordsworth, unfortunately, lived not in communion with
      nature but used it for his own self-cultivation. See
      1882.B46.

24   [PATTISON, MARK]. "Pope and His Editors." British Quarterly
      Review, 55 (1 April), 413-46 (416, 429-30).
          Wordsworth is indebted to Kant for the belief that po-
      etry is ideal.

25   PELAGIUS. "Wordsworth's 'Ode on the Intimations of Immor-
      tality.'" Notes and Queries, 4th ser., 9 (23 March),
      241-42.
          Interprets line in "Ode: Intimations of Immortality."

26   SADLER, THOMAS, ed. Diary, Reminiscences, and Correspondence
      of Henry Crabb Robinson, Barrister-at-law, F.S.A. 2 vols.
      Third edition, with corrections and additions. London and
      New York: Macmillan, passim.
          An expanded edition of 1869.B19.

27 SHAIRP, J.[OHN] C.[AMPBELL]. "Preface to the Second Edition,"
    "Preface to the First Edition," "Wordsworth," "Coleridge,"
    in Studies in Poetry and Philosophy. Second edition.
    Edinburgh: Edmonston and Douglas, pp. vii-xiv (vii-xiii),
    xv-xxi (xvi-xix), 1-103, 104-238 (108-78 [passim]).
        The external object is not obliterated by the meditative
    light Wordsworth pours upon it (vii-xiii). Reprinted from
    1868.B14 (xvi-xix). Reprinted with verbal changes and ad-
    ditions from 1868.B14. Wordsworth needed no external
    sources for his ideas in "Ode: Intimations of Immortality"
    (1-103). Reprinted from 1868.B14 (108-78).

28 THOM, JOHN HAMILTON, ed. Letters Embracing his Life of John
    James Tayler, B.A. 2 vols. Illustrated. London and
    Edinburgh: Williams and Norgate, I:72-74, 86.
        Includes letters in which Tayler records visiting Words-
    worth in 1826 (Wordsworth's simple manners, enthusiastic
    and eloquent conversation, idolizing of Milton, Toryism,
    criticism of Byron and praise of Shelley) and declares
    Wordsworth "the most Christian of poets."

29 WOODWARD, B.[ERNARD] B. and WILLIAM L. R. CATES. "Wordsworth,
    William," in Encyclopaedia of Chronology, Historical and
    Biographical. London: Longmans, p. 1455.
        A brief biographical sketch.

30 YONGE, CHARLES DUKE. Three Centuries of English Literature.
    London: Longmans, pp. 251-72.
        A biographical sketch. The Lake Poets differed en-
    tirely; Wordsworth has influenced succeeding poets the
    most. He sank to poetic depths because of his system; yet
    he kept surprisingly free of vulgarity. He could not plan
    an elaborate work. His philosophy in The Excursion is
    obscure.

1873 A BOOKS - NONE

1873 B SHORTER WRITINGS

1   ADAMS, W. H. DAVENPORT. "Biographical and Critical Authori-
    ties," "William Wordsworth," Notes, in The Student's
    Treasury of English Song. Edited by W. H. Davenport Adams.
    London, Edinburgh, and New York: Nelson, pp. xvii-xxii
    (xxii), 483-85, 485-512.
        A brief secondary bibliography (xxii). A biographical
    sketch. Wordsworth does not merely describe nature but
    shows its inner relations (483-85). Critical notes to the

1873

poems selected, including "The Solitary Reaper," "Laodamia,"
and "Ode: Intimations of Immortality" (485-512).

2   [ALFORD, FANNY, ed.]. Life Journals and Letters of Henry
     Alford. Edited by his Widow. London, Oxford, and
     Cambridge: Rivingtons, pp. 61-66, 113-15.
        Includes H. Alford's description of an evening with
     Wordsworth in 1830: Wordsworth's conversation on Coleridge,
     on a scene reflected on Grasmere Lake, and on the state of
     the country; "Ode: Intimations of Immortality" requires
     study. Records visit to Rydal in 1838.

3   ANON. "Forty Years Ago." All the Year Round, NS 11
     (13 December), 161-64 (163).
        In a portrait Wordsworth appears "absorbed in his own
     excellence."

4   ANON. "Sketch of the Life of William Wordsworth," in The
     Poetical Works of W. Wordsworth: Complete. Illustrated
     [by F. Gilbert]. London: Dicks, pp. [i]-ii.
        A biographical sketch.

5   ANON. "William Wordsworth," in Wordsworth's Excursion: The
     Wanderer [and Longfellow's] The Wreck of the Hesperus.
     London: Marshall, Simpkin, and Hamilton, Adams; Melbourne:
     Laurie [1873], p. 2.
        A biographical sketch. Wordsworth "was pre-eminently
     the poet of nature."

6   BATES, WILLIAM. "Notes," in A Gallery of Illustrious Literary
     Characters (1830-1838) Drawn by the late Daniel Maclise,
     R.A. and Accompanied by Notices Chiefly by the late William
     Maginn, LL.D. Edited by William Bates. London: Chatto
     and Windus [1873], pp. 65, 79-82.
        Wordsworth asks a "funny question" in the "party in a
     parlour" stanza of Peter Bell. He is the poet of nature,
     but for him nature has no life apart from man. Revised
     and expanded in 1883.B9.

7   BOUCHIER, JONATHAN. "Browning's 'Lost Leader.'" Notes and
     Queries, 4th ser., 12 (13 December), 473.
        Browning is reproaching Wordsworth in "The Lost Leader."

8   [COLERIDGE, EDITH, ed.]. Memoir and Letters of Sara Coleridge.
     Edited by her Daughter. 2 vols. London: King, passim.
        Includes autobiographical recollections in which Sara
     Coleridge recalls her life with the Wordsworths at Grasmere:
     Wordsworth's fondness for picturesque clothing. Includes

testimonial to her preference for Wordsworth's earlier poems, and letters in which she discusses Wordsworth's allegiance to the Church of England, his showing us how to endure suffering, the imagery in "Resolution and Independence," the philosophy of The Excursion, his opinion that Shelley and Keats would please young readers only, his treatment of nature compared to Milton's, the comparative merits of his poems, the failure of "Laodamia" (compared with "She was a Phantom of delight"), the decline in his conversation in 1847, his sorrow at the deaths of Dora and of Hartley Coleridge, his final illness, his reputation abroad, the self-revelation of The Prelude, and the absence of pantheism in "Tintern Abbey."

9   COLERIDGE, SIR JOHN DUKE. "Wordsworth." Macmillan's Magazine, 28 (August), 289-302.
    A lecture, delivered before the literary society of Exeter, April 1873: Wordsworth still suffers from the effects of the first critical attacks, especially Jeffrey's. For men immersed in business, the study of Wordsworth's life and works is ennobling and refreshing. His poems reveal the holiness of nature and the dignity of virtue, simplicity, independence, and patriotism; they possess felicity in diction and meter.

10 COOPER, THOMPSON. "Wordsworth, William," in A New Biographical Dictionary. . . . London: Bell, p. 1200.
    A biographical sketch.

11 [COURTHOPE, WILLIAM JOHN]. Review of Forman's Our Living Poets. Quarterly Review, 135 (July), 1-40 (31-34, 38).
    Wordsworth heralded the modern trend of the poet isolated from men. To him poetry "meant Philosophy in metre." His theory of style in the Preface to Lyrical Ballads destroys poetry as art.

12 DALBY, JOHN WATSON. "Browning's 'Lost Leader.'" Notes and Queries, 4th ser., 12 (27 December), 519.
    A reply to 1873.B7. Wordsworth was not a "leader."

13 [DAVIES, WILLIAM]. Review of The Book of the Sonnet, etc. Quarterly Review, 134 (January), 186-204 (188, 201-204).
    Few of Wordsworth's sonnets are perfectly constructed.

14 DEVEY, J.[OSEPH]. A Comparative Estimate of Modern English Poets. London: Moxon, especially pp. 81-106.
    Wordsworth treats nature subjectively. He sympathized only with the rustic poor and hence lost both radical and

conservative readers. He writes to propound his philosophy, which is unclear, even in The Excursion. He believes man and nature are spiritually linked and ignores man's fall. His ignoring of man's intellect has led him to glorify childhood.

15   GIBBON, CHARLES. Note, in The Casquet of Literature. . . .
Edited by Charles Gibbon. 4 vols. London, Glasgow, and Edinburgh: Blackie, I:36.
A biographical sketch; remarks the patronizing tone of 1793.B3.

16   HEWLETT, HENRY G. "English Sonneteers: Mr. Charles Turner."
Contemporary Review, 22 (September), 633-42 (635-37, 639, 642).
Wordsworth was attracted by the sonnet's constraint. His sonnet series are repetitious; some sonnets lack adequate themes.

17   HUNTER, DR. HENRY JULIAN. "William Wordsworth and Joseph Hunter," in Old Age in Bath: Recollections of Two Retired Physicians, Dr. John Sherwen and Dr. Thomas Cogan; to which are Added a few Unpublished Remains of William Wordsworth, the Poet, and Joseph Hunter, F.S.A. Bath: Lewis, pp. 59-75.
Wordsworth was "greedy of judicious admiration." Records Joseph Hunter's admiration of Lyrical Ballads and visit with Wordsworth in 1831: Wordsworth's plain garb and grave countenance, his conversation on early English poets, the Reform Bill, and genealogy.

18   JACOX, FRANCIS. At Nightfall and Midnight: Musings after Dark. London: Hodder and Stoughton, especially pp. 2-4, 13-14, 66, 99-100, 289-90, 314-15.
Notes Wordsworth's diversified studies of twilight, moon-light, and morning; praises Wordsworth's single lines.

19   [KNIGHT, WILLIAM]. "A Contribution towards a Theory of Poetry."
British Quarterly Review, 57 (1 January), 178-89 (181-82, 188).
Wordsworth's poetic theory, "erring through . . . re-strictions of the sphere of imagination," contrasts with his practice. Reprinted in 1879.B16.

20   LONSDALE, HENRY. "William Wordsworth," in The Worthies of Cumberland: William Wordsworth. . . . [Volume IV of 6-vol. series.] London: Routledge, pp. 1-40.

A biographical sketch. A reclusive poet of Nature and philosophy, Wordsworth lacked grand inspiration and knowledge of natural sciences and history. As a man, he was more prized by his neighbors for his negative than his positive qualities. Though like in appearance, Wordsworth and Milton differed as men and poets.

21 MALLESON, THE REV. F.[REDERICK] A. "Wordsworth's 'Westmorland Girl.'" Sunday at Home, no. 997 (7 June), pp. 360–63.
    Records interview with the subject of "The Westmoreland Girl." Reprinted in 1890.B33.

22 MILL, JOHN STUART. Autobiography. London: Longmans, pp. 146–50, 155.
    Records how he felt "better and happier" after reading Wordsworth's shorter poems, including "Ode: Intimations of Immortality," which express "not mere outward beauty, but states of feeling, and of thought coloured by feeling, under the excitement of beauty," and records debate with J. A. Roebuck and John Sterling on the merits of Wordsworth and Byron.

23 MORLEY, HENRY. A First Sketch of English Literature. London, Paris, and New York: Cassell, Petter, & Galpin [1873], pp. 866–92.
    A biographical sketch.

24 MUNBY, ARTHUR J. "Browning's 'Lost Leader.'" Notes and Queries, 4th ser., 12 (27 December), 519.
    Browning's "The Lost Leader" is unfair to Wordsworth.

25 NICHOLS, THE REV. W.[ILLIAM] L.[UKE]. The Quantocks and their Associations: A Paper Read before the Members of the Bath Literary Club on the 11th December, 1871. Bath: privately printed, passim.
    A biographical survey of Wordsworth's work and association with Coleridge in Somerset. Expanded in 1891.B33.

26 NOEL, RODEN. "Lord Byron and His Times." Saint Pauls Magazine, 13 (December), 618–38 (620–22).
    Wordsworth has distilled the "essence of Nature's gentler moods" and felt the "power of northern mountains"; yet he largely lacks "the Titanic diabolic element." Reprinted with minor addition in 1886.B36.

27 [OLIPHANT, MARGARET]. "A Century of Great Poets, from 1750 Downwards: No. IX.—Johann Friedrich Schiller." Blackwood's Edinburgh Magazine, 114 (August), 183–206 (204).

1873

No one any longer credits Wordsworth's foolish arrangement of his poems announced in the Preface to The Excursion.
See 1882.B46.

28 PATER, WALTER H. "Preface," in Studies in the History of the
Renaissance. London: Macmillan, pp. vii-xiv (x-xi).
The virtue of Wordsworth's poetry, much of which should
be forgotten, lies in Wordsworth's "mystical sense of a life
in natural things."

29 RUSKIN, JOHN. "Appendix," in The Crown of Wild Olive: Four
Lectures on Industry and War. [Volume VI in The Works of
John Ruskin.] London: Smith, Elder, and Allen,
pp. 175-210 (179-80).
Wordsworth's portrait in "Character of the Happy Warrior"
is literal, not metaphorical.

30 SHAIRP, J.[OHN] C.[AMPBELL]. "Wordsworth's Three Yarrows."
Good Words, 14:649-56.
Traces the biographical and factual background to the
Yarrow poems. Reprinted in 1881.B30.

31 WILTON, THE REV. RICHARD. "Gray at Grasmere (1769) and
Wordsworth's Grave (1869)" (poem), in Wood-notes and
Church-bells. London: Bell and Daldy, p. 274.
Wordsworth sang "of Nature, Man, and Duty."

1874 A BOOKS

1 SHAIRP, J.[OHN] C.[AMPBELL], ed. Recollections of a Tour Made
in Scotland A.D. 1803. By Dorothy Wordsworth. Edinburgh:
Edmonston and Douglas, 360 pp.
Includes Dorothy Wordsworth's record of her tour with
Wordsworth and Coleridge. Includes "Preface" in which
Shairp sketches Wordsworth's and Dorothy's lives, and notes
that Wordsworth's frugal life at Dove Cottage directly affected his poems and that his later Christianity was an ad-
vance, not a retrogression. Includes "Appendix" in which
Shairp compares "Stepping Westward" with "The Trosachs,"
and explanatory notes to Dorothy's journal.

1874 B SHORTER WRITINGS

1 ANON. "The Cycle of English Song." Temple Bar, 40 (March),
478-94 (490-93).
Wordsworth lived divorced from man, hence his happiness.
His mind was insular.

WRITINGS ABOUT WILLIAM WORDSWORTH, 1793 - 1899

2   ANON. Review of D. Wordsworth's Recollections of a Tour Made
    in Scotland. Athenaeum, no. 2437 (11 July), pp. 41-42.
       Wordsworth's relations with Dorothy compare with Lamb's
    with Mary Lamb. Wordsworth did not sufficiently return his
    sister's devotion.

3   ANON. "Miss Wordsworth's Tour in Scotland." Saturday Review,
    38 (22 August), 248-49.
       "Miss Wordsworth is always accumulating possible sug-
    gestions for her brother's work."

4   ANON. Review of D. Wordsworth's Recollections of a Tour Made
    in Scotland. Christian Observer, 73 (September), 678-90.
       Wordsworth's use of low subjects costs him admirers.
    Discusses Dorothy's influence on Wordsworth.

5   ANON. "Contemporary Literature." Westminster Review, NS 46
    (October), 515-90 (544).
       Dorothy Wordsworth saw the hidden secrets in nature and
    detailed them to Wordsworth, who published them.

6   ANON. "Introduction," "Notes," in Lyrical Ballads. By
    William Wordsworth. London and Glasgow: Collins, pp. 3-4,
    29-32.
       A biographical sketch (3-4). Notes on the poems se-
    lected, including "Hart-leap Well," "We Are Seven," "The
    Fountain," and "Tintern Abbey" (29-32).

7   ANON. "Introduction," "Notes," in The Excursion: Book I:
    The Wanderer. London and Glasgow: Collins, pp. 3-6,
    31-40.
       The Excursion is the greatest philosophic poem in English
    literature (3-6). Critical notes (31-40).

8   ANON. "Life of Wordsworth," Notes, in Selections from
    Wordsworth's Poems. London: Allman [1874], pp. iii-iv,
    passim.
       A biographical sketch. Wordsworth's poems are marked by
    purity of language, originality of thought, beauty in oc-
    casional lines, perfect knowledge of nature, and high moral
    aim (iii-iv). Brief notes to the poems selected, including
    "Ruth" (passim).

9   ARTHUR-A-BLAND. "They Are Three" (poem). Shotover Papers,
    Or, Echoes from Oxford, no. 11 (28 November), pp. 167-68.
       Parody of "We Are Seven."

1874

10   ASPLAND, T. LINDSEY. "Memoir," in The Poets of Lakeland:
      Wordsworth. . . . London: Simpkin Marshall; Windermere:
      Garnett, pp. 1–137.
          A full biographical sketch, including discussion of
      Wordsworth's early reception and political and religious
      views. In early life Wordsworth defied received opinions
      simply because they were received.

11   BOUCHIER, JONATHAN. "Browning's 'Lost Leader.'" Notes and
      Queries, 5th ser., 1 (14 February), 138; (14 March), 213.
          A reply to 1873.B12 (138). Browning is reproaching
      Wordsworth in "The Lost Leader" (138, 213).

12   BROOKE, STOPFORD A. Theology in the English Poets: Cowper--
      Coleridge--Wordsworth and Burns. London: King, pp. 93–286.
          To Wordsworth the natural world has a life separate from
      man's thought, a personality formed of the living spirit of
      God. Hence Wordsworth sees in nature not himself but God,
      and nature can educate man to a love of itself, to a politi-
      cal love of man, and to a hope for immortality, as Words-
      worth traces in The Prelude, The Excursion, "Elegiac Stan-
      zas Suggested by a Picture of Peele Castle," "Ode: Intima-
      tions of Immortality," "Yew-trees," and "Composed upon an
      Evening of Extraordinary Splendour and Beauty."

13   C.[HAMBERS], W.[ILLIAM]. "William and Dorothy Wordsworth."
      Chambers's Journal, 4th ser., 11 (15 August), 513–16.
          A biographical sketch of Wordsworth's and Dorothy's
      helping of each other. Attribution: W. Knight in 1896.B36,
      VIII:371.

14   CLARKE, CHARLES COWDEN. "Recollections of John Keats."
      Gentleman's Magazine, NS 12 (February), 177–204 (196–97).
          Records Wordsworth's preference for his own poetry. Re-
      printed in Recollections of Writers (1878).

15   COLLINS, [EDWARD JAMES] MORTIMER. "Browning's 'Lost Leader.'"
      Notes and Queries, 5th ser., 1 (7 March), 192.
          A reply to 1873.B7. Wordsworth's final faith was that
      which all great minds in time attain.

16   COLLINS, [EDWARD JAMES] MORTIMER. "Introduction," in
      Transmigration. 3 vols. London: Hurst and Blackett,
      I:[vii].
          Notes his interest in metempsychosis originated during
      a visit with Wordsworth.

17 COLLYER, ROBERT. "The Wordsworths." Notes and Queries,
      5th ser., 1 (21 February), 143-44.
         Describes Wordsworth memorabilia and prints letter in
      which Dora Wordsworth in 1827 comments upon Wordsworth's
      editing and the state of his eyes.

18 D., J. S. "Browning's 'Lost Leader.'" Notes and Queries,
      5th ser., 1 (24 January), 72.
         Wordsworth did not possess the characteristics of
      Browning's "The Lost Leader."

19 D.[ENNIS], J.[OHN]. "English Lyrical Poetry." Cornhill
      Magazine, 29 (June), 698-719 (699, 713, 715, 717).
         Even though Wordsworth lacks passion, his strength lies
      in his lyrics, not in his philosophy. Byron's noblest po-
      etry is inspired by Wordsworth. Reprinted in Studies in
      English Literature (1876).

20 DIRCKS, HENRY. "On Shakespeare's Dramas as Affording Evidence
      of the Poet's Nature-study, and his Varied Practice in
      Assimilating its Results with the Matter of his Literary
      Compositions." Transactions of the Royal Society of
      Literature of the United Kingdom, NS 10:521-45 (527).
         Wordsworth did not pursue a definite study of nature.

21 E., J. W. "Browning's 'Lost Leader.'" Notes and Queries,
      5th ser., 1 (24 January), 71-72.
         Wordsworth affected not a few disciples but a multitude,
      including Byron. He could not be Browning's model in "The
      Lost Leader."

22 ENTWISLE, ROYLE. "'Transmigration.'" Notes and Queries,
      5th ser., 1 (31 January), 84.
         Wordsworth in "Ode: Intimations of Immortality" echoes
      Vergil and Pindar.

23 GREVILLE, CHARLES C. F. The Greville Memoirs: A Journal of
      the Reigns of King George IV and King William IV. Edited
      by Henry Reeve. 3 vols. London: Longmans, II:120.
         Records Wordsworth's eloquent, animated conversation in
      1831, including his admiration of Brougham.

24 HAZLITT, W. CAREW. "New Illustrations of the Life and
      Character of Charles Lamb," in Mary and Charles Lamb:
      Poems, Letters, and Remains: Now First Collected, with
      Reminiscences and Notes. Edited by W. Carew Hazlitt.
      Illustrated. London: Chatto and Windus, pp. 131-232
      (215-16, 229-30).

1874

> Notes Lamb's later neglect of his friendship with Words-
> worth; "Written after the Death of Charles Lamb" is unworthy
> of Wordsworth.

25   HORNE, R.[ICHARD] H.[ENGIST]. "Letters from Elizabeth Barrett
     Browning to the Author of 'Orion' on Literary and General
     Topics: II." Contemporary Review, 23 (January), 281-302
     (281-83).
          Wordsworth originated the project of publishing The Poems
     of Geoffrey Chaucer, Modernized, though he refused to edit
     it.

26   HUTCHINSON, THOS. "The Poet's Stone." Hereford Times, 43
     (26 December), 16.
          Relates Wordsworth's visits and associations in Here-
     fordshire.

27   [HUTTON, RICHARD HOLT]. "Dorothy Wordsworth's Scotch Journal."
     Spectator, 47 (1 August), 980-81.
          A "hardy imaginative simplicity" characterizes Words-
     worth's genius. Wordsworth adds his "brooding power" to
     Dorothy's descriptions in her journal.

28   MANT, FREDERICK. "Transmigration." Notes and Queries,
     5th ser., 1 (14 February), 126-27.
          Notes parallel between "Ode: Intimations of Immortality"
     and lines from Charles Mackay and Tennyson.

29   MAURICE, THE REV. [JOHN] F.[REDERICK] D.[ENISON]. "Milton,"
     in The Friendship of Books and Other Lectures. Edited by
     Thomas Hughes. London: Macmillan, pp. 244-70 (244-48,
     269).
          In "London, 1802" Wordsworth calls upon Milton the man,
     not the writer. Wordsworth's arrangement of his own poems
     is artificial.

30   MORLEY, JOHN. "Mr. Mill's Autobiography." Fortnightly Review,
     NS 15 (1 January), 1-20 (14).
          Wordsworth is "a poet austere yet gracious." Reprinted
     in Critical Miscellanies (Second series, 1877).

31   [MOZLEY, ANNE]. "The Poets at Play." Blackwood's Edinburgh
     Magazine, 115 (June), 678-95 (680).
          Wordsworth held poetry too sacred to write ephemeral
     jingles.

32   MUNBY, ARTHUR J. "Browning's 'Lost Leader.'" Notes and
     Queries, 5th ser., 1 (11 April), 292.

Wordsworth "led us . . . in the spiritual conflicts of
our college days," though he is little read now, even in
the Lake District.

33   N. "The Wordsworths." Notes and Queries, 5th ser., 2
         (4 July), 9-10.
         Includes "Peter Thompson" (poem), a parody of The Excur-
         sion, reprinted from the Chaplet of Concord (c. 1834).

34   N. "Wordsworth and Hogg." Notes and Queries, 5th ser., 2
         (22 August), 157-58.
         Recounts incident of Wordsworth showing Hogg the Lakes.

35   [PALGRAVE, FRANCIS TURNER]. Review of Mill's Autobiography.
         Quarterly Review, 136 (January), 150-79 (157-58, 171).
         Wordsworth rarely portrays a passion without also giving
         the thought to which it is allied. Mill's understanding of
         Wordsworth lacked insight.

36   PATER, WALTER H. "On Wordsworth." Fortnightly Review, NS 15
         (1 April), 455-65.
         In his higher moods, Wordsworth quietly observed natural
         things and approached human life through a view of a spir-
         itually ennobled nature. He was attracted to local sanc-
         tities, distinguishing passions in characters, and bold
         speculative ideas. To him meter is but an accessary grace
         to the music of words. He teaches the importance of con-
         templation. Recast as "Wordsworth" in 1889.B49.

37   PROWETT, C. G. "Browning's 'Lost Leader.'" Notes and Queries,
         5th ser., 1 (11 April), 292.
         Browning could not have meant to refer to Wordsworth in
         "The Lost Leader."

38   [REEVE, HENRY]. Review of Mill's Autobiography. Edinburgh
         Review, 139 (January), 91-129 (113-15).
         Wordsworth's poetry is best fitted to restore the in-
         fluence of the heart to a mind overcome by false reasoning.

39   [RICHARDSON, MARY FLETCHER, ed.]. Autobiography of Mrs.
         Fletcher, of Edinburgh, with Selections from her Letters
         and Other Family Memorials. Edited by the Survivor of Her
         Family. Carlisle: privately printed, pp. 70-71, 97-98,
         184-266 (passim).
         Includes autobiography in which Eliza Fletcher records
         the tranquilizing effect of Lyrical Ballads (1798), her
         intercourse with the Wordsworths in the 1830's (Wordsworth's
         gloom over public affairs), and Dr. Chalmers's attraction to

1874

Wordsworth's love for the common people. Includes letters
in which she remarks the high moral tone of The Excursion
though objecting to the poem's length, and records testimonies to the solace of Wordsworth's poems, and Wordsworth's
account of the origins of "Ode to Lycoris." Includes entries from a notebook in which Mary Fletcher Richardson records Wordsworth's reactions to Italy and France in 1837,
his pain at reading of Scott's weaknesses, his denunciation
of despotism in Europe, and his mixed reaction to Crabbe and
praise of Cowper's and Burns's letters. Includes poems by
Eliza Fletcher: "Thoughts on Leaving Grasmere Churchyard,
April 27, 1850, after the Funeral of William Wordsworth"
(Wordsworth's "was no narrow creed"; he lifted men above
sordid cares) and "On the Union and Companionship between
Wordsworth and His Sister, after Reading her Grasmere Journal" (without Dorothy, Wordsworth "had idly gazed"). Includes letter in which J. Baillie notes Wordsworth "taught
much in his own peculiar way." Expanded in 1875.B16.

40 RUSSELL, WILLIAM CLARK. The Book of Table-talk: Selections
    from the Conversations of Poets, Philosophers, Statesmen[,]
    Divines, &c. London and New York: Routledge, pp. 250-56.
       A biographical sketch, with extracts from Wordsworth's
    table talk.

41 SHAIRP, J.[OHN] C.[AMPBELL]. "Wordsworth's 'White Doe of
    Rylstone': A Lecture delivered in St. Salvator's College,
    St. Andrews." Good Words, 15:269-78.
       Wordsworth's handling of the story in The White Doe of
    Rylstone is unlike Scott's manner. Wordsworth gives to
    nature and to the soul's own power too great a healing
    power. The charm of the poem arises from Wordsworth's
    imaginative use of the doe. Revised with omissions in
    1881.B30.

42 SIMCOX, EDITH. Review of D. Wordsworth's Recollections of a
    Tour Made in Scotland. Academy, 6 (25 July), 91-93.
       Wordsworth cannot always assume his particular associa-
    tions are typical.

43 SMITH, GEORGE BARNETT. Review of Masson's Wordsworth, Shelley,
    Keats, and other Essays. Examiner, no. 3470 (1 August),
    p. 823.
       Though Wordsworth falters in tune and lacks grand passion,
    his reputation will grow.

44 THORNBURY, WALTER. "Browning's 'Lost Leader.'" Notes and
    Queries, 5th ser., 1 (14 March), 213.

252

1875

Reports Browning's identification of Wordsworth as the lost leader.

45 TOMLINSON, CHARLES. The Sonnet: Its Origin, Structure, and Place in Poetry. London: Murray, pp. 76-78.
   Criticizes Wordsworth's use of the sonnet in The River Duddon.

46 TURNER, H.[AWES] H. "Life," "Introduction," "Notes," in Wordsworth's Excursion: The Wanderer. Edited by H. H. Turner. London, Oxford, and Cambridge: Rivingtons, pp. 5-15, 17-18, 43-77.
   A biographical sketch. Wordsworth's life was singular for its unconventionality. His theory of the language of poetry, as expressed in the Preface to Lyrical Ballads, is unsound. His genius is not dramatic; he is rarely puerile, is only superficially a poet of nature. He is remarkable for the completeness of his life, for his friendships, and for his originality. He stands aloof between the eighteenth and nineteenth centuries. Revised in 1886.B53 (5-15). In The Excursion he made no great effort to obtain dramatic effect (17-18). Includes critical notes. Revised in 1886.B53 (43-77).

47 TURNER, H.[AWES] H. "Notes," in Selections from the Poetical Works of William Wordsworth. Edited by H. H. Turner. London, Oxford, and Cambridge: Rivingtons, pp. 43-87.
   Brief critical notes to the poems selected. Revised in 1881.B33.

48 WORDSWORTH, CHRISTOPHER [FELLOW OF PETERHOUSE, CAMBRIDGE]. Social Life at the English Universities in the Eighteenth Century. Cambridge: Deighton, Bell; London: Bell, pp. 116, 171-72, 589-90.
   Records Wordsworth's life at and opinions about Cambridge. Includes extracts from the diary of Christopher Wordsworth (Master of Trinity College, Cambridge) in 1793: Wordsworth's first published poems should have been aimed at popular taste; Wordsworth is esteemed at Exeter, according to Coleridge.

1875 A BOOKS - NONE

1875 B SHORTER WRITINGS

1 ANON. Review of D. Wordsworth's Recollections of a Tour Made in Scotland. London Quarterly Review, 45 (October), 248-49.

1875

Wordsworth, a "calm giant of intelligence," did all he
could to stifle the lyric poet unquestionably in him.

2   ANON. Review of The Prose Works of William Wordsworth.
    Athenaeum, no. 2502 (9 October), pp. 467-69.
    "A Letter to the Bishop of Llandaff" shows Wordsworth's
    generous sympathies rather than argumentative powers, and
    his mastery of prose. In Concerning . . . the Convention
    of Cintra Wordsworth eloquently insists on pursuing the
    right course, regardless of consequences. In "Essay upon
    Epitaphs" his specimens do not come up to his ideal.

3   ANON. Review of The Prose Works of William Wordsworth.
    Examiner, no. 3533 (16 October), pp. 1165-66.
    There was a "falling off" in Wordsworth's later political
    writings.

4   ANON. "Wordsworth's Prose Works." Saturday Review, 40
    (6 November), 590-91.
    In his political prose Wordsworth moves from spirited
    Republican maxims in 1793 to non-constructive stock phrases
    in 1818. Though at times too hasty and exclusive in his
    attack on artificial poetry, he did effect a poetic revo-
    lution.

5   ANON. Review of The Prose Works of William Wordsworth.
    Dublin University Magazine, 86 (December), 756-60.
    Prose was not Wordsworth's forte. "A Letter to the
    Bishop of Llandaff" abounds in crude reasoning and prin-
    ciples Wordsworth later disavowed. "Essay upon Epitaphs"
    contains searching, discriminating criticism. Wordsworth
    did not excel in letter writing.

6   ANON. "William Wordsworth," in Gleanings from the Sacred
    Poets. Edinburgh and London: Gall & Inglis [1875],
    pp. 166-67.
    A biographical sketch.

7   DE V.[ERE], A.[UBREY THOMAS]. "Memoir," in Sonnets. By Sir
    Aubrey De Vere. A new edition. London: Pickering,
    pp. xi-xix (xii, xiv, xvi).
    Records Sir A. De Vere's friendship with Wordsworth.
    (According to "Advertisement" [p. v], the "Memoir" was
    first prefixed to the republication in 1875 of Sir A. De
    Vere's Mary Tudor, a volume not located.)

8   DOWDEN, EDWARD. "The Prose Works of Wordsworth." Fortnightly
    Review, NS 18 (1 October), 449-70.

The opinion of Mill notwithstanding, there is in Wordsworth's poetry "an entire consentaneity of thought and feeling." Wordsworth's political prose may be divided into that
of his youthful republicanism (in "A Letter to the Bishop of
Llandaff"), his patriotic enthusiasm (in Concerning . . .
the Convention of Cintra), and "his uncourageous elder
years." After the French Revolution Wordsworth chose to
work to correct the errors of the eighteenth century rather
than to ally with the progressive thought of the time. Reprinted in Studies in Literature (1878).

9   HALES, J.[OHN] W.[ESLEY]. Review of The Prose Works of
    William Wordsworth. Academy, 8 (6 November), 469-71.
        Discusses Wordsworth's influence on Byron and Shelley;
    his reputation is spreading.

10 MARTIN, THEODORE. The Life of His Royal Highness the Prince
    Consort. Illustrated. 5 vols. London: Smith, Elder,
    I:391-97.
        Though not the equal of "Ode: Intimations of Immortal-
    ity," "Ode on the Installation of His Royal Highness Prince
    Albert" contains "a succession of vivid images." Includes
    Queen Victoria's testimony to the applause that greeted the
    performance of the ode at Cambridge.

11 MASON, JAMES, ed. The Great Triumphs of Great Men.
    Illustrated. London and Edinburgh: Nimmo, pp. 194-97.
        Wordsworth had, through life, extraordinary good luck.

12 MOREHEAD, CHARLES, ed. Memorials of the Life and Writings of
    the Rev. Robert Morehead, D.D. Edited by his Son.
    Edinburgh: Edmonston and Douglas, pp. 102, 169-71.
        Includes letter in which F. Jeffrey notes he has "been
    enchanted with a little volume of poems, lately published,
    called 'Lyrical Ballads.'"

13 PALGRAVE, FRANCIS TURNER. "Notes," in The Children's
    Treasury of English Song. Edited by Francis Turner
    Palgrave. First part. London: Macmillan, pp. 143-46
    (145).
        In "Written in Early Spring" Wordsworth makes his ori-
    ginal thought seem familiar. "To the Cuckoo" ("O blithe
    New-comer! I have heard") can be appreciated only by the
    highly imaginative.

14 PALGRAVE, FRANCIS TURNER. "Notes," in The Children's Treasury
    of English Song. Edited by Francis Turner Palgrave.
    Second part. London: Macmillan, pp. 144-48 (144).

"Lucy Gray" is not strictly a pathetic poem because the child's character is ideal.

15   POLLOCK, SIR FREDERICK, ed. Macready's Reminiscences, and Selections from His Diaries and Letters. 2 vols. London: Macmillan, I:284-85, 358; II:32-33, 277, 353-54, 364.
      Records Macready's admiration of Wordsworth's poems and visits with Wordsworth in 1823, 1836, and 1846.

16   [RICHARDSON, MARY FLETCHER, ed.]. Autobiography of Mrs. Fletcher: with Letters and other Family Memorials. Edited by the Survivor of Her Family. Edinburgh: Edmonston and Douglas, pp. 78-79, 109-10, 213-308 (passim).
      Expanded from 1874.B39. Adds letters in which Eliza Fletcher gives an account of Wordsworth's funeral and notes the likeness of Wordsworth's face to Dante's.

17   [SEELEY, JOHN ROBERT]. "Natural Religion." Macmillan's Magazine, 32 (October), 481-89 (483-84, 486-87); 33 (November), 1-9 (3-8).
      Wordsworth worships trees and flowers for themselves, unconnected with the Supernatural; his view of the universe is Judaic rather than Hellenic (483-84, 486-87). Up to a point Wordsworth and Goethe agree in their way of regarding the universe. Wordsworth's pantheism did not dull his sense of duty. His life was pious; he mastered the art of plain living, triumphing over sorrow. He was a Christian; nature inspired him with faith (3-8). Recast as 1882.B56.

18   [STORY, WILLIAM WETMORE]. "In a Studio.--Conversation No. II." Blackwood's Edinburgh Magazine, 117 (June), 713-41 (736).
      Wordsworth wrote his best poems later in life.

19   [STORY, WILLIAM WETMORE]. "In a Studio.--Conversation No. IV." Blackwood's Edinburgh Magazine, 118 (December), 674-95 (689-92).
      Except in "Why art thou silent! Is thy love a plant" and "Surprised by joy--impatient as the Wind," Wordsworth does not sing of personal love.

20   SWINBURNE, ALGERNON CHARLES. "Matthew Arnold's New Poems," "Byron," "Coleridge," in Essays and Studies. London: Chatto and Windus, pp. 123-83 (145-54, 173), 238-58 (239, 244-45, 257), 259-75 (259, 269, 271).
      Reprinted from 1867.B11 (145-54, 173). Expanded from 1866.B16. After an early delight in nature, Wordsworth turned to moralizing (239, 244-45, 257). Reprinted from 1869.B22 (259, 269, 271).

21 WARREN, C. F. S. "Wordsworth." Notes and Queries, 5th ser.,
    4 (17 July), 54.
       Interprets "Stanzas: Suggested in a Steamboat off Saint
Bees' Heads." (A reply to A. L. Mayhew, "Wordsworth,"
Notes and Queries, 5th ser., 3 [12 June], 468.)

1876 A BOOKS - NONE

1876 B SHORTER WRITINGS

1 ANON. "Wordsworth's Prose Works." Spectator, 49
    (22 January), 113-14.
       Wordsworth's "fame is happily too well established to be
affected by the incapacity of biographers or the blunders
of editors."

2 ANON. Review of The Prose Works of William Wordsworth.
    London Quarterly Review, 47 (October), 102-18.
       Wordsworth wrote his political prose from deep convic-
tion. His opinion on the Catholic Relief Bill is prepos-
terous. He was a pioneer of the co-operative movement. He
repeats in the Fenwick notes the sin of his poems: the
"desire to set everything right by recounting his own
experiences."

3 BOUCHIER, JONATHAN. "Wordsworth: 'The child is father of the
    man.'" Notes and Queries, 5th ser., 6 (25 November), 439.
       Notes parallel between "My heart leaps up when I behold"
and Milton.

4 BROOKE, STOPFORD. English Literature. London: Macmillan,
    pp. 151-57.
       A biographical sketch. The root of Wordsworth's thought
lies in his seeing nature possessing a personality distinct
from man; his love of nature led to a love of man. Revised
in 1880.B13.

5 [BROWN, JAMES BUCHAM] J. B. S. "Culture and Modern Poetry."
    Cornhill Magazine, 34 (December), 664-79 (673-76).
       Wordsworth wrote "rhymed prose," exhibits an "oriental
quietism." Reprinted in Ethics and Aesthetics of Modern
Poetry (1878).

6 [COLLINS, W. LUCAS]. "In My Study Chair: No. II."
    Blackwood's Edinburgh Magazine, 119 (January), 21-33
    (30-31).

1876

It formerly was the proper thing to admire Wordsworth.
Wordsworth's personal amiability is irrelevant to his merit
as a poet.

7   [COURTHOPE, WILLIAM JOHN]. Review of The Prose Works of
     William Wordsworth. Quarterly Review, 141 (January),
     104-36.
     The features that repel the reader from Wordsworth's
     verse are more pronounced in his prose, which is all like a
     sermon. His attack in the Preface to Lyrical Ballads on
     Gray represents the quarrel between the romantic and classi-
     cal schools of poetry over the liberty of the imagination.

8   DE VERE, AUBREY [THOMAS]. "Recollections of Wordsworth," in
     The Prose Works of William Wordsworth: For the First Time
     Collected, with Additions from Unpublished Manuscripts.
     Edited by the Rev. Alexander B. Grosart. 3 vols. London:
     Moxon, III:486-99.
     Praises Wordsworth's manly simplicity and lofty recti-
     tude. Records Wordsworth's remarks that a true description
     of nature is at once real and ideal, and that Shakespeare
     fails to give due importance to man's religious sentiment.
     Wordsworth was a man of strong affections and political
     passions, diffident of writing on religious themes, pessi-
     mistic about the future of English poetry. Records Sir
     Aubrey de Vere's and his own admiration of Wordsworth's
     poems, especially "Laodamia," and Wordsworth's visits to
     London. Wordsworth viewed death as "the taking of a new
     degree in the University of Life." He never resented a jest
     at his own expense. Condensed in 1887.B19.

9   FITZGERALD, PERCY, ed. The Life, Letters and Writings of
     Charles Lamb. 6 vols. London: Moxon, I-III (passim).
     Reprints, with additions, the account of Lamb's friend-
     ship with and opinions of Wordsworth, in his correspondence,
     in 1837.B24 and 1848.B11.

10 GOSTWICK, JOSEPH. English Poets: Twelve Essays. Illustrated.
     London: Bruckmann, pp. 3-12, 135-56.
     A biographical sketch. Wordsworth sometimes wrote ser-
     mons in verse; his "use of an unaccented syllable instead
     of a true rhyme," especially in the sonnets, is a blemish.
     His characters each represent mostly one sentiment.

11 GRAVES, R.[OBERT] P.[ERCEVAL]. "Further Reminiscences of
     Wordsworth by the Same, Sent to the Present Editor," in
     The Prose Works of William Wordsworth: For the First Time
     Collected, with Additions from Unpublished Manuscripts.

Edited by the Rev. Alexander B. Grosart. 3 vols. London:
Moxon, III:471-75.
Wordsworth advocated making only minor revisions in the
translation of the Bible and in the Book of Common Prayer.
Records Wordsworth's opinion that the strongest passion to
be found in his poems is in "Song at the Feast of Brougham
Castle," his rejection of the chronological arrangement of
his poems as being too egotistical, and his criticism of
Southey's poems.

12 GROSART, THE REV. ALEXANDER B. "To the Queen," "Preface,"
    "Notes and Illustrations," Notes, in The Prose Works of
    William Wordsworth: For the First Time Collected, with
    Additions from Unpublished Manuscripts. Edited by the Rev.
    Alexander B. Grosart. 3 vols. London: Moxon, I:v,
    vii-xxxviii, 357-60 and II:343-47 and III:505-10, passim.
        Wordsworth is supreme as Poet and Thinker (I:v). In-
    cludes Bishop Charles Graves's verse tribute to Wordsworth
    as philosopher, "To Wordsworth" (vii-xxxviii). Gives bibli-
    ographical and explanatory notes to the prose works, in-
    cluding a letter in which Browning identifies Wordsworth as
    a model for "The Lost Leader" (vii-xxxviii, 357-60;
    II:343-47; III:505-10). Includes footnotes throughout the
    volumes (passim).

13 HARE, AUGUSTUS J. C. Memorials of a Quiet Life. Supplementary
    Volume. Illustrated. London: Daldy, Isbister, pp. 224-25.
        A continuation of 1872.B15. Records Julius Hare's visit
    to Wordsworth in 1833.

14 HAYDON, FREDERIC WORDSWORTH, ed. Benjamin Robert Haydon:
    Correspondence and Table-Talk. With a Memoir by his Son.
    Illustrated. 2 vols. London: Chatto and Windus, passim.
        Records Wordsworth's admiration of Haydon and the aged
    Wordsworth's invective against Jeffrey. Includes letters
    in which Haydon expresses his gratitude for Wordsworth's
    support and Keats's and Hunt's reverence for Wordsworth,
    explains Hazlitt's anger at Wordsworth, and calls Words-
    worth, though elevated, "insufferably obscure, starched,
    dowdy, anti-human," lacking constructive power. Includes
    table-talk in which Haydon notes that Wordsworth perceives
    human feelings by analyzing his own and finds, in opposition
    to Shakespeare, the positive in death and grief, and com-
    ments on Wordsworth's appearance at Court in 1845. In-
    cludes letters in which Barron Field expresses admiration
    of Wordsworth, C. H. Townshend finds Wordsworth "prosy in
    real life," T. N. Talfourd defends Wordsworth's attending
    Court, Keats says that Wordsworth is too proud, and M. R.
    Mitford defends Wordsworth against Byron.

1876

15   HORNE, R.[ICHARD] H.[ENGIST]. "Elizabeth Barrett Browning on
      Some of her Contemporaries." St. James's Magazine and
      United Empire Review, [3rd ser.,] 2:21-31 (25-26).
          Includes correspondence with E. B. Browning over Words-
      worth's choice of low subjects.

16   MORLEY, HENRY, ed. Shorter English Poems. Illustrated.
      London, Paris, and New York: Cassell [1876], pp. 417-20,
      427-28, 434-37, 449, 458-60.
          A biographical sketch.

17   PAUL, C.[HARLES] KEGAN. William Godwin: His Friends and
      Contemporaries. Illustrated. 2 vols. London: King,
      II:3, 8, 78-79.
          Includes Coleridge's praise of Wordsworth in letters to
      Godwin.

18   R., B. "Wordsworth's Originality." Notes and Queries,
      5th ser., 6 (21 October), 326.
          Notes echoes in "My heart leaps up when I behold" from
      Dryden, in The Excursion from Horace, and in "Walton's Book
      of Lives" from Henry Constable.

19   [REEVE, HENRY]. Review of Benjamin Robert Haydon:
      Correspondence and Table-Talk. Edinburgh Review, 144
      (July), 33-52 (42-49).
          Wordsworth's character and life contrast with Haydon's.
      Wordsworth's prose style is labored and cold; but he shows
      in his letters to Haydon a "delicate perception of beauty
      in painting" and a noble patriotism. His advice to a young
      poet (in a letter of 1830) contains "delicate irony."

20   RICHARDSON, LADY [MARY]. "Additional [Reminiscences] Sent to
      the Present Editor," in The Prose Works of William
      Wordsworth: For the First Time Collected, with Additions
      from Unpublished Manuscripts. Edited by the Rev. Alexander
      B. Grosart. 3 vols. London: Moxon, III:437-38.
          Recalls Wordsworth's conversation in 1841 on the effects
      of Jeffrey's criticism and on the separation of rich and
      poor.

21   ROSSETTI, W.[ILLIAM] M.[ICHAEL]. "William Bell Scott and
      Modern British Poetry." Macmillan's Magazine, 33 (March),
      418-29 (419).
          Wordsworth's "power was more individual and special than
      some enthusiasts supposed."

22 RUSKIN, JOHN. "Preface," in A Protest against the Extension
of Railways in the Lake District. . . . By Robert
Somervell. Windermere: Garnett; London: Simpkin,
Marshall [1876], pp. 1-9 (2, 7).
Wordsworth painted the Border peasantry with "absolute
fidelity" (e.g., in "Michael"). Reprinted in On the Old
Road (1885).

23 [RUSSELL, CHARLES WILLIAM]. "Critical History of the Sonnet."
Dublin Review, NS 27 (October), 400-30 (402, 406-407,
421-26).
Wordsworth avoids the doctrine of the immaculate concep-
tion in "The Virgin." He restored the sonnet form in
England.

24 S., J. B. See 1876.B5.

25 SOMERVELL, ROBERT. A Protest against the Extension of
Railways in the Lake District. . . . Windermere: Garnett;
London: Simpkin, Marshall [1876], pp. 11-19, 43-46.
Recalls Wordsworth's efforts against the railway in 1844.
Prints anonymous article to the same effect from the Daily
News of 17 January 1876.

26 [STEPHEN, LESLIE]. "Hours in a Library: No. XIII.--
Wordsworth's Ethics." Cornhill Magazine, 34 (August),
206-26.
Wordsworth is a good poet because he is a good philosopher. In "Ode: Intimations of Immortality" he recognizes
the "mysterious efficacy of our childish instincts"; he
strove to find a continuity between these instincts and
man's later reasoned convictions. He at times overlooked
the dark side of nature. To him, mountains provide the
background of domestic affections rather than anti-social
feelings. He realizes man's being must not be fragmented.
He teaches us to turn grief into strength. Expanded in
1879.B20.

27 STEPHEN, LESLIE. History of English Thought in the Eighteenth
Century. 2 vols. London: Smith, Elder, I:14-15; II:448,
451-52, 457.
Wordsworth errs in regretting Proteus in "The world is
too much with us; late and soon." His pantheism, based upon
immediate intuition, differs from Pope's and Cowper's.

28 TODHUNTER, I.[SAAC]. William Whewell, D.D.: Master of
Trinity College, Cambridge: An Account of His Writings

1876

<u>with Selections from his Literary and Scientific</u>
<u>Correspondence</u>. 2 vols. London: Macmillan, I:356, 411;
II:196.
 Includes Whewell's criticism of the lack of interest,
false philosophy, and weak reasoning of <u>The Excursion</u>, and
a letter expressing satisfaction with Wordsworth's company.

29 TREVELYAN, GEORGE OTTO. <u>The Life and Letters of Lord Macaulay</u>.
2 vols. London: Longmans, I:77, 335; II:133, 279, 321,
323, 471.
 Records Macaulay's opinions of Wordsworth: <u>The Prelude</u>
contains Wordsworth's same old faults and beauties, "the
old flimsy philosophy about the effect of scenery on the
mind"; the poem is Socialist.

<u>1877 A BOOKS - NONE</u>

<u>1877 B SHORTER WRITINGS</u>

1 ANON. "The Wordsworths at Brinsop Court." <u>Temple Bar</u>, 49
(January), 110-16.
 Describes Wordsworth's associations with Brinsop Court.

2 ANON. "We Are Seven" (poem). <u>Funny Folks</u>, 3 (21 July), 21.
Parody of "We Are Seven."

3 ANON. "English Poets." <u>Poets' Magazine</u>, 3 (September),
137-45 (138-39).
 Wordsworth discovered that poetry could be extracted from
common life and cast his lyrics and idylls in novel forms.

4 ANON. "Introduction," "Notes," in <u>The Excursion: Book III:</u>
<u>Despondency</u>. London and Glasgow: Collins, pp. 3-4, 29-32.
 The interest in <u>The Excursion</u> is philosophical and didactic rather than narrative (3-4). Brief critical notes
(29-32).

5 ANON. "Wordsworth, William," in <u>The Popular Encyclopedia; or,</u>
<u>Conversations Lexicon: Being A General Dictionary of Arts,</u>
<u>Sciences, Literature, Biography, and History</u>. New edition.
Illustrated. 14 vols. London, Glasgow, and Edinburgh:
Blackie [1877], XIV:793-94.
 A biographical sketch, revised from 1862.B3.

6 ARMSTRONG, EDMUND J. "Coleridge," "Remarks on Some of the
Characters in Wordsworth's Poems," in <u>Essays and Sketches</u>

of Edmund J. Armstrong. Edited by George Francis Armstrong.
London: Longmans, pp. 38-96 (46-49), 97-126.
    Wordsworth and Coleridge "mutually aided one another:
Coleridge gave light, and Wordsworth reality" (46-49).
Though Wordsworth's portraits are ideal because Wordsworth
himself lived in retirement, they are still realistic--es-
pecially, De Quincey's criticism notwithstanding, in The
Excursion. Wordsworth's characters are of unblemished
morality, as was Wordsworth's own life (97-126).

7   ARMSTRONG, GEORGE FRANCIS. The Life and Letters of Edmund J.
    Armstrong. London: Longmans, pp. 25-26, 37, 545, 552, 555.
        Recounts E. Armstrong's attraction to the tenderness and
    love of nature in Wordsworth's poems.

8   [ARNOLD, MATTHEW]. Review of Macaulay's "Essay on Milton,"
    etc. Quarterly Review, 143 (January), 186-204 (201).
        Wordsworth's blank verse lumbers; in The Prelude ("at the
    Hoop alighted") Wordsworth tries "to render a platitude en-
    durable by making it pompous." Reprinted as "A French
    Critic on Milton" in Mixed Essays (1879).

9   ARNOLD, MATTHEW. "A Guide to English Literature." Nineteenth
    Century, 2 (December), 843-53 (849-50, 852-53).
        Wordsworth's natural descriptions are unlike Milton's
    or Scott's. "No one will be much helped by Wordsworth's
    philosophy of Nature, as a scheme in itself and disjoined
    from his poems." Reprinted in Mixed Essays (1879).

10 AUSTIN, ALFRED. "The Poetic Interpretation of Nature."
    Contemporary Review, 30 (November), 961-80 (967, 973,
    977-79).
        Wordsworth consciously altered scientific fact in "The
    Pet-lamb." Those who most admire Wordsworth admire him be-
    cause he reinforces their own beliefs. His poetry deteri-
    orates as he introduces his Christian creed into it.

11 [BOWRING, LEWIN B., ed.]. Autobiographical Recollections of
    Sir John Bowring: with a Brief Memoir by Lewin B. Bowring.
    London: King, pp. 60, 355-56.
        Includes recollections in which J. Bowring claims author-
    ship of 1813.B4, notes Byron's debt to Wordsworth, Words-
    worth's political apostasy, and his preference for his own
    poems.

12 DAVIS, WILLIAM. "William Wordsworth: 1770-1850," in The
    Junior Book of Poetry, for Schools and Families. Edited by

1877

   William Davis. London: Simpkin, Marshall; Edinburgh:
   Oliver & Boyd, and Menzies, p. 21.
    A biographical sketch.

13 DOWDEN, EDWARD. "The French Revolution and Literature."
   Contemporary Review, 30 (June), 120-41 (121, 123-29).
    Wordsworth's earlier teaching exhibits transcendentalism.
   Sternness characterizes his joy at the French Revolution.
   After the Revolution failed, Wordsworth retained a true
   reverence for democracy. Reprinted in Studies in Literature
   (1878).

14 DOWDEN, EDWARD. "The Transcendental Movement and Literature."
   Contemporary Review, 30 (July), 297-318 (301, 305-10, 312).
    Wordsworth's impassioned contemplation involves the har-
   monious action of diverse mental faculties. The tendencies
   of Wordsworth at his imaginative best are adverse to Anglo-
   Catholicism. Reprinted in Studies in Literature (1878).

15 DOYLE, SIR FRANCIS HASTINGS. "Wordsworth," in Lectures on
   Poetry Delivered at Oxford. Second series. London:
   Smith, Elder, pp. 1-77.
    Wordsworth's suppression of The Prelude is significant
   in light of his love of fame. His best poems were those
   written before 1806 in moments of rest from working on The
   Prelude; "The Brothers" is his finest poem. His poetic
   failure arose from his retirement, his lonely nature, the
   critics' response, and the death of Lucy. Discusses Wordsworth's life as chronicled in The Prelude. Wordsworth
   should have devoted himself less to didacticism and more to
   passion. His praise of Burke and of the French revolu-
   tionaries is inconsistent. The Prelude is too long and un-
   revised. The Excursion is The Prelude over again in looser,
   more didactic form; the poem is best before the introduction
   of the Pastor. Wordsworth is a master of the sonnet.

16 FORMAN, HARRY BUXTON. Note, in The Poetical Works of Percy
   Bysshe Shelley. Edited by Harry Buxton Forman. 4 vols.
   London: Reeves and Turner, III:224.
    Prints expanded text of letter (see 1860.B12) in which
   Shelley blasts Wordsworth's apostasy.

17 FRANK, FATHER. "A Descendant of Wordsworth." Notes and
   Queries, 5th ser., 8 (13 October), 289.
    Describes a woman named Keeling claiming to be a de-
   scendant of Wordsworth.

18 GIBSON, T. H. "Studies in Poetry." Poets' Magazine, 3
    (September), 157-68 (166).
        Wordsworth makes nature and rustic life appear vividly
    before us.

19 [JAPP, ALEXANDER H.] H. A. PAGE. Thomas De Quincey: His Life
    and Writings: With Unpublished Correspondence. 2 vols.
    London: Hogg, passim.
        Records De Quincey's appreciation of Wordsworth's poems
    and intercourse with the Wordsworths. Wordsworth's lack of
    sympathy, which alienated De Quincey, is integral to his
    value as a teacher. Includes letters in which De Quincey
    reacts to the deaths of Wordsworth's children and discusses
    the similarity of Wordsworth's and Plato's thoughts on im-
    mortality. Revised with omissions in 1890.B29.

20 [KINGSLEY, FRANCES E., ed.]. Charles Kingsley: His Letters
    and Memories of His Life. Edited by his Wife. Illustrated.
    2 vols. London: King, I:120.
        Includes letter in which C. Kingsley praises Wordsworth
    as a light in a dark age, preaching a simple faith in man
    and God.

21 MACKAY, CHARLES. Forty Years' Recollections of Life,
    Literature, and Public Affairs: from 1830 to 1870.
    2 vols. London: Chapman & Hall, I:231-46.
        Gives his own and S. Rogers's criticism of Wordsworth's
    views in Kendal and Windermere Railway and Rogers's opinion
    that Wordsworth lived too much alone and that his characters
    mingled simplicity and vanity. Records visit to Rydal
    Mount in 1846: Wordsworth's preference for his own poems,
    his refusal to converse with Dorothy.

22 [MACKENZIE, A. W.]. "Poets of Past-times on Pas-times of the
    Present: By the Author of 'Idylls of the Rink.'" Mirth,
    no. 7, pp. 229-30 (230).
        Includes "Rink, pretty creature, rink" (poem), a parody
    of "The Pet-lamb." Attribution: W. Hamilton in 1888.B19,
    V:96.

23 MARTINEAU, HARRIET. Autobiography. With Memorials by Maria
    Weston Chapman. Illustrated. 3 vols. London: Smith,
    Elder, II:233-44.
        Records her early response to Wordsworth and her later
    visits with him. He combined "odd economies" with "neigh-
    bourly generosity." He is not a philosopher, nor are his
    writings poems. He did not understand mankind. He grew
    more liberal in politics and religion in his later years.

1877

His reception of visitors to Rydal Mount was impersonally routine.

24 MAYER, S. R. TOWNSHEND, ed. Letters of Elizabeth Barrett Browning Addressed to Richard Hengist Horne, With Comments on Contemporaries. 2 vols. London: Bentley, I:92, 95–97, 100–101, 108, 117, 135, 176–80, 185; II:35–42, 172–73.
Includes Horne's account of the publishing of The Poems of Geoffrey Chaucer, Modernized, and of his collaborating with E. B. Browning on 1844.B22. Includes E. B. Browning's remarks on Wordsworth's opposition to the Windermere railway.

25 MORLEY, HENRY. "Recent Literature." Nineteenth Century, 2 (August), 124–48 (131–33, 136).
Wordsworth first expressed the master-thought of English life in the nineteenth century--the hope for the future through individual education.

26 MORLEY, HENRY. Illustrations of English Religion. London, Paris, New York, and Melbourne: Cassell [1877], pp. 402–405.
Wordsworth felt deeply "the place of man in the great harmony of creation." In the Ecclesiastical Sonnets he testifies to "the power of a calm religious influence."

27 PAGE, H. A. See 1877.B19.

28 [PATMORE, COVENTRY, ed.]. Bryan Waller Proctor (Barry Cornwall): An Autobiographical Fragment and Biographical Notes, with Personal Sketches of Contemporaries, Unpublished Lyrics, and Letters of Literary Friends. London: Bell, pp. 59, 128–29, 136–44, 183, 202, 205.
Records Proctor's comment that in the 1860's "Wordsworth is no longer widely read" and his recollections of Wordsworth: he was grave, inferior in ordinary talk, a meditative poet of nature and common man; he faced early poverty. Includes letter in which he reports Lamb mocking Wordsworth.

29 PLATT, WILLIAM. "Wordsworth's Originality." Notes and Queries, 5th ser., 7 (13 January), 39.
A reply to 1876.B18. Notes parallels to The Excursion, "Walton's Book of Lives" and "My heart leaps up when I behold."

30 SHAIRP, JOHN CAMPBELL. On Poetic Interpretation of Nature. Edinburgh: Douglas, pp. 113–14, 225–70.

1878

Wordsworth makes us partake in his interpretation of nature as possessing a life independent of himself, a view that grew out of experiences, told in The Prelude, of his school years and the French Revolution. His later poems fittingly reflect a moral tendency resulting from his increased experience and sorrow.

31   [SHEPHERD, RICHARD H.]. "Memoir of Samuel Taylor Coleridge," Note, in The Poetical and Dramatic Works of Samuel Taylor Coleridge. . . . [Edited by Richard H. Shepherd.] 4 vols. London: Pickering, I:ix-cxviii (passim), 82.
     Recounts Wordsworth's relations with Coleridge: doubts Wordsworth and Coleridge met in 1795.

32   SMITH, GEORGE BARNETT. Shelley: A Critical Biography. Edinburgh: Douglas, pp. 1-4, 9, 124, 198-99, 226-29, 244-45.
     Conservative instincts underlay the Communistic spirit the early Wordsworth shared with Shelley. Traces Shelley's admiration of Wordsworth.

33   STARKIE, G. "Sonnet: Written in a Copy of Wordsworth." Poet's Magazine, 3 (November), 312.
     Pays tribute to Wordsworth, the philosopher of truth, inspired by nature.

34   SULLY, JAMES. Pessimism: A History and a Criticism. London: King, pp. 15-16.
     To Wordsworth, suffering is tied to man's deepest happiness.

35   TREVELYAN, W. C. "Autographs of Wordsworth and Kenyon." Notes and Queries, 5th ser., 7 (14 April), 285-86.
     Transcribes autograph of Wordsworth.

1878 A BOOKS

1   KNIGHT, WILLIAM. The English Lake District as Interpreted in the Poems of Wordsworth. Edinburgh: Douglas, 272 pp.
     Aims "to interpret the poems, by bringing out the singularly close connection between them, and the district of the English Lakes, and by explaining Wordsworth's numerous allusions to the locality." Includes "A Lecture on Wordsworth" reprinted from 1878.B16. Revised in 1891.A1.

1878

1878 B   SHORTER WRITINGS

1   ADAMS, W.[ILLIAM] DAVENPORT. Dictionary of English Literature.
    London, Paris, and New York: Cassell Petter & Galpin
    [c. 1878], pp. 700-701.
       A brief bibliographical notice.

2   ANON. "Biographical Sketches," in Poetical Gleanings. London
    and Edinburgh: Chambers, pp. 153-59 (159).
       A biographical sketch. Wordsworth loved nature as a
    personal being.

3   ARNOLD, THOMAS. "English Literature," in The Encyclopaedia
    Britannica: A Dictionary of Arts, Sciences, and General
    Literature. Ninth edition. 24 vols. Edinburgh: Black,
    VIII:403-35 (433-35).
       Wordsworth lived a simple and serene life as nature's
    poet-priest.

4   B.[ETHAM]-E.[DWARDS], M.[ATILDA]. "Letters of Coleridge,
    Southey, and Lamb to Matilda Betham." Fraser's Magazine,
    NS 18 (July), 73-84 (76-78, 81, 83).
       Includes letters in which Coleridge indicates his friend-
    ship with Wordsworth, Southey praises Concerning . . . the
    Convention of Cintra, and Mrs. Coleridge reports "the Words-
    worths are woeful destroyers of good books." Reprinted in
    Six Life Studies of Famous Women (1880).

5   BOUCHIER, JONATHAN. "Portrait of Wordsworth by Haydon."
    Notes and Queries, 5th ser., 10 (23 November), 407.
       Describes a portrait of Wordsworth.

6   COMPTON, EDWARD. "'I've Got Seven'" (poem). Touchstone,
    NS 4 (16 November), 7.
       Parody of "We Are Seven."

7   DOWDEN, EDWARD. "The Text of Wordsworth's Poems."
    Contemporary Review, 33 (November), 734-57.
       Discusses poems not retained by Wordsworth in later edi-
    tions and textual alterations, especially in The Excursion,
    "Ode to Duty," "Louisa," "I wandered lonely as a cloud,"
    and "Ode: 1815." Wordsworth made a real attempt to re-
    solve the facts of life into a spiritual harmony. In
    "Andrew Jones" the misery is relieved only by a frank es-
    cape of indignation. "Power of Music" and "Star-gazers"
    make companion statements about the emotions. Wordsworth
    lost his early enthusiasm for the adjective "sweet" and the
    verb "to be." Reprinted with minor changes in Transcripts
    and Studies (1888).

8   DOWDEN, EDWARD. "Wordsworth's 'Glowworm'; Lucy; and Miss
     Wordsworth." Academy, 14 (9 November), 454.
          A note to 1878.B7. Points out Wordsworth's "imaginative
     re-handling" of material in D. Wordsworth's journal.

9   EDMONDS, HERBERT. Well-Spent Lives: A Series of Modern
     Biographies. London: Paul, pp. 1-29.
          A biographical sketch. Nature was Wordsworth's teacher;
     Wordsworth taught men purer thoughts.

10   FLEMING, CHARLES. "To Wordsworth, on his being Appointed Poet
     Laureate" (poem), in Poems, Songs, and Essays. Edited by
     Robert Brown. Paisley: Cook, p. 78.
          Remarks the incongruity of Wordsworth's mild muse ac-
     cepting the laureateship.

11   HODGSON, THE REV. JAMES T. Memoir of the Rev. Francis Hodgson,
     B.D.: Scholar, Poet, and Divine: With numerous Letters
     from Lord Byron and Others. By his Son. 2 vols. London:
     Macmillan, II:75, 173-74, 225.
          Includes letters in which Byron attacks Wordsworth as a
     renegade and Dr. Samuel Butler criticizes Wordsworth's
     prosing.

12   HORATIO. "Wordsworth's Portmanteau." Notes and Queries,
     5th ser., 9 (16 February), 140.
          Questions who would want Wordsworth's portmanteau adver-
     tised for sale.

13   HUTCHIESON, J. C. "Introduction," in Fugitive Poetry: 1600-
     1878. Edited by J. C. Hutchieson. London: Warne [1878],
     pp. 1-5 (4).
          Reveres simple Wordsworth, master of the Lake School.

14   [HUTTON, RICHARD HOLT]. "The Poetic Place of Matthew Arnold."
     Spectator, 51 (20 July), 918-19 (919).
          Arnold, though indebted to Wordsworth, did not fully un-
     derstand Wordsworth's exultation from discerning the divin-
     ity of this unintelligible world; where Wordsworth says
     "rejoice," Arnold says "endure."

15   KNIGHT, WILLIAM. "The Doctrine of Metempsychosis."
     Fortnightly Review, NS 24 (1 September), 422-42 (425,
     428-29, 441-42).
          Pre-existence is the central thought of "Ode: Intima-
     tions of Immortality." Reprinted with minor addition in
     1879.B16.

1878

16   KNIGHT, WILLIAM. "Wordsworth." Transactions of the Cumberland
      Association for the Advancement of Literature and Science,
      Part III, pp. 203-29.
          Wordsworth's poems possess a directness compared with
      Pope's, a healthful naturalness compared with Byron's.
      Though he did not understand the complexity of nineteenth-
      century life, Wordsworth found the cure for its fever. Dis-
      cusses his early critical reception and his view of his own
      poetry. He advocates the use of the language not of common
      but of unaffected life. He tells us that the key to under-
      standing the kinship and the calm of nature lies in improv-
      ing the perception of our inward eye; the secret of his
      power lies in his asking the meaning of individual natural
      details. He did not interpret nature subjectively. His
      poetry of nature is unaffected by the advance of science.
      Reprinted in 1878.A1 and 1879.B16.

17   [MEW, JAMES]. "Literary Coincidences." Cornhill Magazine, 37
      (March), 303-15 (315).
          Mockingly notes verbal echo of Milton in The Prelude.

18   ROSSETTI, WILLIAM MICHAEL. "William Wordsworth," in Lives of
      Famous Poets. London: Moxon, pp. 203-18.
          Briefly expanded from 1870.B13. Wordsworth, in contrast
      to Shelley, fails to excite sympathy in others.

19   RUSKIN, JOHN. "The Three Colours of Pre-Raphaelitism."
      Nineteenth Century, 4 (November), 925-31 (930); (December),
      1072-82 (1077-78).
          The Pre-Raphaelite movement was headed, in literary
      power, by Wordsworth. Reprinted in On the Old Road (1885).

20   SCOTT, R.[OBERT] PICKETT. The Place of Shelley among the
      English Poets of His Time: Being the Essay which Obtained
      the Members' Prize, 1877. Cambridge: Deighton, Bell;
      London: Bell, pp. 5-6, 14, 31, 48-50.
          Wordsworth teaches the calm Nature bestows and the one-
      ness of rich and poor. Unlike Shelley, he was disillusioned
      by the Reign of Terror. He is "a man of method," "lacking
      in fire."

21   SHAIRP, J.[OHN] C.[AMPBELL]. "The Aim of Poetry." Princeton
      Review, 54th Year (September), 449-70 (452, 455, 463-65).
          Wordsworth passes through distress to a higher illumina-
      tion. In "Resolution and Independence" his diction moves
      with his thought; his manner contrasts with Tennyson's.
      Reprinted as "The Province of Poetry" in 1881.B30.

22 [SKELTON, JOHN]. "Above the Clouds: A Reverie on the Bel
    Alp." Blackwood's Edinburgh Magazine, 123 (February),
    172-81 (173-74).
       Wordsworth's scenery is local. Phrases from his poems
    have become proverbial.

23 [STEPHEN, LESLIE]. "Hours in a Library: No. XVIII.--The
    First Edinburgh Reviewers." Cornhill Magazine, 38
    (August), 218-34 (226-27, 233).
       "Wordsworth's wilful and ostentatious inversion of ac-
    cepted rules" invited attack, though Jeffrey's was incom-
    petent. Reprinted in 1879.B20.

24 SYMONDS, JOHN ADDINGTON. Shelley. London: Macmillan,
    pp. 55-56, 86, 130, 183.
       Discusses Shelley's relationship with Wordsworth.
    "Wordsworth, the very antithesis to Shelley in his reverent
    accord with institutions, suits our meditative mood" but
    lacks Shelley's magnetism.

25 TAYLOR, HENRY. "Essay on the Poetical Works of Mr. Words-
    worth," "Essay on Mr. Wordsworth's Sonnets," in The Works
    of Henry Taylor. 5 vols. London: Paul, V:1-52, 53-122.
       Revised from 1849.B13.

26 VEITCH, JOHN. The History and Poetry of the Scottish Border:
    Their Main Features and Relations. Glasgow: Maclehose,
    pp. 518-24.
       In the Yarrow poems Wordsworth investigates the ideal
    versus the real.

27 [VENABLES, GEORGE S.]. Review of The Collected Works of Sir
    Henry Taylor in Prose and Verse. Edinburgh Review, 148
    (October), 504-27 (507-509).
       Except for "a misty pantheism," Wordsworth had no
    philosophic opinions.

28 WALPOLE, SPENCER. A History of England from the Conclusion of
    the Great War in 1815. 5 vols. London: Longmans,
    I:356-60.
       Wordsworth "shrank from the bustle of humanity." Re-
    vised in 1890.B47.

1879

1879 A   BOOKS - NONE

1879 B   SHORTER WRITINGS

   1   ANDERSON, ALEXANDER. "Dedication: To Archibald Cameron
       Corbett" (poem), in Ballads and Sonnets. London:
       Macmillan, pp. v-vii.
          Wordsworth leads us to a spiritual level in which we
       view nature with a sacred awe.

   2   ANON. "Scott and Wordsworth on Highland Scenery." Builder,
       37 (26 July), 821-22.
          In contrast to Scott, Wordsworth makes the landscape the
       main object of his poetry. His descriptions possess com-
       pleteness of detail.

   3   ANON. "Life of William Wordsworth," "Notes to 'The Excursion,'"
       in The Excursion: Book I: With Life and Notes. By
       William Wordsworth. Manchester and London: Heywood
       [1879], pp. iii-iv, 27-32.
          A biographical sketch. After the hostile reviews of
       Lyrical Ballads, Wordsworth wrote on, undaunted (iii-iv).
       Brief critical notes (27-32).

   4   ARNOLD, MATTHEW. "Wordsworth." Macmillan's Magazine, 40
       (July), 193-204.
          Wordsworth's popularity was at its height between 1830
       and 1840, at Cambridge. Wordsworth has left a great body
       of work "superior in power, in interest, in the qualities
       which give enduring freshness." His shorter poems are
       best, though unequal. An editor should abandon Wordsworth's
       flat and dull poems and his system of classification. Words-
       worth's superiority lies in the fact that his poetry is a
       criticism of life; it is great not because he expresses a
       formal system of thought but because he makes us share his
       joy in nature and in the primary affections. At his best
       he has no style. Slightly expanded in 1879.B6.

   5   ARNOLD, MATTHEW. "The French Play in London." Nineteenth
       Century, 6 (August), 228-43 (228, 232).
          Wordsworth's poetry is superior to V. Hugo's. Reprinted
       in Irish Essays and Others (1882).

   6   ARNOLD, MATTHEW. "Preface," in Poems of Wordsworth. Edited
       by Matthew Arnold. London: Macmillan, pp. v-xxvi.
          Slightly expanded from 1879.B4. Reprinted with minor
       changes twice in 1879 and in 1886; reprinted as thus re-
       vised in Essays in Criticism: Second Series (1888).

7   BOWEN, H. COURTHOPE. "William Wordsworth," in Simple English
     Poems: English Literature for Junior Classes. Edited by
     H. Courthope Bowen. Part I. London: Paul, pp. 48-52.
         A biographical sketch. Wordsworth's simple poems are
     remarkable for their feeling rather than their description.
     Includes critical notes on "Lucy Gray" and "Hart-leap Well."

8   C., E. A. "Wordsworth's Limits." Spectator, 52 (19 July),
     914.
         A reply to 1879.B15. Wordsworth's lack of popularity
     stems from his failure to seek a sympathetic response in
     his reader and to use similes.

9   DOWDEN, EDWARD. Review of Knight's The English Lake District
     as Interpreted in the Poems of Wordsworth and Calvert's
     Wordsworth: a Study. Academy, 15 (1 February), 92-93.
         For Wordsworth, the literal reality is but the material
     of poetry. Identifies scene of "There is a little unpre-
     tending Rill."

10   DOWDEN, EDWARD. "Wordsworth and Burns." Academy, 15
     (31 May), 479-80.
         A reply to 1879.B23. Wordsworth reacted to Burns's un-
     tamed elements with sympathy.

11   DOWDEN, EDWARD. "Waifs and Strays of S. T. Coleridge and
     Wordsworth." Academy, 15 (14 June), 523.
         Notes appearance of "The Birth of Love" in Wrangham's
     Poems (1795).

12   DOWDEN, EDWARD. Southey. London: Macmillan, especially
     pp. 31, 84, 136, 148-49, 157-58, 191.
         Contrasts Wordsworth's poetic temperament with Southey's.
     They shared a prophetic political spirit.

13   EDWARDS, AMELIA B. "Notes," in A Poetry-Book of Modern Poets.
     Edited by Amelia B. Edwards. London: Longmans, pp. 319-27
     (320, 322-23).
         Critical notes to the poems selected, including "'Tis
     said that some have died for love," "Ode: Intimations of
     Immortality," and "Written in March."

14   HAMILTON, WALTER. The Poets Laureate of England: Being a
     History of the Office of Poet Laureate, Biographical
     Notices of its Holders, and a Collection of the Satires,
     Epigrams, and Lampoons Directed against Them. London:
     Stock, pp. xxiv, xxvii, 243-62.

A biographical sketch. Few have or will admire Wordsworth's poetry of commonplace remarks in very blank verse.

15 [HUTTON, RICHARD HOLT?]. "How to Popularize Wordsworth."
    Spectator, 52 (12 July), 879-81.
        Wordsworth's intellectual world is more wholesome than
    Milton's. Wordsworth cannot be popular; he does not give
    readers an immediate imaginative stimulus, but gives pic-
    tures of simple beauty and passion.

16 KNIGHT, WILLIAM. "The Doctrine of Metempsychosis," "Theism--
    Desiderata in the Theistic Argument," "A Contribution
    towards a Theory of Poetry," "Wordsworth," "Nature as
    Interpreted by Wordsworth," in Studies in Philosophy and
    Literature. London: Paul, pp. 119-54 (125, 130-31,
    152-54), 155-224 (217-20), 264-82 (270, 281), 283-317,
    405-26.
        Reprinted with minor addition from 1878.B15 (125, 130-31,
    152-54). Reprinted with verbal changes from 1871.B9
    (217-20). Reprinted from 1873.B19 (270, 281). Reprinted
    from 1878.B16 and 1878.A1 (283-317). Wordsworth's reflec-
    tive interpretation of Nature as being in harmony with man
    unites "the conclusions of Science and Philosophy, of
    Poetry and Religion" (405-26).

17 LOCKER[-LAMPSON], FREDERICK. Patchwork. London: Smith,
    Elder, p. 216.
        Notes manuscript variant in "The Brothers." Wordsworth's
    second thoughts were best.

18 MARSHALL, ED. "Wordsworth's Greek Poet." Notes and Queries,
    5th ser., 12 (8 November), 376.
        Wordsworth echoes Vergil in "After-thought" ("I thought
    of Thee, my partner and my guide"). (A reply to query of
    R. F. S., "Wordsworth's Sonnet, 'After-thought,'" Notes and
    Queries, 5th ser., 12 [4 October], 269.)

19 [ROBINSON, FRANK WALLACE]. "The Private Libraries of
    Philadelphia: Ninth Paper: The Library of George W.
    Childs, Esq." Robinson's Epitome of Literature, 3
    (15 June), 91-93 (92).
        Prints Byron's manuscript parody of Peter Bell, "Epi-
    logue" ("There's something in a stupid ass"). Attributed
    when reprinted in The Private Libraries of Philadelphia:
    The Library of George W. Childs (1882).

20 STEPHEN, LESLIE. "The First Edinburgh Reviewers,"
    "Wordsworth's Ethics," in Hours in a Library. Third series.
    London: Smith, Elder, pp. 138-77 (157-61, 175), 178-229.

Reprinted from 1878.B23 (157-61, 175). Expanded from
1876.B26. The emotions Wordsworth voiced will remain,
though the system he believed in should perish (178-229).

21   SYMONDS, J.[OHN] A.[DDINGTON]. "Matthew Arnold's Selections
     from Wordsworth." Fortnightly Review, NS 26 (1 November),
     686-701 (691-701).
         Arnold's opinion notwithstanding, no moral sentiment
     can redeem Wordsworth's banal lines. His poems are at once
     sedative and stimulative. He passes too readily from poet
     to moralizer. He is the poet of man's dependence upon Na-
     ture and of the simple and permanent in social life. Re-
     printed with omissions as "Is Poetry at Bottom a Criticism
     of Life?" in 1890.B45.

22   TRUMAN, J.[OSEPH]. "Chamouni and Rydal" (poem). Macmillan's
     Magazine, 39 (April), 530-32 (531).
         Wordsworth's pure influence endures. Reprinted in
     Afterthoughts (1889).

23   WALLACE, WILLIAM. Review of Shairp's Robert Burns. Academy,
     15 (24 May), 448-49.
         Wordsworth's austerity made him incapable of sympathizing
     fully with Burns.

24   WALLACE, WILLIAM. "Burns and Wordsworth." Academy, 16
     (19 July), 52.
         A reply to 1879.B10. Wordsworth is a poet for "the
     elect."

1880 A   BOOKS - NONE

1880 B   SHORTER WRITINGS

1   ACLAND, HENRY W. Introductory Address Delivered before the
     Devonshire Association for the Advancement of Science,
     Literature, and Art. Oxford: privately printed, pp. 34-38.
         Wordsworth's thoughts in "The Solitary Reaper" and "Ode:
     Intimations of Immortality" are unlike those of the scien-
     tist.

2   ADAMS, W. H. DAVENPORT. Plain Living and High Thinking; or,
     Practical Self-Culture: Moral, Mental, and Physical.
     London: Hogg, pp. 142-46.
         A biographical sketch. Wordsworth is his own subject;
     his inquisition into nature and men is intellectual, not
     emotional.

1880

3   [ALLARDYCE, ALEXANDER]. "Beattie." Blackwood's Edinburgh
      Magazine, 128 (July), 17-36 (33-34).
         Wordsworth is indebted to Beattie in The Excursion.

4   ANON. "Milton and Wordsworth." Temple Bar, 60 (September),
      106-15.
         Though differing in style and attitude toward nature,
      Wordsworth and Milton, both sincere and egotistical, share
      a Puritan point of view. Wordsworth is at once dull and
      inspiring, prosaic and lofty.

5   ANON. "A New Edition of Wordsworth." Athenaeum, no. 2763
      (9 October), p. 465.
         Summarizes the new features in Knight's edition of Words-
      worth and reports on the first meeting of the Wordsworth
      Society.

6   ANON. "The Wordsworth Society." Spectator, 53 (16 October),
      1311-12.
         Reports on the first meeting of the Wordsworth Society,
      including remarks by Bishop Charles Wordsworth, William
      Knight, Edward Dowden, and Dr. Cradock, outlining the
      origin and purposes of the Society.

7   ANON. Note, in The Code Poetical Reader, for School and Home
      Use. London: Burns and Oates, p. 7.
         A biographical sketch.

8   ANON. "Notice," "The Life of Wordsworth," in Poems of
      Wordsworth. 2 vols. London: Kent, I:iii, v-viii.
         Wordsworth's greatness lies in a few of his shorter
      pieces (iii). A biographical sketch (v-viii).

9   ANON. "William Wordsworth, 1770-1850," in Wordsworth. London:
      Simpkin, Marshall; Leeds: Bean, and Arnold; Manchester:
      Greenwell, and Heywood; Hull: Browne [1880], pp. 1-2.
         A biographical sketch.

10 ARNOLD, MATTHEW. "Introduction," in The English Poets. . . .
      Edited by Thomas Humphry Ward. 4 vols. London:
      Macmillan, I:xvii-xlvii (xviii, xxxiii, xxxvii).
         The charm is gone in "The Prioress' Tale." Wordsworth's
      authority does not weigh much with the young generation.
      Reprinted as "The Study of Poetry" in Essays in Criticism:
      Second Series (1888).

11 BAYNE, PETER. "Studies of English Authors: Charlotte Brontë."
      Literary World (London), NS 21 (16 April), 248-50 (248-49).

Depicts Wordsworth reacting to a letter from Branwell
Brontë with "serene cynicism." Reprinted in 1881.B8.

12   BREWER, E.[BENEZER] COBHAM. The Reader's Handbook of
     Allusions, References, Plots and Stories: with two
     Appendices. London: Chatto and Windus, p. 1168.
     A brief primary bibliography. Revised in 1884.B4.

13   BROOKE, THE REV. STOPFORD. English Literature. [Second
     edition.] London: Macmillan, pp. 169–75.
        Revised from 1876.B4. When he drags in formal Christian-
     ity, Wordsworth becomes prosaic. (Second edition first
     appeared in 1879 and was reprinted in 1880 [see note in
     1896.B12, p. 2]; no copy of the 1879 edition has been lo-
     cated.) Revised in 1896.B12.

14   CAIRD, EDWARD. "Wordsworth." Fraser's Magazine, NS 21
     (February), 205–21.
        Wordsworth's poetry, dealing with the essentials of hu-
     manity, can never be popular. Wordsworth took his vocation
     seriously; his poetry is original. He encourages the mis-
     taken view that the world itself is poetic. He brought
     poetry back to nature. His later political views and poems
     are feeble. His thoughts grew out of Rousseau's. Reprinted
     in Essays on Literature and Philosophy (1892).

15   [CARR, FRANK] LAUNCELOT CROSS. "Wordsworth." New Monthly
     Magazine, [4th ser.,] 2 [April], 350–71.
        Traces the growth of his personal admiration of Words-
     worth, a poet who exalts and strengthens by revealing the
     Soul of Nature. Wordsworth's cheerful faith rests on Love.
     Attribution: British Museum catalogue.

16   CHURCH, R.[ICHARD] W.[ILLIAM]. "William Wordsworth," in The
     English Poets. . . . Edited by Thomas Humphry Ward.
     4 vols. London: Macmillan, IV:1–15.
        A biographical sketch. Wordsworth was foremost a philo-
     sophical thinker. He will never please all men; his defense
     of his own work is inadequate. His uniqueness lies in see-
     ing poetry and truth in familiar and humble things. He ob-
     serves nature as Turner does. Wordsworth always aims at
     direct, truthful expression. His strength lies in short
     passages, not long poems; his poems suffer from a lack of
     art, from too much of his own presence, and from his one-
     sided interests. Reprinted in Dante and Other Essays
     (1889).

1880

17   COLVIN, SIDNEY. "Literature and the Manual Arts."
        Fortnightly Review, NS 27 (1 April), 580-97 (582-83).
        Wordsworth quietly unlocks the heart of a matter in
        language luminous and majestic.

18   CROSS, LAUNCELOT. See 1880.B15.

19   DE VERE, AUBREY [THOMAS]. "The Genius and Passion of
        Wordsworth." Month and Catholic Review, 38 (April),
        465-89; 39 (May), 1-30.
        Wordsworth's poetry gives profound insight into human
        nature as influenced by external nature. To him the world
        was a Divine language. One cannot properly charge Words-
        worth with a lack of passion: his poems, especially The
        Excursion, "Michael," and "Resolution and Independence,"
        contain moral passion and a strong pathos (465-89, 1-30).
        In "Yew-trees" Wordsworth "leaves behind him the actual
        scene, to follow and grope after its meanings." Like Tur-
        ner, he paints the soul of natural scenes (1-30). Condensed
        and recast in 1887.B19.

20   G., W. E. "'They Are Five.'--After Wordsworth" (poem), in
        "They Are Five," and other Humorous Reminiscences in Verse.
        Edited by the Author of "The Scarecrow"; "The Lay of the
        Last Minstry"; etc. London: Bogue, pp. 7-8.
        Parody of "We Are Seven."

21   GAUSSERON, HENRI. "Wordsworth's 'Prelude.'" Notes and
        Queries, 6th ser., 1 (24 April), 343.
        Suggests Chaumont as the castle referred to by Words-
        worth in The Prelude (Book IX). (A reply to query by
        William George Black, "Wordsworth's 'Prelude,'" Notes and
        Queries, 6th ser., 1 [21 February], 155. See also J. K.,
        "Wordsworth's 'Prelude,'" Notes and Queries, 6th ser., 1
        [27 March], 260.)

22   [HASELL, ELIZABETH J.]. "A Talk about Sonnets." Blackwood's
        Edinburgh Magazine, 128 (August), 159-74 (163, 171-73).
        Analyzes "Thought of a Briton on the Subjugation of
        Switzerland," "It is a beauteous evening, calm and free,"
        and "Ejaculation."

23   HAWEIS, THE REV. H.[UGH] R.[EGINALD]. Poets in the Pulpit.
        London: Low, Marston, Searle, & Rivington, pp. 241-60.
        Wordsworth hears the voice of God in the soul of natural
        objects. Despondent at observing men in cities, he turned
        to the pure lives of children and the rural poor. He "re-
        mained to the end of his life the champion of oppressed

nationalities," though he feared a revolution at home. His
spirituality is attractive in an age of materialism.

24 HERFORD, C.[HARLES] H.[AROLD]. The Essential Characteristics
    of the Romantic and Classical Styles: with Illustrations
    from English Literature: Being the Essay which Obtained
    the Members' Prize, 1879. Cambridge: Deighton, Bell;
    London: Bell, pp. 14, 36, 49.
        On the whole Wordsworth's poems are "marked by a classic
    selectness of phrase and thought."

25 [HUTTON, RICHARD HOLT]. "Mr. Ruskin on Wordsworth."
    Spectator, 53 (7 August), 1001-1003.
        Ruskin's opinion notwithstanding, Wordsworth is not
    content with superficial natural intimations of immortality
    in "Ode: Intimations of Immortality," does probe the mys-
    tery of suffering, and does not have a vivid sense of
    beauty. Reprinted in Criticism on Contemporary Thought and
    Thinkers (1894).

26 [HUTTON, RICHARD HOLT]. "Wordsworth the Man." Spectator, 53
    (11 December), 1581-82.
        Wordsworth was a powerful figure, moody, with a passion-
    ate tenderness and the habit of musing over his own feel-
    ings. Reprinted in Criticism on Contemporary Thought and
    Thinkers (1894).

27 KNIGHT, WILLIAM. Review of Wordsworth's Poems (ed. Arnold).
    Modern Review, 1 (January), 235-38.
        Arnold's opinion notwithstanding, Wordsworth's poetic
    failures are not due to his philosophy.

28 MAIN, DAVID M. "Notes," in A Treasury of English Sonnets.
    Edited by David M. Main. Manchester: privately printed,
    pp. 235-451 (365-90).
        Full critical notes to the sonnets selected.

29 MORLEY, HENRY, ed. Shorter Works of English Prose.
    Illustrated. London, Paris, New York, and Melbourne:
    Cassell [1880], p. 378.
        Notes Wordsworth's sorrow at the death of his brother
    John.

30 MYERS, ERNEST. "Wordsworth" (poem), in The Defence of Rome
    And other Poems. London: Macmillan, pp. 58-60.
        Wordsworth leads one to nature, where "thy still soul in
    free exulting awe / Shall feel the majesty of duteous law."

1880

31   NICHOL, JOHN. Byron. London: Macmillan, especially
          pp. 82-84, 203-204, 211, 214, 216.
              Records Byron's relations with Wordsworth. Wordsworth
          submitted himself to a self-imposed literary law and to es-
          tablished institutions. His influence is limited because
          he "had no feverish blood."

32   NOBLE, JAMES ASHCROFT. "The Sonnet in England." Contemporary
          Review, 38 (September), 446-71 (passim).
              In "It is a beauteous evening, calm and free" Wordsworth
          creates a unity out of two moods. By virtue of his strong
          humanity, he makes us feel with him. His "effects are all
          explicable and calculable." In his sonnets his style is
          its finest. Reprinted in The Sonnet in England (1893).

33   OWEN, F.[RANCES] M.[ARY]. John Keats: A Study. London:
          Paul, pp. 25-29, 34, 172-73.
              A comparison of their poems on Greek subjects shows that,
          as opposed to Keats, Wordsworth meant to be a teacher; yet
          they both strove to reconcile the spirit's discordant ele-
          ments into harmony.

34   PATER, WALTER H. "Samuel Taylor Coleridge," in The English
          Poets. . . . Edited by Thomas Humphry Ward. 4 vols.
          London: Macmillan, IV:102-14 (103-109).
              Wordsworth was "the chief 'developing' circumstance" of
          Coleridge's poetic life. Recast as "Coleridge" in 1889.B49.

35   PETERSON, PETER. Notes, in The Golden Treasury of the Best
          Songs and Lyrical Poems in the English Language. Edited by
          Francis Turner Palgrave and Peter Peterson. Book fourth.
          Bombay: privately printed, passim.
              Critical notes to the poems selected.

36   POLLOCK, FREDERICK. Spinoza: His Life and Philosophy.
          London: Paul, pp. 400-403.
              Spinoza's thought, transmitted by Coleridge, may have
          fostered the impulse of artistic nature-worship in Words-
          worth.

37   RUSKIN, JOHN. "Fiction--Fair and Foul." Nineteenth Century,
          8 (August), 195-206 (204-206); (September), 394-410
          (394-97, 399-400, 406-407); (November), 748-60 (748-49,
          755, 760).
              "Wordsworth is simply a Westmoreland peasant," lacking
          humor, with a sense of natural beauty and a pretty turn for
          medicinal reflections: "A measured mind, and calm; inno-
          cent, unrepentant; helpful to sinless creatures" (204-206).

He is no more pious than Byron, and not so true (394–97, 399–400, 406–407). Though a poet of homely virtues, he often wrote verses neither musical nor profound (for example, in "Scene in Venice") (748–49, 755, 760). Reprinted in On the Old Road (1885).

38   RUSKIN, JOHN. Elements of English Prosody for Use in St. George's Schools: Explanatory of the Various Terms Used in "Rock Honeycomb." Orpington: Allen, p. 58.
      In The Excursion, a "sententious epic," the characters' speech is arranged to make it memorable.

39   SHAIRP, J.[OHN] C.[AMPBELL]. "Poetry versus Agnosticism." Princeton Review, 56th Year (March), 286–302 (292–93, 298–300).
      Wordsworth in The Excursion describes scenes by the feeling they awaken. Mill delighted in Wordsworth's imaginative emotions yet rejected the spiritual beliefs upon which they depend. Revised as "The Spiritual Side of Poetry" in 1881.B30.

40   SHAIRP, J.[OHN] C.[AMPBELL]. "Poetic Style with Special Reference to Modern English Poetry." Princeton Review, 56th Year (September), 207–30 (210, 214–22, 226–28).
      Wordsworth's critical theories enhanced his poetry. Wordsworth does have a style—direct, plain, and severe. Reprinted with verbal changes in 1881.B30.

41   [WIFFEN, MARY ISALINE]. "The Life of Jeremiah Holmes Wiffen," in The Brothers Wiffen: Memoirs and Miscellanies. Edited by Samuel Rowles Pattison. London: Hodder and Stoughton, pp. 1–76 (33–41).
      Recounts visit of J. H. and B. B. Wiffen to Rydal Mount in 1819: Wordsworth's conversation about Campbell, Crabbe, his own poetry, and Ossian; Wordsworth in appearance and conversation has nothing of the puerile simplicity of his early writings.

1881 A BOOKS

1   BEDFORD, EDWIN JACKSON. Genealogical Memoranda relating to the Family of Wordsworth, with an Elaborate Pedigree. London: privately printed, 27 pp.
     Traces Wordsworth's genealogy.

2   MYERS, F.[REDERIC] W.[ILLIAM] H.[ENRY]. Wordsworth. London: Macmillan, 190 pp.
     A full biographical study.

1881

*3   NELSON, JAMES HENRY. William Wordsworth: A short study of
         his Life and Work: To which are Added Remarks upon the
         System of Theology as Expressed in his Writings.
         Manchester: privately printed, 32 pp.
             Not located. Cited in Thomas J. Wise, A Bibliography of
         the Writings in Prose and Verse of William Wordsworth
         (London: privately printed, 1916), p. 246.

4   SHORTHOUSE, J.[OSEPH] H.[ENRY]. On the Platonism of
         Wordsworth: A Paper Read to the Wordsworth Society,
         July 19th, 1881. Birmingham: Cornish [c. 1881], 17 pp.
             Wordsworth is a safe guide, a poet of man. Notes simi-
         larities between the thoughts of Plato and Wordsworth, es-
         pecially in "Tintern Abbey" and The Excursion.

5   SYMINGTON, ANDREW JAMES. William Wordsworth: A Biographical
         Sketch, with Selections from his Writings in Poetry and
         Prose. 2 vols. London, Glasgow, Edinburgh, and Dublin:
         Blackie, 268 pp., 266 pp.
             A full biographical and critical study, designed to
         illustrate Wordsworth as an elevating teacher, with sound,
         progressive social principles.

1881 B   SHORTER WRITINGS

1   ANON. Review of Myers's Wordsworth. Literary World (London),
         NS 23 (7 January), 2-4.
             Wordsworth represents the Transcendental in the literary
         and social revolution of his time.

2   ANON. "Literary Gossip." Athenaeum, no. 2804 (23 July),
         pp. 114-15 (115).
             Reports on the annual meeting of the Wordsworth Society.

3   ANON. "Biographical Notes," in Poetry for the Young: A
         Graduated Collection in Four Parts. London: Griffith and
         Farran; New York: Dutton, pp. 631-38 (638).
             Wordsworth owes his fame to his shorter pieces; he has
         exercised a transforming influence on modern thought.

4   ANON. "Wordsworth, William," in The Globe Encyclopaedia of
         Universal Information. Edited by John M. Ross. 6 vols.
         Edinburgh: Jack, VI:553-54.
             A biographical and bibliographical sketch. Wordsworth
         turned in disgust from his own age to the sanctities of
         Nature; he is indebted to no other poet.

282

5   ARNOLD, MATTHEW. "Byron." Macmillan's Magazine, 43 (March),
     367-77.
          Wordsworth gains by having his poetry presented in a
     volume of selections. His work is often pompous and pon-
     derous. His poetry, because of its sense of joy, is su-
     perior to Leopardi's and Byron's. Slightly expanded in
     1881.B6.

6   ARNOLD, MATTHEW. "Preface," in Poetry of Byron. London:
     Macmillan, pp. vii-xxxi.
          Slightly expanded from 1881.B5. Byron's poetry will al-
     ways find more readers than Wordsworth's. Reprinted in
     Essays in Criticism: Second Series (1888).

7   AUSTIN, ALFRED. "Old and New Canons of Poetical Criticism:
     I." Contemporary Review, 40 (December), 884-98 (889, 892).
          The orthodox assume Wordsworth is right in The Excursion
     because he led a blameless life and meant well. Wordsworth
     does not rank above Shelley.

8   BAYNE, PETER. "Essay on Poetry," "Charlotte Brontë and Her
     Sisters," in Two Great Englishwomen: Mrs. Browning &
     Charlotte Brontë; with an Essay on Poetry, illustrated from
     Wordsworth, Burns, and Byron. London: Clarke,
     pp. ix-lxxviii, 155-340 (172-73).
          As Wordsworth's poems illustrate, poetry is an imitation,
     not, as Arnold argues, a criticism of life. Arnold also
     errs in claiming for Wordsworth the power of displaying and
     making us share in simple joy; his poems are depressing.
     He lacks the imaginative power to rise above mere facts,
     especially in "Ellen Irwin." He gives commonplace reflec-
     tions on commonplace subjects. His poems contrast with
     Burns's and Byron's (ix-lxxviii). Reprinted from 1880.B11
     (172-73).

9   BELL, CHARLES D. "Wordsworth." Churchman, 3 (March), 417-30.
          Wordsworth has never been and is not popular, even with
     the young. He is a Christian but not a theological poet.
     Expanded in 1895.B10.

10   BOOTH, JAMES. Note, in Poetical Reader. . . .   Edited by
     James Booth. London: Longmans, p. 170.
          A biographical sketch.

11   CARLYLE, THOMAS. Reminiscences. Edited by James Anthony
     Froude. 2 vols. London: Longmans, II:330-41.
          Records he did not much reverence the work of Wordsworth,
     a man of strong, meditative character and "a fine limpid

style," yet "a rather dull, hard-tempered, unproductive" man. Records Wordsworth's conversation: his deprecation of other poets, his recollections of the French Revolution, his opinion of Wilberforce; records Wordsworth's behavior when visiting London.

12 COCHRANE, ROBERT. "Biographical Notices," in The Treasury of English Literature. . . . Illustrated. Edinburgh: Nimmo, pp. 539-72 (572).
    A biographical sketch.

13 COLVIN, SIDNEY. Landor. London: Macmillan, passim.
    Records Wordsworth's praise of Landor and Landor's mixed appreciation of Wordsworth. Landor was incapable of Wordsworth's "parochial rusticity" and narrow social judgments.

14 DOUGLAS, MRS. STAIR. The Life and Selections from the Correspondence of William Whewell, D.D. . . . London: Paul, pp. 28-34, 66-67, 75-77, 94, 96, 159, 267, 273.
    Includes letters in which Whewell relates his initial repulsion by Wordsworth's poems, his visits with Wordsworth in the 1820's to 1840's (and his being puzzled that a man of Wordsworth's good sense could write poems about such odd heroes), and his dislike of Wordsworth's sonnets. Includes his verse tribute to Wordsworth's recalling poetry from erring ways, "To Dora Wordsworth."

15 DOWDEN, EDWARD, ed. The Correspondence of Robert Southey with Caroline Bowles: to which are Added: Correspondence with Shelley, and Southey's Dreams. Dublin: Hodges, Figgis; London: Longmans, especially pp. 124-25, 164, 225, 231-32, 288-90, 348.
    Includes letters in which Caroline Bowles expresses her admiration of Wordsworth's poetry, and letters in which Southey records Wordsworth's mixed response to the Howitts, his trouble with his eyes, and his disgust with a letter from Branwell Brontë.

16 FLETCHER, JOSEPH S. "The Birthplace of Wordsworth." Academy, 19 (18 June), 456; 20 (19 November), 386.
    Questions whether Wordsworth was really born at Cockermouth (456). Though born at Cockermouth, he was not born in the "Wordsworth house" (386).

17 GILES, THE REV. DR. [JOHN ALLEN]. "Introduction," in Poetic Treasures: or, Passages from the Poets. Edited by the Rev. Dr. Giles. London: Ward, Lock [1881], pp. xxvii-li (xlix).
    Wordsworth is the poet of his own mind, of sentiment.

Writings about William Wordsworth, 1793 - 1899

18 [HASELL, ELIZABETH J.]. "A Talk about Odes." Blackwood's
    Edinburgh Magazine, 129 (June), 783-802 (795-96).
        In contrast with Shelley's, Wordsworth's odes, especially
    "Ode: Intimations of Immortality," elevate as well as
    please.

19 HENDERSON, FRANK, ed. Sketches Literary and Theological:
    Being Selections from an Unpublished MS. of the late Rev.
    George Gilfillan[,] Dundee. Edinburgh: Douglas,
    especially pp. 2, 5-6, 31, 164, 168, 186.
        Includes Gilfillan's remarks that Wordsworth is a great
    poet even though he wrote but small pieces, that he read
    his poems with "pealing power," that he fails as a story-
    teller but excels in probing Nature, and that he does not
    borrow from other writers.

20 [HENLEY, WILLIAM ERNEST]. Review of Poetry of Byron
    (ed. Arnold). Athenaeum, no. 2800 (25 June), pp. 839-40.
        Contrasts Byron's and Wordsworth's life and work. Re-
    printed in Views and Reviews (1890).

21 HODGSON, SHADWORTH H. "The Supernatural in English Poetry:
    Shakespeare; Milton; Wordsworth; Tennyson," in Outcast
    Essays and Verse Translations. London: Longmans,
    pp. 99-180 (149-57, 179).
        Wordsworth argued from experience to prove the existence
    of God.

22 MASSON, DAVID. De Quincey. London: Macmillan, pp. 28,
    37-38, 42-55, 67, 91-92, 182.
        Recounts Wordsworth's intercourse with and influence
    upon De Quincey.

23 MILNER, GEORGE. "The Literature and Scenery of the English
    Lake District," in Papers of the Manchester Literary Club.
    Volume VII. Manchester and London: Heywood, pp. 243-63.
        Wordsworth describes the Lakes truly both in his poems
    and A Guide through the District of the Lakes; he is es-
    pecially alert to, and was influenced by, the sound of
    water.

24 MORLEY, HENRY. Of English Literature in the Reign of Victoria:
    With a Glance at the Past. Leipzig: Tauchnitz, pp. 97,
    104, 108-12, 116, 121-36, 139, 144, 164-65.
        A biographical sketch.

25 MORLEY, HENRY. Sketches of Longer Works in English Verse and
    Prose. Illustrated. London, Paris, and Melbourne:
    Cassell [1881], pp. 372-79.

1881

> Wordsworth in The Excursion reveals his pure ideal of an
> elevated humanity.

26 MORTIMER, JOHN. "Concerning One of Wordsworth's Sonnets," in
    Papers of the Manchester Literary Club. Volume VII.
    Manchester: Heywood, pp. 85-96.
    Wordsworth, as opposed to Keats, ties nature with moral-
    ity. In "Composed upon Westminster Bridge" he confesses
    the failure of his faith.

27 RAWNSLEY, HARDWICKE D. "Wordsworth's Seat, Rydal" (poem), "On
    Seeing a Telegraph Wire and Pillar-Post Below Wordsworth's
    House" (poem), "A Tree Planted by William Wordsworth at
    Wray Castle" (poem), "Wordsworth's Tomb" (poem), Note, in
    Sonnets at the English Lakes. London: Longmans, pp. 9,
    35, 51, 62, 75.
    Wordsworth's poems give the "knowledge of peace that
    human goodness brings" (9). Wordsworth wrought into concord
    "The poet's passion and the postman's lot" (35), gave a
    lasting glory to the rocks of Wray Castle (51), and sang
    "'of Humble Themes and Noble Thought'" (62). Suggests
    Crinkle Crags as the scene in "Composed upon an Evening of
    Extraordinary Splendour and Beauty" (75).

28 SHAIRP, J.[OHN] C.[AMPBELL]. "The Prophetic Power of Poetry."
    Fraser's Magazine, NS 23 (January), 53-66 (60-65).
    Wordsworth revealed the freshness of nature. Though he
    is not optimistic in poems dealing with human life, he
    never loses himself entirely in suffering. Revised as
    "The Poet as a Revealer" in 1881.B30.

29 SHAIRP, J.[OHN] C.[AMPBELL]. "English Poetry in the Eighteenth
    Century." Princeton Review, 57th Year (July), 30-50 (35,
    42-43, 45-46, 48).
    Wordsworth was indebted to Pope, though he did not know
    it. He criticizes Gray too harshly.

30 SHAIRP, JOHN CAMPBELL. "The Province of Poetry," "The
    Spiritual Side of Poetry," "The Poet as a Revealer,"
    "Poetic Style in Modern English Poetry," "The Three
    Yarrows," "The White Doe of Rylstone," in Aspects of Poetry:
    Being Lectures delivered at Oxford. Oxford: Clarendon
    Press, pp. 1-36 (8, 12, 24-28), 66-93 (75-77, 79, 87-89),
    94-121 (108-19), 122-58 (passim), 316-44, 345-76.
    Reprinted from 1878.B21 (8, 12, 24-28). Revised from
    1880.B39 (75-77, 79, 87-89). Revised from 1881.B28. Words-
    worth's "plain and severe imagination wanted nimbleness and
    versatility" (108-19). Reprinted with verbal changes from

1880.B40 (122-58). Reprinted from 1873.B30 (316-44). Revised with omissions from 1874.B41 (345-76).

31   SHAPCOTT, REUBEN. See 1881.B35.

32   TAYLOR, HENRY. "Carlyle's 'Reminiscences.'" Nineteenth
     Century, 9 (June), 1009-25 (1010-12).
          Carlyle's picture of Wordsworth's conversation is based
     on partial knowledge. Though helpless in the little trans-
     actions of life, Wordsworth "keeps tumbling out" the highest
     thoughts in conversation.

33   TURNER, HAWES [and FRANCIS STORR]. "Notes," in Selections
     from the Poetical Works of William Wordsworth. A new
     edition. Edited by Hawes Turner. London: Rivingtons
     [1881], pp. 37-84.
          Critical notes, revised from 1874.B47. Attribution:
     Preface to volume.

34   WADDINGTON, SAMUEL. "The Sonnet: Its History and Composition,"
     in English Sonnets by Living Writers. Edited by Samuel
     Waddington. London: Bell, pp. 181-211.
          Wordsworth's sonnets, the best in English, combine
     strength and simplicity, truth and earnestness, majestic
     thought and diction.

35   [WHITE, WILLIAM HALE] REUBEN SHAPCOTT, ed. The Autobiography
     of Mark Rutherford, Dissenting Minister. Edited by his
     Friend. London: Trübner, pp. 23-24.
          Records the effect of reading Lyrical Ballads. Words-
     worth substituted a living God of the hills for the old God
     of the Church.

36   Z., X. Y. "De Omnibus Rebus." Carlisle Patriot, 65
     (2 December), pp. 4-5 (4).
          A reply to 1881.B16. Includes letter from William Words-
     worth (son of the poet) confirming Wordsworth's birthplace
     at Cockermouth.

1882 A   BOOKS - NONE

1882 B   SHORTER WRITINGS

1   ANON. "Literary Gossip." Athenaeum, no. 2845 (6 May),
     pp. 571-73 (571).
          Reports on the annual meeting of the Wordsworth Society.

WRITINGS ABOUT WILLIAM WORDSWORTH, 1793 - 1899

1882

2   ANON. "News of the Week." Spectator, 55 (6 May), 581-83
    (583).
      Reports on meeting of the Wordsworth Society, including
    John Duke Coleridge's recollections of Bishop Thirlwall's
    admiration of Wordsworth.

3   ANON. Review of Oliphant's The Literary History of England in
    the End of the Eighteenth and Beginning of the Nineteenth
    Century. Athenaeum, no. 2848 (27 May), pp. 659-60.
      Wordsworth was too close to the poetic revolution to
    assess it accurately in the Preface to Lyrical Ballads. He
    only at moments escaped from "eighteenth century didactics"
    to the romantic temper.

4   ANON. Review of The Poetical Works of William Wordsworth
    (ed. Knight, Volumes I-II). Modern Review, 3 (October),
    861-65.
      Wordsworth's textual revisions are usually improvements.

5   ANON. "A French Critic on Wordsworth." Saturday Review, 54
    (28 October), 565-66.
      Wordsworthians try to "palm off" Wordsworth's "desperate
    platitudes" as his "noblest title to praise." His greatness
    lies in his power to make men better and happier.

6   ANON. "Biographical Appendix," in The Poetical Reader.
    Part I. London, Edinburgh, and New York: Nelson, pp. 47-48
    (48).
      A biographical sketch.

7   ANON. Note, in The Poetical Reader. Part III. London,
    Edinburgh, and New York: Nelson, p. 26.
      Commends the true picture of the Scottish peasantry
    Wordsworth gives in The Excursion (Book I).

8   ARNOLD, THOMAS. Note, in English Poetry and Prose. Edited by
    Thomas Arnold. London: Longman, p. 370.
      "The Solitary Reaper" appeals "to every organ of sense
    and perception."

9   AUSTIN, ALFRED. "Old and New Canons of Poetical Criticism:
    II." Contemporary Review, 41 (January), 124-41 (125-33,
    137-38, 140).
      Wordsworth's verse rises to poetry only when the literal
    is spiritually transfigured. Wordsworth does not deal
    enough with life. "It was not till the critics of life dis-
    covered how orthodox were [Wordsworth's] views, that they
    discovered how exquisite was his Poetry."

1882

10   [AUSTIN, ALFRED]. Review of Poems of Wordsworth (ed. Arnold),
     Poetry of Byron (ed. Arnold) and Scherer's Wordsworth et
     La Poésie Moderne de l'Angleterre. Quarterly Review, 154
     (July), 53-82.
          To do Wordsworth justice, an editor must suppress three-
     fourths of his poems, from which the essence of poetry is
     absent. Wordsworth writes nothing about the clash of human
     passions. In "Ode: Intimations of Immortality" he de-
     scribes his own, not universal, experience. Arnold's
     opinion not withstanding, Wordsworth has not written an
     "ampler body of powerful work." Wordsworth errs in taking
     the function of poetry to be to talk about things.

11   BUCKLAND, ANNA. The Story of English Literature. London,
     Paris, and New York: Cassell, Petter, Galpin, pp. 476,
     480-505.
          A biographical sketch. Wordsworth's simple stories
     (e.g., in "We Are Seven") illustrate great truths. In The
     Excursion Wordsworth shared Milton's vision of an ideal
     state.

12   CAINE, T.[HOMAS] HALL. "Notes," in Sonnets of Three Centuries:
     A Selection including Many Examples hitherto Unpublished.
     Edited by T. Hall Caine. London: Stock, pp. 269-320
     (284-88).
          Critical notes to the sonnets selected, including "Com-
     posed upon Westminster Bridge" and "It is a beauteous
     evening, calm and free." Wordsworth receives his poetic
     impulses from the external world, not from within. His
     sonnets have from the first been universally approved.

13   CAINE, T.[HOMAS] HALL. Recollections of Dante Gabriel
     Rossetti. London: Stock, pp. 135, 147-51, 240-41, 246.
          D. G. Rossetti's objection to "proseman's diction" lay
     at the heart of his criticism of Wordsworth. He "'grudge[d]
     Wordsworth every vote he gets,'" thought Wordsworth "was too
     much the High Priest of Nature to be her lover," did not
     recognize Wordsworth's greatness in "The Affliction of
     Margaret ----" or "Ode to Duty" (praised by Theodore Watts
     [-Dunton]), and thought his sonnets should be judiciously
     selected.

14   CARR, MARY. "Thomas Wilkinson." Friends' Quarterly Examiner,
     16 (April), 181-205 (186, 198, 201-205); (July), 328-54
     (333, 336, 338).
          Relates biographical incidents involving Wordsworth. In-
     cludes letters in which Wilkinson in 1799 describes Words-
     worth as rejecting preferment and choosing a sober life

1882

among the Lakes; in 1807 recounts incident of Wordsworth and
Scott at an inn at Patterdale; and in 1802 relates that
Dorothy Wordsworth wrote Wordsworth's love letters for him.
Gives background to "To the Spade of a Friend" (186, 198,
201-205). Includes references by Wilkinson in letters to
meetings with Wordsworth (333, 336, 338).

15 COTTERILL, H.[ENRY] B.[ERNARD]. An Introduction to the Study
    of Poetry. London: Kegan Paul, Trench, especially
    pp. 208-41.
        A biographical sketch. Wordsworth has recreated the
    common world around us. He is original in adopting lowly
    subjects and natural language. He uses minute description
    to convey feeling.

16 DOWDEN, EDWARD. Review of The Poetical Works of William
    Wordsworth (ed. Knight, Volumes I-II). Academy, 22
    (12 August), 111-12.
        Points out errors in Knight's dating and printing of
    poems.

17 DOWDEN, EDWARD. "Wordsworth's 'Selections from Chaucer
    Modernised.'" Transactions of The Wordsworth Society,
    no. 3 [c. 1882], pp. 47-55.
        Wordsworth's modernization of Chaucer is frank and
    faithful, though not without failings.

18 [FITZGERALD, EDWARD]. "Introduction," in Readings in Crabbe:
    "Tales of the Hall." London: Quaritch, pp. iii-xiv (xii,
    xiv).
        Notes Wordsworth's honest compliment to Crabbe.

19 FLETCHER, JOSEPH S. "The Birthplace of Wordsworth." Academy,
    21 (7 January), 11.
        A reply to 1881.B36. See 1881.B16.

20 FROUDE, JAMES ANTHONY. Thomas Carlyle: A History of the
    First Forty Years of His Life 1795-1835. 2 vols. London:
    Longmans, II:338-39.
        Records Carlyle's report that Wordsworth was character-
    ized by others in 1833 as "full of English prejudices,"
    gossip, and, rarely, wisdom.

21 GOSTWICK, JOSEPH. German Culture and Christianity: Their
    Controversy in the Time 1770-1880. London: Norgate;
    Edinburgh: Williams & Norgate, pp. 136-37, 155, 196, 251,
    380, 402-403.

1882

Notes similarity between the religious faith of Wordsworth, Jacobi, and Kant. Wordsworth shows his wide sympathies in Postscript (1835). His poems are rarely directly
Christian. His speculative philosophy, echoing Coleridge
and Schelling, did not disturb his religious belief.

22 GRAVES, ROBERT PERCEVAL. Life of Sir William Rowan Hamilton. . . . 3 vols. Dublin: Hodges, Figgis; London:
Longmans, I:passim.
Records Hamilton's visits and correspondence with Wordsworth. Includes Eliza Mary Hamilton's memoir of Wordsworth's
visit to Ireland in 1829: Wordsworth's "rusticity and constraint" and "indescribable superiority" in manner, his defense of himself from a charge of lacking respect for
science. For Volume II, see 1885.B24; for Volume III, see
1889.B33.

23 [HAMLEY, EDWARD BRUCE]. "False Coin in Poetry." Blackwood's
Edinburgh Magazine, 131 (June), 727-40 (728-33, 736).
Wordsworth writes poorly when he abandons the theme of
the influence of nature on man. Closely analyzes "Composed
upon Westminster Bridge," "Laodamia," "Anecdote for Fathers,"
and "Ruth." Reprinted in Shakespeare's Funeral (1889).

24 HELPS, EDMUND ARTHUR. "Notes," in Poetry for Children.
Edited by Edmund Arthur Helps. Second book. London:
Bell, pp. 191-206 (204).
Suggests a line in "The Oak and the Broom" refers to a
passage in the Sermon on the Mount.

25 HOSKYNS-ABRAHALL, JOHN. "A Greek Epitaph and Wordsworth's
'Lucy Gray.'" Academy, 21 (25 March), 214.
Notes similarity between an epitaph and "Lucy Gray."

26 HUTCHINSON, THE REV. THOMAS. "On the Structure of the Sonnets
of Wordsworth." Transactions of The Wordsworth Society,
no. 2 [1882], pp. 27-31.
Though he took Milton as his model, Wordsworth did not
always follow Milton's order of rhymes.

27 [HUTTON, RICHARD HOLT]. "The Wordsworth Society's
Publications." Spectator, 55 (18 February), 238-39.
A reply to 1881.A4. Wordsworth did not intend to teach
Platonism but faith in God. (See rebuttal by J. Henry
Shorthouse, "'The Platonism of Wordsworth,'" Spectator, 55
[25 February], 263.)

1882

28 [HUTTON, RICHARD HOLT]. "The Weak Side of Wordsworth."
    Spectator, 55 (27 May), 687-88.
        A reply to 1882.B46. In "Anecdote for Fathers" Words-
    worth extracts too much out of a trifle. Though affectedly
    simple, "The Idiot Boy" shows Wordsworth's grasp of basic
    passions. Wordsworth's weakness lay in his difficulty in
    recognizing when he had failed to fuse language with
    passion.

29 HUTTON, RICHARD HOLT. "Wordsworth's Two Styles." Modern
    Review, 3 (July), 525-38.
        In his rhymed verse Wordsworth has two styles, that of
    fresh energy of his youth and that of stately feeling of
    his age. Both achieve an effect of "limpid coolness."

30 [HUTTON, RICHARD HOLT]. "The Critical Edition of Wordsworth."
    Spectator, 55 (2 September), 1141-42.
        Wordsworth usually wisely revised his poems, though not
    Peter Bell.

31 I., C. M. "Scott and Wordsworth." Notes and Queries,
    6th ser., 6 (9 September), 204-205.
        Notes parallel between Scott and "Memory."

32 INGLEBY, C.[LEMENT] M.[ANSFIELD]. "An Estimate of Wordsworth."
    Hibernia, 1 (September), 129-31.
        Many of Wordsworth's subjects (e.g., in "Goody Blake and
    Harry Gill") are unfit for poetry. Splendid single lines
    illumine otherwise bad poems; prosaic and puerile passages
    mar otherwise good ones.

33 IRELAND, ALEXANDER. "Recollections of George Dawson and His
    Lectures in Manchester in 1846-7." Manchester Quarterly, 1
    (April), 181-204 (202-204).
        Recounts visit to Wordsworth in 1846: Wordsworth's con-
    versation on his library, his neighbors, and the death of
    B. R. Haydon.

34 KEMBLE, FRANCES ANNE. Records of Later Life. 3 vols. London:
    Bentley, I:108.
        Records her recollections of Wordsworth's conversing with
    Rogers and his fondness for his own poems.

35 KINDON, JOSEPH. "Wordsworth's Weakness." Spectator, 55
    (3 June), 722.
        A reply to 1882.B28. Wordsworth's elevated thought and
    lonely spirit cause his lapses into prose.

36 KNIGHT, WILLIAM. "Constitution of the Wordsworth Society,"
"Bibliography of the Poems of Wordsworth," "Minute of
Meeting at Grasmere, 20th July 1881." Transactions of The
Wordsworth Society, no. 1 [1882], pp. 4, 5-15, 15-16.
Gives purposes of the society (4), primary bibliography
to 1850 (expanded in 1882.B40) (5-15), and list of papers
read (15-16).

37 [KNIGHT, WILLIAM]. "The Wordsworth Society." Transactions of
The Wordsworth Society, no. 2 [1882], pp. 19-22.
Describes Dorothy Wordsworth's journals, and papers read;
includes John Duke Coleridge's recollections of Bishop
Thirlwall's admiration of Wordsworth.

38 KNIGHT, WILLIAM. "On the Portraits of Wordsworth."
Transactions of The Wordsworth Society, no. 3 [c. 1882],
pp. 56-76.
Describes portraits of Wordsworth. Revised in 1882.B39.

39 KNIGHT, WILLIAM. "Portraits of Wordsworth." Transactions of
The Wordsworth Society, no. 4 [c. 1882], pp. 79-91.
Supplements 1882.B38 and prints five portraits. Expanded
in 1889.B38.

40 KNIGHT, WILLIAM. "Preface," "Chronological Order of the
Poems," "Note," in The Poetical Works of William Wordsworth.
Edited by William Knight. 8 vols. Edinburgh: Paterson,
I:ix-1, 1i-lxxxiii, [315-16].
Discusses editing Wordsworth's poems, including their
chronological arrangement and the printing of textual revisions; includes a primary bibliography, expanded from
1882.B36 (ix-1). Lists poems in order of composition
(1i-lxxxiii); announces discovery of the publication of
"Sonnet, on Seeing Miss Helen Maria Williams Weep at a Tale
of Distress" ([315-16]). Includes textual, critical, and
biographical notes to the poems throughout the eight
volumes (1882-86), including extracts from Dorothy Wordsworth's letters and journals and Mary Wordsworth's letters.
For Volume III, see 1883.B25; for Volume VI, see 1884.B16.

41 L'ESTRANGE, THE REV. A. G., ed. The Friendships of Mary
Russell Mitford: as Recorded in Letters from Her Literary
Correspondents. 2 vols. London: Hurst and Blackett,
II:110, 137, 176, 184.
Includes letters in which Ruskin remarks that Wordsworth
does not understand the mountains of Switzerland, Digby
Starkey notes that Wordsworth failed to sympathize with his
portrayal of Judas, and Mitford notes Wordsworth's worship
of his own poetry and of "mere rank and riches in others."

1882

42 Mac DONALD, GEORGE. Orts. London: Sampson Low, Marston,
    Searle, & Rivington, pp. 245-63.
        Wordsworth's "inner life was full of conflict, discovery,
    and progress." He expressed a Christian pantheism. He
    found amusement, joy, lessons, and a higher teaching in na-
    ture. He adhered to his poetic theory to the last.

43 [MAITLAND, BROWNLOW]. Review of Natural Religion. Quarterly
    Review, 154 (October), 425-47 (441-42).
        Wordsworth does not attest to an atheistical natural
    religion.

44 [MALLOCK, WILLIAM HURRELL]. Review of Ecce Homo and Natural
    Religion. Edinburgh Review, 156 (October), 508-51 (528-29,
    541-43).
        Wordsworth's life and views were not the result of
    natural religion. Reprinted in Atheism and the Value of
    Life (1884).

45 MATHESON, A. "Sonnets after Coppée: To William Wordsworth"
    (poem). Journal of Education (London), NS 4 (1 April),
    126.
        Salutes Wordsworth's calm greatness, his faith in his
    own powers.

46 OLIPHANT, MRS. [MARGARET]. The Literary History of England
    in the End of the Eighteenth and Beginning of the Nineteenth
    Century. 3 vols. London: Macmillan, especially I:7, 78,
    240-42, 260-95, 305-32, 341, 343-44, 350-51; II:111-16;
    III:59-60, 67, 82-84, 128-29.
        Recast and expanded from 1871.B12-B14; 1872.B22-B23;
    and 1873.B27. Wordsworth and Pope are dissimilar in every
    point. In contrast with Cowper, Wordsworth wilfully de-
    scends to use mean language. There is little affinity be-
    tween Wordsworth, Coleridge, and Southey. A biographical
    sketch and discussion of Lyrical Ballads, "The Idiot Boy,"
    Peter Bell, the Lucy poems, the Preface to Lyrical Ballads,
    The Excursion, and The Prelude. "Ode: Intimations of Im-
    mortality" is masterful; Wordsworth's classical poems and
    sonnets are overrated. Compares Wordsworth, and discusses
    his relations, with other nineteenth-century writers, es-
    pecially Coleridge, Southey, Scott, Byron, and Shelley.

47 OWEN, MRS. [FRANCES MARY]. "Notes": "On the Seeming
    Triviality of Some of Wordsworth's Subjects," "On
    Wordsworth's View of Death." Transactions of The
    Wordsworth Society, no. 2 [1882], pp. 32-44.

294

1882

Wordsworth's vision of common humanity justifies his choice of subjects. Wordsworth views death calmly. Reprinted in 1887.B39.

48   PRICE, BONAMY. "On the Ode of Immortality." Transactions of The Wordsworth Society, no. 2 [1882], pp. 25-26.
         Gives Wordsworth's explanation, in conversation, of the "fallings from us, vanishings" in "Ode: Intimations of Immortality."

49   PYM, HORACE N., ed. Memories of Old Friends: Being Extracts from the Journals and Letters of Caroline Fox of Penjerrick, Cornwall From 1835 to 1871. London: Smith, Elder, especially pp. 18-20, 66, 131, 138, 156-63, 182, 193-98, 258, 264.
         Includes C. Fox's record of Hartley Coleridge's admiration of Wordsworth's "mixing himself up with everything that he mentions," though admitting Wordsworth is an unpleasant travelling companion and unpopular neighbor; of discussing that Wordsworth inserts emotion into reflection; of William Ball's account of Wordsworth's conversation about his own poetry; of Lady Holland's depreciation of Wordsworth and John Sterling's attributing Wordsworth's obscurity to his attempt to reconcile philosophical insight with received opinions; of Carlyle's opinion of Wordsworth's limitations; of Wordsworth's withholding The Prelude to preserve the copyright; of Anna Braithwaite's report that Wordsworth at the end of his life desired to become "poor in spirit"; and of her meetings with Wordsworth: Wordsworth's appreciation of the beauty of the city, his opinion of Hartley and S. T. Coleridge and Shelley, his speaking of the necessity of Faith, his trust that the "money-getting spirit" ruling England is exhausting itself, his insistence that a sound philosophy contain both Plato and Aristotle, and his opinions on railroads, health, German literature, and France.

50   PYM, HORACE N., ed. "Appendix," in Memories of Old Friends: Being Extracts from the Journals and Letters of Caroline Fox of Penjerrick, Cornwall From 1835 to 1871. Second edition: To Which Are Added Fourteen Original Letters from J. S. Mill Never Before Published. 2 vols. London: Smith, Elder, II:311-42 (322, 324).
         Adds to 1882.B49 letters in which Mill interprets "Tintern Abbey" and notes that Wordsworth has kept alive the tradition of contemplation in a hostile age.

1882

51   RAWNSLEY, THE REV. H.[ARDWICKE] D.[RUMMOND]. "Memorandum: in
     reference to the Memorial Stone at Grisedale Tarn."
     Transactions of The Wordsworth Society, no. 2 [1882],
     pp. 23-24.
          Describes memorial to mark Wordsworth's parting from his
     brother John.

52   ROBINSON, PHIL. "The Poets' Birds." Gentleman's Magazine,
     252 (January), 40-48 (41-42); (February), 171-88 (173,
     187); (March), 322-41 (323-24, 328, 331, 336-39); (April),
     487-92 (489).
          Notes Wordsworth's use of birds in his poems. Reprinted
     in 1883.B50.

53   ROBINSON, PHIL. "The Birds of Poetry." Gentleman's Magazine,
     253 (September), 316-35 (321, 328).
          Notes Wordsworth's use of birds in his poems. Reprinted
     in 1883.B50.

54   ROBINSON, PHIL. "Birds of Beauty and of Song." Gentleman's
     Magazine, 253 (November), 591-617 (592-93, 596, 606).
          Notes Wordsworth's use of birds in his poems. Reprinted
     in 1883.B50.

55   SCOTT, WILLIAM BELL. "Wordsworth" (poem), in A Poet's Harvest
     Home. London: Stock, p. 123.
          Wordsworth has made his life earth's hymn of praise.

56   [SEELEY, JOHN ROBERT]. Natural Religion. By the Author of
     "Ecce Homo." London: Macmillan, pp. 79, 84, 99-109.
          Recast from 1875.B17.

57   SHAIRP, J.[OHN] C.[AMPBELL]. "Aesthetic Poetry: Dante
     Gabriel Rossetti." Contemporary Review, 42 (July), 17-32
     (21, 29).
          "The modern beauty-worshippers" consider Wordsworth "a
     tiresome proser." His sonnets are transparently clear
     compared to Rossetti's.

58   [SHELLEY, LADY JANE, ed.]. Shelley and Mary. 4 vols.
     [London:] privately printed [1882], I:188; II:295;
     III:497, 779; IV:972.
          Adds, to previously published Shelley correspondence,
     letters in which Charles Clairmont envies Wordsworth's
     life, in which Peacock attacks Wordsworth's participation
     in the election of 1818, and in which Mary Shelley notes
     (in 1823?) that Wordsworth was in town, "publishing, and
     looking old."

59   SWINBURNE, ALGERNON CHARLES. "After Looking into Carlyle's
     Reminiscences: (1)" (poem), in Sonnets of Three Centuries:
     A Selection including Many Examples hitherto Unpublished.
     Edited by T. Hall Caine. London: Stock, p. 208.
     Wordsworth's "clear spirit . . . hung / Between the
     mountains hallowed by his love / And the sky stainless as
     his soul above." (The lines are identified as referring
     to Wordsworth by Thomas James Wise, A Bibliography of the
     Writings in Prose and Verse of Algernon Charles Swinburne
     [London: Heinemann; New York: Wells, 1927], p. 185.) Re-
     printed in Tristram of Lyonesse and Other Poems (1882).

60   WEDMORE, FREDERICK. "My Rare Book." Gentleman's Magazine,
     252 (May), 531-39.
     Describes the origins and his copy of Lyrical Ballads
     (1798).

1883 A   BOOKS - NONE

1883 B   SHORTER WRITINGS

1   ANON. Review of The Poetical Works of William Wordsworth
     (ed. Knight, Volume III). Modern Review, 4 (July), 640-42.
     Most of Wordsworth's textual revisions are improvements.

2   ANON. "In Wordsworth's Country: Some extracts from the diary
     of Miss Nellie Paton." Yorkshire Illustrated Monthly, 1
     (December), 32-40.
     Records interview with an old man who knew Wordsworth:
     he "used to go about with his hands behind him, looking at
     the flowers and listening to the birds singing." Records
     Henry Leigh's interpretation of lines in Peter Bell.

3   ANON. "List of Letters by Wordsworth in the South Kensington
     Museum." Transactions of The Wordsworth Society, no. 5
     [1883], pp. 127-32.
     Includes letters to J. Cottle and A. Dyce.

4   ANON. "Introduction," in The Brothers, and Other Poems
     Founded on the Affections. . . .   London and Glasgow:
     Collins [1883], pp. 3-5.
     A biographical sketch.

5   ANON. "Wordsworth, William," in Cassell's Concise Cyclopaedia.
     Edited by William Heaton. Illustrated. London, Paris, and
     New York: Cassell, p. 1333.
     A biographical sketch.

1883

6   ARCHER-HIND, R.[ICHARD] D.[ACRE]. Note, in The Phaedo of
     Plato. Edited by R. D. Archer-Hind. London: Macmillan,
     p. 85.
          Notes difference between Plato's thought and Wordsworth's
     in "Ode: Intimations of Immortality."

7   ARNOLD, MATTHEW. "Address to the Wordsworth Society: May 2nd,
     1883." Macmillan's Magazine, 48 (June), 154-55.
          Wordsworth preached and practiced a monastic discipline;
     his spiritual passion exceeds Milton's. He has something
     to say.

8   AUSTIN, ALFRED. "On the Relation of Literature to Politics."
     National Review, 2 (September), 81-95 (83-84, 88-89).
          Wordsworth would have been a more admirable poet had he
     mingled more fully with his fellow men.

9   BATES, WILLIAM, ed. The Maclise Portrait-Gallery of
     "Illustrious Literary Characters" with Memoirs Biographical,
     Critical, Bibliographical & Anecdotal Illustrative of the
     Literature of the Former Half of the Present Century.
     Illustrated. London: Chatto and Windus, pp. 138-43.
          Revised and expanded from 1873.B6. Blake anticipated
     Wordsworth's new school of poetry. The site of Wordsworth's
     grave is in a state of decay.

10   [BOYLE,] THE VERY REV. [G. D.,] THE DEAN OF SALISBURY. "A
     Few Words on Wordsworth's Position as an Ethical Teacher."
     Transactions of The Wordsworth Society, no. 5 [1883],
     pp. 37-42.
          Wordsworth's value is as an ethical teacher.

11   BROOKE, STOPFORD. "On Wordsworth's Guide to the Lakes."
     Transactions of The Wordsworth Society, no. 5 [1883],
     pp. 23-35.
          In A Guide through the District of the Lakes Wordsworth
     sees nature differently from Gray. Though accurate in de-
     scribing, Wordsworth also brings in his belief that the
     universe is alive.

12   BROWNING, ROBERT. "A Letter of Leigh Hunt's." Athenaeum,
     no. 2906 (7 July), pp. 15-18 (16).
          Prints letter in which Hunt in 1857 confesses not to
     have read The Prelude, calls Wordsworth "barren and
     prosaic."

13   BUCHANAN, ROBERT [WILLIAMS]. "Prose and Verse: A Stray
     Note," in A Poet's Sketch-Book: Selections from the Prose

Writings of Robert Buchanan. London: Chatto and Windus,
pp. 165-79 (175-78).
  Though theoretically correct in the Preface to Lyrical
Ballads, Wordsworth habitually used rhythmic speech for non-
rhythmic moods. The Excursion suffers from an unnatural
form: it should have been written as a poem in prose.

14   CAINE, T.[HOMAS] HALL. Cobwebs of Criticism: A Review of the
     First Reviewers of the "Lake," "Satanic," and "Cockney"
     Schools. London: Stock, pp. 3-29, 32-35, 86, 92-93,
     261-62.
        Wordsworth was consistently maligned in early reviews;
     he ignored the criticism and eventually triumphed. Southey
     and Wordsworth, but not Byron, belong to the same poetic
     school. Wordsworth's "mind never went to work on its own
     vision."

15   [CARR, FRANK] LAUNCELOT CROSS. Hesperides. London: Trübner,
     passim.
        Remarks Wordsworth's dedicating himself to poetry,
     and parallels between Wordsworth and Alfieri, Goethe,
     Rousseau, Schiller, and Swedenborg. Wordsworth embodies
     pure and devout imagination; his verse, including The Ex-
     cursion and "Ode: Intimations of Immortality," elevates
     and soothes. The Prelude is daring in concept. The ex-
     ample of his harmonious life has been influential. He is
     passionate in his communion with nature. "He despises the
     worldling." He "sees in Nature a representation of the
     human mind."

16   COLERIDGE, SARA. "Letter from Mrs. H. N. (Sara) Coleridge to
     Mr. Henry Reed." Transactions of The Wordsworth Society,
     no. 5 [1883], pp. 111-20.
        Records her friendship with Wordsworth. Wordsworth's
     later poems, including "The Triad," are inferior. Includes
     letter from A. de Vere defending Wordsworth's later poetry.

17   COTTERILL, H.[ENRY] B.[ERNARD]. "Wordsworth," in Ueber
     Wordsworth und Walt Whitman: Zwei Vorträge gehalten vor
     dem Literarischen Verein zu Dresden. Von H. B. Cotterill
     und T. W. Rolleston. Dresden: Tittmann, pp. 5-37.
        A biographical sketch and introduction to Wordsworth's
     poetic theories. His poems produce a tranquillity of soul.
     (In German.)

18   CROSS, LAUNCELOT. See 1883.B15.

1883

19   DENNIS, JOHN. <u>Heroes of Literature: English Poets: A Book</u>
     <u>for Young Readers</u>. London and Brighton: Society for
     Promoting Christian Knowledge; New York: Young, pp. 170-71,
     278-99.
          In criticizing Dryden, Wordsworth took too narrow a view
     of poetry. A biographical sketch. Wordsworth's poems are
     demanding, happy, truthful. His use of common language mars
     "She was a Phantom of delight." He teaches best when he
     teaches indirectly. His poetry contrasts with Burns's, ex-
     cels Blake's. He writes memorable single lines; he did his
     best work between 1799 and 1809. Includes bibliographic
     note.

20   DE VERE, AUBREY [THOMAS]. "Remarks on the Personal Character
     of Wordsworth's Poetry." <u>Transactions of The Wordsworth</u>
     <u>Society</u>, no. 5 [1883], pp. 11-21.
          Wordsworth united mental faculties in contemplating na-
     ture and man spiritually; hence his classification of his
     poems is arbitrary. Reprinted with minor additions in
     <u>Essays Chiefly Literary & Ethical</u> (1889).

21   DOWDEN, EDWARD. Review of <u>The Poetical Works of William</u>
     <u>Wordsworth</u> (ed. Knight, Volume III). <u>Academy</u>, 24
     (14 July), 20.
          Discusses dating of "To the Cuckoo" ("O blithe New-
     comer! I have heard") and Wordsworth's use of the word
     "machine" in "She was a Phantom of delight."

22   EMERSON, RALPH WALDO. "Letter from Ralph Waldo Emerson to
     Professor Henry Reed, Philadelphia." <u>Transactions of The</u>
     <u>Wordsworth Society</u>, no. 5 [1883], p. 124.
          Wordsworth did not succumb to those around him.

23   F. "The Scene of 'Lucy Gray.'" <u>Notes and Queries</u>, 6th ser.,
     7 (12 May), 365-66.
          Suggests location of the setting of "Lucy Gray."

24   FARRAR, F.[REDERIC] W.[ILLIAM]. "Preface," in <u>With the Poets:</u>
     <u>A Selection of English Poetry</u>. Edited by F. W. Ferrar.
     London: Suttaby, pp. v-xxvii (vi-vii, xxv-xxvii).
          Praises Wordsworth, in contrast to Byron, as a moral
     teacher.

25   FLETCHER, J. S. "An Introductory Memoir," in <u>Selections from</u>
     <u>Wordsworth</u>. Edited by J. S. Fletcher. London and Paisley:
     Gardner, pp. 13-37.
          A biographical sketch. Wordsworth was not a good judge
     of the quality of his own work. After reading his poems,

especially amidst the scenery in which they were written,
one feels "that life, after all, is well worth living."

26   FLINT, THE REV. ROBERT.   "Norman Macleod," in Scottish Divines
     1505-1872. . . .   Edinburgh: Macniven and Wallace,
     pp. 425-60 (433-34).
          Notes Macleod's early appreciation of and debt to
     Wordsworth.

27   FORMAN, HARRY BUXTON, ed.   The Poetical Works and Other
     Writings of John Keats. . . .   4 vols.   London: Reeves &
     Turner, I:82, 132, 334; II:129, 305; III:95-96, 101, 163;
     IV:74.
          Notes parallels between Keats's poems and "The world is
     too much with us; late and soon" and "Thoughts Suggested
     the Day Following, on the Banks of Nith, near the Poet's
     Residence."   Prints "The Gadfly" ("All gentle folks who owe
     a grudge"), mocking Wordsworth.   Adds, to previously pub-
     lished Keats correspondence, letter in which Keats praises
     The Excursion and letter in which Charles Brown transcribes
     Keats's "On Oxford" ("The Gothic looks solemn"), burlesquing
     Wordsworth.

28   GILCHRIST, MRS. [ANNE].   Mary Lamb.   London: Allen,
     especially pp. 41-48.
          Records the Lambs's intercourse with the Wordsworths,
     noting parallels in Wordsworth's and Lamb's relations with
     their sisters.

29   HALL, S.[AMUEL] C.[ARTER].   Retrospect of a Long Life: From
     1815 to 1883.   2 vols.   London: Bentley, II:36-42.
          A recasting of 1866.B7.   Recalls Wordsworth's objecting
     to Scott's misquoting "Yarrow Unvisited."   Wordsworth was,
     above all, a good man.

30   HAVERFIELD, F.   "George Herbert and Wordsworth."   Notes and
     Queries, 6th ser., 8 (15 September), 206.
          Wordsworth was indebted to Herbert in "Ode: Intimations
     of Immortality."

31   HUTCHINSON, THE REV. THOMAS.   "Local Note on Hart Leap Well."
     Transactions of The Wordsworth Society, no. 5 [1883],
     p. 126.
          Describes visit to the scene of "Hart-leap Well."

32   [HUTTON, RICHARD HOLT].   "Professor Knight's Wordsworth:
     Volume III."   Spectator, 56 (12 May), 614-15.

When one understands the background to "To the Spade of a Friend" and "Louisa," one can understand Wordsworth's blindness to the faults in the poems.

33 KNIGHT, WILLIAM. "The Wordsworth Society." Athenaeum, no. 2900 (26 May), p. 668.
A defense of the Wordsworth Society.

34 [KNIGHT, WILLIAM]. "Report of Meeting Held on May 2, 1883." Transactions of The Wordsworth Society, no. 5 [1883], pp. 3-9.
Minutes of the meeting.

35 KNIGHT, WILLIAM. "Note III.--The Hawkshead Beck," "Note VII.-- 'The meeting-point of two highways,'" "Note VIII.-- Coleridge's Lines to Wordsworth on Hearing 'The Prelude' Recited at Coleorton in 1806," in The Poetical Works of William Wordsworth. Edited by William Knight. 8 vols. Edinburgh: Paterson, III:410-13, 416-20, 420-24.
Includes H. D. Rawnsley's accounts of Wordsworth at Hawkshead (410-13, 416-20). Prints Coleridge's early drafts of "To William Wordsworth" (see 1817.B6) and "Dejection: an Ode" (addressed to Wordsworth) (see 1817.B6 and 1895.B13) (420-24). For Volume I, see 1882.B40; for Volume VI, see 1884.B16.

36 LAMB, CHARLES. "Extract from an Unpublished (and Undated) Letter of Charles Lamb to Miss Wordsworth." Transactions of The Wordsworth Society, no. 5 [1883], p. 123.
Praises The River Duddon.

37 [LE BRETON, ANNA LETITIA]. Memories of Seventy Years. By One of a Literary Family. Edited by Mrs Herbert Martin. London: Griffith & Farran; New York: Dutton, pp. 53-54, 78.
Recollects seeing Wordsworth at a party in Hampstead.

38 M., T. C. "Wordsworth as a Teacher." Progress, 1 (January), 46-51.
Wordsworth's didactic purpose is too conscious. His philosophy is based on the false beliefs that joy in nature is strongest in childhood and that emanations proceed from natural objects. Wordsworth viewed only the lovely aspects of nature.

39 MALLESON, THE REV. F.[REDERICK] A.[MADEUS]. "Wordsworth and the Duddon: A Holiday Study." Good Words, 24:573-81.
Traces Wordsworth's path in The River Duddon. Expanded in 1890.B33.

40 NICOLL, HENRY J. Landmarks of English Literature. London:
    Hogg, pp. 295–302.
        A biographical sketch. Wordsworth thought highly of
    himself; his poems are unequal. To him, nature was not
    dead.

41 [NORTON, CHARLES ELIOT, ed.]. Correspondence of Thomas
    Carlyle and Ralph Waldo Emerson 1834–1872. 2 vols. Boston:
    Osgood, I:71–72, 199; II:160–61.
        Includes letters in which Carlyle records his impression
    of Wordsworth as "a natural man," though he talks plati-
    tudes, and in which Emerson records meeting Wordsworth in
    1848. Expanded in 1886.B38.

42 POOLE, W.[ILLIAM] F.[REDERICK]. "Bibliography of Review and
    Magazine Articles in Criticism of Wordsworth." Transactions
    of The Wordsworth Society, no. 5 [1883], pp. 93–100.
        A bibliography of English and American articles.

43 RAWNSLEY, H.[ARDWICKE] D.[RUMMOND]. "The Proposed Permanent
    Lake District Defence Society." Transactions of The
    Wordsworth Society, no. 5 [1883], pp. 43–58.
        Notes Wordsworth's spirit behind efforts to save the
    Lake District from unwanted change.

44 RIX, HERBERT. "Notes on the Localities of the Duddon Sonnets."
    Transactions of The Wordsworth Society, no. 5 [1883],
    pp. 59–78.
        Topographical notes to The River Duddon. Revised in
    1884.B16.

45 ROBERTSON, J. "Preface," in Winnowings from Wordsworth.
    Edited by J. Robertson. Edinburgh: Nimmo, pp. vii–xxvii.
        Only a very few of Wordsworth's poems—fewer than Arnold
    selected—are stylistically faultless. Wordsworth's lapses
    stem from his solitary life. In the Preface to Lyrical
    Ballads Wordsworth erred in arguing, not for common sub-
    jects, but for commonplace language. If one tries to de-
    fend him as a teacher, one finds his teaching questionable.
    Yet, in the midst of dull poems he writes memorable lines.

46 ROBINSON, PHIL. "Asses and Apes." Belgravia, 51 (July),
    99–113 (99–101, 103, 105).
        Notes Wordsworth's use of the ass in his poems. Re-
    printed in 1885.B38.

47 ROBINSON, PHIL. "The Heptarchy of the Cats." Belgravia, 51
    (August), 219–31 (226–27).

Notes Wordsworth's use of the leopard and panther in his poems. Reprinted in 1885.B38.

48 ROBINSON, PHIL. "Some Poets' Dogs." Belgravia, 51 (October), 494-512 (507, 509).
Notes Wordsworth's use of dogs in his poems. Reprinted in 1885.B38.

49 ROBINSON, PHIL. "The King of Beasts: (A Sketch from our Poets)." Gentleman's Magazine, 255 (October), 359-76 (364-66).
Notes Wordsworth's use of the lion in his poems. Reprinted in 1885.B38.

50 ROBINSON, PHIL. The Poets' Birds. London: Chatto and Windus, passim.
Recast and reprinted from 1882.B52-B54. Notes Wordsworth's use of birds in his poems.

51 RUSKIN, JOHN. The Art of England: Lectures Given in Oxford. . . : Lecture VI: The Hill-side. Orpington: Allen, pp. 223, 233-35.
Mountains were the first motive of inspiration in Wordsworth. His description of clouds in The Excursion (Book II) is feeble though sincere.

52 RUSKIN, JOHN. Fors Clavigera: Letters to the Workmen and Labourers of Great Britain: Letter the 92nd. (Eighth of New Series): November, 1883: Ashestiel. Orpington: Allen, p. 203.
In "Ode: Intimations of Immortality" Wordsworth associates heaven with infancy only.

53 RUSKIN, JOHN. Fors Clavigera: Letters to the Workmen and Labourers of Great Britain: Letter the 93rd. (Ninth of New Series.): Christmas, 1883: Invocation. Orpington: Allen, p. 226.
Reports on a working girl who quotes Wordsworth.

54 RUSKIN, JOHN. Modern Painters: Vol. II: "Of Ideas of Beauty," and "Of the Imaginative Faculty." Revised. 2 vols. Orpington: Allen, I:97 (Section II, Chapter i, Paragraph 2).
Expanded from 1846.B13. Wordsworth is without appeal "as to the impressions of natural things on the human mind; but by no means as to the logical conclusions to be surely drawn from them."

55   [SKELTON, JOHN]. "A Little Chat about Mrs Oliphant."
     Blackwood's Edinburgh Magazine, 133 (January), 73-91
     (84-85, 89, 91).
        Wordsworth's simple style is a symptom of the change in
     poetry to a romantic and revolutionary spirit. Notes J.
     Wilson's early advocacy of Wordsworth. Young men today no
     longer follow Wordsworth.

56   SPEED, JNO. GILMER, ed. The Letters of John Keats. New York:
     Dodd, Mead, p. 3.
        Adds to previously published Keats correspondence letter
     in which Keats records dining with Wordsworth in London.

57   WHATELY, EDWARD. "Personal Recollections of the Lake Poets."
     Churchman, 8 (September), 436-49.
        Wordsworth contrasts with Southey in appearance and mode
     of living. His poems produce "a feeling of uneasiness"
     because he never plunges directly into his subject. Hartley
     Coleridge both praised and satirized Wordsworth.

58   WHITTIER, J.[OHN] C. [i.e., GREENLEAF]. "Wordsworth: Written
     on a blank leaf of his Memoirs" (poem). Transactions of
     The Wordsworth Society, no. 5 [1883], p. 125.
        Wordsworth led a life "calm and good," sang "Of Nature's
     simple joys!"

59   YARNALL, F. C. "Letter from F. C. Yarnall, on Wordsworth's
     Influence in America." Transactions of The Wordsworth
     Society, no. 5 [1883], pp. 79-92.
        A discussion of American editions and secondary studies
     of Wordsworth.

1884 A   BOOKS - NONE

1884 B   SHORTER WRITINGS

1   ANON. Review of The Poetical Works of William Wordsworth
     (ed. Knight, Volume IV). Modern Review, 5 (January),
     194-95.
        Despite Wordsworth's revisions, many prosaic lines re-
     main in The White Doe of Rylstone.

2   ANON. "Wordsworth in Germany," in Papers of the Manchester
     Literary Club. Volume X. Manchester: Heywood, pp. 432-33.
        Reports on a paper by Dr. Adolph Samelson on German
     translations of Wordsworth's poems.

1884

3   ARNOLD, MATTHEW. "Emerson." Macmillan's Magazine, 50 (May),
    1-13 (5, 11-13).
        Wordsworth's later revisions were generally not improve-
    ments. His and Emerson's work is important because they
    knew the value of hope. Reprinted in Discourses in America
    (1885).

4   BREWER, THE REV. E.[BENEZER] COBHAM. Authors and their Works
    with Dates: Being the three Appendices to "The Reader's
    Handbook." London: Chatto and Windus, p. 1357.
        A brief bibliography, revised from 1880.B12.

5   BRIGHT, HENRY A. "Unpublished Letters from Samuel Taylor
    Coleridge to the Rev. John Prior Estlin," in Miscellanies
    of the Philobiblon Society. Volume XV. London:
    privately printed [1884], pp. 6, 32-33, 39, 42.
        Includes letters in which Coleridge notes his admiration
    of Wordsworth's intellectual powers, Wordsworth's love of
    Christianity, and Wordsworth's praise of Osorio.

6   BROOKSBANK, B. "Poetic Emotion and Affinities." National
    Review, 3 (June), 528-39 (535, 537-39).
        Wordsworth experienced an intense affinity with nature;
    some poetic emotion was closed to him.

7   COURTHOPE, WILLIAM JOHN. "The Liberal Movement in English
    Literature: III.--Wordsworth's Theory of Poetry."
    National Review, 4 (December), 512-27 (515-27).
        The revolution in English literature began with Lyrical
    Ballads (1798). Wordsworth's real innovation lay in pre-
    senting unusual associations; yet the poems fail just in
    proportion as Wordsworth intrudes his personality upon the
    reader. He erred in thinking the mind can make any subject
    poetical. Though incessantly introspective, he extended
    men's social ideas. Revised in 1885.B19.

8   [DE VERE, AUBREY THOMAS]. "The Wisdom and Truth of Wordsworth's
    Poetry." Catholic World, 38 (March), 738-54; 39 (April),
    49-58; (May), 201-16; (June), 335-55.
        Wordsworth wrote philosophic rather than didactic poems
    characterized by wisdom and truth. He champions man's
    spiritual over his animal nature (e.g., in "Ode to Duty,"
    "Character of the Happy Warrior," "Resolution and Inde-
    pendence," "Laodamia"). He loved liberty from first to
    last, as shown in his sonnets and "Dion" (738-54). His
    poetry flies from the vulgar world to bask in the presence
    of the beauty of creation. He presents a mature wisdom,
    based on a knowledge of suffering (49-58). He observes

nature imaginatively, seeing what others fail to notice.
He returns by memory to idealize scenes. He blends inner
and outer worlds, intellect and emotion (201-16). In "Ver-
nal Ode," "On the Power of Sound," "Ode: Intimations of
Immortality" and The Excursion he discusses the origin of
things in Orphic strains. "The plainness of Wordsworth's
style results from the greatness of his thoughts" (335-55).
Condensed with verbal changes in 1887.B19.

9 FROUDE, JAMES ANTHONY. Thomas Carlyle: A History of His Life
in London 1834-1881. 2 vols. London: Longmans, I:31-32,
45.
    Includes Carlyle's record of meeting Wordsworth in 1835:
Wordsworth's speech is sincere but prolix, his handshake
feckless. "He has fallen into the garrulity of age," is
"a genuine but a small diluted man."

10 GARROD, HERBERT B. "To Wordsworth" (poem). Spectator, 57
(2 February), 155.
    Wordsworth "trod the mystic ways / That lead through
common things to Nature's shrine."

11 [GATHORNE-HARDY, GATHORNE, EARL OF] CRANBROOK. "Christopher
North." National Review, 3 (April), 151-60.
    Records Wordsworth's remarks criticizing Carlyle's
writing and praising Tennyson's artistry and Byron's letters. Gives J. Wilson's recollections of Wordsworth's dig-
nified tone in reciting poems, of reading The Prelude, and
of Wordsworth's quarrel with Coleridge.

12 HOFFMANN, FREDERICK A. Poetry: its Origin, Nature, and
History. . . . London: Thurgate, pp. 11-12, 359-75, 378,
389, 877.
    Wordsworth's works unite all the faculties of mind; they
are characterized by earnestness. Wordsworth loves the
universe as a symbol of God; he sees past common forms to
beauty. His works compare and contrast with Coleridge's.
A biographical sketch.

*13 KERR, R. N. Our English Laureates and the Birds. Dundee:
Leng, pp. 29-51.
    Not located. Listed in 1896.B36, VIII:359.

14 [KIPLING, RUDYARD]. "Jane Smith" (poem), in Echoes. By Two
Writers. Lahore: The "Civil and Military Gazette" Press
[1884], pp. 30-31.
    A burlesque.

1884

15   [KNIGHT, WILLIAM]. "Report of the Fifth Annual Meeting,
       May 10, 1884," "Letters from Wordsworth to John Kenyon,"
       "On the Yew-trees of Borrowdale." Transactions of The
       Wordsworth Society, no. 6 [c. 1884], pp. 7-70, 71-116,
       149-55.
         Describes Wordsworth manuscripts recently collected.
       Includes addresses: 1) by J. R. Lowell. Wordsworth did
       not swerve from, but rather redefined, his early faith in
       freedom. He has been too often studied as a philosopher
       rather than as a poet. He found nature more interesting
       than man, has no dramatic power, and is parochial in sub-
       ject. His poems console and purify. 2) by Roden Noel,
       "On the Poetic Interpretation of Nature, with examples
       taken Chiefly from Wordsworth." Wordsworth values neither
       nature nor man alone; he observes landscape closely. Re-
       printed with omissions in 1886.B36. 3) by W. A. Heard on
       "Wordsworth's Treatment of Sound." Wordsworth was sensi-
       tive to sounds, retained memories of them, and used them
       imaginatively. 4) by the Rev. Alfred Ainger on "Wordsworth
       and Charles Lamb." Discusses Lamb's review of The Excur-
       sion. 5) by the Dean of Salisbury [the Rev. G. D. Boyle].
       As the poet of common life, Wordsworth will someday be the
       poet of the many as well as of the few (7-70). Includes
       textual notes by Frederick L. Hutchins to Wordsworth's let-
       ters to John Kenyon (71-116). Gives H. D. Rawnsley's ac-
       count of the destruction of the trees celebrated in "Yew-
       trees" (149-55).

16   KNIGHT, WILLIAM. "Laodamia," "Dion," Notes, "Note H," in The
       Poetical Works of William Wordsworth. Edited by William
       Knight. 8 vols. Edinburgh: Paterson, VI:1-13 (9-13),
       14-23 (20-23), 305-48 (passim), 374-79.
         Includes W. A. Heard's notes to "Laodamia" (9-13) and
       "Dion" (20-23), Herbert Rix's notes on The River Duddon
       (revised from 1883.B44; expanded in 1891.B39) (305-48), and
       H. D. Rawnsley's topographical notes to The River Duddon
       (374-79). For Volume I, see 1882.B40; for Volume III, see
       1883.B25.

17   MAURICE, [JOHN] FREDERICK, ed. The Life of Frederick Denison
       Maurice: Chiefly Told in His Own Letters. Edited by his
       Son. Illustrated. 2 vols. London: Macmillan, I:65, 176,
       199, 317; II:59.
         Records J. F. D. Maurice's admiration for Wordsworth and
       his reporting of Wordsworth's qualified praise of Shelley's
       "To a Skylark" and of Chatterton. The Prelude is the dying
       utterance of the preceding half century.

18 MORTIMER, JOHN. "The Story of the White Doe of Rylstone."
    Manchester Quarterly, 3 (July), 283-99.
        Wordsworth exercised "the poet's licence in dealing with
    his materials" when writing The White Doe of Rylstone. It
    is not clear how the doe helped Emily look towards God.

19 NICHOLSON, ALBERT. "The Literature of the English Lake
    District." Manchester Quarterly, 3 (October), 330-39
    (334-36, 339).
        Notes Wordsworth's attack on whitewash and larches in A
    Guide through the District of the Lakes. Wordsworth's poems
    are "addressed to the cultured few."

20 NOBLE, J. ASHCROFT. "Pens and Pencils: Wordsworth and Sir
    George Beaumont." Magazine of Art (London), 7:206-208.
        Traces Wordsworth's relations with Sir George Beaumont.

21 PALGRAVE, FRANCIS TURNER. "Notes," in The Golden Treasury of
    the Best Songs and Lyrical Poems in the English Language.
    Edited by Francis Turner Palgrave. London: Macmillan,
    pp. 319-36 (335).
        Expanded from 1861.B14. Commends "Ode: Intimations of
    Immortality."

22 [PAYN, JAMES]. "Some Literary Recollections." Cornhill
    Magazine, NS 2 (January), 33-41 (36-37); (February), 148-59
    (149).
        Records H. Martineau's reverence for Wordsworth (36-37),
    and her report of Wordsworth only once experiencing the
    sense of smell (149). Reprinted in Some Literary Recollec-
    tions (1884).

23 RAWNSLEY, THE REV. H.[ARDWICKE] D.[RUMMOND]. "Reminiscences
    of Wordsworth among the Peasantry of Westmoreland."
    Transactions of The Wordsworth Society, no. 6 [c. 1884],
    pp. 157-94.
        Wordsworth kept apart from the poor of Westmorland. Re-
    cords the recollections of Wordsworth by former servants and
    townspeople: Wordsworth's composing outdoors, his appear-
    ance, his unsociable and plain habits, the unpopularity of
    his poems, and his relations with Hartley Coleridge.

24 RIX, HERBERT. "A Stroll up the Brathay." Good Words,
    25:392-98 (395-96, 398).
        Wordsworth allowed himself license in his descriptions
    in The Excursion. Reports a tourist's ignorance of Words-
    worth.

1884

25 SHAIRP, J.[OHN] C.[AMPBELL]. "Henry Vaughan, Silurist."
   North American Review, 138 (February), 120-37 (121, 132-36).
      Compares Vaughan's "The Retreat" and "Ode: Intimations
   of Immortality." Reprinted in 1887.B48.

26 SHAIRP, J.[OHN] C.[AMPBELL]. "Friendship in English Poetry."
   North American Review, 139 (December), 580-98 (588-93).
      "Extempore Effusion upon the Death of James Hogg" is
   worthy of Wordsworth's earliest inspiration. Wordsworth
   and Scott respected each other.

27 SHAIRP, PRINCIPAL [JOHN CAMPBELL]. "Wordsworth and 'Natural
   Religion.'" Good Words, 25:307-13.
      A response to 1882.B56. Wordsworth was not satisfied by
   nature alone. To him, God speaks through nature. Later in
   life he was more conscious of Christian truths.

28 SKIPSEY, JOSEPH. "Prefatory Notice," in The Poems of Samuel
   Taylor Coleridge. Edited by Joseph Skipsey. London and
   Newcastle-on-Tyne: Scott, pp. 9-31 (16-21).
      Wordsworth did not understand Coleridge's genius. Their
   account of their reasons for writing Lyrical Ballads (1798)
   is suspect.

29 STANSFIELD, ABRAHAM. "Rambles in the West Riding (With a
   Glance at the Flora): II.--In the Track of the 'White
   Doe.'" Manchester Quarterly, 3 (April), 155-72 (163-67).
      Describes the setting of The White Doe of Rylstone, a
   "most ethereal, subtile" poem.

30 SWINBURNE, ALGERNON CHARLES. "Wordsworth and Byron."
   Nineteenth Century, 15 (April), 583-609 (583-87, 591-93,
   605-607); (May), 764-90.
      A response to Arnold's criticisms of Wordsworth, Byron,
   and Shelley. Wordsworth was not overwhelmed by Milton's
   influence (583-87, 591-93, 605-607). "Devotion to Wordsworth . . . infatuate[s] the judicial sense . . . of his
   disciples," including Henry Taylor. Wordsworth's genius
   lay in "meditation and sympathy, not action and passion."
   The Borderers is eccentric in motive and morality. Wordsworth "was wrong in thinking himself a poet because he was
   a teacher, whereas in fact he was a teacher because he was
   a poet." "The Solitary Reaper" contains lines of perfect
   beauty that none of Wordsworth's theories can explain. He
   never ceased to be a republican. As a poet of suffering
   he is unequalled, though the story of Margaret in The Excursion and "The Thorn" fail, and his other work is unequal. He is "sublime by the very force of his tenderness."

"He was the heroic poet of his age." His best poems possess "seeming spontaneity" (764-90). Reprinted in Miscellanies (1886).

31 TRAILL, H.[ENRY] D. Coleridge. London: Macmillan, especially pp. 14-15, 25, 42-54, 64-68, 105, 156-57.
    Discusses Wordsworth's life and work as it touches Coleridge's. Coleridge took more from Wordsworth than he gave. Wordsworth's "primary function is to interpret nature to man."

32 WADDINGTON, SAMUEL. Review of The Sonnets of William Wordsworth. Academy, 25 (16 February), 108.
    Though usually staid, Wordsworth's muse could at times be sportive, as in "The Same Subject" ("Not so that Pair whose youthful spirits dance").

33 WATSON, R. SPENCE. "Wordsworth's Relations to Science." Macmillan's Magazine, 50 (July), 202-209.
    Though in The Excursion he frequently condemns science, Wordsworth objects only to those who see with their eyes rather than their minds. In Kendal and Windermere Railway he argues calmly, sensibly.

34 WATSON, WILLIAM. "Byron and Wordsworth" (poem), in Epigrams of Art, Life, and Nature. Liverpool: Walmsley, no. lvi.
    Wordsworth's song was "An earthborn coolness colour'd with the sky."

35 WATTS, ALARIC ALFRED. Alaric Watts: A Narrative of His Life. By His Son. 2 vols. London: Bentley, I:185-86, 235-42, 247, 252, 261-62, 270-71; II:286-87, 330.
    Records Wordsworth's befriending of M. J. Jewsbury, Watts's efforts to find Wordsworth a publisher, Mrs. Watts's recollections of Wordsworth's admiration for Burns and for his own poems and his criticism of "Christabel," and Wordsworth's contributions to the annuals. Wordsworth's political conservatism "did not proceed from want of liberality, but from apprehension of change." Wordsworth fled Paris when warned that his life was in danger.

1885 A BOOKS - NONE

1885 B SHORTER WRITINGS

1 ANDREWS, WILLIAM. "Talks about Authors and Books." Wakefield Free Press, no. 1470 (25 April), p. 8; no. 1471 (2 May), p. 5.

1885

Includes J. R. Tutin's cataloguing of Wordsworth's poems about Yorkshire.

2   ANON. "The Ballad of the 'Bus" (poem). <u>Punch</u>, 88 (18 April), 190.
      Parody of "We Are Seven."

3   ANON. "Windermere As It Was and Is." <u>Literary World</u> (London), NS 32 (28 August), 206-207 (206).
      Recounts story of J. Wilson playing a prank on Wordsworth. Reprinted from the <u>Times</u> of 22 August 1885.

4   ANON. "Wordsworth's Influence in Scotland." <u>Spectator</u>, 58 (3 October), 1292-93.
      Wordsworth is "the high priest of pure Nature-worship." "The first love" of Wordsworth is "an intoxication of the soul." Wordsworth's influence is felt more in morals than in poetry; his creed and Scotch Calvinism have much in common.

5   ANON. "They Are Seven: (A Warble After Wordsworth)" (poem). <u>Fun</u>, NS 42 (2 December), 243.
      Parody of "We Are Seven."

6   ANON. "We Are Seven" (poem). <u>Judge: A Weekly Journal for the Nation</u>, 1 (5 December), 140.
      Parody of "We Are Seven."

7   ANON. "Ralph Rattat: A Wordworthian Warble" (poem). <u>Funny Folks</u>, 11 (Christmas Supplement), 427.
      A burlesque.

8   ANON. "The Reverie of a Poor Squeezed 'Un" (poem). <u>Punch</u>, 89 (26 December), 302.
      Parody of "The Reverie of Poor Susan."

9   ANON. <u>Archbishop Sandys' Endowed School, Hawkshead, Near Ambleside: Tercentenary Commemoration, Thursday, September 17th, 1885</u>. Kendal: privately printed [1885], pp. 7, 20-21.
      Notes Wordsworth's association with the school and memorials to him there.

10 ANON. "Life of Wordsworth," Notes, in <u>Tintern Abbey[,] Ode to Duty[,] Ode on Intimations of Immortality[,] and The Happy Warrior</u>. London and Edinburgh: Chambers, pp. 3-4, passim.
      A biographical sketch (3-4). Includes full critical notes on the four poems (passim).

11   ANON. Notes, in Poetry for Recitation. 4 parts. London:
     Moffatt & Paige [1885], pp. 18, 106-107.
        A biographical sketch and critical note to "Characteris-
     tics of a Child Three Years Old."

12   ANON. "Publishers' Preface," "Memoir," in The Poetical Works
     of Wordsworth: with Memoir, Explanatory Notes, Etc.:   The
     'Albion' Edition. London and New York: Warne [1885?],
     pp. [v], xxviii-xliv.
        The Prelude is not considered equal to Wordsworth's other
     poems ([v]). A biographical sketch (xxviii-xliv).

13   ANON. "Wordsworth, William," "Wordsworth, Mrs. (Mary
     Hutchinson)," "Wordsworth, Dorothy," in Men of the Reign:
     A Biographical Dictionary of Eminent Persons of British and
     Colonial Birth who have Died during the Reign of Queen
     Victoria. Edited by Thomas Humphry Ward. London and
     New York: Routledge, pp. 973-76.
        Biographical sketches.

14   ARDEN, MAURICE. Undercurrent & After-glow: An Elegy of
     England (poem). London: Bell; Clifton: Baker [1885],
     pp. 93, 95-99.
        Celebrates Wordsworth's brotherhood with Coleridge, his
     transfiguring of earth.

15   ASHE, T.[HOMAS]. "Introduction," Notes, in The Poetical Works
     of Samuel Taylor Coleridge. Edited by T. Ashe. 2 vols.
     London: Bell, pp. xiii-clxxxvi (passim), passim.
        Discusses Wordsworth's life as it touches Coleridge's.
     Wordsworth's definition of a poet does not adequately ac-
     count for Coleridge as a poet (xiii-clxxxvi). Includes
     brief critical notes to Coleridge's poems connected with
     Wordsworth (passim).

16   CAMPBELL, J.[AMES] DYKES. "Coleridge, Lamb, Leigh Hunt, and
     Others in 'The Poetical Register.'" Athenaeum, no. 2994
     (14 March), pp. 344-45 (345).
        Wordsworth loved his system "better, if possible, than
     its results."

17   COURTHOPE, WILLIAM JOHN. "The Liberal Movement in English
     Literature: V.--Poetry, Music, and Painting: Coleridge
     and Keats." National Review, 5 (June), 504-18 (505-12,
     516-18).
        In the Preface to Lyrical Ballads Wordsworth mistakenly
     applies to poetry "the Revolutionary theory of perpetual
     Progress." Wordsworth is deficient in invention. He

1885

contrasts with Coleridge and Keats. By basing poetry on
its own impressions, he deprives it of social influence.
Reprinted in 1885.B19.

18   COURTHOPE, WILLIAM JOHN. "The Liberal Movement in English
      Literature: VI.--Conclusion: The Prospects of Poetry."
      National Review, 5 (August), 770-86 (770-73, 780-82, 785).
          Wordsworth was dogmatic in his deprecation of Gray.
      What really inspired Wordsworth was not common life but as-
      sociations connected with his birthplace. His theory of
      poetic language is unpoetic. Reprinted in 1885.B19.

19   COURTHOPE, WILLIAM JOHN. "Wordsworth's Theory of Poetry,"
      "Poetry, Music, and Painting: Coleridge and Keats,"
      "Conclusion: The Prospects of Poetry," in The Liberal
      Movement in English Literature. London: Murray,
      pp. 69-108, 157-94 (162-80, 189-94), 195-240 (198-204,
      224-29, 237).
          Revised from 1884.B7. Wordsworth contends for the right
      of the poet to assert his own imagination without reference
      to the imagination of society (69-108). Reprinted from
      1885.B17 (162-80, 189-94). Reprinted from 1885.B18
      (198-204, 224-29, 237).

20   CROSS, J.[OHN] W.[ALTER], ed. George Eliot's Life as Related
      in Her Letters and Journals. Edited by her Husband.
      3 vols. Edinburgh and London: Blackwood, I:61, 388-89.
          Records George Eliot's lasting admiration for Wordsworth's
      poems. Includes letters in which she confesses that Words-
      worth expresses her own feelings and praises The Prelude
      and Wordsworth's single lines.

21   CURZON, GEORGE N. "Poetry, Politics, and Conservatism."
      National Review, 6 (December), 502-18.
          Wordsworth, like Tennyson, championed Conservative
      principle, though in a different manner.

22   ELLWOOD, THE REV. T. "The Poets and Poetry of Cumberland,
      including the Cumbrian Border." Transactions of the Cumber-
      land & Westmorland Association for the Advancement of
      Literature and Science, no. 9 (1883-84), pp. 137-67
      (156-57).
          Wordsworth saw everything at its best and brightest.

23   [ELWIN, WHITWELL]. Review of Glenaveril. Quarterly Review,
      161 (July), 1-28 (1-2, 15-16).
          Criticizes Wordsworth's classification of "the metrical
      Novel" in the Preface (1815).

24   GRAVES, ROBERT PERCEVAL. <u>Life of Sir William Rowan Hamil-</u>
     <u>ton</u>. . . . 3 vols. Dublin: Hodges, Figgis; London:
     Longmans, II:passim.
         Records Hamilton's visits and correspondence with and
     about Wordsworth: Wordsworth "requires a little previous
     <u>tuning</u> of the reader's mind"; his classifying of his poems
     is objectionable. Includes correspondence over Wordsworth's
     election as an Honorary Member of the Royal Irish Academy,
     and "Recollections" (poem) recording Hamilton's meetings
     with Wordsworth. Includes Aubrey de Vere's comments that,
     in the 1830's, Wordsworth had lost none of his power and
     that his poems are unified, and his report of Wordsworth's
     remark that he first began writing poetry to fill up blank
     pages in a book. For Volume I, <u>see</u> 1882.B22; for Volume
     III, <u>see</u> 1889.B33.

25   HAMERTON, PHILIP GILBERT. <u>Landscape</u>. London: Seeley, pp. 28,
     30-31, 46-48, 70-77.
         Wordsworth's "intellectual liberty was in great part
     sacrificed to his interest in the English Lake district";
     his interest in humanity saved him from being entirely con-
     quered by landscape. Wordsworth often simply versified
     prose. He possessed a landscape painter's knowledge of
     landscape, a delicacy of observation. To him the magnifi-
     cent in nature at once suggests the lowly; when he describes
     buildings, he ties them with landscape.

26   [HUTTON, RICHARD HOLT]. "Wordsworth and Professor Huxley on
     the Narrowness of Specialists." <u>Spectator</u>, 58 (5 December),
     1611-12.
         Wordsworth thought poetry and religion the only guaran-
     tees against the narrowing effect of scientific analysis.

27   [KNIGHT, WILLIAM]. "Report of the Sixth Annual Meeting,
     July 8, 1885," "A List of Wordsworth's Poems Arranged in
     Chronological Order." <u>Transactions of The Wordsworth</u>
     <u>Society</u>, no. 7 [1885], 7-33, 53-117.
         Includes: 1) an address by R. M. Milnes. Recalls his
     enthusiasm for Wordsworth at Cambridge in the 1830's, and
     confirms Rawnsley's observations in 1884.B23. 2) a paper
     by Harry Goodwin on "Wordsworth and Turner." Wordsworth and
     Turner both loved nature and led a return to simplicity;
     both sympathized with human sorrow. 3) remarks by James
     Bryce. Notes Wordsworth's reputation and the state of the
     school at Hawkshead. 4) remarks by R. H. Hutton. Words-
     worth is not entirely without humor in <u>Peter Bell</u> (7-33).
     Lists Wordsworth's poems in order of composition, based on
     the list in 1882.B40; reprinted in <u>The Poetical Works of</u>

1885

William Wordsworth (ed. Knight, Volume VIII, 1886)
(53-117).

28 LANG, ANDREW. "Poetry and Politics." Macmillan's Magazine,
    53 (December), 81-88 (85-87).
        A response to 1885.B19. The charm of Wordsworth's lines
    in "The Solitary Reaper" does not depend on their context.

29 LEE, EDMUND. "Dorothy Wordsworth." Christian World Magazine,
    [21] (April), 314-19; (May), 360-67; (June), 464-72;
    (July), 548-57.
        Discusses Wordsworth's life and relations with Dorothy.
    Dorothy consecrated her life to Wordsworth. Revised and
    expanded as 1886.B32.

30 NOEL, RODEN. "The Poetry of Tennyson." Contemporary Review,
    47 (February), 202-24 (205, 207).
        Wordsworth's delineating Margaret's grief through the
    neglect of her garden in The Excursion is not characteris-
    tic. Reprinted in 1886.B36.

31 NOEL, RODEN. "The Poetry of Shelley." British Quarterly
    Review, 82 (1 October), 277-87 (278-80, 282).
        Wordsworth sees the spirituality through the veil of the
    material world; nature and man form a vital unity. Re-
    printed with minor changes as "Shelley" in 1886.B36.

32 [PROTHERO, ROWLAND]. Review of Traill's Coleridge. Edinburgh
    Review, 162 (October), 301-51 (305, 313-14, 320, 324-26,
    331-32).
        Discusses Wordsworth as he touches Coleridge's life and
    work. To Wordsworth, nature was the outward manifestation
    of a personal God.

33 RHYS, ERNEST. "A Little Academe." Gentleman's Magazine, 259
    (October), 371-89.
        Visits Stowey and Alfoxden and recalls Wordsworth's and
    Coleridge's lives there.

34 ROBINSON, PHIL. "Some Poets' Horses." Gentleman's Magazine,
    258 (February), 156-62 (157, 161).
        Notes Wordsworth's use of horses in his poems. Re-
    printed in 1885.B38.

35 ROBINSON, PHIL. "Beasts of Chase." Gentleman's Magazine, 258
    (May), 442-56 (443).
        Wordsworth lacks sympathy with sport. Reprinted in
    1885.B38.

36   ROBINSON, PHIL. "Poets' Reptiles." Gentleman's Magazine, 259
        (November), 465-71 (467).
            Wordsworth uses the term "reptile" incorrectly. Re-
        printed in 1893.B52.

37   ROBINSON, PHIL. "'The Tuneful Frog.'" Gentleman's Magazine,
        259 (December), 570-79 (575, 578).
            Wordsworth's knowledge of frogs is faulty. Reprinted in
        1893.B52.

38   ROBINSON, PHIL. The Poets' Beasts: A Sequel to "The Poets'
        Birds." London: Chatto and Windus, passim.
            Mostly reprinted from 1883.B46-B49 and 1885.B34-B35.
        Briefly notes Wordsworth's use of animals in his poems.

39   [ROSS, JOSEPH CARNE, ed.]. John Carne: Letters 1813-1837.
        N.p.: privately printed, pp. 133-38, 206.
            Includes letters in which Carne details a visit to Words-
        worth in 1823 (commends Wordsworth as a judge of picturesque
        beauty, conversationalist, and reader of his own poems) and
        Wordsworth's arrangements to contribute to The Keepsake
        (1829).

40   RUSKIN, JOHN. Bibliotheca Pastorum: Vol. IV: A Knight's
        Faith: Passages in the Life of Sir Herbert Edwardes.
        Part III: The Patience of Kineyree. Orpington: Allen,
        p. 249.
            Recalls Sir Herbert Edwardes's interpretation of "Charac-
        ter of the Happy Warrior" as a literal rather than imaginary
        portrait.

41   SCRYMGOUR, E.[DWARD] P.[HILLIPS]. A Few Words on the Study of
        Literary History. N.p.: privately printed [1885], pp. 5-7.
            Wordsworth is the poet of the Idealist movement.

42   SHAPCOTT, REUBEN. See 1885.B47.

43   SYMINGTON, ANDREW JAMES. "Prefatory Notice," in The Poetical
        Works of William Wordsworth. London and Newcastle-on-Tyne:
        Scott, pp. 9-46.
            A biographical sketch. Wordsworth, the great, healing
        poet-teacher, persevered despite his reception in calm con-
        fidence of his mission. His just estimate of his own works
        is unique in literary history. After he threw off his early
        revolutionary opinions, he became a shrewd political pro-
        phet, warning of the tyranny of democracy. He lays great
        stress on Moral Force. There is less of the exuberance of
        genius in his later work. An upright man, he was singularly
        free from prejudice, took a catholic view of most subjects.

44   TAYLOR, HENRY. Autobiography of Henry Taylor: 1800–1875.
     2 vols. London: Longmans, I:178–82, 185, 188–92, 210–12,
     323–24, 334–39; II:8, 41–42, 44, 55–61, 180–81.
         Scott and Wordsworth were unlike in aspect and genius.
     Though he wrote too much, Wordsworth molded the mind of at
     least one generation. Records Thomas Spring Rice's and the
     Rev. Richard Whately's judgments of Wordsworth's poems and
     Isabella Fenwick's admiration of Wordsworth and discussion,
     in her letters, of his depression after Dora's death and
     of plans for the writing of his biography and for erecting
     a monument. Wordsworth delighted in gossip.

45   TULLOCH, JOHN. Movements of Religious Thought in Britain
     during the Nineteenth Century: Being the Fifth Series of
     St. Giles' Lectures. London: Longmans, pp. 5–6, 225, 238.
         Wordsworth lays the foundation of religion "in the na-
     tural instincts of man." He did not initiate any distinc-
     tive religious movement.

46   WATTS[-DUNTON], THEODORE. "Poetry," in The Encyclopaedia
     Britannica: A Dictionary of Arts, Sciences, and General
     Literature. Ninth edition. 24 vols. Edinburgh: Black,
     XIX:256–73 (258, 271).
         When he moves away from iambic meter, Wordsworth writes
     doggerel. The length of lines and arrangement of rhymes
     in "Ode: Intimations of Immortality" are not always in-
     evitable.

47   [WHITE, WILLIAM HALE] REUBEN SHAPCOTT, ed. Mark Rutherford's
     Deliverance: Being the Second Part of his Autobiography.
     Edited by his Friend. London: Trübner, p. 6.
         Records how Lyrical Ballads impressed upon him the im-
     portance of country landscape.

48   WOODHOUSE, RICHARD. "Notes of Conversations with Thomas De
     Quincey," in Confessions of an English Opium-Eater. By
     Thomas De Quincey. Edited by Richard Garnett. London:
     Kegan Paul, Trench, pp. 189–233 (191–93, 198, 200, 218–25).
         Records De Quincey's admiration of Wordsworth, who was
     otherwise ridiculed in Oxford; his praise of Wordsworth's
     reading poetry; his objection to J. Clare's comparing of
     Wordsworth and Crabbe and describing Wordsworth as a nursery
     poet; and his defense of Wordsworth's style from the charge
     of meanness. Identifies Wordsworth as the subject of an
     anecdote related by Hazlitt in 1821.B19.

1886 A BOOKS

1   ANON. Commentary, in <u>Wordsworth's Country: A Series of Five
     Etchings of the English Lake District</u>. By David Law.
     London: Dunthorne.
          Wordsworth's poems contain the truest interpretation of
     nature among the Lakes. Describes Rydal and Grasmere.

1886 B SHORTER WRITINGS

1   ALEXANDER, SIDNEY A. "To Wordsworth" (poem). <u>Academy</u>, 30
     (18 December), 411.
          Praises Wordsworth as the voice of Nature.

2   ANON. "On Auberon Herbert" (poem). <u>Punch</u>, 90 (5 June), 266.
          Parody of "She was a Phantom of delight."

3   ANON. "'We Are Seven': (The Birmingham Version)" (poem).
     <u>Figaro</u>, no. 1587 (10 July), pp. 9-10.
          Parody of "We Are Seven."

4   ANON. Review of Lee's <u>Dorothy Wordsworth</u>. <u>Athenaeum</u>,
     no. 3070 (28 August), pp. 266-67.
          Discusses Dorothy's life with and influence on Words-
     worth.

5   ANON. "Dorothy Wordsworth." <u>Saturday Review</u>, 62
     (18 September), 402-403.
          The "sublime egotist" Wordsworth was "fortunate in his
     womankind," especially Dorothy.

6   ANON. "Henry Vaughan." <u>Spectator</u>, 59 (18 September),
     1245-47 (1246).
          Wordsworth received "the first hint" for "Ode: Intima-
     tions of Immortality" from Vaughan.

7   ANON. "William Wordsworth," in <u>Wordsworth</u>. London, Belfast,
     and New York: Ward [1886], pp. [5-6].
          A biographical sketch. Except during his early revolu-
     tionary fervor, Wordsworth lacked "warm human sympathies."

8   ANON. "Wordsworth," in <u>The Book of the Poets; from Chaucer
     to Montgomery</u>. . . . Illustrated. London: Blackwood
     [1886], pp. 483-84.
          A biographical sketch.

1886

9   [BROWN, JAMES BUCHAM] J. B. SELKIRK. "The Secret of Yarrow."
        Blackwood's Edinburgh Magazine, 140 (July), 27-36 (29-31).
        Notes Wordsworth's reaction to the Yarrow.

10   CAINE, T.[HOMAS] HALL. Review of Dowden's The Life of Percy
        Bysshe Shelley. Academy, 30 (4 December), 371-74 (371-72).
        Wordsworth is not describing Coleridge in "Stanzas
        Written in My Pocket-copy of Thomson's 'Castle of Indo-
        lence.'"

11   CAINE, T.[HOMAS] HALL. "'A Noticeable Man with Large Grey
        Eyes.'" Academy, 30 (18 December), 412.
        A reply to 1886.B22. Wordsworth's portrait in "Stanzas
        Written in My Pocket-copy of Thomson's 'Castle of Indo-
        lence'" is of neither Coleridge nor W. Calvert.

*12 [CARR, FRANK] LAUNCELOT CROSS. "Thinkers of the World in
        their Relation to the New Church." [c. 1886-88.]
        Not located. Listed in 1896.B36, VIII:360: a series of
        periodical articles. One installment, "Childhood as Re-
        vealed in Wordsworth," exists as a clipping in the library
        at Dove Cottage: Wordsworth was "largely inspired by the
        inward light which shone in his childhood," as he reveals
        in The Prelude and the Lucy poems.

13   [COLLINS, J. CHURTON]. Review of Gosse's From Shakespeare to
        Pope. Quarterly Review, 163 (October), 289-329 (316-17).
        One must know Plato to understand much of Wordsworth's
        poetry.

14   COURTHOPE, WILLIAM JOHN. "Poetry and Politics: Form and
        Subject." National Review, 6 (January), 640-50 (644-45).
        A reply to 1885.B28. Questions Lang's ability to appre-
        ciate lines from "The Solitary Reaper" out of context.

15   COWAN, WILLIAM. "Wordsworth and Nature." Churchman, 14
        (September), 418-30.
        Wordsworth did not please early readers because he is not
        dazzling but serene. He spiritually apprehends the meaning
        of natural objects. His poetry purges, refreshes, and calms.
        He is a Christian, not a pantheist.

16   CREIGHTON, THE REV. M.[ANDELL]. "The Story of the English
        Shires: VI.--Westmorland." Leisure Hour, 35 [November],
        723-28 (728).
        Wordsworth has sketched the "historic character of the
        people" of Westmorland; yet his works, by making the Lakes
        fashionable, have led to the dalesman's demise. Reprinted
        in The Story of Some English Shires (1897).

17   CROSS, LAUNCELOT. <u>See</u> 1886.B12.

18   DAWSON, GEORGE. <u>Biographical Lectures</u>. Edited by George St
     Clair. London: Kegan Paul, Trench, pp. 251-307, 353-55.
         Wordsworth devoted himself to his revolutionary mission
     in life, ignoring public censure. His valuing of inner
     worth over outer appearances (e.g., in <u>Peter Bell</u>) is
     Christian. He teaches us the calming power of nature; he
     is "to a certain extent" a mystic. Compares Wordsworth,
     Coleridge, and Shelley.

19   DAWSON, W.[ILLIAM] J.[AMES]. "Wordsworth and His Message,"
     "The Poetry of Despair," in <u>Quest and Vision: Essays in
     Life and Literature</u>. London: Stock, pp. 45-85, 196-248
     (216-19).
         Wordsworth lacks the Byronic personality that appeals to
     young and sensationalist minds. He was a quiet, decent
     man, as is reflected in the healing calm of his poetry
     (45-85). He was saved from pessimism by his belief in God,
     his simple tastes, and his love of nature (216-19).

20   DOVETON, F. B. "To the Coming Comet!" (poem), "Emancipation"
     (poem), in <u>Sketches in Prose and Verse</u>. London: Sampson
     Low, Marston, Searle, & Rivington, pp. 398-99, 436-37.
         Parody of "To the Cuckoo" ("O blithe New-comer! I have
     heard") (398-99). Parody of "She dwelt among the untrodden
     ways" (436-37).

21   DOWDEN, EDWARD. "The Interpretation of Literature."
     <u>Contemporary Review</u>, 49 (May), 701-19 (704-707, 709, 717).
         "The poetry of Wordsworth brought a new thing into Eng-
     lish literature"; hence it was ridiculed. Wordsworth de-
     lighted little in music, had no sense of smell. Reprinted
     in <u>Transcripts and Studies</u> (1888).

22   DOWDEN, EDWARD. "'A Noticeable Man with Large Grey Eyes.'"
     <u>Academy</u>, 30 (11 December), 395-96.
         A reply to 1886.B10. Reviews opinions concerning the
     identity of Wordsworth's portraits in "Stanzas Written in
     My Pocket-copy of Thomson's 'Castle of Indolence.'"

23   DOWDEN, EDWARD. <u>The Life of Percy Bysshe Shelley</u>. 2 vols.
     London: Kegan Paul, Trench, I:209-10, 225-26, 471, 485;
     II:20, 26, 32, 156, 218, 288-89, 295.
         Notes Wordsworth's friendship with W. Calvert, whom
     Wordsworth describes in "Stanzas Written in my Pocket-copy
     of Thomson's 'Castle of Indolence.'" Includes letters in
     which Shelley expresses his enthusiasm for Wordsworth in

1811-12. Notes Shelley's later disappointment, especially with The Excursion and Wordsworth's political activity in 1818. Notes Wordsworth's influence on Byron.

24 DOYLE, SIR FRANCIS HASTINGS. Reminiscences and Opinions of Sir Francis Hastings Doyle: 1813-1885. London: Longmans, pp. 164-65.
    Recalls Wordsworth's vigorous conversation during three meetings in London.

25 FINDLAY, JOHN RITCHIE. Personal Recollections of Thomas De Quincey. Edinburgh: Black, pp. 35-36, 47-51, 55-56.
    Records De Quincey's recollections of Wordsworth's disgust over Wilhelm Meister, his ridiculing of J. Wilson's tales, his scorn of public opinion, and his rejecting of De Quincey's offer to contribute to A Guide through the District of the Lakes. Records De Quincey's opinions that the titles of Wordsworth's longer poems were inappropriate and that The Excursion contains commonplace religious sentiments.

26 HAWEIS, THE REV. HUGH REGINALD. "Introduction," in Select Poems. Edited by the Rev. Hugh Reginald Haweis. London and New York: Routledge, pp. 5-6.
    Wordsworth wrote everything that came into his head; yet his poems contain a simple pathos for a sated age.

27 HODGSON, WILLIAM. "The Cuckoo." National Review, 7 (April), 239-49 (240, 243-44).
    One cannot take Wordsworth's remarks on the cuckoo in "To the Cuckoo" ("O blithe New-comer! I have heard") too literally.

28 [HUTTON, RICHARD HOLT]. "Professor Knight's Wordsworth [Volumes VI-VIII]." Spectator, 59 (13 March), 355-56.
    A "very considerable mass" of Wordsworth's verse does not contribute to his fame.

29 HUTTON, R.[ICHARD] H.[OLT]. "Newman and Arnold: II. Matthew Arnold." Contemporary Review, 49 (April), 513-34 (534).
    As opposed to Arnold, Wordsworth taught us to bear, not to put by, "The cloud of mortal destiny." Reprinted in Essays on Some of the Modern Guides of English Thought in Matters of Faith (1887).

30 JOHNSON, CHARLES F. "Wordsworth." Temple Bar, 77 (July), 336-55.
    Wordsworth, liberal in poetic theory but otherwise conservative, is "an eminently safe poet." His democratic

spirit should make him of interest to Americans. In Peter
Bell he gives a startling insight into the abnormal development of a social outlaw. He can sympathize with all, especially children; his originality lies in his power to
divine the influence of environment over men's characters.
His insularity kept him from a full understanding of life,
though he shows a wider range in his sonnets; his poems are
tedious, his sense of landscape unequalled.

31 LANG, ANDREW. "Letters on Literature: Introductory.--Of
    Modern Poetry." Independent (New York), 38 (28 October),
    1364.
        Despite Wordsworth's "inspired greatness," "creeping
    prose" invades even "Tintern Abbey." Reprinted in 1889.B39.

32 LEE, EDMUND. Dorothy Wordsworth: The Story of a Sister's
    Love. London: Clarke, passim.
        Revised and expanded from 1885.B29. Revised in 1894.B22.

33 MORLEY, HENRY. A First Sketch of English Literature. New and
    enlarged edition. London, Paris, New York, and Melbourne:
    Cassell, pp. 866-921 (passim).
        A biographical sketch, revised from 1873.B23 and
    1881.B24.

34 [MORRIS, MOWBRAY]. "English Literature at the Universities."
    Macmillan's Magazine, 55 (December), 124-32 (127, 129).
        A reply to 1886.B13. The bulk of Wordsworth's lyrical
    poems have slight connections with the classics.

35 NICHOLSON, CORNELIUS. Wordsworth and Coleridge: Two Parallel
    Sketches: A Lecture, delivered at Ambleside, June, 1886.
    [N.p.: privately printed,] pp. 5-16, 19-21.
        A biographical sketch. Wordsworth, the poet of child-
    hood, is unique in his harmonizing of mind and the external
    world and in the moral elevation of his muse. He was
    neither a materialist nor an agnostic. The number of his
    lines that have become household phrases is the test of his
    fame. His impulses were external, Coleridge's internal.

36 NOEL, RODEN. "On the Poetic Interpretation of Nature," "Lord
    Byron and His Times," "Shelley," "Wordsworth," "The Poetry
    of Tennyson," in Essays on Poetry and Poets. London:
    Kegan Paul, Trench, pp. 1-35 (1, 4-15, 25-26), 50-113
    (86-89, 112), 114-31 (115-17, 120), 132-49, 223-55 (227,
    231).
        Combined with omissions from 1866.B10 and 1884.B15 (1,
    4-15, 25-26). Reprinted with minor addition from 1873.B26

1886

(86–89, 112). Reprinted with minor changes from 1885.B31
(115–17, 120). Wordsworth's poetry breathes comfort and
courage, "a kind of inarticulate, still-life pathos," a
glorification of common humanity. At times Wordsworth is
too peculiar and uninspired; he spiritualizes nature
(132–49). Reprinted from 1885.B30 (227, 231).

37 NORTON, CHARLES ELIOT, ed. Early Letters of Thomas Carlyle:
    1814–1826. London and New York: Macmillan, pp. 267, 294.
      Includes letter in which Carlyle notes Wordsworth was
    "much talked of" in Edinburgh in 1823.

38 [NORTON, CHARLES ELIOT, ed.]. The Correspondence of Thomas
    Carlyle and Ralph Waldo Emerson 1834–1872. Revised edition.
    2 vols. Boston: Ticknor, I:71–72, 199, 254; II:190–91.
      Expanded from 1883.B41. Includes letter in which
    Carlyle describes Wordsworth as garrulous and genuine.
    (Added reference also published in The Correspondence of
    Thomas Carlyle and Ralph Waldo Emerson 1834–1872: Supple-
    mentary Letters [Boston: Ticknor], p. 14.)

39 PALGRAVE, FRANCIS T. "The Province and Study of Poetry."
    Macmillan's Magazine, 53 (March), 332–47 (336, 338, 342–43,
    345–46).
      The Preface to Lyrical Ballads contains reasoned convic-
    tions, not rhetorical phrases. In "The Solitary Reaper"
    Wordsworth transmutes the commonplace into novelty and
    beauty.

40 [PATER, WALTER]. "Four Books for Students of English
    Literature." Guardian, no. 2098 (17 February), pp. 246–47
    (247).
      The simple stories of Lamb and Wordsworth possess seren-
    ity, a tragic power. Reprinted as "English Literature" in
    Essays from The "Guardian" (1896).

41 [PROTHERO, ROWLAND]. Review of Tennyson's Tiresias and
    Courthope's Liberal Movement in English Literature.
    Edinburgh Review, 163 (April), 466–98 (466–71, 477–81, 484).
      Wordsworth founded a poetic revival rather than a revo-
    lution. His view of the poet was aristocratic; his exces-
    sive insistence on plain language was an offense against
    taste. He believed every subject capable of poetic treat-
    ment.

42 Q.[UILLER-COUCH, ARTHUR THOMAS]. "Anecdote for Fathers"
    (poem). Oxford Magazine, 4 (1 December), 406–407.

1886

Parody of "Anecdote for Fathers," announced as by "the
late W. W. (of H. M. Inland Revenue Service)." Reprinted
in Green Bays (1893).

43 ROBINSON, PHIL. "Snakes in Poetry." Gentleman's Magazine,
    261 (July), 36-48 (43).
       Wordsworth transforms the hackneyed image of a serpent
    in The Excursion (Book VII). Reprinted in 1893.B52.

44 ROBINSON, PHIL. "Night-Moths and Day-Moths." Gentleman's
    Magazine, 261 (November), 483-94 (489).
       Wordsworth's descriptions of butterflies are suspect.
    Reprinted in 1893.B52.

45 RUSKIN, JOHN. Praeterita: Outlines of Scenes and Thoughts
    perhaps Worthy of Memory in My Past Life: Chapter XII:
    Roslyn Chapel. Orpington: Allen, pp. 403-405.
       Wordsworth idly takes childish love of nature for an
    intimation of immortality. Compares his love of nature
    with Wordsworth's.

46 RUSSELL, JAMES. Reminiscences of Yarrow. With a Preface by
    Professor Campbell Fraser. Edinburgh and London:
    Blackwood, pp. 229-35.
       Records visit with Wordsworth in 1842: Wordsworth's
    conversation about Yarrow and contemporary poets.

47 RUSSELL, PERCY. The Literary Manual; or, A Complete Guide to
    Authorship. London: London Literary Society, pp. 27,
    56-57.
       Wordsworth sees nature clearly, can write sublime
    thoughts.

48 SELKIRK, J. B. See 1886.B9.

49 SHARP, WILLIAM. "The Sonnet: Its Characteristics and
    History," "Notes," in Sonnets of This Century. Edited by
    William Sharp. London and Newcastle-on-Tyne: Scott,
    pp. xxi-lxxxi (lxvi, lxxi-lxxii, lxxix), 267-324 (323-24).
       Wordsworth initiated the revival of interest in the son-
    net; his work is uneven (lxvi, lxxi-lxxii, lxxix). Though
    Wordsworth's habit of rhyming on everything produced The
    River Duddon and the Ecclesiastical Sonnets, his sonnets
    are in general free from his characteristic flaws (323-24).

50 [STORR, FRANCIS]. "Preface," in Wordsworth's Excursion: The
    Wanderer. New edition. Edited by Hawes Turner. London:
    Rivington's [1886], pp. vii-viii.

1886

The Excursion provides a lesson on the differences between poetry and prose. Its beauty can be enjoyed without
entering into Wordsworth's philosophy. Attribution: Storr
edited series; see also 1881.B33.

51 TALFOURD, SIR THOMAS NOON and W. CAREW HAZLITT, eds. Letters
    of Charles Lamb: with Some Account of the Writer, his
    Friends and Correspondents, and Explanatory Notes. New
    edition, revised and enlarged. 2 vols. London: Bell,
    passim.
        Reprints, with additions by W. C. Hazlitt, the account
    of Lamb's friendship with and opinions of Wordsworth and
    his correspondence in 1837.B24 and 1848.B11.

52 TILLEY, ARTHUR. "The Poetic Imagination." Macmillan's
    Magazine, 53 (January), 184-92 (188-90).
        Wordsworth's sonnets are characterized by a high degree
    of penetrative imagination.

53 TURNER, HAWES [and FRANCIS STORR]. "Life," "Notes," in
    Wordsworth's Excursion: The Wanderer. New edition.
    Edited by Hawes Turner. London: Rivington's [1886],
    pp. 9-22, 47-77.
        A biographical sketch, revised from 1874.B46. During
    his life and now, Wordsworth was a poet "rather honoured
    than popular." He cannot give characters (e.g., in The Ex-
    cursion) an individuality distinct from himself; he lacks
    humor and is uniformly reflective (9-22). Critical notes,
    revised from 1874.B46 (47-77). Attribution: Storr edited
    series; see also 1881.B33.

1887 A BOOKS

1 GOODWIN, HARRY, and PROFESSOR [WILLIAM] KNIGHT. Through the
   Wordsworth Country. London: Sonnenschein, Lowrey, 287 pp.
       Descriptive text by Knight to sketches by Goodwin of
   Wordsworthian localities in the Lake District.

2 PARK, JOHN. A Greenockian's Visit to Wordsworth: From
   Journals of Late Reverend Dr Park of St. Andrew's.
   Greenock: privately printed, 18 pp.
       Records visit to Rydal in 1842 and Wordsworth's conver-
   sation on the Scotch church and the Oxford movement, translating Chaucer, the sale of his works in cities, Burns,
   Shakespeare, Spenser, writing to elevate the reader, and
   touring the Lakes.

3   SUTHERLAND, JAMES MIDDLETON. William Wordsworth: The Story
     of His Life, with Critical Remarks on his Writings.
     London: Stock, 239 pp.
          A full biography, aiming to present "a popular story" of
     Wordsworth's life. Wordsworth offers needed withdrawal and
     reflection "in these nineteenth-century days of life-at-
     high-pressure." His poetry is wholesome, correct in lan-
     guage; he gives us eyes and ears to see the natural world.
     He excels in lyrics, sonnets, and blank verse. Includes
     "At the Grave of Wordsworth (November 9, 1887)" (poem):
     the world sadly needs Wordsworth's love for Man. Revised
     as 1892.A1.

1887 B   SHORTER WRITINGS

1   [ABBOTT, EVELYN]. "Peacock." Temple Bar, 80 (May), 35-52
     (52).
          Men are now turning to Wordsworth in reaction to arti-
     ficiality in life. Attribution: Richard Haven et al.,
     eds., Samuel Taylor Coleridge: An Annotated Bibliography
     of Criticism and Scholarship, Volume I (Boston: Hall,
     1976), p. 213.

2   AINGER, ALFRED. "The Letters of Charles Lamb." Macmillan's
     Magazine, 55 (January), 161-73 (163-65, 168).
          Records Lamb's admiration of "Tintern Abbey" and Lyrical
     Ballads (1800).

3   AINGER, ALFRED. "Coleridge's 'Ode to Wordsworth.'"
     Macmillan's Magazine, 56 (June), 81-87.
          Cites evidence for identifying Edmund in Coleridge's
     "Dejection: An Ode" with Wordsworth. "Resolution and In-
     dependence" is an appropriate response.

4   ANON. "Poets' Pictures." Temple Bar, 80 (June), 232-40
     (232-34).
          Though Wordsworth was interested in the life within na-
     ture rather than its external beauty, his works contain
     memorable brief descriptions. He had graphic power but no
     sense of color.

5   ANON. "Fine Passages in Verse and Prose; Selected by Living
     Men of Letters." Fortnightly Review, NS 42 (1 August),
     297-316 (301, 307); (1 September), 430-54 (437-39, 444);
     (1 October), 580-604 (591, 596, 600); (1 November), 717-39
     (719-20, 729, 731, 735-36, 738).
          F. C. Burnand, W. S. Lilly (301, 307), Edward Henry
     Stanley (Lord Derby), Edward Dowden, Ernest Rhys (437-39,

1887

444), Frederic Harrison, Frederic W. H. Myers, H. D. Traill
(591, 596, 600), Sidney Colvin, Mrs. Louise Chandler
Moulton, the Rev. R. W. Church, William Sharp, and Edmund
Yates (719-20, 729, 731, 735-36, 738) note favorite passages in Wordsworth's poems and prose.

6 ANON. "Memorials of Coleorton." Saturday Review, 64
(19 November), 710-11.
   Records Wordsworth's relations with Sir George Beaumont.
Wordsworth's letters show how thoroughly he was concerned
with his poetry.

7 ANON. Review of Through the Wordsworth Country. Spectator,
60 (Suppl., 19 November), 1591.
   Wordsworth is associated with the Lake District in a way
without parallel in literature.

8 ANON. Proceedings (18 October 1886), in Papers of the
Manchester Literary Club. Volume XIII. Manchester and
London: Heywood, pp. 408-10 (408-409).
   Reports debate between W. E. A. Axon and John Mortimer
on Wordsworth's interest in man as opposed to nature; includes account of Wordsworth's dreaming of himself as a
large bird soaring above other birds.

9 ANON. "William Wordsworth," in Literary Celebrities:
Biographies of Wordsworth--Campbell--Moore--Jeffrey.
[Illustrated.] London and Edinburgh: Chambers, pp. 7-73.
   Reprinted, adding a brief secondary bibliography, from
1850.B36.

10 AXON, WILLIAM E. A. "Wordsworth in London." Manchester
Quarterly, 6 (October), 310-13.
   Wordsworth was inspired by nature not by man, and so
drew little stimulus from London.

11 B., J. T. "Wordsworth: 'Vagrant Reed.'" Notes and Queries,
7th ser., 4 (30 July), 95.
   Interprets "The Resting-place."

12 BOUCHIER, JONATHAN. "Wordsworth: 'Vagrant Reed.'" Notes and
Queries, 7th ser., 4 (30 July), 95; (17 December), 491.
   Interprets "The Resting-place."

13 CAINE, [THOMAS] HALL. Review of Memorials of Coleorton.
Academy, 32 (17 December), 399-400.
   Discusses Wordsworth's relations with Coleridge concerning
opium and Coleridge's wife.

14 CAINE, [THOMAS] HALL. Life of Samuel Taylor Coleridge.
    London: Scott, passim.
        Discusses Wordsworth as he touches Coleridge's life and
    work.

15 CLAYDEN, P.[ETER] W. The Early Life of Samuel Rogers.
    London: Smith, Elder, pp. 68, 116-17, 156-57, 217-19,
    236, 291.
        Compares Rogers's initial failure with that of Lyrical
    Ballads (1798), Rogers's and Wordsworth's reaction to the
    French Revolution and reputation.

16 COLVIN, SIDNEY. Keats. London and New York: Macmillan,
    passim.
        Records the associations of Keats and his circle with
    Wordsworth. Wordsworth's poetry of nature, which is sub-
    jective, differs from Keats's and Shelley's.

17 D. "Wordsworth: 'Vagrant Reed.'" Notes and Queries,
    7th ser., 4 (24 December), 511.
        A reply to 1887.B12 concerning "The Resting-place."

18 DENNIS, JOHN. "Robert Southey." National Review, 8
    (February), 765-76 (766, 771-72, 775).
        Wordsworth and Southey admired each other. Wordsworth,
    as opposed to Southey, tended to disregard all books save
    his own. Reprinted as "Introduction" in Robert Southey
    ([1887]).

19 DE VERE, AUBREY [THOMAS]. "The Genius and Passion of
    Wordsworth," "The Wisdom and Truth of Wordsworth's Poetry,"
    "The Two Chief Schools of English Poetry: Poetic
    Versatility: Shelley and Keats," "Recollections of
    Wordsworth," in Essays Chiefly on Poetry. 2 vols. London
    and New York: Macmillan, I:101-73, 174-264; II:100-42
    (122-23), 275-95.
        Condensed and recast from 1880.B19 (I:101-73). Con-
    densed with verbal changes from 1884.B8 (174-264). Con-
    densed and recast from 1849.B5 (II:122-23). Condensed from
    1876.B8 (275-95).

20 DOWDEN, EDWARD. "Victorian Literature." Fortnightly Review,
    NS 41 (1 June), 835-67 (836-37, 853, 864).
        Wordsworth looks on the loss of his youthful glory with-
    out self-pity. He was the poet of order and wonder. Re-
    printed in Transcripts and Studies (1888).

1887

21   [EASTLAKE, ELIZABETH]. Review of Brandl's Samuel Taylor
     Coleridge, etc. Quarterly Review, 165 (July), 60-96 (63,
     69-70, 80-84, 87).
          Discusses Wordsworth's life as it touches Coleridge's.
     Wordsworth's and Coleridge's poetic temperaments differed.

22   EWART, HENRY C. "Wordsworth, the Poet of Nature." Sunday
     Magazine (London), 16 [March], 166-73.
          Pre-Raphaelite painting found its inspiration in Words-
     worth. Wordsworth "proceeds like the landscape painter"
     in Peter Bell and "Ode: Intimations of Immortality."

23   FORSTER, JOSEPH. "John Ruskin." London Society, 52
     (November), 532-45 (534-35).
          Ruskin shared Wordsworth's worship of nature but lacked
     his calm and manly strength. Reprinted with additional
     note in 1890.B26.

24   GILCHRIST, HERBERT HARLAKENDEN. "Anne Gilchrist," "A
     Confession of Faith," in Anne Gilchrist: Her Life and
     Writings. Edited by Herbert Harlakenden Gilchrist.
     London: Unwin, pp. 1-284 (275), 331-62 (332-33).
          Includes letter in which A. Gilchrist praises the "gener-
     ous ardour, clear-sightedness, grasp" and eloquence of
     Concerning . . . the Convention of Cintra (275). Includes
     essay in which she notes that Whitman is a more daring in-
     novator, and hence even less well received by his own
     generation, than Wordsworth (332-33).

25   GRESWELL, WILLIAM. "Coleridge and the Quantock Hills."
     Macmillan's Magazine, 56 (October), 413-20.
          Wordsworth and Coleridge hatched a conspiracy against
     classicism while living amidst the Quantocks.

26   H., W. "Wordsworth: 'Vagrant Reed.'" Notes and Queries,
     7th ser., 4 (30 July), 95.
          Interprets "The Resting-place."

27   HALLIDAY, JOHN. "Wordsworth: 'Vagrant Reed." Notes and
     Queries, 7th ser., 4 (2 July), 16.
          Interprets "The Resting-place."

28   HOGBEN, JOHN. "The Mystical Side of Wordsworth." National
     Review, 9 (August), 833-34.
          Wordsworth's mystical associations, when he is unaffected
     by reason, and his mystic sense of continuity, lie at the
     core of his life.

1887

29   [HUTTON, RICHARD HOLT]. "The Mystical Side of Good Sense."
      Spectator, 60 (6 August), 1051-52.
          Wordsworth's "mystical insights" are nothing more than
      propositions proven by common sense.

30   [HUTTON, RICHARD HOLT]. Review of Memorials of Coleorton.
      Spectator, 60 (3 December), 1656-57.
          Wordsworth's letters to the Beaumonts are characterized
      by "sturdy self-respect."

31   [KNIGHT, WILLIAM]. "Prefatory Note," "Report of Proceedings
      . . . ," "Letters from Wordsworth, His Wife, and Sister to
      Henry Crabb Robinson, and Others." Transactions of The
      Wordsworth Society, no. 8 [c. 1887], pp. iii-vi, 9-68,
      81-200.
          Includes letter from George Wilson defending "Words-
      worthians" (iii-vi). Surveys the Society's work including:
      1) address by Roundell Palmer, Earl of Selborne. Records
      his devotion to Wordsworth's poems, which teach us about
      human sympathy and contain nothing repugnant to Christian-
      ity; Wordsworth is a true artist. 2) address by John
      Veitch on "The Theism of Wordsworth." Wordsworth's mind
      was open equally to the world of sense and of the infinite;
      he sought to unify all existence. 3) address by Alfred
      Ainger on "The Poets Who Helped to Form Wordsworth's
      Style." Discusses the influence on Wordsworth's style of
      Anne Finch, Countess of Winchilsea, and James Thomson.
      4) remarks by Aubrey de Vere. Wordsworth was eminently a
      statesman; recalls Wordsworth's conversation on descriptive
      and religious poetry; Wordsworth celebrates a theologically
      acceptable, ideal Nature (9-68). Includes letters in which
      Dorothy and Mary Wordsworth discuss the daily goings-on of
      Wordsworth's life, with brief textual and critical notes
      by Knight (81-200).

32   KNIGHT, WILLIAM, ed. Memorials of Coleorton: Being Letters
      from Coleridge[,] Wordsworth and his Sister[,] Southey[,]
      and Sir Walter Scott to Sir George and Lady Beaumont of
      Coleorton, Leicestershire[,] 1803 to 1834. 2 vols.
      Edinburgh: Douglas, passim.
          Discusses Wordsworth's associations with the Beaumonts
      and Coleorton. Includes bibliographic and critical notes
      to Wordsworth's letters. Includes letters in which Cole-
      ridge notes that Wordsworth's "mind and body are both of a
      stronger texture than mine," mentions a loan from Words-
      worth in 1804, and criticizes The Excursion as containing
      commonplace truths; in which Dorothy Wordsworth reports on
      Wordsworth's daily life and work; in which Southey reports

1887

urging Coleridge to defend Wordsworth in 1807, and discusses Wordsworth's property at Applethwaite and Wordsworth's portrait; and in which Scott describes visiting
Wordsworth in 1825.

33   M., A. J.   "Wordsworth's Lines on 'Lucy.'" Notes and Queries,
      7th ser., 4 (3 December), 456.
           Lucy in "She dwelt among the untrodden ways" was Words-
      worth's first love. (A reply to Jonathan Bouchier, "Words-
      worth's Lines on 'Lucy,'" Notes and Queries, 7th ser., 4
      [29 October], 348-49; see also E. V., "Wordsworth's Lines
      on 'Lucy," Notes and Queries, 7th ser., 4 [19 November],
      416.)

34   MILES, ALFRED H.   "Introduction," in The English Reciter:
      William Wordsworth to John Clare. Edited by Alfred H.
      Miles. London: Simpkin, Marshall, and Hamilton, Adams;
      Manchester: John Heywood, and Abel Heywood; Edinburgh:
      Menzies [1887], pp. 3-4 (3).
           Wordsworth founded the Lake School, wrote with a lofty
      aim.

35   MORTIMER, JOHN.   "Wordsworth on Beggars." Manchester
      Quarterly, 6 (October), 314-23.
           Wordsworth, the poet of humanity rather than of nature,
      was attracted to wanderers and vagrants. "The Old Cumber-
      land Beggar" should be read with Lamb's "A Complaint of the
      Decay of Beggars in the Metropolis."

36   M.[OUNT], C. B.   "Wordsworth: 'Vagrant Reed.'" Notes and
      Queries, 7th ser., 4 (2 July), 16.
           Interprets "The Resting-place." (A reply to query of
      R. D. W., "Wordsworth: 'Vagrant Reed,'" Notes and Queries,
      7th ser., 3 [4 June], 449.) Attribution: see 1888.B28.

37   NOBLE, JAMES ASHCROFT.   "In a Selection from the Poems of
      Wordsworth" (poem), in Verses of a Prose-writer.
      Edinburgh: Douglas, p. [115].
           Commends Wordsworth's "happy dower of Faith and Rest."

38   NODAL, JOHN H.   "Recent Work on Wordsworth." Manchester
      Quarterly, 6 (October), 297-309.
           Arnold is wrong in saying that Wordsworth's reputation
      was still declining in 1879. Commends Knight's editing of
      Wordsworth; discusses Wordsworth's textual alterations, es-
      pecially those to "At the Grave of Burns" and "The Foun-
      tain." Wordsworth's life and work parallel Turner's.

1887

39   OWEN, FRANCES MARY. "Two Papers Read before the Wordsworth
         Society: I. On the Seeming Triviality of Some of Words-
         worth's Subjects; II.--On Wordsworth's View of Death,"
         "Wordsworth," in Essays and Poems. London: Bumpus,
         pp. 44-60, 132-62.
              Reprinted from 1882.B47 (44-60). Wordsworth leads us to
         a larger life through sympathy with both nature and man.
         He studies his own life as he studies nature. He "was as
         receptive to the beauty of sound as to that of sight." A
         biographical sketch (132-62).

40   PALGRAVE, F.[RANCIS] T.[URNER]. "On the Direct Influence over
         Style in Poetry, Exercised by the other Fine Arts, Sculpture
         and Painting especially; with Illustrations Ancient and
         Modern." National Review, 10 (October), 202-18 (214-15,
         218).
              Wordsworth's pictorial poetry possesses directness, a
         "sweet severity."

41   POLLOCK, SIR FREDERICK. Personal Remembrances of Sir
         Frederick Pollock. 2 vols. London and New York:
         Macmillan, I:182; II:188.
              Recounts visit to Rydal Mount in 1841 (Wordsworth's
         pride in his hollyhocks), Wordsworth's reaction to Miss
         Carr's singing of "The Force of Prayer," and his distress
         at Scott's misquoting "Yarrow Unvisited."

42   [RAWNSLEY, HARDWICKE DRUMMOND]. "From Skiddaw Top on Jubilee
         Bonfire Night." Cornhill Magazine, NS 9 (August), 154-64
         (156-57, 163).
              Describes Wordsworth and Southey celebrating England's
         victory in 1815.

43   RAWNSLEY, H.[ARDWICKE] D.[RUMMOND]. "Wordsworth and Japan."
         Murray's Magazine, 2 (October), 538.
              Includes note from a Japanese testifying to his appre-
         ciation of Wordsworth.

44   RAWNSLEY, MR. [HARDWICKE DRUMMOND]. "The Humanity of
         Wordsworth," "Note." Transactions of The Wordsworth
         Society, no. 8 [c. 1887], pp. 69-78, 79-80.
              Though Wordsworth does not celebrate "man in action,"
         the "mind of man" pervades his poems. He could not separate
         men from their surroundings (69-78). Discusses plans for
         preserving the Rock of Names and establishing a museum
         (79-80).

1887

45   ROBERTSON, JOHN. "The Art of Tennyson." <u>Our Corner</u>, 9
       (1 February), 87-97 (92); (1 March), 167-80 (167-68,
       173-76).
           Wordsworth did not improve his poems by revising them.
       Reprinted in 1889.B53.

46   SAINTSBURY, GEORGE. "Francis Jeffrey." <u>Macmillan's Magazine</u>,
       56 (August), 256-67 (262).
           One would willingly give up most of Wordsworth's poems;
       yet Jeffrey's criticism of Wordsworth is inconsistent. Re-
       printed in <u>Essays in English Literature 1780-1860</u> (1890).

47   SAUNDERS, FREDERICK. <u>The Story of Some Famous Books</u>. London:
       Stock, pp. 125-28.
           An adaptation of 1866.B14. Wordsworth, living seques-
       tered, must have had few cares.

48   SHAIRP, JOHN CAMPBELL. "The Ettrick Shepherd," "Henry Vaughan,
       Silurist," in <u>Sketches in History and Poetry</u>. Edited by
       John Veitch. Edinburgh: Douglas, pp. 317-49 (333, 336-38),
       350-76 (351, 368-75).
           In "Extempore Effusion upon the Death of James Hogg"
       Wordsworth compensates for his earlier insult of Hogg (333,
       336-38). Reprinted from 1884.B25 (351, 368-75).

49   SONNENSCHEIN, WILLIAM SWAN. <u>The Best Books: A Reader's</u>
       <u>Guide. . . .</u> London: Swan Sonnenschein Lowrey,
       especially pp. 180, 187, 301, 311, 509-10, 530-31, 540.
           A primary and secondary bibliography. Expanded in
       1891.B42.

50   TROLLOPE, THOMAS ADOLPHUS. <u>What I Remember</u>. 3 vols. London:
       Bentley, II:15-17.
           Records visit to Wordsworth in 1839: Wordsworth was not
       popular with his neighbors, talked solely of his own
       poetry.

51   UNDERHILL, GEORGE F. <u>Literary Epochs: Chapters on Noted</u>
       <u>Periods of Intellectual Activity</u>. London: Stock,
       pp. 181-83.
           The poems of Wordsworth and the Lake Poets are "redundant
       with pantheistic principles."

52   VEITCH, JOHN. <u>The Feeling for Nature in Scottish Poetry</u>.
       2 vols. Edinburgh and London: Blackwood, I:16, 21, 25-26,
       75-76; II:186, 196, 218, 238, 244, 275, 302.
           In Wordsworth, the yearning for a union of invisible and
       visible results in symbolism. His tediousness is pardonable

because it provides a rest between luminous flashes. Notes
Wordsworth's similarities with and influence upon Scottish
poets.

53 WALKER, H. "Wordsworth, William," in Celebrities of the
Century: Being A Dictionary of Men and Women of the
Nineteenth Century. Edited by Lloyd C. Sanders. London,
Paris, New York and Melbourne: Cassell, pp. 1067-69.
A biographical sketch. In Lyrical Ballads Wordsworth
carries simplicity, learned from Burns, too far. He gives
poetic expression to Rousseau's cry for a return to nature;
he becomes dull when he reduces his opinions to a theory.

54 WATSON, WILLIAM. "Wordsworth's Grave" (poem). National
Review, 10 (September), 40-45.
Wordsworth's poems give us peace. Reprinted in
1890.B51.

55 WHEELER, A. F. "An Unpublished Letter of Wordsworth."
Academy, 32 (1 October), 221.
Notes the writing of the letter (of 4 October 1830) is
"rough and careless" though the expression is polished.

1888 A BOOKS

1 ANON. The Home of William Wordsworth. London: Walker
[1888?], [10] pp.
A series of plates illustrating Wordsworth's associations with the Lake District.

1888 B SHORTER WRITINGS

1 AINGER, ALFRED, ed. The Letters of Charles Lamb. Newly
arranged, with additions. 2 vols. London and New York:
Macmillan, passim.
Adds, to Lamb's correspondence previously printed, letters in which Lamb reports Wordsworth's reaction to his
criticism of Lyrical Ballads (1800), notes that the new
volume in 1800 "too artfully aims at simplicity of expression," and praises The River Duddon. Includes explanatory
notes to Lamb's comments concerning Wordsworth.

2 [ALGER, JOHN G.]. Review of Record Office MSS., etc.
Edinburgh Review, 168 (July), 139-70 (139, 168-69).
Though enraptured with the French Revolution, Wordsworth
was "fated to become an ultra-Conservative."

1888

3   ANON. Review of Sutherland's William Wordsworth. Notes and
     Queries, 7th ser., 5 (12 May), 379.
          Wordsworth is a great poet, but he has equals.

4   ANON. Review of The Prelude (ed. George). Literary World
     (London), NS 37 (29 June), 604.
          The Prelude, a relatively unknown work, impresses one
     with Wordsworth's lofty aim. Attacks George's notes to the
     poem.

5   ANON. "Wordsworth's Poems." Scots Observer, 1 (22 December),
     136-37.
          The Recluse contains Wordsworth's characteristic virtues
     and vices of bathos and platitude.

6   ANON. "Wordsworth," in Cassell's Miniature Cyclopaedia.
     Part 6. London, Paris, New York, and Melbourne: Cassell
     [1888], p. 760.
          Brief biographical sketch.

7   ANON. "Wordsworth," in The Pocket Encyclopaedia: A Compendium
     of General Knowledge for Ready Reference. London: Sampson
     Low, Marston, Searle, and Rivington, p. 1196.
          Brief biographical sketch.

8   B., C. C. "Wordsworth: 'Vagrant Reed.'" Notes and Queries,
     7th ser., 5 (11 February), 114-15.
          Interprets "The Resting-place."

9   BAYNE, THOMAS. "Wordsworth and Scott." Athenaeum, no. 3178
     (22 September), pp. 386-87.
          Points out that Wordsworth's criticism of Scott's mis-
     quoting of "Yarrow Unvisited" refers to Scott's note in
     Marmion.

10   BELLASIS, EDWARD. Westmorland Church Notes: Being the
     Heraldry, Epitaphs, and other Inscriptions in the Thirty-two
     Ancient Parish Churches and Churchyards of that County.
     2 vols. Kendal: Wilson, I:217-18, 236-37.
          Describes Wordsworth family graves at Grasmere.

11   BOUCHIER, JONATHAN. "Wordsworth: 'Vagrant Reed.'" Notes and
     Queries, 7th ser., 5 (10 March), 197.
          A reply to 1888.B28. Interprets "The Resting-place."

12   CATTY, CHARLES. Dedication, "How privileged the man who in
     sweet verse" (poem), "There is a path leads under lofty
     oaks" (poem), in Poems in the Modern Spirit: with The

1888

Secret of Content: A Song for the Hour. London: Scott,
pp. [iii], 109-10, 111-12.
Expresses his reverence for Wordsworth ([iii]). Wordsworth's gentle muse has interpreted the eloquence of the
hills to men (109-10); Wordsworth is a "grave philosopher"
(111-12).

13 COLVIN, SIDNEY. "On Some Letters of Keats." Macmillan's
Magazine, 58 (August), 311-20 (314-16).
Prints letter in which Keats notes Wordsworth's perver-
sity in publishing Peter Bell and includes original text of
his review of Reynolds's parody (see 1819.B43).

14 DEES, R. R. "'Stepping Westward.'" Notes and Queries,
7th ser., 5 (7 April), 265.
Notes echo of "Stepping Westward" in Scott.

15 DOWDEN, EDWARD, ed. Correspondence of Henry Taylor. London
and New York: Longmans, passim.
Includes letters in which Taylor records Wordsworth's
mixing with London society in the 1830's and 1840's, Wordsworth's helplessness in everyday transactions combined with
profound discourse, and Wordsworth's remarks that writing
"Why art thou silent! Is thy love a plant" was "merely
'an act of the intellect'" and that memory aids the poet in
forming a congruous picture. Includes letters in which
Isabella Fenwick notes that Wordsworth's servants deem him
"'their fellow-man,'" describes his illness and his revising
of The Prelude in 1838-39, his "fearfully strong" feelings,
his conviction of his own greatness combined with a desire
for sympathy, and his visits to his rooms at Cambridge and
to Oxford in 1839. Includes James Spedding's jibe in 1842
at Wordsworth's writing on public issues, Aubrey de Vere's
recording of Wordsworth's fresh enthusiasm in 1845, Dr.
John Brown's remark that Wordsworth too often drivels, and
A. C. Swinburne's acknowledging Shelley's debt to Wordsworth.

16 FAWCETT, MRS. HENRY. "Dorothy Wordsworth." Mothers'
Companion, 2:101-103.
A biographical sketch of Wordsworth and Dorothy. She did
not sacrifice herself to him in vain. Reprinted in Some
Eminent Women of Our Times (1889).

17 GRAVES, THE REV. R.[OBERT] P.[ERCEVAL]. "Coleridge's Opium-
Eating." Athenaeum, no. 3143 (21 January), pp. 85-86.
Records Wordsworth's conversation about Coleridge's
bodily pain in 1797-98.

1888

18   HALES, JOHN W. "Victorian Literature." Gentleman's Magazine,
       264 (April), 400-14 (402-404); (May), 460-74 (465).
         Wordsworth's reputation might have been greater had he
       kept silent the last half of his life. Yet for the early
       Victorians he was a great deliverer and high priest (402-
       404). He helped awaken the sense of brotherhood that dis-
       tinguishes the Victorian age (465). Reprinted in Folia
       Litteraria (1893).

19   HAMILTON, WALTER. "William Wordsworth," in Parodies of the
       Works of English and American Authors. 6 vols. London:
       Reeves & Turner, V:88-106.
        It seems unlikely that Mary Hutchinson contributed a
       stanza to "She dwelt among the untrodden ways." Reprints
       parodies of Wordsworth, including the following poems the
       previous printings of which have not been located: "The
       Trustee" (parody of "We Are Seven"), "A Simple Lay"
       (parody of "We Are Seven"), "More Than Seven" (signed A.
       St. J. A.; parody of "We Are Seven"), "We Are One" (parody
       of "We Are Seven"), "The M.A. Degree" (parody of "She was
       a Phantom of delight"), "Cuckoo Notes" (signed F. B. Dove-
       ton; parody of "To the Cuckoo" ["O blithe New-comer! I
       have heard"]), "What Women make of Man" (signed Wm. E.
       Doubleday; parody of "Lines Written in Early Spring"), and
       "An American Parody" ("Scorn not the meerschaum, Housewives,
       you have croaked") (parody of "Scorn not the Sonnet; Critic,
       you have frowned").

20   [HUTTON, RICHARD HOLT]. "Mr. Morley on Wordsworth."
       Spectator, 61 (22 December), 1807-1808.
        Where Wordsworth becomes didactic, his poetry falls off.
       He expresses the highest passion, a rapture that exalts him
       into lofty regions.

21   [HUTTON, RICHARD HOLT]. "Wordsworth." Spectator, 61
       (29 December), 1852-53.
        The Recluse contains too many of Wordsworth's typical
       "little egotistic condescensions," yet expresses his "un-
       fathomable joy in Nature."

22   KNIGHT, WILLIAM. "Preface," "Notes," in Selections from
       Wordsworth. Edited by William Knight and Other Members of
       the Wordsworth Society. London: Kegan Paul, Trench,
       pp. v-xv, 305-309.
        The masses do not know Wordsworth. His "elevating and
       tranquillising" influence is especially needed now. His
       poems are best read chronologically, as opposed to being
       read as Wordsworth himself or Arnold classifies them. Re-
       views editions of selections from Wordsworth already

published; quotes letters from Browning revealing his admiration for Wordsworth's earlier poems (v-xv). Brief
critical notes to the poems selected, including "A Poet's
Epitaph," "A Complaint," "Even as a dragon's eye that feels
the stress," "Scorn not the Sonnet; Critic, you have
frowned" (305-309).

23 KNIGHT, WILLIAM. Principal Shairp and His Friends. London:
    Murray, pp. 11-12, 33, 47-48, 66, 155-56, 204, 226-29, 282,
    421-22.
        Includes Shairp's tribute, in his poem "Retrospect," to
    Wordsworth's revealing of the unexpected beauty in the
    world. Records Shairp's admiration and opinions of Words-
    worth: Wordsworth's pantheism is unconscious; though his
    poems could contain more of Christianity, they do evidence
    Wordsworth's charity. Includes Shadworth Hodgson's and
    John Veitch's recollections of Shairp's appreciation of
    Wordsworth, and Vernon Lushington's tribute to Wordsworth's
    tying of nature to man and his feelings for domestic affec-
    tions and the humble.

24 LINTON, E.[LIZA] LYNN. "The Irresponsibilities of Genius."
    Fortnightly Review, NS 44 (1 October), 521-36 (526-27,
    529).
        Wordsworth stands midway between Coleridge's irresponsi-
    bility and Southey's industry. Wordsworth did nothing base
    if nothing heroic. He held himself apart from Southey.

25 M., A. J. "Wordsworth: 'Vagrant Reed.'" Notes and Queries,
    7th ser., 5 (14 January), 34.
        Interprets "The Resting-place."

26 MINTO, WILLIAM. "William Wordsworth," in The Encyclopaedia
    Britannica: A Dictionary of Arts, Sciences, and General
    Literature. Ninth edition. 24 vols. Edinburgh: Black,
    XXIV:668-76.
        A biographical sketch. Poetically, "The Idiot Boy" is
    a success. Coleridge's criticism of the Preface to Lyrical
    Ballads is based on false assumptions. Wordsworth's poems
    do correspond to his poetic theories. His best poems were
    written in breaks of excitement from his normal quiet life.
    The early, just criticism of The Excursion helped deaden
    Wordsworth's poetic powers.

27 MORLEY, JOHN. "Introduction," in The Complete Poetical Works
    of William Wordsworth. London and New York: Macmillan,
    pp. xlix-lxv.
        A biographical sketch. During the political and social
    tumult and the artistic activity of the first half of the

century, Wordsworth lived sequestered. The Prelude lacks a "sympathetic quality"; yet, contrary to Macaulay's opinion, Wordsworth's description of his life, especially connected with the French Revolution, is sincere and impressive. After Waterloo, Wordsworth's grasp of social issues--and hence the glow of his poetry--failed; his church pieces are ecclesiastical, not religious. His achievement lay in advocating simplification without also advocating, as Byron did, the destruction of the traditional social order. Much of Wordsworth's writing is not poetical: it is too deliberately didactic, prolix, and solemn, and lacks sweetness and spontaneity. His greatness lies in "his direct appeal to will and conduct" (though his poems, especially "Ode: Intimations of Immortality," do not contain a system of philosophy), and in his insight into the natural world (though he was blind to its cruelties and to the ugliness painted by Millet). Though "deficient in clear beauty of form and in concentrated power," Wordsworth has the power to effect quietness and strength of purpose in the reader.

28 MOUNT, C. B. "Wordsworth: 'Vagrant Reed.'" Notes and Queries, 7th ser., 5 (11 February), 115.
    A reply to 1888.B25. Interprets "The Resting-place."

29 NORTON, CHARLES ELIOT, ed. Letters of Thomas Carlyle 1826–1836. 2 vols. London and New York: Macmillan, II:296-97, 305-306.
    Adds to correspondence previously published letters in which Carlyle records his mixed impressions of Wordsworth in 1835.

30 [OLIPHANT, MARGARET and ALEXANDER ALLARDYCE]. "The Old Saloon." Blackwood's Edinburgh Magazine, 143 (June), 831-52 (832-34).
    Wordsworth now receives a little less personal devotion than he did earlier in the century. His criticism of Byron and his image as it emerges in 1888.B15 are distasteful.

31 OVERTON, JOHN HENRY and ELIZABETH WORDSWORTH. Christopher Wordsworth: Bishop of Lincoln 1807-1885. Illustrated. London: Rivingtons, pp. 2-3, 9, 38, 46, 58-68, 72, 77-78, 126-27, 130, 400-402, 493-94.
    Records Christopher Wordsworth's intercourse with the Wordsworths. Includes letters in which Priscilla Lloyd Wordsworth notes the fortitude of the Wordsworth family in the face of sorrow, and Christopher Wordsworth urges Wordsworth in 1849 to write about the Reformation. Includes

1888

entries from his journal in which Christopher Wordsworth
records Wordsworth's efforts to republish his poems in
1825.

32 P.[AIN], B.[ARRY] E. O. "The Poets at Tea" (poem). Cambridge
    Fortnightly, 1 (7 February), 6-8 (7).
        Includes parody of "We Are Seven." Reprinted in Play-
    things and Parodies (1892).

33 PALGRAVE, FRANCIS T. "Preface," in Glen Desseray and Other
    Poems Lyrical and Elegiac. By John Campbell Shairp.
    Edited by Francis T. Palgrave. London and New York:
    Macmillan, pp. vii-xxii (viii, xiii-xvii, xix).
        Compares Shairp's lyrics with Wordsworth's: Wordsworth
    saw his own thoughts and emotions mirrored in nature; he
    has "an impersonal personality"; dalesmen are rarely part
    of his landscape.

34 PATER, WALTER. "Style." Fortnightly Review, NS 44 (December),
    728-43 (728-29, 732).
        "The range of the poetic force in literature was effec-
    tively enlarged by Wordsworth." Reprinted in 1889.B49.

35 [PROTHERO, ROWLAND]. Review of Bowen's Virgil in English
    Verse. Edinburgh Review, 167 (April), 448-81 (460).
        Wordsworth abandoned in despair his attempt to translate
    the Aeneid.

36 [PROTHERO, ROWLAND]. Review of Arnold's The Strayed Reveller,
    etc. Edinburgh Review, 168 (October), 337-73 (344, 347-48,
    358, 362, 370-71).
        Arnold was both indebted to, and differed from, Words-
    worth's attitudes towards poetry, man, and nature. Words-
    worth devoted himself to self-cultivation.

37 [RAWNSLEY, HARDWICKE DRUMMOND]. "A Coach Drive at the Lakes."
    Cornhill Magazine, NS 11 (September), 255-70; (October),
    390-404; (November), 483-98.
        Points out places in the Lake District associated with
    Wordsworth's life and poems. Recalls Wordsworth's clutching
    at a gate, to be assured of reality, to illustrate his mean-
    ing in "Ode: Intimations of Immortality." Expanded in
    1890.B39.

38 RUSSELL, CONSTANCE. "Wordsworth: 'Vagrant Reed.'" Notes
    and Queries, 7th ser., 5 (14 January), 34; (10 March), 197.
        Replies to 1887.B12, B17 concerning "The Resting-place."

341

1888

39   SANDFORD, MRS. HENRY. Thomas Poole and his Friends. 2 vols.
     London and New York: Macmillan, passim.
          Discusses Poole's and Coleridge's life with, and cor-
     respondence about, Wordsworth.

40   [SHORTER, CLEMENT KING]. "Wordsworth, William," in The
     National Encyclopaedia: A Dictionary of Universal
     Knowledge. By Writers of Eminence in Literature, Science,
     and Art. 14 vols. London, Edinburgh, and Glasgow:
     Mackenzie [1888], XIV:468-70.
          Revised and expanded from 1868.B4. A biographical
     sketch. When Wordsworth lost his enthusiasm for human
     progress, his poetry declined; yet his later conservatism
     is partially valid. He opposed eighteenth-century poets in
     simplicity and spirituality. He is a poet of humanity. In-
     cludes secondary bibliography. Attribution: W. Knight in
     1896.B36, VIII:359.

41   SWEET, HENRY. Shelley's Nature-Poetry. London: privately
     printed, pp. 8-9, 19, 22-24, 29, 35.
          Shelley is a poet of nature more than Wordsworth, a poet
     of "the common-place in nature as in man" who bullies na-
     ture and man to suit his moral lessons.

42   [TRENCH, MARIA, ed.]. Richard Chenevix Trench Archbishop:
     Letters and Memorials. Edited by the Author of "Charles
     Lowder." 2 vols. London: Kegal Paul, Trench, I:8-10,
     186, 216, 221, 235; II:30, 216.
          Includes letters in which John Sterling remarks that
     Wordsworth's conversation, as opposed to Coleridge's,
     springs from his immediate circumstances and that Words-
     worth's range is narrow; in which Christopher Wordsworth
     (Bishop of Lincoln) notes Wordsworth's tenacity in pursuing
     any poetic labor; in which R. C. Trench records his friend-
     ship with Wordsworth; and in which the Rev. W. H. Thompson
     declares Wordsworth "a half-despairing penitent."

43   TUTIN, J.[OHN] R.[AMSDEN]. "The Bibliography of Wordsworth,"
     in The Complete Poetical Works of William Wordsworth.
     Introduction by John Morley. London and New York:
     Macmillan, pp. 897-912.
          A primary and secondary bibliography.

44   TYRER, C. E. "A Note on Mr. William Watson's 'Wordsworth's
     Grave.'" Manchester Quarterly, 7 (October), 380-87.
          Compares Watson's poem with Arnold's "Memorial Verses:
     April 27, 1850." Wordsworth is not the poet of nature
     divorced from man.

45   [VERNON, THE REV. JOHN RICHARD]. "The Cradle of the Lake
      Poets: By the Author of 'The Harvest of a Quiet Eye' Etc."
      Leisure Hour, 37:585-90; 663-68.
          It is now difficult to realize the personal bitterness
      Wordsworth faced when he exchanged "artificiality for real
      human beings, and . . . fresh English scenery." Describes
      the Quantock hills and Alfoxden. Attribution: Dictionary
      of Anonymous and Pseudonymous Literature (Samuel Halkett
      and John Laing), new ed., 9 vols. (Edinburgh: Oliver and
      Boyd, 1926-62), III:14.

1889 A BOOKS

1   KNIGHT, WILLIAM. The Life of William Wordsworth. 3 vols.
      Edinburgh: Paterson, 429 pp., 437 pp., 535 pp.
          A full biography. Includes letters in which Coleridge
      notes Wordsworth's happiness despite "occasional fits of
      hypochondriacal uncomfortableness," praises Wordsworth as
      a philosophic poet, discusses his quarrel with Wordsworth
      and his disappointment with The Excursion and Wordsworth's
      translation of Vergil; in which Southey complains that
      Wordsworth finds subjects for philosophizing in every vaga-
      bond he meets; in which A. de Vere objects to Wordsworth's
      classifying of his poems and discusses their meditative
      unity; in which Talfourd, Gladstone, and others discuss the
      copyright bill; in which Gladstone recalls Wordsworth's
      "freedom from the worldly type"; in which Mrs. Thomas
      Arnold notes the Wordsworths's happiness in old age; in
      which Christopher Wordsworth, J. C. Hare, and Adam Sedgwick
      commend "Ode on the Installation of His Royal Highness
      Prince Albert"; and in which Mrs. Davy gives details of
      Wordsworth's death. Includes letters and journals in which
      Dorothy and Mary Wordsworth and H. C. Robinson comment upon
      Wordsworth's life, tours, and poems. Includes extracts
      from Barron Field's memoirs of Wordsworth, Ellis Yarnall's
      reminiscences, and separate essays by Knight on "Words-
      worth's View of Education and Its Methods" and "On the
      Portraits of Wordsworth" (expanded from 1889.B38).

1889 B SHORTER WRITINGS

1   ADAMS, WILLIAM DAVENPORT. "Poetic Eccentrics," "The Married
      Muse," in Rambles in Book-land: Short Essays on Literary
      Subjects. London: Stock, pp. 112-19 (112-13), 170-78
      (175-76).
          Even Wordsworth could give poems ridiculously long
      titles (112-13). He was fortunate in marriage (175-76).

1889

2   AINGER, ALFRED. "Nether Stowey." Macmillan's Magazine, 59
    (February), 254-63.
        Recounts Wordsworth's and Coleridge's lives and writing
    in the west of England.

3   ANON. Review of Memorials of Coleorton (ed. Knight) and
    Brandl's Samuel Taylor Coleridge. Church Quarterly Review,
    27 (January), 316-31 (317, 322-23, 327).
        One respects Wordsworth for his purity of life. He was
    "pious, unselfish, truly Christian and orthodox."

4   ANON. Review of The Complete Poetical Works of William
    Wordsworth (intro. Morley) and The Recluse. Literary
    World (London), NS 39 (11 January), 28.
        Though The Recluse will not add to Wordsworth's reputa-
    tion, it does contain fine short passages.

5   ANON. "The Recluse." Saturday Review, 67 (12 January),
    43-44.
        Wordsworth's blank verse in The Recluse is magnificent,
    though not the language of ordinary life.

6   ANON. "Mr. J. Morley on Wordsworth." Christian World and
    News of the Week, 33 (17 January), 51.
        Wordsworth is often too prosy and mystical; yet his high
    moral purpose and belief in the ethical influence of nature
    lie at the heart of his greatness.

7   ANON. Review of The Recluse. Murray's Magazine, 5
    (February), 285.
        As does all Wordsworth's verse, The Recluse contains
    passages both tedious and splendid.

8   ANON. Review of Wordsworthiana. Athenaeum, no. 3200
    (23 February), pp. 237-38.
        Reports humorous retort by Wordsworth, his efforts to
    make his poems easy to understand, and his political preju-
    dices during a visit to Durham.

9   ANON. "A Modern Poetic Seer." Christian World and News of
    the Week, 33 (28 February), 171.
        Wordsworth's healing and calming power arises from his
    faith in God.

10 ANON. "A Recollection of Wordsworth." Leisure Hour, 38
    [April], 285.
        Relates incident, from a letter of Mrs. S. C. Hall, of
    Wordsworth telling M. J. Jewsbury of his laboring over his
    poems.

11 ANON. Review of Knight's The Life of William Wordsworth.
Athenaeum, no. 3215 (8 June), 719-21.
No one can understand Wordsworth's poetry without know-
ing the circumstances under which it was written. Wordsworth "was much more lovable and loving than is usually
supposed."

12 ANON. "The Life of William Wordsworth." Saturday Review, 67
(15 June), 732-33.
Wordsworth the Poet (lofty, inspired) and the Man (narrow, conceited, dogmatic) "were constantly thwarting and
overlapping each other." Wordsworth became a timid aristo-
crat who "did not present his later ideas more pleasingly
than his earlier fanaticisms."

13 ANON. "Professor Knight's Life of Wordsworth." Spectator,
63 (3 August), 143-44.
Wordsworth responded to Shelley's criticism in a "good-
tempered way." He spoke even when he knew nothing of his
subject. His zeal for the Church of England is suspect.
He was warm-hearted, not a self-contained prig.

14 ANON. "Tourists in Scotland Before Scott: Dorothy
Wordsworth." Scots Observer, 2 (21 September), 489-90.
Describes D. Wordsworth's influence on Wordsworth and
their tour in Scotland in 1803: the tour illustrates
Wordsworth's tenacity.

15 ANON. "The Poet and the Philosopher in the Lake District."
Eagle: A Magazine Supported by Members of St John's
College, 16 (December), 34-44.
Jocularly recalls Wordsworth's associations with scenes
in the Lake District.

16 ANON. "Memoir," in The Poetical Works of William Wordsworth.
8 vols. Glasgow: Bryce [1889], I:ix-xxii.
A biographical sketch. Wordsworth constantly strove
after perfection in literary form.

17 B., C. C. "Wordsworth's 'Ode on the Intimations of
Immortality.'" Notes and Queries, 7th ser., 7 (6 April),
278; (25 May), 417; 8 (9 November), 370.
Interprets lines in "Ode: Intimations of Immortality"
(278, 417, 370). Replies to 1889.B31 (417, 370). (A reply
to A. L. Mayhew, "Wordsworth's 'Ode on Intimations of Immortality,'" Notes and Queries, 7th ser., 7 [2 March],
168.)

1889

18   B., C. C. "Wordsworth." Notes and Queries, 7th ser., 7
     (8 June), 458.
         Traces Wordsworth's acquaintance with Keats.

19   B., C. C. "Osmunda." Notes and Queries, 7th ser., 8
     (3 August), 87.
         Suggests identity of Queen Osmunda in "A narrow girdle
     of rough stones and crags." (See replies by J. F. Mansergh
     and Ed. Marshall, "Osmunda," Notes and Queries, 7th ser., 8
     [28 September], 251-52.)

20   B., W. "Wordsworth's 'Ode on the Intimations of Immortality.'"
     Notes and Queries, 7th ser., 8 (9 November), 370.
         Interprets line in "Ode: Intimations of Immortality."

21   BIRDWOOD, GEORGE. "Wordsworth." Athenaeum, no. 3201
     (2 March), p. 281.
         Reports interviews that support Rawnsley's evidence in
     1884.B23.

22   BOUCHIER, JONATHAN. "Wordsworth." Notes and Queries,
     7th ser., 7 (18 May), 397-98.
         Traces Wordsworth's acquaintance with Keats.

23   BOYCE, ANNE OGDEN. Records of a Quaker Family: The
     Richardsons of Cleveland. . . . London: Harris, pp. 31,
     44, 80.
         Records Wordsworth's friendship with Thomas Wilkinson
     and the Richardsons' sympathy with Wordsworth's poetry.

24   CLAYDEN, P.[ETER] W. Rogers and His Contemporaries. 2 vols.
     London: Smith, Elder, passim.
         Records Wordsworth's intercourse with Rogers, including
     the tour in Scotland in 1803, Rogers's visits with Words-
     worth in 1812, 1816, 1826, 1834, and Wordsworth's trips to
     London. Recounts Rogers's efforts to procure Wordsworth
     a publisher.

25   COURTHOPE, WILLIAM JOHN. The Life of Alexander Pope. London:
     Murray, pp. 370-75.
         Wordsworth's theories in the Preface to Lyrical Ballads,
     indebted to Rousseau and seventeenth-century poets, are
     radically opposed to Pope's. Wordsworth's poems do not
     satisfy Coleridge's definition of a poem. His criticism of
     Pope's diction is unjust; because he was a recluse, his own
     diction is removed from spoken language. (Also issued as
     Volume V of The Works of Alexander Pope, new edition, edited
     by Whitwell Elwin and William John Courthope.)

26   CROSSE, CORNELIA A. H. [MRS. ANDREW]. "Thomas Poole."
      Temple Bar, 87 (November), 354-70 (361-63, 366-67).
      Wordsworth's early poems show the influence of Quantock
      scenery. Records Wordsworth's life in the west of England.
      Reprinted in 1892.B11.

27   DENNIS, JOHN. "Dorothy Wordsworth." Leisure Hour, 39
      [December], 121-25.
      A biographical sketch of Dorothy Wordsworth and her life
      with Wordsworth.

28   DOWDEN, EDWARD. Review of The Recluse and The Complete
      Poetical Works of William Wordsworth (intro. Morley).
      Academy, 35 (12 January), 17-18.
      Wordsworth's poems should be presented as he arranged
      them, with a chronological table.

29   DOWDEN, EDWARD. Review of Wordsworthiana. Academy, 35
      (6 April), 229-30.
      Notes existence of a portrait of Wordsworth by Jane
      Pasley. Wordsworth's distinction is that he combines an
      appeal to conduct with a sense of joy.

30   DOWDEN, EDWARD. "Coleridge as Poet." Fortnightly Review,
      NS 46 (1 September), 342-66 (344, 346-48, 354-58, 364).
      Wordsworth's poems deal with the men and women among
      whom he dwelt. Wordsworth's and Coleridge's contribution
      in Lyrical Ballads (1798) was the combining of the two
      strains then powerful in literature: realism and romance.
      Reprinted in New Studies (1895).

31   EWING, THOMAS J. "Wordsworth's 'Ode on Intimations of
      Immortality.'" Notes and Queries, 7th ser., 7 (4 May),
      357; 8 (3 August), 89-91.
      Replies to 1889.B17, B65 (357), and to 1889.B41 (89-91).
      Interprets lines from "Ode: Intimations of Immortality."

32   G., S. G. "William Wordsworth." Leisure Hour, 38
      [August], 519-27.
      The Recluse is interesting as indicating the scenes that
      formed Wordsworth's lifelong purposes. Wordsworth's beliefs
      are distinct from pantheism and the "pathetic fallacy."
      His "healing power" comes from a study of ideal humanity
      rather than from a knowledge of the wants and sorrows of
      the actual world. His popularity is hindered by his lack
      of a sense of the ludicrous and failure to be more com-
      pletely Christian.

1889

33 GRAVES, ROBERT PERCEVAL. Life of Sir William Rowan Hamil-
      ton. . . . 3 vols. Dublin: Hodges, Figgis; London:
      Longmans, III:passim.
          Records Hamilton's and A. de Vere's correspondence about
      Wordsworth: Wordsworth claimed to be a descendant of
      Alfred, admired Burns and Tennyson. For Volume I, see
      1882.B22; for Volume II, see 1885.B24.

34 GRESWELL, W.[ILLIAM] H. "A Poet's Corner." National Review,
      12 (February), 807-17 (809-17).
          Joy and sympathy with poor humanity were the keynotes of
      Wordsworth's life in the west of England. He can teach us
      philanthropy.

35 GRESWELL, WILLIAM. "Wordsworth and the Quantock Hills."
      National Review, 14 (September), 67-83.
          Wordsworth's life in the west of England, with Dorothy
      and Coleridge, is more interesting than that in the north.
      Wordsworth's early poems foreshadow his later ones.

36 HOWITT, MARGARET, ed. Mary Howitt: An Autobiography.
      Edited by her Daughter. 2 vols. London: Isbister,
      I:111, 174, 196-97, 221, 224-25, 243, 254-55, 267; II:32-33.
          Records Mary and William Howitt's admiration for Words-
      worth, during his visit in 1831, and his poems. Wordsworth
      has helped to bring about the social changes he now dreads
      in his latter days. Records William Howitt's visit to
      Wordsworth in 1845: Wordsworth's attacking slavery in
      America.

37 [HUTTON, RICHARD HOLT]. Review of Wordsworthiana. Spectator,
      62 (16 March), 369-70.
          Cowper prepared the way for Wordsworth's revolutionary
      poems.

38 KNIGHT, WILLIAM. "Preface," "On the Portraits of Wordsworth,"
      in Wordsworthiana: A Selection from Papers Read to The
      Wordsworth Society. Edited by William Knight. London and
      New York: Macmillan, pp. v-xxi, 29-60.
          Gives a record of the meetings of the Wordsworth Society
      (v-xxi). Expanded from 1882.B39; expanded again in
      1889.A1 (29-60).

39 LANG, ANDREW. "Introductory: Of Modern English Poetry,"
      "Appendix I: Reynolds's Peter Bell," in Letters on
      Literature. London and New York: Longmans, pp. 1-14 (5,
      12-13), 195-98 (195-96).

Reprinted from 1886.B31 (5, 12-13). Wordsworth in 1819 was not yet "a kind of solemn shade . . . , chanting the swan song of the dying England" (195-96).

40   LOW, W.[ALTER] H.[UMBOLDT] and A. J. WYATT. The Intermediate Text-book of English Literature. Part II (from 1660 to 1832). London: Clive [1889], especially pp. 127, 202-13, 227.
     A biographical sketch. Wordsworth's sonnets are remarkable. Wordsworth cleansed poetic diction and extended the range of poetic subjects. He offers moral and spiritual consolation. He contrasts with Shelley.

41   M., A. J. "Wordsworth's 'Ode on the Intimations of Immortality.'" Notes and Queries, 7th ser., 7 (25 May), 416-17.
     A reply to 1889.B31, B62. Interprets line in "Ode: Intimations of Immortality."

42   M., C. "Wordsworth and Shelley." Notes and Queries, 7th ser., 7 (25 May), 417.
     Notes Wordsworth's revisions to Peter Bell.

43   M'CORMICK, WILLIAM S. "Preface," "Wordsworth," in Three Lectures on English Literature. Paisley and London: Gardner, pp. 5-8, 63-122.
     Wordsworth and R. Browning illustrate, respectively, the contemplative and penetrative imagination; in the poetry of both, transcendentalism is mingled with bare realism (5-8). Wordsworth's poetry is reflective; much of it, elaborating a philosophical system based on the communion of man and nature, should have been written in prose. In his later works, as opposed to "Tintern Abbey," he consciously lapses into description. In "Ode: Intimations of Immortality" his subject is "our own idealised memories"; hence Arnold misunderstands the poem. Wordsworth's portraits of women give not insight into character but a pure ideal. "The Idiot Boy" fails not because of Wordsworth's use of words but because of his imaginative conception. Wordsworth falsely limits his ideals to rustics. Because he addresses the understanding through the heart, he is difficult to understand and not popular (63-122).

44   MALLESON, W. T. "Shelley and Wordsworth." Spectator, 63 (14 September), 334.
     A reply to 1889.B13. Most of Shelley's writings attack rather than praise Wordsworth.

1889

45   MASSON, DAVID. Editorial Prefaces and Notes, in The Collected
      Writings of Thomas De Quincey. New and enlarged edition.
      Edited by David Masson. 14 vols. Edinburgh: Black,
      II:4-6, 136-37, passim.
         Wordsworth, "with his massive serenity," tossed aside
      De Quincey's criticisms. Wordsworth's feeling for Burns
      was "enthusiastic." Includes explanatory notes to De Quin-
      cey's writings about Wordsworth throughout the volume. For
      Volumes III-XIV, see 1890.B34.

46   MINTO, WILLIAM. "Wordsworth's Great Failure." Nineteenth
      Century, 26 (September), 435-51.
         The publication of The Recluse has aroused little inter-
      est; people are not prepared to see Wordsworth's life as
      one of unfulfilled ambition. The project of The Recluse
      gives unity and dramatic interest to Wordsworth's career.
      "Home at Grasmere" is the buoyant expression of Wordsworth's
      prime. In The Excursion Wordsworth does not present a
      philosophy. He found his true expression in his lyrics,
      though even here he did not fulfill his ambition of being
      a poet of men rather than of nature. His returning to The
      Recluse after 1807 led to his poetic decline. He wrote his
      best when not in rural seclusion.

47   [PATER, WALTER]. Review of The Complete Poetical Works of
      William Wordsworth (intro. Morley), The Recluse, and
      Selections from Wordsworth (ed. Knight et al.). Athenaeum,
      no. 3196 (26 January), pp. 109-10.
         Adapted from 1874.B36. The study of Wordsworth, with
      his sense of a life in natural objects, is needed "to cor-
      rect the faults of our bustling age." Recast as "Words-
      worth" in 1889.B49.

48   [PATER, WALTER]. Review of The Complete Poetical Works of
      William Wordsworth (intro. Morley), The Recluse, and
      Selections from Wordsworth (ed. Knight et al.). Guardian,
      no. 2256 (27 February), pp. 317-18.
         Adapted from 1874.B36 and 1889.B47. Recast as "Words-
      worth" in 1889.B49. Reprinted as "Wordsworth" in Essays
      from The "Guardian" (1896).

49   PATER, WALTER. "Style," "Wordsworth," "Coleridge," in
      Appreciations: With an Essay on Style. London and
      New York: Macmillan, pp. 1-36 (2-4, 12), 37-63, 64-106
      (83-96).
         Reprinted from 1888.B34 (2-4, 12). Combines 1874.B36
      and 1889.B47-B48 (37-63). Combines 1866.B12 and 1880.B34
      (83-96).

50 PRIDEAUX, W. F. "Wordsworth's 'Ode on the Intimations of
    Immortality.'" Notes and Queries, 7th ser., 8
    (9 November), 369.
        Notes parallel to line in "Ode: Intimations of Immor-
    tality."

51 [PROTHERO, ROWLAND]. Review of The Recluse, The Complete
    Poetical Works of William Wordsworth (intro. Morley), and
    Wordsworthiana. Edinburgh Review, 169 (April), 415-47.
        Wordsworth's own arrangement of his poems is "far-
    fetched." Wordsworth has succeeded in reaching an audience.
    His poetry, often uneven, is a protest against utilitarian-
    ism. He did not destroy the conventions of the followers
    of Pope; he unites eighteenth century and Revolutionary po-
    etic qualities. In his moral statements, he tries to recon-
    cile experience with ideal truths. The sense of the dignity
    of man and the moral kinship between man and nature forms
    the core of his ethical teaching, as illustrated especially
    in The Prelude and The Recluse.

52 [RAWNSLEY, HARDWICKE DRUMMOND]. "The Duddon Vale as It Is
    and Is To Be." Cornhill Magazine, NS 13 (August), 151-63
    (152-55, 161-63).
        Describes Wordsworth's visits to the Duddon; Wordsworth's
    sonnets act as a guide.

53 ROBERTSON, JOHN M.[ACKINNON]. "Science in Criticism," "The
    Art of Tennyson," in Essays toward a Critical Method.
    London: Unwin, pp. 1-148 (36-37, 147), 233-82 (244,
    254-55, 264, 269, 271).
        Wordsworth's prose criticisms are more creative than
    nine-tenths of his verse (36-37, 147). Reprinted from
    1887.B45 (244, 254-55, 264, 269, 271).

54 S., M. "Wordsworth's Sense of Fate." Spectator, 62
    (5 January), 15.
        A reply to 1888.B20. Wordsworth did have a sense of
    fate.

55 SAINTSBURY, GEORGE. "George Crabbe." Macmillan's Magazine,
    60 (June), 99-110 (99-100, 105, 108).
        Notes Wordsworth praise of Crabbe. Though he can write
    doggerel and platitudes, Wordsworth can also write musical
    lines. Reprinted with minor revision in Essays in English
    Literature 1780-1860 (1890).

56 SHAIRP, JOHN CAMPBELL. "Norman Macleod," in Portraits of
    Friends. . . . Boston and New York: Houghton, Mifflin,
    pp. 149-68 (152-54).

Recalls his and Macleod's study of Wordsworth at a time when he was little appreciated in Glasgow.

57   SMITH, G. C. M. "Wordsworth's 'Recluse.'" Academy, 35 (9 March), 167-68.
Objects to entitling the poem The Recluse.

58   S.[MITH], G. C. M. Review of The Recluse. Eagle: A Magazine Supported by Members of St John's College, 15 (June), 461-68.
Wordsworth uses memory "to lighten the dark hours of life and to connect the parts of life into an harmonious whole." He was sustained by a spring of inner happiness.

59   [STORY, WILLIAM WETMORE]. "Recent Conversations in a Studio." Blackwood's Edinburgh Magazine, 145 (May), 591-616 (601).
Notes similarity between "Elegiac Stanzas Suggested by a Picture of Peele Castle" and Shelley's "Evening: Ponte al Mare, Pisa."

60   [STORY, WILLIAM WETMORE]. "Recent Conversations in a Studio." Blackwood's Edinburgh Magazine, 146 (September), 381-407 (383-84).
Landor's image of the shell is not followed by reflection, as is Wordsworth's use of it in The Excursion. Reports conversations in which Landor criticizes Wordsworth and Wordsworth criticizes Byron.

61   [STRACHEY, EDWARD]. Review of Marci Tullii Ciceronis Cato Major and Tennyson's Works. Quarterly Review, 169 (July), 42-71 (64-65, 68, 70).
Wordsworth errs in expressing the regrets of old age in "The Fountain."

62   ST. SWITHIN. "Wordsworth's 'Ode on Intimations of Immortality.'" Notes and Queries, 7th ser., 7 (4 May), 357.
Interprets line in "Ode: Intimations of Immortality."

63   [STUART, MARY, ed.]. Letters from the Lake Poets, Samuel Taylor Coleridge, William Wordsworth, Robert Southey, to Daniel Stuart, Editor of the Morning Post and The Courier, 1800-1838. London: privately printed, passim.
Records William Erskine's opinion that Wordsworth's letters reveal him unacquainted with the trading world. Includes letters to Stuart in which Coleridge discusses Wordsworth's health, Stuart's interest in Lyrical Ballads, the production of The Borderers, the publication of Concerning . . . the Convention of Cintra, and Wordsworth's

contributions to the Friend; and in which Southey records
Wordsworth's views on Austria in 1814. Attribution:
British Museum catalogue.

64 SYMONDS, JOHN ADDINGTON. "A Comparison of Elizabethan with
Victorian Poetry." Fortnightly Review, NS 45 (1 January),
55-79 (60, 63-64, 68, 70, 75-77).
Wordsworth participated in the return to Elizabethanism
that has marked Victorian poetry. His lyrics may not, perhaps, be sung. Reprinted in 1890.B45.

65 TERRY, F. C. BIRKBECK. "Wordsworth's 'Ode on the Intimations
of Immortality.'" Notes and Queries, 7th ser., 7
(6 April), 278.
Interprets line in "Ode: Intimations of Immortality."

66 WARD, C. A. "Coleridge." Notes and Queries, 7th ser., 8
(3 August), 89.
Chastises Wordsworth for putting on the appearance of
understanding Coleridge's conversation.

67 WARD, C. A. "Wordsworth's 'Ode on the Intimations of
Immortality.'" Notes and Queries, 7th ser., 8
(9 November), 369-70.
A reply to 1889.B31. Interprets line in "Ode: Intimations of Immortality."

68 WATSON, WILLIAM. "Dr. Johnson on Modern Poetry." National
Review, 13 (July), 593-604 (594-96).
Wordsworth's range is as narrow as his subjects are un-
edifying. Wordsworth is credited with being a great conversationalist. Reprinted in Excursions in Criticism
(1893).

69 WRIGHT, J.[OHN] C.[HARLES]. Outline of English Literature.
Manchester and London: Heywood, pp. 113-20.
A biographical sketch. The Excursion, though dull,
teaches brotherhood.

70 WRIGHT, WILLIAM ALDIS, ed. Letters and Literary Remains of
Edward Fitzgerald. 3 vols. London and New York:
Macmillan, I:15, 17, 30-31, 70, 73, 381-86, 451, 454, 468,
471.
Includes letters in which Fitzgerald comments that Wordsworth's philosophy connects melancholy with humanity, criticizes the sonnets of "Daddy Wordsworth," recalls Wordsworth's
reputation at Cambridge and his opinion of Scott and
Crabbe, and notes that Wordsworth made little of his inspiration.

1890

1890 A BOOKS

1 ANON. Wordsworth in 1798. Bristol: George's Sons, [4] pp.
An advertisement for a portrait of Wordsworth by W.
Shuter.

2 BROOKE, STOPFORD A. Dove Cottage: Wordsworth's Home from
1800-1808: December 21, 1799 to May --, 1808. London and
New York: Macmillan, 75 pp.
Recalls Wordsworth's associations with Grasmere and Dove
Cottage, and describes scheme to purchase the cottage.
Wordsworth's life there proves the value of a poor, simple
existence.

3 DAVEY, SIR HORACE. Wordsworth: An Address Read to the
Stockton Literary and Philosophical Society, on January 8th,
1890. Stockton-on-Tees: privately printed, 24 pp.
A biographical sketch. "To Wordsworth nature was the
giver and creator, not the recipient" of man's thoughts.
Wordsworth was also the poet of man.

1890 B SHORTER WRITINGS

1 ANON. "A New Wordsworth." Scots Observer, 3 (25 January),
272-73.
The arid flats in Wordsworth's verse are interminable.

2 ANON. Review of Lyrical Ballads (ed. Dowden). Athenaeum,
no. 3263 (10 May), pp. 599-600.
Only by studying the poems as a group can one grasp the
full significance of Lyrical Ballads. Dorothy gave Wordsworth and Coleridge eyes and ears. All things considered,
the initial publication of the poems did not fare badly.

3 ANON. "A Classic Stream." Scots Observer, 4 (30 August),
385-86.
"Without the true Wordsworthian drunkenness," one cannot
appreciate the Yarrow poems.

4 ANON. "In Wordsworth's Footsteps." Spectator, 65
(1 November), 596-97.
Wordsworth shows only a casual knowledge of Wharfdale
in "The Force of Prayer." He at one time did lapse into
scepticism.

1890

5   ANON. "Wordsworth, William," in <u>Blackie's Modern Cyclopedia
     of Useful Information</u>. Edited by Charles Annandale.
     8 vols. London, Glasgow, Edinburgh, and Dublin: Blackie,
     VIII:482.
          A biographical sketch.

6   AUSTIN, ALFRED. "Wordsworth at Dove Cottage" (poem).
     <u>Spectator</u>, 64 (14 June), 833-34.
          Wordsworth was wise to avert his ken from the bustle of
     men to his humble life with Mary and Dorothy. Reprinted in
     <u>English Lyrics</u> (1890).

7   B., C. C. "Wordsworth's 'Ode on the Intimations of
     Immortality.'" <u>Notes and Queries</u>, 7th ser., 10
     (9 August), 109.
          Gives Canon Overton's interpretation of "Ode: Intima-
     tions of Immortality."

8   B., W. C. "Scott and Wordsworth." <u>Notes and Queries</u>,
     7th ser., 10 (6 December), 446.
          Notes parallel between <u>The Recluse</u> and Scott.

9   BELLASIS, EDWARD. "Cardinal Newman and Wordsworth."
     <u>Spectator</u>, 65 (8 November), 646.
          Notes Newman's appreciation of Wordsworth.

10   BLACK, C. I. "Wordsworth's 'Ode on Intimations of
     Immortality.'" <u>Notes and Queries</u>, 7th ser., 10
     (8 November), 376.
          Interprets line in "Ode: Intimations of Immortality."

11   BLACK, MARY LUCY. "To Wordsworth" (poem). <u>English
     Illustrated Magazine</u>, 7 (June), 685.
          Wordsworth's power to evoke beautiful scenes compensates
     for the "smoke-grimed ugliness" of life.

12   BORLAND, R.[OBERT]. <u>Yarrow: Its Poets and Poetry</u>.
     Dalbeattie: Fraser, pp. 77-83.
          A biographical sketch. Wordsworth reacted to the failure
     of <u>Lyrical Ballads</u> and the hostility of critics with "im-
     perturbable serenity." Though he tried to dignify objects
     that were too lowly, he followed Cowper and Burns in il-
     luminating nature.

13   BOUCHIER, JONATHAN. "Wordsworth's 'Ode on Intimations of
     Immortality.'" <u>Notes and Queries</u>, 7th ser., 10
     (9 August), 109-10.
          A reply to 1889.B67. Interprets line in "Ode: Intima-
     tions of Immortality."

355

1890

14   BROMLEY, JAMES. "The Story of a Sonnet." Athenaeum,
      no. 3264 (17 May), p. 641.
           Records the background and suggests probable dates of
      composition of "Filial Piety."

15   C.[AMPBELL], J.[AMES] D.[YKES]. "Wordsworth's Verses in his
      Guide to the Lake Country." Athenaeum, no. 3277
      (16 August), pp. 225-26; no. 3278 (23 August), p. 255.
           Calls attention to the poems first published in A De-
      scription of the Scenery of the Lakes (1823) (225-26, 255).
      Notes that the title-page of that edition erroneously
      states "'now first printed separately'" (255).

16   C.[AMPBELL], J.[AMES] D.[YKES]. "Some Early Poems of
      Wordsworth." Athenaeum, no. 3280 (6 September), pp. 320-21.
           Describes variants of poems--including "Hart-leap Well,"
      "The Two Thieves," "The Idle Shepherd-boys," "Strange fits
      of passion have I known," "Lucy Gray," "The Reverie of
      Poor Susan," "There was a Boy," "Written with a Slate Pen-
      cil upon a Stone, the Largest of a Heap Lying Near a De-
      serted Quary, upon One of the Islands at Rydal," "The
      Waterfall and the Eglantine," and "For the Spot where the
      Hermitage Stood on St. Herbert's Island, Derwent-Water"--
      contained in manuscripts once the property of Thomas Poole
      and the Rev. W. L. Nichols. Wordsworth's versification of
      Poole's story of John Walford is a failure.

17   C.[AMPBELL], J.[AMES] D.[YKES]. "The 'Lyrical Ballads' of
      1800." Athenaeum, no. 3291 (22 November), pp. 699-700.
           Discusses the texts of the early manuscripts and 1800
      printing of "Michael," and the text of "Gipsies."

18   DAWSON, W.[ILLIAM] J.[AMES]. The Makers of Modern English:
      A Popular Handbook to the Greater Poets of the Century.
      London: Hodder and Stoughton, pp. 91-154 and passim.
           Wordsworth initiated a return to simplicity, though his
      theory of poetic expression is absurd. His poetry must be
      studied in connection with his life and that of the Cumbrian
      dalesman. He differs from other poets in having formed an
      ideal of what life might be, and in stressing the moral in-
      fluence of nature. He was little aware of literary culture.
      His stylistically best poems were written between 1798 and
      1818. He paints nature as the Impressionists do; he does
      not project his mood onto Nature, but lets Nature create
      the mood in him: hence the accuracy of his descriptions.
      Although he resisted new ideas later in life, he was far
      from a fossilized Tory. He is only now receiving due

recognition. His philosophy, summed up in "Ode: Intimations of Immortality," is based on the belief that man has
in himself all necessary for a perfect life, if he will but
learn to adjust himself to his environment. Wordsworth
compared, throughout the volume, with the major nineteenth-
century poets.

19 DENNIS, JOHN. "Children and the Poets." Leisure Hour, 39
    [January], 182-86 (183, 186).
        Wordsworth enlarges upon Vaughan's thought in "Ode:
    Intimations of Immortality." He never played with children
    but understood them poetically.

20 DENNIS, JOHN. "The Poetry of the Century: A Retrospect and
    Anticipation." Leisure Hour, 39 [April], 378-82 (378, 381).
        "Gladness of song" distinguished Wordsworth's poetry.
    His own perversity and a want of humor hindered his fame.

21 [DOUGLAS, DAVID, ed.]. The Journal of Sir Walter Scott: From
    the Original Manuscript at Abbotsford. 2 vols. Edinburgh:
    Douglas, I:268, 333-35, 358; II:34, 179-84, 189-90, 411-14.
        Includes entries in which Scott declares Wordsworth,
    though a sensible man, has injured his fame by adhering to
    his system of poetry and that Wordsworth has a freshness
    lacking in Southey, and records Wordsworth's visit in 1831.

22 DOW, JOHN G. "Poets and Puritans." Macmillan's Magazine, 61
    (April), 457-64 (461).
        Wordsworth echoes Vaughan's thought and language in
    "Ode: Intimations of Immortality."

23 DOWDEN, EDWARD. "Preface," "Notes," in Lyrical Ballads:
    Reprinted from the first edition of 1798. Edited by Edward
    Dowden. London: Nutt, pp. v-xv, 213-27.
        Discusses printing history of Lyrical Ballads; Wordsworth
    was first only partly conscious of his tendencies in writing
    these poems. Expanded in 1891.B15 (v-xv). Includes notes,
    mainly textual, on the poems. Reprinted in 1891.B15
    (213-27).

24 EWING, THOMAS J. "Wordsworth's 'Ode on Intimations of
    Immortality.'" Notes and Queries, 7th ser., 9 (12 April),
    297-98; 10 (27 September), 258-59.
        Replies to 1889.B17, B20 (297-98), and 1890.B7, B13
    (258-59). Interprets lines from "Ode: Intimations of
    Immortality."

1890

25 FORMAN, H. BUXTON, ed. Poetry and Prose by John Keats: A
Book of Fresh Verses and New Readings—Essays and Letters
lately Found—and Passages formerly Suppressed: and
Forming a Supplement to the Library Edition of Keats's
Works. London: Reeves & Turner, pp. 42-44, 48-52, 73,
78-79, 83, 85, 89, 141, 145, 149-50.
    Includes letters and extracts omitted from 1883.B27 in
which Keats clarifies that "On Oxford" ("The Gothic looks
solemn") burlesques Wordsworth's "style of school exer-
cises," notes his friendship with Wordsworth and his dining
with him in London, and regrets that Wordsworth "left a bad
impression wherever he visited in town by his egotism."

26 FORSTER, JOHN. "John Ruskin," in Four Great Teachers: John
Ruskin, Thomas Carlyle, Ralph Waldo Emerson, and Robert
Browning. Orpington and London: Allen, pp. 1-38 (8-11,
37-38).
    Reprinted from 1887.B23. Adds note quoting a comment
from the Birmingham Daily Post of 29 October 1887, question-
ing Ruskin's debt to Wordsworth.

27 GALE, MARY W. "Wordsworth's 'Ode on Intimations of
Immortality.'" Notes and Queries, 7th ser., 10
(8 November), 376.
    Interprets line in "Ode: Intimations of Immortality."

28 [HUTTON, RICHARD HOLT]. Review of Lyrical Ballads (ed.
Dowden). Spectator, 64 (5 April), 479-80.
    Wordsworth, more than Coleridge, in Lyrical Ballads
forewarned the world against a physical view of natural
things.

29 JAPP, ALEXANDER H. ("H. A. PAGE"). Thomas De Quincey: His
Life and Writings: With Unpublished Correspondence. A new
edition, revised. Illustrated. London: Hogg, passim.
    Revised with omissions from 1877.B19.

30 LINTON, E.[LIZA] LYNN. "Literature: Then and Now."
Fortnightly Review, NS 47 (1 April), 517-31 (520).
    Wordsworth wrote honestly as he thought, "from cogitation
rather than from books."

31 M., A. J. "Wordsworth's 'Ode on the Intimations of
Immortality.'" Notes and Queries, 7th ser., 10
(6 September), 196-97.
    A reply to 1890.B7, B13. Interprets line in "Ode:
Intimations of Immortality."

32 Mc WILLIAM, R.[OBERT]. Longman's Handbook of English
    Literature: Part V: From Burke to the Present Time.
    London and New York: Longmans, especially pp. 14-25, 34,
    141-42.
        A biographical sketch of Wordsworth and the Lake Poets.

33 MALLESON, THE REV. F.[REDERICK] A. "Bolton Abbey and Woods,"
    "Wordsworth's 'Westmorland Girl,'" "Wordsworth and the
    Duddon," in Holiday Studies of Wordsworth By Rivers, Woods,
    and Alps: The Wharfe, the Duddon, and the Stelvio Pass.
    London, Paris, and Melbourne: Cassell, pp. 11-35 (21-24),
    37-49, 51-75.
        Wordsworth interweaves history with romance in The White
    Doe of Rylstone (21-24). Reprinted from 1873.B21 (37-49).
    Expanded from 1883.B39 (51-75).

34 MASSON, DAVID. Editorial Prefaces and Notes, in The Collected
    Writings of Thomas De Quincey. New and enlarged edition.
    Edited by David Masson. 14 vols. Edinburgh: Black,
    V:2-5; XI:3-4; XIV:386-87; III-XIV: passim.
        De Quincey's admiration of Wordsworth was not blind
    idolatry; he admired Wordsworth to the last. Details De
    Quincey's collaboration on Concerning . . . the Convention
    of Cintra. Includes explanatory notes to De Quincey's
    writings about Wordsworth throughout Volumes III-XIV. For
    Volume II, see 1889.B45.

35 [NICHOLSON, CORNELIA]. A Well-spent Life: Memoir of
    Cornelius Nicholson, with a Selection of his Lectures and
    Letters. Kendal: Wilson, pp. 4, 13, 71, 107, 157, 176-77.
        Records Wordsworth's election as honorary member of the
    Kendal Natural History and Scientific Society, and notes
    his opposition to the Windermere railway. Records Nichol-
    son's friendship with Wordsworth and prints passages from
    his lectures praising Wordsworth's poems. Attribution:
    British Museum catalogue.

36 [POLLITT, CHARLES]. De Quincey's Editorship of the Westmor-
    land Gazette, with Selections from his Work on that Journal
    from July, 1818, to November, 1819. Kendal: Atkinson and
    Pollitt; London: Simpkin, Marshall, Hamilton, Kent,
    pp. 6-9, 25-27, 33, 45-46, 61, 65, 70.
        Details Wordsworth's involvement in the election of 1818
    and his relations with De Quincey and contributions to the
    Westmorland Gazette. Reprints De Quincey's comments on
    Wordsworth from the Westmorland Gazette in 1818 and 1819:
    the feelings Wordsworth expresses in "November, 1813"
    ("Now that all hearts are glad, all faces bright") never

1890

become obsolete; praises Wordsworth's "severe accuracy of logic"; recalls conversation in which Wordsworth defines a tarn. Attribution: Introduction to volume.

37   [RAWNSLEY, HARDWICKE DRUMMOND]. "The Last of the Calverts." Cornhill Magazine, NS 14 (May), 494-520 (495-500, 505-508, 518).
       Discusses Wordsworth's ties with the Calvert family. Raisley Calvert admired Wordsworth's "serious earnestness." Records Mrs. Joshua Stanger's (Mary Calvert's) recollections of Wordsworth's casual dress and her opinion that Wordsworth combined portraits of her father and Coleridge in "Stanzas Written in My Pocket-copy of Thomson's 'Castle of Indolence.'"

38   [RAWNSLEY, HARDWICKE DRUMMOND]. "The Last of the Rydal Dorothys." Blackwood's Edinburgh Magazine, 147 (June), 815-21.
       Recounts Wordsworth's affection for Dorothy, daughter of Richard Wordsworth of Whitehaven, and her memory of Wordsworth's solemnity.

39   RAWNSLEY, H.[ARDWICKE] D.[RUMMOND]. A Coach Drive at the Lakes: Windermere to Keswick. Keswick: Bakewell, pp. 85-86.
       Expanded from 1888.B37. Describes places near Keswick associated with Wordsworth's life.

40   REID, T.[HOMAS] WEMYSS. The Life, Letters, and Friendships of Richard Monckton Milnes, First Lord Houghton. 2 vols. London, Paris, and Melbourne: Cassell, I:62, 72-74, 119, 171, 192, 326, 445; II:433-34.
       Records Milnes's interest in Wordsworth at Cambridge in 1829, Wordsworth's repartée concerning the State Ball in 1844, his reputation in 1836 and 1850, and Henry Taylor's comment that one of Wordsworth's letters in 1837 resembled "the journal of a schoolgirl on her first visit to foreign parts."

41   RYLAND, FREDERICK. Chronological Outlines of English Literature. London and New York: Macmillan, p. 350 and passim.
       A brief primary bibliography.

42   SAINTSBURY, GEORGE. "De Quincey." Macmillan's Magazine, 62 (June), 101-12 (107-108, 112).
       "Wordsworth's arrogance was inhuman." Reprinted in Essays in English Literature 1780-1860 (1890).

43 SHARP, WILLIAM. "Introductory Note," in Great Odes: English
    and American. Edited by William Sharp. London: Scott
    [1890], pp. vii–xlv (ix–xi, xxvi–xxvii).
        In "Ode: Intimations of Immortality" and "Ode to Duty"
    Wordsworth writes best when he forgets the metrical con-
    ventions of the ode.

44 ST. SWITHIN. "Wordsworth's Sonnet composed upon Westminster
    Bridge, Sept. 3rd, 1802." Notes and Queries, 7th ser., 10
    (13 December), 465.
        A reply to 1890.B49. Questions the hour when Wordsworth
    wrote "Composed upon Westminster Bridge." (See reply by
    Thomas Bayne, "Wordsworth's Sonnet Composed upon Westminster
    Bridge, September 3rd, 1802," Notes and Queries, 7th ser.,
    11 [17 January 1891], 53.)

45 SYMONDS, JOHN ADDINGTON. "The Art of Style," "Democratic Art:
    with Special Reference to Walt Whitman," "Landscape," "Is
    Poetry at Bottom a Criticism of Life?: A Review of Matthew
    Arnold's Selection from Wordsworth," "A Comparison of
    Elizabethan with Victorian Poetry," in Essays Speculative
    and Suggestive. 2 vols. London: Chapman and Hall,
    II:11–29 (12), 30–77 (74–75), 78–125 (81, 110–17, 121–22),
    150–80 (161–80), 225–77 (235–36, 242–46, 253–54, 258,
    268–71).
        Wordsworth's style is appropriate in "Ode to Duty" (12).
    His democratic sympathy is too condescending (74–75). His
    mysticism gave tone to his description of landscape in The
    Prelude (81, 110–17, 121–22). Reprinted with omissions
    from 1879.B21 (161–80). Reprinted from 1889.B64 (235–36,
    242–46, 253–54, 258, 268–71).

46 TUTIN, J.[OHN] R.[AMSDEN]. "Wordsworth in Yorkshire."
    Yorkshire Notes and Queries, 2:257–67.
        Provides topographical and biographical notes to Words-
    worth's poems set in Yorkshire.

47 WALPOLE, SPENCER. A History of England from the Conclusion of
    the Great War in 1815. New and revised edition. 6 vols.
    London and New York: Longmans, I:237–40.
        Revised from 1878.B28. There is nothing in Burns or
    Paine that compares with Wordsworth's "ardour for liberty"
    during the French Revolution.

48 WARREN, KATE M. "The 'Dove Cottage' Scheme." Speaker, 1
    (24 May), 570.
        An appeal for funds to purchase Dove Cottage.

1890

49   WATSON, G. "Wordsworth's 'Ode on Intimations of Immortality.'"
      Notes and Queries, 7th ser., 10 (8 November), 375-76.
      Suggests method of interpreting "Ode: Intimations of
      Immortality."

50   WATSON, WILLIAM. "Preface," in English Lyrics. By Alfred
      Austin. Edited by William Watson. London and New York:
      Macmillan, pp. vii-xxvi (x-xi, xvi-xvii).
      "The mature Wordsworth is Wordsworth the rehabilitated
      patriot."

51   WATSON, WILLIAM. "To James Bromley, of Lathom, Lancashire"
      (poem), "Wordsworth's Grave" (poem), "To Professor Dowden,
      On Receiving from Him 'The Life of Shelley'" (poem), in
      Wordsworth's Grave and other Poems. London: Unwin,
      pp. 7-8, 11-22, 73-76.
      Praises Wordsworth's "simple themes," "his sincere large
      accent nobly plain," his "immediate soul" (7-8). Reprinted
      from 1887.B54 (11-22). Pays tribute to Wordsworth, the
      poet "Of lowly sorrows and familiar joys" (73-76).

52   [WISE, THOMAS J., ed.]. Letters from Percy Bysshe Shelley to
      Elizabeth Hitchener. 2 vols. London: privately printed,
      I:132, 140, 157-59; II:8.
      Adds to previously published Shelley correspondence let-
      ters in which Shelley announces his expectation of meeting
      Wordsworth, expresses his admiration of Wordsworth in 1812
      and notes that Wordsworth yet retains his integrity but
      lives in poverty.

1891 A BOOKS

1   KNIGHT, WILLIAM. The English Lake District as Interpreted in
     the Poems of Wordsworth. Second edition, revised and
     enlarged. Edinburgh: Douglas, 286 pp.
     Revised from 1878.A1, expanding the notes on the locali-
     ties mentioned in Wordsworth's poems and omitting "A Lec-
     ture on Wordsworth."

2   TUTIN, J.[OHN] R.[AMSDEN]. The Wordsworth Dictionary of
     Persons and Places: With the Familiar Quotations from His
     Works (including full index) and a Chronologically-Arranged
     List of His Best Poems. Hull: Tutin, 216 pp.
     A concordance of persons and places mentioned in Words-
     worth's poems, and chronological list of titles. Includes,
     in an Appendix, a bibliographic description and text of a
     cancelled version of "Ode to Duty" and a concordance of

birds and plants mentioned in Wordsworth's poems, the latter expanded in 1892.A2.

3   WORDSWORTH, ELIZABETH. <u>William Wordsworth</u>. London: Percival, 242 pp.
        A full biography. Wordsworth's value to an age of un-
    certainty and shallow feeling lies in his sincerity, up-
    rightness, and fixed purpose. Wordsworth did for poetry
    what Turner did for painting--teach us to see. His images
    are drawn from ideas, Tennyson's from sensations.

<u>1891 B   SHORTER WRITINGS</u>

1   ANON. "Notes and News." <u>Oxford Magazine</u>, 9 (4 February),
    176-78 (178).
        Notes breakfast given for Wordsworth at Oxford in 1839.

2   ANON. Review of Bussière and Legouis's <u>Le Général Michel
    Beaupuy</u>. Athenaeum, no. 3316 (16 May), pp. 630-32.
        Until he met Beaupuy, Wordsworth viewed the French Revo-
    lution with indifference.

3   ANON. "The Lake District Revisited." <u>Eagle: A Magazine
    Supported by Members of St John's College</u>, 16 (June),
    527-32.
        Jocularly refers to Wordsworth's depiction of natural
    scenes.

4   ANON. "Wordsworth and Wool." <u>National Observer</u>, 6
    (8 August), 304-305.
        Wordsworth shows good sense in "Steamboats, Viaducts,
    and Railways." His "style reminds us of some fine statu-
    esque figure dressed in severe and massive drapery." He
    was a poet (though devoid of humor), not a prophet.

5   ANON. "Coleridge's 'Friend.'" <u>Athenaeum</u>, no. 3337
    (10 October), pp. 484-85.
        Notes Wordsworth's kindness in promoting Coleridge's
    <u>Friend</u>.

6   ANON. Note, in <u>The Northern Poetry Cards: The Traveller's
    Dog</u>. Leeds: Pedley [1891], p. [1].
        A biographical sketch.

1891

7   ANON. Portraits of English Poets from Drawings Made for
     Joseph Cottle of Bristol Reproduced in Photogravure from
     the Originals. . . . Bristol: George's Sons, pp. [3, 9].
     Portrait "after Hancock, 1798."

8   BLAKENEY, EDWARD HENRY. "William Wordsworth." Churchman,
     NS 6 (November), 80-92.
         The poems in Lyrical Ballads, though defective in exe-
     cution, contain "a grave exultation." Good phrases are
     buried in the middle of prosaic poems; Wordsworth's shorter
     poems are best. Wordsworth brought poetry back to the
     elemental truths of Nature: hence his power to give peace
     and joy. Yet he also understands the necessity of duty.
     He is not a pantheist, is the poet of man as well as of
     nature.

9   BOUCHIER, JONATHAN. "Wordsworth's 'Ode on Intimations of
     Immortality.'" Notes and Queries, 7th ser., 11 (28 March),
     255-56.
         Wordsworth is not dull.

10   BOUCHIER, JONATHAN. "Swift: Bernardin de Saint-Pierre:
     Wordsworth." Notes and Queries, 7th ser., 12 (18 July),
     43-44 (44).
         Poems on the Naming of Places may have been suggested
     by a passage in Saint-Pierre.

11   BRADSHAW, JOHN. Notes, in An English Anthology: From Chaucer
     to the Present Time. Third edition. Edited by John
     Bradshaw. London: Bell; Madras: Aiyar, pp. 384-404,
     422-23, 481-82.
         Brief critical notes to the poems selected, including
     "On the Extinction of the Venetian Republic," "Thought of
     a Briton on the Subjugation of Switzerland," "Stepping
     Westward," "The world is too much with us; late and soon,"
     "To Sleep" ("A flock of sheep that leisurely pass by"), and
     "Ode: Intimations of Immortality." (Earlier editions,
     dated in Prefaces 1885 and 1887, not located.)

12   CHANCELLOR, E.[DWIN] BERESFORD. Essays and Studies (Literary
     and Historical). Illustrated by Val R. Prince. London:
     Bemrose, pp. 1-36.
         Describes Wordsworth's life at Dove Cottage and his
     friendship with Coleridge. Wordsworth's admirers refuse to
     admit his faults, his detractors his beauties. His love
     for Dorothy illustrates his character. He is a poet of the
     mind, rather than the senses. His sonnets excel; his
     blank verse is too didactic and verbose.

364

13   COLLINGWOOD, W. G.   Note to "The Iteriad," in The Poems of
     John Ruskin. . . .   Edited by W. G. Collingwood.   2 vols.
     Orpington and London: Allen, I:276.
          Notes Ruskin's disappointment on seeing Wordsworth in
     1830.

14   DE QUINCEY, THOMAS.   "Paganism and Christianity--the Ideas of
     Duty and Holiness," "Literary," "Philosophy Defeated," in
     The Posthumous Works of Thomas De Quincey.   Edited by
     Alexander H. Japp.   2 vols.   London: Heinemann, I:185-93
     (185-87), 292-305 (293-94), 317-19 (318).
          Wordsworth wrongly understands paganism in "Ode to Ly-
     coris" and Christianity in "Ode to Duty" (185-87).   He
     records "phenomena as they are enjoyed."   His social
     philosophy is shallow, his poetry spontaneous (293-94).
     Praises Wordsworth's reading of blank verse (a variant of
     passage in 1821.B15) (318).   For Volume II, see 1893.B22.

15   DOWDEN, EDWARD.   "Preface," "Notes," in Lyrical Ballads:
     Reprinted from the first edition (1798).   Second edition.
     Edited by Edward Dowden.   London: Nutt, pp. v-xv, 213-27.
          Expanded from 1890.B23.   Adds bibliographical remarks
     on Southey's copy of Lyrical Ballads (x-xv).   Reprinted
     from 1890.B23 (213-27).

16   EWING, THOMAS J.   "Wordsworth's 'Ode on Intimations of
     Immortality.'"   Notes and Queries, 7th ser., 11 (6 June),
     453.
          A reply to 1889.B67 and 1891.B47.   Interprets lines in
     "Ode: Intimations of Immortality."

17   F., W. J.   "We Are [Gated After] Seven" (poem).   Oxford
     Magazine, 10 (2 December), 123.
          Parody of "We Are Seven."

18   F., W. R.   "Wordsworth, Keble, and Dr. Bloxam."   Oxford
     Magazine, 9 (25 February), 242.
          A reply to 1891.B1.   A further account of the breakfast
     given for Wordsworth at Oxford in 1839.

19   "FILIA."   "Wordsworth's 'Immortal Ode.'"   Parents' Review, 1
     (January), 864-70.
          "Ode: Intimations of Immortality" is a powerful "pro-
     test against materialism."

20   GEDDES, W.[ILLIAM] D.   "George Mac Donald as a Poet."
     Blackwood's Edinburgh Magazine, 149 (March), 361-70
     (361-62, 366).

1891

> The secret of Wordsworth's power as the priest of wonder
> is his linking of the visible world with the eternal. His
> influence can be traced in Byron and George Macdonald.

21 GOSSE, EDMUND. "Gossip in a Library.--II: Peter Bell and his
      Tormentors." Black and White, 1 (2 May), 398.
        In Peter Bell Wordsworth pushes his theories their fur-
      thest; hence he delayed its publication, which even in 1819
      met with ridicule. The tale is improbable, the narrative
      clumsy, the attempts at wit ludicrous. Expanded in
      1891.B22.

22 GOSSE, EDMUND. "Peter Bell and his Tormentors," in Gossip in
      a Library. London: Heinemann, pp. 251-67.
        Expanded from 1891.B21. Records Barron Field's noting
      of the hostile reception of Peter Bell.

23 GRAHAM, P.[ETER] ANDERSON. Nature in Books: Some Studies in
      Biography. London: Methuen, pp. 174-94.
        In "Ode: Intimations of Immortality" Wordsworth cor-
      rectly analyzes a child's love of nature. He--perhaps too
      optimistically--expresses the joy of earth.

24 GRAVES, R.[OBERT] P.[ERCEVAL]. "Wordsworth and Shakespeare."
      Academy, 40 (8 August), 116.
        Lamb's jesting over Wordsworth's lack of enthusiasm for
      his predecessors should not obscure the fact that Words-
      worth revered Shakespeare.

25 HARDY, THOMAS. "Tess of the D'Urbervilles." Graphic, 44
      (18 July), 74-76 (74); (12 September), 302-303 (302);
      (12 December), 694-95 (694).
        Questions Wordsworth's philosophy in "Lines Written in
      Early Spring" (74) and "Ode: Intimations of Immortality"
      (694). Notes it was fashionable to read Wordsworth (302).
      Reprinted with verbal changes in Tess of the D'Urbervilles
      (1891) (Chapters iii, xxv, and li).

26 HELPS, MRS. EDMUND. "Introduction," "Life of Wordsworth,"
      "Notes," in Wordsworth's Shorter Poems. Edited by Mrs.
      Edmund Helps. London: Percival, pp. ix-xi, xii-xiv,
      43-52.
        The study of Wordsworth helps make one wise, good, and
      happy, with a high sense of duty. He is the poet of nature
      and of family life (ix-xi). A biographical sketch (xii-xiv).
      Critical notes to the poems selected, including "Written in
      March," "To My Sister," and "Stepping Westward" (43-52).

27   [JAPP, ALEXANDER H.] H. A. PAGE. "Early Intercourse of the
     Wordsworths and De Quincey: By De Quincey's Biographer:
     with hitherto Unpublished Letters." Century Magazine, 41
     (April), 853-64.
          Notes De Quincey's admiration of and debt to Wordsworth
     and records his intercourse with the Wordsworths.

28   JAPP, ALEXANDER H., ed. De Quincey Memorials: Being Letters
     and Other Records, Here First Published: with Communica-
     tions from Coleridge, the Wordsworths, Hannah More,
     Professor Wilson, and Others. 2 vols. London: Heinemann,
     passim.
          Wordsworth's correspondence with De Quincey is charac-
     terized by a wise reserve, lofty moral tone, and fine in-
     sight. De Quincey's labor on Concerning . . . the Conven-
     tion of Cintra illustrates his devotion to Wordsworth.
     Wordsworth's early prose shows his keen interest in true
     liberty. Includes letters in which Coleridge praises Words-
     worth, Mary De Quincey testifies to the comfort she re-
     ceived from Wordsworth's poems, and Jane De Quincey
     testifies to De Quincey's admiration of Dorothy Wordsworth
     and of Wordsworth's gardening. De Quincey admired The
     Excursion in spite of its philosophy.

29   KNIGHT, WILLIAM. "Introduction," "Notes," in Wordsworth:
     The White Doe of Rylstone with the Song at the Feast of
     Brougham Castle etc. Edited by William Knight. Oxford:
     Clarendon, pp. 1-8, 103-12.
          Discusses the composition of The White Doe of Rylstone.
     Wordsworth's "genius was not great in construction, as in
     imagination": he valued the story only as he could use it
     for his purposes (1-8). Includes critical notes (103-12).

30   LANG, ANDREW. "Introduction," in The Blue Poetry Book.
     Edited by Andrew Lang. Illustrated by H. J. Ford and
     Lancelot Speed. London and New York: Longmans,
     pp. vii-xiii (x-xi).
          Wordsworth's poems about and for children appeal more
     to older readers.

31   M., W. "A Literary Causerie." Speaker, 4 (8 August),
     171-73 (172-73).
          Wordsworth has not succeeded in creating the taste by
     which he is to be enjoyed; readers now admire the same
     poems the first critics did.

32   MILES, ALFRED H. "William Wordsworth," in The Poets and the
     Poetry of the Century: George Crabbe to Samuel Taylor

1891

Coleridge. Edited by Alfred H. Miles. London: Hutchinson
[1891], pp. 211-28.
A biographical sketch. Wordsworth's initial unpopularity
was caused by his challenge to established taste and by the
lack of the dramatic element in his poems. His poems are
characterized by noble purpose, truth, and intercourse with
nature.

33 NICHOLS, THE REV. WILLIAM LUKE. The Quantocks and their
Associations. Second edition. London: Sampson Low,
Marston; Bath: Mundy, pp. 15, 37-47, 57-58, 99-100.
Expands discussion of Alfoxden from 1873.B25, adding a
description of a manuscript poem by Wordsworth on John
Walford, "a romance of humble life" in the stern tones of
Crabbe.

34 NOBLE, JAMES ASHCROFT. "The Poetry of Common Sense."
Macmillan's Magazine, 64 (October), 431-38 (436, 438).
The poetry of common sense is not absent in Wordsworth's
meditatively observant poems or in his sane and reverent
mysticism. Reprinted in The Sonnet in England (1893).

35 ORR, MRS SUTHERLAND [ALEXANDRA]. Life and Letters of Robert
Browning. London: Smith, Elder, pp. 83, 105, 132-33,
354-56.
Records Browning's acquaintance with Wordsworth and his
testimony, in letters, to taking Wordsworth for his model
in "The Lost Leader" and to disliking Wordsworth's textual
revisions in "To the Daisy" ("In youth from rock to rock I
went") and Wordsworth's later poems.

36 PAGE, H. A. See 1891.B27.

37 PHILLIPPA. "Wordsworth's 'Immortal Ode.'" Parents' Review, 1
(February), 944-49.
In "Ode: Intimations of Immortality" Wordsworth states
experiences common to children and gives lessons in how to
raise children.

38 R., M. "Wordsworth's 'Immortal Ode.'" Parents' Review, 2
(March), 70-73.
"Ode: Intimations of Immortality" contains, in the best
words, lessons a mother should tell her child.

39 RIX, HERBERT. "The Duddon Sonnets." Athenaeum, no. 3325
(18 July), p. 98.
Additions to the topographical notes to The River Duddon
in 1884.B16.

40 SMILES, SAMUEL. A Publisher and His Friends: Memoir and
    Correspondence of the late John Murray, with an Account of
    the Origin and Progress of the House, 1768-1843.
    Illustrated. 2 vols. London: Murray, II:245-46.
        Records Wordsworth's dealings with Murray in 1826. In-
    cludes letter in which Lockhart notes that Wordsworth's
    poems "must become more popular" and reports on Wordsworth's
    vanity.

41 S.[MITH], G. C. M. "The College Days of William Wordsworth."
    Eagle: A Magazine Supported by Members of St John's
    College, 16 (March), 425-43.
        A biographical sketch of Wordsworth's life at Cambridge.

42 SONNENSCHEIN, WILLIAM SWAN. The Best Books: A Reader's
    Guide. . . . Second edition. New York: Putnam's;
    London: Sonnenschein, especially pp. 326, 328, 714-17,
    726, 757, 759, 761, 769, 790.
        Expanded from 1887.B49. A primary and secondary bibli-
    ography. Expanded in 1895.B36.

43 S.[TEPHEN], J.[AMES] K.[ENNETH]. "A Sonnet" ("Two voices are
    there: one is of the deep"). Granta, 4 (12 June), p. 379.
        Parody of "Thought of a Briton on the Subjugation of
    Switzerland." Reprinted in Lapsus Calami (new edition,
    1891).

44 S.[TEPHEN], J.[AMES] K.[ENNETH]. "Of W. W. (Britannicus):
    Poetic Lamentation on the Insufficiency of Steam Locomotion
    in the Lake District" (poem), in Lapsus Calami. Cambridge:
    Macmillan and Bowes, pp. 44-45.
        A burlesque. (Originally published in the Pall Mall
    Gazette, November 1882.)

45 TUCKWELL, THE REV. W.[ILLIAM]. Tongues in Trees and Sermons
    in Stones. London and Orpington: Allen, pp. 119-21.
        Wordsworth was no naturalist.

46 VALENTINE, L.[AURA]. Picturesque England: Its Landmarks and
    Historic Haunts, as Described in Lay and Legend, Song and
    Story. London and New York: Warne, pp. 400-401, 405-406.
        Describes Wordsworth's associations with Grasmere and
    Rydal. "The Somnambulist" can be better understood if
    read near its setting at Ara Force.

47 WARD, C. A. "Wordsworth's 'Ode on the Intimations of
    Immortality.'" Notes and Queries, 7th ser., 11
    (31 January), 94.

1891

       A reply to 1890.B49. Coleridge overly praises Words-
worth, a dull writer.

48   WARREN, T. H. "Wordsworth, Keble, and Dr. Bloxam." Oxford
    Magazine, 9 (11 February), 203-204 (203).
       A reply to 1891.B1. A further account of the breakfast
given for Wordsworth at Oxford in 1839.

49   WILDE, LADY [JANE FRANCESCA]. Notes on Men, Women, and Books:
    Selected Essays. First series. London: Ward & Downey,
    pp. 247-60.
       Wordsworth led men to a higher spiritual life. His life
was untouched by sorrow. He solved the problem which Byron
and Shelley could only utter, by interpreting the outer
world as an allegory of the inner. "He draws not men but
Man." "His thoughts speak so directly to the human soul
that he has no need of images." He patiently endured ridicule until men were prepared to receive his work.

50   WORDSWORTH, CHARLES. Annals of My Early Life 1806-1846: with
    Occasional Compositions in Latin and English Verse. London
    and New York: Longmans, especially pp. 93, 107-108, 112-19,
    156, 244, 271-76.
       Records Gladstone's admiration of Wordsworth, Words-
worth's dislike of Brougham, Wordsworth's visit with Scott
in 1831, Walter Kerr Hamilton's admiration of The Excursion,
Wordsworth's praise of Emmeline Fisher's and Keble's poems,
and Wordsworth's statement that he did not feel qualified
to write on religious subjects. Includes letter in which
Thomas Arnold notes in 1837 Wordsworth's anticipation of
his trip to Italy.

51   YOXALL, J.[AMES] H.[ENRY]. Note, in A New Choice of Standard
    Recitations for Use in Schools and Homes; Book C, for
    Standard IV. Edited by J. H. Yoxall. London: Simpkin,
    Marshall, Hamilton, Kent; St. Andrews: Holden, p. 23.
       "Hart-leap Well" teaches us to sympathize with animals.

1892 A BOOKS

1   SUTHERLAND, JAMES MIDDLETON. William Wordsworth: The Story
    of His Life, with Critical Remarks on His Writings. Second
    edition, revised and enlarged. London: Stock, 258 pp.
       A full biography, revised from 1887.A3. The masses still
do not know Wordsworth. Includes "On Revisiting the Same
[the grave of Wordsworth] (September 17, 1889)" (poem):
Wordsworth was the friend of all; his poems dispel care.

2   TUTIN, J.[OHN] R.[AMSDEN]. <u>An Index to the Animal and
    Vegetable Kingdoms of Wordsworth</u>. Hull: Tutin, 20 pp.
        Wordsworth's delineations of animals and plants are un-
    erringly truthful in detail. Gives an index to references
    to animals and plants in Wordsworth's poems, expanded from
    1891.A2. Expanded in 1897.B68.

3   WINTRINGHAM, WILLIAM H. <u>The Birds of Wordsworth: Poetically,
    Mythologically, and Comparatively Examined</u>. London:
    Hutchinson, 426 pp.
        Catalogues and discusses Wordsworth's references to
    birds in his poems.

<u>1892 B   SHORTER WRITINGS</u>

1   ANON. "Our Library Table." <u>Athenaeum</u>, no. 3356
    (20 February), pp. 243-44 (243).
        Of Wordsworth's works, the half may be greater than the
    whole.

2   ANON. "Dove Cottage." <u>Athenaeum</u>, no. 3371 (4 June),
    pp. 727-28.
        Reports on the meeting of the trustees of Dove Cottage:
    the number of visitors, gifts received, condition of the
    house.

3   ANON. "Notes and News." <u>Academy</u>, 42 (9 July), 29-30 (30).
        Notes gifts to Dove Cottage.

4   ANON. "Wordsworth's Prefaces." <u>Literary World</u> (London),
    NS 46 (18 November), 411.
        Wordsworth's prefaces, in which he enunciated his prin-
    ciple of poetic sincerity, are masterpieces of prose.

5   ANON. "Wordsworth, William," in <u>Cassell's New Biographical
    Dictionary: Containing Memoirs of the Most Eminent Men and
    Women of All Ages and Countries</u>. London, Paris, and
    Melbourne: Cassell, p. 735.
        A biographical sketch.

6   BAYNE, THOMAS. "'Hart-leap Well.'" <u>Notes and Queries</u>,
    8th ser., 2 (26 November), 425.
        The hart did not jump in a well in "Hart-leap Well."

7   CAINE, RALPH H. Note, in <u>Love Songs of English Poets 1500-
    1800</u>. Edited by Ralph H. Caine. London: Heinemann,
    p. 214.

1892

A biographical sketch. Wordsworth freed himself from the influence of previous generations.

8   CORKRAN, ALICE. The Poets' Corner, or Haunts and Homes of The Poets. Illustrated by Allan Barraud. Introduction by Fred E. Weatherly. London: Nister; New York: Dutton [1892], pp. [37-42].
    A plain man who saw clearly, Wordsworth consciously led a poetic revolution. He sanctified the Lake District. A biographical sketch.

9   CROSSE, MRS. ANDREW. "The Wedded Poets." Temple Bar, 94 (January), 29-46 (29-30, 32-34, 45-46).
    Wordsworth saw the merit only of his own poems. Reprinted in 1892.B11.

10 CROSSE, MRS. ANDREW. "Hours Counted on the Sundial." Temple Bar, 95 (July), 373-92 (373-75).
    Wordsworth, contrary to his own impression, could not have remained a tenant at Alfoxden. Reprinted in 1892.B11.

11 CROSSE, MRS. ANDREW. "Hours Counted on the Sundial," "Thomas Poole," "Walter Savage Landor," "The Wedded Poets," in Red-letter Days of my Life. 2 vols. London: Bentley, I:1-62 (2-8), 63-121 (88-94, 101-106), 187-224 (209-10), 225-80 (225-26, 229, 236-41, 278).
    Reprinted from 1892.B10 (2-8). Reprinted from 1889.B26 (88-94, 101-106). Landor was inconsistent in his criticism of Wordsworth (209-10). Reprinted from 1892.B9 (225-26, 229, 236-41, 278).

12 DOWDEN, EDWARD. "Preface," "Memoir," "Notes," in The Poetical Works of William Wordsworth. Edited by Edward Dowden. 7 vols. London and New York: Bell, I:v-xvi; xxi-lxxiv; 353-408, II:259-344, III:327-476.
    Defends Wordsworth's latest texts and arrangement of poems. Wordsworth uses punctuation to aid both meaning and meter (I:v-xvi). His work is characterized by a return to nature, a recognition of the spiritual aspect of nature, and a reverence for the past. "He at once calms and quickens." He harmoniously united conflicting mental qualities. An extended biographical sketch (xxi-lxxiv). Includes textual and critical notes to the poems (353-408, II:259-344, III:327-476). For Volumes IV-VII, see 1893.B26.

13 DUFFY, C.[HARLES] GAVAN. "Conversations and Correspondence with Thomas Carlyle: Part First." Contemporary Review, 61 (January), 120-52 (144-45).

1892

Records Carlyle's opinion that Wordsworth gave a faithful and vivid picture of things he had seen with his own
eyes, that his conversation was meaningful except when on
poetry, and that he was a practical, cold, and silent man.
Reprinted in Conversations with Carlyle (1892).

14 GOSSE, EDMUND. "Tennyson." New Review, 7 (November), 513–23
(515).
Contrasts Wordsworth's quiet funeral with Tennyson's.

15 HALES, JOHN W. "The Last Decade of the Last Century."
Contemporary Review, 62 (September), 422–41.
His scientific studies at Cambridge may have influenced
Wordsworth more than he thought. He participated in the
revival of interest in the Greek and the gothic. He led
the movement in literature to the democratic and to a new
perception of the beauty of the natural world. Reprinted
in Folia Litteria (1893).

16 HILL, GEORGE BIRKBECK. Writers and Readers. London: Unwin,
pp. 17–24, 31, 56–58, 100–101, 106, 177–78, 194–95.
Early critics, including Jeffrey, treated the great poet
of Nature with contempt. Wordsworth's study of contemporary
writers led him into feebleness and tediousness. Records
his personal admiration of Wordsworth. Wordsworth clung
to the past, looked on education with the eye of a solitary
poet.

17 LANG, ANDREW. "Lives of Authors of Poems," in The Blue Poetry
Book. New edition. Edited by Andrew Lang. London and
New York: Longmans, pp. 239–64 (262–63).
A biographical sketch.

18 LEE, EDMUND. Some Noble Sisters. London: Clarke, pp. 155–75.
Dorothy Wordsworth aided Wordsworth intellectually. A
biographical sketch of Wordsworth's relations with Dorothy.

19 M., A. "'The Birds of Wordsworth.'" Athenaeum, no. 3369
(21 May), p. 666.
Wordsworth's description of the dor-hawk is inaccurate.

20 MARSHALL, ED. "John de Clapham." Notes and Queries, 8th ser.,
1 (20 February), 151–52.
Notes a source of The White Doe of Rylstone. (A reply
to the query of Sidney F. Green, "John de Clapham," Notes
and Queries, 7th ser., 12 [19 December 1891], 488.)

1892

21   MATHER, J. MARSHALL. "Wordsworth, the Naturalist," "Coleridge,
     the Metaphysician," in Popular Studies of Nineteenth
     Century Poets. London and New York: Warne, pp. 1-26,
     51-73 (53-57).
         Wordsworth revolted against the poetry of the eighteenth
     century. He was favored by fortune with the leisure to
     pursue poetry, though consequently he lived free from
     struggle and doubt. He stood between pantheism and trans-
     cendentalism, urging men to admiration, hope, and love.
     "We Are Seven" is profound, not a nursery rhyme. Words-
     worth preaches nobly in his sonnets; in his narrative poems
     he is more prosaic (1-26). Notes Wordsworth's friendship
     with Coleridge: Wordsworth is a realist, Coleridge a ro-
     manticist (53-57).

22   MILNER, GEORGE. "The Influence of Burns on Wordsworth."
     Manchester Quarterly, 11 (July), 285-90.
         Wordsworth's own comments refute Hazlitt's remarks on
     Wordsworth and Burns in 1818.B18. Wordsworth was in-
     fluenced by Burns in choice of subjects and diction (e.g.,
     in "Extract: From the Conclusion of a Poem, Composed in
     Anticipation of Leaving School").

23   M.[ORLEY], H.[ENRY]. "Introduction," in Selected Poems from
     Wordsworth. [Edited by Robert Fletcher Charles.] London,
     Paris, and Melbourne: Cassell, pp. 3-6.
         A biographical sketch. God-given genius and firmness of
     resolution made Wordsworth the poet-prophet of the nine-
     teenth century. Every poem embodies a simple truth.
     Attribution: British Museum catalogue.

24   [OLIPHANT, MARGARET]. "Tennyson." Blackwood's Edinburgh
     Magazine, 152 (November), 748-66 (750).
         Wordsworth was "a recluse, never influential as a man
     among men."

25   OLIPHANT, MRS. [MARGARET] and F.[RANCIS] R. OLIPHANT. The
     Victorian Age of English Literature. 2 vols. London:
     Percival, I:2-4, 235, 258; II:134.
         Wordsworth's poetic career was over by 1837. Notes
     Wordsworth's influence on Arnold.

26   PALGRAVE, PROFESSOR [FRANCIS TURNER]. "Wordsworth, William,"
     in Chambers's Encyclopaedia: A Dictionary of Universal
     Knowledge. New edition. 10 vols. London and Edinburgh:
     Chambers; Philadelphia: Lippincott, X:737-40.
         A biographical sketch, noting striking parallels between
     Wordsworth's life and Tennyson's. Critics have exaggerated

1892

Wordsworth's arguments in the Preface to Lyrical Ballads;
still, his poems often fail in execution. He excelled in
sympathy for his fellow men and in imaginative power.
"His subjectivity is itself objective." Includes a brief
primary and secondary bibliography.

27 RAWNSLEY, THE REV. H.[ARDWICKE] D.[RUMMOND]. "The Story of
Gough and His Dog." Transactions of the Cumberland and
Westmorland Association for the Advancement of Literature
and Science, no. 16 (1890-91), pp. 95-124.
Investigates the background to "Fidelity."

28 SAINTSBURY, GEORGE. "Introduction," in A Calendar of Verse.
London: Percival, pp. v-xxiii (xx-xxi).
No poet is so well represented by brief excerpts and
aphorisms as Wordsworth.

29 SHORTER, CLEMENT KING. "A Bibliographical Note," "Introduction," in Lyrics and Sonnets of Wordsworth. Edited by
Clement King Shorter. London: Stott, pp. xix-xxiii,
xxv-xxxiv.
Notes that Knight's Selections from Wordsworth was issued
as a "protest on the part of the Wordsworth Society against
Arnold's volume"; includes a primary and secondary bibliography (xix-xxiii). Wordsworth, as the poet not of nature
but of human life, has made converts among men of widely
different outlooks. Because he wrote of men, he has a
message for those living in cities (xxv-xxxiv).

30 STRACHEY, SIR EDWARD. "Wordsworth on Old Age." Literary
Opinion: An Illustrated Review of English and Foreign
Literature, 7 (January), 186-87.
Wordsworth explores the interaction of youth and age in
"Matthew," "The Two April Mornings," and "The Fountain."
His picture of old age is a true, but not a general, one.

31 SWANWICK, ANNA. Poets The Interpreters Of Their Age. London
and New York: Bell, pp. 268-80.
Wordsworth's work is unequal. His love of nature differed from Burns's: nature reveals God and educates man.
In celebrating the lowly, Wordsworth blends the picturesque
and the human.

32 VEITCH, J.[OHN]. "The Yarrow of Wordsworth and Scott."
Blackwood's Edinburgh Magazine, 151 (May), 638-50.
Describes Wordsworth's visits to the Yarrow and the Yarrow poems. Scott's description does not rise to the sym-
bolism of Wordsworth's. Reprinted in Border Essays (1896).

1892

33   WATSON, GEORGE. "Notabilia of Old Penrith.--Part II."
        Transactions of the Cumberland and Westmorland Association
        for the Advancement of Literature and Science, no. 16
        (1890-91), pp. 55-91 (72-86).
           Traces ancestry of the Cooksons and Wordsworths and
        Wordsworth's early contacts with his relatives.

34   WRIGHT, HENRIETTA C. Children's Stories in English Literature
        from Shakespeare to Tennyson. London: Unwin, pp. 428-34.
           A biographical sketch. Wordsworth uniquely saw the
        spiritual beauty of nature; his poetry contrasts with
        Coleridge's.

1893 A BOOKS - NONE

1893 B SHORTER WRITINGS

1   ANON. Review of The Poetical Works of William Wordsworth
        (ed. Dowden, Volume I). Athenaeum, no. 3404 (21 January),
        pp. 77-78.
           Corrects details in the standard accounts of Words-
        worth's early life.

2   ANON. "Literary Gossip." Athenaeum, no. 3420 (13 May),
        pp. 606-607 (607).
           Reports on the present state of Wordsworth's rooms at
        Cambridge.

3   ANON. "Our Poets' Corner: Wordsworth (1770)." Girl's Own
        Paper, 14 (13 May), 523.
           A biographical sketch.

4   ANON. Review of The Poetical Works of William Wordsworth
        (ed. Dowden). Athenaeum, no. 3433 (12 August), pp. 218-20.
           Wordsworth was not an artist in words. Points out the
        sources of Wordsworth's quotations from other authors and
        suggests datings for several poems. In "Ruth" Wordsworth
        is indebted to Bartram's Travels.

5   ANON. "Prof. Dowden's Edition of Wordsworth." Athenaeum,
        no. 3434 (19 August), pp. 259-60.
           A reply to 1893.B24.

6   ANON. "New Books and Reprints." Saturday Review, 76
        (11 November), 553-54 (554).
           "The prose of the most prosy of great poets is anything
        but inspiriting."

7   ANON. "The Aldine Wordsworth." Saturday Review, 76
      (18 November), 574.
          Wordsworth's arrangement of his poems is arbitrary.

8   ANON. "Wordsworth's Room in St John's." Eagle: A Magazine
      Supported by Members of St John's College, 18 (December),
      61-62.
          Describes Wordsworth's room at Cambridge.

9   ANON. Note, in Pedley's Northern Poetry Cards: The Idle
      Shepherd Boys. Leeds: Pedley [1893], p. [1].
          A biographical sketch. Points out with approval the
      moral in "The Idle Shepherd-boys."

10   ARDENSTONE, JAMES. "The Orientation of Churches." Builder,
      64 (4 March), 179.
          A reply to 1893.B56. Suggests Wordsworth's source for
      his note to "On the Same Occasion" ("When in the antique
      age of bow and spear") is Bartram's Travels of a City
      Gentlemanne thorough the Shire of Yorke.

11   BAYNE, THOMAS. "'Dame.'" Notes and Queries, 8th ser., 3
      (7 January), 14.
          Identifies the "frugal dame" in "Nutting." (A reply to
      query of C. B. Mount, "'Dame,'" Notes and Queries, 8th
      ser., 2 [17 December 1892], 487.)

12   BEECHING, H.[ENRY] C.[HARLES]. "Notes," in A Paradise of
      English Poetry. Edited by H. C. Beeching. 2 vols.
      London: Percival, I:301-12 (304-305, 307, 312); II:357-62
      (360-62).
          The beginning and ending of "Ode: Intimations of Im-
      mortality" deal with particular experiences and so may be
      omitted. Notes echo of Vaughan in The Excursion (Book IV)
      and "Ode: Intimations of Immortality."

13   BLAKENEY, EDWARD HENRY. "Caird's Essays." Churchman, NS 7
      (August), 591-96 (594-95).
          Wordsworth exhibits the constructive rather than nega-
      tive results of the French Revolution. A "flavour of as-
      tringency" pervades his work, resulting from his vision of
      the union of man, nature, and God.

14   BROOKE, STOPFORD A. The Development of Theology as Illustrated
      in English Poetry From 1780 to 1830: The Essex Hall
      Lecture, 1893. London: Green, pp. 18, 27-33.
          Wordsworth's theology was wider in his poetry than in
      his life. He replaced the idea of God as the creator of a

1893

machine with the perception that God is immanent in all
things. He escaped pantheism.

15   C.[AMPBELL], J.[AMES] D.[YKES]. "'Some Unpublished Letters of
Wordsworth.'" Athenaeum, no. 3415 (8 April), p. 443.
A response to 1893.B58. Mary Wordsworth was not only
an affectionate wife but an inspiring influence as well.
Discusses dating of "Oh what a Wreck! how changed in mien
and speech!"

16   C.[AMPBELL], J.[AMES] D.[YKES]. "'Goody Blake and Harry
Gill.'" Athenaeum, no. 3439 (23 September), p. 418.
A letter to the Ipswich Magazine in 1799 (see 1799.B7)
shows that "Goody Blake and Harry Gill" was tolerated as a
poem for the sake of its moral.

17   CAMPBELL, JAMES DYKES. "Introduction," "Notes," in The
Poetical Works of Samuel Taylor Coleridge. Edited by James
Dykes Campbell. London and New York: Macmillan,
pp. xi-cxxiv (passim), 561-654 (passim).
Discusses Wordsworth's life and work as they touch
Coleridge's. Revised as 1894.B10 (xi-cxxiv). Notes in-
fluence of and reference to Wordsworth in Coleridge's poems
(561-654).

18   COLERIDGE, ERNEST HARTLEY. "Unpublished Letters of Samuel
Taylor Coleridge: Edited by his Grandson." Illustrated
London News, 102 (22 April), 500; (27 May), 634; (10 June),
698; (24 June), 766.
Includes letters in which Richard Reynell notes that
Wordsworth had "physiognomical traits of genius" (500),
Coleridge records in 1800 that Wordsworth "meditates a
novel" and notes the appearance of Lyrical Ballads (1800)
(634), and Coleridge records Wordsworth's agreement with
Jeffrey concerning Coleridge's review of Clarkson (698)
and blames charges of simplicity against himself on the
Preface to Lyrical Ballads (766). Reprinted in 1895.B13.

19   C.[OLERIDGE], E.[RNEST] H.[ARTLEY]. "Note on Wordsworth."
Athenaeum, no. 3438 (16 September), p. 388; no. 3443
(21 October), p. 556.
"To a Young Lady who had been Reproached for Taking Long
Walks in the Country" was addressed to Mary Hutchinson.

20   C.[OLERIDGE], E.[RNEST] H.[ARTLEY]. "Wordsworth and the
'Morning Post.'" Athenaeum, no. 3445 (4 November),
pp. 627-28.

Details Wordsworth's contributions to the <u>Morning Post</u> in 1801-1803, including "Sonnet" ("I find it written of Simonides") and "Written in a Grotto."

21 COLERIDGE, SAMUEL TAYLOR. "Ad Vilmum Axiologum" (poem), in <u>The Poetical Works of Samuel Taylor Coleridge</u>. Edited by James Dykes Campbell. London and New York: Macmillan, p. 138.

Wordsworth's "song creates a thousand-fold echo!"

22 DE QUINCEY, THOMAS. "Conversation and S. T. Coleridge," "Mr. Finlay's History of Greece," "Shakespeare and Wordsworth," "Criticism on Some of Coleridge's Criticisms of Wordsworth," "Wordsworth and Southey: Affinities and Differences," in <u>The Posthumous Works of Thomas De Quincey</u>. Edited by Alexander H. Japp. 2 vols. London: Heinemann, II:7-59 (38-43, 49-50), 60-90 (85), 197-200, 201-207, 208-12.

Objects to Wordsworth's portrait of the Rev. Robert Walker (38-43, 49-50) and Wordsworth's depreciation of the present age (85). Wordsworth has affinities with both Shakespeare and Milton (197-200). Defends Wordsworth's choice of a pedlar as philosopher in <u>The Excursion</u>. Wordsworth should not have yielded to Coleridge's perverse criticisms (201-207). Praises Wordsworth's early opposition to Napoleon. His literary theory differs from Southey's (208-12). For Volume I, <u>see</u> 1891.B14.

23 DE VERE, AUBREY [THOMAS]. "Wordsworth," in <u>The Household Poetry Book</u>. Edited by Aubrey De Vere. London: Burns & Oates, pp. 189-90.

A biographical sketch. Wordsworth writes of ideal human nature. His interest in himself is not egotism; his interest in the natural world is not pantheism. His poems are moral and Christian, though the diction sometimes suffers from a "thoughtful diffuseness."

24 DOWDEN, EDWARD. "Prof. Dowden's Edition of Wordsworth." <u>Athenaeum</u>, no. 3434 (19 August), p. 259.

A reply to 1893.B4. Points out the existence of the parody, <u>The Battered Tar</u>.

25 DOWDEN, EDWARD. "Wordsworth's 'Grace Darling.'" <u>Athenaeum</u>, no. 3440 (30 September), pp. 453-54.

Describes the privately-printed pamphlet, <u>Grace Darling</u>.

26 DOWDEN, EDWARD. "Notes," "Bibliography," "Chronological Table," in <u>The Poetical Works of William Wordsworth</u>. Edited by Edward Dowden. 7 vols. London and New York:

1893

Bell, IV:283-387, V:325-66, VI:313-87, VII:259-62, 359-62;
305-28; 329-58.
Includes textual and critical notes to the poems (IV:283-
387, V:325-66, VI:313-87, VII:259-62, 359-62), a primary
bibliography (305-28), and chronological table of the poems
(329-58). For Volumes I-III, see 1892.B12.

27 EWART, HENRY C. "Wordsworth," in In the Footsteps of the
Poets. By David Masson and Others. Illustrated. London:
Isbister [1893], pp. 203-33.
Pre-Raphaelite painting found its inspiration in Wordsworth's devotion to nature. Wordsworth's dealings with
human passion are slight compared with his insight into
nature, even in Peter Bell and "Ode: Intimations of Immortality." A biographical sketch.

28 G-Y. Review of The Poetical Works of William Wordsworth (ed.
Dowden). Bookman, 4 (September), 180-81.
Wordsworth's greatest poems contain few textual revi-
sions. Wordsworth "cures us of the scorn of life."

29 HUTCHINSON, T.[HOMAS]. "Coleridgiana." Academy, 43 (3 June),
481; (10 June), 505.
Points out errors concerning Coleridge and the Wordsworths in 1893.B17.

30 HUTCHINSON, T.[HOMAS]. "Notes on Two Recent Editions of
Wordsworth." Academy, 44 (26 August), 170-72; (9 September),
211-14; (21 October), 340-43; (4 November), 391-92;
(2 December), 486-88.
Points out the inaccuracy of Knight's dating and col-
lating of Wordsworth's poems (170-72, 211-14). Wordsworth's
method was classical, Tennyson's romantic (211-14). Notes
a boom in interest in Wordsworth since Arnold's edition of
1879. Wordsworth classified his poems in groups of rela-
tive importance (340-43). Commends Dowden's editing of
Wordsworth's poems (340-43, 391-92). Traces Wordsworth's
use of the words "frame," "towards," "sombre," and "sweet"
(486-88).

31 INNES, ARTHUR D. "Five English Poets." Monthly Packet, NS 5
(January), 28-36; (March), 255-65; (April), 388-97 (388-89);
(May), 498-508 (500-503); (June), 615-25 (615-16, 620-21).
Wordsworth as a poet, like Arnold, of lofty serenity,
differs from Tennyson and the Brownings (28-36). All that
is best in Wordsworth's work is dependent on his love of
nature, especially the spiritual elevation when contem-
plating the grand aspects of nature that separates him from

other nineteenth-century poets (255-65). Wordsworth's love
poems do not show strong feeling (388-89). In "Ode: Intimations of Immortality" Wordsworth expresses not regret
but triumphant expectations (500-503). Reading him produces "a healing and refreshing calm" because he "restores
our mental and moral balance" (615-16, 620-21). Reprinted
with minor revisions in 1893.B32.

32 INNES, ARTHUR D. Seers and Singers: A Study of Five English
    Poets. London: Innes, especially pp. 1-25, 75-98,
    152-53, 179-85, 199, 201, 211-14, 222.
        Reprinted with minor revisions from 1893.B31. Words-
    worth, contrary to appearances, must have valued reading.
    He struggled long for fame.

33 JAPP, ALEXANDER H. "Wordsworth" (poem), in Occasional Verses:
    with some Miscellaneous Sonnets. [London and Aylesbury:]
    privately printed, p. 94.
        Wordsworth's "judgment with excess would ever break, /
    And joy from sorrow secret tribute take."

34 KNIGHT, WILLIAM. "Wordsworth's Rooms at Cambridge."
    Athenaeum, no. 3421 (20 May), p. 639.
        Protests the impending destruction of the rooms at Cam-
    bridge "once occupied by our great Nature-Poet."

35 KNIGHT, WILLIAM. "Preface," "Bibliography of Wordsworth's
    Prose Writings," in Prose Writings of Wordsworth. Edited
    by William Knight. London: Scott [1893], pp. ix-xxiv,
    xxv-xxix.
        Wordsworth's prose, not all of which is worth reading,
    is characterized by lucidity, freshness, wholesomeness,
    elevation, and truth. There is perfect consistency between
    his views on the worth of man as man in "A Letter to the
    Bishop of Llandaff" and his later conservatism (ix-xxiv).
    A bibliography (xxv-xxix).

36 LEE, EDMUND. "Note on Wordsworth." Athenaeum, no. 3442
    (14 October), p. 523.
        A reply to 1893.B19. "To a Young Lady who had been Re-
    proached for Taking Long Walks in the Country" was addressed
    to Dorothy Wordsworth.

37 [LEE, ELIZABETH]. Review of Angellier's Robert Burns.
    Blackwood's Edinburgh Magazine, 154 (August), 215-23
    (222-23).
        Wordsworth was removed from particular phenomena in his
    attitude towards equality and nature.

1893

38 LITHGOW, R. A. DOUGLAS. "The Lake School, and Its Influence
on English Poetry," in Royal Society of Literature:
Afternoon Lectures on English Literature: Delivered by
Members of the Council from January to June, 1893. London:
Asher [1893], pp. 99-134.
    A biographical sketch. The Lake Poets carried forth the
principles initiated by Cowper and Burns. Wordsworth devoted himself to teaching others his calm, earnest, and en-
nobling faith in the worship of God through nature. Though
sometimes his subjects are too puerile, he is the master
at writing good single lines. All succeeding poets have
been influenced by him.

39 LYSTER, THOMAS W. "Introduction: The Nature of Poetry,"
Notes, in Select Poetry for Young Students. Second edition.
Edited by Thomas W. Lyster. Dublin: Browne & Nolan;
London: Simpkin, Marshall, Hamilton, Kent, pp. ix-xv
(xi-xii), 20-33, 178-93.
    Contrary to Wordsworth's view, poetry and prose are dis-
tinct (xi-xii). Critical notes to the poems selected, including "The Two April Mornings," "Fidelity," and "Hart-
leap Well." Wordsworth's poems are not concerned with the
natural objects described but with the human interest at-
tached to them. Compares Shelley's "To a Skylark" with
"To a Sky-lark" ("Up with me! up with me into the clouds!")
(20-33, 178-93). (First edition, also 1893, not located.)

40 MACMILLAN, MALCOLM KINGSLEY. "Dialogue between Blake and
Wordsworth (Unfinished)," in Selected Letters of Malcolm
Kingsley Macmillan. London: privately printed, pp. 301-
309.
    The spirit of Blake accuses Wordsworth of being "a rene-
gade, a presumer, a blasphemer," who "fled to Nature";
Wordsworth's use of nature contrasts with Byron's.

41 MARSHALL, EDWARD H. "'Dame.'" Notes and Queries, 8th ser., 3
(7 January), 14.
    Interprets "frugal dame" in "Nutting."

42 MARSHALL, EDWARD H. "'We are seven.'" Notes and Queries,
8th ser., 3 (6 May), 346.
    Notes parallel between Genesis and "We Are Seven."

43 MEUSCH, ROBERT A. J. "Goethe and Wordsworth." Publications
of the English Goethe Society, no. 7, pp. 85-107.
    Wordsworth and Goethe both kept the faith to strive while
realizing the limitations of human nature. To Wordsworth,
as opposed to Goethe, man was but a part of nature.

44   MYERS, FREDERIC W. H.   "Modern Poets and the Meaning of Life."
      Nineteenth Century, 33 (January), 93-111 (93, 105-106).
         Wordsworth, ignorantly hostile to science, intuited "the
      interpenetration of the spiritual and the material worlds."

45   PATER, WALTER. Plato and Platonism: A Series of Lectures.
      London and New York: Macmillan, p. 64.
         In "Ode: Intimations of Immortality" Wordsworth made
      the concept of metempsychosis his own.

46   PAYN, JAMES. "Some Unpublished Letters of William Wordsworth."
      Independent (New York), 45 (2 March), 284; (9 March),
      315-16.
         Wordsworth's letters exhibit "honest simplicity and
      directness of purpose," solicitude for others, and lack of
      playfulness. Wordsworth paid little attention to how he
      dressed (284). His letters show the care with which he
      studied poems, his dislike of "literary ladies," and his
      awareness of his poetic decline (315-16).

47   Φ   "Reminiscences of Scott, Campbell, Jeffrey, and
      Wordsworth." Bookman, 4 (May), 47-48 (48).
         Records visit to Rydal Mount: Wordsworth resembled "a
      Lowland farmer of the better class."

48   RAWNSLEY, H.[ARDWICKE] D.[RUMMOND]. "Last of the Dorothys that
      Rydal knew" (poem), Note, in Valete. Glasgow: Mac Lehose,
      pp. 134, 174-75.
         Dorothy Wordsworth, daughter of Richard Wordsworth of
      Whitehaven, helped Wordsworth overcome his grief at the
      deaths of his children.

49   RENTON, WILLIAM. Outlines of English Literature. London:
      Murray, pp. 194-95.
         Wordsworth blends the physical, the spiritual, and the
      psychological.

50   RIX, HERBERT. "Down the Duddon with Wordsworth." Leisure
      Hour, 42 (June), 532-39.
         Traces Wordsworth's path in The River Duddon.

51   ROBINSON, PHIL. "In the Poets' Garden." Contemporary Review,
      63 (June), 825-42 (835, 837-40).
         Traces Wordsworth's use of flowers. "To a Snowdrop" is
      marred.

52   ROBINSON, PHIL. The Poets and Nature: Reptiles, Fishes, and
      Insects. London: Chatto & Windus, passim.

1893

Mostly reprinted from 1885.B36–B37 and 1886.B43–B44.
Notes Wordsworth's use of reptiles, fish, and insects.

53 SANDYS, J. E. "Prof. Dowden's Edition of Wordsworth."
    Athenaeum, no. 3434 (19 August), p. 259.
        Identifies allusion to Moschus in "After-thought" ("I
    thought of Thee, my partner and my guide").

54 SPENCER, J. HOUGHTON. "The Orientation of Churches."
    Builder, 64 (11 February), 115.
        Wordsworth [in his note to "On the Same Occasion" ("When
    in the antique age of bow and spear")] is responsible for
    the idea that ancient church builders took measurements
    from the rising sun.

55 SYDNEY, WILLIAM CONNER. "The Cradle of the Lake Poets."
    Gentleman's Magazine, 275 (December), 590–605 (590–91,
    596–99, 601).
        Retells story of Wordsworth and Coleridge in the west
    of England.

56 T., H. E. "The Orientation of Churches." *Builder*, 64
    (18 February), 135.
        A reply to 1893.B54. Questions Wordsworth's authority
    for his note to "On the Same Occasion" ("When in the an-
    tique age of bow and spear").

57 WARD, C. A. "Dowden's 'Wordsworth.'" *Athenaeum*, no. 3435
    (26 August), p. 289.
        Identifies allusion to Young in "Tintern Abbey."
    Wordsworth lacked wit.

58 [WILLIAMS, MRS. E. BAUMER]. "Some Unpublished Letters of
    William Wordsworth." *Cornhill Magazine*, NS 20 (March),
    257–76.
        Wordsworth's poems exhibit his humanitarianism. His
    letters are characterized by honest simplicity, directness,
    lack of playfulness. Annotates the letters printed.

59 WOOD, MILWARD. "Dove Cottage, Grasmere." *Girl's Own Paper*,
    14 (2 September), 772–73.
        Describes Dove Cottage. One wonders how Wordsworth
    could write in such a small, noisy house. Dorothy, a prac-
    tical woman, was a blessing to Wordsworth.

60 WORDSWORTH, CHARLES. *Annals of My Life 1847–1856*. Edited by
    W. Earl Hodgson. London and New York: Longmans, pp. 19,
    49–50, 89–90.

Attests to Wordsworth's belief in Christianity and promise to revise the title of "Glen Almain" and lines in "William the Third." Describes Wordsworth's funeral, quoting Hall Caine's account from the Times of 17 October 1892.

61   WRIGHT, J.[OHN] C.[HARLES]. "Preface," "Wordsworth," "Notes," in Wordsworth for the Young. Edited by J. C. Wright. London: Jarrold [1893], pp. v, vii-viii, 81-98.
     Wordsworth's "aim was to teach people to love the common objects around them . . . so that their lives might be peaceful and happy" (v). A biographical sketch (vii-viii). Includes critical notes to the poems selected (81-98).

62   WRIGHT, J.[OHN] C.[HARLES]. "William Wordsworth," in Readings from Great English Writers. Edited by J. C. Wright. London: Allen [1893], p. 253.
     A biographical sketch.

1894 A   BOOKS

 1   SOMERVELL, ARTHUR. The Power of Sound: Cantata. London and New York: Novello, Ewer, 74 pp.
     A cantata, the words taken from "On the Power of Sound."

1894 B   SHORTER WRITINGS

 1   ANON. Review of Masson's In the Footsteps of the Poets. Speaker, 9 (3 March), 256-57.
     The prophet Wordsworth, in contrast to Cowper and Thomson, saw natural objects as the symbols of a new revelation.

 2   ANON. "The Wordsworths in Scotland." Spectator, 72 (12 May), 658-59.
     Dorothy Wordsworth's journal illustrates Wordsworth's "perfect equableness."

 3   ANON. Review of The Poetical Works of William Wordsworth (ed. Dowden). Speaker, 9 (19 May), 565.
     Wordsworth's alterations to his texts repay investigation.

 4   ANON. Review of Prose Writings of Wordsworth (ed. Knight). Speaker, 10 (1 September), 251.
     Wordsworth's prose is lucid, fresh, wholesome, elevated, and full of insight.

1894

5   ANON. "Unpublished Letters of Wordsworth and Coleridge."
       Athenaeum, no. 3502 (8 December), p. 791.
            Wordsworth's unpublished letters to F. Wrangham shed new
       light on his collaboration with Wrangham on a satire, on
       his first meeting with Coleridge, and on his relations with
       Mary Hutchinson.

6   ANON. Middleton's Illustrated Handbook to Grasmere. Amble-
       side: Middleton, passim.
            Records Wordsworth's associations with Grasmere.

7   BROWN, J. MACMILLAN. Manual of English Literature: Era of
       Expansion, 1750-1850. Christchurch, Dunedin, and London:
       Whitcombe and Tombs, especially pp. 282-302.
            Surveys Wordsworth's life and works. An Evening Walk
       and Descriptive Sketches contain almost all the qualities
       of Wordsworth's poetic revolution. In Lyrical Ballads
       Wordsworth dwells too much on the commonplace. His poems
       reveal his awareness of the beauty of the world, the soul
       that informs it, and "the purifying influence of intercourse
       with it." In the Preface to Lyrical Ballads he does not
       realize he is but the culmination of a movement rather than
       its leader.

8   C.[AMPBELL], J.[AMES] D.[YKES]. "The Philadelphia Reprint of
       the 'Lyrical Ballads.'" Athenaeum, no. 3460 (17 February),
       pp. 213-14.
            A bibliographic description of the edition published by
       Humphreys in 1802.

9   C.[AMPBELL], J.[AMES] D.[YKES]. "Wordsworth and Allston."
       Athenaeum, no. 3480 (7 July), pp. 33-34.
            Discusses Wordsworth's debt to Washington Allston in
       "Composed upon an Evening of Extraordinary Splendour and
       Beauty."

10   CAMPBELL, JAMES DYKES. Samuel Taylor Coleridge: A Narrative
       of the Events of his Life. London and New York:
       Macmillan, passim.
            Revised from 1893.B17.

11   CAPPER, EDITH. "A Century of Wordsworth." Sunday at Home,
       no. 2102 (11 August), pp. 646-51.
            A biographical sketch. Includes personal recollections
       of Wordsworth by his neighbors, testifying to his kind-
       heartedness.

12   CHOTZNER, A. J. "The English Lakes" (poem). Eagle: A
     Magazine Supported by Members of St John's College, 18
     (June), 246–52 (250–52).
          Wordsworth lived a life of peace, receiving joy from
     nature.

13   C.[OLERIDGE], E.[RNEST] H.[ARTLEY]. "Wordsworth on Wordsworth
     and Coleridge." Athenaeum, no. 3500 (24 November),
     pp. 716–17.
          A reply to 1894.B19. The portraits in "Stanzas Written
     in My Pocket-copy of Thomson's 'Castle of Indolence'" de-
     pict Coleridge and an idealized combination of Wordsworth
     and Coleridge.

14   DIRCKS, W. "Prefatory Note," in Passages from the Prose and
     Table Talk of Coleridge. Edited by W. H. Dircks. London:
     Scott [1894], pp. vii–xiii.
          The Preface to Lyrical Ballads "is a passionately and
     closely reasoned statement," which drew Coleridge's best
     criticism.

15   DIXON, WILLIAM Mac NEILE. English Poetry from Blake to
     Browning. London: Methuen, pp. 8, 74–102.
          In the Preface to Lyrical Ballads Wordsworth argued that
     "thought was not disassociated from feeling." Wordsworth
     and Coleridge were diverse in character and temperament.
     Wordsworth fought not simply against conventional diction
     but against "conventionalism of the heart and mind," favor-
     ing simple elemental feelings. In his sonnets, not his
     longer poems, he is his artistic best. He helps readers
     to a habit of thoughtfulness.

16   [DOUGLAS, DAVID, ed.]. Familiar Letters of Sir Walter Scott.
     2 vols. Edinburgh: Douglas, I:27–29, 40, 52, 85, 97,
     334, 415; II:335–43.
          Includes letters in which Scott comments upon "Yarrow
     Unvisited" and The White Doe of Rylstone, expresses his
     fear that Wordsworth seeks to write simply what is differ-
     ent, praises Wordsworth's morality, and records his visits
     with Wordsworth in 1805 and 1825. Includes letters in
     which F. Jeffrey inquires of Wordsworth in 1806, J. Baillie
     criticizes Wordsworth's personifications of nature, and
     Lockhart remarks in 1825 that Wordsworth "is old and
     pompous, and fine, and absurdly arrogant" and records Words-
     worth's opinion of Canning, Crabbe, and contemporary poets.

17   DOWDEN, EDWARD. "Notes on Wordsworth." Athenaeum, no. 3461
     (24 February), pp. 246–47.
          Notes Wordsworth's debt to books of travels.

1894

18   E., A. "The Library at Hawkshead Grammar School, and the
         School-Days of Wordsworth." Eagle: A Magazine Supported
         by Members of St John's College, 18 (December), 383-88.
              Describes the library at Wordsworth's school. Lines in
         The Prelude (Book V) cannot refer to William Raincock.

19   HUTCHINSON, T.[HOMAS]. "Wordsworth's 'Castle of Indolence
         Stanzas.'" Fortnightly Review, NS 56 (1 November), 685-
         704.
              Discusses the identity of the portraits in "Stanzas
         Written in My Pocket-copy of Thomson's 'Castle of Indo-
         lence.'"

20   HUTCHINSON, T.[HOMAS]. "Wordsworth on Wordsworth and
         Coleridge." Athenaeum, no. 3503 (15 December), p. 829.
              A reply to 1894.B13. Wordsworth is purposefully hyper-
         bolic in "Stanzas Written in My Pocket-copy of Thomson's
         'Castle of Indolence'"; stanzas 1-4 describe Wordsworth,
         not Coleridge.

21   [KEBBEL, THOMAS EDWARD]. Review of Leslie's Letters to Marca,
         etc. Edinburgh Review, 179 (January), 61-75 (61, 64-67,
         70).
              Wordsworth carried a new interest in nature to all
         classes of readers; as opposed to eighteenth-century poets,
         he brought nature into more immediate contact with man.

22   LEE, EDMUND. Dorothy Wordsworth: The Story of a Sister's
         Love. New and revised edition. Illustrated. London:
         Clarke [1894], passim.
              Revised from 1886.B32.

23   MANN, A. H. "Wordsworth, William," in Cassell's Storehouse
         of General Information. 48 parts. London, Paris, and
         Melbourne: Cassell, Part 48, pp. 376-77.
              A biographical sketch.

24   MINTO, WILLIAM. The Literature of the Georgian Era. Edited
         by William Knight. Edinburgh and London: Blackwood,
         pp. 140-84.
              A biographical sketch. The Preface to Lyrical Ballads
         did not initiate a change in literary taste but described
         one that had already taken place. Wordsworth's own artis-
         tic development from eighteenth-century poets can be traced
         in his early poems. Coleridge in Biographia Literaria mis-
         interprets Wordsworth's arguments about the language of
         poetry and prose. One must have a preliminary sympathy be-
         fore one can appreciate Wordsworth's poems. Though the

emotional motive to Wordsworth's poetry is simple, the
imaginative structure is elaborate. Wordsworth wrote of
the new thoughts that occurred to him when minutely ob-
serving nature. He differs from Coleridge and Southey,
though Coleridge influenced him markedly.

25 PARSON, A COUNTRY. The Annals of a Quiet Valley. Edited by
John Watson. London: Dent, pp. 140-41, 169.
Recounts incident of Wordsworth, Coleridge, and John
Gough; describes visit to Wordsworth's grave.

26 RAWNSLEY, THE REV. H.[ARDWICKE] D.[RUMMOND]. Literary
Associations of the English Lakes. 2 vols. Glasgow:
Mac Lehose, passim.
Discusses Wordsworth's life and poems in their contexts
in the Lake District.

27 RINDER, EDITH WINGATE. "Introduction," in Poems and Lyrics
of Nature. Edited by Edith Wingate Rinder. London and
New York: Scott [1894], pp. xvii-xlvi (xxxvii-xxxix).
Wordsworth teaches us not to describe nature but to
interpret it impressionistically.

28 ROBERTSON, J.[AMES] LOGIE. A History of English Literature
for Secondary Schools. Edinburgh and London: Blackwood,
especially pp. 248-51, 254-58.
Wordsworth interprets nature spiritually in a style un-
conventionally free. He completed the return of poetry to
nature begun by eighteenth-century poets. A biographical
sketch.

29 ROBERTSON, JOHN M. "Coleridge." Free Review, 1 (1 January),
305-29 (311-13, 316); (1 February), 470-91 (476-78, 483,
490).
"The Rime of the Ancient Mariner" is "un-Wordsworthian"
(311-13, 316). "On the stimulus of Wordsworth . . .
Coleridge produces rarer and subtler poetry than Wordsworth's." Wordsworth devoted himself to a great poetic
plan but succeeded "only in some of the unforeseen by-ways
of the task" (476-78, 483, 490). Expanded in 1897.B62.

30 RUSKIN, JOHN. "Candida Casa," in Verona and Other Lectures.
Illustrated. Orpington and London: Allen, pp. 77-108
(79-80).
"Lucy Gray" best describes "the local English character
of which [Wordsworth's] works are the monument at once,
and epitaph."

1894

31 VALENTINE, MRS. [LAURA]. Note, in Cameos of Literature from
    Standard Authors: A Modernised and Revised Edition of the
    "Half-hours with the Best Authors." Edited by Mrs.
    Valentine. 12 vols. London and New York: Warne, I:171.
    A biographical sketch.

1895 A BOOKS

*1 ANON. In Lakeland, a Wordsworthic Pilgrimage, Easter 1895.
    Not located. Cited in 1896.B36, VIII:364.

2   MEDBOROUGH, JAMES. Some Wordsworth Finds? London: Unicorn,
    47 pp.
    Claims to have discovered some new poems and fragments
    by Wordsworth.

1895 B SHORTER WRITINGS

1   ANDERSON, G. F. REYNOLDS. "Wordsworth" (poem), in The White
    Book of the Muses. Edinburgh: Johnston, p. 67.
    An anchorite, Wordsworth sang of nature freshly and
    clearly.

2   ANON. Review of The Letters of Samuel Taylor Coleridge.
    London Quarterly Review, NS 25 (October), 58-76 (65-67, 70).
    Wordsworth's poetic realism "penetrates to the essential
    verities of things." In "Dejection: An Ode" Coleridge
    attacks Wordsworth's philosophy.

3   ANON. "Wordsworth and Carlyle--a Literary Parallel."
    Temple Bar, 106 (October), 261-67.
    Wordsworth and Carlyle shared a spiritual kinship, recog-
    nizing the importance of the imaginative faculty, the poet,
    the "seeing eye," childhood, emotion, honest toil, and duty.

4   ANON. "The Poet-Laureateship." Temple Bar, 106 (December),
    498-516 (513-15).
    Recounts Wordsworth's appointment as Poet Laureate.

5   ANON. Note, in Pedley's Northern Poetry Cards: Alice Fell.
    Leeds: Pedley [1895], p. [1].
    Wordsworth's poetry is true to nature and possesses a
    simple gracefulness. Points out the moral in "Alice Fell."

6   ANON. Note, in Pedley's Northern Poetry Cards: The Pet-Lamb.
    Leeds: Pedley [1895], p. [1].
    Points out with approval the moral in "The Pet-lamb."

7   ANON. Notes, in <u>Pedley's Northern Poetry Cards: Grace
     Darling</u>. Leeds: Pedley; London: Simpkin, Marshall
     [1895], pp. [1], [3].
          A biographical sketch. Points out with approval the
     lessons in <u>Grace Darling</u> and "Rob Roy's Grave."

8   ARMITT, ANNIE. "Haunts of the Poets: I.--Wordsworth and
     Westmorland." <u>Atalanta</u>, 9 (November), 82-91.
          Describes Wordsworth's associations with the Lake
     District.

9   BEECHING, H.[ENRY] C.[HARLES]. "Notes," in <u>Lyra Sacra: A
     Book of Religious Verse</u>. Edited by H. C. Beeching. London:
     Methuen, pp. 337-56 (351-52).
          Wordsworth is most religious when he makes least effort
     to be so. Includes critical note to "Ode: Intimations
     of Immortality."

10   BELL, THE REV. CHARLES D. "Wordsworth," in <u>Some of Our
     English Poets</u>. London: Stock, pp. 245-80.
          Expanded from 1881.B9, adding a biographical sketch.

11   BROOKE, STOPFORD A. "Introduction," in <u>The Golden Book of
     Coleridge</u>. Edited by Stopford A. Brooke. London: Dent,
     pp. 1-64 (10, 26-28, 38-40, 46-47, 51, 59-64).
          Wordsworth's poetry was original from the beginning.
     His influence on Coleridge sprang from his simpler, steadier
     soul.

12   COLERIDGE, ERNEST HARTLEY, ed. <u>Anima Poetae: from the Un-
     published Note-books of Samuel Taylor Coleridge</u>. London:
     Heinemann, p. 30.
          Includes S. T. Coleridge's expression of pleasure in
     seeing Wordsworth turn from shorter poems to his great
     work.

13   COLERIDGE, ERNEST HARTLEY, ed. <u>Letters of Samuel Taylor
     Coleridge</u>. 2 vols. London: Heinemann, passim.
          Discusses date of Coleridge's first meeting Wordsworth,
     and Coleridge's later estrangement from Wordsworth. Re-
     prints 1893.B18 and adds to previously printed Coleridge
     correspondence letters in which Coleridge describes Words-
     worth in 1796 as a republican and semi-atheist; praises
     Wordsworth and his poems; records Wordsworth's life at Al-
     foxden, sea-sickness and life in Germany, and objection to
     the want of books at Stowey; speculates that in "A slumber
     did my spirit seal" Wordsworth was fancying Dorothy's
     death; records alarms over Wordsworth's health in 1799;

praises <u>Lyrical Ballads</u> (1800); discusses his plans of
settling with Wordsworth in the North; records Wordsworth's
preference of Lake scenery to the Alps; notes in 1802 that
he and Wordsworth begin to suspect their poetic creeds dif-
fer; records his visit to Scotland with the Wordsworths in
1803; commends <u>Concerning . . . the Convention of Cintra</u>;
and recounts his quarrel with Wordsworth. Includes variant
text of "Dejection: an Ode" addressed specifically to
Wordsworth: hails Wordsworth's rejoicing in the living
world (<u>see</u> 1817.B6 and 1883.B25).

14 DENT, W.[ALTER]. "Biographical Sketch," "Notes," in <u>William
Wordsworth: Shorter Poems</u>. London, Glasgow, and Dublin:
Blackie, pp. 5-9, 28-32.
  A biographical sketch. Wordsworth's theory of diction
is too extreme, <u>The Excursion</u> a great failure. Yet Wordsworth succeeds in minute observation and in seeing lessons
everywhere (5-9). Brief critical notes to the poems selected, including "Composed upon Westminster Bridge"
(28-32).

15 DOWDEN, EDWARD. "Introduction," in <u>Poems</u>. By Robert Southey.
Edited by Edward Dowden. London and New York: Macmillan,
pp. vii-xxvi (ix, xvii, xxiv).
  In political writings Wordsworth deals with principles,
Southey with heroic action.

16 [EDWARDS, CHARLES]. "The Valley of the Duddon." <u>Cornhill
Magazine</u>, NS 25 (July), 78-86.
  Traces and comments upon Wordsworth's descriptions in
The River Duddon.

17 FORMAN, H. BUXTON. "Thomas Wade: The Poet and His Sur-
roundings," in <u>Literary Anecdotes of the Nineteenth
Century: Contributions towards a Literary History of the
Period</u>. Edited by W. Robertson Nicoll and Thomas J. Wise.
2 vols. London: Hodder & Stoughton, I:43-67 (46-47).
  In his later life Wordsworth tried hard not to be a
poet, though unsuccessfully.

18 GOSSE, EDMUND. "Wordsworth, William," in <u>Johnson's Universal
Cyclopaedia</u>. New edition. Edited by Charles Kendall
Adams. 8 vols. New York: Appleton, and Johnson,
VIII:836.
  A biographical sketch.

19 GOW, JAMES. "Correspondence of the Lloyd Family." Athenaeum,
    no. 3514 (2 March), pp. 281-82 (282).
        Prints letter in which Charles Lloyd reveals, in 1809,
    Wordsworth's contempt for Horace, preoccupation with po-
    litical subjects and indifference towards others' literary
    efforts.

20 GRESWELL, WILLIAM. "The Witchery of the Quantock Hills."
    Temple Bar, 104 (April), 523-36 (526-28, 532-36).
        Did the Quantock Hills themselves foster original thought
    in Wordsworth, Coleridge, and Andrew Crosse?

21 HIRON, M. F. "The Charm of Wordsworth." Great Thoughts, 4
    (23 March), 399.
        Unlike Milton, Wordsworth writes of the commonplace.
    His poems possess a simple grandeur. His sympathy with the
    simple life never waivered.

22 HUTCHINSON, THOMAS. "Preface," "Chronological Table of the
    Life of William Wordsworth," "Notes," in The Poetical Works
    of William Wordsworth. Edited by Thomas Hutchinson.
    London: Frowde, pp. vii-x, xxv-xxxii, 897-933 and passim.
        Outlines his editorial procedure (vii-x), includes a
    chronology and primary bibliography (xxv-xxxii), and gives
    brief critical and bibliographical notes (897-933 and
    passim).

23 [HUTTON, RICHARD HOLT]. "Wordsworth and Mr. Watson."
    Spectator, 75 (27 July), 107-108.
        In most poems, including "Thoughts Suggested the Day
    Following, on the Banks of Nith, near the Poet's Residence,"
    Wordsworth accompanies his "soaring" with "clumsy prelud-
    ings" giving his theme. He influenced William Watson.

24 JAPP, ALEXANDER H. "Thomas De Quincey: His Friends and
    Associates," in De Quincey and His Friends: Personal
    Recollections, Souvenirs and Anecdotes of Thomas De Quincey
    His Friends and Associates. Edited by James Hogg. London:
    Sampson Low, Marston, pp. 1-70 (40-48).
        Records De Quincey's admiration of and correspondence
    with Wordsworth.

25 LANG, ANDREW. "Preface," in Border Ballads. Illustrated by
    C. O. Murray. London: Lawrence and Bullen; New York:
    Longmans, pp. v-xxv (xxiii-xxiv).
        Condemns "Ellen Irwin" as doggerel.

1895

26   LEE, EDMUND. "Memoir of Dora Wordsworth," in Journal of A
     Few Months' Residence in Portugal and Glimpses of the South
     of Spain. By Dora Wordsworth (Mrs. Quillinan). New
     edition. Edited by Edmund Lee. London and New York:
     Longmans, pp. ix-xxxix.
         Discusses Wordsworth life as it touches Dora's.

27   LENDRUM, W. T. "Wordsworth and Martial." Academy, 47
     (16 March), 238.
         Notes parallel between "They dreamt not of a perishable
     home" and Martial.

28   MORRISON, ALFRED. The Collection of Autograph Letters and
     Historical Documents: Second Series: 1882-1893: The
     Blessington Papers. [London:] privately printed,
     pp. 101-102, 114, 124, 141.
         Includes letters from Landor to Lady Blessington in which
     Landor comments that the inner depths of Wordsworth's mind
     contain "many coarse, intractable, dangling threads," and
     remarks Wordsworth's receipt of an honorary degree at Ox-
     ford in "Wordsworth has well deserved of late" (poem).

29   NOBLE, J. ASHCROFT. "Some Skylark Poems," in Impressions &
     Memories. London: Dent; New York: Putnam's, pp. 77-90
     (83-85).
         In "To a Sky-lark" ("Up with me! up with me into the
     clouds!") Wordsworth uncharacteristically achieves "a cer-
     tain effusive gaiety."

30   Q.[UILLER-]C.[OUCH], A.[RTHUR] T.[HOMAS]. "A Literary
     Causerie: Poets on Their Own Art." Speaker, 11 (11 May),
     520-21 (521).
         Wordsworth's prose in the Preface to Lyrical Ballads,
     though too rhetorical, is good. Reprinted in Adventures in
     Criticism (1896).

31   RHYS, ERNEST. "Introduction," in The Prelude to Poetry: The
     English Poets in the Defence and Praise of their own Art.
     Edited by Ernest Rhys. London: Dent [1895], pp. vii-xx
     (xi-xiii).
         Wordsworth represents a "slow, deliberate, lyric method."

32   ROSSETTI, WILLIAM MICHAEL. Dante Gabriel Rossetti: His
     Family-Letters with a Memoir. 2 vols. London: Ellis and
     Elvey, I:75, 410, 415, 421; II:330.
         Records D. G. Rossetti's opinions of Wordsworth: his
     "conventionally compliant" character and his surprising in-
     sight into Italian art.

394

1895

33   RUSSELL, GEORGE W. E., ed. Letters of Matthew Arnold 1848–
     1888. 2 vols. New York and London: Macmillan,
     especially I:8, 11, 47, 278, 280; II:58, 126, 190–92,
     213–14.
        Prints letters in which Arnold records his admiration
     for and opinions of Wordsworth: Goethe's range of experi-
     ence surpasses Wordsworth's; Wordsworth could not comply
     with his own teaching when Dora died.

34   SHERARD, ROBERT H. "Letter from Paris." Author, 5 (1 March),
     265–68 (266–67); (1 May), 313–14 (314).
        Wordsworth was overwhelmed with manuscripts sent by as-
     piring writers (266–67). Quotes report denying Wordsworth
     charged visitors for refreshments (314).

35   SMALL, ALEXANDER. "Dorothy Wordsworth." Great Thoughts,
     3rd ser., 5 (27 April), 56–59.
        That Wordsworth's life was so calm was due to his wife
     and sister. Dorothy's self-sacrifice was rewarded, for
     her spirit is wrought into Wordsworth's poems.

36   SONNENSCHEIN, WILLIAM SWAN. A Reader's Guide to Contemporary
     Literature: Being the First Supplement to The Best Books.
     . . . London: Sonnenschein; New York: Putnam's,
     especially pp. 548, 550–52, 562, 589–90, 598, 616–17.
        A primary and secondary bibliography, expanded from
     1891.B42.

37   STEPHEN, LESLIE. "Coleridge's Letters." National Review, 25
     (May), 318–27 (319, 325–26).
        Records Coleridge's admiration of and quarrel with
     Wordsworth.

38   [SYMONDS, EMILY M.]. "The Old Criticism." Cornhill Magazine,
     NS 24 (February), 151–57 (151, 153).
        Points out the initial critical reaction to Wordsworth's
     poems.

39   WALKER, HUGH. The Greater Victorian Poets. London:
     Sonnenschein; New York: Macmillan, especially pp. 204–205,
     221–22, 234–35.
        Wordsworth, unlike Tennyson, theorizes about the relation
     of man to nature; unlike Arnold, he ignored certain elements
     of life.

40   WEDGWOOD, JULIA. "Samuel Taylor Coleridge." Contemporary
     Review, 67 (April), 548–68 (548, 551–54, 560–62).

1895

The Excursion contains echoes of Kant, which Wordsworth
must have received from Coleridge. Wordsworth is never in-
timate with his reader. His political sympathies were
robust but not dominant. Discusses Wordsworth's estrange-
ment from Coleridge.

1896 A BOOKS

1   RAWNSLEY, THE REV. H.[ARDWICKE] D.[RUMMOND], ed. A
    Reminiscence of Wordsworth Day, Cockermouth, April 7,
    1896. . . . Illustrated. Cockermouth: Brash, 88 pp.
        Includes: 1) Rawnsley's tributary sonnet, "Well met in
    glad commemorative throng"; 2) H. J. Palmer's description
    of Cockermouth and Wordsworth's associations there; 3) com-
    memorative speeches by Joseph Straughton, Rawnsley (the
    names of Wordsworth and Dorothy must not be separated;
    Wordsworth aimed to keep men's lives simple and pure),
    Palmer, Edwin Jackson, and Sir Wilfrid Lawson; 4) "Letters
    Read at the Meeting from Distinguished Admirers of the
    Poet," including (among others) Walter Crane, W. E. Glad-
    stone, Harry Goodwin, J. H. Shorthouse, and the Rt. Rev. W.
    Walsham How, Bishop of Wakefield (containing a poem "To
    Wordsworth" saying Wordsworth transfigured nature); 5) an
    address by Rawnsley: Wordsworth "not only unfolded a new
    philosophy, but he made men desire it"; he discovered the
    harmony that exists between man and nature; he combined deep
    feeling with profound thought; 6) an essay by Rawnsley,
    "Wordsworth & Cockermouth"; 7) addresses by T. P. Whittaker
    and W. L. Alexander: Wordsworth espoused the brotherhood
    of man; and 8) "Wordsworth: A Sketch of his Life and Work"
    by the Rev. J. Llewelyn Davies.

1896 B SHORTER WRITINGS

1   ANON. "Wordsworth's 'Parson Sympson.'" Temple Bar, 107
    (January), 63-75 (63-66, 72-74).
        Describes the intercourse of the Wordsworths and Sympsons.

2   ANON. Review of The Poetical Works of William Wordsworth (ed.
    Knight, Volumes I-II). Athenaeum, no. 3575 (2 May),
    pp. 575-76.
        Wordsworth's poems should not be arranged chronologically.

3   ANON. "Wordsworth." Athenaeum, no. 3578 (23 May), pp. 681-82.
        A reply to 1896.B13, B26, and B33, defending charges made
    against Knight in 1896.B2.

4 ANON. "Professor Knight's Wordsworth." Saturday Review, 81 (30 May), 559-60.
Wordsworth's classification of his poems is fanciful. Many of his textual revisions are unfortunate.

5 ANON. Review of The Poetical Works of William Wordsworth (ed. Knight, Volumes I-II). Speaker, 14 (29 August), 226-28.
Wordsworth's singular spiritual music is becoming drowned in his own commentary. Wordsworth changed little, even politically, during his life. Editors should respect his arrangement of his works.

6 ANON. Review of The Poetical Works of William Wordsworth (ed. Knight, Volumes III-VII). Athenaeum, no. 3609 (26 December), pp. 893-94.
Objects to the chronological arrangement of poems for studying Wordsworth's development.

7 ANON. Notes, in Pedley's Northern Poetry Cards: Simon Lee, the Old Huntsman. [Leeds: Pedley, 1896], pp. [1-2].
Points out morals in "Simon Lee" and "The Redbreast Chasing the Butterfly."

8 B. "A Vision of Judgment.--I." Speaker, 13 (22 February), 211-12 (211).
Judges Wordsworth "arrogant, ecstatic, pantheistic, namby-pamby, highest and sometimes lowest of singers."

9 B., C. C. "Wordsworth's 'Ecclesiastical Sonnets.'" Notes and Queries, 8th ser., 9 (22 February), 158; (25 April), 332.
Explains textual revisions in "Elizabeth." (A reply to query of Edward H. Marshall, "Wordsworth's 'Ecclesiastical Sonnets,'" Notes and Queries, 8th ser., 9 [1 February], 89. See also the reply of H. Buxton Forman, "Wordsworth's 'Ecclesiastical Sonnets,'" Notes and Queries, 8th ser., 9 [22 February], 157-58) (158). Notes dates of additions to Ecclesiastical Sonnets and Wordsworth's care in revising "Crusaders." (A reply to query of Edward H. Marshall, "Wordsworth's 'Ecclesiastical Sonnets,'" Notes and Queries, 8th ser., 9 [28 March], 253) (332).

10 BAYNE, THOMAS. "'On sea or land.'" Notes and Queries, 8th ser., 9 (27 June), 506.
Wordsworth's punctuation deepens the significance in "Elegiac Stanzas Suggested by a Picture of Peele Castle."

11 BRIERLY, HARWOOD. "The Village where Wordsworth was Married." Notes and Queries, 8th ser., 9 (25 January), 62-64.
Describes Brompton.

1896

12   BROOKE, STOPFORD A. English Literature from A.D. 670 to A.D.
     1832. [Third edition.] London and New York: Macmillan,
     pp. 151-56.
          A biographical sketch, revised from 1880.B13.

13   CRAIK, GEO. LILLIE. "Wordsworth." Athenaeum, no. 3578
     (23 May), p. 681.
          A defense of Knight against attacks in 1896.B2.

14   CRAWFURD, OSWALD. "Notes," in Lyrical Verse From Elizabeth to
     Victoria. Edited by Oswald Crawfurd. London: Chapman &
     Hall, pp. 423-37 (434).
          Wordsworth's fame as a lyric poet rests on his sonnets.
     Discusses the reference of "she" in "A slumber did my
     spirit seal."

15   [DIXON, WILLIAM Mac NEILE]. Review of De Vere's Julian the
     Apostate, etc. Quarterly Review, 183 (April), 310-38
     (310-13).
          Wordsworth's "theory that greatness in art is greatness
     in conception" rather than in expression is true, though
     little in vogue since 1850. Reprinted as "The Poetry of
     the De Veres" in In the Republic of Letters (1898).

16   ELLIS, A.[DELE]. "Wordsworth," "Notes: Wordsworth," in
     Chosen English: Selections from Wordsworth, Byron, Shelley,
     Lamb, Scott. Edited by A. Ellis. London and New York:
     Macmillan, pp. 11-14, 106-24.
          A biographical sketch. Wordsworth's poems are charac-
     terized by feeling for inanimate nature, and simplicity
     (11-14). Notes to the poems selected, including "Lines
     Written in Early Spring," "To a Skylark" ("Ethereal min-
     strel! pilgrim of the sky!"), and "She was a Phantom of
     delight" (106-24).

17   ELLIS, HAVELOCK. "The Colour-Sense in Literature."
     Contemporary Review, 69 (May), 714-29 (716, 718, 722-23,
     726, 728).
          Green, yellow, and gray predominate in Wordsworth's
     poems. Wordsworth was not keenly sensitive to the joy of
     color.

18   FÖRSTER, MAX. "Wordsworth, Coleridge, and Fredericke Brun."
     Academy, 49 (27 June), 529-30.
          Wordsworth has added a Scottish atmosphere to Brun's
     poem in "The Seven Sisters."

19 FRIEND, THE REV. HILDERIC. "The Flower of the Month: Celan-
    dine: Wordsworth's Favourite Flower." Great Thoughts,
    3rd ser., 6 (14 March), 381-82.
        Approves of Wordsworth's celebrating of the celandine.

20 GRESWELL, WILLIAM. "Wordsworth's Quantock Poems." Temple
    Bar, 107 (April), 530-48.
        Describes Alfoxden and Wordsworth's life and work there,
    work expressing nature's gladness and human sadness. Words-
    worth differed from Crabbe in language, thought, and in-
    tention. He is indebted to his neighborhood for scenes and
    characters, especially in "Simon Lee," "The Old Cumberland
    Beggar," "Ruth," "The Thorn," and the poem on John Walford.

21 HERFORD, C.[HARLES] H.[AROLD]. Review of The Poetical Works
    of William Wordsworth (ed. Knight, Volumes I-III).
    Bookman, 10 (July), 111.
        Wordsworth had "a kind of official punctiliousness and
    precision in dealing with the outer circumstances of his
    poetry."

22 HILL, GEORGE BIRKBECK. "Letters of D. G. Rossetti." Atlantic
    Monthly, 77 (June), 744-54 (746); 78 (August), 242-55
    (242-43, 245).
        Records Rossetti's comment that one might read Crabbe
    more often and later than Wordsworth (746), and that much
    of Wordsworth, who is good but unbearable, is "'puffy-
    muffy'" (242-43, 245). Reprinted in Letters of Dante
    Gabriel Rossetti to William Allingham 1854-1870 (1897).

23 HORTON, ROBERT F. "Grasmere Revisited" (poem). Good Words,
    37:466.
        Records his new appreciation of Wordsworth's "thoughts
    too passionate for passionate speech" and "condescension to
    the weak and worn."

24 HUTCHINSON, THOMAS. "Professor Knight and His Revisers."
    Academy, 49 (18 April), 324-25.
        Quarrels with Knight's editing.

25 HUTCHINSON, THOMAS. "Prof. Knight and Mr. T. Hutchinson--An
    Explanation." Academy, 49 (2 May), 366.
        A reply to 1896.B32.

26 HUTCHINSON, THOMAS. "The Eversley Wordsworth: Errata in Vol.
    II." Athenaeum, no. 3576 (9 May), p. 620.
        A reply to 1896.B2. Briefly discusses chronology of
    early poems.

1896

27 HUTCHINSON, T.[HOMAS]. "Wordsworth." Athenaeum, no. 3580
        (6 June), p. 746.
            A reply to 1896.B13, B33. Questions the existence of a
        third issue of Volume II of Lyrical Ballads (1800). See
        1896.B29.

28 HUTCHINSON, THOMAS. Review of The Poetical Works of William
        Wordsworth (ed. Knight, Volumes I-II, III-VI). Academy,
        50 (4 July), 5-7; (3 October), 233-34.
            Finds fault with Knight as an editor of Wordsworth's
        poems.

29 HUTCHINSON, THOMAS. "The Text of Wordsworth." Athenaeum,
        no. 3584 (4 July), pp. 35-36.
            A continuation of 1896.B27. Discusses the printing of
        Lyrical Ballads (1800) and describes a copy of Volume II
        containing a corrected half-sheet.

30 [HUTTON, RICHARD HOLT]. "What is a Lyric?" Spectator, 76
        (23 May), 735-36.
            Lyrical Ballads are neither lyrical nor ballads.

31 JACKSON, FRANCIS W. "The Village where Wordsworth was Married."
        Notes and Queries, 8th ser., 9 (22 February), 150.
            A reply to 1896.B11. Records entry of Wordsworth's mar-
        riage in the register at Brompton.

32 KNIGHT, WILLIAM. "Prof. Knight and Mr. T. Hutchinson--An
        Explanation." Academy, 49 (2 May), 366.
            A reply to 1896.B24.

33 KNIGHT, WILLIAM. "Wordsworth." Athenaeum, no. 3578 (23 May),
        p. 681.
            A defense against attacks in 1896.B2.

34 KNIGHT, PROFESSOR [WILLIAM]. Memoir of John Nicol: Professor
        of English Literature in the University of Glasgow.
        Glasgow: Mac Lehose, pp. xvi, 8, 42, 67, 229, 303.
            Includes Nichol's recollection of his early appreciation
        of Wordsworth and his remarking of the unequal quality of
        his poems.

35 KNIGHT, WILLIAM. "Preface," Notes, in The Prose Works of
        William Wordsworth. Edited by William Knight. 2 vols.
        London and New York: Macmillan, I:vii-xv, passim.
            Finds fault with Grosart's edition of 1876 on which he is
        dependent since manuscripts have not survived; includes a
        list of prose works (I:vii-xv). Reprints poem by M., "To

William Wordsworth," from the Morning Post of 18 December 1844: commends Wordsworth's stand on the Kendal and Windermere Railway. Includes bibliographic notes throughout the volumes (passim).

36   KNIGHT, WILLIAM. "Preface," "Prefatory Note," "A Wordsworth Bibliography," Notes, in The Poetical Works of William Wordsworth. Edited by William Knight. 8 vols. London and New York: Macmillan, I:vii-lxiv; VIII:xvii-xxiii, 327-429; passim.
      Discusses editorial procedures, including arranging the poems chronologically and printing textual revisions (I:vii-lxiv; VIII:xvii-xxiii). Includes primary and secondary bibliography of British, American, and French works (327-429) and textual, critical, and biographical notes to the poems throughout the volumes (passim).

37   LE GALLIENNE, RICHARD. "William Wordsworth: Shorter's Selections," in Retrospective Reviews: A Literary Log. 2 vols. London: Lane; New York: Dodd Mead, I:39-48.
      Wordsworth's lack of a sense of humor stands in the way of his fame. His attempt in "Michael" to apply realism to the pastoral fails. Wordsworth is a poet of human nature. (Dated February 1892; reprinted from a source not identified.)

38   LOCKER-LAMPSON, FREDERICK. My Confidences: An Autobiographical Sketch Addressed to My Descendants. [Edited by Augustine Birrell.] London: Smith, Elder, pp. 161-62, 177-79.
      Records Landor's ranking of Southey with Wordsworth, and his own admiration of Wordsworth's "meditative rapture, spiritual passion," and imagination.

39   LUCAS, E.[DWARD] V. "Some Notes on Poetry for Children." Fortnightly Review, NS 60 (1 September), 391-407 (391-92, 400).
      Disapproves of including Wordsworth in anthologies for children.

40   [LYALL, ALFRED]. Review of The Letters of Charles Lamb, etc. Edinburgh Review, 183 (April), 306-35 (308-309, 312).
      Wordsworth's letters lack the free outpouring of doubt and affection.

41   Q.[UILLER-]C.[OUCH], A.[RTHUR] T.[HOMAS]. "A Literary Causerie: The Miltonic Sonnet.--II." Speaker, 14 (22 August), 200-201.
      Wordsworth's sonnets are further removed than Milton's from the thought of the Guittonian model, though they approach it in form.

1896

42   Q.[UILLER-]C.[OUCH], A.[RTHUR] T.[HOMAS]. "A Literary
         Causerie: Ossian's Centenary." Speaker, 14 (26 December),
         696-97 (696).
              His invocation to Ossian in Essay (1815) shows the
         length to which Wordsworth, a giant of common sense, would
         go when he lost his temper.

43   R., W. "Books from Wordsworth's Library." Athenaeum,
         no. 3579 (30 May), p. 714.
              Describes books from Wordsworth's library to be sold at
         auction, including presentation copies with tributes to
         Wordsworth from Elizabeth Barrett and Keats.

44   RHYS, ERNEST. "Introduction," in The Lyric Poems of William
         Wordsworth. Edited by Ernest Rhys. London: Dent [1896],
         pp. xiii-xxvi.
              A biographical sketch. Lyrical Ballads contains the
         first sign of the new impulse that was to affect English
         poetry through the century. Fortunately, Wordsworth fol-
         lowed his genius rather than his theories. His poetic de-
         cline began when his fellowship with Coleridge ended. His
         lyrics are written to the music of the mind rather than of
         the ear.

45   ROBERTSON, J.[AMES] LOGIE. English Verse for Junior Classes.
         2 parts. Edinburgh and London: Blackwood, Part II,
         pp. 95-98, 113-20.
              The Excursion, "long and laborious," is on the whole
         "the noblest philosophical poem" in English. The style does
         not suit the characters. Includes critical notes to The
         Excursion (Book I).

46   [ROSCOE, EDWARD STANLEY]. Review of Letters of Samuel Taylor
         Coleridge. Edinburgh Review, 183 (January), 99-128 (108,
         122-23).
              Wordsworth did not appreciate Coleridge's friendship.

47   SAINTSBURY, GEORGE. A History of Nineteenth Century Literature
         (1780-1895). London and New York: Macmillan, pp. 49-56.
              A biographical sketch. Wordsworth's character was not
         wholly amiable. He borrowed his diction from Burns and
         Milton. His merits consist in his felicity of phrase, his
         power of describing natural objects, and his "half-panthe-
         istic mysticism."

48   SHERARD, ROBERT HARBOROUGH. "Notes from Paris." Author, 7
         (2 November), 119-21 (120).
              Recounts circumstances of the composition of "Ode on the
         Installation of His Royal Highness Prince Albert."

402

49   [SMITH, G. C. M.]. "Notes," in The Prelude: or Growth of a
      Poet's Mind. By William Wordsworth. [Edited by G. C. M.
      Smith.] London: Dent, pp. 260-64.
          Brief critical notes. Attribution: note, p. 257.

50   STEAD, W.[ILLIAM] T.[HOMAS]. "Preface," "Appendix: The
      Doctrine of Reincarnation," in Wordsworth: Selected Poems.
      Part I. Edited by W. T. Stead. London: "Review of
      Reviews" Office [1896], pp. iii-iv, 55-58 (58).
          Wordsworth's poetry on the tie between man and nature is
      meditative and calm, yet vital. In his sonnets he expresses
      the highest patriotism. The melody of his lines haunts the
      memory (iii-iv). Includes note signed E. D.[ixon] pointing
      out that Wordsworth adds Christian implications to Plato's
      thoughts on a former existence (58).

51   STEAD, W.[ILLIAM] T.[HOMAS]. "Preface," in Wordsworth:
      Selected Poems. Part II. Edited by W. T. Stead. London:
      "Review of Reviews" Office [1896], p. [2].
          Wordsworth's poems should be read in the Lake Country,
      or at least away from the city.

52   T. "A Literary Causerie: White of Selborne." Speaker, 13
      (29 February), 242-43 (242).
          Wordsworth was no naturalist; he discerned the meanings
      in the forms of Nature.

53   TRAILL, H.[ENRY] D.[UFF]. Social England: A Record of the
      Progress of the People. . . . By Various Writers. Edited
      by H. D. Traill. 6 vols. London, Paris, and Melbourne:
      Cassell, V:446, 580-84.
          Lyrical Ballads (1798) is too celebrated as an epoch-
      making publication. Wordsworth's theory of the language
      of poetry cannot be upheld.

54   VAUGHAN, C.[HARLES] E.[DWYN]. "Introduction," in English
      Literary Criticism. Edited by C. E. Vaughan. London,
      Glasgow, and Dublin: Blackie, pp. ix-cii (lxv, lxxv-lxxvii).
          Wordsworth's poetic theory is foreshadowed by Goldsmith.
      Recounts Jeffrey's attacks on Wordsworth.

55   WHITE, W.[ILLIAM] HALE. "Wordsworth's 'Convention of Cintra.'"
      Athenaeum, no. 3591 (22 August), pp. 258-59.
          Notes source in Bacon of the motto to Concerning . . .
      the Convention of Cintra.

56   WRIGHT, J.[OHN] C.[HARLES]. The Poets Laureate: From the
      Earliest Times to the Present. London: Jarrold, pp. 43-67.

1896

A biographical sketch. In The Excursion Wordsworth preaches a Browning-like optimism; man's regeneration can come only from constant intercourse with nature. Wordsworth teaches brotherhood and peace; "yet it was not so much his work as his life that was an inspiration."

1897 A BOOKS

1 KNIGHT, WILLIAM, ed. Journals of Dorothy Wordsworth. 2 vols. London and New York: Macmillan, 272 pp., 292 pp.
   Adds to extracts previously published, Dorothy's accounts of Wordsworth's life, tours, and poems. In editorial preface, records the circumstances surrounding the Journals; includes editorial notes throughout the volumes.

2 MAGNUS, LAURIE. A Primer of Wordsworth: with a Critical Essay. London: Methuen, 235 pp.
   A full biography and critical study. Includes, in "A Critical Essay," a detailed comparison of Wordsworth and Tennyson; Wordsworth "showed us the spiritual sources of joy under the new conditions of our social life"; his "religion was an intellectual paganism." Includes a primary and secondary bibliography.

3 WHITE, W.[ILLIAM] HALE, ed. A Description of the Wordsworth and Coleridge Manuscripts in the Possession of Mr T. Norton Longman. Illustrated. London, New York, and Bombay: Longmans, 78 pp.
   Describes manuscripts of letters and poems by Wordsworth relating to Lyrical Ballads (1798, 1800, 1802) and Poems (1807).

4 WILSON, RICHARD. Helps to the Study of Arnold's Wordsworth. London and New York: Macmillan, 88 pp.
   Includes a biographical sketch and critical notes to the poems in Arnold's selection of 1879. Wordsworth's ballads are uniquely introspective. His retirement to a life of simple piety was self-chosen; he was devoted to family and country. Nature to him was little less than human and was united with the soul of man and with God. His work was essentially homely in subject and manner, though he did use recognizable figures of speech and versification.

1897 B   SHORTER WRITINGS

1   ANON. Review of The Poetical Works of William Wordsworth (ed.
      Knight, Volumes III-IV). Speaker, 15 (2 January), 18-20.
          Wordsworth could never judge his own work. The White Doe
      of Rylstone is a confused and misty narrative. Wordsworth's
      music is grave, miraculous, spiritual, clear, and harmoni-
      ous, even in The Prelude.

2   ANON. Review of The Prose Works of Wordsworth (ed. Knight).
      Academy, 51 (10 April), 394.
          Wordsworth, in his prose, was content "with the just and
      sufficient epithet, without aiming at the magical epithet";
      his style is abstract.

3   ANON. Review of The Poetical Works of William Wordsworth (ed.
      Knight, Volumes V-VI). Speaker, 15 (17 April), 432-34.
          The later Wordsworth, contemplative and self-centered,
      lacked the faculty of ingenuous criticism or dramatic in-
      sight. The direct realism, daring Christianity, and depth
      of thought of The Excursion, especially the first four
      Books, outweigh its diffuseness and discursiveness.

4   ANON. "The Age of Wordsworth." Saturday Review, 83
      (17 April), 417-18.
          Wordsworth's works "are historically speaking unintel-
      ligible except when viewed in reference to the age." See
      1897.B35.

5   ANON. Review of Herford's The Age of Wordsworth. Spectator,
      78 (Supp., 24 April), 567-68.
          Wordsworth surpasses his contemporaries in imaginative
      thought. His poems are not for all moods nor all men.

6   ANON. "Wordsworth and Coleridge Manuscripts." Saturday
      Review, 83 (12 June), 665-66.
          Wordsworth reveres happiness and a playful wisdom.

7   ANON. Review of Palgrave's Landscape in Poetry from Homer to
      Tennyson. Speaker, 15 (26 June), 709-10.
          Wordsworth is the master, the Turner, of landscape.

8   ANON. Review of White's A Description of the Wordsworth and
      Coleridge Manuscripts. . . . Athenaeum, no. 3636 (3 July),
      pp. 31-32.
          Suggests John Wordsworth as the writer of a letter of
      15 September 1800 and Sir James Mackintosh as the subject
      of the motto to Lyrical Ballads (1800).

1897

9   ANON. Review of White's <u>A Description of the Wordsworth and</u>
     <u>Coleridge Manuscripts</u>. . . . <u>Academy</u>, 52 (17 July), 43–44.
        Had Wordsworth not revised <u>Poems</u> (1807) before publica-
     tion, the critical hostility would have been greater than
     it was. He was indebted to Ben Jonson for the meter of
     "To the Daisy" ("Bright Flower! whose home is everywhere"),
     "To the Daisy" ("In youth from rock to rock I went"), and
     "To the Same Flower" ("With little here to do or see"), and
     to Drayton.

10   ANON. Review of <u>The Prose Works of William Wordsworth</u> (ed.
     Knight). <u>Speaker</u>, 16 (17 July), 72–73.
        Notes discrepancy between Wordsworth's early and later
     political opinions; commends his calm, deep, passionless,
     edifying prose.

11   ANON. Review of <u>The Poetical Works of William Wordsworth</u> (ed.
     Knight, Volume VIII). <u>Academy</u>, 52 (4 September), 176–77.
        Wordsworth's systematic and philosophical arrangement of
     his poems is artificial; he was the most occasional of
     poets. As his inspiration failed later in life, so did
     his poetry.

12   ANON. "Professor Knight's Edition of Wordsworth." <u>Spectator</u>,
     79 (18 September), 375–76.
        Wordsworth's poems should be printed in chronological
     order, without elementary notes.

13   ANON. "School-books." <u>Athenaeum</u>, no. 3647 (18 September),
     p. 384.
        Suggests a German influence on the diction of "There was
     a Boy" and "Nutting."

14   ANON. Review of <u>The Poetical Works of William Wordsworth</u> (ed.
     Knight, Volume VIII). <u>Athenaeum</u>, no. 3648 (25 September),
     pp. 412–13.
        Wordsworth's work does not culminate in "Ode: Intimations
     of Immortality"; his poems cannot be condensed into a dogma.

15   ANON. Review of <u>The Poetical Works of William Wordsworth</u> (ed.
     Knight, Volume VIII). <u>Scottish Review</u>, 30 (October), 416.
        Wordsworth's poems do not all lead up to "Ode: Intima-
     tions of Immortality."

16   ANON. Review of White's <u>A Description of the Wordsworth and</u>
     <u>Coleridge Manuscripts</u>. . . . <u>Speaker</u>, 16 (2 October),
     373–74.
        Wordsworth's best work was published by 1807.

17   ANON. "Dorothy Wordsworth." Saturday Review, 84
      (30 October), 470.
          "The imagination of Dorothy underwent much the same
      fossilization as did that of her brother."

18   ANON. Review of Worsfold's The Principles of Criticism.
      Speaker, 16 (13 November), 539-40.
          Notes similarity between passages from Addison and
      "Elegiac Stanzas Suggested by a Picture of Peele Castle."

19   ANON. "The Early Life of Wordsworth." Spectator, 79
      (13 November), 689-90.
          Wordsworth's poetry is intrinsically English. It is
      difficult to reconcile "the Wordsworth of revolt" with the
      older poet "whose calm estimate of life we revere."

20   ANON. "Wordsworth Literature." Athenaeum, no. 3655
      (13 November), pp. 671-72.
          Wordsworth's textual changes in "Beggars" did not reflect
      a lessened sympathy with vagrants.

21   ANON. "Reprints." Literature (London), 1 (11 December),
      233-34.
          In Poems (1807) Wordsworth abandons the principles of
      the Preface to Lyrical Ballads and, more than in Lyrical
      Ballads, calls us back to nature.

22   ANON. "Preface," "Biographical Note," in The Poetical Works
      of William Wordsworth. London: Bliss Sands [1897],
      pp. vii-viii, ix-xii.
          Wordsworth's attitude towards Nature is today "the com-
      mon inheritance of all educated people" (vii-viii). A
      biographical sketch (ix-xii).

23   [BEECHING, HENRY CHARLES]. "Pages from a Private Diary."
      Cornhill Magazine, 3rd ser., 2 (May), 692-701 (695, 698);
      (June), 836-45 (842-44); 3 (July), 114-25 (116-18).
          The impulse to aspiration (in "The Tables Turned") is not
      the only impulse to come from a vernal wood. The most
      Wordsworthian lines in "I wandered lonely as a cloud" were
      written by Wordsworth's wife (695, 698). Peter Bell is mis-
      understood: he did notice primroses (842-44). Discusses
      the identities of the portraits in "Stanzas Written in My
      Pocket-copy of Thomson's 'Castle of Indolence'" (116-18).
      Reprinted in Pages from a Private Diary (1898).

24   BROOKE, STOPFORD A. "Introduction," in Poems Dedicated to
      National Independence and Liberty: Reprinted on behalf of

1897

the Greek struggle for the Independence of Crete. By
William Wordsworth. London: Isbister, pp. 9-32.
   After 1810 Wordsworth's political poetry fails. His desire to see Napoleon overthrown led Wordsworth into un-
qualified support for England, which hardened into "a stony
conservatism." His earlier sonnets and Concerning . . . the
Convention of Cintra, in which he appeals to the soul of
England, are applicable to England's relations with Crete
today.

25   COLLINS, J. CHURTON. "Wordsworth and Liberty." Saturday
     Review, 84 (28 August), 226-27.
        A reply to 1897.B24. It was because they loved liberty
     that Wordsworth and Burke became conservatives.

26   CORNISH, FRANCIS WARRE, ed. Extracts from the Letters and
     Journals of William Cory. Oxford: privately printed,
     pp. 97, 239, 245-47, 353, 451.
        Includes extracts from his journal and letters in which
     Cory notes that Wordsworth achieves "Virgilian harmony of
     words" and produces in readers "that yielding of ourselves
     to running water and to still clouds" that disposes us to
     appreciate life.

27   COURTHOPE, W.[ILLIAM] J.[OHN]. "Life in Poetry: Poetical
     Expression." Nineteenth Century, 41 (February), 270-84
     (275-78, 283).
        Wordsworth's analysis in the Preface to Lyrical Ballads
     of the function of meter is wrong.

28   DE VERE, AUBREY [THOMAS]. Recollections. New York and London:
     Arnold, pp. 49-50, 59-60, 89, 121-33, 182, 185-87, 194-205,
     268, 273-74, 302.
        Records his and Sir Aubrey de Vere's admiration for
     Wordsworth's poems and his visits with Wordsworth in the
     1840's. Wordsworth exorcised his Byronic sulk. Words-
     worth's meaning penetrates to the soul through the sense,
     not by the sense: Nature was a language that could not be
     translated. Wordsworth refrained from writing love poems
     because they would express only one limited aspect of love.
     He admired only Coleridge among contemporary poets. He
     prayed nightly; his poetic mind was Catholic. His later
     poems deserve appreciation. His face resembled Dante's.
     Records Augustus Stafford's, Lord Chancellor Cranworth's,
     and Cardinal Manning's admiration for Wordsworth.

29   DOWDEN, EDWARD. "Preface," "Introduction," "A Bibliographical
     Note," "Notes," in Poems. By William Wordsworth. Edited by

Edward Dowden. Boston and London: Ginn (Athenaeum Press), pp. vi-viii, xvii-cxiv, cxv-cxvii, 353-516.
Wordsworth's latest texts are on the whole the best (vi-viii). A biographical sketch. Wordsworth's faculties acted in unison. He interpreted rather than described, was an original thinker (though a poet of his age), felt deeply, and lacked humor. "Memory and hope are fellow-workers" in his poems. Traces Wordsworth's poetic development. Wordsworth was a careful craftsman in revising his poems. His prose writings illuminate his poems (xvii-cxiv). Includes a brief primary and secondary bibliography (cxv-cxvii) and bibliographic, textual, and critical notes to the poems selected, based, with additions, on the notes in 1892.B12 and 1893.B26 (353-516). Revised in 1898.B16.

30   DOWDEN, EDWARD. The French Revolution and English Literature: Lectures Delivered in Connection with the Sesquicentennial Celebration of Princeton University. London: Kegan Paul, Trench, Trübner, pp. 156, 160, 195-239, 245-48.
The French Revolution roused equally Wordsworth's intellect and passions; all the aspects of his mind worked together in harmony. He moved from revolutionary fervor but preserved a true understanding of men and liberty.

31   EMERSON, EDWARD WALDO. "John Sterling, and a Correspondence between Sterling and Emerson." Atlantic Monthly, 80 (July), 14-35 (16-17, 22, 33).
Includes letters in which Sterling notes that around 1821 Wordsworth and Coleridge were unknown "mystagogues" and that Wordsworth is satisfied not with the Ideal but with his own feelings about it. Reprinted in A Correspondence between John Sterling and Ralph Waldo Emerson (1897).

32   GARNETT, R.[ICHARD]. "Authors and Publishers." Academy, 51 (2 January), 29.
Wordsworth's translation of a sonnet by Tasso shows his regard for Camoens.

33   HAZLITT, W.[ILLIAM] CAREW. Four Generations of a Literary Family: The Hazlitts in England, Ireland, and America: Their Friends and Their Fortunes 1725-1896. 2 vols. London and New York: Redway, I:80, 84-85, 233-34.
Records W. Hazlitt's appreciation of Wordsworth, who was apparently offended by his discriminating criticism.

34   HAZLITT, WILLIAM CAREW. The Lambs: Their Lives, their Friends, and their Correspondence: New Particulars and New Material. London: Mathews; New York: Scribner's, pp. 136, 216.

1897

Prints letters in which Lamb praises The Excursion and
records sending books to Wordsworth.

35   HERFORD, C.[HARLES] H.[AROLD].   "'The Age of Wordsworth.'"
     Saturday Review, 83 (8 May), 513.
          A reply to 1897.B4. The source of Wordsworth's highest
     poetry does not lie in the French Revolution but in the
     thought it kindled. (Includes a rebuttal by "The Reviewer.")

36   HERFORD, C.[HARLES] H.[AROLD].   The Age of Wordsworth.
     London: Bell, pp. xx-xxix, 146-68, 178-82, 217-18, and
     passim.
          Places Wordsworth in the context of the writers and in-
     tellectual movements of his age, in an effort to define
     "romanticism." A biographical sketch. Wordsworth expressed
     "the dignity of man in himself, and the moral and intel-
     lectual strength which comes to him in communion with Na-
     ture." For him, the speech of rustics is but a negative
     ideal. As his poetic vigor declined, he treated social
     problems more dogmatically. Reprinted with minor correc-
     tions, 1897 and 1899.

37   HUTCHINSON, T.[HOMAS]. "The 'Eversley Wordsworth,' Vol. VIII:
     A Personal Explanation." Athenaeum, no. 3649
     (2 October), p. 456.
          Attacks Knight's "self-satisfaction" as an editor of
     Wordsworth.

38   HUTCHINSON, T.[HOMAS]. "Matthew Arnold's 'Poems of Words-
     worth.'" Athenaeum, no. 3661 (25 December), p. 886.
          Wordsworth altered "The Redbreast Chasing the Butterfly"
     as a result of criticism in The Simpliciad.

39   HUTCHINSON, THOMAS. "Preface," "Appendix: Note on the
     Wordsworthian Sonnet," "Editor's Notes on the Poems," in
     Poems in Two Volumes. By William Wordsworth. Edited by
     Thomas Hutchinson. 2 vols. London: Nutt, I:v-xxxix,
     208-26, 161-207 and II:171-233.
          In the poems written 1802-1807 Wordsworth shows diversity
     and artistic growth in the use of the sonnet and of meter
     (especially in "Song at the Feast of Brougham Castle"), the
     latter due to his study of the Elizabethans. He later al-
     tered passages in the poems that attracted criticism, which
     arose because he seems purposefully to have set out in 1802
     to illustrate the theories of the Preface to Lyrical Ballads
     (I:v-xxxix). The literary conditions of the time and his
     university training combined to form Wordsworth's early
     contempt of the sonnet. Wordsworth followed Milton's

practice, though he occasionally imitated Dante and
Petrarch in the rhymes of the octave. His sestets are
sadly marred (208-26). Includes critical, textual, and
biographical notes (161-207 and II:171-233).

40   [HUTTON, RICHARD HOLT]. "Self-Consciousness in Poetry."
      Spectator, 78 (12 June), 830-32 (831).
          Though his poems contain individual oddities, Words-
      worth's self-consciousness at its best achieves a universal
      quality.

41   KEEN, E. H. "Lines Written in an Album by Wm. Wordsworth."
      Notes and Queries, 8th ser., 12 (6 November), 368.
          Describes autograph (lines from Burns) by Wordsworth.

42   KENYON, FREDERIC G., ed. The Letters of Elizabeth Barrett
      Browning. 2 vols. New York and London: Macmillan,
      I:passim.
          Includes letters in which E. B. Browning records her ob-
      servation of a "reserve" in Wordsworth's face and her ad-
      miration for his poems. Wordsworth is "a philosophical and
      Christian poet." Grace Darling is inferior. Wordsworth
      "took the initiative in a great poetic movement." Records
      Queen Victoria's confession she had not read Wordsworth.

43   KNIGHT, WILLIAM. "A Reminiscence of Tennyson." Blackwood's
      Edinburgh Magazine, 162 (August), 264-70 (265-66).
          Tells of burning a copy of Wordsworth's unpublished poem,
      "an unworthy record of a revolting crime" [about John Wal-
      ford]. Reprinted in Retrospects (1898).

44   LANG, ANDREW. "Introduction," in Wordsworth. Edited by
      Andrew Lang. Illustrated by Alfred Parsons. London,
      New York, and Bombay: Longmans, pp. ix-xxxii.
          A biographical sketch. Wordsworth's direct morals,
      stemming from his view that he wished to be a teacher, in-
      jure him with a generation that believes in art for art's
      sake. Yet what is truly great in his poetry is not his
      moral ideas but the unconscious flashes of genius, evident
      in the poems written 1798-1808, when he was in sympathy with
      life and nature. Because he was too attached to his the-
      ories, he suffered critical abuse and failed to appreciate
      others (especially Scott). "Intellectually he was self-
      absorbed." The poetry of The Excursion needs to be disen-
      tangled from the sermons in not very good blank verse.

45   LANG, ANDREW. The Life and Letters of John Gibson Lockhart.
      Illustrated. 2 vols. London: Nimmo; New York: Scribner's,
      I:81, 102-103, 123-24, 354-55; II:73, 274-83, 336.

1897

> Records Lockhart's observations on Wordsworth: adds, to
> his previously published correspondence, letters in which
> Lockhart praises The Excursion, remarks Wordsworth's pros-
> ing, lack of variety, and self-esteem, and voices his dis-
> appointment at the heaviness and rhetorical declamation in
> The Prelude; a "manliness" separates Wordsworth from
> Southey. Records J. Wilson's dislike of Wordsworth.

46 LILLY, W.[ILLIAM] S. "The Mission of Tennyson." Fortnightly
Review, NS 61 (1 February), 239-50 (239, 241-42).
Wordsworth, though a high prophet, drivels; he cannot
appeal to a wide audience.

47 M., L. "A Literary Causerie: The Psychology of Wordsworth's
Text." Speaker, 16 (11 September), 292-93.
Until Pater, critics did not recognize the passionate
character of Wordsworth's poetry and hence the psychological interest in examining Wordsworth's transition from the
pre-Raphaelitism of Descriptive Sketches to the excessive
reaction of Lyrical Ballads and his later jealous and un-
critical revisions of his texts.

48 M'DONNELL, A. C. "Wordsworth," in XIX.-Century Poetry.
London: Black, pp. 12-19.
A biographical sketch. Wordsworth's life and poetry are
characterized by a "steady determination of purpose."
Wordsworth teaches a lesson in both "Goody Blake and Harry
Gill" and "Laodamia," though in the first poem his manner
is inappropriate.

49 MEYNELL, ALICE. "Notes," in The Flower of the Mind: A Choice
among the best Poems. Edited by Alice Meynell. London:
Richards, pp. 331-48 (345-46).
Discusses textual emendation in "Surprised by joy--
impatient as the Wind." Wordsworth misrepresents the sympathy of nature in "Hart-leap Well."

50 MILNER, GEORGE. "The Criticism of Wordsworth and Some Recent
Additions to Wordsworth Literature." Manchester Quarterly,
16 (July), 195-216.
Wordsworth's poems serve as touchstones of literary
taste. Traces early reviews and recent studies of Wordsworth: his fame has been recovering since 1879.

51 OLIPHANT, MRS [MARGARET]. Annals of a Publishing House:
William Blackwood and His Sons: Their Magazine and Friends.
3 vols. Edinburgh and London: Blackwood, I:171, 278-86,
410; II:158, 199.

Notes J. Wilson's early appreciation and treatment of
Wordsworth in Blackwood's Edinburgh Magazine. Includes
letters in which Coleridge reports on Wordsworth's dealings
with Longman, and Alexander Blackwood reports meeting Wordsworth in Italy in 1837 (Wordsworth's conversation on the
copyright act).

52 PALGRAVE, FRANCIS T. Landscape in Poetry from Homer to
    Tennyson. London and New York: Macmillan, pp. 179,
    231-49.
        The influence of Rousseau can be seen in Wordsworth's
    letter to J. Wilson in 1802. Wordsworth is characterized
    by intenseness of sensibility. He sees landscape spiritual-
    ized and allied with human morality. Like Turner, he gives
    not the copy but the idea of his object. In his best poems
    he blends the picture with the didacticism.

53 PEABODY, A. P. "William Wordsworth." Forum, 23 (July),
    622-28.
        Wordsworth is a priest of nature, a poet of the humble,
    and a philosopher of immortality.

54 PRATT, TINSLEY. "Wordsworth at Rydal" (poem), in Wordsworth
    at Rydal; and other Poems. Manchester and London:
    Heywood, pp. 11-15.
        Wordsworth, free from the taint of earth, found deep
    truths in beauteous scenes.

55 Q.[UILLER-]C.[OUCH], A.[RTHUR] T.[HOMAS]. "A Literary
    Causerie: Suggested by a Volume of Verse." Speaker, 15
    (13 March), 299-300.
        Critics err in valuing Wordsworth's simplistic lyrical
    ballads.

56 Q.[UILLER-]C.[OUCH], A.[RTHUR] T.[HOMAS]. "A Literary
    Causerie: Notes on Mr. Henley's Anthology." Speaker, 16
    (13 November), 538-39 (538).
        "Simon Lee" is not a lyric.

57 Q.[UILLER-]C.[OUCH], A.[RTHUR] T.[HOMAS]. "A Literary
    Causerie: Mr. William Watson's 'The Hope of the World.'"
    Speaker, 16 (24 December), 716-17 (717).
        Wordsworth was moved to poetry by sympathy with nature
    and common life, not by reason; his intellectual principles
    are mere scaffolding to his poems.

58 QUILLER-COUCH, A.[RTHUR] T.[HOMAS]. "Introduction," in
    English Sonnets. Edited by A. T. Quiller-Couch. London:
    Chapman & Hall, pp. v-xx (xvii-xix).

1897

Wordsworth's sonnets combine the "'alive-ness'" of
Milton's with a more general applicability.

59 QUINN, M.[ICHAEL] T.[HOMAS]. "Biographical Sketch,"
"Introduction," "Notes," in Wordsworth: Excursion, Book I.
London and Bombay: Bell, pp. ix-xxv, xxvi-xlii, 43-77.
A biographical sketch. Wordsworth's poetry provides "a
place of refuge for the heart." Wordsworth imported into
English a new element in recognizing the kinship between
nature and man. He never was, and is not now, a popular
poet (ix-xxv). The Excursion bridges conventional genres;
its teaching is of permanent value. The scenery of Book I
is that of the southwest of England. The story of Margaret
has no necessary connection with the rest of the poem, or
with its main idea (xxvi-xlii). Critical notes (43-77).

60 RHYS, ERNEST. "Introduction," in Literary Pamphlets: Chiefly
Relating to Poetry from Sidney to Byron. Edited by Ernest
Rhys. 2 vols. London: Paul, I:9-40 (36-40).
Wordsworth chose to publish his remarks on Burns as a
letter rather than as a traditional pamphlet.

61 ROBERTSON, J.[AMES] LOGIE. Outlines of English Literature for
Young Scholars: with Illustrative Specimens. Edinburgh
and London: Blackwood, pp. 122-25.
A biographical sketch.

62 ROBERTSON, JOHN MACKINNON. "Coleridge," in New Essays toward
a Critical Method. London and New York: Lane, pp. 131-90
(139-41, 145, 150, 170-73, 180, 190).
Expanded from 1894.B29. Coleridge's "physiological experience . . . carried him past at once the theory and the
practice of Wordsworth."

63 S.[HORTER], C.[LEMENT] K.[ING?]. "Notes on New Books."
Illustrated London News, 111 (20 November), 728.
Wordsworth's invigorating influence can be felt by those
unable to appreciate his intense beauty.

64 SHORTER, CLEMENT [KING]. Victorian Literature: Sixty Years of
Books and Bookmen. London: Bowden, pp. 5-9, 13.
Wordsworth has exercised a vital influence over the most
interesting people of the past age. He proclaims liberty,
befriends the poor and oppressed. We now have no time for
his longer poems.

65 [SICHEL, WALTER S.]. Review of Kipling's The Seven Seas, etc.
Quarterly Review, 186 (October), 323-56 (323, 327, 339).

Wordsworth's laborers, insufferably virtuous, are himself, not real rustics.

66 STEPHEN, LESLIE. "Wordsworth's Youth." National Review, 28 (February), 769-86.
    In The Prelude Wordsworth plunges into generalities concerning his experiences in France, the precise applications of which are not clear. He was not at home in metaphysical subtleties, because his philosophy was made up of intuitions. He explores Godwinian moral problems in "Guilt and Sorrow" and The Borderers; he came to realize that "Godwinism meant the 'individualism' of the later economists," with its reckless competition that was destroying English society. Reprinted in Studies of a Biographer (1898).

67 [TENNYSON, HALLAM]. Alfred Lord Tennyson: A Memoir. By His Son. 2 vols. London and New York: Macmillan, I:71-72, 208-10, 265, 338; II:69-71, 288, 484, 491, 504-505.
    Records Wordsworth's visit to Cambridge in 1831 (Wordsworth's fear of revolution, criticism of Coleridge's "Christabel"). Includes A. T. de Vere's recollections of Tennyson's reverence for Wordsworth, admission that Wordsworth was deficient in artistic skill, and visits to Wordsworth (when Tennyson failed to rouse Wordsworth's imagination); Dr. Ker's recollections of the poets' mutual admiration; F. Locker-Lampson's recollections of Tennyson's praise of Wordsworth and criticism of Wordsworth's artistry (e.g., in "Tintern Abbey"); and F. T. Palgrave's reporting of Tennyson's conversation on Wordsworth: Wordsworth's poems are often unequal, heavy.

68 TUTIN, J.[OHN] R.[AMSDEN]. "An Index to the Animal and Vegetable Kingdoms of Wordsworth," in The Poetical Works of William Wordsworth. London: Bliss Sands [1897], pp. 675-81.
    A list of Wordsworth's references to animals and plants, expanded from 1892.A2.

69 W., W. "Tennyson and Wordsworth." Academy, 52 (23 October), 331.
    Notes Wordsworth's early use of an image which later, according to Tennyson, did not move him.

70 WALKER, HUGH. The Age of Tennyson. London: Bell, pp. 216-17, 223.
    To Arnold, Wordsworth's calm was unattainable. Wordsworth did not write long poems well.

1897

71 WEBB, W.[ILLIAM] T.[REGO]. "General Introduction," "Notes,"
    in Selections from Wordsworth. Edited by W. T. Webb.
    London and New York: Macmillan, pp. ix-xlix, 93-208.
        A biographical sketch. Wordsworth's character combined
    austere self-control, child-like responsiveness, sympathy
    with women and children, and love of order. The defects of
    his poems are inequality, restricted range, including ab-
    sence of love poetry, and lack of humor. The merits include
    purity of style, austere naturalness (in which "To a Sky-
    lark" ["Ethereal minstrel! pilgrim of the sky"] contrasts
    with Shelley's poem), seriousness and sanity, uncompromising
    morality (e.g., in "Character of the Happy Warrior"), sym-
    pathy for man as man, sympathy for animal and vegetable
    life, and vivid and truthful imagery. To Wordsworth nature
    is a living presence; nature comes first, man second (con-
    trary to its role in the works of Pope and Tennyson).
    Wordsworth, in contrast with Shelley, views nature as law,
    unified, and often commonplace. His complacent optimism
    arises from his oversight of the cruelties of nature. He
    lacks Tennyson's scientific interest in nature (ix-xlix).
    Full critical notes to the poems selected (93-208).

72 WHEELER, STEPHEN, ed. Letters and Other Unpublished Writings
    of Walter Savage Landor. London: Bentley, pp. 63, 153-61.
        Includes manuscript passages in which Landor notes that
    Wordsworth is prosaic in "To the Right Honourable William,
    Earl of Lonsdale, K.G." ("Oft, through thy fair domains,
    illustrious Peer!") and that Scott excelled Wordsworth.
    Notes Landor's early praise and later detraction of Words-
    worth.

1898 A BOOKS

1   WHITE, WILLIAM HALE. An Examination of the Charge of Apostasy
    Against Wordsworth. London, New York, and Bombay:
    Longmans, 63 pp.
        The charge that Wordsworth changed from a revolutionary
    republican to a commonplace Tory is unfounded.

1898 B SHORTER WRITINGS

1   ANON. Review of Journals of Dorothy Wordsworth. Spectator,
    80 (15 January), 93.
        Wordsworth was "rather exacting" in drawing upon
    Dorothy's devotion.

2   ANON. Review of <u>Selections from Wordsworth</u> (ed. Webb).
      <u>Academy</u>, 53 (15 January), 66.
            Wordsworth's revived fame was due to Palgrave and
      Arnold. His poetry possesses "evenness."

3   ANON. Review of <u>The Poetical Works of William Wordsworth</u> (ed.
      Knight, Volumes VII-VIII). <u>Speaker</u>, 17 (22 January),
      111-12.
            Wordsworth's later poems are failures; the Ecclesiasti-
      cal Sonnets belong to the Oxford Movement. Wordsworth's
      world consisted of a few lonely figures.

4   ANON. Review of <u>Journals of Dorothy Wordsworth</u>. <u>Speaker</u>, 17
      (5 February), 171-73.
            Dorothy humanized the lonely, misanthropic Wordsworth.

5   ANON. Review of White's <u>A Description of the Wordsworth and</u>
      <u>Coleridge Manuscripts. . . .</u> <u>Spectator</u>, 80 (26 February),
      313.
            Wordsworth bestowed much thought on perfecting his work.

6   ANON. Review of White's <u>An Examination of the Charge of</u>
      <u>Apostasy Against Wordsworth</u>. <u>Athenaeum</u>, no. 3678
      (23 April), p. 528.
            Wordsworth owes his reputation as apostate to Shelley
      and Browning. Wordsworth admired Burns.

7   ANON. Review of White's <u>An Examination of the Charge of</u>
      <u>Apostasy Against Wordsworth</u>. <u>Speaker</u>, 18 (2 July), 20-21.
            Wordsworth's change in political views is excusable.
      Wordsworth was a pantheist, agreeing with Christian revela-
      tion only so far as it agreed with him.

8   ANON. Review of <u>Lyrical Ballads</u> (ed. Hutchinson). <u>Athenaeum</u>,
      no. 3690 (16 July), pp. 87-88.
            Wordsworth's emphasis on low and rustic life has in-
      fluenced literature since his day. Gloom often darkens
      Wordsworth's poetry in late as well as early years.

9   ANON. Review of <u>Lyrical Ballads</u> (ed. Hutchinson). <u>Literary</u>
      <u>World</u> (London), NS 58 (5 August), 84.
            If he was overly zealous in preaching his gospel of sim-
      plicity, still Wordsworth effected a poetic revolution.

10   ANON. Review of <u>Lyrical Ballads</u> (ed. Hutchinson). <u>Literature</u>
      (London), 3 (27 August), 174-75.
            <u>Lyrical Ballads</u> (1798) was both symptom and cause of a
      literary revolution.

1898

11 ANON. Review of <u>Lyrical Ballads</u> (ed. Hutchinson). <u>Oxford
    Magazine</u>, 17 (23 November), 104.
        Wordsworth did not in practice follow his theory, set
    forth in the Preface to <u>Lyrical Ballads</u>, about the language
    of poetry and prose.

12 ANON. Proceedings (21 February 1898), in <u>Papers of the
    Manchester Literary Club</u>. Volume XXIV. Manchester:
    Heywood, pp. 471-87 (485-87).
        Includes burlesque, "Wordsworth on a Bicycle," by the
    Rev. A. W. Fox.

13 ANON. "William Wordsworth," in <u>Cassell's Poetry for Children</u>.
    Illustrated. London, Paris, New York, and Melbourne:
    Cassell [1898], p. v.
        Wordsworth celebrates nature and the common.

14 ARMSTRONG, RICHARD A. <u>Faith and Doubt in the Century's Poets</u>.
    London: Clarke, pp. 23-42.
        Wordsworth beheld the face of God and the mind of man
    reflected in nature. His poems urge men to duty and action.

15 BOGG, EDMUND. <u>Two Thousand Miles of Wandering in the Border
    Country, Lakeland and Ribblesdale</u>. Illustrated. Leeds:
    Bogg; York: Sampson, [Part I,] pp. 256-57, 282-83;
    Part II, especially pp. 178-79, 192-93, 216-18.
        Praises the "tender strains" of "On the Departure of Sir
    Walter Scott from Abbotsford, for Naples" and the Yarrow
    poems. Describes Rydal Mount, Wordsworth's birthplace at
    Cockermouth, and Hawkshead.

16 DOWDEN, EDWARD. "Preface," "Addenda," "Introduction," "A
    Bibliographical Note," "Notes," in <u>Poems</u>. By William
    Wordsworth. Edited by Edward Dowden. Boston and London:
    Ginn (Athenaeum Press), pp. vi-viii, viiia-b, xvii-cxiv,
    cxv-cxvii, 353-516.
        Reprinted from 1897.B29 (vi-viii, xvii-cxiv, cxv-cxvii,
    353-516). Corrects and expands notes to the poems selected
    (viiia-b).

17 GARNETT, RICHARD. "Was Wordsworth an Apostate?" <u>Bookman</u>, 14
    (May), 41-42.
        Wordsworth's intellectual error in opting for expediency
    does not justify the charge of political apostasy. His
    later Anglicanism resulted from a decline in his poetic
    faculty.

18 GARNETT, RICHARD. <u>A History of Italian Literature</u>. London:
    Heinemann, pp. 200, 277, 402.

Writings about William Wordsworth, 1793 - 1899

1898

Wordsworth's sonnets, more elevated than Milton's, are
flawed in form. Suggests parallel between "The Thorn" and
a passage in Chiabrera.

19 GARNETT, RICHARD. "Introduction," "Notes," in The Poetry of
    Samuel Taylor Coleridge. Edited by Richard Garnett.
    London: Lawrence & Bullen; New York: Scribner's,
    pp. xiii-lii, 283-313 (283-303, 307).
        The inequality of his poems arises chiefly from Words-
    worth's self-esteem. Coleridge owed his poetical emancipa-
    tion to Wordsworth and Dorothy, though Wordsworth could not
    sympathize fully enough with Coleridge's poetry (xiii-lii).
    Includes notes pointing out Wordsworth's associations with
    Coleridge's poems (283-303, 307).

20 GEIKIE, SIR ARCHIBALD. The Romanes Lecture 1898: Types of
    Scenery and their Influence on Literature: Delivered in
    the Sheldonian Theatre, June 1, 1898. London and New York:
    Macmillan, pp. 39, 54-57.
        Praises Wordsworth's descriptions of the natural world.
    Wordsworth suffused landscape "with an ethereal glow of
    human sympathy," foresaw the interest added to scenery by
    modern scientific knowledge.

21 GOSLOWLY, GIDEON. "'Peter Bell.'" Speaker, 17 (5 February),
    180-81.
        Allegorizes Peter Bell: Peter represents the poet, the
    ass the reading public.

22 GOSSE, EDMUND. A Short History of Modern English Literature.
    London: Heinemann, pp. 276-90, 303-305.
        The romantic school began, the classic school disappeared,
    with the publication of Lyrical Ballads (1798). Though they
    resemble one another closely, Wordsworth and Coleridge do
    differ as poets. The spirit of political revolt was only
    mildly awakened in Wordsworth.

23 GREENLAND, W. KINGSCOTE. "A Tramp through the Wordsworth
    Country." Great Thoughts, 4th ser., 2 (4 June), 149-51.
        Young men do indeed appreciate Wordsworth. Describes
    tour of scenes with Wordsworthian associations.

24 HOGBEN, JOHN. "The Birds of Wordsworth." Gentleman's
    Magazine, 284 (June), 532-40.
        Details Wordsworth's portrayal of birds.

25 HUTCHINSON, T.[HOMAS]. "Untraced Mottoes in Wordsworth."
    Athenaeum, no. 3713 (24 December), pp. 897-98.

419

1898

> Traces the motto to "Ode to Duty" to Seneca and that on
> the half-title in Lyrical Ballads (1802, 1805) to Quin-
> tilian; discusses the mottoes on the title pages of Lyrical
> Ballads (1800, 1802, 1805) and Poems (1807).

26 HUTCHINSON, THOMAS. "Introduction," "Bibliographical Note,"
>   "Notes," in Lyrical Ballads: 1798. By William Wordsworth
>   and S. T. Coleridge. Edited by Thomas Hutchinson. London:
>   Duckworth, pp. ix-liii, lv-lx, 205-63.
>   Recounts the publishing history and reception of Lyrical
>   Ballads. Wordsworth ventured too far in choosing subjects
>   and language from rustic life. By the term "language" in
>   the Preface to Lyrical Ballads Wordsworth means simply
>   "words," not "style." He expended in his levelling theory
>   of diction all the revolutionary ardor that had failed to
>   find an outlet in public affairs. The homely subjects of
>   Lyrical Ballads were not new; Wordsworth's investigation in
>   such poetry of the psychology of the passions, resulting in
>   part from his study of Godwin, was (ix-liii). Includes a
>   bibliography of editions of Lyrical Ballads (lv-lx) and
>   critical and textual notes (205-63).

27 KNIGHT, WILLIAM. "Professor Knight and Dove Cottage."
>   Bookman, 15 (November), 35.
>   A reply to 1898.B37. Defends activities at Dove Cottage.

28 KNIPE, J. W. "The Development of Literary Criticism in
>   England." Transactions of the Royal Society of Literature
>   of the United Kingdom, NS 19:223-54 (224, 244-46, 251).
>   The communing of the Wanderer with Nature in The Excur-
>   sion should appeal to all. With Lyrical Ballads romanticism
>   was infused into literature.

29 LUCAS, E.[DWARD] V. Charles Lamb and the Lloyds. Illustrated.
>   London: Smith, Elder, pp. 233, 273-75, 288.
>   Points out the incongruity of Wordsworth's criticizing
>   the railway while seeking to invest in it.

30 M., L. "Primroses." Academy, 53 (23 April), 449.
>   Wordsworth belongs to April. The lesson of the primrose
>   (in Peter Bell and "The Primrose of the Rock") was deeply
>   graven on his mind.

31 MERIVALE, JUDITH ANNE, ed. Autobiography & Letters of Charles
>   Merivale, Dean of Ely. Illustrated. Oxford: privately
>   printed, pp. 98, 167.
>   Includes C. Merivale's recollection of the Cambridge
>   Apostles' worshipping of Wordsworth and a letter in which

he reports on a visitor's reaction to Wordsworth as a pleasant man but unlike a poet.

32   OSBORN, F. W. "Wordsworth's Poems of Children and Childhood." Education, 19 (October), 93-99.
      Wordsworth's power to idealize what is familiar and to kindle sympathy are especially conspicuous in his poems relating to childhood. Wordsworth was a careful observer of children and their emotions.

33   PRITCHARD, TUDOR. "Wordsworth," "Appendix," in Prophets of the Century. Edited by Arthur Rickett. London, New York, and Melbourne: Ward Lock [1898], pp. 9-32, 325-37 (325-26).
      Before he died Wordsworth had become a cult; today critics tend to approach his poems for their message rather than to study them as poems. Though he changed his political and religious views, Wordsworth remained committed to lofty ideals. Nature to him is the great mother, the great consoler. His pictures of the poor and lowly are true and complete (9-32). Includes brief primary and secondary bibliography (325-26).

34   Q.[UILLER-]C.[OUCH], A.[RTHUR] T.[HOMAS]. "A Literary Causerie: Wordsworth's 'Ode.'" Speaker, 17 (14 May), 611-13.
      The belief, from Plato and Vaughan, that knowledge is recollection, is the motive of "Ode: Intimations of Immortality."

35   Q.[UILLER-]C.[OUCH], A.[RTHUR] T.[HOMAS]. "A Literary Causerie: A Note on 'Lyrical Ballads.'" Speaker, 18 (13 August), 205-206.
      Wordsworth was disloyal but not treacherous to Coleridge in his note on "The Rime of the Ancient Mariner" in Lyrical Ballads (1800).

36   SAINTSBURY, GEORGE. A Short History of English Literature. London and New York: Macmillan, pp. 553, 562, 657-61.
      Wordsworth's remarks in Essay (1815) on the natural imagery of eighteenth-century poets are not true. A biographical sketch. Wordsworth's work is unequal because his poetic theories are narrow. He excelled in sonnets.

37   SHORTER, CLEMENT. "A Literary Causerie." Bookman, 15 (October), 6-8 (7).
      A Guide through the District of the Lakes is beautifully written. Dove Cottage has lost its unkempt character due to Knight's efforts.

1898

38 SPEIGHT, ERNEST E. "On Literary Introductions, with Especial
    Reference to Wordsworth." Parents' Review, 9 (March),
    171-77.
        Wordsworth teaches that one should have faith in children
    and surround them with things of beauty. Suggests how to
    present Wordsworth to children.

39 THOMPSON, A.[LEXANDER] HAMILTON. Cambridge and Its Colleges.
    Illustrated by Edmund H. New. London: Methuen, pp. 15,
    169-70, 197.
        Briefly describes Wordsworth's life at Cambridge.

40 WHEELER, ETHEL. "Great Men's Visions of Womanhood:
    Wordsworth's Vision." Great Thoughts, 4th ser., 1
    (22 January), 270.
        Wordsworth's beauty and joy are solemn; his healing power
    resembles Nature's. His ideal woman, in "Three years she
    grew in sun and shower," is molded by Nature: she is happy,
    because in tune with Nature.

41 WILLIAMS, MRS. E. BAUMER. "Some Unpublished Letters of Robert
    Southey." Blackwood's Edinburgh Magazine, 164 (August),
    167-85 (184).
        "Oh what a Wreck! how changed in mien and speech!"
    refers to Edith Southey.

1899 A BOOKS

1 FOTHERINGHAM, JAMES. Wordsworth's "Prelude" as a Study of
   Education. London: Marshall, 73 pp.
        The Prelude was coldly received in 1850. It is "a sound
   and healthy record," heavy at times, proudly sincere, a
   treatise on education teaching us to respect the natural,
   individual evolution of a child's creative mind. Compares
   Wordsworth's theories with Rousseau's and later educational
   theorists'. Wordsworth believes that "all necessary good
   is possible."

1899 B SHORTER WRITINGS

1 ANON. "England's Debt to Wordsworth." Spectator, 83
   (5 August), 181-82.
        Wordsworth was responsible for our recognition of Na-
   ture's interaction with man, its healing power and its reve-
   lation of the divine. He saw "the fundamental beneficence
   of the world."

WRITINGS ABOUT WILLIAM WORDSWORTH, 1793 - 1899

2   BLAKENEY, E.[DWARD] H.[ENRY]. "Poetry in the Nineteenth
    Century." Churchman, NS 13 (July), 528-39 (530-33).
       The secret of Wordsworth's arresting power lies in his
    unquestioning search for truth and his consequent mastery
    over language.

3   [BROWNING, ROBERT B., ed.]. The Letters of Robert Browning
    and Elizabeth Barrett Barrett 1845-1846. Illustrated.
    2 vols. London: Smith, Elder, especially I:86-87, 479-80,
    486; II:47-48, 63, 75-76, 118-19, 455-56.
       Records Browning's and Barrett's correspondence on Words-
    worth's going to Court, his worldly cunning, W. Howitt's
    visit to Wordsworth, and Browning's lack of enthusiasm for
    Wordsworth.

4   CAIRD, EDWARD. "Preface," in Selections from the Poetry of
    William Wordsworth. Edited by E. E. Speight. London:
    Marshall, pp. v-viii.
       Wordsworth, unlike Burns, did not react quickly and pas-
    sionately to outward influences; he was inspired more by
    his own thoughts and feelings. Though the poet of natural
    beauty, he is interested in nature not in itself but as it
    reveals his own soul. His failings include his identity
    of the languages of poetry and prose, and his lack of
    critical power to judge his own poems.

5   COLERIDGE, ERNEST HARTLEY. "The Lake Poets in Somersetshire."
    Transactions of the Royal Society of Literature of the
    United Kingdom, NS 20:105-31.
       Sketches Wordsworth's and Coleridge's lives and work in
    Somerset.

6   COLERIDGE, ERNEST HARTLEY. "Poetry--the Vision and the
    Faculty Divine." Transactions of the Royal Society of
    Literature of the United Kingdom, NS 21:73-95 (89-92).
       The primrose in Peter Bell is a symbol of the kinship of
    man and nature. Dorothy Wordsworth aided Wordsworth with
    her accurate observation of nature.

7   COWPER, HENRY SWAINSON. Hawkshead (The Northernmost Parish of
    Lancashire): Its History, Archaeology, Industries, Folk-
    lore, Dialect, Etc., Etc. London and Derby: Bemrose,
    pp. 27-29, 145, 415-17.
       Questions the accuracy of Wordsworth's memory of Hawks-
    head in The Prelude. In opposing whitewash in A Guide
    through the District of the Lakes Wordsworth felt only "the
    romance of the hills," not the needs of the inhabitants.
    He never meant his poetic descriptions to be scrutinized
    for factual accuracy.

1899

8   DENNIS, JOHN. The Realms of Gold: A Book for Youthful
    Students of English Literature. London: Richards,
    pp. 101-102, 107-108, 130-43.
        Wordsworth is partly responsible for stimulating a pas-
    sion for mountain climbing; but he cared more for man than
    for the loveliest of inanimate objects. He is a happy poet
    with no sense of humor, in contrast to Cowper. His poems
    are not apt to appeal to youthful readers; they give joy
    and elevate. At his best Wordsworth abandons the extremes
    of his poetic theory. His patriotic sonnets deserve
    praise.

9   DOWDEN, EDWARD. "Puritanism and English Literature."
    Contemporary Review, 76 (July), 22-40 (37).
        Notes Wordsworth's verbal debt to Richard Baxter in The
    Excursion (Book IV).

10 FORD, C. LAWRENCE. "Wordsworthiana." Notes and Queries,
    9th ser., 4 (21 October), 321-23; (28 October), 342-43.
        Notes sources and parallels to thirty passages in Words-
    worth's poems.

11 HARRISON, FREDERIC. "Tennyson," in Tennyson, Ruskin, Mill and
    Other Literary Estimates. London and New York: Macmillan,
    pp. 1-50 (passim).
        Wordsworth speaks truisms in "Ode: Intimations of Im-
    mortality," yet rouses the soul. Notes Wordsworth's use
    of polysyllables in "Tintern Abbey." "Wordsworth was
    capable of goody-goody drivel," yet influenced his genera-
    tion.

12 HAYES, THOMAS R. Flora of the Wordsworth Country. Keswick:
    Bakewell, pp. 9-13, 16-17.
        Describes plants growing at Dove Cottage, Rydal Mount,
    and Helvellyn, to which Wordsworth refers in his poems.

13 HUTCHINSON, THOMAS. "Wordsworthiana." Notes and Queries,
    9th ser., 4 (25 November), 439-40.
        A reply to 1899.B10. Points out additional sources and
    parallels to passages in Wordsworth's poems.

14 JUPP, W. J. "Wordsworth." Inquirer: A Weekly Journal of
    Liberal Religious Thought and Life, 58 (13 May), 291;
    (20 May), 307-308.
        Wordsworth maintained a singleness of purpose and a
    happiness of heart throughout life (291). He teaches "that
    life is meant for joy," the unity of man and nature, and
    the spiritual reality of life (307-308).

1899

15   NEWELL, E.[BENEZER] J.   "Man's Love for Nature."   Macmillan's
        Magazine, 80 (August), 300-306 (301, 305-306).
        Wordsworth's healing power is still effective.

16   PALGRAVE, GWENLLIAN F.   Francis Turner Palgrave: His Journals
        and Memories of His Life.   London, New York, and Bombay:
        Longmans, pp. 37, 65-66, 137, 204, 217.
             Includes the Rev. G. D. Boyle's recollection that Pal-
        grave's publishing of Wordsworth in The Golden Treasury had
        revived the taste for Wordsworth's poetry, and Palgrave's
        recording of Gladstone's praise of Wordsworth's "simplicity
        and openness" of character, Newman's quoting a parody of
        Wordsworth, and Tennyson's naming of Wordsworth as the
        greatest poet of the century.   Records Palgrave's disap-
        pointment at "the undercurrent of 'preachiness'" in Words-
        worth's work.

17   POTTS, R. A.   "'Lyrical Ballads, 1798.'"   Athenaeum, no. 3716
        (14 January), p. 51.
             Describes a copy of Lyrical Ballads (1798) with the
        Bristol imprint and verses by Dr. Thomas Beddoes.

18   PROTHERO, ROWLAND E.   "Appendix II: Three Letters from James
        Hogg, the Ettrick Shepherd," in The Works of Lord Byron.
        New, revised, and enlarged edition.   Edited by Rowland E.
        Prothero.   Illustrated.   Letters and Journals: Volume III.
        London: Murray; New York: Scribner's, pp. 392-96 (394).
             Includes letters in which Hogg notes in 1814 that The
        Excursion is little talked of and notes Wordsworth's bad
        influence on J. Wilson.

19   RAWNSLEY, THE REV. H.[ARDWICKE] D.[RUMMOND].   "Daffodil Day
        at Cockermouth: April 7th, 1898," in Life and Nature at
        the English Lakes.   Glasgow: Mac Lehose, pp. 188-92.
        Records ceremony in tribute to Wordsworth.

Index

In addition to authors of entries, helpful titles of entries, and names mentioned in the annotations, the index includes, under the heading "Wordsworth, William," a listing of references in the annotations to Wordsworth's works and a listing of principal discussions on selected topics. References to major poets may be found either under their individual names or under groupings by century or school (e.g., Elizabethan poets, Eighteenth-century poets, Lake School).

M., C., 1889.B42

M., C. B., 1887.B36

M., G., 1821.B26-B28; 1822.B42.
    See also Moultrie, John

M., H., 1892.B23

M., I. A., 1833.B14

M., L., 1897.B47; 1898.B30

M., M., 1821.B29

M.--R., G., 1859.B17

M., R. M., 1844.B27

M., T. C., 1883.B38

M., T. Q., 1827.B9

M., W., 1891.B31

Macaulay, Thomas Babington, Baron
    Macaulay, 1824.B16; 1831.B21;
    1870.B5; 1876.B29; 1888.B27

M'Cormick, William S., 1889.B43

M'Dermot, Martin, 1824.B17

Macdonald, George, 1868.B12;
    1869.B3; 1882.B42; 1891.B20

M'Donnell, A. C., 1897.B48

Mac Farlane, Charles, 1858.B5

M'Gilchrist, John, 1857.B2

Mackay, Charles, 1851.B24;
    1874.B28; 1877.B21

Mackenzie, A. W., 1877.B22

Mackenzie, Robert Shelton,
    1837.B19; 1850.B67; 1855.B6;
    1870.B9

Mackintosh, Sir James, 1835.B38;
    1897.B8

Mackintosh, Robert James,
    1835.B38

Macleod, Norman, 1883.B26;
    1889.B56

Macmillan, Malcolm Kingsley,
    1893.B40

Mac Neill, Sir John, 1866.B7

Macnish, Robert, 1830.B8

Macpherson, James, 1835.B10;
    1839.B22. See also Ossian

Macready, William Charles,
    1875.B15

Mc William, Robert, 1890.B32

Madge, Mr., 1843.B13

Maginn, William, 1819.B47;
    1820.B25, B31-B33;
    1822.B43-B44, B46; 1824.B15;
    1831.B22; 1832.B16, B21;
    1836.B20; 1837.B17; 1855.B6;
    1873.B6

Magnus, Laurie, 1897.A2

Mahony, Francis, 1836.B20

Main, David M., 1880.B28

Maitland, Brownlow, 1882.B43

Makrocheir, 1869.B16

Malagrowther, Malachi. See
    Scott, Sir Walter

Malden, Henry, 1823.B27

Malleson, the Rev. Frederick
    Amadeus, 1873.B21; 1883.B39;
    1890.B33

Malleson, W. T., 1889.B44

Mallock, William Hurrell,
    1872.B20; 1882.B44

Mann, A. H., 1894.B23

Manners, George, 1809.B14

Manning, Henry E., Cardinal,
    1897.B28

Manning, Thomas, 1837.B24

Mansergh, J. F., 1889.B19

Mant, Frederick, 1874.B28

Mant, Richard, 1808.B6

Marshall, Ed., 1879.B18;
    1889.B19; 1892.B20

Marshall, Edward H.,
    1893.B41-B42; 1896.B9

Martial, 1895.B27

Martin, Mrs. Henry, 1883.B37

Martin, Theodore, 1841.B13;
    1843.B11; 1845.B11; 1875.B10

Martineau, Harriet, 1850.B61;
    1860.B3; 1869.B17; 1877.B23;
    1884.B22

Mason, James, 1875.B11

Massey, Gerald, 1855.B7

Massinger, Philip, 1844.B14

Masson, David, 1850.B62;
    1852.B22; 1853.B21; 1881.B22;
    1889.B45; 1890.B34; 1893.B27

Mather, J. Marshall, 1892.B21

Matheson, A., 1882.B45

Mathetes. See Blair, Alexander;
    Wilson, John

Maunder, Samuel, 1851.B25;
    1866.B9; 1867.B8

Maurice, John Frederick,
    1884.B17

Maurice, John Frederick Denison,
    1826.B16-B17; 1828.B15-B16;
    1874.B29; 1884.B17

Mayer, S. R. Townshend, 1877.B24

dejection freed," 1819.B46;
1841.B16
"The Germans on the Heights
of Hochheim," 1822.B39
"Gipsies," 1815.B20; 1820.A1;
1847.B12; 1848.B6; 1864.B4;
1867.B9; 1890.B17
"Glen Almain," 1831.B27;
1832.B1; 1834.B9; 1893.B60
"Gold and Silver Fishes in a
Vase," 1835.B33
"Goody Blake and Harry Gill,"
1798.B4; 1799.B6-B7;
1812.B2, B4; 1820.B13;
1829.B18; 1851.B27;
1882.B32; 1893.B16;
1897.B48
Grace Darling, 1893.B25;
1895.B7; 1897.B42
"A Gravestone upon the Floor
in the Cloisters of Wor-
cester Cathedral," 1829.B1
"Great men have been among
us; hands that penned,"
1826.B9; 1833.B12; 1841.B13;
1842.B24
"Grief, thou hast lost an
ever-ready friend," 1832.B7
A Guide through the District
of the Lakes, 1838.B17;
1849.B7; 1866.B7; 1881.B23;
1883.B11; 1884.B19;
1886.B25; 1898.B37; 1899.B7.
See also A Description of
the Scenery of the Lakes;
A Description of the Sce-
nery of the Lakes (1823);
"Topographical Description
of the Country of the Lakes"
"Guilt and Sorrow," 1817.B5;
1842.B6; 1843.B3; 1897.B66
"Hart-leap Well," 1871.B5;
1874.B6; 1879.B7; 1883.B31;
1890.B16; 1891.B51;
1892.B6; 1893.B39; 1897.B49
"The Idiot Boy," 1798.B4;
1803.B1; 1809.B6; 1820.B13,
B42; 1829.B18; 1832.B15,
B21; 1834.B19, B27;
1871.B13; 1882.B28, B46;
1888.B26; 1889.B43

"The Idle Shepherd-boys,"
1890.B16; 1893.B9
"If this great world of joy
and pain," 1853.A1
"Influence of Natural Ob-
jects," 1829.B18
"The Italian Itinerant,"
1822.B55
"It is a beauteous evening,
calm and free," 1880.B22,
B32; 1882.B12
"It was an April morning:
fresh and clear," 1853.A1
"I wandered lonely as a
cloud," 1811.B5; 1816.B14;
1878.B7; 1897.B23
Kendal and Windermere Railway,
1844.B8-B9; 1877.B21;
1884.B33; 1896.B35
"Lament of Mary Queen of
Scots," 1853.B32
"Laodamia," 1823.B23;
1824.B10; 1825.B5, B7;
1826.B10; 1827.B1; 1830.B5;
1831.B27; 1832.B15;
1833.B10; 1837.B2, B21;
1842.B24; 1845.B6; 1848.B6;
1849.B11; 1854.B6; 1869.B11;
1872.B14; 1873.B1, B8;
1876.B8; 1882.B23; 1884.B8,
B16; 1897.B48
"The Last of the Flock,"
1799.B6
"The Last Supper, by Leonardo
da Vinci," 1822.B39
A Letter to A Friend of Robert
Burns,
reviews of, 1816.B4-B5;
other references to,
1817.B26-B28; 1818.B15, B18;
1833.B19; 1837.B13; 1849.B9;
1897.B60
"A Letter to the Bishop of
Llandaff," 1875.B2, B5, B8;
1893.B35
"Lines Left upon a Seat in a
Yew-tree," 1834.B27
"Lines Written in Early
Spring," 1875.B13; 1888.B19;
1891.B25; 1896.B16
"London, 1802," 1829.B18;

1801.B3; 1803.B1; 1808.B4;
1809.B14; 1811.B2; 1812.B2,
B7; 1813.B1, B3, B7;
1814.B13; 1816.B29, B34;
1818.B8; 1819.A1-A3, B34,
B47-B48; 1820.A1, B20, B22,
B31-B33, B39; 1821.B1, B6,
B31; 1822.B6, B45-B46, B52,
B57; 1823.B27; 1824.B6;
1825.B6; 1826.B2, B21;
1827.B4-B5; 1831.B10-B11,
B22; 1832.B5, B13, B23;
1836.B2; 1837.B20;
1838.B18-B19, B22; 1839.B13;
1840.B20; 1841.B13;
1842.B23-B24; 1843.B11;
1847.B7; 1851.B32; 1856.B6;
1860.B9; 1865.B11, B14;
1869.B16; 1872.B12, B19;
1874.B9, B33; 1877.B2, B22;
1878.B6; 1879.B19; 1880.B20;
1883.B27; 1884.B14; 1885.B2,
B5-B8; 1886.B2-B3, B20, B42;
1888.B19, B32; 1891.B17,
B43-B44; 1893.B24; 1898.B12
--philosophical and religious
  opinions of, 1803.B2;
1814.B10-B11; 1815.B4,
B25-B26; 1816.B43;
1818.B33-B34; 1819.B40, B57;
1820.B48; 1821.B3; 1822.B9,
B11; 1825.B5; 1826.B1;
1827.B15; 1828.B6, B19;
1829.B5; 1830.B15; 1831.B30;
1832.B9; 1833.B13; 1834.B27;
1835.B33, B45-B46; 1836.B1,
B7, B15; 1837.B16; 1838.B1;
1841.B15-B16; 1842.B9, B11,
B16, B19, B31, B33; 1843.B10;
1844.B4, B17; 1847.B5, B17;
1849.B4, B11; 1850.B7, B12,
B50, B53; 1851.B10, B18, B21,
B27; 1852.B29; 1853.A1;
1854.B2, B9; 1856.B9;
1858.B8, B13; 1859.B4;
1861.B1; 1862.B11; 1864.B5,
B12; 1865.B1, B6, B16;
1868.B9; 1869.B13-B14, B18;
1871.B11, B13; 1872.A1, B8;
1873.B9, B14; 1874.A1, B10,
B12, B36; 1875.B8, B17;

1876.B8, B26; 1877.B14, B23,
B30; 1878.B16, B27; 1879.B4,
B16, B21; 1880.B14, B19,
B23, B37; 1881.B9, B21, B28;
1882.B21, B27, B42; 1883.B15,
B38, B45; 1884.B8, B12, B27;
1885.B41, B43, B45;
1886.B18-B19, B30; 1887.A2,
B28, B31; 1888.B23, B27;
1889.B32, B43, B51; 1890.B18;
1891.B8, B23, B49; 1892.B12,
B21, B26; 1893.B14, B23;
1894.B15; 1897.B28, B36, B66,
B71; 1898.B3, B7, B14, B26,
B33
--political opinions of, 1799.B3,
  B6; 1802.B3; 1809.B5, B17;
1813.B4; 1815.B2, B12, B18;
1816.B11, B24-B25, B27-B28,
B31, B40, B42; 1817.B5,
B9-B11, B19; 1818.B10, B13,
B15, B20, B55; 1820.B17,
B51; 1821.B5, B11, B19, B23,
B25; 1822.B14, B23, B33,
B39, B43, B55; 1823.B8, B24,
B30; 1824.B4, B18; 1826.B5;
1827.B1; 1828.B11; 1831.B16,
B26; 1832.B21; 1833.B5, B19;
1834.B27; 1835.B6, B25, B35,
B41; 1836.B4, B16, B19;
1837.B20; 1838.B3-B4, B25;
1840.B20; 1841.B16; 1842.B2;
1844.B31; 1845.B5, B13;
1846.B2, B9; 1850.B8, B18, B46,
B67; 1851.B1, B5; 1852.B2;
1853.B31; 1858.B13; 1859.B4;
1860.B12; 1861.B1, B6;
1862.B11; 1864.B9; 1865.B16;
1868.B11; 1869.B14, B18;
1870.B4, B13; 1872.B28;
1873.B2, B17; 1874.B10, B12,
B39; 1875.B2-B4, B8;
1876.B2, B8, B19; 1877.B11,
B13, B15, B32; 1878.B11;
1879.B12; 1880.B14, B23;
1882.B58; 1884.B8, B15, B30,
B35; 1885.B21, B43; 1888.B27,
B40; 1889.B8, B12, B36;
1890.B18, B36, B47, B50;
1893.B35, B37, B40; 1895.B15,
B19, B21, B40; 1896.B5;